INDIA

THE DEFINITIVE HISTORY

INDIA

THE DEFINITIVE HISTORY

D. R. SARDESAI

UNIVERSITY OF
CALIFORNIA AT LOS ANGELES

Westview
PRESS

A Member of the Perseus Books Group

Find us on the World Wide Web at www.westviewpress.com.

Westview Press books are available at special discounts for bulk
purchases in the United States by corporations, institutions,
and other organizations. For more information, please contact
the Special Markets Department at the Perseus Books Group,
2300 Chestnut Street, Philadelphia, PA, or call (800) 255-1514,
or e-mail special.markets@perseusbooks.com.

Designed by Trish Wilkinson
Set in 11 point Adobe Caslon

Library of Congress Cataloging-in-Publication Data

SarDesai, D. R.
    India : the definitive history / D.R. SarDesai.
        p.   cm.
    Includes bibliographical references and index.
    ISBN-13: 978-0-8133-4352-5 (alk. paper)
    ISBN-10: 0-8133-4352-6 (alk. paper)
    1. India—History. I. Title.
DS436.S23 2007
954—dc22   2007009972

10 9 8 7 6 5 4 3 2 1

For
ARNAV
and
the New Generation of Indians

CONTENTS

CHRONOLOGY

BCE

ca. 2600–1300	Indus-Saraswati Civilization
ca. 1200–1000	The Vedas
ca. 1200–600	Vedic Age
ca. 1000–800	Brahmanas
817	Traditional date of the birth of Parshvanath, Jain savior
ca. 800–600	Aranayakas and Upanishads
ca. 600–527	Mahavira Vardhamana
ca. 563–483	Gautama Buddha
ca. 542–491	Bindusara, king of Magadha
ca. 491–458	Ajatasatru, king of Magadha
ca. 480	First Buddhist General Council held at Rajagriha
327–326	Alexander invades India
325	Alexander leaves India
ca. 322	Kautilya writes *Arthasastra*
ca. 321–297	Chandragupta Maurya, king of Magadha
ca. 321–185	The Maurya dynasty
ca. 300	Megasthenes, ambassador of Seleucus Nikator, visits Chandragupta
ca. 297–273	Bindusara, king of Magadha
ca. 273–231	Asoka's reign
200–200 CE	Period of Hindu lawbooks, epics, six systems of philosophy

ca. 185–172	The Sunga dynasty
ca. 185–149	Pushyamitra Sunga
ca. 150	Menander or Milinda, greatest of the Indo-Greek kings, meets with the great Buddhist monk Nagasena
ca. 100–100 CE	Composition of Bhagavad Gita
58 Vikrama era begins	

CE

Early first century	Kushanas invade India
40–64	Kadphisis I Kushana
78	Saka era begins
ca. 78–101	Kanishka's reign
ca. 79 or 82	Jains split into Digambaras and Svetambaras
ca. 100–200	Buddhists split into Mahayana and Theravada (Hinayana)
ca. 100–200	Law Code of Yajnavalkya
ca. 300–500	Syrian Christian community in Cochin
320–540	The Guptas
ca. 320–335	Chandragupta I
ca. 335–376	Samudra Gupta
ca. 376–415	Chandra Gupta II
ca. 400–500	Foundation of the Buddhist monastery/ university at Nalanda
401–410	Chinese traveler Fa Hsien in India
415–455	Kumara Gupta I, contemporary of Kalidasa
ca. 454	Jain Council at Vallabhi in Saurashtra
ca. 454	The first Hun invasion
455–467	Reign of Skanda Gupta
476	Aryabhata (astronomer) born
477–544	The later Guptas
606–612	Conquest of northern India by Harsha
606–647	Harshavardhana, king of Kanauj and Thanesar
622	Muhammad's Hegira, flight from Mecca to Medina; Islamic era begins
629–645	Chinese traveler Hsuan Tsang in India
630	Muhammad reconquers Mecca

632	Muhammad the Prophet dies
643	Harsha's meeting with the Chinese traveler Hsuan Tsang
671–695	Chinese traveler I-tsing in India and Southeast Asia
675–685	Chinese scholar-traveler I-tsing at Nalanda
700–800	Buddhism spreads to Nepal and Tibet
ca. 700–800	Tamil Saint Manikkavachar in Mathura
712	Arab conquest of Sind
731	Yasovarman's embassy to China
ca. 750–1142	Pala rule in Bengal and Bihar
753	Rise of the Rashtrakutas
765–815	Pandya Varaguna I
788–820	Sankaracharya
ca. 800–900	Bhagavata Purana; Jinasena's Mahapurana; Shaiva Nayanar of South India
1000–1026	Muhammad of Ghazni's raids into India
1026	Muhammad of Ghazni's raid against Somnath temple
1191	First Battle of Tarain
1192	Second Battle of Tarain; Prithviraj Chauhan defeated
1193	Muhammad of Ghur leaves; Qutb-uddin Aibek in charge in Delhi
1206–1210	Reign of Qutb-uddin Aibek in Delhi as sultan
1206–1290	The Slave Dynasty
1210–1236	Reign of Iltutmish
1221	Invasion of Chingiz Khan
1236–1239	Reign of the first female Muslim ruler, Raziya
1246–1266	Nasir-uddin Mahmud's reign
1266–1287	Ghyas-uddin Balban's reign
1275–1296	Jnyanadeva's Jnyaneswari
1290–1296	Jalal-uddin Khalji's reign
1290–1320	Khalji Dynasty
1294	Ala-uddin Khalji captures Deogiri
1296–1316	The reign of Ala-uddin Khalji
1302–1303	Ala-uddin's capture of Chitor
1306	Malik Kafur's capture of Deogiri

1309–1312	Malik Kafur's expedition to South India and defeat of the Kakatiyas, Hoysalas, and Pandyas
1320–1325	Ghiyas-uddin Tughluq's reign
1325–1351	Muhammad bin Tughluq's reign
1327	Transfer of capital from Delhi to Daulatabad
1333–1334	Traveler Ibn Battutah arrives
1336–1646	Vijayanagar Empire
1351–1388	Firuz Shah Tughluq's reign
1389–1414	Later Tughluqs
1398	Timur invades Delhi
1414–1451	The Sayyids rule in Delhi
1424–1446	Devaraya II of Vijayanagar
1429	Bahmani capital transferred from Gulbarga to Bidar
1440–1518	Kabir, prominent leader of the *bhakti* movement
1451–1526	Lodi dynasty in Delhi
1451–1489	Buhlul Lodi's reign
1469–1539	Guru Nanak
1475–1531	Vallabha, Vedanta philosopher
1481	Mohammad Gawan exeuted
1485	End of the Sangama dynasty in Vijayanagar
1485–1505	Saluva dynasty
1505–1646	Tuluva and Aravidu dynasties
1489–1517	Sikandar Lodi's reign
1489–1686	Dynasty of Adil Shahi of Bijapur
1489–1510	Reign of Yusuf Adil Khan of Bijapur
1490–1633	Dynasty of Nizam Shahi of Ahmednagar
1497	Accession of Prataprudra Gajapati in Orissa
1498	Vasco da Gama lands in Calicut
1498–1547	Mirabai, *bhakti* saint in Rajasthan
1509–1529	Krishnadeva Raya's reign in Vijayanagar
1510	Afonso de Albuquerque occupies Goa
1518–1686	Dynasty of Qutb Shahi of Golkonda
1517–1526	Ibrahim Khan Lodi's reign
1526	First Battle of Panipat
1526–1530	Babar's reign
1530–1540	First part of Humayun's reign

1540	Sher Shah defeats Humayun; Humayun goes into exile
1540–1545	Sher Shah's reign
1542	Birth of Akbar
1552	Guru Angad dies
1555–1556	Second part of Humayun's reign
1556–1605	Akbar's reign
1562	Akbar marries Jodhabai, princess of Amber
1564	Vijayanagar defeated at the Battle of Talikota
1568	Akbar's capture of Chitor
1569	Prince Salim (Jahangir) born
1571	Construction of Fatehpur Sikri begins
1572	Akbar annexes Gujarat
1574	Guru Amar Das dies
1574–1581	Guru Ramdas
1579	Akbar issues declaration making himself arbiter on religious questions
1581–1606	Guru Arjan
1597	Rana Pratap dies
1600	Queen Elizabeth I issues charter to the East India Company
1605–1627	Jahangir's reign
1606–1644	Guru Har Govind
1608–1612	William Hawkins at Agra
1611	Jahangir marries Nur Jahan
1615	English open the first factory at Surat
1616	The Dutch open a factory in Surat
1627–1658	Shah Jahan's reign; Shah Jahan dies in 1666
1630	Birth of Shivaji
1631	Mumtaz Mahal dies
1633–1653	Taj Mahal's construction
1636	Aurangzeb appointed viceroy of the Deccan
1636	Ahmednagar's Nizam Shahi ended
1644–1661	Guru Har Rai
1646	Shivaji captures Torna Fort
1653	Aurangzeb reappointed viceroy of the Deccan
1657–1659	War of succession for the Mughal throne
1658	Shah Jahan imprisoned by Aurangzeb in Agra Fort

1659–1707	Aurangzeb's reign
1661	Portugal gives Bombay as part of the dowry to King Charles II
1661–1664	Guru Har Kishan
1664	Shivaji sacks Surat
1664–1675	Guru Tegh Bahadur
1666	Shivaji and Sambhaji visit Agra, escape and return to Maharashtra
1674	The French establish Pondicherry; Shivaji's coronation at Raigad
1675–1708	Guru Govind Singh
1680	Shivaji dies
1680–1689	Sambhaji's reign
1689	Sambhaji blinded and executed by Aurangzeb
1689–1700	Rajaram crowned in 1689 but moves to Jinji
1707	Death of Aurangzeb
1708	Shahu crowned as *chhatrapati* (king)
1708	Death of Guru Govind Singh
1712	Death of Bahadur Shah
1713	Farrukhsiyar proclaimed emperor
1714	Balaji Viswanath formally appointed *peshwa*
1716	The Sikh leader Banda executed
1720	Death of Balaji Viswanath; Bajirao I appointed *peshwa*
1739	Nadir Shah sacks Delhi
1739	Marathas conquer Bassein and Salsette from the Portuguese
1740	Death of Bajirao I; Balaji Bajirao becomes *peshwa*
1740–1748	War of the Austrian Succession
1749	Death of Shahu
1751	Clive's defense and occupation of Arcot
1756	Death of Alivardi Khan; accession of Siraj-ud-Daula
1756–1763	Seven Years' War
1757	Sack of Delhi by Ahmad Shah Abdali
1757	Battle of Plassey; Mir Jafar becomes nawab
1758	Clive becomes governor of Bengal

1760	Mir Jafar deposed; Mir Kasim made nawab
1761	Death of Tarabai; Third Battle of Panipat; Shah Alam II becomes emperor
1761–1772	Madhavrao I is *peshwa*
1763	Mir Kassim deposed; Mir Jafar becomes nawab again
1764	Battle of Buxar; Mughal emperor's forces defeated
1765	Diwani of Bengal conferred by the Mughal emperor on the East India Company
1765	Nawab Mir Jafar dies
1772	Warren Hastings appointed governor of Bengal
1773	Regulating Act passed
1774	Hastings becomes governor-general
1774	Birth of Narayanrao; made Peshwa Madhavrao II
1775–1782	The First Anglo-Maratha War
1775–1862	Bahadur Shah Zafar II
1780–1784	The Second Mysore War
1782	Treaty of Salbai; Hyder Ali dies
1784	Pitt's India Act passed
1785	Warren Hastings resigns as governor-general
1786–1793	Lord Cornwallis is governor-general
1789–1814	French Revolution and Napoleonic Wars
1790–1792	The Third Mysore War
1792	Permanent Settlement in Bengal
1792	Ranjit Singh succeeds his father as leader of a *misl*
1793	East India Company's charter renewed
1794	Death of Mahadji Scindia
1795	Marathas defeat the Nizam at Kharda; death of Peshwa Madhavrao II
1795	Ahalyabai Holkar dies
1798–1805	Marquis of Wellesley is governor-general
1799	Ranjit Singh appointed as governor of Lahore
1799	Fourth Mysore War; death of Tipu Sultan
1800	Nana Phadnavis dies
1802	Treaty of Bassein between the East India Company and Bajirao II

1803–1805	The Second Anglo-Maratha War
1806	Mutiny at Vellore
1806	Death of Shah Alam II
1808	Treaty of Alliance between Ranjit Singh and the English
1809	Treaty of Amritsar
1813	East India Company's charter renewed
1817–1818	The Third Anglo-Maratha War; Bajirao II surrenders and is deported to Bithur
1819	Mountstuart Elphinstone, governor of Bombay
1828–1835	William Bentinck is governor-general
1828	Brahmo Samaj founded
1829	Bentinck abolishes sati
1833	East India Company's charter renewed for twenty years
1835	Macaulay's approves English as the medium of instruction
1837–1858	Bahadur Shah II's reign
1839	Ranjit Singh dies
1839–1842	The First Afghan War
1843	British annex Sind
1845–1846	The First Anglo-Sikh War and the Treaty of Lahore
1848–1856	Dalhousie is governor-general
1849	The Second Anglo-Sikh War
1852–1853	Second Anglo-Burmese War
1853	East India Company's charter renewed for an indefinite period
1853	First railway, Bombay to Thane; first telegraph line, Calcutta to Agra
1854	Charles Wood's Education Dispatch
1856	New army recruits made liable for overseas service; annexation of Oudh
1857–1859	The Great Uprising
1857	Universities of Bombay, Madras and Calcutta established
1858	East India Company's rule ends; Act for the Better Government of India
1861	Indian Councils Act

1861–1941	Rabindranath Tagore
1862	Bahadur Shah II dies in Burma
1869	Suez Canal opened
1875	Arya Samaj founded by Dayanand Saraswati
1875–1880	Lord Lytton is viceroy
1877	Anglo-Oriental College founded at Aligarh
1877	Queen Victoria proclaimed empress of India
1878	Lytton approves the Vernacular Press Act (the Gagging Act)
1883	Ilbert Bill; Ripon's Resolution on Local Self-Government
1884–1888	Lord Dufferin is viceroy
1885	Indian National Congress founded
1885–1886	Third Anglo-Burmese War
1892	Indian Councils Act
1905–1910	Partition of Bengal; Lord Minto is governor-general
1906	Indian Muslim League founded; memorandum to Lord Minto
1907	Tata Iron and Steel Company founded
1909	Indian Councils Act; Morley-Minto reforms
1916	Indian National Congress and Muslim League pact
1917	Montagu's announcement on responsible government
1919	Montagu-Chelmsford reforms; dyarchy introduced
1919	Jalianwala Bagh massacre; Khilafat movement begins
1928	Simon Commission's visit to India
1930	Simon Commission Report published; Gandhi launches Salt Satyagraha
1930–1931	First Round Table Conference
1931	Gandhi-Irwin Pact; Second Round Table Conference
1932	Third Round Table Conference
1935	Government of India Act; Reserve Bank of India founded
1937	Burma politically separated from India

1937	Provincial elections; ministries formed
1939	World War II begins; Congress ministries resign
1942	Cripps Mission to India; Gandhi launches "Quit India" movement
1945	Subhash Chandra Bose dies in a plane crash in Taiwan
1946	Cabinet Mission to India; Interim Government formed
1946–1949	Constituent Assembly at work
1947	Partition and the birth of Pakistan on August 14; India attains freedom on August 15
1947–1964	Jawaharlal Nehru prime minister of India
1947–1948	Mountbatten becomes India's first governor-general
1948	First India-Pakistan War (Kashmir War)
1948	Mahatma Gandhi assassinated
1948–1950	C. Rajagopalachari becomes the first Indian governor-general
1950	India's Constitution becomes effective on January 26
1950–1962	Rajendra Prasad, the first president of India
1954	India-China Agreement over Tibet
1954	France hands over its Indian colonies to New Delhi
1955	Untouchability Act passed
1955	Asian-African Conference at Bandung
1959	Dalai Lama and 35,000 followers given refuge in India
1961	Liberation of Goa from Portuguese rule
1962–1967	Sarvepalli Radhakrishnan, president of India
1962	China invades India
1964	Nehru dies on May 27
1964–1966	Lal Bahadur Shastri, prime minister of India
1965	Second India-Pakistan War
1966	Lal Bahadur Shastri dies in Tashkent
1966–1977	Indira Gandhi, prime minister of India
1967–1969	Zakir Hussain, president of India (dies in office)

1969–1974	V. V. Giri, president of India
1971	Indo-Soviet Treaty of Friendship and Co-operation
1971	Third India-Pakistan War; Bangladesh becomes independent
1972	India-Pakistan Agreement (Simla Agreement)
1974	India tests an underground nuclear device
1974–1977	Fakhruddin Ali Ahmed, president of India (dies in office)
June 1975–March 1977	Indira declares emergency
1977–1982	Neelum Sanjeeva Reddy, president of India
March 1977–June 1980	Janata Party rule
March 1977–July 1979	Morarji Desai, prime minister of India
July 1979–January 1980	Charan Singh, prime minister of India
January 1980–October 1984	Indira Gandhi, prime minister of India
1982–1987	Giani Zail Singh, president of India
1984	Operation Blue Star at the Golden Temple of Amritsar
1984	Indira Gandhi assassinated on October 31
1984–December 1989	Rajiv Gandhi, prime minister of India
1987–1992	R. Venkataraman, president of India
December 1989–November 1990	V. P. Singh (National Front), prime minister of India
November 1990–June 1991	Chandra Shekhar (Janata), prime minister of India
1991	Rajiv Gandhi assassinated in May
1991–1996	Narasimha Rao, prime minister of India
1991	Economic liberalization; Manmohan Singh as finance minister
1992–1997	Shanker Dayal Sharma, president of India
June 1996–April 1997	Janata Party forms government; Deve Gowda as prime minister
1997–2002	K. R. Narayanan, president of India
April 1997–December 1997	Inder Kumar Gujral, prime minister of India (Janata Party)
1998	India and Pakistan launch nuclear tests
1998–April 1999	Atal Bihari Vajpayee, prime minister of India (BJP-NDA)

1999	Vajpayee-Sharif Declaration at Lahore in February
October 1999–May 2004	Atal Bihari Vajpayee, prime minister of India (BJP-NDA)
1999	Fourth India-Pakistan War (Kargil Conflict)
2000	President Clinton visits India
2001	Terrorists attack the Indian Parliament building in December
2002–present	A. P. J. Abdul Kalam, president of India
May 2004–present	Manmohan Singh, prime minister of India

PREFACE

This book has been long in the making. It received special impetus during 1998–2001, when I became the first holder of the newly endowed Navin and Pratima Doshi Chair in Pre-Modern Indian History at the University of California at Los Angeles (UCLA). The lecture and seminar courses in Indian history I offered during that period and the numerous conferences I planned and directed provided me with a useful forum for testing many ideas in the historiography concerning India. I am most grateful to scores of bright students and conference participants who helped sharpen my ideas, for which they do not, indeed, bear any responsibility.

Most general histories of India give an inordinate amount of space and consideration to the colonial period. Although the actual period of British rule was short, the impact on the political, economic, and educational spheres has been very deep and consequential. A treatment of that period, however, does not warrant a blow-by-blow account of each governor-general's tenure in India. I have limited myself to the main ideas and goals motivating those who concerned themselves with the extension of British power and the administration of the Indian Empire. It is notable that despite the colonial impact, most pre-British Indian modes of thought, social behaviors, political idioms, and religious practices persisted and continue to prevail in Indian society and politics. I have, therefore, dealt elaborately with the premodern period, the so-called Hindu and Muslim periods, during which times such ideas and practices were born and sustained.

There has been a phenomenal literary output in the past half century on India in all aspects, most notably in history, politics, anthropology, and economics. To take note of all the publications of books, monographs, articles, and conference papers is an almost impossible task. I have tried my best to identify various points of view, keeping in mind the need to avoid making the reading dense and cluttering the text with footnotes. An indication of the works I have consulted is provided by the extensive bibliography at the end of the volume.

I want to express my gratitude to Hubert Ho and his team of experts in the computer laboratory of UCLA's History Department for the extensive assistance they provided, with patience at all times. I am grateful to the research staff of UCLA's Young Research Library and, in India, to the able staff of the library of the Asiatic Society of Mumbai. My special thanks to executive editor at Westview Press Steve Catalano and production editor Kay Mariea for their continued interest in my writings. Finally, I owe an immense obligation to my wife, Bhanu, for dozens of discussions on many controversial issues, particularly affecting religious thought and practices and their impact on the society and politics of India. She will soon complete a half century as the best unpaid critic of my writings and other activities.

INDIA
States and Union Territories

TAJIKISTAN

AFGHANISTAN

PAKISTAN

JAMMU & KASHMIR
Srinagar

HIMACHAL PRADESH
Chandigarh • Shimla
PUNJAB
Dehradun
HARYANA
UTTARAKHAND
DELHI

CHINA

TIBET

NEPAL

SIKKUM

BHUTAN

ARUNACHAL PRADESH
Itanagar

UTTAR PRADESH
Jaipur •
Lucknow •

RAJASTHAN

BIHAR
Patna

Dispur ASSAM
Shillong •
MEGHALAYA

NAGALAND
• Kohima
• Imphal
MANIPUR

BANGLADESH

JHARKHAND
Ranchi

WEST BENGAL

Agartala
TRIPURA

• Aizawl
MIZORAM

Gandhinagar •

Bhopal •

MADHYA PRADESH

Raipur •

CHHATTISGARH

Kolkata

GUJARAT

Diu Daman
DADRA & NAGAR HAVELI

ORISSA

Bhubaneshwar

MYANMAR

Mumbai (Bombay) •

MAHARASHTRA

• Hyderabad

Bay

of

Bengal

ANDAMAN ISLANDS

Panaji •
GOA

ANDHRA PRADESH

KARNATAKA
Bengaluru •
• Channai
• Puducherry

LAKSHADWEEP

KERALA

TAMIL NADU

Andaman Sea

Laccadive Sea

an Sea

Thiruvananthapuram

NICOBAR ISLANDS

SRI LANKA

Indian

Ocean

Strait of Malacca

Map not to Scale

Some statistical indicators may be relevant to appreciate the importance of the study of India for the modern world. Some of its distinctions are laudable, whereas others are clearly of dubious value. India is the second most populated country in the world, behind China, with an estimated population in 2006 of 1.3 billion, making Indians between one-fifth and one-sixth of the human race. Its economy, the second fastest growing in the world, is also the fourth largest. India constitutes the largest democracy and has one of the freest presses in the world. Indians are proud that their country is a member of the "nuclear club," has a space program, and has the third largest scientific human-resources pool in the world. (page 1)

1

LAND AND THE
HUMAN FABRIC

The history of India is the story of a civilization whose past is well incorporated into its present. No major civilization in the world, with the possible exception of China, has demonstrated a greater continuity from ancient to contemporary times than India. Other major riverine civilizations such as Egypt on the banks of the Nile and the Sumerian, Babylonian, Assyrian, and Chaldean on the banks of the Tigris and Euphrates were radically altered in terms of their human fabric and cultural content over the millennia. The present-day people in those riverine civilizations and their ways of life are, in so many respects, so different from their ancient past. By contrast, the people of the Indian subcontinent, in its different segments and spaces, have cultural elements drawn all the way from the Neolithic period to the present.

Some statistical indicators may be relevant to appreciate the importance of the study of India for the modern world. Some of its distinctions are laudable, whereas others are clearly of dubious value. India is the second most populated country in the world, behind China, with an estimated population in 2006 of 1.3 billion, making Indians between one-fifth and one-sixth of the human race. Its economy, the second fastest growing in the world, is also the fourth largest. India constitutes the largest democracy and has one of the freest presses in the world. Indians are proud that their country is a member of the "nuclear club," has a space program, and has the third largest scientific human-resources pool in the world.

India covers an area of roughly 1.2 million square miles (about one-third the area of the United States, with more than four times its population), about 2,008 miles from north to south and about 1,833 miles from west to east at its widest points, with a land frontier of 9,425 miles and a coastline of 3,535 miles.[1] Located in the Northern Hemisphere and extending between latitudes 8 and 37 degrees north and longitudes 61 and 97 degrees east, the country has a single time zone based on the longitude of 87.5 passing through Allahabad (Prayag). The single time zone is annoying to at least one group in India, the cricket lovers (which includes almost everyone), for the visibility is reduced early in the day in the eastern parts of the country, notably Calcutta (Kolkata), where so many test matches are played. Apart from the mainland, India includes numerous islands, the largest of which are the Lakshadweep in the Indian Ocean and the Andaman and Nicobar Islands in the Bay of Bengal. It has land borders with six countries: Bangladesh (2,533 miles), China (2,122 miles), Pakistan (1,820 miles), Nepal (1,056 miles), Myanmar (914 miles), and Bhutan (378 miles).

GEOGRAPHY

Does the lay of the land have an influence on the historical development of its people? In the nineteenth century, two major scholars agreed with the proposition but not on the details. Carl Ritter (1779–1859), a German geographer, held that the form and shape of continents are responsible for their general cultural growth. Diversified geographical conditions and an irregular coastline are ideal for an exuberant culture, in his view. Likewise, the more compact and homogenous a continent, the more backward its inhabitants, breeding stagnation. He had Europe and the Indian subcontinent, respectively, as contrasting entities in mind. On the other hand, Henry Thomas

Buckle (1821–1862), an English historian, emphasized two factors: those that stimulate the imagination and those that sharpen understanding. As an example of the first category, he pointed to India, where the works of nature—be they the perpetually snowcapped mountains or mighty rivers, tropical forests or long coastline, torrential rains or water-starved deserts—are overawing enough to make human beings feel insignificant. Human beings in such environments tend to become pessimists and fatalists, he said, denying all value to life and repudiating the ability of man to understand and control the world.

The Indian Constitution recognizes two names for the country, both of which have geographical significance: India and Bharat. The latter is a short form for *Bharatvarsha,* the land of Bharata, a famous king in ancient India. The subcontinent was regarded in Bharata's time as part of a larger unit called Jambudwipa, innermost of the seven concentric island-continents into which the earth as conceived by Hindu cosmographers was divided. (The Indian subcontinent, shaped like an irregular quadrilateral, appeared to some ancient Indian writers in Sanskrit as a "many-sided diamond.") The name India comes from the Greek *Indos,* which itself is derived from the river Indus, whose ancient name was Sindhu; the land watered by Indus and its tributaries was called Saptasindhava (Hapta Hindu in Greek), meaning "the seven Sindhus."

Four Main Divisions

The subcontinent, the area of historical development under our consideration, has four major geographical divisions, the first of which is the Himalayan and sub-Himalayan region. Looking at a map, South Asia, specifically the Indian subcontinent, appears separated from the rest of Asia. Geographers tell us that the subcontinent was at one time a mass of land attached to the southeastern part of the African continent or a loose entity in the Indian Ocean until it became attached to the Asian geographical plate. In a mountain-building movement, beginning violently about 70 million years ago, sediments and basement rocks rose to dramatic heights, in the process forming one of the youngest major mountain systems in the world: the Hindu Kush Range in the west; the Arakan Yoma in the east; and the highest, perpetually snowcapped mountains in the world, the Himalayas (*Hima* for snow and *alaya* for abode or home) in the north. Among the Himalayas' peaks is Mount Everest, the highest in the world at roughly 29,000 feet. The mountain ranges stretch from the Baluchistan-Iran border in the west, northward toward Tibet, and eastward all the way to Myanmar, a distance of more than 4,000 miles. The mountains protect the subcontinent from the cold winds of China and central Asia and are the birthplace of its principal rivers—the Indus, Ganges (Ganga), Jumna (Yamuna), and Brahmaputra—which bring rich alluvial soil to the plains below. The mountains fence the subcontinent but do not protect it from external enemies, some of whom have used the major passes as pathways for invasion and for trade. Some of the major passes include the Khyber, Khurram, Gumal, Bolan (near Quetta in Baluchistan), and Jelep La and Nathu La through the Chumbi and the Satlej valleys.

The second major division may be designated the great northern plains, from the Arabian Sea in Sind to the Bay of Bengal and between the Himalayas and the Vindhyas. Of these plains, the Indus valley (mostly in today's Pakistan) and the Punjab (*Punch* for five, *aab* for water) would be barren but for the mighty river Indus and its five main tributaries. The Indian part of the plains here covers the Indian Punjab and Haryana. The Ganges and the Jumna form the Doab (which means "land between two rivers"), an important and fertile part of the great northern plains. Thanks to the moderate rainfall and perennial river water supply, agriculture flourishes and presently supports a population of more than 300 million. The two rivers meet at Allahabad and flow as one river, the Ganges, all the way to Bengal, where it meets the Brahmaputra River and forms a combined delta. The region is at once notorious for the disasters caused by the annual flooding occasioned by heavy monsoons as well as for the delta's very fertile soil, annually replenished by two rivers bringing down rich alluvium. The Indus-Ganges plain has a very low, almost imperceptible, gradient of about six inches per mile, making the vast area cultivable and easy for transportation.

The Ganges flows through Uttar Pradesh, Bihar, West Bengal, and Bangladesh and is joined, besides the Jumna at Allahabad, by relatively smaller streams such as the Ghāghara, Gomti, Gandak, and Kosi. The Jumna's principal tributaries include the Chambal, Betwa, and Ken. The Brahmaputra rises in eastern Tibet and, flowing along the eastern Himalayas, drops south into Assam and continues roughly between the Naga Hills on the east and the Khasi and Garo Hills on the west to Bengal. The Ganges-Jumna-Brahmaputra basin is the largest river basin in the country, roughly 1,000 miles long from Delhi to Bengal, covering one-quarter of the country's total area. The basin forms a phenomenal plain with a drop of only six hundred feet in elevation, averaging six inches per mile. Whereas the northern rivers are perennial thanks to the melting of snow in the Himalayas as well as the monsoon rains, the peninsular rivers are completely dependent on the monsoon rains and, though they are generally well fed, remain starved of water for parts of the year.

The two major river basins—the Indus-Saraswati and Ganges-Jumna—gave rise to two major prehistoric civilizations. The Indus Valley Civilization (IVC), whose beginnings lie around 6000–5000 BCE, was notable for its urban culture from about 2600 BCE to 1300 BCE. Although the development in the Saraswati Valley paralleled that of the Indus Valley, the economic and cultural development in the Doab, between the Ganges and the Jumna rivers, was contemporaneous with the later phase of the Indus-Saraswati Civilization.

The third major geographical component is the Great Indian or Thar Desert, which is a poor southwestern extension of the Indus-Ganges plain. Most of the desert lies in India, with a smaller portion in Pakistan. Divided into two segments, the desert extends from the Rann of Kutch northward up to the Luni River, while the smaller desert portion covers the region north of the Luni to Jaisalmer and Jodhpur, with a small stretch between the two deserts marked by rocky terrain and limestone ridges. Both the great and the little deserts, in their western flanks, mark the boundary between India and Pakistan.

The fourth major segment is peninsular India, which is separated from the north by the Vindhya Mountains, or Satpura Range, stretching from the west and declining eastward, more or less along the Tropic of Cancer. It has two subdivisions: the Deccan tableland and the two coastal strips in the west and the east. In contrast to the youthful Himalayan range, the mountains of peninsular India are ancient, estimated to be 3.8 billion years old, creating a region of relative stability and providing the Deccan with very fertile lava soil.

The incline of the Vindhyas eastward has determined the west-east flow of the major rivers in peninsular India, including the Godavari, which has the second-largest river basin, covering 10 percent of the country's area, and the Mahanadi, the third-largest river basin. The Narmada flows east to west, mostly along the Vindhyas in the northern part of the Deccan. The Krishna and the Kāveri are the two other principal rivers of peninsular India. Two west coast rivers—the Tapti (Tāpi) in the north and the Penner in the south—are together responsible for 10–11 percent of the country's water resources. The Vindhyas along with the Western Ghats (also known as the Sahyadri Mountains) and the Eastern Ghats form a triangle enclosing the Deccan plateau and, meeting in the south, forming the Nilgiri Hills.

The two Ghats (literally "steps") drop sharply to the sea in the west, forming a narrow coastal strip with the Arabian Sea, known as the Konkan in the north and central region and as the Malabar Coast and Cardamom Hills in the south; in the east, the Ghats form a broader coastal strip, known as the Coromandel Coast. The Western Ghats have an average elevation of 3,000 to 4,000 feet, whereas the Eastern Ghats are lower, averaging only about 2,000 feet above sea level. The relatively infertile coastal strips, as compared to the very fertile Deccan, have compelled their inhabitants to look to the sea for their livelihood, through fishing or maritime trade.

The southernmost point of the Indian subcontinent is Cape Comorin, where the Indian Ocean, the Bay of Bengal, and the Arabian Sea meet.

CLIMATE

The climate on the subcontinent is as varied as its flora and fauna, its people and their dress and cuisine. It varies from the year-round snowcapped mountains in the north to the year-round hot weather in the south. Although the entire country falls in the tropical monsoon region, the length of the season and the amount of precipitation vary from place to place with the direction of the monsoon. There are two monsoons: southwest from June to September and northeast from November to January. The former starts in the Indian Ocean as a northwest monsoon in May. Then its clouds change direction due to the equatorial tilt to the southwest. There have been different theories about the phenomenon of the monsoons. The one most favored presently is that the low-pressure areas created by the intense summer heat of April and May attract the cooler, precipitation-laden winds from the Indian Ocean. They hit the entire west coast and in attempting to cross the Western Ghats drop a large part of their precipitation, amounting to between 100 and 120 inches from late May or early June until mid-September. As the monsoon winds advance northward, the news of them hitting Sri Lanka and then Kerala, generally in the beginning of June, gives much awaited notice of their impending arrival in Goa and Bombay (Mumbai), four to ten days thence. Across the Western Ghats, the Deccan plateau gets between 20 and 40 inches of rain, depending on the distance from the Ghats.

Another "branch" of the monsoon, by passing Sri Lanka, advances northward through the Bay of Bengal to India's West Bengal and Bangladesh, to Assam and the Arakan Yoma, making Cheerapunji the wettest spot on earth, with precipitation averaging 456 inches annually. Here it does not rain, it pours—in sheets.

The second monsoon, moving to the northeast, is relatively much milder, with a much shorter season. It operates more like a "retreating" monsoon, covers the early winter months, blows over the Bay of Bengal, and hits the Coromandel Coast, Orissa, and southern Bengal. While Bombay enjoys its much desired mild winter, the southern metropolis of Madras (Chennai) could be experiencing a flood thanks to the northeastern monsoon.

Despite all the industrial development in India and its recent globalization and increased lucrative employment owing to outsourcing, India's economy is overwhelmingly agricultural and depends heavily on the monsoon rains. It is no wonder that throughout the ages, the Indian people have been god-fearing, praying to the gods for early, plentiful, but not too plentiful, precipitation. The Indian way of life—the seasonal cycle of the people's activities, their religious observances and festivals, as well their marriage "season"—is principally based on the expected timing of the rains. A timely monsoon and a good harvest translate into substantial purchasing power in India's villages, where nearly three-quarters of its population live.

DRESS AND CUISINE

Generally, North Indians, with Punjabis leading, are a wheat-producing and wheat-consuming people, whereas for most of the coastal population, as well as all over South India, Orissa, Bengal, and Assam, rice is the staple crop and food; they tend to eat rice for their major meals and derivatives of rice for breakfast and snacks. The coastal population and Bengalis (not necessarily coastal), Keralites, and Konkani-speaking people add fish to their diet, and the popular belief is that it accounts for their well-acknowledged cerebral power.

Brahmans all over the country except in the Konkan and Bengal are vegetarians; so are Jains and upper-caste people, particularly Vaishyas in Gujarat. There are a hundred different cuisines all over the country, each claiming to be the best in the country, if not in the world, yet two styles have become popular among visitors to most major cities and towns countrywide: *Mughlai*, which is vegetarian and nonvegetarian, largely Punjabi, with a somewhat liberal use of ghee (clarified butter) and the use of a tandoor (an oven usually implanted in the ground), and South Indian vegetarian cuisine, which is somewhat less oily but spicier. Although the homogenization of food in the two styles has dominated the urban restaurant scene, households continue to be loyal to the different cuisines that have come down by tradition, possibly through the centuries.

There is a greater homogenization in women's dress in cities and towns. Whereas women in the countryside and in tribal communities continue to wear traditional or regional dress, most urbanite young females and college coeds sport *salwar* (loose pants) and a *khameez* (long shirt), in the latest designer styles for the affluent; the not-so-young women tend to wear saris, in the preferred Bengali style. Not a little of this homogenization is owed to Bollywood movie and television stars, who, as anywhere else, wield enormous influence over the youth and those who think young.

Speaking of homogenization contributing to national unity are two elements, completely unplanned by politicians and unforeseen by the constitution. These are Bollywood Hindi movies and popular television serials and the game of cricket. More has been done, unwittingly, by Hindi movies than all the well-planned government campaigns to popularize Hindi. And most Indians think cricket was invented by the English but is really an Indian sport, played all over the country, not only on the formal (battle)fields but also in the lanes and by-lanes of the cities and even villages. Its one-day matches and the tradi-

tional five-day tests in which the country is represented by the best players from all over the nation invoke and confirm nationalism, patriotism, and unity among all, regardless of caste, creed, or gender. Every activity stops or at least becomes secondary or worse when it comes to a popular television serial or watching cricket.

POLITICAL STRUCTURE

Officially, the Republic of India or Bharat (its ancient name) consists of twenty-nine states and six union territories. The latter do not have a parliamentary democracy in the same sense as the states, where the executive is responsible to and removable by an elected legislature. The territories are administered "centrally" for special reasons. The chief executive there, usually a lieutenant governor, is appointed by and responsible to the central or union government. The union territories include Chandigarh, Daman and Diu, Dadra and Nagar Haveli, Pondicherry, Lakshadweep, and Andaman and Nicobar Islands. Until 2004, as the capital of the country, Delhi (like Washington, D.C.) was centrally administered. It was conferred the status of a state on certain conditions, such as that federally owned lands and structures are outside its jurisdiction. There are also restrictions on its authority in regard to law and order and the security provided the central government ministers, high officials, members of parliament, and diplomats.

Chandigarh, which serves as the common capital of two states, Punjab and Haryana, is, for that reason, centrally administered. Dadra and Nagar Haveli, as well as Daman and Diu, were, along with Goa, parts of Portuguese holdings in India. Goa, which was a union territory, became a state in 1987. Pondicherry was one of the five "pockets" under France. Whereas the other four are integrated into the neighboring states, Pondicherry is still centrally governed. The Lakshadweep and Andaman and Nicobar Islands are retained under central control largely because they are physically isolated and are strategically important for the maritime defense of the country.

All twenty-nine states enjoy the same measure of autonomy under the constitution, except Jammu and Kashmir, which have more autonomy than others. There is a special provision in the constitution, article 370, that disallows non-Kashmiris from buying land in that state. It protects the state from being swamped by people from outside the state becoming voters there and thus having a government led by non-Kashmiris. There is no such protection for any other state in the union, every citizen being free to move from one state to another and to buy property, set up a business or industry, run for election, and hold office. All the states have elected assemblies (some are bicameral), with everyone over the age of eighteen eligible to vote. All have executives (cabinets) headed by a chief minister, responsible to the elected assembly. A governor, appointed by the central government, serves as the ceremonial head of state and assumes executive authority only in case of a constitutional breakdown and until fresh elections are held.

India boasts of being the largest democracy in the world, with a free press, radio, and the Internet. There is a censor board both to rate movies and to order "cuts" before being certified fit for public exhibition. The Indian film industry, dubbed Bollywood, produces more movies than Hollywood and has a large audience overseas. Many of the movies have song and dance sequences but are not permitted to show smooching and stop far short of sexual scenes. The actors and actresses are so popular that many of them run for elective positions at the state and central levels and move back and forth between the real and the fictional with great ease.

As for politics, it is a free field for parties of all kinds of opinions, including communists, who range all the way from the ultraviolent, radical Naxalites to the communist government of West Bengal, whose policies are more friendly to capitalism, both domestic and foreign, than any other state of the Indian Union or, for that matter, the country's central government. In the history of independent India, only two states have formed communist governments, Kerala and West Bengal, the latter being under communist rule since 1977. There is a well-founded belief that when communism is wiped out everywhere else (it is nearly so), India will still have communist parties pursuing noncommunist goals!

Since India adopted a constitution in 1950, there have been fourteen general elections held by the Election Commission, which is highly regarded for its integrity and efficiency. In the fourteenth elections, in 2004, there were 675 million registered voters, of whom 56 percent, or about 378 million, cast their ballots. The voting, by and large, is fair and free, with all the contesting parties having a right to have their official representatives present at every stage of the electoral process to ensure fairness. The counting of ballots is also done in their presence, and the results are announced promptly, often within hours of closing the polls. Large numbers of voters are illiterate but not politically so and have changed governments at the local, state, and national levels.

SECULARISM AND RELIGIOUS TOLERANCE

India is a plural society, with people of different colors and creeds. The constitution specifically makes the state a secular institution, which gives rights to all regardless of their religious persuasion or racial origin. Is Indian secularism an altogether Western import or, as many have claimed, an Indian tradition? Those who support the latter contention point to the country's long tradition of offering refuge to persons of all religions and allowing them to follow their beliefs and traditions on Indian soil. Thus, they talk

of Christianity arriving in India long before it did so in the Western world and the convert families of the Syrian Church today tracing their tradition to the first century CE when the apostle Saint Thomas arrived in Kerala and built his first church, in Mylapore near Madras. So, too, the first batch of Jews arrived in India in the first century CE. Their descendants lived and prospered in Cochin, where their temple, built and rebuilt several times, enjoyed the patronage of the Hindu rulers through the centuries. More batches of Jews arrived later, both in Kerala and in the Konkan, where their descendants live to this day, although large numbers of them emigrated to Israel after that state was created in 1948. The third religious group that arrived in India, possibly in the eighth or the tenth century (there are two traditions), and retained its identity and faith through the centuries was the Parsis (Zoroastrians). Though the community's largest presence is in Bombay, their origins were in the coastal Sanjan in Gujarat, where the persecuted Parsis first arrived from Persia and asked for and received refuge from the local Hindu ruler. It is believed that the torch of fire they brought with them provided the source of fire in all Parsi temples in India. All three communities—Syrian Christians, Jews, and Parsis—contributed their best to the country of their adoption.

That same tradition, that of providing refuge to those who ask for it regardless of their origins, led to the

Indian government's prompt decision in 1959 to admit the Dalai Lama and his estimated 35,000 followers fleeing Communist Chinese persecution. The action invited Chinese reproach and was cited as the main reason for China's war with India in October 1962. The Tibetan Buddhists were settled in Dharmasala, a cool hill station where they have established their religious and cultural presence over the past half century.

Enthusiasts of Hinduism's tolerant, secular tradition ascribe it to the Upanishadic belief that all paths lead to the same god or absolute truth. God manifests periodically in different forms, as avatar or incarnation, to guide the human race on the track of morality and righteousness. Therefore, the founders of all religions are saintly persons, God's messengers, who should be revered without a competitive or rival spirit. It is possible to say that such a tolerant tradition has helped independent India make secularism a part of its constitution and system of laws, which are largely based on their Western counterparts.

POPULATION

Most modern literature on India focuses on its appalling poverty and rightly links it to its burgeoning population. With a current annual rate of increase in population at 1.4 percent, or about 18 million people, India adds the equivalent of Australia's population every year. There has been an impressive decline in the rate of births over the past two decades, but at the same time there has been an even greater decrease in deaths thanks to better health care and especially the decline in the number of infant deaths. Promising news is that the population growth in Tamil Nadu, Kerala, and Goa is less than what it takes to replace the dead. At the other end of the spectrum are the "Hindi Belt" states, notably Uttar Pradesh, Bihar, Rajasthan, and Madhya Pradesh. Bihar's former chief minister Lalu Prasad Yadav was not exactly a good model for the state's population, with a score of nine children, while the central government's Ministry of Family Planning has, for the past three decades, plastered on billboards throughout the country its catchy slogan: "We two, ours two."

The 2001 census showed India's population past the 1 billion mark, at 1,027,015,247. Nearly three-quarters of its population, 72.2 percent, live in its more than 500,000 villages, primarily dependent on agriculture. Its urban component of more than 285 million, or 27.8 percent, is almost the equivalent of the total population of the United States or Western Europe. Its middle class, rural and urban, potential consumers of modern manufactures such as electronics and appliances, is estimated at more than 100 million, a market comparable to that of Europe.

The states with at least one-third of the population urbanized are Delhi (93 percent), Goa (49.7 percent), Mizoram (49.5 percent), Tamil Nadu (43.8 percent), Maharashtra (42.4 percent),

Gujarat (37.3 percent), Punjab (33.9 percent), and Karnataka (33.9 percent); the union territories are Chandigarh (89.7 percent), Pondicherry (66.5 percent), and Daman and Diu (36.9 percent). The least urbanized are the states Himachal Pradesh (9.79 percent), Bihar (10.4 percent), Sikkim (11.1 percent), Assam (12.7 percent), and Orissa (14.9 percent). There are two megacities with a population exceeding 10 million: Bombay and Calcutta; three with more than 5 million: Bangalore, Delhi, and Madras; and seventeen with more than 1 million: Agra, Ahmadabad, Allahabad, Baroda (Vadodara), Bhopal, Cochin, Coimbatore, Indore, Jaipur, Kanpur, Lucknow, Madurai, Nagpur, Patna, Pune, Surat, and Vishakhapatnam.

LANGUAGES

The Indian Constitution of 1950 recognized fourteen languages: Assamese, Bengali, Gujarati, Hindi, Kannada, Kashmiri, Malayalam, Marathi, Oriya, Punjabi, Sanskrit, Tamil, Telugu, and Urdu. Hindi was declared the official national language, with English as an additional official language for fifteen years. In 1965, because of the riots in South India against the exclusive use of Hindi as the official language at the central or federal level, English was declared the "associate additional official language" until such time that a "duly appointed" committee decides on a full-scale transition to Hindi. This may take several periodic reviews of the situation.

Meanwhile, the federal government may send a communication in Hindi and English, leaving it to the state government to reply in English and its state language. It is clearly a way of avoiding the embarrassment of retaining the colonial language as an official language long after the attainment of independence. The fact is, however, that more Indians than ever before are using English for national, political, commercial, and communication purposes. Though the number of speakers of English as a "mother tongue" is negligible, the international *Ethnologue: Languages of the World* lists India as having the second-largest group of nationals knowing and using the English language, next only to the United States, and almost twice that of the United Kingdom, at 100 million.[2] This is enabled in India by an increasing number of parents sending their children to "English medium schools" because of the improved prospects for employment, particularly of the international type, whether located overseas in the English-speaking world or in the "outsourcing" enterprises in India itself.

Although the list of fourteen languages included Sanskrit, it has not been the official language of any state because there are only a handful, no more than 3,000, who use it as a "mother tongue." Sanskrit is the language in which the ancient Indian texts were written and is one of the world's oldest languages, believed by some scholars to be the oldest language to be recorded as such. Like Latin, it is a "dead" language, known only to scholars of ancient India and to priests officiating at rituals, whether in temples or homes on special religious occasions.

The agitation in the 1950s for reorganizing India administratively into units based on language cautioned the national leaders of the importance of language as a powerful tool for inducing both harmony and disharmony among people. In July 1969, the Central Institute of Indian Languages (CIIL) was established to "coordinate the development of Indian languages to bring about the essential unity of Indian languages through scientific studies ... [and to] contribute to mutual enrichment of languages and thus contribute towards emotional integration of the people of India." It also has the contrary aim of protecting and documenting "minor, minority, and tribal" languages. The CIIL lists eighteen languages as "scheduled" (that is, spoken by 96.29 percent of the total population) and ninety-six others as "nonscheduled" (responsible for the remaining 3.71 percent). In addition to the original fourteen languages listed in the 1950 constitution, the Indian Parliament subsequently added four as amendments to the constitution: Sindhi, Konkani, Manipuri, and Nepali.

Except for Manipuri, the other seventeen languages belong to two main groups of languages: Indo-Aryan and Dravidian. Thirteen of the eighteen "scheduled" languages belong to the Indo-Aryan group, all drawing from Sanskrit. The Indo-Aryan languages

collectively are used by a little less than 75 percent of the population, with Hindi being the mother tongue of more than 300 million people in the "Hindi Belt" composed of six states—Himachal Pradesh, Haryana, Rajasthan, Uttar Pradesh, Bihar, and Madhya Pradesh— all of which have adopted it as their official state language. So has Delhi, the nation's capital, not usually included in the "Hindi Belt" or "Cow Belt."

The other Indo-Aryan languages, most of them holding recognition as states' official languages, are Assamese in Assam; Bengali in West Bengal and Tripura; Gujarati in Gujarat; Kashmiri in Jammu and Kashmir; Konkani in Goa; Marathi in Maharashtra; Nepali in portions of Northwest Bengal; Oriya in Orissa; Punjabi, written in the Gurmukhi script in the Punjab; Sindhi, in the Devanagari script, which is used by the inhabitants of Kutch, a part of Gujarat bordering Pakistan, and by Sindhi immigrants and their families who emigrated in very large numbers to India following the subcontinent's partition in 1947; and Urdu, written in Perso-Arabic script, holding the status of an official language in Uttar Pradesh and Bihar, where large numbers of Muslims use it as their primary language, and understood by many Muslims in the country. There is extensive literature read by millions in each of these languages, with an active theater in most but notably in Bengali, Hindi, and Marathi.

Of the four main Dravidian languages, Tamil, the oldest, is the majority language of Tamil Nadu, with a tradition of literature going back to some centuries before the Common Era. Malayalam, the youngest of the Dravidian languages, is the state language of Kerala. The others are Kannada, the state language of Karnataka, and Telugu, the state language of Andhra Pradesh. All four languages have a large percentage of vocabulary drawn from Sanskrit. Additionally, there are Dravidian speakers among the Gond tribal peoples in Madhya Pradesh, and the Brahui-speaking people in Baluchistan (Pakistan). The speakers of the main four Dravidian languages constitute about 25 percent of the country's population.

Based on the *States Reorganization Commission Report* in 1957, the Indian Parliament reconstituted the country into states based on language, while continuing to use Hindi and English as the link languages. Ironically, the number and percentage of those who know how to write and speak English, in addition to their "mother tongue," have increased dramatically over the decades. Equally dramatic is the use of Hindi in major cities, notably Bombay, the capital of Maharashtra, where Hindi is spoken not with the perfection the northern Indian purists would like but as a link language in a city where the majority do not speak Marathi, the state language. Given the trend, the southern city of Bangalore, India's "cybercity," will be increasingly inhabited by speakers of languages other than Kannada, the state language. India's growing urbanization may partly change the linguistic configuration, making English and Hindi, in that order, the languages more used than ever before.

Apart from these eighteen languages, it is officially admitted that the total number of "mother tongues" (languages and dialects) spoken in India is 1,683, about half of that number being in daily use. Several hundred of these are tribal languages and dialects, most of them with fewer than 100,000 speakers. Most tribal people live in hilly areas, speakers of one tribal language living in a particular valley being separated from those speaking another tongue by a hill. The tribal people, almost as a rule, know the language of the state in which they are located besides, of course, their own language.

———

NOTES _____

1. Unless specifically otherwise, by "India" I mean the republic, not the subcontinent.

2. See Raymond G. Gordon Jr., *Ethnologue: Languages of the World*.

All early civilizations, including the Indus Valley Civilization, had some unique characteristics. Thus, the IVC was the first major urban civilization with architectural, street, and drainage planning not found anywhere else in the ancient world. Its technical skills were of a very high order, and so was its metallurgical talent for making bronze as hard as steel. For all its expanse, there was hardly any security except for the citadel walls, which were in some cases a protection against high tides or floods. It was par excellence a peace-loving civilization. Nowhere among its 1,500 sites has any evidence been found of armies or caches of weapons, or a major battle or the taking of prisoners of war.   (page 18)

2

INDIA IN
PREHISTORIC TIMES

In the world of countries vying to be in the league of the oldest, India does not lag behind. The Indian subcontinent is, like East Africa, a region known for its grassland environment, where, several millennia ago, early hominids are believed to have lived. Although no fossils of hominids have been found in India, the stone-tool assemblages discovered at several sites indicate that there were hominids there in the Lower Pleistocene age roughly 1.2 million years ago.

Considerable excavation activity in the postcolonial period, in the second half of the twentieth century, has enabled the reconstruction of India's dim past, well before the time of the well-known Harappan Civilization in the Indus-Saraswati River valleys.

Several sites belonging to the Lower Paleolithic period have been found in different parts of the subcontinent: Tamil Nadu, Punjab, Deccan, and the Rohri Hills bordering the Great Indian or Thar Desert. There are also excava-

tions of other Paleolithic sites such as at Hungsi in Karnataka, at Shanghao Cave in the Northwest Frontier Province (NWFP) (Pakistan), and in the Vindhya Range, whose findings are currently available only in a tentative form. Competing claims among those working on different sites make it hard to determine which of the excavated sites is the oldest.

According to the archaeologists of the famed Deccan College, in Pune, the sites at Bori, Morgaon, Chirki-Nevasa, Saswad, and Gunore, all in the so-called Deccan Trap, are notable for the existence of both Early as well as Late Acheulian technology,[1] which was characterized by bifacial tools, representing a pre–hand ax industry. Although the artifacts are associated with extremely rich sedimentary evidence and fossil fauna, no "correlative" hominid remains have been found. In the same region, the earliest hand axes (of the type commonly called Acheulian, after an early find in France) have been dated paleomagnetically to about 500,000 years ago.

Also dated about a half million years old are the Acheulian hand axes at Western Siwalik Hills near Rawalpindi, Pakistan.[2] Of great interest are the findings at Attirampakkam in Tamil Nadu that show a "layered sequence" that includes Middle and Upper Paleolithic and Mesolithic artifacts.[3] Further excavations at the same site have revealed evidence of the Lower Paleolithic age, which would make it perhaps the only site in India recording a continuity all the way from the Lower Paleolithic to the Mesolithic, an "entire stratigraphy" of the Pleistocene Age.[4]

Of similar interest are the hand axes at Didwana, Rajasthan, which can be traced to about 400000 BCE. Taken along with the finds in the Rohri Hills in Jacobabad District, located at the Indus River margins of the Great Indian Desert, there is a continuity with the Middle Paleolithic period and Upper Paleolithic stage of 15,000 years ago. Considering the later development of urbanism in the Indus Valley Civilization in Mohenjo Daro, there is the possibility of links between it and the artifacts of a much earlier date in the Rohri Hills. Archaeologists have found in the latter evidence of abundant quantities of chert, used in the making of weapons, and have deduced that it must have been a major manufacturing center for weapons during the Middle Paleolithic. The continuity of material development in the region may have been interrupted by some radical environmental changes from the alluvial to

drier plains during the Upper Paleolithic period. The findings of the earliest rock paintings in the region also offer new possibilities of discovering human habitation, perhaps as a precursor to the Neolithic age in the lower Indus Valley.

As evidence of even closer connection with the Neolithic phase in India is the large number of Mesolithic sites throughout the country, which chronologically mark the end of the Paleolithic and the beginning of the Neolithic. Associated with the Mesolithic are a wide variety of subsistence patterns linked with hunting and food gathering, fishing, and, in the latter stages, the beginnings of agriculture and the domestication of animals. The Mesolithic hunters used progressively smaller tools with diminutive two-sided blades and tiny microliths, which they attached to bone or wooden handles to make knives, arrows, spears, and such weapons and tools, and often interacted with communities that had already moved to the pastoral and agricultural stages.

One of the most interesting legacies of the Mesolithic hunters is their cave paintings, which are found at some 150 sites in India and show the artwork of the artists of the late Stone Age or Mesolithic period, mostly 10,000 to 15,000 years ago. They are in the form of rock paintings, a large number of them in central India in the Vindhya Mountains—for example, at Bhimbetka in Madhya Pradesh. That single site alone offers 642 rock shelters where people lived. Nearly 400 of them have rock paintings, in some twenty-one colors, including different shades of yellow, purple, green, red, black, and white, their favorite colors being white and light red. They may have made brushes from animal fur or squirrel tail and paints by grinding various kinds of rock and minerals and mixing them with animal fat, gum, or resin. It is likely that they made white from the limestone, green from chalcedony stone, and the most widely used red from hematite, the iron oxide called *"geru"* still used in the region as well as all over India.

Predictably, the Mesolithic hunters-painters depicted a wide variety of hunting situations in which men chased wild animals or vice versa. They also painted a variety of fish, birds, lizards, and squirrels but not snakes, which they possibly feared. There are large paintings close to the ceilings of caves, which most likely were not used for habitation. Such paintings represent large hunting scenarios and show both compassion on the faces of the hunters as well as fear and ferocity depending on the animals and the situation.[5]

India abounds in Neolithic sites, known for the new kind of stone weaponry and tools and, important for human civilization, the sure beginnings of agriculture, animal domestication, and dairy farming. Among the larger Neolithic sites were the Indus-Saraswati valleys in Punjab, the lower Indus in Sind, and the middle reaches of the Jumna-Ganges rivers.

THE INDUS-SARASWATI RIVERS CIVILIZATION

For a long time, until the 1920s, Indian history was deemed to begin with the Vedas, the renowned Books of Knowledge dated by most scholars to about 1200–1000 BCE. Then, in 1921–1922, the Archaeological Survey of India (ASI) announced the discovery of two ancient cities, Harappa and Mohenjo Daro. The first was discovered by Daya Ram Sahni at Harappa on the banks of the Ravi River, a tributary of the Indus, in Punjab, the second by R. D. Banerji at Mohenjo Daro in the lower Indus in Sind. Separated by several hundred miles, the two sites testify to an urban civilization with a population each of about 35,000 to 50,000. For the next quarter century, while the British still ruled the subcontinent, there were no major excavations, and the knowledge of the Indus Valley Civilization, as it was called, was principally limited to those two cities. However, the dating and analysis of the findings, speculation of the people who inhabited the sites, and the possible destruction of the urban cultures by external invaders were all carried out under the direction of two British directors of the ASI: John Marshall from the time of the discovery until 1931 and Mortimer Wheeler for a brief period after World War II. Their frustration in deciphering the script of the Indus Valley Civilization compelled the initiation of some theories, which had the burden of rationalizing its chronology to fit that of Egypt, Meso-potamia, and biblical events. The task of the succeeding generations of archaeol-ogists both Indian and Western, notably American and French, became that much more onerous inasmuch as those who had new theories had first to dis-prove those that had been current over some decades.

All early civilizations, including the Indus Valley Civilization, had some unique characteristics. Thus, the IVC was the first major urban civilization with architectural, street, and drainage planning not found anywhere else in the ancient world. Its technical skills were of a very high order, and so was its met-allurgical talent for making bronze as hard as steel. For all its expanse, there was hardly any security except for the citadel walls, which were in some cases a protection against high tides or floods. It was par excellence a peace-loving civ-ilization. Nowhere among its 1,500 sites has any evidence been found of armies or caches of weapons, or a major battle or the taking of prisoners of war.

In the second half of the twentieth century, after the emergence of India and Pakistan as independent states, the desire to know more about the region's past goaded the archaeological depart-ments of both countries to invest sub-stantially in new diggings. They were joined by archaeologists in other coun-tries, notably the United States and France, who helped in opening some more chapters of the subcontinent's pre-history. The combined efforts have re-sulted in the uncovering of some 1,500 settlements, the majority of them, more than 1,000, along the Hakra-Ghaggar or the dried-up Saraswati River.

The Vedas talked about the Saraswati as a mighty river flowing from the "mountains to the sea," now identified as the Rann of Kutch; when the river dried up is still not known. A noted British geologist of the late nineteenth century, R. D. Oldham, pointed out in 1887 that the Saraswati was responsible in some remote time for broadening some of the Indus tributaries and even creating new channels.[6] In more recent times, several studies of the satellite images produced by the Indian Space Research Organiza-tion (ISRO) of Cholistan and the cen-tral Rajasthan region clearly showed the old course of the Saraswati River and the remains of a flourishing civilization on its banks and those of its tributaries. Expert analysis of the satellite images shows that the Saraswati flowed east-ward to join the Ganges. This is signifi-cant, because when the Indus-Saraswati Civilization declined or was destroyed by natural calamities, the surviving in-habitants most likely fled or moved to the vast plains of the Ganges River val-ley to the east.

Among the most notable new sites on the Indus and the Saraswati rivers are Dholavira in Kutch, in northwestern Gu-jarat; Ganwariwala and Kalibangan (Kali Banga) along the Hakra-Ghaggar (old Saraswati River) in central Rajasthan;

Lothal, a port city in the Gulf of Khambhat in Gujarat; Dwarka, a submerged city in northwestern Gujarat; Banawali and Rakhigarhi, farther east of Kalibangan in northeastern Rajasthan; Naushahro Firoz in northern Kutch; and Shortughai in the Amu Dar'ya (Oxus) Valley in Afghanistan. The findings at these major sites and the more than 1,500 minor ones, whether along the Indus or the Saraswati, show a remarkable similarity that has led many scholars, South Asian and Western, to name the entire region the Indus-Saraswati Civilization. As Jonathan Mark Kenoyer of the University of Wisconsin, the foremost archaeologist of South Asia, explained when the cities of Mohenjo Daro and Harappa were first discovered, "The Indus river dominated the alluvial plain, hence the name Indus Valley civilization. However, now that we know of the presence of the ancient Saraswati river (also known as the Hakra-Ghaggar along its central stretches), some scholars refer to this culture as the Indus-Saraswati civilization."[7]

However, because the Harappan Civilization is a model for most of the sites, many scholars prefer to designate the entire development the Harappan Civilization. Whether Indus-Saraswati or Harappan, the corpus of these 1,500 archaeological sites covers portions of present-day India, Pakistan, and Afghanistan, an area of more than 500,000 square miles. Putting it into the context of other riverine civilizations of prehistoric times, the Indus-Saraswati Civilization enveloped an area larger than the Egyptian, Mesopotamian, or Chinese cultures.

Since the 1980s, archaeologists have labored to unravel the preurban stages, the times anterior to the development of cities in the Harappan Civilization. The process has been dramatically helped by major advancements in the field of archaeology, especially radiocarbon dating and the techniques of thermoluminescent and paleomagnetic analysis. It is well known that all major riverine civilizations went through a long process of Neolithic agriculture and pastoral life before the development of an urban culture and commercial interaction with one another. With some variations, most scholars agree on the following stages in the development from Neolithic agriculture to urbanism in the Indus-Saraswati or Harappan Civilization: the early agricultural or Neolithic/Chalcolithic period, ca. 8000 to 5000 BCE; the regionalization or pre-Harappan era, ca. 5000 BCE to 2600 BCE; the Harappan era proper, ca. 2600 BCE to 1900 BCE; and the disintegration era, ca. 1900 BCE to 1300 BCE.

The Early Agricultural or Neolithic/Chalcolithic Period, ca. 8000 to 5000 BCE

The earliest period shows the beginnings of agriculture, notably in barley and wheat, and domestication of animals such as water buffalo, cattle, sheep, and goats. Some centuries later, following the pattern in all Neolithic cultures, the institution of family developed, which led to the rise of small settlements. The use of material objects increased, and religious symbols slowly evolved during this phase.

The best site that shows this early progression is Mehrgarh, south of the Bolan Pass, about one hundred miles from Quetta in Baluchistan, the southwestern province of Pakistan. Here at the earliest levels, wild barley has been found, suggesting that it may have been present in that region during the Upper Paleolithic period immediately before the Neolithic stage. According to Jean-François Jarrige, director of the French Excavation Project in Mehrgarh from 1974 to 1986, the presence of domesticated wheat and barley, cattle, sheep, and goats there lays to rest the previous hypothesis that these grains and animals had spread to the Indus Valley from Mesopotamia through Iran and Baluchistan.[8] That was an essential ingredient of the so-called diffusion theory, first propounded by British archaeologists such as Sir John Marshall in 1931, linking the Harappan development to the Mesopotamian Civilization. Supporting the new thinking emphasizing the indigenous development is substantial evidence of earlier human habitation in an area close to the IVC. These are the Upper Paleolithic (30000 to 10000 BCE) and Mesolithic (10000 to 8000–7000 BCE) sites in the forests and deserts of northwest-

ern Gujarat and Rajasthan. Such finds have encouraged archaeologists to dig more in the region to find the links showing the transition from the Mesolithic to the Neolithic period.

The Regionalization or Pre-Harappan Era, ca. 5000 to 2600 BCE

Numerous settlements belonging to this period show characteristics of a larger region having a distinct style, notably in ceramics. Thus, in Harappa, there was a development of new techniques first in hand-built and then wheel-thrown pottery, copper metallurgy, stone bead making, and seal carving. As Jonathan Mark Kenoyer comments on the new developments: "Geometric seals were made from terracotta, bone and ivory, and the beginning of writing is seen in the form of graffiti on pottery. Extensive trade networks were established along the major river routes and across mountain passes to connect settlements to each other and facilitate the movement of goods and raw materials."[9]

In sum, the development over nearly a half millennium since 8000 BCE in agriculture, animal breeding, and the use of metallurgy in the manufacture of diverse material objects may have given rise to early commercial interaction and communication by land and water. All this must have promoted regionalization, the growth of a lifestyle over a geographical region, creating a substantial base for a common civilization such as the Indus-Saraswati Civilization.

The Harappan Era Proper, 2600–1900 BCE

The outcome of such activities over an extended period of several centuries increasingly using navigation along the Indus and Saraswati rivers produced a sophisticated urban culture exemplified by Harappa and Mohenjo Daro. By about 2600 BCE, cultural homogeneity had developed over a large geographical area of several hundred square miles, which has rightly been called the Indus-Saraswati Civilization. Also, some of the important sites such as Dholavira, Kalibangan, Banawali, and Shortughai in the Amu Dar'ya Valley in Afghanistan show a common Harappan pattern in their town planning, citadel walls, and granary, producing the same kind of pottery, art objects, and jewelry.

The entire region watered by the Indus and its tributaries (the Jhelum, Chenab, Ravi, and Beas) and the Saraswati and its tributaries (the Sutlej and Drishadwati) would later be called Saptasindhawa, meaning "the region of seven rivers." It was one of the two most fertile regions of the time, the other being the Ganges-Jumna (later called the Doab, "the land of two rivers"). To the east of the Indus, originating in the Himalayas and passing through the forested Shiwalik Hills and flowing in some parts parallel to the Indus, the Saraswati enabled a large number of agricultural and pastoral settlements. The ISRO's image studies have shown that the ancient bed of the now extinct Saraswati was, in some parts, so close to the northern Ganges reaches that it may have emptied itself into the Ganges stream at some point in time. The Indus and Saraswati river systems, mainly fed by the snows and glaciers melting in the Himalayas and by the seasonal monsoon rains, more often than not, caused the two rivers and most of their tributaries to overflow their banks. When the waters receded, they left behind rich alluvial silt and created numerous natural lakes in the oxbow bends of the rivers. Additional alluvial land also became available as the rivers changed courses over long periods of time. The rich soil enabled bountiful crops and furnished material for bricks and pottery. The large network of the two principal rivers and their tributaries was used by the dozens of communities, upstream and downstream, to create an interactive network of boat traffic, carrying surplus grain and minerals as well as manufactured goods to towns and cities, contributing substantially to the growth of trade and commerce in the entire region. It is this interactive network that brought about a homogeneity of culture over such a large region extending to more than a half-million square miles.

A major exhibit, Great Cities, Small Treasures: The Ancient World of the Indus Valley, which was shown among other places at Pasadena's Asia-Pacific Museum in 1997, showed vividly how much the common person's life in contemporary Sind and Punjab resembles the society and its material culture in the third millennium BCE. Among the elements of continuity from the time of the Harappan era proper to the present date are the modes of transportation such as the canopied bullock cart still used in small towns and rural areas and water transportation such as large, sailless cargo-bearing riverboats. The continuity is also seen in the jewelry used by women, including bangles and nose rings. In the spiritual area, too, we see continuities such as the statues resembling the god Siva meditating in a yogic sitting position.

The Harappan Civilization.   Among the most distinguishing features of the urban Harappan Civilization was its city planning. Divided into two parts, most of the cities had a citadel and a lower town, including a granary. The citadels varied in length and height, most of them constructed with mud or mud brick. The streets formed a grid pattern laid along east-west, north-south corridors. Unique among the riverine civilizations, the Harappan Civilization had an underground drainage system, with, at one time, "soakage jars" placed outside each house or structure. The houses usually opened on the sides, with bare walls facing the street in order to keep the traffic dust from entering the dwellings.

Most independent houses had a courtyard in the center, much like an atrium, bringing in fresh air and light; the four sides of the courtyard served as common spaces for household work and group recreation, whereas the rooms opening out from these common inner verandahs served as family quarters or bedrooms. These kinds of plans for single-residence homes that admit light but keep out the dust to combat the summer duststorm season are still popular in Punjab, Haryana, and Delhi.

Unlike the other riverine civilizations, there is an absence in the Harappan Civilization of palaces or very large mansions, which would indicate the absence of kingdoms or powerful principalities. This goes well also with the absence of weaponry and therefore the lack of large-scale warfare and conquest of large territories to bring them under a single ruler. Yet there were different sizes of dwellings, which suggests a certain amount of social stratification. There were independent houses with their own wells as well as multiple tenement structures with common facilities.

The most notable of such public facilities is the Great Bath in Harappa, which must have been a common facility for the common people. Ancient Mesopotamian texts talk of a culture called Meluha in neighboring India in the third millennium BCE in which bathing played a crucial role. One wonders if they were referring to the Great Bath, which offered residents a bath before performing rituals or a convenience to cool themselves in during the insufferable summer. Whatever it was, the Great Bath was an engineering marvel for the time. It measured thirty feet long, twenty-three feet wide, and eight feet deep. It was placed in an open quadrangle with verandahs backed by galleries and rooms on all sides, with a flight of steps to go in and out of the bath. The construction of the water tank showed impressive engineering skills, as it was lined with brick laid in gypsum mortar and reinforced by a wall of burned bricks, creating an enclosure akin to a sauna facility. The walls of the houses were built with kiln-fired or sun-baked bricks, mostly in the ratio of four in length, two in width, and one in height, which "enabled the masons to build the walls in alternate courses of headers and stretchers, a technique that gave them the necessary strength."[10]

Theories of External Stimulus and Cultural Diffusion. Who were the people of the Harappan cities, well populated for the times, connected with each other by road and waterway transportation, engaged in trade and exchange of goods over a stretch of a thousand miles? Trade seals with signs from the Harappan writing system have been found not only in the major cities of the Indus-Saraswati Civilization but also overseas or overland at Ur in Babylon (South Iraq), at Ebla in North Syria, and at numerous ports in the ancient Persian Gulf. When archaeologists first discovered Harappa and Mohenjo Daro, there was a whole body of knowledge regarding the Mesopotamian people and their trading activities thanks to the ability to read their clay tablets written in cuneiform script. There was also the question of setting the IVC finds in the chronological context of the other riverine civilizations. Sir John Marshall and his team may have found an easy way out by propounding the diffusion and migration theories suggesting the IVC was developed by the expanding Mesopotamian culture.

Such interpretations, based on an external stimulus, also held that the IVC people were monoethnic and monolinguistic. With the data from a much larger number of sites, the studies since the 1980s show the presence of numerous ethnic groups. Studies based on radiocarbon dating in the second half of the twentieth century have also led to the abandonment of the theories of migration and diffusion by most scholars, who emphasize instead indigenous development.[11]

Trade and Writing. An impressive aspect of the Harappan cities spread over an area of 500,000 square miles is the existence of a common script and a common system of weights and measures. Thus, the merchants all the way from Harappa in the Punjab to those in the port of Lothal in Gujarat used a binary system for the lower denominations of weights (1, 2, 4, 8, 16, 32, 64) and a decimal system for the larger weights (160, 200, 320, 640, 1,600, 3,200, 6,400, 8,000, and 12,800), with the units of weight equal to 0.8565 grams. As for linear measurements, these were multiples of 1.32 inches up to and including 13.2 inches as well as the use of a bronze rod marked in lengths of 0.367 inches up to 20.7 inches. These weights and measures were enforced both in domestic trade as well as in exports. A major continuity between the time of the Indus-Saraswati Civilization and later times is the widespread use of the decimal system for which India came to be known, the knowledge of the decimal system passing to the West through the intermediary of the Arabs toward the close of the first millennium CE.

We have only a limited knowledge of the Harappan people and their ways of thinking in the absence of an agreement among scholars on the decipherment of their writing system. More than 500 symbols, some of them apparently compounds, as in the later Devanagari script, on pottery and trading seals and on signboards such as the one over the inner citadel of Dholavira have been found. The more than 2,000 inscriptions discovered so far range from a single sign to the longest having twenty-six symbols.

Although very few such short inscriptions have survived, they have been found in numerous sites separated from each other by hundreds of miles, all of

them in the same Harappan script. It is possible given the occurrence of frequent floods that very few of these clay tablets and seals outlasted the ravages of time.

There is no agreement on whether the symbols are ideographic or logographic or some other system. The claims for decipherment vary from S. R. Rao of India, a computer-assisted attempt by Soviet scholars led by Yuri Knorozov, and another by a Scandinavian team led by Asko Parpola. On the other hand, Steve Farmer and Michael Witzel dispute calling the Harappan writing system a script; they argue that the symbols were a "non-linguistic sign system" prevalent in the Near East. In any case, it is only when some sense is made of these signs or symbols that more light will be shed on the social organization, trading practices, methods of government, and, perhaps, thinking processes of the people of the Indus-Saraswati Civilization.

Religion. In the absence of script decipherment, our perceptions of the religion followed by the Indus-Saraswati Civilization can be based only on conjecture. Based on a study of the numerous terra-cotta statuettes, seals, and amulets, experts believe that the religious system of the time had points in common with the later Hindu religion. One such commonality is the seals showing Siva, one of the trinity in the Hindu religion, shown seated like a

Yogi in a meditative posture and surrounded by beasts. A large number of terra-cotta figurines of Mother Goddess have also been found, suggesting to some Siva's consort, Parvati or Uma; others see in them the cult of the Mother Goddess.

Additionally, people may have believed in tree spirits and in an animal cult involving the bull (regarded in Hinduism as Siva's mount), buffalo, or tiger. Some mythological animals are also found in the seals, such as a bull-elephant and a bull-man with horns and a tail. There are some additional symbols, which would show a remarkable continuity in the belief systems of the Indian people all the way from the Harappan times through the Vedic Age to the modern. These are the pipal leaf and the swastika, widely used to this day by Hindus, Jains, and Buddhists.

A large variety of sculptures, mostly of clay, with a smaller number of cast-bronze figures, have been found at numerous Harappan sites. These include small chariots and carts, more like children's toys, perhaps used for religious rituals. Also found are bronze figurines of dancing girls and animals, which represent a highly developed stage of working in bronze. The largest number are terra-cotta figures of males and females, the males with beards and horns, the females standing and decked out with jewelry. The largest number are children's toys. Art of the time is also represented in the steatite seals, a large

number showing a unicorn without a hump, humped bulls, elephants, tigers, and rhino. These seals were used in trade as well as for cult amulets.

There is no common agreement among scholars on the disposal of the bodies among the people of the Harappan Civilization. One thing is certain: the cemeteries were separated from the settlements, whether at Harappa on the Ravi River, Kalibangan on the Saraswati, or Lothal, a port more than a thousand miles away in Gujarat. All of them show the widespread practice of inhumation. The corpse was kept, in some cases, in a brick chamber serving as a grave, on its back, with the head pointing north. Some had ornaments on their bodies, and most had a variety of pottery.

The Disintegration Era, 1900 to 1300 BCE

Sometime around 1900 BCE, the Indus-Saraswati culture disintegrated into smaller groups that lacked the extensive trading networks of the past centuries. As the Saraswati River dried up, the inhabitants of the eastern part of the Indus-Saraswati region moved farther east along the Saraswati's tributaries to the Ganges and Jumna basin. There they maintained continuity with their common past but evolved new styles of pottery and material objects.

No one knows how such a remarkable civilization declined and then totally disappeared. Scholars now completely

discard the theory of an external invasion by Aryans first propounded by John
Marshall, then director of the ASI.
First, there is no agreement that the
Aryans came from outside the subcontinent. Second, if they destroyed the
Harappan Civilization spread over a
large region, there would be some evidence of weapons used, mass deaths, or
the taking of prisoners of war.

What is now generally agreed upon is
that the remarkable civilization suc-
cumbed to a single major natural disaster
such as a massive flood or a disastrous
earthquake of incalculable magnitude,
wiping out a civilization that enveloped a
half-million square miles. The decline
and disappearance of the cities were in all
areas of the Indus-Saraswati Civilization. The excavators find in this phase of

disintegration a dramatic decline in the
use of writing and trading seals; without
the ability to decipher the writing, however, we do not know the reasons for
such a decline. The guess is that it was a
combination of several factors, the principal factor being the shifts in climatic
patterns leading to long-term drought,
repeated floods, and recurring famines.
Perhaps there was a series of epidemics
following such climatic disasters.

Following the disastrous earthquake
on India's Republic Day in 2001 in the
Kutch region, there has been speculation among geophysicists that a similar
or worse tectonic movement may have
occasioned a massive tsunami-style
flooding of the Indus or the shifting of
the course of the Saraswati River to the
point of it drying up totally.

NOTES

1. Sheila Mishra, Sonali Naik, Sushama
Deo, and S. N. Rajaguru, "The Geological
Context of Lower Pleistocene Palaeolithic
Sites in Peninsular India," *Current Anthropol-
ogy* 33 (1992): 118–24.

2. A. Jah, "Palaeoecologic Reconstruction of
Floodplain Environments Using Palaeosols
from Upper Siwalik Group Sediments, Northern Pakistan," in *Himalaya to the Sea: Geology,
Geomorphology, and the Quaternary*, edited by
J. F. Schroeder, 213–26 (London: Routledge,
1993).

3. S. Pappu, *A Re-examination of the Palae-
olithic Archaeological Record of Northern Tamil
Nadu, South India*, BAR-International Series
(Oxford: Oxford University Press, 2001).

4. Y. Gunnell, C. Rajshekhar, S. Pappu,
M. Taieb, and A. Kumar, "On the Depositional
Environment of Lower Palaeolithic Horizons
at the Pre-historic Site of Attirampakkam,
Tamil Nadu," *Current Science* (July 10, 2006):
114.

5. Most of this information is based on
Upinder Singh, "Bhimbetka," http://www
.4to40.com/discoverindia/places/index.asp?
article=discoverindia_places_bhimbetka9/4/
2006.

6. R. D. Oldham, "On Probable Changes in
the Geography of Punjab and Its Rivers."

7. Jonathan Mark Kenoyer, *Ancient Cities of
the Indus Valley Civilization*, 29. See also S. P.
Gupta, *The Lost Saraswati and the Indus Civi-*

lization; and B. B. Lal, *The Saraswati Flows On: The Continuity of Indian Culture* (New Delhi: Aryan Books International, 2002).

8. Jean-François Jarrige, "Excavations at Mehrgarh: Their Significance for Understanding the Background of the Harappan Civilization," in *Harappan Civilization*, edited by Gregory L. Possehl, 79–84.

9. Kenoyer, *Ancient Cities,* 26.

10. B. B. Lal, *New Light on the Indus Civilization* (New Delhi: Aryan Books International, 1998), 22.

11. Jean-François Jarrige and Richard H. Meadow, "The Antecedents of Civilization in the Indus Valley," *Scientific American* 243, no. 2 (1980): 122–33.

The Upanishads (literally, to "sit down near someone") are also known as the Vedanta, or the end of the Vedas, marking the conclusion of the Vedic literature. It is fittingly so because the Upanishads mark the high point of a line of evolution of thought from the time of the Rig-Veda through the Brahmanas and Aranyakas, from a pantheistic faith centered on nature gods to an all-encompassing cosmic reality with the agnostic notion of identification of the individual soul with its cosmic counterpart. Unlike some who argue that they mark a departure from the Brahmanas, others see in the Upanishadic collection of texts a commendable exercise in the interpretation of the cosmogonic data contained in the largely ritualistic Brahmanas by speculating on the connection between the divine and human worlds. Most agree that the Upanishads represent the quintessence of Vedic knowledge.   (pages 38–39)

3

THE VEDIC AGE,
CA. 1200 BCE–600 BCE

POST-HARAPPAN EARLY HISTORY OF INDIAN SOURCE MATERIAL

The discovery of the extensive Indus-Saraswati Civilization and, in general, the Neolithic cultures in different parts of the subcontinent opened new chapters in the story of India's past, but the discoveries cannot be regarded as part of its history proper, in the absence of documents and, in the case of the Indus-Saraswati Civilization, ability to decipher them. There is a different kind of problem in looking at India's past in the succeeding period, the so-called Vedic Age, because the voluminous Vedic literature that gives us so much information about the society of the times was not written down as such but stored in human memory from generation to generation for close to a millennium before being committed to writing. Historical purists who insist on written documents do not easily admit that such caches of "documents," committed to memory and transmitted through the centuries, qualify as historical archives. The entire body of Vedic literature, not just the four Vedas, but all the Vedangas and Upavedangas, amounting to multigigabytes, underwent a process of pruning and weeding, selecting and compiling, all in the human computers, the heads of the gurus and disciples, until sometime around the fourth century BCE, when scholars, rulers, bureaucrats, and others began to put these "archives" into writing. If history is a record of events and changes (and their analysis) in the political, social, economic, artistic, and intellectual fields, to name only a few, then the vast Vedic lore, extending roughly from 1200 BCE to 600 BCE, is replete with historical and topographical information, names of tribes and states, issues of war and peace, of administration and policymaking, of trade and interstate relations.

Two Indian eras, to count the passage of years, were born in the succeeding centuries. There is no record of any system of dating before that time, except the regnal year of the ruling king who ordered a particular inscription to record an event or proclaim a policy. The Vikrama era, which began in 58 BCE, was started by King Vikramaditya of Ujjaini in central India to mark his victory over the Sakas. The second era, called the Saka era, began in 78 CE and was founded in the same Ujjaini, by a Saka king, who marked his reconquest of that city and kingdom. There are some other eras, far less used than these two, such as the Buddha era beginning in 488 BCE (in Sri Lanka from 544 BCE), the Mahavira era, beginning in 528 BCE, and the now obsolete ones such as the Gupta era, the Harsha era, and the Kalachuri era, to name only a few. The Vikrama era and the Saka era are still used by people, mostly for religious purposes. Before the growing use of the Christian era during the British administration and its widespread use by the general public beginning in the late nineteenth century, most historical events as well as historical writing in India used either the Vikrama or the Saka era.

Most ancient civilizations have a mythical history. Writers on India's hoary past show their appreciation of the concept of timelessness when speaking about the beginning of the universe itself. Thus, they speak of the cosmos passing through cycles within cycles. The basic cycle is a *kalpa* of 4,320 million years; each *kalpa* has fourteen *manvantaras*, or secondary cycles, each lasting 306,720,000 years.

There are relatively brief intercycle intermissions during which a Manu appears or is sent down by the creator God, Brahma, as a progenitor of humankind. According to this theory, the world is currently in the seventh *manvantara*, with Manu Vaivasvata as the progenitor. Each *manvantara* has seventy-one aeons, or *mahayugas*, each of them divided into four ages, or *yugas*. The *yugas* of the current *mahayuga* are marked by the progressive decline of the "just" society from *Krta* (or *Satya*), when there was justice and no evil, followed by *treta, dvapara,* and the present "evil" *Kali Yuga*, which began in 3102 BCE.

There are several traditions about how the civilization in India progressed from primitivism to the organization of states. The highly regarded political treatise of the fourth century BCE, *Arthasastra*, endorsed the mythical origin of the king. In the midst of recurring chaos, presumably during the *Treta Yuga*, humans approached Brahma, the creator God, and prayed for a solution. Thereupon, Brahma sent down Manu Swayambhu (self-born), a hermaphrodite, whose female half produced a progeny of two sons and three daughters, from whom came a series of ten Manus. Brahma's dispatching a king, Manu, in response to the human prayers suggests *Arthasastra*'s acceptance of the social-contract theory, made popular in the Western world by John Locke and Jean-Jacques Rousseau, with the former writing about the state of Leviathan, of anarchy, followed by a king who came in as a result of a social contract. In mythical India as in most early societies, once a monarch was consecrated, he was regarded as divine, yet his powers were subject to public approval from time to time.

During the rule of the tenth Manu, there was, in a tradition similar to many early societies, including the Babylonian, Jewish, and Christian, a great flood in North India that washed away everything and everyone except Manu, his family, and seven sages. Their survival was helped by the god Vishnu, who assumed the form of a mighty fish and tugged their boat to higher, safer ground. It was the surviving Manu and his family that produced the human race. The eldest of the tenth Manu's sons, Ikshavaku, was again a hermaphrodite and was regarded as the progenitor of all kings claiming descent from the solar line (Suryavamsha, *Surya* for the sun, *vamsha* for dynastic origin), the last of the great kings being Rama, the hero of the Ramayana. Ikshavaku's daughter, Ila, married to the Moon God, created the lunar (*Chandravamsh, Chandra* for the moon) line. This tradition of tracing their genealogical line from the solar or lunar line continues in most Indian princely families today.

There are three major sources of a genealogical account of Indian history in ancient times: the Puranas and the Buddhist and Jain accounts. Interestingly, there were two separate genealogies, of kings and sages, though not equally consistently for the sages.[1] All

three do not agree on all genealogical details, and, importantly, each one of them has a distinct ethical angle from which the lists are presented. Thus, the Puranas sing the praises of those who conform to the ideal of a king as the protector of society in accordance with dharma. The Buddhist accounts give more space to the republics than the Puranas, which is understandable, since Gautama Buddha himself was born in a republic. Again, the Buddhist authors were interested only in the exceptional, highly ethical kings who were extolled as upholders of the Buddhist moral order. The Jain list is the least exhaustive of the three, with large chronological gaps, perhaps explained by the fact that many of the Jain texts are missing. Moreover, there is an extra emphasis in the Jain texts on the twelve "universal" emperors of the Jain tradition and of the twenty-four *tirthankaras*.

The eighteen Puranas, compiled between 200 BCE and 200 CE, are sometimes, because of their comprehensiveness and historical importance, referred to as the fifth Veda. They drew on all the Vedic literature (the Vedas, Brahmanas, Aranyakas, and Upanishads) to compile genealogies (also providing some details of the principal events in the rule of some of the prominent kings), identifying as many as 153 kings all the way from the first king, Manu Vaivasvata, through a hundred generations, up to the Mahabharata War, which they state took place in 3102 BCE, and continuing down to the rise of the Mauryas.[2] The

Puranas are available in English, in two books by the famous scholar F. E. Pargiter. The importance of these Puranic genealogies is underlined by the fact that almost all of the non-Muslim ruling families in India, in post-Mauryan, medieval, and modern times, used them for authenticating their right to rule based on linear descent.

The Buddhist texts, notably the Vinaypitaka of the Tripitaka (The Three Baskets), are notable for a detailed political account of Buddha's time, with side glances at the society and economy of the time. The Jatakas, stories of Buddha's previous births, are useful not so much for political history as for the understanding of the society in pre-Buddha times. Both the accounts do mention some kings, but far fewer than in the Puranas, instead giving more space to those who were close to the Buddha in his lifetime and in his previous births. Significantly, the Sri Lankan Mahavamsa accounts of Buddhism and its spread give details of the succession of teachers of the Theravada sect. One should use caution in handling such Buddhist historical writing because of the beliefs of such Buddhist writers that no human act is accidental, that all acts are conditioned by past actions in accordance with the Buddhist doctrine of moral causality. Moreover, they believe that "just as an action is related to past events, so it is pregnant with its future consequences." Such an approach "naturally led secondary Buddhist historians

to select, distort and imagine events in such a way as to improve the ethical picture of history presented."[3]

VEDIC LITERATURE

The corpus of Vedic literature consists broadly of two kinds—ritualistic and intellectual—and is classified into four groups: the Vedas, Brahmanas, Aranyakas, and Upanishads. Whereas the Brahmanas and the Aranyakas fall into the category of ritualistic texts, the Upanishads are noted for their wide-ranging philosophical speculation on a variety of subjects, especially concerning the relationship of humans and the cosmos. The Vedic corpus incorporates early human spiritual experience, all the way from being one with nature to the metaphysical world of identification of the self with the abstract cosmic ultimate reality. As for the time when the Vedic literature came into being, there is no agreement among scholars; the chronology adopted here is the one widely in use at present:

The Vedas	1200–1000 BCE
The Brahmanas	1000–800 BCE
The Aranyakas	800–700 BCE
The Upanishads	700–600 BCE

The Vedas and Their Significance

Of the four Vedas, the oldest and most basic is the Rig-Veda. It was composed in Sanskrit in the form of hymns, 1,017 of them, arranged in ten mandalas, or books, of unequal size. Books 2 to 10 claim to be a "record" of what was revealed by the gods to certain ancient families of sages and seers who had been practicing *tapas,* or austerity, over long periods of time. The sages are supposed to have interacted with the gods and "heard" them, hence the generic term for Vedic literature, *Shrutis,* which means "those that were heard." The ancient practice was to indicate somewhere in the body of the text, mostly in the last hymn or paragraph, the identity of the particular seer who had heard it, in the same fashion as an artist would sign his name or rubric in the corner of a painting or work of art. They passed such revelations on to their sons or pupils, who memorized them through habitual recitation, forming a "national" bank of hymns. These hymns fall into a number of genres, from the ritual to the secular, in the process delivering varied materials reflecting the cosmogony and the gods, social and political order, and early economic activity. Some hymns indulge in the theory of politics and philosophical speculation.

The materials in the Vedas underwent numerous revisions and were compiled over a long period of time before the first of them, the Rig-Veda, was completed around 1200 BCE. The first to be compiled were Rig-Veda's books 2 to 7, composed by six of the most respected priestly families: Grtsamada,

Visvamitra, Vamadeva, Atri, Bharadvaja, and Vasistha. Books 1 and 8 were compiled in the second stage, whereas the ninth and tenth were finished in the third stage. The three other Vedas—the Sama Veda, Atharva Veda, and Yajur Veda—were compiled over the next two centuries, from 1200 BCE to 1000 BCE.

Yaska, who lived in the seventh century BCE, classified the Vedic materials into three types: *pratyaksa* (direct transmission), *paroksa* (indirect transmission), and *adhyatmiki* (loosely translated as those with metaphysical or philosophical content). Of all the commentaries on the Vedas, the most comprehensive and arguably the highest regarded is the one by Sayana from Karnataka in South India in the fourteenth century CE.

The significance of the three other Vedas was specific and limited. Thus, the second Veda, the Sama Veda, in 1,810 stanzas, or *rks,* consists of hymns set to music for singing in a chorus led by the Udgatr priest at the sacrifices. With the exception of some seventy-five of them, the bulk of the Sama Veda hymns were drawn from the eighth and ninth mandalas of the Rig-Veda.

The third Veda, the Yajur Veda, contains the formulas and prayers of the chief priest, the Adhvaryu, in a sacrifice. It is a kind of guidebook for the Adhvaryu when performing rituals, be they domestic or royal sacrifices such as the *asvamedha* (horse sacrifice). Though meant for priests, the contents of some of the Yajur Veda texts are important for their content reflecting the social mores of the time. Among the gods mentioned is Agni (Fire), who holds the highest position, because he is regarded as the priest of the gods and as the bridge between humanity and divinity.

The fourth Veda, the Atharva Veda, is a combination of religious and magical formulas. Of its 731 hymns, at least one-seventh were drawn directly from the Rig-Veda. *Atharva* means "holy magic bringing happiness." Scholars hold that the Atharvan charms and incantations reflect the strength of the non-Aryan tribal practices on the minds of those following the Vedas. Thus, along with witchcraft and magic, quite a few of the charms that were believed by the tribal members—for example, how to cure diseases—found a place in the Atharva Veda. In that sense, the Atharva Veda reflects a time when the Aryans worked out a conciliation between their gods and those held sacred by the non-Aryan tribal people. Hence the prevalence of such practices in India through the centuries to this date. The Atharva Veda has a distinct place in Vedic literature as an important source of history and sociology, particularly of the pre-Aryan and non-Aryan society. The contents of the Atharva Veda are varied: songs and spells for healing diseases; benedictions for farmers, shepherds, and merchants; spells for harmony with one's master, at a general assembly, or in a court of law; songs of marriage and love; and songs in aid of royalty and important courtiers.

Creation and Gods. The *Purusa-sukta* of the Rig-Veda's tenth mandala (10.90) speaks of a unique sacrifice that created a social order, which in its basic formulation remains the structure of Hindu society. Since it appeared in the last mandala, it would be reasonable to assume that the basically tribal organization of the Aryan people was long in seeking to organize itself and that by the end of Rig-Veda, it had managed to do so. In order to make it acceptable to all in the growing Aryan community, the sages of the time may have felt it necessary or prudent to make the social structure an outcome of a cosmic sacrifice, thereby making it sacred and immutable. The *Purusa-sukta* was considered so basic and important that it was copied in the three other Vedas.

The *Purusa-sukta* speaks of Prajapati (Lord of Beings), later called Brahma (the creator God), who, not unlike many other early belief systems, was a primeval man, or *purusa*. As A. L. Basham points out, "In the Edda, the god Wodan, in order to obtain magic power, is sacrificed by himself to himself."[4] In the *Purusa-sukta,* in the Great Sacrifice of Creation, Prajapati made an offering of the cosmic being, *purusa,* as a sacrifice to himself. What followed that sacrifice has been regarded as basic and is at the root of the social division into four *varna*s, or classes, later leading to the caste system, a persistent and pernicious element of Hindu society through the ages. It has had a tremendous grip over the Hindu social mind because of its implication of a "divine sanction" for the ordering of society.

From the body of the sacrificed *purusa*, the whole universe was believed to have been created, including the four great classes or four orders of Indian society, each being made from different parts of his body: mouth (Brahman); arms (Kshatriya); thighs (Vaishya); and feet (Sudra). The four vital points—mouth, arms, thighs (loins), and feet—symbolize the four social functions: speech or communication, protection, procreation, and physical action. Again, the four social segments (*varnas*, or classes)—Brahman, Kshatriya, Vaishya, and Sudra—represent the external ordering of the human being. The four divisions of human society parallel the four main cosmic functions in nature: the Sun and the Moon, the Fire (Agni), and the Wind (Vayu). Thus, the first two—the Sun and the Moon—refer to the phenomena of sustenance and constant change and emergence into a new being. They move in the sky, "the one seeing all and the other shaping itself ever anew." As for the Fire and the Wind, their pride of place in the Rig-Veda is an acknowledgment of their prime importance to human existence and civilization. Wind is analogous to breath *(prana)*, constant and essential, whereas human civilization dawned with the use of fire. Here are the relevant hymns of the Rig-Veda regarding the creation of the world and human society:

When the gods made a sacrifice
With the Man as their victim,
Spring was the melted butter,
  Summer the fuel,
And Autumn the oblation.

~

From that all-embracing sacrifice
Were born the hymns and chants,
From that the metres were born,
From that the sacrificial spells were born.

~

When they divided the Man
Into how many parts did they
  divide him?
What was his mouth, what were
  his arms,
What were his thighs and his feet called?

~

The Brahman was his mouth,
Of his arms was made the warrior,
His thighs became the vaisya,
Of his feet the sudra *was born.*

~

The moon arose from his mind,
From his eye was born the sun,
From his mouth the Indra and Agni,
From his breath the wind was born.

~

From his navel came the air,
From his head there came the sky,
From his feet the earth, the four
  quarters from his ear,
Thus they fashioned the worlds.[5]

Thus, the structural constitution of human society mirrored the very structure of the world.

A major distinction of the Vedas is their message to humans to seek identity with nature and accommodate their thinking and way of life with natural changes, whether seasons, signifying harmony, or nature's wrath, in the form of fire and flood, drought and famine, earthquake and tsunami. In that sense, it has closeness with the core of Taoism. All gods (small *g*) are identified with the forces of nature. Their external forms are anthropomorphic, and it is up to human beings to please them with offerings through fire, which serves as the bridge between humanity and divinity. The central theme of the Vedas is to enable humans to conduct their journey of life toward a meaningful and purposeful end. Those may be the factors that have helped the Vedas to endure in India to this day, because the Indian natural environment has basically remained the same, with the people's dependence on the forces of nature—its mountains and rivers, the sun and stars, its monsoons and seasonal changes.

Except for the Upanishads, in which the Godhead, or Absolute Truth, is spoken of in monistic terms, the Aryan society believed in a multiplicity of gods. Thus, the Vedic gods were classified into three groups: *samraj, viraj,* and *svaraj,* representing the regions of heaven, earth, and the middle region between the two, respectively. The Sun, or Mitra-Varuna, presided over the heaven; Agni (Fire) presided over the earth; and Indra, or Vayu (Wind), presided over the middle region (atmosphere). Indra was in the category of *svaraj* (*sva* for self, *raj* for shine or rule), a self-luminous god, the principal god of the Vedas. "He is everywhere and sees everything." Agni was the god of sacrifice (*yajna*), "its eternal preserver, and the one in whom all the gifts of the sacrifice are contained." Indra, however, had a specific responsibility: "to engage himself in a continuous effort to guide the course of the world."

It was important for human beings to establish a harmonious relationship with nature and its various manifestations. The Vedas denote this harmony by the notion of *rta,* the universal order, the cosmic harmony. Individuals sought the good offices of the Agni, to make sacrifices to the gods, particularly every day—twice a day at sunrise and sunset to the Sun and to Indra as the chief of the gods—so that the natural order, the balance between good and evil, was maintained and the "cosmic harmony" was not disturbed. The Vedas held that the universe was governed by laws of nature, which could not be changed even by the gods, who held their high ground through their commitment to keeping the world order, *Rta,* balanced and going. The *Rta*'s manifestation was the Sun, the Moon, the planets, and the cycle of seasons. In the ancient Greek system, a planned order was the charge of the creator god. As the remarkably prescient D. P. Singhal explains, "Vedic *rta* was the functional balance of an already existent single phenomenon in which each part functioned according to its own law of activity, and all of them together balanced each other in the general rhythm of the universe." To the noted French Indologist Jean Filliozat, *Rta* stood not only for the natural order but also for the moral order, and, therefore, represented "an overall determinism. It differs from strict scientific determinism in that it rejects all apparent irregularities out of hand, simply because they are irregular. It is less concerned with physical laws than with norms, less with order, as such, than with 'good' order."[6] It was Indra's special responsibility to maintain the *Rta,* or world order.

The Brahmanas

Chronologically, the Brahmanas followed the Vedas and were, in fact, prose commentaries on them. The Brahmanas represented ritual texts, a kind of manual to help the Brahmans in their task of officiating as priests at different rituals and sacrifices. Although specific Brahmanas were associated with specific Vedas, there were some Brahmans who were experts in two, three, or all four Vedas, known, for that reason, respectively, as Dwivedi, Trivedi, and Chaturvedi. The Brahmanas provide information about a variety of sacrifices,

each directed toward a specific purpose, performed by a prescribed number of priests, or groups of four priests.

Although for the most part the Brahmanas are ritualistic, mechanical, and dull, some portions of them do have merit, chiefly sociological, particularly when the authors used illustrations from social life to make a point or paused to narrate some beautiful, mythological, or semihistorical stories using the ballad form. Thus, included in them are the *gathas* (accounts) in narrative verse form, bringing out legends such as that of the great flood *(pralaya)* and the stories of Creation. Some of them are theological treatises that not only give details of a particular Vedic sacrifice but also speculate about the deep significance of such rituals. At times, the Brahmanas explain the prevalent social and political institutions, including the origin of the state and kingship. Of the Brahmanas, the most valuable in terms of the variety of its contents, and the most quoted, is the Satapatha Brahmana.

The Brahmanas, for the first time, speak of the concept of karma, without specifically using the word. Thus, they say that after an individual's death, he or she will receive a reward or retribution for the good or bad acts done during his or her lifetime. The law of moral causality, though not as well stated as in the later Upanishads, however, does not extend to one's place in the *varna* system. Thus, although there was social mobility during the time of the Vedas by which one could change one's *varna* by changing one's occupation, the Brahmanas increasingly closed such options. One had to be born to a Brahman family to qualify as a Brahman and perform the priestly function.

With such a rigid attitude on the part of the Brahmans, the social mobility of the previous centuries wherein a person's *varna* or class was determined not by birth but by his profession gradually ended. The Brahmans not only refused to teach the sacred lore to persons from the other three *varnas* but also preached that it would be sinful on their part, particularly the Sudras, to learn the Sanskrit language and recite the sacred texts. The Brahmans could be very wrathful and curse the "culprits" to damnation. The uttered word had a lot more power, since nothing was available in written form. Increasingly, therefore, social rigidity crystallized, making birth the determinant of one's *varna*. This was still far different from the later caste *(jati)* system, the groupings and subgroupings within each *varna*.

Yet despite all the attempts of the Brahman class to formalize the religion and close the door to study of the Vedas to non-Brahmans, some Brahmans themselves managed to think and live outside the straitjacket of rigid rituals and the *varna* system. They were liberal and more intellectually oriented than the others. They probed deeper to understand the metaphysical aspects of the sacrificial practices and relate them to philosophical speculation of the here and the hereafter, matter and mind, the relationship of an individual to the cosmos. They were few in number, but their impact was very consequential; they were to be the precursors of the creators of the Upanishads.

The Aranyakas

The Aranyakas (literally, "Forest Books") formed the concluding portions of the Brahmanas. As such, no rigid line can be drawn between the Brahmanas and Aranyakas as between those two and the Upanishads. The Aranyakas were so called because the philosophical and mystical character as well as symbolism of their contents were held to require the solitude of the forests for their proper study. Some others hold that those Brahmans who disliked the excessive stress on the rituals to attain their spiritual and material objectives retired to the forests for deeper thinking on the meaning of those rituals. Hence, the Aranyakas offered a mystic interpretation of Brahmanical rites, rituals, and sacrifices.

The Upanishads

The Upanishads (literally, "to sit down near someone") are also known as the Vedanta, or the end of the Vedas, marking the conclusion of Vedic literature. It is fittingly so because the Upanishads mark the high point of a line of evolution of thought from the time of the Rig-Veda through the Brahmanas and

Aranyakas, from a pantheistic faith centered on nature gods to an all-encompassing cosmic reality with the agnostic notion of identification of the individual soul with its cosmic counterpart. Unlike some who argue that they mark a departure from the Brahmanas, others see in the Upanishadic collection of texts a commendable exercise in the interpretation of the cosmogonic data contained in the largely ritualistic Brahmanas by speculating on the connection between the divine and human worlds. Most agree that the Upanishads represent the quintessence of Vedic knowledge.

The Upanishads were the result of the sessions between the teacher and the taught, very much in the Socratic fashion, supposedly taking place a little before the great Greek guru. Numbering more than 120, the Upanishads have been divided by scholars into three categories. The first category includes the Chandyogya, Aitareya, Kausitaki, Taittiriya, and Kena. The second category includes the Katha, Mahanarayana, Isa, Mundaka, and Prasna. The third category includes the Maitrayaniya and Mandukya. These last two were composed in the post-Buddha period. All the Upanishads were regarded as part of Vedic literature. The teaching sessions between the guru and his pupils were often conducted with the help of parables and maxims.

In general, the Upanishads frown on the sacrificial ceremonial as the means to attain salvation. Instead, they prefer knowledge obtained through meditation and discussion as the means to understand and absorb the Truth. Essential for such a goal is the understanding of the true nature of the ultimate reality, of the Absolute Truth, of the Brahman (not to be confused with the Brahman priests), the universal soul. The goal is deliverance from one's mundane existence through the absorption of the individual soul, or the *atman,* into the world soul, *brahman.*

What is the ultimate basis of things? From the time of the Vedas to the Upanishads, there was always a search for the single universal truth, similar to that in Aegean philosophy. Correspondingly, there was the shift from belief in pantheism to monotheism to monism. Thinking in monistic terms, they sought some one principle as the governing principle for the entire world. They followed the logic by ruling out the various alternatives, one by one—*neti, neti, neti*—not this, not this, they said. Thus, they speculated that it was not matter, mind, life, or intelligence. They held the truth to be beyond or removed from the process of thinking; the ultimate truth lay beyond the world of experience. Some of them sought to identify the cosmic self or the *brahman* with the Creation, distinguished from individual self, although the individual self is also part of the Creation. Therefore, the famous dictum of identity: *Tat tvam si* ("You are that," or "You, as *atman,* are a part of the cosmic *Brahman*"). The identity of the *brahman* and the *atman* has been explained by Paul Deussen: "The *brahman*, the power which presents itself to us materialized in all existing things, which creates, sustains, preserves and receives back into itself against all the worlds, eternal, infinite, divine power identical with the *atman*, with that which, after stripping off everything external, we discover in ourselves as our real most essential being, our individual self, the soul."[7]

The Upanishads present still another approach—the subjective analysis. The Chandogya Upanishad contains an inquiry into the nature of the self. First, it says what the true Self is not and then proceeds to identify it. Thus, it says that the true self is not the body that is born, grows up, decays, and dies. The true self is not the dreaming self, since it is subject to accidents or experience. The self is not the unity of the ever growing and changing mental experiences; neither is it the one in dreamless sleep, since it is empty of all content and is a bare abstraction. The true self is the universal consciousness existing both in itself and for itself.

The Mandukya Upanishad observes that the three states of the soul—waking, dreaming, and sleeping—are included in a fourth *(turiya)*, which is intuitional consciousness, where there is no knowledge of objects, internal or external. Such an intuitional consciousness continues in the midst of all change. It is the *atman*.

Atman and *brahman* are one. The essence of the universal nature is the same as our innermost self: *Tat tvam asi* ("That art Thou"), meaning that you as an individual are part of that *brahman* or the ultimate reality. The nature of this ultimate reality cannot be defined. It can be grasped, however, through intuition, which is not objective like perceptual experience or communicable to others like inferential knowledge. A formal exposition cannot be given. To any suggested definition of reality, we can say only, "not this, not this." In other words, one can say only what it is not because we cannot define it in narrow terms.

By the time of the Upanishads, Aryan society had extended itself farther east toward modern eastern Uttar Pradesh, Bihar, and northern parts of Madhya Pradesh. There were growing conflicts between the Aryan rulers, be they monarchs or chiefs of republics, and their non-Aryan counterparts with different languages and ways of life. Aryan efforts to bring them into their polity and culture would involve increasing conflicts and material losses, as multiple fighting groups marauded fields and pastures, increasing the insecurity among the common people regarding life and property. Continuing with the Brahman-led rituals, sacrifices to gods, and adherence to life based on dharma did not explain the growing incidents of political anarchy and life's uncertainties, which affected "good" people. There had to be an explanation. In the latter part of the Upanishadic period, a small group of ascetics had created the doctrine of karma and the cycle of births and rebirths, or samsara.

The Doctrine of Karma and Samsara. The doctrine of rebirth is essential to the doctrine of karma. Karma is translated as "deed" as well as "willed activity," activities that are the result of will for which the doer is responsible. The migration of the soul of the dead into another body and after death again into still another body is called samsara (literally, "wheel of existence"). The cycle of birth, death, and rebirth repeats itself until the karma attached to the soul helps it to break through and attain a release from the cycle and achieve *moksha* (liberation). The differences in the condition of individuals at birth are explained by their respective past actions, the results of which come in the form of the individual's karma at birth.

Some seers differentiated between the accumulation of karma from a series of previous cycles of births and deaths, calling it *sancita,* and a portion of the *sancita* that a newly born baby brings with birth, known as *prarabdha.* As the child grows into a man or woman, its actions are partly predetermined by its *prarabdha* and partly by its will. The law of karma follows the fundamental law of causation: Every action has consequences, good and bad. However, all the consequences may not be explicit or visi-

ble during one's lifetime. Some will become a part of the accumulation, or *sancita,* and may be evident in the next birth if it comes with the *prarabdha* of the reborn. The body serves as a receptacle for the soul, "a vehicle of mind and character," that moves after the death of a body to another body, which serves as its new receptacle. The Katha Upanishad states, "Like corn does a mortal ripen; like corn does he spring to life again." Later, the Bhagavad Gita puts it similarly: "As a person casts off worn-out garments and puts on others that are new, so does the soul cast off worn-out bodies and enter into others that are new."[8]

The doctrine of rebirth or of the transmigration of the soul thus involves repeated passage of the soul from one life to another for an indefinite period of time until it is able to break the chain. This unbroken process of incarnation applies to all sentient beings—humans and beasts, birds and insects alike. Like Albert Schweitzer's concept of reverence for all life, some ancient Indian seers spoke of the systematic unity of creation, of the minute molecules of dust, air, and water having the same souls as humans. One's rebirth in a new species or the same one would be subject to one's karma. As the Brhadaranyaka says, "According to the quality of their work and degree of knowledge, souls enter various forms of existence, from man to worm."[9] The soul itself never perishes; it is eternal. Once its evil karma is destroyed and it attains *moksha*, there is no more rebirth for it and no more return to samsara.

The twin doctrines of samsara and karma were crucial to most Indian thought from about the sixth century BCE. Their hold over spiritual life in India is such that they still influence if not govern the life of a majority of its people. So much of the human suffering there, and there is surfeit of it, so much of the inequity or lack of logic in rewards or retribution, which would ordinarily lead to depression or suicide, become clearer and perhaps bearable to people because of their belief in samsara and karma. On the other hand, many individuals who lead a life of crime and corruption throw up their hands and ascribe their actions to fate and predetermination.

Are human beings free to do whatever they like, commit thefts or murders and explain them on the basis of their *prarabdha* or karma that predetermined their actions? No, said the sages. A human being is not a helpless tool of karma, for he is the one that wills and acts and is, therefore, "mightier than the Karma." In this respect, karma is different from the Islamic concept of kismet or the Western destination for all human beings, heaven or hell, depending on the nature of the acts and the intercession of the confessors. Sarvepalli Radhakrishnan, a professor of Indian philosophy at Oxford before he became India's vice president and later presi-

dent, explained: "The cards in the game of life are given to us. We do not select them. They are traced to our past karma but we can call as we please, lead what suit we will, and as we play, we gain or lose. And there is freedom."[10]

Individual freedom and free will are parts of the human baggage; all actions are not predetermined, because part of the consequences of actions in this birth determines the *prarabdha* in the next birth. The Nyaya Vaisesika school argued that an individual may not escape deeds, but he can control them by self-discipline in thought and deed; he can strengthen good impulses and weaken the bad ones.

Was the concept of karma an altogether new one and, therefore, outside Vedic thought? Scholars point out that the doctrine of karma is foreshadowed in the concept of the *rta* of the Rig-Veda. *Rta*, or the universal order, applied not only to uniformity of nature but also to moral order, which applied to human beings. T. M. P. Mahadevan explained the link between the thinking on *rta* and the later doctrine of karma:

> The gods were called "guardians of *rta*" and "practitioners *of rta*." They rewarded the good and punished the wicked. The good are those who follow the path of *rta* and keep their vows. Varuna, the ethical god of the Rig-Veda is the upholder of the physical as well as the moral order. . . . Each sacrificial rite has its own re-

ward. . . . Both these concepts, *rta* and *yajna* [sacrifice], anticipate the theory of karma in so far as they imply that each action carries its own reward.[11]

Traditionally, the Upanishads have been regarded as the high point of Hindu philosophy. Among those influenced in the Western world was Arthur Schopenhauer, who regarded them as "the solace of his life" and said they would be the "solace of his death." For years before his death, he read excerpts from them every night before going to bed. The age of the Upanishads closed in around 600 BCE.

CONCLUSION

None of the early Vedic literature was put into writing. It was only with the Jain and the Buddhist canons that the materials began to be written down. Until then, vast materials such as the Vedas were memorized and passed on from generation to generation. Partly the reason for not writing was that the writing materials, such as palm leaves, were prone to perish in a tropical or flood environment, whereas the human memory, passed on from the guru to the pupil, would last indefinitely.

Many of the beliefs and practices of Vedic times, whether in the form of rituals, the conception of the universe or the world order, or norms for the life of the individual, family, and the society, passed on to later times and to Hin-duism and remain extant in present-day India. Some of the spiritual thinkers and religious reformers have regarded Vedic thought and life as the purer form of Hinduism, devoid of the caste system and the pernicious practice of untouchability. They point to the high place of morality and of women in Vedic society and the obligation of the rulers to hold on to ethical norms.

Two very important concepts in the early Vedic literature that held a firm place and constituted anchors of Indian society were *rta* and *dharma*. The Vedic sages were conscious of the fine balance of diverse forces in the universe and were concerned that the world order, or *rta*, be maintained. They believed that it was the god Indra's special responsibility to deal with the forces of nature, such as the wind and the rain, and that the god Siva meditated in the Himalayan heights on Mount Kailasa in order to retain *rta*. Human beings had to pray and propitiate the gods, who represented the diverse natural forces, to keep the *rta* in balance for the good of all. In order to maintain the *rta*, they offered sacrifices to the gods and chanted the sacred mantras because they believed in the power of the spoken word, provided they were uttered in a certain order and cadence.

By the time of the Brahmanas, the ritual overwhelmed the reasoning that gave the Brahmans—officiating priests and scholars, astronomers and astrologers, social and royal advisers—the highest place in the societal hierarchy. The sacrifices had to be performed according to a set procedure, known only to the specialist priests. The mantras had to be recited only in a certain order and tone by those whose life and daily routine spelled purity, conforming as they did to a prescribed regimen, the knowledge of which was passed on from generation to generation by the gurus to the pupils who lived with them as part of their households. All this, the sages and the masses believed, made for an integrated life in which each individual, family, and the society's components carried out their duties or observed the dharma—all directed to the maintenance of the *rta*.

—————— APPENDIX ——————

VEDIC PEOPLE AND THE ARYAN INVASION THEORY

For most of Indian history, until the British extended their territorial and administrative control over large parts of the subcontinent from 1757 to 1848, there was no dispute about the indigenous Indian authorship of Vedic literature. Beginning in the late eighteenth century when British rule began in earnest and more so in the second half of the nineteenth century, when social Darwinism gripped the British colonial mind, some British scholars and a prominent German scholar, Max Muller, then living in Britain and benefiting from the subsidies periodically provided by the India Office, chose to ascribe the authorship of the Vedas to the "Aryans," who, they maintained, invaded India somewhere around 1500 BCE. According to the so-called Aryan invasion theory, the language of the Vedas, Sanskrit, had close affinity not only to the Avesta of the Iranians but also to some older European languages such as Old Greek, Illyrian, Tarentino, Gaulish, Irish, Welsh, Gothic, Umbrian, and, importantly, Latin. Lists of words in such "Indo-European" languages were compiled to underline their commonality with Sanskrit, and it was hypothesized that a common pre-Sanskrit language existed among the Indo-European people before they migrated from their homelands.

Most proponents of the Aryan invasion-migration theory argued that the homeland of the Aryans was located near the Caspian Sea. Despite the passing of more than one and a half centuries since the postulation of the theory, to date scholars have not been able to identify that common language.

The demographic movement occurred in two principal directions–westward to Europe and southwest to Iran, from which one stream invaded India. The event was dated around 1500 BCE to synchronize with the chronology of the movement of some other "Indo-European" groups, the Mittanians, Hittites, and Kassites in the Middle East.

Later in the discourse, some scholars preferred to see the process of the Aryan movement all the way to India as migration rather than use the offensive term *invasion*. It was held that the light-skinned invaders, or immigrants, used horse-driven chariots and weaponry made of iron to overwhelm easily the pre-Aryan inhabitants of the Punjab and northwestern Pakistan. These were the dark-skinned *dasyus* or *dasas*, who were pushed to the eastern and southern parts of the subcontinent. A couple of centuries later, the newcomers, who called themselves the *Aryas*, or Aryans, began composing the Vedas.

The theory helped the British colonial rulers in a variety of ways. First, following their practice of divide and rule, they used the theory to divide the subcontinent's population among the Aryans, mainly in the North, and the Dravidians, in the South. Second, by identifying the higher classes among the Hindus as Aryans, they created a gulf between them and the lower classes who did not read Vedic literature. Third, the theory removed the odium of British alien rule by indicating that they were fellow "Indo-Europeans," doing nothing different from what the ancestors of the upper-class Indians, the Aryans, had done some two and a half millennia earlier. The British colonial rulers would carry on their "civilizing mission" with the help of their historical cousins in India.

After defeating the *dasyus*, the Aryans were alleged to have settled in the Saptasindhava, "the land of seven rivers," five constituting the Punjab (*punch* for five, *aab* for water or rivers) in addition to the Saraswati and the Drishadwati. Later, they moved eastward to the Doab, or "the land between the two rivers," namely, the Ganges and Jumna. By the time of the Upanishads, the combined region of the Saptasindhava and the Doab was called the Aryavarta, "the land of the Aryans," whose distinction was that the people there, Aryans and non-Aryans alike, followed Vedic culture. Many of the beliefs of the Vedic period passed on to the Sanatana Dharma (the orthodox religion), or Hinduism, the dominant religion of the subcontinent throughout its history.

The Aryans (meaning "noble" in Sanskrit) regarded themselves as "noble" in spirit and character. Because the Nazis called themselves Aryans, the term has come into disrepute. The preferred term is, therefore, *Indo-Europeans*, although that term properly refers to language, not a race. To quote Romila Thapar, a well-known historian of ancient India:

> Aryan is in fact a linguistic term indicating a speech-group of Indo-European origin, and is not an ethnic term. To refer to the coming of the Aryans is therefore inaccurate. However, this inaccuracy has become so current in historical studies of early India that it would sound unduly pedantic to refer to the Aryans as "the Aryan-speaking people." Their ethnic identity is not known on the basis of the Indian evidence.[12]

The most common affinity, however, is with Avestan, the language of ancient Iran. The two peoples had common gods, common organization of society into four *varnas* (classes), the religious initiation of youth *(upanayana* or *nawroj),* the pantheon of thirty-three gods, the religion based on sacrifice, and most of the technical terms employed in it such as *yajna, mantra, soma, hotar,* and so on. Yet there were differences. In the Avestan language, *asuras* were gods, and *devas* were evil spirits, exactly the opposite of what they were and have always been in India.

Criticism of the Aryan Invasion–Migration Theory

Much water has passed through the Indus-Saraswati and Ganges-Jumna rivers since the Aryan invasion theory was first enunciated and later modified as the Aryan migration theory. The best work summarizing the debate and critiquing it is Edwin Bryant's work *The Quest for the Origins of Vedic Culture: The Indo-Aryan Migration Debate.* Here is how he summarized the centrality of the debate for Indian history:

> The solution to the Indo-European problem has been one of the most consuming intellectual projects of the last two centuries. It has captivated the imagination and dedication of generations of archaeologists, linguists, philologists, anthropologists, historians, and all manner of scholarly, and not so scholarly, dilettantes.[13]

In the process, many scholars and politically oriented nonscholars have muddied their hands, lost their balance, and revealed their egos—a lot of sound and fury, but very little light. The discourse has at times been unsavory, unproductive, and, indeed, inconclusive.

The critique of the Aryan invasion-migration theory covers several grounds. First is the lack of textual evidence in the Rig-Veda to a "conscious memory" of an Aryan warrior past or of their homeland outside the Indian subcontinent, as most immigrants in a diaspora would have. The recorded migrations of a later date such as that of the Bactrians and Scythians in the three or four centuries before the Common Era as well as the invasions and migrations of the different hordes of Afghans, Mongols, and Turks from the seventh to the sixteenth centuries maintained contact with the lands of their origin and left nostalgic references to them in individual memoirs, travel accounts, and historical accounts. The Vedic people, if they did migrate from central Asia, left no such references to their homeland in their extensive literature. Nor did any other people outside the Indian subcontinent develop any literature, religious or secular, in Sanskrit, the language of the Vedas. For the migration theory to be valid or plausible, one would have to assume that *all* Sanskrit-speaking people migrated in one small time segment into the Indian subcontinent, leaving no links behind. In fact, there is no evidence in any of the Vedic hymns to suggest that the Vedic people were intrusive to the area. Importantly, there is a complete lack of any archaeological evidence whether in northwestern India or Afghanistan corroborating the fact of an Indo-Aryan invasion or migration. The lack of such a connection is the weakest point in the Aryan invasion-migration theory.

Second, the invaders or immigrants are supposed to have dominated the indigenous people by virtue of their use of horse-driven chariots and iron weapons. More recent archaeological evidence of horse bones in Lothal, Kalibangan, Surkotada, and Ropar and of iron in the later Vedic period in the Ganges-Jumna region prove that horse and iron were not introduced from outside the subcontinent. As for the use of horse-drawn chariots by invaders or immigrants, such a possibility belies the unsuitability of the mountainous and desert terrain the invaders would have had to traverse before reaching the Punjab plains. Moreover, there is no archaeological

evidence of a military interaction between outsiders and the indigenous inhabitants. Nor is there evidence of the alleged massacre of the inhabitants, prisoners of war, or iron weaponry supposedly used to overwhelm the pre-Aryan inhabitants.

Third, there is reason to assume that some of the practices of the Vedic people were the same as those in the later stages of Harappan civilization, showing a continuity and lack of any input from outside the subcontinent. Thus, the sacrificial rites and rituals elaborated in the Vedic texts, particularly in the Atharva Veda, are similar to the practices in the Indus-Saraswati Civilization. For example, the fire altars at Kalibangan, Lothal, and some archaeological sites in Rajasthan closely resemble Vedic sacrificial fire altars. Further, the bones of oxen, potsherds, shell jewelry, and other items used by the Vedic Brahmans are strikingly similar to those used in the Harappan civilization. All this suggests continuity of religious practices from the Harappan civilization to the Vedic Age and that the Brahmans of Vedic times were successors to the Harappan priests. Considerable compelling evidence of many items such as chess pieces, dice, terra-cotta animal and goddess figurines, decimal weights and measures, and figures in yogic *asanas* (positions) in the Harappan civilization show vital links between Harappan and later "Aryan" settlements in the Gangetic plain.

Fourth, the structural commonality of the Indo-European languages does not have to be a product of Aryan invasion. It may have been a by-product of the trade contacts between the Harappan civilization and Babylon, Egypt, and Crete in the third and second millennia BCE. It is possible that such a linguistic commonality developed as traders and others traveled from the Middle East and the Mediterranean to Europe during the Roman and Byzantine empires in the first millennium and a half CE.

Fifth, after the discovery of the Harappan and Mohenjo Daro sites in the 1920s, it was assumed that the Indus Valley Civilization was derived from the civilization of the Middle East, probably Sumerian, as antecedents of the IVC were not found in India. Recent excavations, notably at Mehergarh by French archaeologists, have shown that all the antecedents of the IVC were present within the subcontinent going back to the time before 6000 BCE.

Last, the critics of the Aryan invasion-migration theory point out recent genetic-research findings in regard to the subcontinent's people. *National Geographic* reported in January 2006 that a study made by the government-owned National Institute of Biologicals in Noida of thirty-two tribal and forty-five caste groups throughout India had revealed that the large majority of modern Indians descend from South Asian ancestors who lived on the Indian subcontinent more than 10,000 years ago.[14]

In conclusion, the Aryan invasion-migration theory seems to have imploded. However, one needs to explain the commonality between the vocabulary of Sanskrit and some European languages, the so-called group of Indo-European languages.

NOTES

1. The Puranic genealogical lists more or less agree with those compiled by the Greek writers Arrian and Diodorus and the Greek ambassador to the Magadha court in the fourth century BC, Megasthenes. The total covered by these lists was 6,042 years, very close to the later accounting by Pliny the Elder, who put it at 6,451 years and 3 months. There were several fairly long intermissions, lasting some generations, when monarchy was supplanted by democratic republics.

2. A. K. Warder, *An Introduction to Indian Historiography* (Bombay: Popular Prakashan, 1972), 30.

3. A. L. Basham, *The Wonder That Was India: A Survey of the History and Culture of the Indian Sub-continent Before the Coming of the Muslims,* 240.

4. Ibid., 240–41.

5. RV 10.90 quoted in ibid., 240–41.

6. D. P. Singhal, *India and World Civilization,* 1:157; Jean Filliozat quoted in Rene Taton, ed., *Ancient and Medieval Science,* 134–35.

7. Paul Deussen, *Philosophy of the Upanishads,* translated by Rev. A. S. Geden (Edinburgh: T. T. Clark, 1906).

8. Katha, II, 6; Bhagavad Gita, II, 22.

9. Brhadaranyaka, IV, iv, 5.

10. Sarvepalli Radhakrishnan, *The Hindu View of Life* (London: George Allen and Unwin, 1927), 75.

11. T. M. P. Mahadevan, *Outlines of Hinduism*, 3d ed. (Bombay: Chetana, 1999), 55–56.

12. Romila Thapar, *A History of India*, 27.

13. Edwin Bryant, *The Quest for the Origins of Vedic Culture: The Indo-Aryan Migration Debate* (Oxford: Oxford University Press, 2001), 7.

14. *National Geographic News,* January 10, 2006.

The Buddha did not nominate his successor. When he was asked who would succeed him, he answered, "The truths and the rules of Order which I have set forth and laid down for you, let them, after I am gone, be the Teacher for you." A council met at Rajagriha after his death to make as complete and authentic a collection of the teachings of the master as was possible. It was not until two centuries later that the teachings were available in the form of Tripitaka (The Three Baskets) . . .   (page 56)

4

BIRTH OF TWO RELIGIONS
Buddhism and Jainism

Buddhism and Jainism were both products of similar social, political, and spiritual milieus, particularly on the frontiers of the Aryanized areas, representing an anti-Brahmanical movement. Both religions were born and prospered in the less Aryanized area of the time, in Magadha, modern-day Bihar. The reaction from within the Vedic fold to Brahmanical supremacy and a life dominated by mechanistic rituals and sacrifice came up in the form of Upanishadic philosophy and an approach to life as a pursuit of Absolute Truth in which the brahman (the Universal Soul) and the *atman* (the individual soul) were regarded as parts of the same cosmos. All Upanishads were a reaction against ritualistic Brahmanism; some of them taught a pantheistic philosophy, seeking Universal Reality as the Truth behind the multiplicity of gods and advocating an intellectual and spiritual approach aimed at deliverance by the union with that reality. From outside the Vedic field came at least sixty-three identifiable schools of philosophy, some of them influenced by South Indian Dravidian thought, which protested against the orthodox Brahmanical ritual sacrifice–based approach. Not all of them had a large following. In fact, most of such protest faiths merged into the emerging Hinduism. Only Buddhism and Jainism were successful in securing a large following and maintaining their identity to this date as separate religions.

By the sixth century BCE, the Brahmans had practically closed the sacred Vedic learning to non-Brahmans. Most people, including the followers of Jainism and Buddhism, believed in the twin Vedic (Hindu) doctrines of karma and samsara (the cycle of births, deaths, and rebirths). Where they would differ with the orthodox Brahmans would be in the prescription for breaking the cycle of births, deaths, and rebirths and attaining salvation. The intellectual approach to salvation was denied to most people because Sanskrit, the language of that learning, had become too stylized and the scholars declared Prakrit as lacking the sophistication required for any fine-tuned intellectual discourse. Buddhism would be preached in Pali and Jainism, for the most part, in Ardha-Magadhi.

Both Jainism and Buddhism enjoyed the patronage of the Maurya rulers, Jainism at the hands of Chandragupta Maurya and Buddhism during the reign of the more powerful Asoka. Of the two, Buddhism would become a world religion and remains to this date the majority faith in Sri Lanka, Tibet, mainland Southeast Asia (Myanmar, Thailand, Laos, Cambodia, and Vietnam), and East Asia (China, Korea, and Japan). As for the subcontinent, Buddhism was, for the most part, absorbed by Hinduism, except for about 2 million people in India's border areas, including Ladakh, and about 1 million people who converted to that faith following the conversion of the eminent leader of the harijans, or *dalits*, B. R. Ambedkar, in October 1956. They are styled Nav-Buddhas (new Buddhists) and are predominantly in Maharashtra. As for Jainism, it exists today mostly in Gujarat, Maharashtra, and Rajasthan, with somewhat lesser numbers in Karnataka and Madhya Pradesh, and in the Indian diaspora, totaling a little more than 4 million people. Until very recently, when the Jains began to reassert their separate religious identity, the Hindus, particularly in Gujarat, had tended to downplay their separateness because of many interfaith (Hindu and Jain) marriages and similar dietary and sociocultural habits.

BUDDHISM

Today, Buddhism is a world religion with 708 million people of that faith. One out of about nine people on earth is a Buddhist belonging to the two main sects of Buddhism: Mahayana and Theravada (Hinayana).

Buddhism was a revolt against the formalized, mechanical, sacrificial Brahmanism. It sought a deeper solution to the problems of the inner life. It rejected the authority of the Vedas, teaching an independent morality that could attain liberation of the soul from the bondage of samsara, the seemingly endless cycle of births, deaths, and rebirths. That, the Buddhists said, was the Buddha's contribution to the world of the suffering.

The Life Story of Buddha

The facts of the Buddha's life are presented in the *Book of the Great Decease*. As in most cases of founders of religions, his "biography" was written in about 70 BCE, over 200 years after his death, or *parinirvana*. It came down, generation after generation, through oral tradition. Fact and fiction were mixed in the narrative, which was committed to writing in about 70 BCE.

Buddha means "the Enlightened One." He was born Gautama Siddhartha, son of Suddhodana, a Sakya chieftain of Kapilavastu, a small principality near the ancient site of Lumbini on the border of India and Nepal, in about 563 BCE. When his mother, Mahamaya, was pregnant with him, she had a dream in which an elephant with a lotus flower entered her side. The court astrologer interpreted the dream to mean that the child would be a son and that he would be either a universal emperor or a universal teacher. One soothsayer added that when the child grew up, he would be so impressed by four "sights" or "visions" that he would decide to become a universal teacher.

In the Lumbini groves where he was born, the baby stood up, took seven steps, sang seven verses, and said: "This is my last birth—henceforth there is no birth for me." The creator God, Brahma, came down, held him on a cloth of gold, and bathed him in waters of a spring that suddenly gushed forth. Serpents and *nagas* (cobras) attended the event in honor of the divine child's birth. As the child grew up, he was trained in all arts appropriate to a prince. As a Kshatriya prince, Gautama showed himself to have superior qualities of strength and intelligence. He was married with great pomp to the beautiful and accomplished Yashodhara, whom he had won in a contest. Gautama's father continued, however, to be concerned about the prophesy that Gautama would not become a universal ruler if he saw misery.

Young Gautama led a normal life but did not appear happy. One day, as he was having a chariot ride in the city's park, he saw four "sights," three of them—an aged man, a sick man, and a corpse—all representations of pain and misery. The fourth "sight" was an ascetic, calm and serene. With the last sight, Gautama felt relieved.

He was concerned with the question of pain and misery and how to end it for all.

When the charioteer reported the event to Gautama's father, he took extra precautions, multiplying the pace of pleasures for Gautama. There were great festivities as Yashodhara delivered a son, Rahul. On the same night, after his wife and son were fast asleep, Gautama took leave of them and left for the forests with Channa, his charioteer. Before disappearing into the forests, Gautama removed his jewelry and gave it to Channa; he exchanged his own clothes for those of his charioteer. Buddhist annals call the event "the Great Renunciation." When Gautama's father came to know of what had happened, he was aghast; there is no mention of the fate of the charioteer.

During the next fourteen years, Gautama tried a variety of ways to realize the Truth and solve the riddle of misery. He met many hermits and sages. Most of them refused to teach him Vedic lore because he was not a Brahman. Finally, one sage, Alara Kalama, agreed, and Gautama devoted himself to learning everything from the Vedas to the contemporary Upanishads. He concluded that the solution to the problem of forever ending human misery would not come from self-discipline and knowledge. Therefore, he joined a group of five ascetics who were practicing fasting and self-mortification. He tried it for six years. Instead of seeing light, he fainted. Finally, at the age of thirty-five, he sat cross-legged under a large pipal tree (now called the Bodhi Tree, a sacred site) at Gaya (since called Bodh Gaya), in Magadha (today's Bihar). After forty-nine days of meditation, Gautama resolved the riddle of suffering. Legend has it that toward the end of that period, he was surrounded by gods and spirits. Mara, the evil spirit representing temptation, offered him all kinds of wealth and pleasures including, finally, the Universal Empire. The gods, who wanted Gautama to succeed, helped him in the opposite direction. Gautama was unmoved by Mara's temptations. The gods won; Gautama won. Gautama attained Enlightenment; he became the Buddha.

After spending an additional seven weeks contemplating the great Truths he had just encountered in his Enlightenment, the Buddha went to Varanasi (Benares) or Sarnath, and delivered his First Sermon in the Deer Park to five ascetics or, in Buddhist phraseology, set in motion the Wheel of Law or enunciated the Doctrine of Righteousness *(Dharma-chakrapravartan)*. Buddhists regard four events as the most important and sacred in the life of the Buddha: his birth, Enlightenment, First Sermon, and death.

Thereafter, for the next forty-five years, the Buddha had a regular schedule of moving about to spread the message for eight months and staying in one place for four months of the monsoon. This was called the *vasa*. It would be the same schedule for the monks he ordained. As a mendicant preacher, Buddha converted large numbers of people, including his wife, son, and father. He had two types of disciples: monks (*bhikkus*, literally, "beg-gars," in Pali) and lay disciples *(upasakas)*. The monks wore yellow robes; their worldly possessions were limited to a begging bowl, staff, razor, and toothpick. They would, as they do today, visit the homes of people, collecting alms, which would be brought to the *vihara* (monastery), eat one meal before noon, and spend the rest of the day in meditation, reading, and discourse. At the insistence of his foster mother and aunt, Krsa-Gautami, but most reluctantly, Buddha agreed to admit women as nuns. Together with the monks and nuns, the Buddhist Order or the Samgha was established.

The Buddha and his monks preached not in Sanskrit but in Pali, the language of the masses in that part of India. He performed no miracles. When a woman, distraught over the death of her child, asked the Buddha to give it life, he asked her to bring some rice from a home that had never experienced death.

He died at the age of eighty in 483 BCE after eating a meal at Kusinagara. The meal consisted of whatever was dropped into his bowl that day. The texts say that he died from eating *sukara-maddava*, which is translated as "sweetness of pig" but also as truffles, poisonous underground fleshy fungi. Either way, it did not matter for the vegetarian Buddha, who had renounced violence. He had no appetite, only hunger, and his practice was to eat whatever was offered by his followers in the form of alms in early morning when he begged from house to house. He was beyond enjoyment of a meal. With his death, he broke the cycle of births and deaths and achieved *parinirvana.* As he is supposed to have said at his birth, there would be no more rebirths for him.

Buddhist Philosophy

Crucial to the understanding of Buddha's message is his First Sermon at Sarnath. It enunciated what the Buddhists call the Four Noble Truths: (1) existence is suffering whether it be birth, death, sickness, or old age (manifestations of pain); (2) suffering is born of desire; craving for lust and unfulfilled desires lead to rebirth (Cause of Pain); (3) the Cessation of Desire (forsaking, relinquishment, release, and detachment from desire) leads to the Cessation of Pain; and (4) when desire ceases, rebirth ceases, which is the highest good—one attains Nirvana; the Cessation of Desire is attained by following the Noble Truth of the Path.

The Cessation of Desire is attained by following the good law that comprises purity in deed, word, and thought; the observance of the ten injunctions; and pursuit of the Eightfold Path *(asthangika marga)*: Right Belief, Right Thought (freedom from lust, incest, ill-will, and untruthfulness), Right Speech (no lying, harsh language, or vain talk), Right Action (nonviolence, no stealing, and no sexual misconduct), Right Means of Livelihood, Right Effort (avoid evil thoughts and arouse good thoughts), Right Mindfulness (or vigilant attention to every state of the body, feeling, and mind), and Right Meditation or Con-

centration (on a single object for special consciousness in deep meditation). The Right Path is the Middle Path. By following the path, a disciple aims at complete purity of thought and life, hoping to become an *arahat,* one freed from the necessity of rebirth, ready for Nirvana. The ten injunctions are not to kill, not to steal, not to commit adultery, not to lie, not to speak ill of other people, not to indulge in faultfinding, not to indulge in profane language, to abstain from covetousness, to abstain from hatred, and to avoid ignorance.

Buddha accepted the concept of karma, according to which each event brought its own consequences and placed value on the moral improvement of an individual. Karma is autonomous and functions independently as a law. Though he accepted a modified concept of karma, he denied the Hindu and Jain concept of intact transmigration of the soul. At the same time in what appears as a contradiction, he agreed that the newly born does suffer from the actions of the life that has ended. He said that individuals, like everything else, are constantly in flux; life is an ever-flowing stream of events. Rebirth is not transmigration but "a continuity in life series, in which process karma serves as a causal connection." He denied the existence or the immortality of an individual soul (the *atman*) as well as the Upanishadic concept of the Universal Soul (the *brahman*). Therefore, his three basic propositions were that life is transitory in a state of continual unrest, that life is pure misery, and that no being, including human, has a soul. He said if these three basic facts were understood, a human being "will break all ties with life to obtain complete extinction or Nirvana (from the Pali word *Nibbana* or bliss)." Freed from lust, hatred, ambition, and ignorance, he will upon death be completely free, because his separate existence will cease: "One thing only do I teach, o monks," said the Buddha, "sorrow, and the ending of sorrow."

There are various elaborations and interpretations of the state of conditions called Nirvana. Its other names are *Nirodha, Nirmoksa, Nivritti,* and *Nirveda. Nirvana* means the annihilation of passion, hatred, and delusion. It is a transcendental state from craving, suffering, and sorrow. Its positive character is inexpressible in any terms of finite experience, for its reality transcends the realms of birth and death. As an ethical proposition, Nirvana came as a result of retrospection, through reevaluation of one's action or self-purification through self-restraint. Nirvana is not easily comprehended, yet the Theravada collections, or Nikayas, advance some propositions in terms of both positive and negative attributes that must be overcome or acquired for the attainment of Nirvana. The negative part involves the eradication of attachment *(raga),* envy *(dvesa),* delusion *(moha),* impurities *(klesas),* pollutants *(asravas),* and ignorance *(avidya).* The positive part includes the cultivation of those attributes that make for the perfection of *prajna* (mindfulness or experiential insight). The eradication of the

negative and attainment of the positive attributes lead to the end of desire for material things or existence.

The Buddhist society was to be a classless, casteless society where there was no room for rituals and sacrifices. The emphasis was only on ethical conduct without the aid of any priests.

After the Buddha

The Buddha did not nominate his successor. When he was asked who would succeed him, he answered, "The truths and the rules of Order which I have set forth and laid down for you, let them, after I am gone, be the Teacher for you." A council met at Rajagriha after his death to make as complete and authentic a collection of the teachings of the master as was possible. It was not until two centuries later that the teachings were available in the form of Tripitaka (The Three Baskets): Vinaypitaka, consisting of 227 rules and regulations binding on the Buddhist monks and for the guidance of the management of the *samgha* (association); Suttapitaka, a collection of more than 10,000 religious discourses of the Buddha with his disciples; and Abhidhammapitaka, which was an exposition of the philosophical principles underlying the religion. It is partly psychological and helps in the elucidation of the terms and ideas found in the first two baskets.

The Samgha. The Buddha did not establish a "church" in the Western sense. Instead, he established an association of followers called the *samgha*, whose membership was open to all, male or female above the age of fifteen, irrespective of any distinction based on caste or class. The only ones excluded were lepers, criminals, and slaves.

The organization was democratic, in spirit. A new convert needed a preceptor who led him before an assembly of monks and made a formal proposal for admitting him into the *samgha*. When the members present consented, the initiate was fully ordained and told what kind of life he was expected to lead and the vows he was expected to repeat regularly. These were in the form of refuge in the Three Jewels: Buddha, *dhamma*, and *samgha*. Buddha used the term *dhamma* not in the same Brahmanical sense of religious duties but in the sense of the moral laws prescribed by him. The instruction was to last for sixteen years under a preceptor; thereafter, the initiate became a part of the *samgha*, with full voting rights. There were chapters of the *samgha* all over the Buddhist world. Since the monks were expected to travel for eight months a year and stay in one place for four (*vasa*, or retreat, during the monsoon season), any member of the *samgha* could attend the meetings of any local *samgha*. In effect, they were all parts of one universal *samgha*. Decisions could be made by any assembly of members by vote on any matter including the conduct of any monk. Every local assembly prescribed that the *dhamma* be recited on the eighth, fourteenth, and fifteenth days of every fortnight. On the fifteenth day, additionally, there would be a recitation of *Patimokkhar*, a treatise listing crimes and offenses to be avoided by Buddhist monks. At the end of the assembly session, the offenders confessed the guilt and were tried for their transgressions.

The shortcomings of the lack of central authority in Buddhism caused an absence of uniformity in decisionmaking, unfairness in justice to the monks for their transgressions, and a difference in opinion on what is right and what is not even within the same geographical area or period of time. Mostly, the *samgha* did not favor the admission of women; most Buddhist monks held the opinion that their admission would destroy "the purity" of the *samgha*.

The Spread of Buddhism

There was a provision in the Buddhist practice to hold periodic meetings of the General Council, the first of which was held soon after the Buddha's death. The second council did not meet until 100 years later, in about 383 BCE, at Vaishali. At that meeting, it was held that the Buddha was not just a living being but a *lokottara*, or supramundane being, who appeared on earth in an apparitional form as Sakyamuni. The third council was called in the third century BCE by Emperor Asoka and the fourth by Emperor Kanishka in 78 CE. By that time, there were eighteen known sects in Buddhism. The fourth council resulted in a major schism establishing Mahayana and Theravada (or Hinayana) as the principal sects.

A major boost to Buddhism and its spread was provided by the Mauryan emperor Asoka. As detailed elsewhere, he had a feeling of remorse and misery after the battle of Kalinga (in Orissa) in which more than 100,000 lost their lives and another 150,000 were injured. According to the Buddhist accounts, the incident led to his conversion to Buddhism and, after a period of thirty months as a lay disciple, to a membership in the Buddhist order as a *bhikku* (monk). This is not corroborated by any of the large number of edicts Asoka issued and have come down as inscriptions on rock and sandstone pillars. He did, however, help the spread of Buddhism in a substantial way. Thus, Asoka appointed *Dharmamahamatras*, special officials to propagate the dharma, counsel the people, and watch over the implementation of the various edicts that had religious significance. He called the third General Council at his capital of Pataliputra (Patna) to settle internal differences among Buddhist monks. He also sent special emissaries to various states, not only to Sri Lanka and Myanmar, where he is believed to have sent, respectively, his son Mahendra and daughter Samghamitra, but also to more distant states in West Asia, Egypt, and eastern Europe.

The Great Schism

The fourth General Council convened by Emperor Kanishka in 78 CE settled many points in the growing body of Buddhist doctrine. There was no agreement, and the council resulted in a major schism among the followers: Mahayana, or the Greater Vehicle or conveyance to salvation, and the Hinayana, or Lesser Vehicle, a pejorative term coined by the Mahayanists. The latter argued that the term *Mahayana* was reserved for those who achieved their own salvation without anyone's help but who had the ability and the merit to help others with appropriate guidance and assistance. Meanwhile, some lesser persons who had, however, the capacity of attaining perfection through practicing their dharma *(dhamma)* in accordance with Buddha's prescriptions may be considered to use the Lesser Vehicle, Hinayana. However, those whom the Mahayanists designated as Hinayanists chose to call themselves Theravada (*Thera* in Pali meant "the Elders"), signifying that they would adhere to the older original faith.

The principal difference between the two sects hinged on the Mahayana concept of bodhisattva ("Buddha in the becoming" or "future Buddhas"), according to which a meritorious person could "save" others. Mahayanists believe that the Buddha himself, in his previous births, was a bodhisattva, a person of tremendous merit, who was on the way to achieving Buddhahood. Such stories about his previous lives were compiled in the Jatakas, numbering about five hundred, in which the future Buddha was shown as a bodhisattva, performing acts of great merit with a moral aim. It was also held that there are among human beings at any time individuals of great note and merit who develop *bod-hicitta*, the motivation to become a bod-hisattva for the sake of compassion, through dedication of their lives to the service of the downtrodden and who do not want to attain salvation just as yet because that would stop them from being useful. The Mahayanan texts carefully laid down the stages by which such persons would mark moral and intellectual attainments. They elaborated on the special attributes, ethical standing, and powers of major bodhisattvas for the guidance of others. Such bodhisattvas were the Avalokitesvara, Manjusri, Vajrapani, and others who could be worshiped with rituals prescribed in these texts. They were given a recognizable form and insignia, in the same manner as the Hindu gods. Such great souls would be reborn in a higher order until they attain Nirvana, or the state of Buddhahood. Bodhisattvas were worshiped and temples built for them. The Mahayana faith naturally appealed to kings, nobility, scholars, and the elite because they could claim to be bodhisattvas, superior to other fellow beings by virtue of the extra merit they had earned through good works toward others.

Mahayana used Sanskrit, whereas Theravada used the languages of the masses, including Pali and Magadhi. Mahayana employed pomp, pageantry, and imagery in sculpted panels around the temples; Theravada had only images of the Buddha in simple religious edifices. Mahayana followers could save themselves as well as others through good meritorious deeds; Theravada followers believed that each individual has to work for his personal salvation and that all human beings are equal.

Beginning in the second century CE, the Mahayana faith spread via India's Northwest along the Silk Trade route and the Bamian Valley in Afghanistan to China, where it was accepted by the Chinese emperors. Thereafter, the religion spread rapidly to Korea, Japan, and Vietnam, countries that were traditionally receptive to anything that came from China.

At the same time, along with Hinduism, Buddhism of both the principal sects—Mahayana and Theravada—spread to Funan (eastern Cambodia and South Vietnam), a kingdom that prospered from the second to seventh centuries CE, Angkor or the Khmer kingdom from the ninth to fifteenth centuries CE, and to Sumatra and Java. It also prospered in Sri Lanka and Pegu in southern Myanmar.

In the eleventh century CE, an upper Myanmar monarch, Anawratha, who conquered Pegu, converted to Theravada and spread the new faith all over central and northern Myanmar. From Myanmar, Theravada spread to the other countries of mainland Southeast Asia, becoming the dominant faith of Thailand, Laos, and Cambodia.

The Decline of Buddhism in India

As centuries rolled on, the number of individuals, royals, and rich, saintly, and scholarly who claimed to be bodhisatt-vas and a large following of devotees increased. When they died, temples were built for them, and their images were regularly worshiped. Rituals and recitals of the holy scriptures with attendant offerings increased among the followers of the Mahayana faith. The number of temples for the Buddha and his previous incarnations as a bod-hisattva also multiplied. The Mahayana Buddhists looked more and more like the Hindus; the gap between the two faiths decreased over time until by the seventh or eighth century CE, Buddha himself was absorbed by Hinduism as an incarnation of Vishnu. Many Bud-dhist temples were converted to Hindu places of worship.

By the end of the first millennium CE, only pockets of Buddhism remained on the Indian subcontinent, mostly in Ladakh and the Himalayan border areas with Tibet. In the postindependence period, B. R. Ambedkar converted to Buddhism in a public ceremony in Nag-pur, India, in October 1956. A large number of *dalits*, notably the *mahars* in Maharashtra, followed his lead and con-verted to Buddhism. Ambedkar died two months later, achieving in the eyes of his followers *parinirvana*. The new converts numbered about 1 million and called themselves Nav-Buddhas.

A major world-acclaimed Buddhist presence in India is marked by the Dalai Lama, who was, along with his 35,000 Tibetan refugees, given asylum in India in 1959, when they fled persecution at the hands of the Communist Chinese government. The refugees were settled in Dharamsala, in the Kangra Valley in Hi-machal Pradesh, about 5,000 feet above sea level, from which the Dalai Lama continues to inspire millions in India and all over the world with his message of peace and nonviolence. He was awarded the Nobel Prize for Peace in 1989.

JAINISM

The founder of Jainism was Mahavira Vardhamana, who was a senior contem-porary of the Buddha, living in the same general region of India and preaching a faith that, like Buddhism, signified a protest against the Brahman-dominated Vedic faith. Again like the Buddha, Ma-havira was born a Kshatriya, the son of Siddhartha, the chief of the republic of Vaishali in modern Bihar in a village, now known as Bashahr, about twenty-seven miles from Patna in ca. 600 BCE. At the early age of twenty-eight, similar to Gautama Buddha, he gave up his family, but unlike the Buddha, he did so with his brother's consent, in order to join the Nirgrantha sect. For twelve years, he wandered as a mendicant, in search of truth, living a life of austerity and spending considerable periods of time meditating on the problems of life and death. Of this, he spent thirteen months without changing clothes, at which point he abandoned all his worldly belongings and became a nude monk. At forty-two, he received full en-lightenment and became a Kevalin, the

Perfect One, and a Jina (the Conqueror). Thereafter, he established the order of naked monks, and as a monk, he taught Jainism for thirty years. During that period he met the Buddha often. In 527 BCE, he died at the age of seventy-two at Pavapuri in Bihar, which has since become a place for Jain pilgrimage.

Jain tradition begins with Rishabhdeva, the first *tirthankara,* who established institutions such as government and society before he turned to asceticism. His son, Bharata, became the first universal emperor, or *chakravartin.* His daughter, Brahmi, invented the alphabets. There were twenty-four *tirthankaras* (literally, "ford-crossers, those who take others across the ocean of samsara"), whose span of life lessened with each successor, reflecting the deteriorating conditions of life on earth. Jains believe in cosmic cycles, each of them divided into two: ascending *(utsarpani)* and descending *(avasarpani).* The world is currently supposed to be in the descending phase. Each of these periods has three stages of happiness and misery, each lasting 21,000 years. Mahavira himself lived in the transitional misery-happy *(duhsama-susama)* phase, which is supposed to have ended three years after his death. Jains believe that things have been getting worse ever since and will do so for 21,000 years since the beginning of the misery *(duhsama),* followed by a third phase of another 21,000 years, when there would be no morality left at all in the world and mankind will revert to the law of the jungle and living in caves. The good part of it all is that the end of that phase will mark the beginning of the age of ascent.

Mahavira was preceded by Parshvanath, the twenty-third *tirthankara.* He belonged to the Nirgrantha (Free from Fetters) sect and died in 776 BCE. The Nirgranthis observed four commands: not to injure life (ahimsa, or nonviolence), not to tell lies (adhere to *satya,* or truth), not to steal, and not to possess any property *(aparigraha* or *asteya).* To these, Mahavira added two: chastity *(brahmacharya)* and renunciation (no material belongings, including clothes; therefore, poverty and, according to some, nudity). After his passing, the Jain order was led by a series of religious heads called *ganadharas* (supporters of communities).

Two Major Sects

For quite some time, there was a dispute among Mahavira's followers in regard to certain regulations for monks. The rift culminated in the first century CE in dividing the followers into two sects: the Digambara (or "sky-clad," that is, "naked") held that a saint needs no food and should own nothing, not even clothes. They also believed that salvation was not possible for women, and, therefore, their religion should not have any nuns. The Svetambara (or "white-clad") differed from the Digambaras on all these points. Today, most Jains in Gujarat and Rajasthan are Svetambaras, whereas those in Karnataka are Digambaras.

Jainism flourished during the reign of Chandragupta Maurya (321 BCE–297

BCE), when he converted to Jainism and became a monk. Tradition says that he gave up his throne and went south to Sravanbelagola in Karnataka, where he died.

The Jain Canon

Jains of both persuasions continued to be led by the *ganadharas*. The eleventh *ganadhara* in line was Bhadrabahu, who in anticipation of a famine in the North led the Digambara monks, including Chandragupta Maurya, south to the Deccan. However, many monks, some of whom had accepted the leadership of a well-known teacher, Sthulabhadra, stayed behind. When Bhadrabahu returned from the South, he was shocked at the practices of some of the monks, who had badly fallen in their morals. Disgusted, he left for Nepal. Thereupon, Sthulabhadra convened a council of monks at Pataliputra, where the Jain Canon was reconstructed. It included texts called the eleven *angas* (limbs). The Jain Canon was preserved by the Svetambara sect. It contains forty-five texts written in Ardha-Magadhi in prose and verse forms. The canon reached its final form in the fifth century CE when another council met in 454, this time in Vallabhi in Saurashtra (Gujarat), and adopted it. The forty-five texts fall into the following categories: eleven *anga*s, twelve *upanya* (secondary limbs), ten *pakirnaka* (miscellaneous texts), six *chedasutra* (separate texts), four *mulasutra* (basic texts), and two individual texts:

Nandisutra (The Blessing) and Anuyoga (Door of Inquiry).

Jain Philosophy and Beliefs

The essence of Jainism is the realization of the highest perfection in man, who then becomes free from such bondage. The perfect man is the highest, the *Kevalin*. Jainism sees "no need" to recognize any God, though it recognizes that "he is." There is no forgiveness from God or anyone; there are no intermediaries from whom to seek penance or forgiveness. The Jains believe in the Three Jewels *(Ratnatraya)*: Right Knowledge *(Samyog Jyana)*, Right Faith *(Samyog Darsha)*, and Right Conduct *(Samyog Charitra)*.

Jainism believes in karma, a substance that clogs the *jiva*, or soul, which remains with it through a series of births and deaths. It is described as substances permeating the soul and weighing it down to a spiritually lower level. Karma is formed as a result of actions of the body, speech, and mind. One can attain *moksha*, or liberation from such bondage, after many lives of strict penance and moral conduct, in the process destroying one's karma. The soul is individual and eternal. Jainism divides souls into three categories: those that are not yet evolved, those in the process of evolution, and those that have attained *moksha* and are liberated. Each individual must conquer and liberate one's soul with one's own efforts. Jainism holds that such a goal is possible only for ascetics; nonascetics and women can hope to attain *moksha* only in another life if they are reborn male and become ascetics.

Jainism is, par excellence, a religion of ahimsa, or nonviolence. Violence must be avoided by its followers not only because it harms the victims but also because it harms the one who commits the violence in the first place. Jains believe souls exist even in plants and in the elements. In order not to commit violence to any sentient beings, Jainism divides all living things into five categories depending on the number of senses they have. Thus, those that have all five senses of touch, taste, smell, sight, and hearing are placed in the first category. These include humans, monkeys, cattle, horses, elephants, parrots, pigeons, and snakes. In the second category are those with four senses—all except hearing. These include flies, wasps, and butterflies. In the third category are those having three senses, all except sight and hearing; these include ants, fleas, other insects, and moths. The fourth category has two senses, only touch and taste, and include worms, leeches, shellfish, and so on. And, finally, there are those that have only one sense, touch. The last category is subdivided into five again: vegetables, earth bodies such as minerals and jewels, water bodies, fire bodies such as lights and flames including lightning, and wind bodies including all kinds of gases and winds.

Jainism recommends not walking around outside at night because of the possibility of stepping on crawling insects. The monks and nuns go to the extent of wearing a piece of cloth over their mouths for fear of inhaling germs in the air. They are not supposed to eat root vegetables such as onions and potatoes. Jains are enjoined not to eat between sunset and sunrise. Laymen are required to fast on the nights of full moon and new moon, fasting again during the Paryusana: eight days for Svetambaras and fifteen for the Digambaras. They must confess their sins, pay all debts, and ask for forgiveness of everyone, particularly their neighbors.

In the detailed rules of daily conduct, a Jain must follow the Agamas and Siddhantas. The most important is, indeed, ahimsa, or nonviolence. Violence or injury is categorized into four types: accidental, occupational, self-defensive, and intentional. Jain laymen must abstain from the last category and try as much as possible to avoid the other three forms of violence. A monk must abstain fully from all four categories of violence—in thought, word, and deed. There is no excuse or concession in the monks and nuns, not even in self-defense to save their own lives. They must carry a bunch of peacock feathers or a broom to drive away small insects from places where they intend to walk or sit.

Jainism has never been an aggressive or competitive faith. Consequently, it did not spread very much. There are an estimated 4.2 million Jains (2001 census) in India today. There is a smaller number among the Indian diaspora overseas.

Despite the history of ancient India for most of the period being one of fragmented polities, there was a clear notion of the subcontinental political aspirations of kings. Afghanistan at least up to the river Oxus was included in this concept of "Bharatavarsha," which much later came to be commonly called India, following the Greek practice of referring to the peoples around and beyond Indus as people of *Indos*, hence the name India. The common use of the name India belongs to the period after the Europeans found their way to it. The Muslims, invaders and rulers, almost invariably called it Hindustan, "the country inhabited by the Hindus."   (page 84)

5

STATE AND POLITICS
IN ANCIENT INDIA

Whether the Aryans were indigenous or not, some ancient Indian texts throw light on how the early
states were formed in ancient India. The
epic *Mahabharata* speaks of a very consequential battle, "the Mother of all
Battles," which took place on the battlefield of Kurukshetra or Panipat, where
in later history three very consequential
battles (1526, 1556, and 1761) were
fought. In the absence of any archival or
reliable archaeological evidence, scholars
have tended to depend on the textual
evidence in the *Mahabharata*. Calculat-
ing on the basis of the events mentioned
in the Puranas, one school avers that
the titanic battle of the *Mahabharata*
between the Pandavas and the Kauravas
took place in 3102 BCE. Most others believe that the dynastic dispute between
two sets of cousins, in which numerous
family elders, learned scholars, and
princely scions were ranged on either
side, must have occurred not before
1000 BCE, which makes it the contem-

porary of the Hellenic struggle described in the Greek epic *The Iliad*.

Regardless of the exact chronology of
events, the materials in the Vedic and
post-Vedic literature enable one to recon-
struct the social and political institutions
of ancient India. Thus, the primary unit
was the extended family, or *kula*, headed
by the *kulap*; many *kulaps* made a village,
or *grama*, headed by a *gramani*. Several
gramas, around twenty *(vis)*, were, for administrative purposes, brought under a
vispati. The larger community, *jana* (literally, "people") was headed by a *rajan*, or
king. This did not completely do away
with the tribal organizations that continued side by side with the monarchies.
Whereas the *rajan* model produced small
kingdoms, the tribal organizations persisted in the form of tribal republics, or
ganas or *ganarajyas*, where decisions were
made by consensus among the elders.

In the later Vedic Age, the *rajans*
built up their power and made their
kingdoms hereditary. However, though

the extended family units were patriarchal, the *rajan*'s authority was circumscribed by tribal tradition in which a tribal assembly could question his acts. Additionally, the Vedic tradition that witnessed the rising power of the Brahmans was brought to bear on the *rajan* as well, overwhelmingly though not necessarily drawn from the Kshatriya class. The *rajan*'s court advisers were Brahmans, who quoted tradition, or dharma, in support of their advice. The *rajan* had, therefore, to bow to the Brahman and the dharma. The third element restricting the *rajan*'s power was the force of public opinion. Thus, immediately after his consecration, the ruler visited the homes of the important Brahmans, including the court advisers, and vowed to conform to the tenets of the dharma. Then he appeared before the assembly of people who acknowledged him as their monarch. In moments of crisis, assemblies of people indicated to the *rajan* what they thought about important issues.

The kings had some form of ministerial council. Members of that prestigious body were called the *ratnins*, or jewels of the kingdom. Time gave them tremendous prestige and authority, which the monarch, particularly if he was young at the time of succession, would not risk ignoring. That constituted a restraint on his authority. It also assured him of sound advice based on generations of experience and wisdom, because the ministers were usually drawn from the same prestigious families of Brahmans.

The *ganas*, or republics, were governed by two bodies: the *sabha* and the *samiti*. Ancient texts state that they were regarded as the twin daughters of *prajapati*, the lord of the people, or the head of the republic. The *sabha* was the larger of the two bodies. It is also the name the two houses of independent India's Parliament adopted for themselves: the Rajya Sabha and the Lok Sabha. The *samiti* was a smaller body, more like a council, whose deliberations were close and confidential.

By the time of the *Mahabharata*, there were two centers of political power: Indraprastha of the Pandavas was based on the Jumna River, Hastinapura of the Kauravas on the Ganges. The battle between the two sets of cousins took place at Kurukshetra in modern Haryana. Other important kingdoms mentioned in that epic include Kosala (Oudh), Kasi (Benares or Varanasi), and Videha (north Bihar, north of the Ganges). Magadha in South Bihar was yet to emerge as a major center of power. Heads of polities of the time, possibly covering all of North India from the Punjab to Bihar, were involved in that *dharmayudh*, or war for righteousness. Most of them were aligned on the side of the Pandavas, who stood for righteousness, as opposed to the Kauravas, who were known for their lack of virtue and limitless greed.

By 700 BCE, two centuries before the birth of the Buddha, the smaller kingdoms were being swallowed up by the bigger ones by what the political commentators call the *matsyanyaya*, the law of the fishes, the bigger variety living at the expense of the smaller. Tribal organizations, based on kinship and familial security, were fast giving way to the impersonal elements of might and military power. Ambitious but insecure Kshatriya warriors were roped in increasingly by well-known Brahmans, who invented new, expensive, and impressive sacrifices accompanied by elaborate and more exacting rituals involving numerous teams of lesser Brahmans, all under the head priest, to increase the royal authority. A Brahman-Kshatriya alliance or axis of power emerged in which the Brahmans stoked the ambitions of royals or potential royals who would like augmentation of their power without the traditional curbs.

Three new sacrifices that were not prevalent at the time of the Rig-Veda were now in vogue. These were the *rajasuya,* or royal consecration, ending in the White Umbrella being raised over the monarch's head; *vajapeya yagna,* during which the drink of potency made the king a king of kings, a *samrat* or sovereign; and the *asvamedha,* or horse sacrifice, in which a consecrated horse accompanied by a picked body of soldiers went from territory to territory whose rulers, unless they challenged the horse, were automatically regarded as vassals. If challenged, a trial of strength ensued. If a ruler successfully acquired large chunks of territory, he was regarded as *cakravartin,* the "world" ruler.

Such trials of vanity produced bitterness lasting generations, involving conflicts that destroyed the lives of peasants, and the fields through which rival armies marched were scorched to deny the enemy any food or fodder. Stories of ruination of royal families engaged the balladeers, who sang the glories of the victors, adding to the insecurity all around affecting the rich and the poor, the mighty and the fallen, the scholars and the illiterates alike. It produced political unrest, intellectual doubts, and spiritual ferment whose outcome was to look for a solution to the perpetual misery and suffering of all.

The center of political activity was still moving farther east. A little before the birth of Gautama Buddha, the Middle Ganges region saw the rise of small political units, called *mahajanapadas,* some of them kingdoms and others called republics, the latter controlled by chiefs who ruled in consultation with the people. Gautama Buddha was born in one such republic, Kapilavastu, where his father was a chieftain of the Sakya tribe; Mahavira, founder of Jainism, was born in the republic of Vaishali in modern Bihar, where his father was the chief. The geographical areas of the activity of these two founders of protest faiths were the kingdoms of Kosala (capital Savatti) and Magadha (capital Rajagriha, later called Pataliputra) in the Middle Ganges region. Soon after, in the sixth century BCE, Magadha grew into a large kingdom, as its king, Bindusara, annexed the surrounding territories. His long rule of fifty-two years ended in 491 BCE when his son, Ajatasatru, assassinated him.

Ajatasatru was an ambitious warrior who annexed to Magadha the kingdom of Kasi, the Lichhavi Republic, and the much larger kingdom of Kosala. He ruled until 458 BCE.

At the time of Alexander's invasion in the latter part of the fourth century BCE, the Nanda dynasty was on the throne of Magadha, ruled by Dhanan and, a particularly obnoxious king, not at all well regarded by subjects and scholars alike.

ALEXANDER'S INVASION

Alexander's invasion in the latter part of the fourth century BCE was of only limited importance to Indian history. After overrunning the Persian empire of Darius III, Alexander (Sikandar, as he was called in the Indian annals) crossed the Hindu Kush Range and entered Northwest India in 327 BCE. He was helped by the king of Taxila, much to the chagrin and pride of most of the scholars and student body, respectively, of the famous university for which the town was known throughout North India. It was located near modern Rawalpindi. Another monarch who helped the foreign invader was the king of Gandhara. Such "traitors," as Kautilya (also known as Chanakya), the leader of the scholars, called them, were exceptions, whereas there were numerous rulers of small kingdoms that opposed an alien invasion. One such state was Pushkalavati near modern Peshawar, which was ruled by Queen Cleophis. Although 7,000 of her soldiers died along with her in the

defense of the state, Alexander himself was hurt, a rare occasion and setback in his eleven-year campaign to conquer the world. However, the first major military confrontation Alexander had was with a valiant monarch from beyond the river Jhelum. His name has stirred many a warrior in India. This was Porus, brave and generous even in war. Seeing Porus's forces, Alexander is said to have exclaimed: "I see at last a danger that matches my courage." Porus's army was overcome by the better-disciplined forces of the Hellenic invader. When the defeated king who had suffered nine wounds was brought into Alexander's presence and asked how he would like to be treated, Porus responded, "As befits me—like a king." Alexander treated with him great respect and left him in charge of his former kingdom.

Soon after that encounter, Alexander decided to end his plans for world conquest and return to his homeland, which was not to be. His army left partly by land and partly by sea. Alexander himself left by sea in 325. He died in Susa in 323 BCE. Before leaving India, he left his deputy in Punjab, which was given the status of a satrapy.

Alexander's decision to end his campaign and return to his homeland was owed to the protests of his top officers as well as significant numbers of troops. For the first time, the troops had met patriotic rather than mercenary forces. A small republic led by a woman, in the then mostly male-chauvinistic world, had inflicted serious losses on Alexander's forces. If this could be so, they wondered what kind of opposition they would encounter in the "real" India much farther east, where they had heard of the Nandas ruling over a large kingdom called Magadha. Some accounts indicate that the troops were weary of being away from home and families for more than a decade. They were tired, and the conditions worsened with the unbearable heat of India's Punjab and the Northwest. Most of these factors, including the Nanda power, are not mentioned in the Greek accounts, which tend to play down Alexander's setbacks in India; on the other hand, the Indian accounts hardly mention Alexander. However, the first major Greek contact did influence Northwest India, notably its art forms. The Gandhara school of art shows drapery in the Greek style on the statues of Hindu gods and the Buddha.

There was no direct conflict between the Nandas and Alexander's forces. Alexander's invasion and annexation of kingdoms and republics in the Northwest and the Punjab, however, let loose forces that resulted in political upheaval in Magadha led by Chandragupta Maurya in 321 BCE. The Nanda rule was ended. The new regime under Chandragupta extended its writ over a much larger area, including the territories conquered by Alexander.

THE MAURYAS

Chandragupta Maurya's mentor and minister was Chanakya or Kautilya,

which name he assumed as the author of the most well-known treatise on politics and diplomacy of the ancient times, *Arthasastra*. Chanakya had spent several years at Pataliputra, where the much-hated Nandas had taken over. At one of the assemblies of the learned, King Dhananand insulted Chanakya, who thereupon quit Pataliputra, vowing both to end the Nanda rule and to make it the center of a polity that should represent India's strength and invulnerability. He joined the Taxila (Takshashila) University in the Northwest (near modern Rawalpindi), also arguably the most famous and well-provided institution of higher learning in Sanskrit and Vedic studies. The event that shocked Chanakya was the king of Takshashila, Ambhi (Omphis in the Greek accounts), surrendering to Alexander and becoming his instrument to forge a Greek polity in the strategic region, which would open the gates to India's plains.

Chanakya played a major role in visiting most of the kings in the Northwest and organizing a confederacy under a young, well-trained student, the future Chandragupta Maurya. Whether Alexander left because of his generals' reluctance to continue his campaign for world conquest, his reverses at Pushkalavati, or the news of the formation of a confederacy led by Chandragupta and guided by the shrewd Chanakya cannot be resolved from the available evidence.

One thing is certain: in 322 BCE Chanakya authored a political treatise under the pen name Kautilya. The treatise,

Arthasastra, speaks of how a king may amass power by playing states against each other. It has remained a classic, and its author has been commemorated by postcolonial independent India by naming the area allocated for foreign embassies in New Delhi Chanakyapuri ("the city of Chanakya"). Often unjustly compared to *The Prince* by Machiavelli, the treatise has both admirers and detractors. Here is what India's first prime minister, Jawaharlal Nehru, who served from 1947 to 1964, had to say while he was in a British jail and authored his prescient *Discovery of India:*

> There was hardly anything Chanakya would have refrained from doing to achieve his purpose; he was unscrupulous enough; yet he was also wise enough to know that this very purpose may be defeated by means unsuited to the end. Long before Clausewitz, he is reported to have said that war is only a continuance of state policy by other means. But he adds, war must always serve the larger ends of policy and not become an end in itself; the statesman's objective must always be the betterment of the state as a result of war, not the mere defeat and destruction of the enemy. If the war involves both parties in a common ruin, that is the bankruptcy of statesmanship.[1]

Toward the end of his life, Chandragupta became very spiritual and abdicated the throne in favor of his son, Bindusara (297–273 BCE). He himself became a monk and migrated south to Sravanbelagola, a very sacred spot for the Jains in today's Karnataka. There he fasted to death in the Jain tradition.

The Account by Megasthenes

From one of the three main divisions into which Alexander's empire was split, Antioch in Syria, the ruler, Seleucus Nikator, sent his ambassador to India, Megasthenes, to the court of Chandragupta Maurya at Pataliputra in 300. Chandragupta had possibly conquered large parts of the former Greek-Asian kingdom and married a Greek princess. The detailed account that Megasthenes left in the form of a volume titled *Indika* has been lost, but it was so well known as a standard work on India that there are many later writers who had copious extracts from *Indika* in their works. It was the first account by a foreigner of the capital city of Pataliputra, its organization, and the pomp of the royal court and compares it favorably with the structures and settings in Susa and Ekbatana. Most of the details of the administration and diverse officials compare well with what is available from Kautilya's *Arthasastra.*

Megasthenes describes the society of the time, which from his perspective was divided into seven castes or professional groups: philosophers, husbandmen (the largest class), herdsmen (mostly from the Sudra class), artisans, armed forces (not necessarily Kshtriyas), spies, and a class of magistrates, councillors, and assessors. Priests, monks, and philosophers were exempt from taxation. The large number of people in the armed forces must have been a burden on the society. In a later work by Pliny the Elder (first century CE), it is stated that in the period of the Nandas, immediately preceding Chandragupta Maurya, the army consisted of 600,000 infantry, 30,000 cavalry, and 9,000 elephants. One may assume that the military was maintained at a comparable or higher level by Chandragupta Maurya, who controlled larger domains.

Asoka Maurya

Historians, Indian and non-Indian, have showered Asoka Maurya (273–231 BCE) with superlative praise as the ablest and noblest ruler of ancient India. In these attributes, only one other ruler in Indian history is compared with him, namely, the Mughal Akbar seventeen centuries later. Both were warriors and excellent administrators whose guidelines were compassion and the well-being of their subjects. Both had a liberal attitude toward followers of religions other than their own, thus promoting a plural and secular society, an attitude far ahead of their times anywhere in the world.

According to Buddhist sources, which are inclined to highlight his transformation to a humane ruler, Asoka's rule started with the most tyrannical of acts: He usurped the throne and killed all his rivals. Though the Asokan inscriptions do not acknowledge such dastardly acts

on his part, they do highlight the dramatic transformation in his personality and as a ruler who was filled with tremendous remorse after the battle of Kalinga, in the present-day Orissa, which saw more than 100,000 killed and more than 150,000 injured. The event took place thirteen years after he ascended the throne, sometime around 260 BCE. According to Asoka's thirteenth rock edict, he decided at that point to pursue a policy of resolving disputes with his neighbors or recalcitrant subordinate rulers through conciliation rather than conflict. Asoka preferred to call himself "Beloved of the Gods" rather than adopting self-glorifying military and political epithets, as was the custom among monarchs in ancient India and elsewhere. He recorded the change in himself:

> Just after the taking of Kalinga, the Beloved of the Gods began to follow Righteousness, to love Righteousness, to give instruction in Righteousness. When an unconquered country is conquered, people are killed, they die, or are made captive. That the Beloved of the Gods finds very pitiful and grievous. . . . Today, if a hundredth or a thousandth part of those who suffered in Kalinga were to be killed, to die, or to be taken captive, it would be very grievous to the Beloved of the Gods. If anyone does him wrong, it will be forgiven as far as it can be forgiven.[2]

Asoka's rule is the first well-documented reign in Indian history.

Besides the archaeological finds, there are the Asokan inscriptions on rock surfaces and pillars all over the country, but more so in the Ganges heartland. Both Brahmanical and Buddhist texts preserve his memory and attest to his role in religion and administration. And then we have the foreign travelers' accounts substantially corroborating the other sources. The numerous inscriptions Asoka left were mostly in the Prakrit language written in Brahmi script, both from left to right and from right to left. There were some others in the Northwest that were in Greek and Aramaic written in the Kharoshti script, which was used in Iran of the time. Apart from their tremendous value to understanding his mind as well as his administration over the first extensive political entity on the subcontinent, his inscriptions constitute the oldest Indian written documents. As for the materials used for these inscriptions, the edicts in the first half of his reign of forty-two years were carved on rock, whereas the later inscriptions were on well-polished pillars made of sandstone. The pillars were adorned with an animal capital on the top, such as the four lions on the Sarnath pillar, adopted by postcolonial independent India's government as its logo, which is seen on most official documents including the nation's currency.

Asoka's edicts constituted official pronouncements of his policy in the form of instructions to his officials and the public at large. Scholars attribute the drafts of the edicts to the emperor himself. Humanity and compassion were the core principles of his administration, which took pride in replacing the usual policy of territorial conquest and aggrandizement with conquest by righteousness. To borrow from the inscription quoted above, "The Beloved of the Gods considers that the greatest of all victories is the victory of Righteousness, and that [victory] the Beloved of the Gods has already won, here and on all his borders, even 600 leagues away in the realm of the Greek king Antiyoka [Syria] and beyond Antiyoka among the four kings of Turamaya [Egypt], Antikini [Macedonia], Maga [Cyrene] and Alikasudara [Epirus] and in the South among the Colas and Pandyas and as far as Ceylon."[3] In A. L. Basham's view, Asoka may have "believed that by setting an example of enlightened government, he might convince his neighbors of the merits of his new policy and gain the moral leadership of the whole world."[4] He by no means gave up his imperial ambitions, but modified them in accordance with the humanitarian ethic of Buddhism.

Asoka's reign saw a number of unusual measures of administration. Among his top officials were *dharma-mahamatras* (officials of righteousness), who toured the empire to enforce the regulations based on compassion to humans and animals alike. Asoka had adopted a principal ingredient of Buddhism, ahimsa, or nonviolence, and approved measures that would drastically reduce violence in his domains. Thus, he banned the traditional practice of animal sacrifice and killing of certain species of animals for human consumption. He preferred a vegetarian diet for himself and encouraged the practice in his palace. He gave up hunting for pleasure; instead, he promoted for his courtiers and the general public pilgrimages to Buddhist holy places. Along the roads to such places, he ordered the planting of trees to provide shade, the digging of wells to provide water, and the building of rest houses to provide shelter. Hospitals were built in his empire both for humans and for animals and encouragement given to research in *ayurveda*, the system of medicine mainly based on herbs and soils.

Was Asoka a complete pacifist? It appears he was a realist in the same sense as modern governments, which maintain standing armies and even nuclear arsenals as instruments for global peace. As one of his inscriptions clearly said: "If anyone does him wrong, it will be forgiven as far as it can be forgiven. The Beloved of the Gods even reasons with the forest tribes in his empire, and seeks to reform them. . . . He is not only compassionate, he is also powerful, and he tells them to repent, lest they be slain. For the Beloved of the Gods desires safety, self-control, justice and happiness for all beings."[5] In political parlance, he must be deemed a "realist," who, may it be noted, for all his nonviolence had not abolished the death penalty.

Asoka and Buddhism. Although there are some scholars who maintain that Asoka embraced Buddhism and even became a monk, none of his inscriptions even hint at such a possibility. Undoubtedly, he was tremendously influenced by Buddhism, at least insofar as he believed that his good deeds on earth would earn him merit, but that was the belief in Hinduism as well. Morality interested Asoka more than metaphysics; his mind seemed not attuned or interested in the finer points of philosophy whether Upanishadic or Buddhist. He wanted to remain "Beloved of the Gods," whether Vedic or not. He was good to all faiths; he provided caves, for instance, to Ajivikas, who were unfriendly to the Buddhists as well as Jains. In his humanity, compassion, and nonviolence, he came closest to Buddhism, but it should be remembered that these attributes were not exclusive to Buddhism in ancient India.

It should be conceded, however, that he had a special feeling for Buddhism. During his reign, he held the third Buddhist General Council at his capital of Pataliputra. He made serious attempts at spreading Buddhism not only in India but outside its borders as well. He sent his son, Mahendra, to Sri Lanka, where its king converted to Buddhism and assumed the name and title Devanamapiya Tissa. Tradition also says that he sent the same son or a daughter to Myanmar to spread Buddhism there. Sri Lanka proudly mentions Asoka as the reason for its conversion to Buddhism and perhaps for getting Buddha's tooth and a portion of the Bodhi Tree. The island country became a major seat for the continued study of Buddhism and providing spiritual links to Buddhist Southeast Asia, most notably to Myanmar, throughout that country's history.

Mauryan Administration

The Mauryan rulers did not have a precedent in the form of administration of a large empire spread from present-day Afghanistan, covering all of North India, and extending to the Deccan and the Konkan in peninsular India. Based on Asokan inscriptions and the account by Megasthenes, one gets a fairly good idea of the administration during the period. What one finds is a combination of a centralized government coexisting with the autonomy of the village as a unit. The official in charge of a village was the *gramika*, with a couple of other officials to help him. A group of ten or twenty villages would be under a higher official called the *gopa*. Still larger units were created consisting of a hundred or two hundred villages, under an official called *sthaniya*, who was, in turn, responsible to a very high official, possibly a member of the royal family, called *sthanika*. The latter's responsibility may extend over one-quarter or one-fifth of the entire empire. At the level of a *sthaniya*, the administration was more complex and elaborate, with responsibility for maintenance of law and order, investigation of crimes, and administration of justice. He had a particular jurisdiction over large tracts of territory lying between villages that may have been uninhabited or lying fallow. The administration of such unproductive lands that could be hideouts for bandits was placed under special officials called *vivitadhaksa*, aided by armed officials called *corajjukas*, specializing in the capture of runaway criminals.

Basically, it was a paternalistic administration that claimed to work for the welfare of the people, both materially and spiritually. In Asokan times, the emperor called himself the "Beloved of the Gods" and believed it was his high duty to guide his subjects, whom he regarded as his children, in living a life of morals, according to the dharma, for which purpose he appointed *dharma-mahamatras* throughout his far-flung empire. In the annals of ancient India, this was perhaps the first time that such a function reserved for the Brahmans was usurped by the monarch and his appointed officials.

The Mauryas raised the land tax from the customary one-sixth to one-fourth and in time of emergency to one-third. The courts at different levels collected fines, and the officials in charge of trade and industry collected toll taxes and excise duties. There were professional taxes paid by artisans of all kinds and fisher-men, foresters, and mine workers. The king had his own private lands that were cultivated by an army of prisoners of war, a kind of forced labor. All un-exploited mineral and forest resources were regarded as state property. Property belonging to persons dying without heirs lapsed to the state.

At the central level, the executive was, indeed, headed by the king, aided by a Mantri-Parisat (Council of Min-isters). It consisted of eighteen *asta-dasatirthas* (fords), mostly heads of the various departments and other high-level executives, headed by the *mantri-nah* (chief minister) and, in order of importance, the *purohita* (head priest), *senapati* (chief of the armed forces), *yu-varaja* (heir apparent), *dandapala* (chief of the police in charge of law and or-der), *durgapala* (keeper of forts), and *an-tapala* (head of the royal household). Such high officials were called the *am-atyas*. The second tier of high officials at the central level were those in charge of collection of revenue, treasury and ac-counts, records, weights and measures, passports, and so on. The king regularly consulted the *mantrinah* and, on his recommendation and depending on the matter under discussion, the relevant *amatya* in charge of a particular admin-istrative division. It was perfectly un-derstood that all ministers including the *mantrinah* served at the king's pleasure, and the latter was not bound to accept their advice.

The monarch indeed headed the sys-tem and was in full charge of the civilian administration, armed forces, and the legal system. All appeals for justice, from the lowest level of the village up through the hierarchy of officials, lay with the king. At the next lower rung of adminis-tration, that of the *sthanikas*, the court was aided by three *amatyas*, of the same level as members of the Mantri-Parisat, and three *dharmasthas*, high-level reli-gious scholars. At this level and in the larger administrative units, there was a core of high-level officials represent-ing the courts, revenue assessment and collection, and law and order. A very distinct appointment was that of *kanta-kasodhaka* (literally, "remover of thorns"), who could not only help eliminate bu-reaucratic bottlenecks in specific cases but also bring a matter of importance or of severe neglect directly to the attention of the *mantrinah* or the king.

The capital Pataliputra (modern Patna, Bihar's capital) had a separate metropolitan administration, which in many respects was copied for the other major cities and towns in the empire. The municipal administration in such large towns was headed by *nagaravy-oharakas*, like modern city commission-ers. The administration of market towns or *nigamas* fell into two categories, those that were controlled by a board or corporation appointed by the king and a central government. They were called *rajakrtasamvit* (established by the king) as distinguished from *samuhakttasamvit* (established by the people), which in effect was controlled by trade and professional associations *(sanghas)* or guilds *(srenis)*. Some of the towns held periodic meetings of councillors called *mahajans* (who may represent a particular trade, industry, or caste) to discuss common policies in regard to general sanitation, space and cleanliness of markets, control of the city gates, and law and order. The day-to-day business of these boards or corporations was conducted by a number of committees of bureaucrats called *karyacintakas* and their heads, the *mukhyas*.

As a paternalistic state or a state with major welfare programs, the Mauryan administration maintained homes for the aged, widows without family support, the handicapped, and orphans. There were regular programs for famine relief, refugees, and those affected by epidemics. At the local level, there were programs to help the peasants with seeds or cattle to tide over a particularly distressful season when the rains failed to arrive on time or were excessive and caused floods. Additionally, at the municipal level, there were pension programs for those working in temples and religious organizations and aid to particular traders or artisans who may have suffered for reasons beyond their control.

India after Asoka

The Mauryan empire collapsed within fifty years of Asoka's death in 231 BCE.

After Asoka's death, his empire was most likely divided among his sons. Details of Asoka's successors are hazy and uncertain except that the last king in the Mauryan dynasty, Brihadrath, was overthrown by his commander, a Brahman, Pushyamitra Sunga. The Maurya dynasty thus ended in 185 BCE, lasting altogether 136 years. With the end of the dynasty, Magadha and the city of Pataliputra declined, because the Sungas preferred the East Malwa region of central India as their center of power.

Being Brahmans, the Sungas revived the Vedic sacrificial rituals, and for a time the patronage to Buddhism declined. In fact, Buddhist sources criticize the Sungas severely for their persecution of the Buddhists, which may seem unfair considering the remarkable Buddhist monuments at Sanchi and Bharhut.

Pushyamitra Sunga (ca. 185 BCE–149 BCE) established control over the entire region, from the Indus to Bihar. After Pushyamitra's death, his successors were able to hold the empire only by dividing it among several feudatories, who ruled their areas like semiautonomous lords. They were not able to maintain the well-knit system of administration of the Mauryas. Such a pattern, in fact, became the norm in the whole of northern India from then until the establishment of the Gupta dynasty.

Meanwhile, northern India was wrecked by invasions from the Northwest—the Bactrians, Parthians, and Scythians—who brought at various times large areas of today's Northwest Frontier Province, Rajasthan, Gujarat, and, for a while, the Deccan under them. The entire movement of such people may have been triggered by the first political consolidation in China under Emperor Ch'in Shih Huang Ti (r. 247–210 BCE) in which many ethnic people were pushed around. Additionally, some severe climatic changes in central Asia may have been responsible for the pastureland of the Yueh-chih drying up. Large bands of Yueh-chih nomads moving in the central Asian region may have pushed the Scythians (Saka), Bactrians, and Parthians from their home bases toward India. All of them, including their armed followers, accepted Hinduism and Vedic culture. Most of them were likely absorbed into the Hindu social fold as Kshatriyas, many of them being the founders of the small princely states of Rajasthan and Kathiawar. All of them lost contact with the lands of their origin, becoming for all intents and purposes Indian.

Some of the significant events of this period of invasions may, however, be listed. For one thing, the most notable Bactrian king, Menander or Milinda, whose capital was Sakala (modern Sialkot), held discussions with the great Buddhist monk Nagasena in 150 BCE. These were recorded in Pali, *par excellence*, the language of Buddhism, and were available to future generations as *The Questions of Milinda*. Other significant events are detailed in the following section.

THE RISE OF THE KUSHANAS

Some Yueh-chih tribes, including a branch called the Kushanas, had lived for more than a century in northeastern Iran, speaking a variant of the Iranian language. They took advantage of the disturbed situation in the trans-Oxus region, consolidated their strength under Kujula Kadphisis (40–64 CE), crossed the Indian borders, and conquered Northwest India in the first century CE. Kujula's grandson, Kanishka, became the mightiest ruler of the line (ca. 78–101 CE), as he established control over an extensive region all the way from central Asia to Oudh and Benares (Varanasi) and including Kashmir in North India. His capital was Purushapura (modern Peshawar). The Kushanas remained a power until the third century CE, when they were defeated by the Sassanian rulers of Persia, who brought Northwest India under their rule for about sixty years.

The contribution of the Kushanas to Buddhism was enormous. Kanishka was a great patron of the Buddhist faith, which under him spread to central Asia and China through the Bamian Valley, as evidenced by the numerous *chaityas* cut into the rocks to serve as places of worship for the Buddhists at Peshawar and in the Bamian Valley. Kanishka called the fourth General Council of Buddhist monks, which formalized the great schism in Buddhism between

Theravada (Faith of the Elders) and Mahayana (Greater Vehicle). The Mahayana followers, called the Theravada followers Hinayana, or "belonging to the Lesser Vehicle." Another major area of Kushana influence is in the Gandhara style of art, which became influential in India and East Asia.

Kanishka founded a new era called the Saka era in 78 CE, although he was not himself a Scythian or Saka. The Saka era is widely used in India to this date including by the Indian government, which publishes it side by side with the Gregorian method. Kanishka also made a mark by issuing coins, including gold coins.

Following the brief reign of the Kushanas, India broke up once again into numerous political units: in western India, the Satavahanas or Andhras (first century BCE–300 CE) were dominant; in Orissa, the Kharavela dynasty dominated in the first century BCE; and in South India, the early Cholas in Tamil Nadu from the first to the fourth centuries CE and the early Cheras in Kerala from the first century BCE to the sixth century CE were in power.

THE GUPTAS

After the collapse of the Mauryan empire in 185 BCE and its ultimate fragmentation into numerous kingdoms, the first major political consolidation, barring the brief rule of the Kushanas, did not come until Chandra Gupta (not Chandragupta Maurya) arose to establish the Gupta dynasty in 320 CE. He and his successors not only restored the great splendor of the Mauryas but also went far beyond it to make their dynastic rule the first golden age for the country. The Gupta dynasty (320–550 CE) also saw the extension of Indian culture beyond India's traditional borders to Southeast Asia.

The Gupta power was importantly based on their alliance with the Lichchavis, who were highly regarded because they were believed to mark the eighth generation from the father of Rama, King Dasharatha. They were powerful in Kasi (Benares) and Kosala. The marriage of Chandra Gupta to the Lichchavi princess Kumaradevi, which cemented the Gupta-Lichchavi alliance in the fourth century CE, was commemorated in the Gupta coins, including some of Samudra Gupta's coins in which he describes himself proudly as the son of the daughter of the Lichchavis.

Samudra Gupta

The greatest ruler of the Gupta dynasty was Samudra Gupta (335–375 CE), whose capital, Pataliputra (same as that of the Mauryas), became once more the center of a great empire. His long reign is fairly well documented by his coins, in an inscription on an Asokan pillar in Allahabad, and in a long poem in Sanskrit by the court poet Harishena. Samudra Gupta's domain was divided into two categories of imperial control, which had the sanction of Kautilya's *Arthasastra:* those that were directly administered being classified as *lobha-vijaya* and those that merely acknowledged his suzerainty and fell under *dharma-vijaya* and followed his morality. The Allahabad inscription indicates that the first category included kings who were killed after the Gupta conquest of their territories, whereas the second category consisted of those kings who were reinstated after conquest as vassals and those who, anticipating the Gupta conquest, submitted to them.

With an empire already stretching from Kamarupa (Assam), Nepala (Nepal), to the borders of the Punjab, Samudra Gupta sent an expedition to South India up to Kanchi (modern Conjeeveram), the first effort by a ruler from the North to tie the southern part of the subcontinent into an imperial system. The expedition route was through the eastern and southern parts of central India, then eastward all the way to Orissa, and roughly following the coastline to the Pallava capital, Kanchi. Including the return journey, it marked a march of 3,000 miles. The Allahabad inscription that gives details of this well-planned military expedition indicates that the kings of South India agreed to become Samudra Gupta's vassals, paying him enormous treasures as tribute.

Samudra Gupta's main military effort was, however, against the Sakas, who had ruled over a kingdom that stretched from Malwa in central India to Kathiawar in the West. For more than 200 years, the Sakas had maintained a hold over the lucrative western trade. Their capital, Ujjaini (modern Ujjain), one of the seven holiest cities of ancient India and a major interstate trading center, was also known as a great center of learning and culture. For all his might and prowess, however, Samudra Gupta was not able to extend his control over the Saka kingdom, a feat achieved later by his son, Chandra Gupta II.

Chandra Gupta II or Vikramaditya

With the defeat of the Sakas, Chandra Gupta II (376–415 CE), famously known as Vikramaditya, the Sun of Prowess, completed his control over all of North India, except the Northwest. His influence was over both sides of the Vindhyas in Madhya Pradesh and northern Deccan (in modern Andhra Pradesh), which was, at that time, ruled by the powerful king of the Vakatakas, Rudrasena. To seal his alliance with him, Vikramaditya gave his daughter in marriage to Rudrasena. The latter's early death left the large kingdom in the hands of his widow, Vikramaditya's daughter, for a long time.

Chandra Gupta II's reign is rightly known for the efflorescence of culture. His patronage of the arts and literature was legendary. It is believed that Kalidasa, the greatest Indian poet and playwright, the author of the famous *Sakuntala,* the work that made the German poet Goethe place it on his head and dance with joy, lived and worked during his time.

Fa Hsien at Nalanda University

Vikramaditya's period is also noted for the first visit by a Chinese Buddhist monk, Fa Hsien (401–410 CE), to India. Traveling westward from China via the Gobi or Taklamakan Desert, he came through the Bamian Valley, across the Pamirs, into India. By that time, Buddhism had won the status of the state religion in China, and Buddhist scholars and monks were most sought after for visits to the celestial kingdom where the emperor and his family paid high respect to them and sought answers to questions troubling them. Fa Hsien would begin a trail for many Chinese monks to come to the Buddhist centers of learning, notably Nalanda University in Bihar. Notable among the monks who came between 401 when Fa Hsien came and 700 CE were Hsuan Tsang (629–645) and I-tsing (675–685). Their aim was to study Buddhism deeply and discuss the subject with scholars at Indian universities, particularly Nalanda, which had been established with munificent grants by successive monarchs of the Gupta dynasty, although the Guptas were not Buddhist. Eventually, by the time of Harsha in the middle of the seventh century, Nalanda University was supported by the income of nearly one hundred villages. The famous university, which had an estimated 10,000 students and several thousand monks and teachers, included a large number of foreigners, mostly monks from China, Vietnam, and Sri Vijaya (Sumatra). It flourished until it was "pillaged" by the invading Muslims.[6] The Chinese monks also spent time in the various monasteries at the places sacred to Buddhism, and, most important, they labored to translate the original texts of Buddhism and take them to their homeland. The Buddhism that spread into China was of the Mahayana faith. From China, it spread to Japan, Korea, and Vietnam (which was until the fifteenth century limited to a little south of the Red River basin). Fa Hsien stayed in India from 401 to 410, collecting manuscripts and Buddhist texts and studying Buddhism. He returned to China by sea from the port at Tamralipti (Tamluk) in Bengal.

Not as observant as Megasthenes, the ambassador of Seleucus Nikator to the court of the Mauryas in the third century BCE, Fa Hsien's account is still valuable as a corroboration of what the Indian sources say about the period. Fa Hsien spoke glowingly about how peaceful India was, noting the rarity of serious crime and the mildness of administration. It was possible, he stated, to travel from one end of the country to the other without a passport and without any fear of molestation. It would appear from his account that the people were very virtuous and nonviolent. His account mentions, for the first time, that there were "untouchables" in ancient India. He attested that Buddhism, both Mahayana and Theravada, was flourishing in the country.

Judging by Fa Hsien's account, it would appear that since the time of the account of Megasthenes, India had become even more humane and mild in the intervening centuries from the Mauryas to the Guptas. Reviewing the cultural conditions of the Gupta period, more particularly during the reign of Vikramaditya, the great scholar A. L. Basham observes: "In the best days of the Gupta Empire, Indian culture reached a perfection which it was never again to attain. At this time India was perhaps the happiest and most civilized region of the world, for the effete Roman empire was nearing its destruction and China was passing through a time of troubles between the two great periods of the Hans and the T'angs."[7]

The Later Guptas

Vikramaditya's successor, Kumara Gupta I (415–455 CE), managed to maintain the political integrity of the empire. Toward the end of his reign, there were fresh invasions across the western borders of India. These were the Huns (in the Indian records, the Hunas), a central Asian people, called the White Huns in the Byzantine Empire. They were a branch of the Turkish-Mongol people

who were threatening Europe at about the same time. After occupying Bactria, the Huns attacked India.

Kumara Gupta died fighting the Huns, whose incursions proved a continuing thorn for the Gupta rulers. His son, Skanda Gupta (455–467 CE), valiantly fought against the Huns and bought peace for a while. His early death was a blow to the Gupta empire. The continued Hun menace weakened the Gupta authority and depleted their treasury. By the end of the fifth century, the Gupta empire was disintegrating; distant monarchs, including the South Indian, stopped sending tributes to their court. Powerful vassals in central India and the northwestern and hilly parts of the empire declared themselves independent. By the middle of the sixth century CE, the Gupta control over their empire had clearly vanished, their writ being limited to Magadha and Bengal.

The Huns

Meanwhile, the Huns were able to establish their control over western India. An account of the Chinese ambassador Sung-yun of around 500 CE speaks of the barbarities of the Huns, which included the tortures of Buddhists. Their notorious leaders were Toramana and his son, Mihirakula, also known as Mihiragula or Mihiradutta. The latter is the more notable, and his exploits are recorded in an inscription dated 530 CE at Gwalior in Madhya Pradesh. Mihi-rakula was a worshiper of Siva and as a fresh convert was fanatical and a known enemy of the Buddhists. An alliance of several monarchs under one Yashodhar-man of Malwa was finally able to van-quish Mihirakula, the scourge of the time. He fled to Kashmir, where he turned against the very king who had given him refuge and became the ruler. Thereafter, he attacked Gandhara, killed a fellow Hun ruler, and became the king. His death in 542 did not erase the memory of his horrors. A century later, when the famous Chinese monk Hsuan Tsang visited India, he went to Mihirakula's capital, Sakala (Sialkot), and wrote about his anti-Buddhist acts.

HARSHAVARDHANA

After the eclipse of the Gupta power, the center of power moved westward to Sthanvisvara (Thanesar) in the water-shed of the Sutlej and the Jumna. A war erupted among the Maukharis (whose capital was Kanauj or Kanyakubja), who had made themselves powerful during the waning days of the Gupta dynasty, and the then king of Thanesar killed both of the principal contestants. In fact, the Maukhari kingdom was left without an heir. The son of the just-killed king of Thanesar, Harshavardhana, or Har-sha, who was just sixteen years of age, succeeded him to the throne at Thanesar in 606 AC. He was to rule for forty-one years, build an empire, and establish for

himself a place in Indian history as one of the greatest kings ever.

Harsha's rule is one of the best-documented reigns in ancient India be-cause of the writings of two eminent men. One was the poet Bana, who was patronized by Harsha and wrote the lat-ter's biography, *Harsha Charita*. The materials in it, at least for the latter part of his reign, are corroborated by the ac-count left by the most highly esteemed among all the Chinese monk-travelers to come and stay in India, Hsuan Tsang. The latter lived in India from 629 to 645 CE, traveling all over the country, visiting Taxila University but spending most of his time at Nalanda University. He also spent some time at Harsha's court at Kanauj, where an assembly was held in his honor in 643 attended by twenty of Harsha's tributary rulers and more than 1,000 learned men from three religions: Buddhism, Jainism, and Hinduism. Harsha's account gives a vivid description of the ceremony last-ing several weeks, with a procession every day of the statue of Buddha and with Harsha himself holding the sacred umbrella over the statue. Hsuan Tsang's account, which has survived intact, pro-vides the most valuable description of India, its seasons, mountains and rivers, flora and fauna, soils and weather con-ditions in different regions appropriate to the crops, society and social stratifi-cation, towns and cities, and adminis-tration and military system. There was not one aspect of human life that he missed. In particular, he gives great credit to India's educational system and details the working of Nalanda University. When Hsuan Tsang returned to China via the Northwest and the Bamian Valley, he took with him 657 volumes of manuscripts; images of the Buddha in gold, silver, and sandalwood; and some relics of the master. After his return to his homeland, with the help of some associates, he worked feverishly on translating some 74 Buddhist works. He returned to China just a year before Harsha's death.

Harsha's empire extended over North India from Bengal to Kathiawar and from the northwest to Malwa. It was feudal in structure, the various kings paying obeisance to him and acknowledging his suzerainty. Harsha himself traveled often throughout his extensive domains. Unfortunately, when he died at the end of his long rule, he left no heir to succeed him. The feeble feudal imperial edifice that he had carefully built and retained with the force of his personality collapsed.

From all accounts, Harsha was a great patron of Buddhism, although he was a Hindu and a worshiper of Siva, as his biographer, Bana, says in *Harsha Charita*. It is possible that under Hsuan Tsang's powerful impact, he may have been swayed significantly to Buddhism, but there is no evidence that he embraced that faith. By nature, he was a very tolerant man, just like Akbar and Shivaji a thousand years later. Harsha

built a *vihara* for monks at Nalanda University and several thousand Buddhist *stupas* along the Ganges. At the same time, he built innumerable temples for Siva, resting houses for the *Saivite* devotees, and living accommodations for the priests.

Harsha has left an imprint on history as a man of great talents. He was a kind, compassionate ruler with concern for the welfare of his subjects. Hsuan Tsang records his practice of carefully listening to the complaints of his subjects with great patience and interest not only in the specially constructed audience hall but also in roadside pavilions during his extensive travels. He loved philosophy and literature and authored three plays of considerable merit: *Ratnavali, Priyadarsika,* and *Nagananda.*

Despite Harsha's patronage, Buddhism, according to the Chinese account, was on the decline. The Mahayana faith, in its use of the images of the Buddha and the bodhisattvas, use of "priests" in conducting rituals in Sanskrit, and depiction of the previous lives of the Buddha on temple walls, had approximated Hindu practices. It was left only for the Hindus to declare that Gautama Buddha was one of the ten incarnations of Vishnu. Buddhism had long been in decline. With the adoption by the Buddhists of Tibetan Tantrism (ca. 600–700 CE), Buddhism would shortly disappear from most of the subcontinent, surviving in the countries to which it had spread from India, including Sri Lanka and Southeast Asia. The Mahayana faith continued to flourish in East Asia and North Vietnam.

CONCLUSION

A panoramic sweep of the political history of ancient India would indicate very few instances of large polities and only two of empires—the Mauryas and the Guptas—which covered most of the subcontinent. Together, the two empires lasted about 470 years. Most empires of the ancient world did not last long, exceptions being the Holy Roman Empire, which, as they say, was neither holy, nor Roman, nor an empire. The Roman Empire, *per se*, including the years of decline, lasted a little more than four centuries. Most Chinese dynasties did not last that long.

The Puranas provide genealogies from the time of the Battle of the Mahabharata, which they place in 3102 BCE, to the Mauryas and the Guptas. The two epics *Ramayana* and *Mahabharata* mention the various kings and kingdoms of the time, but there is no agreement among scholars on the dating of the two epics. It is in the post-Buddhist period that a clearer political image emerges, and there are fairly reasonable details available until the end of the first millennium CE.

Despite the history of ancient India for most of the period being one of fragmented polities, there was a clear notion of the subcontinental political aspirations of kings. Afghanistan at least up to the river Oxus was included in this concept of "Bharatvarsha," which much later came to be commonly called India, following the Greek practice of referring to the peoples around and beyond Indus as people of *Indos*, hence the name India. The common use of the name India belongs to the period after the Europeans found their way to it. The Muslims, invaders and rulers, almost invariably called it Hindustan, "the country inhabited by the Hindus."

The limits of Bharatvarsha were known as being from the Himalayas to the tip of the peninsula in the Indian Ocean, and the country was known to be a part of the continent of Jambudvipa. The area bounded by the four points of the compass to the north, east, west, and south—respectively, Badrinath, Puri, Dwarka, and Rameshwaram—were the limits of Bharatvarsha, which would be the limits of the political ambition of the greatest of the monarchs. There was no desire or ambition to go beyond these "natural" limits and invade other countries and bring them under subjugation. Hence, the influence in Southeast Asia was cultural, not political. Except for one solitary invasion by Rajendra Chola of the Sri Vijaya kingdom in Sumatra, bringing it under his sway in the eleventh century for a brief quarter century, there is no instance of political aggrandizement in ancient India beyond India's borders.

———

NOTES

1. Jawaharlal Nehru, *The Discovery of India* (1946; reprint, New York: Anchor Books, 1960), 80.

2. Quoted in A. L. Basham, *The Wonder That Was India: A Survey of the History and Culture of the Indian Sub-continent Before the Coming of the Muslims,* 53–54, from J. Bloch, *Les inscriptions d'Asoka* (Paris: Éditions Les Belles Lettres, 1950), 125.

3. Ibid.

4. Basham, *Wonder That Was India,* 54.

5. Ibid.

6. Ibid., 164.

7. Ibid., 66.

The era of consolidation [200 BCE to 200 BCE] concluded with the beginnings of the spread of Indian influence in Southeast Asia. Beginning from the second century CE to the thirteenth and fourteenth centuries, all the kingdoms and peoples of Southeast Asia from Myanmar to the myriad islands of Southeast Asia, barring the Philippines, adopted the Indian system of thought, language and script, literature, arts, court protocol, sculpture, and urban architecture and superimposed them on the cultural substructure they already had. The cultural consolidation brought about in India made its transference to Southeast Asia easier than otherwise . . .   (pages 87–88)

6

THE ERA OF CONSOLIDATION
Political and Cultural

For some reason that cannot yet be fathomed, the ancient Indians had used only the human memory for transmission of knowledge and tradition from one generation to the other. Such a practice continued for centuries, from the Vedic times to a little after the birth of Buddhism and Jainism. The earliest texts in the written form were composed about two centuries after those religions were born. The first ruler to provide inscriptions was Asoka, who used the Brahmi script, which, with modification, became the Devanagari script, which was then used for transcribing from memory the whole body of knowledge from the Vedic times to that date.

The period from about 200 BCE to 200 CE may be regarded as the era of consolidation, when a large part of all that was known was put into the form of digests of all kinds. These included the two epics *Ramayana* and *Mahabharata*. They clearly relate to a much earlier period; the stories in them had been re-counted, added to, subtracted from, and revised over and over again until during this period when they were put into writing. The *Mahabharata* included the Bhagavad Gita, the Song of the Lord, consisting of the advice Lord Krishna, as charioteer, gives to Arjuna, the bravest of the Pandavas, on the battlefield of Kurukshetra. The second genre was the Puranas, eighteen in number, some of them repetitive, particularly since they provided the genealogies of important families of kings and the principal courtiers, sages, and teachers. The third category consisted of the six systems of philosophy and the voluminous Dharmasastras, a manual of religious, social, and ritual practice, including the Code of Manu.

The era of consolidation concluded with the beginnings of the spread of Indian influence in Southeast Asia. Beginning from the second century CE to the thirteenth and fourteenth centuries, all the kingdoms and peoples of Southeast Asia from Myanmar to the myriad islands of Southeast Asia, barring the

Philippines, adopted the Indian system of thought, language and script, literature, arts, court protocol, sculpture, and urban architecture and superimposed them on the cultural substructure they already had. The cultural consolidation brought about in India made its transference to Southeast Asia easier than otherwise, as described below.

THE EPICS AND THE PURANAS

With more than 100,000 two-line stanzas, the *Mahabharata* is the longest poem in the world, eight times longer than Homer's *Iliad* and *Odyssey* put together. The *Ramayana* is much shorter, with about 25,000 verses. The importance of both these epics is not merely historical or as sources of information about the polity and society, interpersonal relations, weaponry, and economy of the time. Some scholars might even dispute their historical veracity, but none can dispute that they have been "living" epics, through the millennia to the present, for millions of people of all ranks, rich and poor, policymakers and administrators alike. This is true as much for India as for Buddhist and Muslim Southeast Asia. When two decades ago Indian national television carried episodes from the two epics every Sunday morning, traffic, including railroad traffic, stopped because people did not want to miss the program. With slight variations peculiar to each country, the people of Myanmar and the royal courts and people of Thai-

land, Laos, and Cambodia (the last two in a subdued fashion because they are officially Communist and areligious) recite and enact the stories from those two epics in plays and dances. Indonesia, though predominantly Muslim, boasts of having the best *Ramayana* ballet in the world. Their shadow theater and puppet shows enact stories from the two epics into the early-morning hours. The main square in Jakarta carries a huge sculpture depicting the scene from the *Mahabharata* of Krishna as charioteer telling the meaning of life and death to Arjuna, one of the five Pandavas.

The epics give 3102 BCE as the year of the eighteen-day Battle of Kurukshetra (Panipat). There is no archaeological or documentary evidence in support of that date, which was possibly picked up because it marks the beginning of the fourth age, or *yuga*—the Kali Yuga—the worst of the four ages. Since the *Mahabharata* involves so much duplicity, greed, chicanery, and the ethical fall of great humans, the Puranas considered it representative of the beginning of a bad age, the decline of human character. The bad times would also be the justification for the appearance of Krishna, the godhead, who gives his message in the Bhagavad Gita, or Gita, regarded by Hindus as the Book.

The Bhagavad Gita

The Bhagavad Gita, composed between 100 BCE and 100 CE and translated into more than fifty languages, was available to the Western world for a long time only in its English translation, *The Song Celestial*, by Edwin Arnold. Its importance in India, in the words of Franklin Edgerton, lies in the fact that "it provides its Hindu adherents with the kind of personal, benevolent, tangibly recognizable, and gracious divinity whom they can understand and who they feel can understand them: a god, in essence, who takes upon himself the main burden of the personal salvation of his devotees." Edgerton adds that no religion can survive by "theology, by the philosophically subtle speculative system. . . . If, as Christians, each of us were expected to be a Thomas Aquinas or a Paul Tillich, one wonders what would be the fate of Christianity."[1]

The cult of Krishna became more popular after the fourth century BCE. Common people may not have been satisfied with the austerity of Buddhism, which put the whole burden of salvation on an individual, or the even more strict asceticism of Jainism. Buddhism became more popular only when Mahayana Buddhism, with its belief in the bodhisattvas and popular worship and ritual, resembling Hinduism, became available to them as a means for salvation.

The Gita combines three different strands in its monotheistic core. Krishna, a popular god of a local tribe, appears in a human form; he is at the same time an incarnation of the ancient Vedic god Vishnu, descended in a human guise and subject to hieratic ritual, and represents the metaphysical Absolute of

the Upanishads. His identification with Vishnu helped integrate diverse cults across the country. Thus, Krishna both is a monotheistic deity and has the shapeless, formless attributes of the Upanishadic Absolute, thereby having appeal to the higher intellectual circles as well as those of the lower classes who need some more concrete object for their devotion and worship.

The Upanishadic tradition, toward the end, offered a multiplicity of *margs* (paths) for attaining *moksha*, or liberation of the soul, among them *Gyana* (knowledge) *marg*, *Dhyana* (meditation) *marg*, and *Bhakti* (devotion) *marg*. The Gita did not deny the validity of the other *margs* that emphasized austerity and altruism, asceticism and self-denial, or selfless action. It emphasized *bhakti*, personal devotion to God through constant repetition of his name or his attributes, by men and women, through speech, dance, or music, "losing" oneself in the total dedication to him. In emphasizing the *Bhakti marg*, the Gita offered a feasible path to common people as well as the intellectual classes. This option would become popular later in the thirteenth to seventeenth centuries by the rise of the *bhakti* movement, popularized not only by Brahmans but also by saints drawn from all classes, one of them Chaitanya from Bengal. In the second half of the twentieth century, the Chaitanya cult was revived and made popular in the Western world, notably in the United States, by Swami Prabhupada and the Hare Krishna movement he initiated.

The "chanting Hare Krishnas" became a familiar sight, including at the airports. Scores of temples to Krishna were constructed in various parts of the world, taking the message of Gita, translated and edited by Prabhupada into English and translated into many other languages as well.

The epics speak of the four-class *varna* system, the four *ashramas* (stages) of life, the four goals of life. They do not speak of the caste system or untouchability, but they do mention *karma*, samsara, and rebirth. Together they formed the core of the Sanatana Dharma, popularly called Hinduism.

The Puranas

There were eighteen main Puranas and an equal number of Upa-Puranas, or subsidiary Puranas, most of the latter not extant. The main Puranas include the popular Bhagavata Purana and Vishnu Purana.

The Puranas, for the most part, serve as histories and have five main characteristics *(lakshanas):* history, genealogy of kings and gurus, cosmology, secondary creation, and Manvataras (the cyclical periods of Manu's rule extending more than 3 million years). In covering these five areas of inquiry and record, the Puranas describe the development of religion all the way from the Vedas to the first centuries of the Common Era. This is done through stories and legends, allegories, and chronicles of the principal historical events, written in a language that could be easily understood by commoners. As works of history, they lack a sense of precision and instill a need for documentation to verify the "facts."

The Bhagavad Purana, centered on Vishnu, details the activities of his ten avatars, or incarnations. An avatar is a form that Vishnu assumed to come down to earth to save it from some imminent danger, mostly to destroy evil and protect the virtuous. The ten avatars are: Matsya (Fish), Kurma (Tortoise), Varaha (Boar), Narasimha (Man-lion), Vamana (Dwarf), Parasurama (Rama, not the Rama of the *Ramayana*, with axe), Ramachandra (Rama, the hero of the *Ramayana*), Krishna (the expounder of the Gita), Buddha (the founder of Buddhism), and Kalki (who is expected to arrive at the end of the present Kali Yuga).

The Dharmasastras

There were several Dharmasastras (books of instructions in the sacred law), the most notable of them being that by Manu, which was composed in its extant and final form in the second or third century CE. The work known as *Manava Dharma Sastra* or *Manusmriti* (The Law Book of Manu) deals with the duties of persons of the four different *varnas*, or classes, at different stages of life; of the king and his officials toward the subjects and of the subjects toward the king; of husband and wife, parents and children. In general, they are weighted in favor of the Brahmans, who were their authors. The caste system described in these works shows a rigid social stratification, with no opportunity at all for anyone born in a particular caste to change it during his lifetime. As the invasions from the Northwest increased, bringing in different people such as the Bactrians, Scythians, Parthians, and Huns, who wanted to settle down in India, or as trade with foreign countries increased and some foreigners residing at the bustling port cities wanted to be integrated into Hindu society, the Code of Manu was referred to, and none of them would be absorbed at the highest level of the Brahmans. The difficulty was pervasive; none but those who were born into a particular caste could be allowed to be a member of it. In the case of invaders, a compromise seems to have been made by somewhat winking at the Code of Manu and giving them a place among the fighting class, the Kshatriyas.

The *Manusmriti* enunciates four sources of law: *sruti* (those that were heard), or the Vedas; *smruti* (those that were remembered), or the local texts; customs of holy men; and one's own inclination. The *sruti*, indeed, had primacy over the other three, and *smruti* over the other two. Since the Dharmasastras including the Code of Manu were based on the *sruti*, their authority was derivative. Even so, because of their basis in *sruti*, they were regarded as sacrosanct and divinely ordained.

Manu classified the code under eighteen heads. Eight of them concerned monetary transactions, including debts, gambling debts, partnerships, and payment of wages; disputes between master and servants; felonies such as assault and robbery; relations between husband and wife and questions of adultery; and inheritance. The punishments ranged in order of severity: gentle admonition, harsh warning, a fine, and corporal punishment. The really bad offenders like murderers were to be given the death penalty, and repeat offenders were to be banished.

The kings and administrators had to guard against being too severe in punishment lest they lose their place in heaven; they must be sure not to punish the undeserving and not to let off those who deserved to be punished. As much as possible, kings should preside over the court and be assisted by Brahmans in the interpretation of the Dharmasastras; in the king's absence, a learned Brahman, well versed in the Vedas, should preside over the court. The king was the protector of the dharma; many kings carried the title of Dharmaraja (which was, not coincidentally, the name of the eldest of the Pandavas, who held a reputation for being always just and truthful). Punishments must be both retributive and serve as deterrents. Capital punishment was to be imposed on those who killed Brahmans, women, and children; for treason; and for tampering with the loyalty of the king's ministers. The kings must use the *danda* (literally, "stick"), for, as Manu wrote, "The whole world is controlled by punishment," and *dandaniti* (morality regulated by punishment) is essential for a civilized life.

Manu's work was followed by some others, including Yajnavalkya, Narada, Brihaspati, and Katyayana, but none of them had the enduring value that Manu's Dharmasastra had as a source of reference in settling law cases or family disputes without going to litigation. There were several prestigious commentaries on Manu's Dharmasastra over the centuries as life varied and also became more complex. The commentaries of Medhatithi in the ninth or tenth century, Govindaraja in the eleventh, and Kulluka in the thirteenth are regarded as particularly valuable.

The Six Schools of Hindu Philosophy

Although there was some philosophical material in the Brahmanas, the real growth of philosophical thought begins with the Upanishads. Sarvepalli Radhakrishnan, the greatest Indian philosopher of twentieth-century India, held that the two epics "indirectly" presented philosophical doctrines and that the Bhagavad Gita, a part of the *Mahabharata*, ranks "as one of the three most authoritative texts in Indian philosophical literature."[2] Most of the six Indian philosophical systems had their beginnings from around the time of the rise of Buddhism and Jainism, coinciding with similar movements in Greece, China, and Persia, but were not crystallized until about the second or third century CE.

Hindu philosophy was by then classified into six doctrines, or schools of philosophy. All of them had the same goal of liberation of the soul and freeing it from samsara, the cycle of misery of going from birth to death and to rebirth.

The six systems[3] were presented in the form of sutras (literally, "strings"), in complementary groups of two. First and second were Nyaya (logical realism) and Vaisesika (the school of individual characteristics). The Nyaya school was more inclined to emphasize logic and epistemology and had very little to do with theology. On the other hand, the Vaisesika school was interested in questions of physics, with the belief that the entire physical world consists of atoms *(anu),* as distinct from four other elements—time, space, the soul, and the mind. Each element has individual characteristics, or *visesas,* hence the name of the school, Vaisesika, which talked about the duality of the soul and matter. In some of their analyses, Vaisesika philosophers sounded like atheists.

The third and fourth groups of schools consisted of Sankhya (evolutionary dualism), which resembles Jainism in its rigor, and Yoga, the school that held that psychic disciplined training was the best means of salvation. The Sankhya was the oldest of the six systems, mentioned as it was in an early form in the Upanishads and several times in the Bhagavad Gita. *Sankhya* means counting as well as reasoning. The originator of the Sankhya system was the sage Kapila, who held that "there are two entities, spirit and matter, *purusa* and *prakriti*. The phenomenal world that we see, the beings and their activities, are all manifold manifestations of matter." Matter is nonsentient and is based on three qualities *(guna)*: those that created virtue or purity *(sattva)*, passion *(rajas)*, and darkness *(tamas)*. Human personalities reflect the three *gunas*, and *sattva*, in a high proportion, represents the virtues of truth and the state of being happy. The quality of *rajas* exists more among those who are violent, active, passionate, or forceful. Last, *tamas* accounts for the element of stupidity, gloominess, or the state of unhappiness in a given person. These three *gunas* must be held in equilibrium. When the "equilibrium is disturbed and one or the other constituents gains the upper hand, matter starts evolving into cosmic intellect, egoity, the subtle elements and so on."[4]

The Sankhya system mentions twenty-five principles *(tatva)*, of which twenty-four fall under *prakriti* (matter), which is primary. It is *prakriti* that is responsible for the Creation, not some divine entity, which makes the Sankhya system close to atheism. From *prakriti* rise intelligence *(buddhi)* and self-consciousness *(ahankara)*, which produces five elements: ether, air, light, water, and earth. It also produces the five senses *(jnanendriya)* (hearing, touch, sight, taste, and smell) in addition to five senses involving action *(karmendriya)* (speech, grasping, walking, evacuation of bowels, and procreation). The ten correspond to the ten principal human organs except for the mind *(manas)*, which because of its special nature serves as the link between the ten organs and the outside world. The twenty-fifth principle is the most important: *purusa*, or "the person" but referring to the soul. This is where dualism comes in, because the *purusa* is not created by the *prakriti*, nor is it dependent on it. The world of matter can exist without the *purusa* or soul. Whereas *prakriti* is female, *purusa* is male.

In the same subgroup as Sankhya is the Yoga system, involving discipline of the mind and its control over the body. The basic work of the Yoga system is the yoga sutras of Patanjali, who was most likely not the same as the famous grammarian of that name. The yoga accepts the Sankhya but not its atheism; it believes that God (Iswara) is the supreme omniscient teacher. The royal yoga (rajayoga) outlined the yoga training in eight stages, the first two of which are self-control *(yama)*, dictated by five rules (nonviolence, truthfulness, not stealing, chastity, and nongreed), and observance *(niyama)*, which prescribed details on how to observe the five *yama*. The other six had to with the yogic *asanas* (postures); *pranayama* (control of breath); *pratyahara* (restraint); *dharana* (steadying of the mind) by concentrating on some single object, such as the tip of the nose, the navel, or a sacred symbol such as the syllable "om"; and *samadhi* (meditation).

Over the centuries, some additional yogic systems developed: *mantra* (spells) yoga; *hatha* (force) yoga, involving acrobatics; and *laya* (dissolution) yoga, close to *hatha* yoga and based on ancient Indian knowledge of human physiology. Another type, *kundalini* yoga, is based on the theory that *susumna*, the main vein of the body, runs through the spinal column. There are six points along the *susumna*, which are identified as "wheels," or centers of psychic energy. At the top of the vein in the human skull is *sahasrara*, the main psychic center, and in the lowest *cakra*, behind the genitals, is the *kundalini*, which can be awakened from its generally quiescent state by yogic exercises. The raising of the *kundalini* so it meets *sahasrara* is the aim of the yoga to attain superhuman power and salvation.

The third subgroup, numbers five and six of the system, consists of Mimamsa (inquiry), sometimes referred to as Purva (Early) and Uttar (Later) Mimamsa, also known as the Vedanta, the sixth system. Mimamsa represents an investigation into the Vedas, whereas the Vedanta deals with later Upanishadic thought and literally means "The End of the Vedas." Over time, the Vedantic school was subdivided into several schools. The principal work of the Vedantic system was the Brahma sutras of Badarayana. There have been numerous commentaries on the Vedanta, and it is the single system most read by Indian intellectuals and philosophers.

The greatest among the commentators on the Vedantic system was Sankaracharya (788–820 CE), born in Kaladi, Kerala. An orthodox Brahman, Sankaracharya dealt with the philosophical thought in the Upanishads, the Brahma sutras of Badarayana, and the Bhagavad Gita. He was the first to deal with the dualism in the later Upanishads as *brahman* and *atman*, microcosmos and macrocosmos, mind and matter, waking and dreaming. Sankaracharya postulated that the universe must be perceived on two levels of truth: on the phenomenal level of the Sankhya system, the world as created by the god Brahma, whereas on the highest level of truth, the world was *maya*, illusion, unreal, a product of the imagination. The absolute truth was the Upanishadic or Vedantic reality of the *brahman*, the universal or cosmic soul, which is the same as the individual soul, the *atman*. The first version of truth is meant for the masses, appropriate for popular or sectarian Hinduism, whereas the second one, which stays away from the phenomenal world, is meant for intellectuals and therefore is referred to as "higher Hinduism." Sankaracharya's doctrine was pure monism and was, therefore, known as *advaita* (nondual).

Sankaracharya took note of the contradictions in the 108 Upanishads. His major feat was the interpretation he gave to some of the illustrations and aphorisms, through the use of dialectics, indicating that the disputed contradictory phrases had been used only figuratively and that what were apparent contradictions in the Upanishads were not so at all. Most intellectuals in India continue to abide by Sankaracharya's interpretations and analysis of the Vedanta. In A. L. Basham's view, "The comparison of Sankara in Hinduism with St. Thomas Aquinas in the Roman Catholic Church is a fair one."[5]

Sankaracharya has left a deep imprint on Hinduism through the establishment of *mathas* (monasteries) at Sringeri in Mysore, Dwarka in Saurashtra, Puri in Orissa, and Badrinath in the Himalayas, roughly marking the four points of the compass on the Indian subcontinent. He traveled throughout India to spread the monistic message of the *advaita* doctrine.

Although all six systems of philosophy were led by the orthodox and were based on the acceptance of the Vedas, there were, indeed, some systems of philosophy that did not accept the Vedas. Buddhists and Jains were, by definition, nonbelievers in the Vedas. One system that was not part of those two faiths and still outside the Vedic fold was the Carvaka or Lokayata school. They believed purely and simply in materialism.

India's "Cultural Empire" in Southeast Asia

India had no political ambitions beyond its borders (except Rajendra Chola's solitary invasion much later in the eleventh century and occupation of Sri Vijaya for a quarter century) but was content that the Southeast Asian kings and people desired Indian culture. Beginning in the second century CE with

Funan, all the kingdoms of Southeast Asia—Champa and Angkor; Sukhotai and Ayuthaya; the kingdoms of the Pyus, Mons, and Tibeto-Burmans in Myanmar; Sri Vijaya; and various dynasties of Java—all adopted Indian culture, in fact readily, as it came without any political strings. The initiative was taken by the Southeast Asian monarchs, who sent emissaries to India to request from the courts in India—North, East, and South—that Brahmans, with the cultural package that had been organized and assembled during the era of consolidation, be sent to make the cultural transference possible. These monarchs were most likely motivated to legitimate their polity in the eyes of their own people and also raise themselves to a higher cultural level by having courts that resembled those in India.

Southeast Asians adopted Indian alphabetical scripts, first using Sanskrit in their inscriptions and later switching to their own local languages. They produced literature, codes of law, and court protocol all based on Indian prototypes, not only taking the help of the Brahmans but also sending scholars to Indian universities for further learning. Their works of sculpture show indigenous genius blended with ideas and concepts borrowed from India. Their courts glittered with dances and music, some of it borrowed from India, though they retained their own older forms, such as the *gamelan* in Indonesia. They adopted the ethical content of the *Mahabharata* and the *Ramayana*, some of their kings and scholars producing their own versions, such as the *Ramakien* in Ayuthaya, with changes in the names of some of the characters. The Thai kings, from their beginnings with Rama Khamheng in Sukhotai and later Rama Tibodi (Ramadhipati) in Ayuthaya (Rama's capital in *Ramayana*) to the present dynasty beginning with Rama I in 1782 (the present king is Rama IX), took the title of Rama, known for his valor, moral integrity, and justice, to promise to the people a fair and just rule.

There were at least two areas of reservations that Southeast Asians demonstrated in their adoption of Indian culture. One was in the nonadoption of the *varna* system along with its *jati* (caste) system. This was perhaps because the Brahmans did not allow such a social structure to be transplanted, as it had its origins in the *Purusa-sukta,* the sacrifice of primeval man through an elaborate ritual that could not be replicated in some other geographical milieu. The second area of nonadoption must have been deliberate. Around the time that Indian culture began to be transmitted around Southeast Asia, the Indian cultural consolidation included the Code of Manu, which gave lowly status to women. The tradition in Southeast Asia from the early times to this day has been to give women very high status. This is one more argument to bolster the thesis that the initiative to adopt Indian culture came from Southeast Asians, who were discriminating in their cultural borrowings.

HINDUISM

Hinduism is not a static religion. No religion, in fact, is static, in the sense that interpretations of it over time depend so much on the psychological and moral conditioning of the scholars, scriptural authorities, or religious jurists. Today, Hinduism is an inclusive religion of nearly 1 billion people on the Indian subcontinent and among the majority of about 20 million in the Indian diaspora around the globe.

Hinduism includes beliefs compiled in the *srutis* (those that were heard), mostly the Vedic literature, and the *smritis* (those that were remembered), the epics *(Ramayana* and the *Mahabharata),* the Puranas, and the Dharmasastras—to mention only the most important. In the process, the body of beliefs called Sanatana Dharma, later called Hinduism, emerged, devoid of the aboriginal faiths as well as the specific belief systems of Buddhism and Jainism, though some of the beliefs of those two religions, such as the concept of karma, are primarily integral to Hinduism.

The authority of the *sruti* is regarded as primary. The term is applied mostly to the Vedas and the commentaries thereon, whereas the *smruti* are regarded as secondary. As T. M. P. Mahadevan explains, "*Sruti* is revelation; *smruti* is tradition. As between the two, *Sruti* is primary because it is a form of direct experience whereas the *Smruti* is secondary, since it is a recollection of that experience."[6]

It is difficult to define Hinduism in precise terms. A religion does not have to be what it means in the Western sense, conforming with the Abrahamic faiths—Judaism, Christianity, or Islam—in their essential components of God's revelation, one central book, and monotheism. A religion may be described as a belief or set of beliefs binding the spiritual nature of man to a supernatural being, be it God or Creator or Absolute Truth. It generally involves a feeling of dependence on the supernatural being and responsibility or accountability through ethical behavior as required by the founder of the religion or some principal book, whether it is the Bible, Koran, Tripitaka, Grantha Sahib, or Bhagavad Gita. Religion is the reverent acknowledgment of a divine being and includes worship, whether it is external and formal or the reverence of the human spirit for the divine seeking outward expression. All religions include rituals and worship generally and on special occasions—birth, marriage, and death. The social components of religions include festivals marking solstices, eclipses, movement of the planets, harvesting, and thanksgiving. Most religions provide a concept of the hereafter, what happens to human beings after death, and lay down a way of life governing relationships among members of a family, marriage, and inheritance.

Broadly speaking, Hinduism includes the doctrine of transmigration of souls, known as samsara, with its corollary that all living beings, whether humans, animals, birds, or insects, have a soul; it is an apparent polytheism involving worship of numerous gods and goddesses "subsumed in a fundamental monotheism by the doctrine that all lesser divinities are subordinate aspects of the one God." In the Bhagavad Gita, the incarnate God, Krishna, says: "Whatever god a man worships, it is I who answers the prayer." There is in Hinduism a tendency toward mysticism and monistic philosophy. Last, Hinduism includes a social hierarchical structure signified by *varnas* and *jatis* (classes and castes). In the beginning centuries of the Common Era, numbers of persons were deemed to have lost their caste and were pejoratively pronounced outcastes or untouchables.

Reaction from Within the Vedic Fold

The growing uncertainty and misery of the masses of people around the time of Buddhism and Jainism (the sixth and fifth centuries BCE) were partly caused by the political upheavals of the time. The increasing power and prosperity of the emerging states, whether monarchical or republican, propelled political rivalries and constant warfare. And although the doctrines of samsara and karma seemed to offer relatively satisfactory explanations for the causes of the misery, they could not stem the tide of pessimism and despondency in the public. Scholars and seers were looked up to for a solution to the ending of the painful cycle of births and rebirths. Several different, though related, *margs* (paths) were suggested, any of which or a combination would lead one to *moksha*, or salvation: meditation *(Dhyan marg)*, knowledge *(Gyan marg)*, and devotion *(Bhakti marg)*. There was concern among the sages and thinkers that too many members of the society would adopt the *Dhyan* and *Gyan margs*. They sought a balance in life by dividing its span into four stages that would provide both for materialism and for spiritualism.

The Dharmasastras laid down a way of life for all that would reduce the rigor and severity of life and make for a balanced, peaceful journey on earth. It stipulated duties for four natural stages of life, or *varnasramadharma*: *brahmacharyasrama* during adolescence, *grihasthasrama* during youth and early middle age, *vanaprasthasrama* during later middle age, and *sanyasasrama* during old age until one's death or, if one is very fortunate, the attainment of *moksa*. The four *asramas* corresponded to the spirit of the four parts of the Vedas: Mantra, Brahmanas, Aranyakas, and Upanishads.

Brahmacharyasrama marked the stage when a little boy, after performing the *upanayana*, the sacred thread ceremony, went to the house of the guru, generally at the age of eight. Here children of the rich and the poor lived together without regard to their backgrounds, all dedicated to the pursuit of learning from their teacher. Partly in exchange for the education they received, they served in the teacher's household, helping the teacher's wife in her chores, tending the cattle and the farm. Among the important tasks were collecting fuel (wood and cow-dung cakes), keeping the sacred fire burning, and going from house to house begging for food. Those who gave received merit. The education, mostly in the arts and sciences, included in the case of children from the Kshatriya (warrior) families the martial arts. Students were taught the Vedas and the commentaries thereon, particularly the Brahmanas. They learned the proper way of reciting the mantras. During the *brahmacharyasrama*, the student was to be celibate. The period of training or studentship was generally twelve years, after which the youth returned to his parents' home, ready to take up the responsibilities pertinent to the next *asrama*.

After the studentship, one was expected to get married and take up the responsibilities of life. Marriage was regarded as a sacrament, with the duty to procreate and continue the human race. The wife was to be regarded as a life partner; it was to be a life together according to the tenets of the dharma, with full consciousness of the duties as a *grihasthi*, or householder. He should keep the marriage vows, which included consulting the spouse in matters of dharma, *kama* (sex and material pleasures), *artha* (acquisition and disbursement of wealth), and *moksa*. These included five *yajnas*, or sacrifices: *brahma-yajna*, or sacrifice to *Brahman*, which consisted of study and teaching of the Vedas; *deva-yajna,* or sacrifice to the gods by offering oblations; *pitr-yajna,* or sacrifice to the departed ancestors by making food offerings on the appointed *shraddha* ceremony; *bhuta-yajna,* or the sacrifice to the domestic animals by taking care of them; and *manusya-yajna,* or sacrifice to men by feeding guests, the homeless, and holy wanderers. The *grihasthi* was regarded by Manu, the lawgiver, the pillar of the society, as being as essential as air to living beings, since it was his duty to provide support to the three *asramas.* He should certainly enjoy himself and indulge in different kinds of pleasure but always within the limits of moral law.

Vanaprasthasrama was the third stage of life. After the responsibilities of a householder were taken care of, that is, raising children and getting them married and fairly well settled, a *grihasthi* should decide to withdraw from the routine responsibilities of life, passing them on to his sons. He should retire to the forest with his wife (if she is not willing, he should leave her with his sons) and live a simple life. Manu says, "When the householder notices wrinkles in his skin, gray hair and the son of his son, let him retire to the forest." Married life, or *grihasthasrama,* is not an end in itself. There is a higher life than that. Therefore, when a householder had finished his responsibilities, he was to retire to the forest to devote all his time to spiritual pursuits and undergo his second period of training. In the *vanaprasthasrama,* he did not perform rituals; instead, he devoted his mind to spiritual and intellectual matters, contemplating the hereafter and the universe. As laid down by Manu, the lawgiver, the *vanaprastha* (hermit) was to bathe himself twice or thrice a day; eat simple food consisting of forest produce but only once a day, preferably in the middle of the day; perform the five daily *yajnas;* and generally live a life of continence, refraining from all pleasures, including sexual intercourse. Life in the *vanaprasthasrama* prepared an individual for the fourth and final stage of life, the *sanyasasrama.*

The Dharmasastras do not prescribe an age for this stage of life, when a person became a *sanyasin* (monk) and single-mindedly sought to realize the *Brahman,* or the Absolute Truth, as laid down in the Upanishads. A *sanyasin* completely renounced all worldly possessions and pleasures, except for a change of garments, which were usually two pieces of cloth to cover his middle and the torso, mostly of the saffron color; a staff, a begging bowl, and a water jug completed his "possessions." His sole goal was the attainment of *moksa* (liberation of the soul) and to that end attainment of spiritual perfection and total freedom. He slept little and tried to spend all his waking hours meditating and thinking of life's mysteries and on the unity of the *brahman* and the *atman,* the microcosm and the macrocosm. As Mahadevan observes:

He [*sanyasin*] is the spiritual sentinel of the race. He is the same in honour and dishonour, success and failure. He is the free man of the spirit who has broken through the narrow circles of clan and country. He loves all and hates none. He has no private ambitions or personal desires. He has no wants and is impelled by no desire. He has nothing to accomplish in this world or in the next. . . . He revels in the bliss of God.[7]

A true *sanyasin* was regarded as the perfect man, who had completed the cycle of life and was deserving of *moksa,* his soul liberated from the painful cycle of births and rebirths.

THE *BHAKTI* MOVEMENT

The origins of the *bhakti* movement with its emphasis on devotion and appeal to the masses lie first in South India, where the Brahmans realized that they were losing the masses to Buddhism because of the monks' practice of going to the general public and speaking to them in their own language rather than insisting on the use of Pali, in which the Buddhist texts were originally written. The Brahmans, therefore, began to bring the truths of the Upanishads and other philosophical materials to the masses in simple language they could follow. Additionally, the saintly persons among the Brahmans and later among the non-Brahmans increasingly

resorted to the medium of poetry, witty aphorisms, and stories to convey such truths more pleasingly to the masses. Some of these saints also composed songs in the languages of the masses and set them to music. They encouraged the masses to sing with them and dance in devotion to Siva or Vishnu depending on the affiliation of the saint concerned to Saivism or Vaishnavism.

The beginnings of such devotional singing were found in Tamil Nadu, where a number of such saints arose between the fourth and ninth centuries CE. They traveled on foot from village to village, town to town, temple to temple, singing such philosophical songs in simple language of the masses. From the Pallava country, the devotional, or *bhakti,* movement was carried to Southeast Asia, where Hinduism and Buddhism were spreading rapidly among the common people. The saints of Siva, known as Nayanars, called the devotional hymns *Devaram,* and the saints of Vishnu, known as *Alvars,* called their hymns the *Divya Prabandham.* The saintly, devotional *bhakti* tradition was in full bloom in the eighth and ninth centuries CE, continued thereafter, and has remained alive and popular to this date in Tamil Nadu.

Tamil *bhakti* saints such as Jnanasambandha and Tirunavukkarashu (both in the seventh century CE) and Manikkavaschakar (born in the eighth century) were popular and effective in keeping the followers of the Sanatana Dharma within the Hindu fold. The first of them helped to reconvert the Pallava ruler, Mahendra Varman's sister, Tilakavati, from Jainism to the worship of Siva; a similar reconversion of the Pandya king of the time from Jainism to the worship of Siva is attributed to the second saint. The third was a minister of the Pandya court, who became a saint and reconverted large numbers from Buddhism to Saivism.

The *bhakti* movement spread from Tamil Nadu to Karnataka and Maharashtra. The movement became very popular and was carried by Hindu pilgrims to Varanasi to the North, where Hindi-speaking saints popularized the cult of devotion, or *bhakti,* all over the countryside. Prominent among the Kannada (Karnataka) saints were Basavaraja of the twelfth century, a devotee of Siva, and Purandaradasa of the fifteenth century, a devotee of Vishnu, who is also credited with founding the Karnataka school of music. In Maharashtra, the most celebrated name of the *bhakti* saints is Jnyanadeva (1275–1296), who was one of four saintly siblings. He is credited with the founding of the Marathi language, into which he translated and commented on the Gita, his work being known as the *Jnyaneswari,* which is still popular in Maharashtra. In that state, the *bhakti* tradition is most active at Pandharpur, where hundreds of thousands of singing and dancing devotees called *varkaris* regardless of caste or gender and from all strata of society congregate from

different parts of Maharashtra every year. The movement grew tremendously during the time of Tukaram (sixteenth century), a non-Brahman saint.

The movement became richer with the practice of setting entire texts of the epics *Ramayana* and *Mahabharata* as well as some of the Puranas, notably, the Bhagavata Purana, to a musical recitation by saintly persons. In the process, the *Ramayana* came to be translated into Tamil by Kamban and into Hindi by Tulsidas. The movement contributed to the development of vernacular languages all over the country from about the eleventh or twelfth century onward. The movement also gave impetus to a renaissance in music, as devotional songs, or *bhajans,* were sung not only in temples but also in *bhajan sabhaghars* (devotional singing halls).

It is quite likely that a similar Hindu reaction set in when the Brahmans realized the growing popularity of the Muslim Sufi dervishes and saints, who spoke to the masses in their languages and also sang and danced in devotion to Allah. The *bhakti* movement picked up again during the fourteenth to sixteenth centuries as a result of the need for the Hindus to retain the common masses within the Hindu fold. The independent growth of vernacular languages in this period helped the growth of the *bhakti* movement, as the new saints, coming from non-Brahman castes, appealed to all classes to seek salvation through devotion, singing to their God, and approaching him directly.

Among the most important *bhakti* saints was Mirabai (1498–1547) from Rajasthan in the sixteenth century. As a young widow in a princely family, she gave up the life of seclusion then deemed appropriate to a widow and declared that she was married to Lord Krishna. Mirabai's songs are extremely popular all over India. So is the Hindi translation of *Ramayana* by Tulsidas in the sixteenth or seventeenth century. Excerpts from *The Ramacharitamanas* are musically recited in untold number of households in North India every day and recited before the masses in multiday, usually nine-day, Ram festivals across the land.

From the two ends of the country, West and East, came two saints who made an immense impact on the masses of people of all levels. One was Narsi Mehta from Gujarat, whose song "Vaishnava Jana To" was the one *bhajan* sung by Gandhi every day. The other, from the East, in Bengal, was Chaitanya Mahaprabhu, the dancing and singing saint, whose popularity revived with the establishment of the International Society of Krishna Consciousness by Swami Prabhupada in Los Angeles and its temples all over the world beginning in the mid-twentieth century.

The greatest among the *bhakti* saints from South India in more recent times was Tyagaraja (1767–1847), a Telugu-speaking South Indian music composer living in Tamil Nadu. His compositions, dedicated, for the most part, to Rama, are used most of the time in South Indian concerts and *bharata natyam* (classical dance performances).

Perhaps the best example of a popular *bhakti* saint coming from lowly non-Brahman stock and appealing to the followers of both the Hindus and the Muslims was Kabir in the fifteenth or sixteenth century, born at Varanasi into a weaver family. He established an order of monks and nuns who belonged to a cult called Kabir Panth, which has flourished to this date. Kabir's *dohas* continue to be sung in millions of households, particularly in northern and western India. India's Nobel Laureate, Rabindranath Tagore, translated Kabir's poems, one of which is the following:

> If God be within the mosque, then to
>   whom does this world belong?
> If Ram be within the image which
>   you find upon your pilgrimage,
>   then who is there to know what
>   happens without?
> Hari is in the East: Allah is in
>   the West. Look within your heart,
>   for there you will find both Karim
>   and Ram;
> All the men and women of the world
>   are His living forms.
> Kabir is the child of Allah and of Ram;
>   He is my Guru, he is my Pir.[8]

Gandhi very often included Kabir's songs in his daily public prayer meetings. Kabir's contribution to the evolution of Hindu-Muslim understanding and the secular traditions of India is immense.

THE CASTE SYSTEM

The classification of human society into hierarchical classes is not uniquely or exclusively Indian or Hindu. What is peculiar about the Hindu system is its persistence through a couple of millennia since it began and took hold. It is also notable that its earlier flexibility regarding moving from one class to another was lost in the last centuries before the Common Era and one's birth in a given family became the determinant of his or her caste.

Looking elsewhere in history, one finds Herodotus, who said that in ancient Egypt there were seven classes: priests, fighting men, herdsmen, swineherds, tradesmen, interpreters, and navigators.[9] At least three of them were the same as in India. As for untouchables, the Sandals of Myanmar and the Eta in Japan fitted that class.[10]

It was and is difficult to provide a precise definition of the caste system. The word itself came from the Portuguese *casta,* signifying breed, race, or kind. Scholars have quoted each other and proceeded to demolish their own definitions through descriptions of what they saw in Indian Hindu society. Herbert Hope Risley defined it as follows: "A collection of families or groups of families bearing a common name, claiming a common descent from a mythical ancestor, human or divine; professing to follow the same hereditary calling; and regarded by those who are competent to give an opinion as forming 'a single homogenous community.'"[11] An Indian scholar of great distinction and Risley's contemporary in the beginning of the twentieth century, S. V. Ketkar, defined caste as

a social group having two characteristics: (a) membership is confined to those who are born of members and includes all persons so born; (b) the members are forbidden by an inexorable social law to marry outside the group. Each one of these groups has a special name by which it is so called, several of such small aggregates are grouped together under a common name, while these large groups are but sub-divisions of groups still larger which have independent names. Thus we see that there are several stages of groups and that the word "caste" is applied to groups at any stage. . . . In this way two hundred million Hindus are so much divided and sub-divided that there are castes who cannot marry outside fifteen families.[12]

A quarter century later, N. K. Dutt refrained from defining *caste,* but described its features:

[A] member of a caste cannot marry outside it; there are similar but less rigid restrictions on eating and drinking with a member of another caste; there are fixed occupations for many castes; there is some hierarchical gradations of castes, the best recognized position being that of the Brahmans at the top; birth determines a man's caste for life unless he be expelled for violation of its rules. Otherwise, transition from one caste to another is not possible; the whole system turns on the prestige of the Brahman.[13]

In understanding the caste system, three terms are very important: *endogamous, exogamous,* and *pollution.* The first of these is an anthropological term signifying "customs of marriage within the group, class, caste, or tribe." The next term means exactly the opposite: "the custom of certain peoples forbidding any man to marry within his own tribe or clan or family." *Jatis* are endogamous social units, each *jati* having its own distinct traditions and customs while adhering to the core of Hindu beliefs. Untouchability was determined by the concept of "pollution," which, generally speaking, meant the handling of filth by certain categories of persons involved with the disposal of animal carcasses, including cows; human emissions; tanning and leatherwork; and the making and selling of alcohol, to mention a few. Hindus would feel polluted by touch from this caste (therefore, untouchables, or *achuta* in most of North India), and in some areas even by being approached by a member of the "polluted class."

The Origin of the Caste System

A distinction must first be made between classes and castes, *varnas* and *jatis,* respectively. There were four *var-*nas during the time of the Vedas, originating from the *Purusa-sukta* sacrifice when the Prajapati, Lord of Creatures, is believed to have sacrificed the Cosmic Man to himself. The four *varnas*—Brahmans, Kshatriyas, Vaishyas, and Sudras—emerged from four parts of the Cosmic Man: the mouth, arms, thighs, and feet, respectively. These four parts indicated four main professions, an open class system, which regarded the Brahmans as the most superior and the Sudras, who were mostly menials, at the bottom. It was perfectly in order for an individual to change his identity by switching his profession. Over the course of time, the fourfold division of society became inflexible; one's birth determined one's class, which could be altered only with rebirth, depending on one's karma, a concept that became prevalent during the Upanishadic times. Though the Dharmasastras prescribed specific occupations as falling under these four broad classes, in practice there were any number of exceptions, indicating a certain amount of occupational fluidity in either direction, upward or downward, in the class hierarchy. The same legal treatise stated that a rise in status would result from a woman marrying someone from a higher class *(anuloma),* and correspondingly losing her higher status by marrying a person from a lower caste *(pratiloma).*

The word *varna* literally means "color," which would suggest four different shades, each particular to a class.

In fact, this was never so and is not the case today. At the time of the supposed original cosmic sacrifice, the first three classes were designated by their Aryan and light-skinned origin, whereas the fourth class, the Sudras, was regarded as having come from the Dravidians or the *dasas* mentioned in the Vedas. *Varnas* were supposed to have thereby created a social order in which the Aryans had come to terms with the non-Aryans, including the Dravidians, the original inhabitants of the land, if one accepted the proposition that the Aryans were immigrants from outside of the subcontinent.

To emphasize the twofold division based on color, the first three *varnas* held the privilege of performing the *up-anayana* ceremony, generally carried out at the age of eight before the beginning of *brahmacharyasrama*, the first of the four *asramas*. The ceremony included wearing a sacred thread across the shoulder from right to left, a sort of consecration, which made the person twice-born *(dwija)*. Only those who had completed the ceremony were entitled to recite the sacred *gayatri-mantra* and to study Vedic lore.

The Brahmans also adopted certain restrictions on themselves to emphasize purity in their ordinary routine. Thus, they would not drink or eat anything before cleaning their bodies through a bath. Their food would not be cooked without first taking a bath. They would not worship gods or perform any ritual without a bath and or wear clothes touched by anybody else after they had been washed and put up to dry. The Brahmans also kept their "superior" status by renouncing the consumption of meats and embracing vegetarianism. The proposition that this division was based on color, the literal meaning of the word *varna*, does not hold, considering that so many among the three upper *varnas* are dark-skinned and some among the Sudras and the untouchables are not. It should also be pointed out that many castes in a *varna* lower than that of Brahmans often led a Brahmanical way of life, adopting vegetarianism and generally following the Brahmanical purist routine of cleanliness, thereby creating a new caste or subcaste of a higher rank than the others in the same *varna*.

The contention that the class system was a "benign division of labor" without any moral judgment on the superiority of one over the other is even more contestable. There is absolutely no evidence of this. It succeeded in creating a hierarchy where a whole class looked down on the other, the *dwijas* on the Sudras and all four on the untouchables. Profession-wise, numerous Brahmans departed from their normal occupations as priests, scholars, astronomers, and astrologers to take up martial arts, not just as teachers and trainers but also as warriors, some of whom succeeded in ascending the throne as rulers and established political dynasties. All three other *varnas* and, in some cases, the untouchables produced saints and scholars. The "benign division of labor" is not tenable at all. There is more reason to assume that the class divisions, particularly the Sudras and untouchables, were created and perpetuated more as a form of economic exploitation than by any other rationalization.

Over the centuries, the broad four-fold class system came to be subdivided into several thousand castes or *jatis*. The extensions were approved as a part of the great tradition of the Vedas by stating that they were still within the fourfold *varnas*. Absent in the Vedic literature, castes are mentioned in the Dharmasastras and in the later *smriti* literature. Of the literally thousands of *jatis,* some have a membership of no more than a few hundred, whereas others may have more than a million. The smaller *jatis* find it hard to find brides or grooms within the caste fold; there is also the biological risk associated with inbreeding. Until very recent times and even now in very traditional, orthodox, rural milieus, members of a *jati* would dine together and intermarry only with members of their *jati*. In many cases, they would not eat food cooked by someone from another caste, with the exception that food cooked by a Brahman could be consumed by all *jatis*. Again, the origin of the different *jatis* is not precisely known, though most *jatis* carry the oral tradition of their own origins and how the *jatis* that were at one time part of them became differentiated, an account that may or may not

find corroboration with the ones who were thrown out or moved out of the fold. Most of the time, the *jatis* belonging to a given *varna* are operating within a geographical and linguistic region. Thus, a Brahman from Uttar Pradesh may dine with a Brahman from Maharashtra but may not marry one. The cultural nuances of caste members within a *varna* were often different enough to discourage intermarriages. This, however, does not apply as much to the former princely class in the country, all of them Kshatriyas, who were matrimonially allied with one another across state and linguistic lines.

How did the differentiation leading to different *jatis* come about? Experts relate it to different historical and social conditions, including "an incomplete detribalization." When it became problematical for the lawgivers to give a person or a group of persons an identity, the general course was to accommodate them in the largest *varna* category, the Sudras, and generally give a new caste based on the profession in a certain geographical region. Often, members of a caste threw individuals and families out of their caste for simple transgressions. This could lead to a general meeting of the heads of caste families, *mahajans,* who might decide to condone and contain the transgression or rule against the transgressors, who would band together and form another caste. Examples of this kind compounded all over the country and are a part of the oral traditions.

The origins of untouchability are even more obscure. Untouchability is not mentioned in any of the Vedic literature—the Vedas, Brahmanas, Aranyakas, or Upanishads. That would have been outside the great tradition in the sense that the original *Purusa-sukta* sacrifice has no justification for it. Some hold that the heinous practice of untouchability crystallized around the second century CE. The first mention of it in a written document was in the Chinese traveler Fa Hsien's account of the fourth century CE. Because untouchables did not fit into the Vedic fourfold *varna* system, they were sometimes called "outcastes" or were said to be "without caste" and in some areas were called *Panchama,* the fifth *varna.* If purity and pollution are the basis of Hindu society, as Louis Dumont holds, the Brahmans and the untouchables are at opposite ends of the same pole—either having purity or having a lack of it.[14]

Born in the Vaishya community, Gandhi, who lived among the sweepers, cleaned the latrines just as they did, and worked for their political rights on a par with the caste Hindus, selected a new term for the untouchables after holding a national competition. In 1933, he announced "harijans" (literally, "people of God") as the new name, and it was widely accepted in the country and proudly accepted by millions of untouchables themselves for their self-identity. This did not mean that others were not children of God. Gandhi's weekly, pub-

lished in numerous Indian languages and English, was titled *Harijan,* though its coverage included all kinds of subjects besides the plight and regeneration of the harijans. The term became popular and was generally accepted from the 1930s to the 1970s, when the term *dalit* began, rather rapidly, to replace it. A Marathi word with Sanskrit origins, it means "broken or ground to pieces." Its first use as applied to the oppressed classes is attributed to the nineteenth-century Maharashtrian reformer Jyotiba Phule, who was also known by the respectable title "Mahatma," "the great-souled," showing his standing among the public, then and now. In the 1970s, the term *dalit* was adopted by activists of the untouchable *mahar* caste in Maharashtra.[15] Like *harijan,* the term *dalit* is intensely political. It is not as widely used in other areas such as Bihar, Uttar Pradesh, or West Bengal as it is in Maharashtra, where there is a highly respected genre of literature called *dalit* literature, the most notable exponent of it being Namdeo Dhassal.

The first to bring the untouchables to political prominence were the colonial British, who found them useful as a category to divide the Hindu majority. Already, the separate electorates had become a feature of Indian politics since the Morley-Minto Reforms of 1909 and had come to be accepted by the leading nationalist organization, the Indian National Congress, through the Congress-League Pact of 1916. The 1931 census used the term *Scheduled Castes* (SC) as the official identifying term for the untouchables. In 1936, the government of India enumerated the different castes among the untouchables in a schedule (hence the term *Scheduled Castes*). The castes that would be so regarded would be conferred separate status for assembly and parliamentary seats as well as for special benefits in education and employment. The practice has endured to date because of specific provisions for the Scheduled Castes in the Indian Constitution and considerable legislation thereafter not only for extending the initial period provided in the Constitution but also for making untouchability an offense. Thus, the Untouchability Act of 1955 provides penalties for the offenders. Since the abolition of untouchability in the Indian Constitution, some have used the term *ex-untouchables*, which would be, legally speaking, the correct term.

The general identification of the untouchables with carrying out "unclean" professions is problematic, to say the least. Going by the census figures, the SC number about 15 percent of the Indian population, or roughly 170 million. Such a high number could not have been the biological descendants of the practitioners of the so-called polluting professions. As Oliver Mendelsohn and Marika Vicziany point out, *chamars* (shoemakers or leather workers) have been mostly agricultural laborers, whereas *mahars* (bamboo weavers) in Maharashtra "traditionally performed work that was mostly non-polluting." Generally, the untouchables did not have specialized skills,

mostly working as "village servants and messengers, though sometimes they collected dead animals." Curiously, the untouchables too are subdivided into their own *jatis*. To quote Mendelsohn and Vicziany again: "Untouchables are just as divided from each other along caste, regional, linguistic and general cultural lines as they are from the rest of the Indian society."[16]

WOMEN IN ANCIENT INDIA

Contradictions, the Ideal, and the Real

Most societies are riddled with contradictions, some more so than others. The contradictions sometimes appear at different times but are often contemporaneous. Such is the case with the place of women in ancient India. There is consistency in regarding women, particularly mothers, in an idealized form throughout Indian history. Despite the ups and downs, some attitudes were consistently held by the Hindus throughout their history, both before and after the advent of Islam and the West. Thus, they believed that when the universe was created, two forces emerged: *purush* (male) and *prakriti* (female), both equally important and powerful. When rituals were performed, it was essential to have both husband and wife committing themselves through the mantras to a variety of propositions and making offerings. Husband and wife *(pati* and *patni)* made for one complete entity, with wife mentioned specifically as one-half of the whole *(ardhangini)*. Marriage vows to date have included the groom consulting his soon-to-be spouse in all matters involving dharma (religion and duty), *artha* (material matters), and *kama* (enjoyment of sex). Women were and are respected. Indians are brought up to look at a stranger woman, not necessarily a damsel in distress, depending on her age and mien as his mother, grandmother, sister, or sister-in-law and address her as such. This is true in many societies, particularly Asian. Indians address their elder family members, both male and female, by a respectable honorific title. The literature in all Indian languages, including, indeed, Sanskrit, abounds with poems acknowledging love and gratitude toward mothers.

On a specific day *(Rakshabandhan)*, a sister ties a thread, often ornamented, to her brother's wrist, and the brother offers her sweets and sometimes a token present, assuring her mutual affection and offering to protect her. On another specific day *(Bhaibeej)*, the fourth day after the festival of *Diwali*, a sister makes a lamp offering and then affectionately feeds her brother; after her marriage, she invites him to a meal at her house, makes a lamp offering, and feeds him, and the brother gives her a present. If a woman sends a *rakhi* (string) to a male and he accepts it, he accepts her as a sister, with the attendant obligation to protect her. These observances are, however, subject to dual interpretations, including

the one that sees them as patronizing on the part of the male.

Beginning with the Indus-Saraswati Civilization, there have been mother goddesses throughout Indian civilization. In Vedic times and thereafter, people worshiped goddesses of good attributes, such as Saraswati for learning and Lakshmi for wealth. Mothers are deified. Rivers, as life givers, are goddesses and are often addressed simply as "mother" in India and Southeast Asia. Among the divinities, the goddesses are regarded as the stronger, the *shakti* (strength), and are worshiped in different representations such as Durga or Kali, particularly prevalent in Bengal and Orissa. The goddess was regarded as *shakti*, the strength or potency of her male counterpart. Gods were inactive and transcendent, whereas the *shakti* was active and immanent. Beginning with the Gupta period, the mother-goddess cult was revived, and special temples were built for goddesses. The practice continued until the rise of the *bhakti* movement in the fourteenth to sixteenth centuries.

However, women's rights, religious and political, marital and of inheritance, have differed over time. From a position of complete equality in the times of the Vedas (1200 BCE–1000 BCE) to the time of Manu, the lawgiver (200 CE), woman was shown as a weaker person needing protection. Manu said that a female should, until her marriage, be protected by her father, after marriage by her husband, and as a widowed mother by her adult son. All males, including fathers, husbands, and adult sons, are obligated to offer protection *(raksha)* to all females.[17]

The epics show the gradual decline in the position of the woman in society. Thus, in the *Mahabharata,* women chose their husbands through *swayamvara,* a contest in which she would stipulate the conditions, as described below. The latter portion of the *Mahabharata,* the "Anushasan Parva," says that "Manu, on the eve of his departure from the world, made over women to the care and protection of men, for they are weak and that they fall an easy prey to evils."[18] There was a double standard in regard to the male and female morality and conjugal fidelity. Thus, men could openly keep any number of mistresses; women were punished for infidelity. Women propitiated God, asking for the same husband in the next birth. Savitri would not let the god of death, Yama, take away her husband's body. Women worship Savitri by tying colored sacred threads to the *Vata* (banyan) tree as part of an observance during the rainy season in many parts of India, the occasion being called *Vatasavitri.* There is no corresponding observance for a husband asking for the same spouse in his next birth.

The Historical Role of Women in India

Unique among the major civilizations of the ancient world, India in the Vedic Age had a very high place for women. They were the equals of men in most respects: they performed the *upanayana* ceremony, donned the sacred thread, studied Vedic lore, held discussions, performed rites and rituals, and offered sacrifices. They often chose their mates, sometimes through *swayamvara (swayam* means "by self"; *vara* means "groom"), wherein potential grooms assembled and performed feats of brawn or brain as required by the rules of the competition set in advance by the bride; the winner won the bride's hand in marriage. Marriage through courting *(gandharvivah)* was one of eight acceptable ways. Monogamy was the rule, and polygamy was frowned upon or even condemned.

By the time of the era of consolidation, the place of woman had clearly fallen. No longer did she perform the *upanayana* or thread ceremony, nor was she allowed to study the sacred lore. She did not hold religious events and sacrifices in her own right. Notions of personal physical purity had ruled her out for a religious role during the days of menstruation or for a specific period after giving birth. Progressively, her intelligence was underrated and equaled to that of the Sudras, who were deliberately left illiterate and regarded as incapable of differentiating between right and wrong, dharma from *adharma,* moral and immoral. Her place in the household was subordinated to that of her father, husband, or adult son. Though she was consulted and had a primary voice in routine household matters, in matters of consequence her opinion hardly mattered.

Polygamy was widely practiced; polyandry was rare but not unknown. Monogamy was still best, but taking another wife or multiple wives under certain circumstances was "legally" allowed. Manu, the lawgiver, prescribed the circumstances and a schedule in which an additional wife was morally allowed: if the wife was "barren" for eight years, if all children died by the tenth year, or if the wife delivered only daughters by the eleventh year; if she was quarrelsome, though, it was allowable "without delay." A wife who was superseded may or may not have been given a share of the inheritance. But a wife "who is kind to her husband and virtuous in her conduct may be superseded only with her own consent and must never be disgraced."[19] Another noted lawmaker of ancient India, Yajnavalkya, though of a "liberal" bent, also allowed a second wife, "if wife drinks, is sick, hypocritical, barren, of wasteful habits, quarrelsome and always produces daughters," a situation far from the times when women chose their own mate through a *swayamvara*!

It is no wonder then that male children were preferred over female, a circumstance still prevalent in many societies. The sons inherited the wealth, and the eldest of them had the right and the duty to perform the last rites and to light the funeral pyre. As in most societies, daughters were "given away"

(kanyadan) in marriage. In some societies, dowries were given to get a husband, whose family would take care of the bride for life; in some others, the dowry was given in the form of jewelry and *streedhan* (woman's wealth) to the bride, not to be given to the husband's family except in times of acute financial distress as a loan. In some societies, mostly from the lower *varnas*, there were reverse dowries, given to the bride's family.

As time passed, girls were married early and still later when they were infants. The Sutra literature has numerous references to the marriages of prepubescent girls and even infant girls with grooms much older. Manu recommended "before puberty or three years after," at an age one-third that of men. Yajnyavalkya recommended marriage for girls immediately after the first menses; thereafter, nonmarriage would be considered a *bhrunhatya* (death of a child in the womb!). Men married immediately after their study, *brahmacharyasrama*, normally at the age of nineteen or twenty, to enter the *grihasthasrama*; their brides were much younger. Some ancient Indian writers suggest that this was to arrest "the decay in morals" that had set in with the expansion of society.

It is possible that endemic warfare among rival kingdoms created the need for replacing the slain males, hence the need for early and multiple marriages. By Manu's time, polygamy had become so common that he tried to regulate its incidence by prescribing a descending scale based on one's *varna:* Brahmans, four wives; Kshatriyas, three; Vaishyas, two; and Sudras, one. Demographic problems may have led him to "legislate" marriages between men from the higher *varna* marrying women from the lower. This practice was all right, he said, except that the eldest wife should be from one's own caste. She should be the *dharmapatni* (wife for religious rites). Perhaps he held approval for her membership in the husband's higher caste as bait to the wife from the lower community; conversely, he may have discouraged marriages between women from the upper caste to men from the lower ones by holding that such women stood to lose their higher-caste status. They would be regarded as belonging to the lower caste of their husbands.

EDUCATION IN ANCIENT INDIA

The most common facility for education was the *gurukula*, often the home of a Brahman, who lived there with his own family. Young boys went to such *gurukulas* after their *upanayana* ceremony, which was held around the age of eight. They lived at the guru's house, performing household duties and learning Sanskrit and the sacred lore from the guru.

Notable was the rise of universities in various parts of the country. The most

well known of these were Taxila (or Takshashila) in the Punjab; Nalanda in Bihar; Benares (or Varanasi) in Uttar Pradesh; Vallabhi in Saurashtra, Gujarat; Uddandapura in Bihar (550–1040 CE); Vikramsila in Bihar (ca. 800–1040 CE); Somapura (now in Bangladesh) from the time of the Guptas to the Turkish conquest in the thirteenth century; Jagaddala (from the Pala period of rule to the Turkish conquest); and Kanchi and Bahur (near Pondicherry) in South India, patronized among others by the Pallava kings. Bhoja, the king of Malwa, established Sanskrit College at Dhara, whereas the Yadavas of Deogiri (Daulatabad) founded a reputed college of astronomy. Many of these institutions of higher learning are mentioned in the travel accounts of I-tsing, Fa Hsien, and Hsuan Tsang.

Among all these universities, the most well known were Taxila and Nalanda. Taxila University was possibly established during the period of the Brahmanas, around 800 or 700 BCE. It existed during the time of the Buddha and was the seat of restlessness and revolt during and after the invasion of Alexander. The great scholar Kautilya, or Chanakya, taught there for quite some time. Lying on the busy trade route between India and central Asia and later to China, it was known to the Western world. Pliny and Strabo mentioned its location as a great center of learning and trade. Many of the great scholars of ancient India (besides Chanakya) taught there, including

Atreya, Panini, Nagarjuna, and Brahmadatta. The remains of the great university lie some twenty miles northwest of Rawalpindi in Pakistan.

Nalanda University, much younger than Taxila, was the largest of all the Indian universities, with a student population between 8,000 and 10,000 and about 1,500 teachers. The ruins of Nalanda show a once bustling seat of learning, a mile long and one-half mile broad, sixty-five miles southeast of Patna. Archaeologists tell us of eight large halls and some 300 lecture or seminar rooms where most of the teaching was done either one-on-one or in small groups. There was a substantial number of international students, mostly from the Buddhist world of China, Japan, Korea, Tibet, Mongolia, and Southeast Asia.

HIGHER LEARNING IN ANCIENT INDIA

Although considerable learning in ancient India centered around the Vedic, post-Vedic, Buddhist, and Jain works of religion and philosophy, there were significant advancements in various sciences, notably in astronomy and astrology, mathematics, and medicine.

Astronomy and Altar Construction

One of the most developed sciences in ancient India was astronomy, knowledge of which was essential to learning when the Vedic rituals could be performed most effectively. The most important of all the texts on astronomy was the Vedanga Jyotisha, a subsidiary Veda dealing with astronomy and astrology. Important, therefore, was the knowledge of the movement of the sun and the moon, the full moon and the new moon, solstices and equinoxes. The lunar month, the time between one new moon and the next, was twenty-nine and a half days, each month divided into two fortnights (*paksha*), the waxing half (*shukla*) and the waning half (*vadya*), with each day, or *tithi*, representing the phase of the moon, changing each night by fifty minutes. The 360 such *tithis* made one lunar year, which was a little more than 354 days, whereas the solar year was the equivalent of between 371 and 372 *tithis*. The lunar year was thus found to be lagging behind the solar year, and, therefore, one tradition added 11 days to the lunar year, whereas another added a month every fourth year during the monsoon season.

The movement of the sun and the moon was known to affect the biological clock. All living organisms were influenced by the movements of the sun and the moon, determining the reproductive cycles of animals and marine plants. The menstrual period of human females was known to be a synodic month, and nine synodic months were counted as the full period of pregnancy before the child's delivery.

Subhash Kak, who has written authoritatively on the Astronomical Code of the Rig-Veda, shows that the design of the five Vedic altars was based on the astronomical numbers and was related to the reconciliation of the lunar and solar years. To quote Kak at some length:

The fire altars symbolized the universe and there were three types of altars representing the earth, the space and the sky. The altar for the earth was drawn as circular whereas the sky (or heaven) was drawn as square. The geometric problems of circulature of a square and that of squaring a circle are a result of equating the earth and the sky altars.

The fire altars were surrounded by 360 enclosing stones, of these 21 were around the earth altar, 78 around the space altar and 261 around the sky altar. In other words, the earth, the space, and the sky are symbolically assigned the number 21, 78, and 261. Considering the earth/cosmos dichotomy, the two numbers are 21 and 339 since cosmos includes the space and the sky. . . .

These altars were built in five layers, of a thousand bricks of specified shapes. The construction of these altars required the solution to several geometric and algebraic problems.[20]

Astronomy made great progress. Aryabhatta (b. 473) came up with the calculation of pi as 3.1416 in 499 CE and determined the length of the solar year as 365.358 days. He held that the earth rotated on its own axis, was round, and revolved around the sun. He declared that the eclipses were caused by the earth's shadow falling on the moon.

Indian astronomers, particularly Varahamihira, were aware of the work of their Greek and Roman counterparts. In this, the Indian knowledge of mathematics was most useful and was perhaps ahead of all others. They knew the concept of zero and its use for what would emerge as a decimal system. Baudhayana and Apastamba obtained the *dvi-karani,* or diagonal, which is the side of a square of area twice that of the original square. Some of their calculations vary from the modern at the sixth place of decimals. Baudhayana also showed how to square a circle. All this progress emerged out of the desire to build fire altars in different shapes, sizes, and layers and to know how many and what size of bricks would be needed to construct them. The problem encountered in the effort would lead to the development of algebra.[21]

Medicine

The science of medicine made great strides after the Vedic period, particularly in the era of consolidation, 200 BCE to 200 CE. There was some information on medicine in the Rig-Veda and considerably more in the Atharva

Veda. The belief in the Vedic period was that diseases were caused by evil spirits entering the body or the gods inflicting punishment on a human for transgressions of different kinds. Bodily pains, particularly sharp ones, were attributed to Rudra's spear, whereas Varuna, the god of storms, punished humans with *jalodara* (dropsy). Agni (fire) was, appropriately, responsible for all kinds of fever. The remedies in the Atharva Veda ranged from offerings to penances and purification rituals. Some medical treatment is mentioned, such as enemas and the application of leaches or a torch to the area of a serpent bite.

Schools for the systematic study of medicine were established around the time of the Upanishads and Buddhism. That was the time when *ayurveda* (the science of well-being and longevity) developed and, because of its importance, given the status of a semi-Veda or Upa Veda of the Atharva Veda. Of the eight divisions of *ayurveda,* only one now dealt with the evil spirits, whereas for most practitioners, medicine was rational, not magico-religious.

Even so, the origins of *ayurveda* were regarded as divine. The god Indra was believed to have taught the science of medicine to Punarvasu Atreya, who was regarded as the fount of wisdom in the field of medicine. Atreya taught at Taxila University at the time of Buddha. Six pupils of Atreya compiled all that they learned from the master in a medical encyclopedia. Of the different versions, only those of Bhela (*Bhela Samhita* survived only partly in South India) and Agnivesa have survived. During the era of consolidation, the well-known *Caraka Samhita* was compiled. It was based on the compilation of Agnivesa in its final form. Caraka is believed to have been the court physician to Emperor Kanishka at Peshawar in the first or second century CE.

The *Caraka Samhita* was the most elaborate treatise on medicine.[22] It had eight divisions, each of them further divided into several chapters. It dealt with fetal generation and development, human anatomy, and the bodily functions depending on the three bodily humors known at that time—*vayu* (breath or wind), *pitta* (gall), and *kapha* (phlegm). The treatise discussed the basis of the *tridosa* (or three-humors) theory. The work listed about fifty groups of medicines working on the various systems.

Ayurveda is practiced on a significant scale today in India, which has fifty-eight four-year-degree colleges in *ayurveda* medicine. The basis of this system of medicine is that the human body consists of four humors—phlegm *(kapha),* gall *(pitta),* breath or wind *(vayu),* and blood *(loha)*—in balanced proportion, which can be maintained through proper diet, ingesting solids and liquids at a proper temperature, varying from season to season.

What Caraka did for medicine, Susruta did for surgery. Caraka postulated that the lungs and the palate were "the source of the vessels which carry water through the body." Susruta believed that the navel, surrounded by the tubular vessels *(sira)*, about 700 of them, was central to the body's functioning. He was known to have used innovative techniques in dissecting the human body, for reconstructing noses and earlobes, and for performing abdominal operations and removing dead fetuses from the body. *Susruta Samhita* was later translated into Arabic in the eighth century CE and translated from Arabic into Latin. In 1897, it was first translated into English by the noted Sanskritist A. F. R. Hoernle. Under Susruta's tutelage, surgeons learned their skills. Some information is available on the kind of instruments used in surgery. By the first century CE, instrumentation consisted of twenty types of knives and needles, thirty probes, twenty tubular instruments, and twenty-six types of dressing.[23]

NOTES

1. Franklin Edgerton, *The Bhagavad Gita* (Cambridge, Mass.: Harvard University Press, 1972).

2. Sarvepalli Radhakrishnan and Charles Moore, *History of Indian Philosophy* (Princeton: Princeton University Press, 1957), 40.

3. For details, see A. L. Basham, *The Wonder That Was India: A Survey of the History and Culture of the Indian Sub-continent Before the Coming of the Muslims*, 32–28.

4. William Theodore de Bary, ed., *Sources of Indian Tradition* (New York: Columbia University Press, 1958), 1:296.

5. Basham, *Wonder That Was India*, 328.

6. T. M. P. Mahadevan, *Outlines of Hinduism*, 27.

7. Ibid, 75.

8. Rabindranath Tagore, *Songs of Kabir* (New York: Macmillan, 1915), 112.

9. Herodotus, *Histories* (New York: Macmillan, 1915), 2, 64.

10. J. H. Hutton, *Caste in India* (Cambridge: Cambridge University Press, 1946), 147–48.

11. Herbert Hope Risley, *People of India* (Calcutta: Thacker, 1908), 273.

12. S. V. Ketkar, *History of Caste in India* (Delhi: Low Price Publications, 1990), 15.

13. N. K. Dutt, *Origin and Growth of Caste in India* (London: Kegan Paul, Trench, Trubner, 1931), 3.

14. Louis Dumont, *Homo Hierarchicus* (Chicago: University of Chicago Press, 1970), 33–64.

15. Eleanor Zelliot, *From Untouchable to Dalit: Essays on the Ambedkar Movement*, 267, 271.

16. Oliver Mendelsohn and Marika Vicziany, *The Untouchables: Subordination, Poverty, and the State in Modern India*, 8–9.

17. Manu, IX, 2-3, in P. V. Kane, *History of the Dharmasastras* (Pune: Bhandarkar Oriental Research Institute, 1974), 2:577.

18. *Mahabharata*, 46.14.7.

19. Manu, IX, 81, 82.

20. Subhash Kak, *The Wishing Tree: The Presence and Promise of India* (Delhi: Munshiram Manoharlal, 2001), 45.

21. For details, see Bibhutibhusan Datta, *The Science of the Sulba* (Calcutta: University of Calcutta, 1932).

22. *Caraka Samhita,* translated and edited by P. V. Sharma, 4 vols. (Varanasi: Chowkhamba Orientalia, 2000).

23. *Susruta Samhita*, translated by Kaviraj Bhishagranta, 2 vols. (Varanasi: Chowkhamba Sanskrit Studies, 1999); H. R. Zimmer, *Hindu Medicine* (Baltimore: Johns Hopkins University Press, 1948), 82. See also P. J. Deshpande, K. R. Sharma, and G. C. Prasad, "Contribution of Susruta to the Fundamentals of Orthopaedic Surgery," *Indian Journal of the History of Science* 5, no. 1 (1970): 13–55.

The major gains of the Arab presence in Sind were found in the wide cultural transmission from India to the West. It inaugurated a period of nearly three centuries of peaceful, cultural contacts between India and the Arab world, helping the transmission of Indian knowledge, particularly in mathematics, science, and literature, through Middle Eastern intermediaries eventually to the Western world. During the period, Baghdad, the seat of the caliphate, emerged as one of the major cultural and intellectual centers of the world, well known for art, architecture, and the sciences. Arab scholars thrived in Spanish universities, which became the conduits for transmission of knowledge to universities in France and England. In the process, some of the vital contributions of India to the world passed off as Arabic contributions. Thus, the Indian decimal system and Indian numerals known to the Arabs as *tarikh-i-hind* came to be called Arabic numerals in Europe. Knowledge of the Indian holistic system of medicine, *ayurveda*, was first integrated with the Iranian *unani* system of medicine before transmission to Spain and Europe. Hindu physicians Ganga and Manka were invited to treat the well-known *khalifa* Haroon al-Rashid. A number of Hindu scholars were taken to Baghdad because of the caliph's interest in getting Sanskrit texts in mathematics, sciences, medicine, and literature translated into Arabic. Another major Indian contribution was the game of chess, which became a preferred pastime at Arab and European courts. Translations of literature included the Indian treasuries of stories, the *Panchatantra* and *Katha Sarita Sagar* (Ocean of Stories), which provided the materials for *Aesop's Fables* and the *Arabian Nights*. (pages 126–27)

7

EARLY ISLAM
The Sultanate

Of all the people who came to India through the passes in its Northwest, only the Muslims remained as a separate religious group. The others—Bactrians, Scythians, Huns, and Kushans, to name some of the most prominent groups—sought absorption and were integrated within the Hindu fold, mostly as Kshatriyas. Warriors as they were, they settled, for the most part, in Rajasthan and came to be known as the Rajputs. Some of them left a cultural impact on the mainstream civilization of India such as, for example, the Bactrian influences on Indian art, Hindu and Buddhist.

Historically, there were four major Muslim invasions that resulted in the establishment of long-term political entities: (1) the Arab conquest of Sind in 712 CE and later expansion to neighboring Multan; (2) the invasions of Muhammad of Ghazni, 1000–1026, and his conquest of the Punjab; (3) the establishment of the so-called sultanate, under five different dynasties, centered in Delhi, 1206–1526; and (4) Babar's inva-

sion in 1526 and with a short break from 1540 to 1555 the Mughal rule centered on Delhi-Agra effectively up to 1707, less effectively and over a much reduced "empire" until about 1765, and decreasingly over a nominal area until 1858.

The nineteenth-century British historians of India divided Indian history into three periods: Hindu, Muslim, and British. The labeling of the first two by religion was a convenience for the colonial rulers, who would use the religious categories all through their years of political and administrative ascendancy to divide and rule. The Muslim period was said to have lasted 652 years, from 1206, when Muhammad of Ghur's deputy established the Slave Dynasty in Delhi, until 1858, when the British unceremoniously bundled the last Mughal ruler, Bahadur Shah II, into exile to Burma (Myanmar), where he died in obscurity in 1862.

Several questions come up. How long was this period of "Muslim" rule really Muslim? What areas of the subcontinent

119

were formally included in the Muslim domains under the five different dynasties of the Sultanate of Delhi and under the great Mughal rulers from Babar to Aurangzeb, as contrasted with the later Mughals who followed Aurangzeb? Did the Muslim rulers have a totally Muslim administration, or did their administration include at different levels of government—central, regional, and local—substantial input from non-Muslims? Did such a role entitle the non-Muslim contribution in certain periods in that long 652-year tenure to be called "a partnership"? Did the Muslim rulers follow an unrestrained policy of converting the subject people to their own faith? How does one explain the fact that the demographic concentrations of converts to Islam, in the western and eastern parts of the subcontinent, were far away from the Delhi-Agra region where the political and military power was the most dense? Last, how did the overwhelming majority of common people, particularly those in rural areas, perceive the impact of "Muslim rule" in the daily pursuit of their religion and life's myriad matters? Islam, like all major religions, claims to be a religion of peace that fostered a great civilization. What kind of enduring impression did it leave on the Hindu majority throughout the centuries, "the scratches on the mind," to borrow the well-known title of the book by Harold Isaacs? The answers to some of these questions are significant for the understanding of the creation of Pakistan as a "homeland" for the subcontinent's Muslims, the foundation of Bangladesh disputing the assumption that common religious ties serve as a binding element, by extension the dispute over Kashmir on the grounds of religious separateness, and, importantly, the Indian exercise of state secularism, regardless of the religious, racial, or gender affiliation of its plural citizenry. Before we attempt to consider much less provide answers to such ponderous questions, it would be helpful to understand the basic tenets of Islam (and its principal sects), the religion of a quarter of the population of the subcontinent before its partition in 1947 and of roughly 13–14 percent of present-day India, who are in absolute numbers larger than in Pakistan and only a little less than in Bangladesh.

ISLAM

The founder of Islam, Muhammad (570–632 CE), was born in Mecca, Saudi Arabia, and became an orphan at an early age. Compelled to earn his own living, he joined and later led caravans of traders through the desert northward to the lands of the Fertile Crescent. There, he met followers of Judaism and Christianity, which led to knowledge of those religions. During these desert travels, Muhammad had divine revelations. His teachings infuriated influential people in Mecca, leading to Muhammad's Hegira, or flight, to Medina in 622, an event of tremendous importance in the history of Islam, marking the commencement of the Islamic era. Eight years later, Muhammad returned to Mecca as the head of his armed believers. In 632, two years after he had made Mecca the headquarters of his religion, Muhammad died.

The religion Muhammad preached spread fast; it was simple and easy to follow. The use of the sword helped to bring nonbelievers into the faith. The "five pillars of Islam" require (1) profession of faith in Allah (the Arabic name for God) and in Muhammad as the only prophet; (2) believers to offer prayers five times a day—early morning, midmorning, noon, midafternoon, and evening—facing Mecca; (3) the giving of alms (the recommendation of the pious was to give 2.5 percent of one's earnings to charity [zakat]—if one gave more, God would grant forgiveness, and one could gain exemption from certain requirements, such as fasting, partial or full, during the month of Ramadan); (4) fasting during the holy month of Ramadan (there should be no eating, drinking, smoking, sexual intercourse, or even swallowing of one's own saliva between sunrise and sunset; the fasting was intended to infuse self-restraint and develop self-discipline, the more pious among the followers refraining, during the month, from evil thoughts entering their minds); and (5) making a pilgrimage to Mecca, in the month of Hajj, at least once in a lifetime (under certain circumstances, such as old age or sickness, one could be exempted,

in which case he could deputize someone to go in his place instead). On the last of the five pillars, it is important to note the fact that no Muslim ruler in India (and most of the court elite) ever took the risk of leaving his throne to make the pilgrimage. The essence of the pilgrimage is to establish unity and solidarity among Muslims, who get off whatever transportation has brought them, like a horse or camel, and walk the final distance to the Holy Black Stone of Mecca, using two pieces of plain white cloth to cover the body. The pilgrimage underlines the spirit of equality among the faithful.

Islam preaches brotherhood of all believers and equality of men before God, irrespective of color, race, or class (but not gender). There are specific injunctions against the use of intoxicants and the consumption of pork. No idol worship is allowed. Islam has no "church" or priests. The entire brotherhood is regarded as the *umma*, or community of the faithful. Every Friday at noon, the faithful meet for prayer at the mosque, led by a member of the community.

By 651, the series of divine revelations made by Allah to the Prophet were compiled in the Koran. Additionally, the sayings and deeds of the Prophet were put together as the *hadith*. The Koran has remained ever since the ultimate authority in political, economic, legal, and ethical matters for Muslims.

Muhammad maintained that God had finally and completely revealed himself only to him. The Christian and

Jewish holy books constituted only partial revelations; as such, their followers should be tolerated as "people of the book." Others were termed infidels, to be put to death if they refused to convert to Islam. Muhammad's inspiration led hordes of Arabs out of their homeland "with Koran in one hand and sword in the other" to reduce *dar-ul-harb* (country at war) to *dar-ul-islam* all over the Middle East, North Africa, and the Iberian Peninsula within a century of Islam's birth. The subject peoples, if they were not "people of the book," were given a choice: convert or be ready to be killed.

The Rift: Sunnis and Shias

Islam had no formal church hierarchy. The Prophet had not laid down any rules for succession. He was succeeded by Abu Bakr, the Prophet's father-in-law, the choice of whom, made by the leaders, was endorsed by the whole assembly of followers. He would be known as the imam or the *khalifa* or, in Western literature, caliph. He and three successor *khalifas*, all elected, were called the righteous *khalifas*.

A *khalifa* was both the spiritual and the temporal head of the Muslim community. The first four were not blood relatives of the Prophet but were chosen by consensus of the people. The followers of Islam were divided between its two principal sects—the *Shii*, or Shia (as they are called in India), who believed that the *khalifas* had to be blood

relatives of the Prophet, and the Sunni, who did not. Shias are dominant in Iran and southeastern Iraq. On the subcontinent, the Sunnis outnumber the Shias, both in Pakistan and in India. There are large numbers of Shias particularly in the former Oudh (roughly Uttar Pradesh), Gujarat (Western India), and the Deccan.

An important factor in the growth of Islam was the development of the law. It was held that the Koran had the highest authority; next was the *hadi* or *hadith*, the traditions of the Prophet or the interpretations of the Koran as contained in the sayings and actions of the Prophet. The difficulty was knowing which of these traditions were authentic and which were forgeries. Muslim divines have debated endlessly before arriving at some agreement on this subject and decided what they should be. These are called the sharia and have historically been used for the guidance of the court system.

By the thirteenth century, when Muslim rulers in India were confronted with the question of how to deal with a large number of non-Muslim population, who were not "people of the book," the Sunnis followed four different schools of law: the Hanbali, Maliki, Shafi'i, and Hanafi, named after prominent Islamic scholars in jurisprudence and theology. The first two of these schools were more fundamentalist than the last two, the Hanafi school being the most popular in India because it provided for a liberal attitude toward non-Muslim subjects and also because it provided for clear guidance on the state's share of the agricultural produce in different circumstances.

Sufism

There is no agreement on the origins of Sufism. The term *sufi* derives from *suf,* meaning wool; the *sufi* men were the "dancing dervishes" of medieval times dressed in long woolen garments. Sufism was the mystical philosophy known as Tasawwuf, which for millions of Islam's followers provided a means to bring forth their love of God through a variety of ways, including dance, music, chanting, art, and poetry. Scholars have ascribed the origin of the belief to many sources, including Neoplatonism and Buddhism in the general region of Afghanistan and the Silk Route to China. Some have argued that Sufism helped Islam to accommodate diverse non-Islamic faiths such as Judaism, Manichaeanism, and Christianity in the Middle East and on the Indian subcontinent followers of Hindu, Buddhist, and Zoroastrian religions to the stark and severe demands of Islam by integrating some of those pre-Islamic cultural and intellectual practices perhaps in the same way that Christianity provided transition to Roman and Greek beliefs and ways of life.

Sufism emerged as a low-key protest movement commending the doctrine of love and simple piety in preference to crass materialism and this-worldliness that had characterized the centuries af-ter the completion of Muslim conquests in the Middle East and North Africa. Sufism at once promoted romanticism, meditation, intellectualism, and continuous chanting of the name Allah as the certain means of reaching God. It produced ascetics and intellectuals, poets and philosophers, artists and architects, lending a liberalizing and cultural dimension to Islam. On the Indian subcontinent, its appeal lay in its mysticism and in the chanting of the name of God echoing the Upanishadic path of meditation or of unselfish devotion *(bhakti)* to reach the divine or Absolute Truth. Their ideal of "renunciation, self-abnegation, and poverty" appealed to the Indian mind. Those factors accounted for the success of Sufism in certain parts of India and the myriad islands of Indonesia, to which the mystic Sufi missionaries went on board the trading vessels from India, though one would imagine they were not wearing woolens in those humid islands. In India, Sufis allowed the new converts their beliefs in saints through devotion to Muslim *pirs* (preceptors) and allowed them to continue their age-old Hindu social customs after their conversion.

The farther away from the Middle East and Mecca the converts were, the greater the likelihood that the content of their daily lives reflected their preconversion practices. Thus, the Bengali Muslims remained culturally closer to their Hindu Bengali brethren than to their Punjabi or Middle Eastern coreligionists, which was one of the main divides between the people in the two wings of Pakistan and a principal reason for the movement for the separate state of Bangladesh in 1971. Indonesia, for example, is even farther away geographically from the cultural capital of Islam in the Middle East. Although 90 percent of Indonesians are Muslims, most of them still retain their Sanskrit-based names and their Hindu-Buddhist marriage (and, until recently, coronation) ceremonies. They continue with their addiction to *wayang* puppet shows and shadow theater, where the themes are drawn from the Indian epics *Ramayana* and *Mahabharata*. Java rightly boasts the best *Ramayana* ballet in the world. The Indonesian national airline, Garuda, takes its name from the mount of Vishnu. Jakarta's main square proudly presents a massive representation of Krishna as the charioteer of Arjuna, reciting to him the Bhagavad Gita. It was the Sufis who saw nothing wrong in allowing the new converts to continue with their social and cultural mores after conversion to Islam, thus enhancing the cultural richness and diversity of the Islamic world.

Some scholars see in Sufism a nonviolent means to defy the orthodox Muslim divines, who tried to impose a strict, puritanical, and discriminating code for women. Both men and women could use Sufism and the intense personal closeness and devotion to God to compose and recite some of the most romantic verses, ordinarily denied in a conservative society. Two of the most famous Sufi scholars were women, Rabia and Nuri in the ninth and tenth centuries, respectively, who lay emphasis on renunciation of life's pleasures and single-minded devotion to God as the means to attain salvation. Among the most popular Sufi scholars in India was the thirteenth-century Afghan poet-philosopher Jalaluddin Rumi Balkh. Some of his teachings echoed the Hindu cycle of life, including this one: "I died as inert matter—and became a plant; And as a plant I died and became an animal; And as an animal I died and became a man; So why should I fear losing my human character? I shall die as a man, to rise in angelic form."[1]

In India, many Sufi poets and saints such as Kabir also employed age-old Indian folk stories to bring to the common people wisdom and a message to lead a moral life. It is no wonder that the Sufi missionaries found a fair measure of acceptance of their ways among the lower-class Hindus who converted to Islam, realizing that in doing so they would not have to pay the price of abandoning their previous cultural tradition. Sufism also allowed the Indian fine arts—music and dance, art and architecture, literature and poetry—to be incorporated into the life of the Muslims without any spiritual conflict. Last, Sufism was one of the factors that may have led Hinduism to adopt a syncretic approach and underline the age-old path of devotion, *Bhakti marg*, available to one and all, irrespective of caste or creed, to reach God.

The First Period of Contact with Islam: The Arab Conquest of Sind

Political Islam came to India first with the Arab conquest of Sind (southern Pakistan) in 712 CE, ninety years after it was founded in Saudi Arabia. However, it was not the first contact of India with the Arabs or with Islam. For at least a couple of centuries before the birth of Islam, Arab trading ships and merchants had been visiting the Malabar Coast and Sri Lanka, some of them further bound for ports in Sumatra and southern China. Historical evidence points to small Arab settlements in all the four areas where the small Arab communities practiced their pre-Islamic faiths. Nothing much changed in their relationship with the local Hindu trading communities or with the local rulers after their conversion to Islam. Just like the Jews and Christians before them, the Muslim Arabs on the Malabar Coast were able to practice their new religion without interference from the Hindu rulers of the region.

In 712, the wives and children of some Arab traders and mariners in Sri Lanka were on their way to Mecca when there was a shipwreck that caused them to land in the Gulf of Debal in Sind. They were captured and taken to the local Hindu ruler, Dahir, of the Chach dynasty. The news enraged al-Hajjaj, the Arab governor of Iraq, who sent his nephew and son-in-law, the seventeen-year-old Muhammad bin Kasim, to punish the pirates of Debal as well as King Dahir and retrieve the Muslim victims. Kasim led a huge army overland to Sind, crossed the Indus, killed Dahir, and, despite stiff resistance from Dahir's brave widow, conquered his kingdom. Multan to the north of Dahir's kingdom also fell.

In the new Arab kingdom, all subjects were, to start with, non-Muslim. The Koran had stated that only the "people of the book," such as Jews and Christians, were to be tolerated. Should the Hindu and Buddhist population of Sind be converted to Islam or killed, those being the two choices a Muslim conqueror was supposed to give to a subject people who were not "people of the book"? Without consulting the jurists back home, the young Kasim decided on his own (which made it an act of *ijtihad* or independent reasoning) that the Hindu and Buddhist population would be treated as "people of the book" and given the status of *zimmis* (protected people). Fortunately for him, his stand was later supported by the *ulamas* (learned Islamic scholars) at the *khalifa's* court. This would allow the Hindu and Buddhist population to practice their own religion. Kasim even employed followers of those religions in his administration, particularly continuing some of them in their old posts as revenue collectors. This was a clever move, because the peasants were apprehensive of the new rulers because of their religion.

There are at least two interpretations about the conditions in Raja Dahir's kingdom at the time of the Arab conquest of his kingdom. According to two major Arab accounts—Muhammad Ali bin Hamid bin Abu Bakr and Ahmad bin Yahya bin Jabir—Kasim's adventure was nothing but a piratical attack that sacked Dahir's kingdom and an opportunity to send a large amount of loot and slaves to his uncle in Iraq. The defense of the kingdom was hampered by a certain amount of intercaste and interreligious tension. According to the two writers, Dahir was a Brahman ruler whose family had acquired the kingdom from its Kshatriya Rajput rulers. Another source of tension was the uneasiness among Debal's sizable Buddhist population, although there is no evidence to that effect. The lack of unity in Debal must have made it easier for Kasim to conquer Sind.[2]

The other interpretation is given by Ghulam Murtaza Shah Syed (1904–1995), a prominent native of Sind who specialized in its history. According to him, Islam was not new to Raja Dahir, who had previously allowed some Arab Muslim mariners and traders to settle in the coastal areas. As such, he was a very tolerant, secular-minded ruler who had permitted followers of all faiths—Hindus, Buddhists, Parsis (Zoroastrians), and Arabs—to practice their religions freely without any interference. In Syed's view, the real reason for Kasim's invasion was that Raja Dahir had only recently provided refuge and assistance to some Sassanians who had been defeated by Arabs in Persia. It would seem, therefore, that Kasim's invasion was a preemptive strike to avoid possible Sassanian-Sind retaliation against the Sassanians' Arab conquerors.

The Arab conquest of Sind was limited to it and the neighboring Multan because of the resistance from the Pratiharas and the Rashtrakutas. Arab power at that time was primarily focused on the Middle East, North Africa, and the Iberian Peninsula.

The major gains of the Arab presence in Sind were found in the wide cultural transmission from India to the West. It inaugurated a period of nearly three centuries of peaceful, cultural contacts between India and the Arab world, helping the transmission of Indian knowledge, particularly in mathematics, science, and literature, through Middle Eastern intermediaries eventually to the Western world. During the period, Baghdad, the seat of the caliphate, emerged as one of the major cultural and intellectual centers of the world, well known for art, architecture, and the sciences. Arab scholars thrived in Spanish universities, which became the conduits for transmission of knowledge to universities in France and England. In the process, some of the vital contributions of India to the world passed off as Arabic contributions. Thus, the Indian decimal system and Indian numerals known to the Arabs as *tarikh-i-hind* came to be called Arabic numerals in Europe. Knowledge of the Indian holistic system of medicine, *ayurveda*, was first integrated with the Iranian *unani* system of medicine before transmission to Spain and Europe. Hindu physicians Ganga and Manka were invited to treat the well-known *khalifa* Haroon al-Rashid. A number of Hindu scholars were taken to Baghdad because of the caliph's interest in getting Sanskrit texts in mathematics, sciences, medicine, and literature translated into Arabic. Another major Indian contribution was the game of chess, which became a preferred pastime at Arab and European courts. Translations of literature included the Indian treasuries of stories, the *Panchatantra* and *Katha Sarita Sagar* (Ocean of Stories), which provided the materials for *Aesop's Fables* and the *Arabian Nights*.

Muhammad of Ghazni's Raids

Except for Sind and Multan, there were no further Muslim territorial acquisitions on the subcontinent until the beginning of the eleventh century. On the contrary, a Hindu replaced a Turkish ruling family called the Shahiyas in the Kabul Valley. That the religious divide between the Hindus and the Muslims did not affect the polity was indicated by the fact that a Brahman held the position of *diwan* at the Shahiya court.

He established a kingdom and a dynasty known to history as the Hindu Shahiya dynasty (in honor of his former master), extending over the present Northwest Frontier Province of Pakistan and the Punjab, in effect creating a buffer between the rising Muslim kingdoms in Afghanistan and central Asia, on the one hand, and India, on the other. The kingdom's strength and prosperity were based on the fertility of the vast Punjab plains. Its wealth and revenue base became a target for ambitious adventurers from Afghanistan and central Asia, who could use its riches to build their own mountainous, unfertile kingdoms beyond the Oxus.

This was a period of considerable political and military stability in the western part of the Muslim world, the center of power and of spiritual authority being the caliphate based in Baghdad. By contrast, the region between the present-day Iran and central Asia was populated by military adventurers, recent converts to Islam who did not hesitate to liquidate their fellow coreligionists for material gains. One such opportunist was a Turkish nobleman, Sabuktigin, the founder of Ghazni in Afghanistan. It was the ambition of Sabuktigin's son, Muhammad, to make Ghazni the most powerful kingdom in all of central Asia.

What followed was a period of extremely violent contact between Islam and India. The objective of the invaders was plundering, looting, wanton destruction, and death. Muhammad of Ghazni has remained in Indian history the epitome of cruelty and barbarism. He invaded India seventeen times between 1000 and 1026. In the beginning, his raids were focused on the Shahiya kingdom of Jayapal and, south of it, the city of Multan, a gateway to Lower Indus and Sind, which had been under Arab Muslim rule since 712. These were not his only targets. He was involved in a life-or-death struggle with the neighboring kingdom of Ghur, under a Muslim potentate. Although some of the contemporary accounts, including that by the court historian Utbi, stated that Muhammad's invasions were *jihads* (holy wars) to advance the cause of Islam, in the opinion of the eminent Indian Muslim historian Mohammad Habib, Muhammad of Ghazni's raids were predominantly politically and economically motivated.

Thus, Muhammad of Ghazni attacked the Muslim kingdom in Multan with the same ferocity and greed that he meted out to Hindu kingdoms; he did not bother to convert the indigenous Hindus in the areas he raided. In fact, there were Hindu mercenaries in his large entourage. His main motive was to collect wealth for building the capital of his kingdom, Ghazni, and to finance his campaigns in central Asia. Hindu temples of the Punjab, the Doab region (the land between the Ganges and the Jumna rivers), and Gujarat attracted him more because of their wealth; their destruction would win him support at his own court from Muslim divines. That consideration weighed most in his

wanton destruction of temples after they were looted and in putting large numbers of Hindu devotees and defenders to death. An additional factor was the use of prisoners of war as slaves. The Punjab provided him, and later the Ghurs, with an enormous supply of slaves; after satisfying their own needs, they sold the surplus as a commodity in the markets of central Asia.

In India, the Hindus remember Muhammad of Ghazni's raids with abhorrence, although it has been a millennium since they took place. A particular case was the raid on the Somnath temple, located at the tip of the Kutch peninsula, in 1026. An Arab contemporary wrote the following about the Somnath temple and Muhammad's barbaric atrocities there:

> Somnath was a celebrated city of India situated on the shore of the sea and washed by its waves. Among the wonders of that place . . . was the idol in the middle of the temple without anything to support it from below, or to suspend it from above. It was held in the highest honor among the Hindus, and whoever beheld it floating in the air was struck with amazement, whether he was a Musulman or an infidel. The Hindus would go on a pilgrimage there whenever there was an eclipse of the moon and would assemble there to the number of more than a hundred thousand. . . . The ebb and flow of the tide was considered to be the worship paid to the idol by the

sea. Everything of the most precious was brought there as offerings and the temple was endowed with more than 10,000 villages. . . . The edifice was built upon 56 pillars of teak covered with lead. . . . Near the idol was a chain of gold weighing 200 mans. . . . The sultan [Muhammad of Ghazni] arrived there [in December 1025]. The Indians made a desperate resistance. . . . [T]he numbers of slain exceeded 50,000. The sultan . . . gave orders for the seizing of the spoil.[3]

Muhammad of Ghazni died in 1030. His Indian possessions included only the present Northwest Frontier Province, the Punjab, and the former Arab kingdom in Sind and Multan. His biographers praise him as a lover of culture because of his construction of Islamic monuments in Ghazni. In India, he was the personification of inhumanity and barbarism, an uncivilized human who had no compunction in destroying places of worship and killing fellow human beings. North India and Gujarat heaved a sigh of relief upon his death.

Al-Biruni (973–1048), the most famous chronicler of the period, who accompanied Muhammad to India, praised Muhammad's exploits but also detailed the devastating consequences of his master's military campaigns:

Muhammad utterly ruined the prosperity of the country and performed those wonderful exploits by which the Hindus became like atoms of dust

scattered in all directions. . . . [T]heir scattered remains cherish, of course, the most inveterate aversion towards all Muslims. This is the reason too why the Hindu sciences have retired far away from parts of the country conquered by us and have fled to places, which our hand cannot yet reach, to Kashmir, Benaras and other places.[4]

There were no major incursions from the West for quite some time, the Muslim potentates in Afghanistan and central Asia being involved there with internecine struggles for power.

India According to Al-Biruni

Al-Biruni's account of India, *Kitab-ul-Hind* (The Book of India), has been one of the most perceptive and detailed analyses of India since the turn of the first millennium CE. A great scholar and linguist of the time, he had studied Sanskrit and translated several works in that language into Arabic before he came to India. He was well read in Vedic literature and the epics. He had also acquainted himself with the scientific and philosophical works of ancient India, including medical treatises such as the *Caraka Samhita*.

Al-Biruni's book was divided into eight parts and seventy-six chapters, dealing with all aspects of Indian life and thought: philosophy and literature, customs and laws, mathematics and astronomy, physical sciences and medicine, religions and modes of worship.

He noted a dichotomy in the Hindu personality that allowed "the peaceful co-existence of science and superstition." In his view, the Hindus were self-centered and vain. Thus, he wrote, "The Hindus believe that there is no country but theirs, no king like theirs, no science like theirs." Would the two communities coexist in peace and harmony? In an observation that would support Muslim separatism in the twentieth century, he said, "In all manners and usages, they differ from us to such a degree as to frighten their children, . . . with our dress, and our ways and customs, and to declare us to be the devil's breed, and our doings as the very opposite of all that is good or proper."[5]

Muhammad of Ghur

Almost two centuries later, Muhammad of Ghur, who, by that time, had conquered Ghazni, followed the same economic logic as had moved Muhammad of Ghazni, namely, bringing the wealth from India to build his country. In 1182, he entered India not through the northern Khyber Pass but through the southern Gomal Pass leading to the southern Indus region, hoping to get the cooperation of the Muslim kingdom of Sind. This did not happen. He subjugated that kingdom but failed to get the king's cooperation, although he was a fellow coreligionist. Three years later, Muhammad of Ghur attacked the Northwest and the Punjab through the northern

route, this time with the idea of not just raiding and looting as Muhammad of Ghazni had done but also retaining his conquests and building an Indian empire. He met stiff opposition from Prithviraj Chauhan of Delhi, who was able to rally some of his fellow Rajput kings at the Battle of Tarain in 1191. Prithviraj defeated and captured the Ghur leader, but, following the Rajput martial code, he released his prisoner. He was to regret his decision a few months later, when Muhammad of Ghur returned with a larger force, defeated and killed Prithviraj in 1192 at Tarain, and annexed the kingdom of Delhi.

Muhammad of Ghur returned to his base in Afghanistan, where he was assassinated in 1206 by one of his ambitious associates. The kingdom of Ghur did not last long after his death, but his Indian possessions did. Muhammad of Ghur had left in Delhi one of his slaves, Qutb-uddin Aibek, to rule over the Indian possessions. In 1206, Aibek became the founder of what came to be called the Slave Dynasty, marking the beginning of the so-called Indian sultanate, a rule mostly of Turkish-Afghan adventurers.

Muslim Society

A major impact of Islam on Indian society, which was predominantly Hindu, was through conversion to Islam. S. A. A. Rizvi categorizes the converts to the new faith into five types: persecuted religious minorities; prisoners of war belonging to the ruling classes; village headmen, tax collectors, and the like; artisans dependent on the patronage of Muslim rulers; and the children of slaves. In his view, "the motivations were economic and the driving element could be political."[6] This applied to the early centuries of contact with political Islam. Later, the mystical and devotional Sufism had a major impact on the subcontinent of a genre qualitatively different from the early contacts. The Sufi practices had a lot in common with Hindu mystic practices, and the conversion, for that reason, was not hard on the converts. By and large, the Sufis did not apply political pressure, and their impact on society was close-range, person-to-person contact, especially in villages and small towns. Large numbers of lower-class and rural Hindus were converted to Islam by the Sufi mystics in far-off Bengal, far away from the Delhi-Agra region that was the center of political-military-economic concentration.

How much did the Islamic message of egalitarianism and brotherhood attract Hindus to the new faith? As Rizvi points out, "Even those that chose to convert to Islam were subject to systematic discrimination since the Turkish nobility refused to accept Indian converts to Islam as their equals. India's Turkish invaders thus became like a caste above all castes. Rather than the caste system being undermined by Islamic egalitarianism . . . new all-powerful castes of foreign-origin Muslims lorded over all others."[7] Furthermore, even those few upper-caste Hindus who converted to Islam continued to maintain their distance from converts from the lower classes.

THE SULTANATE OF DELHI

The period of the so-called Sultanate of Delhi extended from 1208 when Muslim rule was, for the first time, established in Delhi to the beginning of the Mughal rule in 1526. Except for some thirty years when the writ of the Sultanate of Delhi extended over almost all of the subcontinent, including South India, the territories under the sultanate were limited. In the period 1208–1526, there were at least a half-dozen sultanates in the country having their own territorial jurisdiction, most often independent of Delhi.

The two short periods during which the Sultanate of Delhi exercised authority over most of the subcontinent were the regimes of Ala-uddin Khalji (1296–1316) and the early Tughluqs (1320–1351). Besides the Sultanate of Delhi, there were seven other sultanates: the Gujarat (1407–1526), Khandesh (1370–1510), Malwa (two dynasties) (1401–1531), Jaunpur (1394–1479), Bengal (four dynasties) (1282–1533), Multan (1444–1525), and the Bahmani Sultanate of the Deccan (1347–1482). Moreover, there were several Hindu kingdoms. Vijayanagar (1336–1565), Mewar (1314–1528), Marwar, Mithila, Orissa, and Assam were not subjugated through-out the period of the so-called sultanate, nor were the Hindu kingdoms of the deep south brought under Muslim rule except briefly during the Khalji rule.

The Sultanate of Delhi was held by five separate dynasties: the Slave Dynasty (1208–1290), the Khaljis (1290–1320), the Tughluqs (1320–1414), the Sayyids (1414–1451), and the Lodis (1451–1526). Thirty-four sultans sat on the Delhi throne during a little more than three centuries. In all the cases of transition from one dynasty to another, there was violence, bloodshed, and in-stability. The same was true for a major-ity of the ordinary successions from one ruler to the other within the same fam-ily or dynasty. The primary reason for the lack of peaceful transfers of power was the lack of laws governing suc-cession in a Muslim state, making it susceptible to palace intrigue and indi-vidual ambition on the part of sons or close relatives within the ruling family. Consequently, the period of the Sul-tanate of Delhi was riddled with shift-ing loyalties, political groupings whose sole binding factor was individual self-interest and little, if any, concern for the ordinary subjects.

The Slave Dynasty

During the lifetime of Muhammad of Ghur, his Indian possessions were gov-erned from his capital in Afghanistan. After his death in 1206, his commander in chief, Qutb-uddin Aibek, declared himself the sultan of Delhi. Although there was some hereditary succession in the dynasty he established, it was known as the "Slave Dynasty," because the founder as well as some of his suc-cessors were slaves before they rose to the highest position of authority. The Slave Dynasty lasted until the establish-ment of the Khalji dynasty in 1290.

Aibek's rule lasted only four years; he was killed in a polo accident. The rule is distinguished, however, for the erection of the famed Qutb Minar. According to Vincent Smith, the materials for the Minar came from some twenty-seven Hindu temples.[8] The work on the pillar, which was started during Aibek's brief reign, was completed by his former Turk-ish slave Iltutmish, who killed Aibek's successor, Aram, to seize the throne.

Iltutmish

By that time, the caliphate in Baghdad was in ruins, as the city was sacked in 1258 by the Mongols, who destroyed Baghdad's many famed centers of cul-ture as well as well-stocked libraries. The significance of the sack of Baghdad for India was that the Muslim rulers on the subcontinent could not fall back on Baghdad for cultural inspiration or mili-tary help. They had to depend on them-selves and on whatever cooperation they could get from the people there. At the least, it would not be politically or mili-tarily prudent to antagonize them all.

An able and powerful ruler of the Slave Dynasty, Iltutmish (1210–1236), raised an important question: What was to be done about the overwhelming numbers of the indigenous Hindu population? According to the Koran, they would have to be regarded as *kafirs,* or infidels, not "people of the book" like the Jews and the Christians. As stated above, by the thirteenth century, Islam had four schools of jurisprudence, with predominance in certain geographic areas of the far-flung Arab empire. Three of them propounded the orthodox position, which would allow only two choices to be given to the Hindus: convert to Islam or be killed. The fourth school—the Hanafi—was liberal. That was the school Iltutmish adopted, much to the chagrin and opposition of the other three schools. The real reason for Iltutmish's action was the Indian reality, in which a small minority of Muslims, mostly born outside the country, would have to face the wrath of tens of millions of Hindus, who might be roused to extreme action if their coreligionists were converted or killed in unacceptable numbers. This constituted a major compromise with the dictates of Islam.

What was the political position of the sultans in India? Thus far, in the interests of Islamic unity and to generate a spirit of pan-Islamism in the territories under Muslim rule, the *khalifas* would reward Muslim adventurers and conquerors of distant lands with the title of sultan, sending them robes of investiture

at the time of their "coronation." In acknowledgment of the *khalifa*'s paramount position, the sultans would read the *khutba* on Fridays in the name of the reigning *khalifa,* reiterating loyalty to the *khalifa.* For this reason, a sultan would not be regarded as being a totally independent monarch, although ordinarily he was fairly autonomous in his decisionmaking. Iltutmish broke this practice altogether and chose to read the *khutba* in his own name, thereby declaring his independence of the *khalifa.* In taking such a position, which went contrary to the conventional arrangement of a pan-Islamic society, subservient to the *khalifas,* who were both the spiritual and the temporal heads, Iltutmish had made a political break with the Islamic world. He had thereby made the sultanate in India independent of the caliphate; thereafter, the seat and sanction of power would lie in India itself. The act made the Slave Dynasty an Indian dynasty.

Throughout the sultanate, the military strength of the rulers depended substantially on importing fighters from where they themselves had come. This ensured the immigrants' loyalty to the sultan. As time moved on, partly because of the turbulent political situation in central Asian lands, the number of foreign recruits declined. Not many Hindus would convert to Islam for the likelihood of recruitment in the Islamic armed forces. Therefore, contrary to the dictates of Islam, the sultans resorted to recruiting Hindus into the army, many of them

Rajputs, who constituted essentially a martial class in India. When some Rajput rulers could not be defeated, the sultans made peace with them and formed alliances, a practice that would become the norm and a high point later under the Mughal emperor Akbar.

Raziya: The First Female Muslim Ruler

Iltutmish's sons were not impressive, at least not to their father, who nominated his able daughter, Raziya (short for Raziat-ud-din), as his successor (1236–1239). Most successions during the entire period of the sultanate had to be implicitly or explicitly acceptable to the principal nobles and commanders. During Iltutmish's reign, they had formed a group known as "the Forty." The group did not agree with Iltutmish's wishes and instead offered the throne to his son Rukh-ud-din, who proved thoroughly incapable of ruling. He was a dissolute young man who spent all his waking hours drinking and on drugs and in the company of dancing girls. Disgusted with Rukh-ud-din's behavior, the same nobles who had put him on the throne now pulled him down and voted unanimously to raise Raziya to the throne.

With her assumption of the title of sultan, Raziya became the first Muslim female to ascend a throne in India. Taking her late father's advice, she dressed as a man and led her troops herself. But soon the nobles found a reason to oppose her: She showed preference to her Abyssinian slave, Yakut Khan, who was the only one privileged to help her physically get on the horse. They rebelled, killed Yakut Khan, and offered the throne to their leader, Altunia, the governor of Sind. Altunia quickly changed his political position with the Forty and married Raziya, which infuriated his previous supporters, who killed the couple. Thus ended the first female Muslim's rule of a little more than three years in November 1239.

Ghyas–uddin Balban: The Ablest Slave Ruler

The assassination of Raziya and her erstwhile husband produced endemic chaos in Delhi. One after the other, Iltutmish's sons were raised to the throne, until Nasir-uddin, the last one to survive, was made sultan in 1246. His only memorable decision was to appoint Ghyas-uddin Balban (1266–1287), a former slave, who had already made his mark as an able administrator of a small fiefdom, to the position of *diwan*, the chief minister of the realm. Balban himself was raised by the noblemen to the position of sultan after Nasir-uddin, who had married Balban's daughter, died (after an illness) in 1266. Balban was to remain the sultan for twenty-one years, in effect running the administration of the Sultanate of Delhi for forty-one years. He died in 1287.

The ablest administrator produced by the Slave Dynasty, Balban gave the Sultanate of Delhi the best stability in a half century. First, he broke up the coterie of power that "the Forty" nobles had created. Second, he effectively checked the Mongol threat by impressive fortifications in Lahore and policing the frontier in Multan. Third, he launched an elaborate campaign to clear the forests around the capital and get rid of highway robbers of different ethnicities who had made the law-and-order situation critical in Delhi itself. The capital then became the refuge for the fallen elite from far and near who had been removed from their positions of power. So also was it for men of literature and artistic abilities who had fallen out of royal favor elsewhere and found Delhi a congenial place to resettle. One of these was the poet Amir Khusrau, the most talented litterateur of the time.

Yet the stability that Balban had provided died with him. Once again, the sultanate became a hotbed of ambition and intrigue, plots and counterplots, the various ethnic groups jockeying for power. One of these groups was the Khaljis, whose leader, though old, was acceptable to a large group of nobles. Jalal-uddin Khalji became at seventy the founder-sultan of the Khalji dynasty.

THE KHALJI DYNASTY

The Khalji dynasty lasted only thirty years (1290–1320). Its only notable ruler was Ala-uddin Khalji (1296–1316), who took over power by killing his uncle and father-in-law and the dynasty's founder, Jalal-uddin Khalji. Ala-uddin was a man of great talents: As a conqueror, he was the first since Asoka and Samudra Gupta to bring most of the subcontinent under his sway, and as an administrator, he was the first among the Muslim rulers to introduce a revenue system. The regrettable aspect of these achievements was that he used, in large measure, his reprehensible attributes of disloyalty, cruelty, and ruthlessness.

Ala-uddin believed in the power of wealth, particularly gold and silver, to facilitate his dreams of conquest and unchallenged authority. Even before he became the sultan, he invaded and looted Deogiri, the fabled capital of the Yadavas in the Deccan, in 1294. He used that treasure to build a larger army and bribe the nobles to win their support. He then killed the sultan along with many of his supporters before crowning himself as the sultan of Delhi. Thereafter, he killed all his cousins and others who could even remotely lay a claim to the throne.

During Ala-uddin's two-decade reign, he brought most of the subcontinent under his control. It was the first time any territory south of the Vindhyas had been brought under Muslim rule. The subjugation of the deep south between 1309 and 1312 was the achievement of his former slave, Malik Kafur. Indeed, the conquest in those days did not mean assuming full administrative responsibility; it involved formal acceptance of the victor's sovereignty and agreement on the part of the vanquished to pay a tribute, which continued as long as the victor was able to enforce the terms. Malik Kafur was able to secure the subjugation of three South Indian kingdoms between 1309 and 1312 besides the Yadavas of Deogiri in 1306. These were the Kakatiyas of Warangal, the Hoysalas of Karnataka, and the Pandyas of Tamil Nadu.

An objective in some of these conquests was the lust for beautiful women, in some cases the wife of the reigning monarch or his daughter. Thus, the defeat of Vaghela king Karnadeva of Gujarat resulted in the abduction of his wife, Kamala Devi, who later became Ala-uddin's favorite wife. The invasion of Chitor in 1302–1303 was motivated by the desire to capture Padmini, the beautiful wife of the ruler, Rana Ratan Singh. In the event, the ruler was defeated, but Padmini led the women inside that famed fort to *jauhar* (leap into the sacrificial fire to death) before the fort fell. After the first defeat of the ruler of Deogiri, Ala-uddin asked for the hand of his daughter in marriage. After the second, his deputy, Malik Kafur, carried Kamala Devi's daughter, who had taken refuge there, to Delhi to be married to Ala-uddin's son.

Another objective was, indeed, the lure of loot, whether it was from the palaces of the defeated or the temples of the Hindus. After the conquest of Gujarat

in 1298, Ala-uddin's generals raided the famed temple of Somnath, first desecrated and looted by Muhammad of Ghazni in the early eleventh century. To please the orthodox, he and his generals took the idols from all the temples they raided to Delhi, there to be trodden upon by the faithful.

Early in his reign, Ala-uddin faced so many rebellions that he decided to end once and for all the possibility of another one. First, as noted before, to set an example to everyone and to remove all potential rebels, he exterminated all the members of the family and supporters of his predecessor—men, women, and children. Second, he established a system of espionage to know all about the "doings of the people." In his view, all conspiracies originated in the "convivial meetings where open political talk followed the wine cup, in the seditious intimacy of the various *amirs* and notables." Therefore, he banned drinking and the use of all intoxicants and, a little later, all social meetings of the elite. Third, in an effort to attack the root of the problem, he decided to rid people of any chance to accumulate wealth, which, in his view, provided the financial wherewithal to start a rebellion. As Zia-uddin Barani, an eminent contemporary historian, wrote:

> Whenever a village was held by proprietary right, in free gift, or as a religious endowment, it was to be brought back into the exchequer by a stroke of the pen. The people were

pressed and money was exacted from them on every kind of pretext. All pensions, grants of land, and endowments were appropriated. The people became so absorbed in trying to keep themselves alive that rebellion was never mentioned.

There were specific instructions from the sultan to reduce his Hindu subjects to penury. To quote Barani again: "The Hindu was to be so reduced as to be unable to keep a horse, wear fine clothes, to enjoy any of life's luxuries. No Hindu could hold up his head and in their houses no sign of gold or silver or any superfluity was to be seen. These things, which nourish insubordination, were not to be found."[9]

Ala-uddin had high personal ambitions beyond being the ruler of India. He wanted to be a world conqueror and, at one point in time, named himself Alexander the Second. He had fresh coins minted with that title. At another time, he thought his spiritualism was of such an order that he should be the prophet of a new religion. He was fortunate in having a true friend and well-wisher in Malik-Alaul-Mulk, the *kotwal,* the chief of law and order in Delhi, who had the courage to advise him to refrain from such vanity. He reminded Ala-uddin that before he could even think of world conquest, he must make sure of fortifications against the Mongols, who were repeatedly transgressing his kingdom's northwest frontiers. The *kotwal* too was fortunate.

Instead of punishing him for such effrontery, Ala-uddin gave up his megalomaniacal projects and focused on building up better security against the Mongols.

The Last Days of the Khaljis

Ala-uddin Khalji died in January 1316. The last three years of his life were marked by miserable health and reports of his sons' life of heavy drinking and womanizing. His own queen, Malika-I-Jahan, pressed for the claims of her dissolute son Khizr Khan. Increasingly, Ala-uddin left the matters of state to his confidant, his former slave Kafur, who had distinguished himself in the southern campaigns and had now become the most important individual in the capital, next only to the sultan. He may have precipitated his master's death and in the prevailing confusion put Khizr Khan's six-year-old son on the throne with himself as the regent. Kafur blinded Khizr Khan and imprisoned all the other sons of the dead sultan. The whole situation caused such rivalries among the nobles that they had Kafur killed a little more than a month after Ala-uddin's death. They also released Ala-uddin's son, the inefficient and incapable Mubarak, from prison and crowned him the sultan.

In the next four years of Mubarak's "rule," Ala-uddin's empire, all the territories in peninsular India—importantly, the kingdoms of Gujarat, Devagiri, and Warangal—disintegrated rapidly. He came to depend increasingly on an obscure slave from Gujarat, Khusrav, both in his campaigns and in the affairs of state in the capital. Four years later, in April 1320, the ambitious Khusrav had Sultan Mubarak Khalji killed, ending the Khalji dynasty.

Immediately, Khusrav captured the throne and made himself the sultan and married a widow of Mubarak, much to the bitter opposition of the nobles, who regarded him as a low upstart. The opposition chose Ghazi Tughluq, governor of Dipalpur, as their leader. With the help of his own son, Malik Jauna (the future sultan Muhammad bin Tughluq), who was at the time "master of the horse" at the capital, Ghazi Tughluq emerged the victor in the battle for Delhi that took place on September 6, 1320. Khusrav was captured and beheaded as Ghazi Tughluq was raised to the throne on September 8 as Ghiyas-uddin Tughluq, the founder of the Tughluq dynasty, which lasted for the next eight decades before it was practically wiped out by the terrible invasion of Timur in 1399.

The two most important rulers of the Tughluq dynasty were Muhammad bin Tughluq (1325–1351) and Firuz Shah Tughluq (1351–1388), two long reigns and between them responsible for losing the empire. The period is very well documented, the first ruler known for his maverick schemes and merciless torture and killing of both Muslims and Hindus on the slightest hint of disobeying the sultan's orders or posing a politi-

cal challenge to the sultan's position. Contemporary accounts of his plans and of his inhumanity differ in their details but not in the essentials. Firuz Shah was known for his public works projects, but his other side was that of an orthodox Sunni Muslim who was severe to the Shias and cruel toward the Hindu population and a destroyer of their temples. Apart from the contemporary accounts, posterity could evaluate his beliefs and acts based on his own account of his reign. The differences between the modus operandi of the two apart, the country had been left so weak that it fell easy prey to the devastation brought to its capital and its environs by Timur Lane in the penultimate year of the fourteenth century.

Both Muhammad and Firuz were talented rulers in the entire history of the Sultanate of Delhi, if one judges persons by their intelligence and erudition. They were both well versed in Arabic and Persian. Muhammad was interested in literature, logic and metaphysics, mathematics, science, and medicine. Firuz was truly a scholar of some distinction, a patron of learning, and a writer.

How does one reconcile these two aspects of their personalities—interest in humanities and being inhuman? Were both of them bipolar? Can one dismiss their cruelties and Firuz's destruction of Hindu temples merely on the grounds that they were different from the other rulers only in the degree of violence, not the fact of it? Was the fratricide and parricide for the throne true of all states in India—for example, the kingdoms of South India, Rajasthan, or Tughluq's contemporary, Vijayanagar (1336–1565)?

Ghiyas-uddin Tughluq

The five years of Ghiyas-uddin's reign (1320–1325) produced some measure of stability in Delhi and its environs. He built new fortifications for the capital, which was renamed Tughlakabad, "the city of the Tughluqs." He earned respect for his regime by his courteous treatment of the Khalji family, particularly the queens and the princesses, who had been literally distributed among the nobles like merchandise during the period of anarchy following the end of the Khalji dynasty. He showed his merit as a military leader by bringing Bengal, which had for at least a quarter century been ruled to be part of the Delhi sultanate. His nemesis, however, was his own eldest son, Jauna, also known as Ulugh Khan and later to be his successor, Sultan Muhammad bin Tughluq, arguably the most controversial and perhaps important ruler of the dynasty. Extremely ambitious and ruthless, he killed his own father, making the fall of a wooden structure meant to be a pavilion for reception look like an accident.

Muhammad bin Tughluq

Two projects of Muhammad bin Tughluq (1325–1351) have evoked much

controversy among historians, including those of his time, Badauni, Barani, and Islami, as well as the famous traveler Ibn Battutah, who was there in 1333–1334. The two projects were the transfer of the capital and the introduction of a token currency. It was not just the projects that have been controversial. It was more the manner of implementation and the severity of punishments to those who stood in the way of their implementation.

Transfer of the Capital from Delhi to Deogiri. In 1326–1327, Muhammad bin Tughluq decided to transfer his capital from the traditional Delhi to Deogiri in the Deccan, which would be more central to his empire, now that he had made conquests in the South. It would also be central for possessions to the west and east—Gujarat and Bengal. It is possible that he thought of moving the capital far from the Mongols, who had already attacked the capital several times. His biographer M. Hussain posits that the intention was to populate central and South India with more Muslims and therefore to make Deogiri, renamed by him Daulatabad, a center of Muslim culture.[10]

The transfer to Daulatabad involved two stages: in 1327 the migration of the elite, and two years later the entire population of Delhi, which was a punitive measure. Accounts differ in regard to the numbers involved. Thus, Barani wrote, "All was destroyed. So complete was the ruin [of Delhi], that not a cat or a dog was left among the buildings of the city, in its palaces or in its suburbs. . . . Thus, this city, the envy of the cities of the inhabited world, was reduced to ruin." Ibn Battutah does not say that Delhi was totally deserted but admits "it was empty and was scantily inhabited." To make sure that his orders to move had been obeyed, the sultan, according to Battutah, would go to the roof of his palace to check to see if there was any light or smoke in the city and express satisfaction when there was neither.[11]

For the ease of the travelers, the sultan had a road constructed and lined with shady trees from Delhi to Daulatabad. There were numerous rest houses and hospices for humans and animals and sufficient arrangements made for everyone to have food and drinks and a few comforts along the way. Despite all the arrangements, many died. Barani wrote of the human toll:

> The people, who for many years and for generations had been natives and inhabitants of the land [Delhi], were broken-hearted. Many, from the toils of the long journey, perished on the road, and those who arrived at Deogir [Daulatabad] could not endure the pain of exile. In despondency they pined to death. All around Deogir, which is infidel land, there sprung up graveyards of Musulmans [Muslims].[12]

The sultan himself had second thoughts about his transfer of the capital. In 1336–1337, he ordered everyone to return to Delhi; more must have died on the way.

The Token Currency Project. In 1329, Muhammad bin Tughluq launched his fictitious currency project. He issued tokens of copper and possibly of brass as the currency equivalent of the existing silver *tanka* of 140 grains. The gold and silver coins, which were current, were not withdrawn. It appears that the sultan had acquainted himself with the paper currency that had been extant in China for a long time and lately introduced in Persia (Iran). The experiment in Muhammad's domains failed, because the people preferred to pay the revenues in the token currency, hoarding the gold and silver coins. Worse, there were private mints working overtime producing the token currency, and the state did not have the means to check the genuine from the spurious. In the three or four years the experiment lasted, the state lost huge amounts because the sultan ordered that the tokens be fully redeemed at their face value.

Again, historians differ. Barani says that the sultan had spent considerable amounts of money on his building and public welfare projects (transferring the capital and building the facilities en route), and he needed funds for his other projects, including "world conquest." Ishwari Prasad maintains that the project was sound and had merit; it failed because of a lack of "proper safeguards."[13] So does Muhammad's biographer M. Hussain, on the grounds that there was a worldwide shortage of silver and Muhammad foresaw the problem and was ahead of his time in introducing the token currency.

Conquests and Rebellions. Muhammad followed in the footsteps of Ala-uddin Khalji in extending his rule to the kingdoms of eastern and peninsular India. While still working for his father, Muhammad (then known as Ulugh Khan) had brought Orissa in the East and Warangal in the South back to the control of Delhi. After succeeding to the office of the sultan, he himself led several expeditions to the Deccan, the very first one being to quell the rebellion led by his own nephew (his sister's son), Bahauddin Gurshasp, and against the Hindu rulers of Kampili (the modern Bellary, Raichur, and Dharwar districts) and Dvarasamudra (Ballala III of the Hoysala dynasty) for giving refuge to Gurshasp. When the sultan laid his hands on the rebel nephew, he showed his barbaric qualities, altogether inhuman for the man of humanities he was known to be. He ordered that the rebel's flesh be cooked with rice and offered to elephants; his skin was to be stuffed and exhibited in all the main cities of the sultanate. The governor of Multan refused to exhibit the skin and was summarily executed.

One of the results of the defeat of Kampili was its annexation to the empire and taking a large number of its elite to Delhi and converting them to Islam. These included two brothers, Harihara and Bukka. Many years later, the brothers would be sent by Muhammad to the South as governors. They would reconvert to Hinduism and become the founders of the Vijayanagar Empire.

In the second half of his reign, Muhammad faced a number of rebellions—in Bengal, Gujarat, Punjab, Warangal, and Malabar—and many smaller ones, including one in Sind. Many of these led to the establishment of independent kingdoms such as in Bengal, Warangal, and Malabar. The sultan would move from one rebellion to another, in each place mercilessly torturing and killing thousands, presumably as a lesson to rebels elsewhere. The victims were mostly fellow Muslims, which did not matter to Muhammad, who was not a religious partisan as such. It was during the efforts to put down one such rebellion in Sind that the sultan fell ill and died at Tattah in March 1351.

A major source of opposition to Muhammad was the Islamic orthodoxy, which is one of the reasons the contemporary Islamic historians were prejudiced against him. Biographer Hussain points out that many of the leaders of the rebellions were Muslim divines of all minds whom Muhammad did not spare when captured. To overcome their opposition, he approached the Abbasid Khalifa of Egypt in 1343 for recognition and robes of honor, thereby reversing the practice since the time of Iltutmish of the sultan's complete political autonomy and his reading the *khutba* in his own name.

Firuz Shah Tughluq

There was chaos and anarchy, looting and plunder in the camp of the dead Muhammad bin Tughluq at Tattah. Muhammad had no son. To stabilize the situation, the nobles raised Firuz Shah, Muhammad's uncle's son, to the throne. The forty-year-old Firuz was the opposite of Muhammad in many respects. He was an orthodox Sunni Muslim, ready and willing to act to the complete satisfaction of the orthodox *ulamas* (the community of learned men) and the *qazis* (judges), discriminating against the liberal Sunnis and the Shias. As for the Hindus and their places of worship, Firuz followed Islamic lines to the letter. In cruelty toward the Hindus and demolishing their temples, including one of the holiest temples, that of Jaggannath at Puri in Orissa, he reminds one of the brutalities and iconoclasm of Muhammad of Ghazni. Unlike Muhammad, who had antagonized the religious leaders, some of whom wrote the largely unfavorable record of his reign, Firuz received high praise from the contemporary historians because of his bigotry.

Unlike Muhammad, Firuz was not a leader in the field of battle. He was allergic to confrontations. He allowed Bengal to become independent, and he never recovered control of the territories in peninsular India. In only one respect did he resemble his cousin Muhammad: He was an avid reader of literature in several languages, including Arabic and Persian.

Firuz has been hailed by historians, contemporary and later, as the first Muslim ruler who had the welfare of the common man, notably peasants, in mind. He was the first to appoint an assessor of land and land revenue based on an estimated production and fix the tax on a permanent basis, so that it was not dependent on the whims and fancies of the revenue collectors. He also abolished the fee that was traditionally charged an appointee to the provincial governorship, on the grounds that it usually translated into an imposition of the peasantry. He also took measures to ensure low prices of food, clothing, and other essentials.

For the general education of his people, Firuz Shah established some thirty *madrasas* and three colleges for higher learning, the first Muslim monarch to do so. He liberally set aside funds for the salaries of the teachers and assistance to needy students. He also encouraged the establishment of libraries, and although he demolished temples, he did not destroy Hindu learning. At the Jwalamukhi temple in the Kangra Valley, he ordered the maintenance of its library of books on Hindu learning and had at least one book translated into Persian, *the Dala il-I-Firuz Shahi*. He brought two Asokan pillars from

Meerut and Topara to Delhi and had one of them installed in Firuz Shah Kotla in Delhi. He left a record of his reign, *Sirat-I-Firuz Shahi*, and the thirty-two-page booklet *Futuhat-I-Firuz Shahi*, which allows one glimpses into his mind.

Among the public works of Firuz Shah Tughluq were 50 river dams, 40 mosques, 100 rest houses, 30 water reservoirs, 100 public baths, 100 hospitals, 150 bridges, and numerous public wells. All public facilities were well endowed with assignments of land revenues for their continued maintenance. In the capital, he built the new city of Firuzabad, the future site of New Delhi.

One of the problematic measures Firuz Shah took was in regard to slaves. He encouraged the nobility throughout the empire to send slaves captured in warfare, particularly those who were good in crafts, to the imperial or provincial capitals, where the sultan created special facilities to use their talents. It appears that out of the 180,000 selected, some 12,000 worked as artisans, while 40,000 worked as security. The good part of the enterprise was that the slaves were well treated, the bad side being a new element that would cause trouble after Firuz died.

Firuz's reign was of comparative peace, devoid of the constant campaigning that had marked his predecessor's rule. There were no repetitive rebellions, because his was a lax rule that allowed autonomy and even independence for distant provinces. Firuz continued as sultan until the age of seventy-seven, when he died in 1388.

Firuz's death was followed by the usual mayhem following a sultan's demise. His grandson Ghiyas-uddin Tughluq II, who succeeded to the throne, was engaged in a civil war first with his own uncle, and then against his own cousin, the situation compounded by rival nobles and leaders of the slaves. Between 1388 and Timur's invasion in 1398, there were five rulers.

Timur's Invasion

Timur, or Timur-I-lang for the Persians and Timur the Lame or Tamer Lane in Western accounts, was so named because he limped due to a leg injury. He was already the ruler of a vast empire that included Afghanistan, Persia, Kurdistan in northern Iraq, Syria, and Asia Minor when, at the age of sixty-three, he decided to invade India. The best source of information about his dastardly exploits is his own memoir, *Tuzuk-I-Timuri*, which clearly states that his twin motives for the Indian invasion in 1398–1399 were religion and the riches of India. His aims included "to war with the infidels [Hindus]" so he could get a "reward in the life to come." He would be Ghazi, a victor or a martyr in the cause of Islam, either way earning for himself a place in Paradise. The other aim was to plunder "the wealth and valuable[s] of the infidels" for the benefit of the "army of Islam."[14]

Leaving Samarkand in April 1398, he reached Delhi in December, where he met weak opposition, since the sultan, Mahmud Tughluq, and his minister Mallu had fled. It does not appear that Timur had plans to build an empire in India. Everywhere along his way, he left a trail of torture and mass killings, enslavement or conversion to Islam of women and children, and loot and plunder of an order that would surpass Muhammad of Ghazni's beastly record four centuries before. It is pointless to chronicle his horrible misdeeds, which were the worst in the history of humankind. A sample from his memoir of the sack of Delhi is instructive:

> On that day, Thursday and all of Friday, nearly 15,000 Turks were engaged in slaying, plundering and destroying. . . . The other booty was immense in rubies, diamonds, garnets, pearls and other gems; jewels of gold and silver; *ashrafis* and *tankas* of gold and silver; . . . vessels of gold and silver; and brocades and silks of great value. Gold and silver ornaments of the Hindu women were obtained in such quantities as to exceed all accounts. Excepting the quarter of the saiyids, the *ulama*, and the other Musulmans, the whole city was sacked.[15]

It would imply that except for the religious leaders, Timur's army did not spare anyone, including Muslims. Ironically, Timur, a Muslim, in the name of Islam, had ruined a city to whose greatness his fellow Muslim rulers had contributed so magnificently over the previous two centuries.

The Last Tughluq and the Sayyids

The fugitive Mahmud Tughluq returned to Delhi almost two years after Timur had left the city desolate. In the remaining little more than a decade of his dismal reign, three individuals vied for power: his own minister Mallu; Khizr Khan, who was supposed to have been nominated a viceroy by Timur; and Daulat Khan Lodi, who briefly became the sultan in 1413 following Mahmud Tughluq's death the previous year. He was displaced by Khizr Khan, who established the Sayyid dynasty in 1414, thereby ending the rule of the Turks.

In the less than four decades of the Sayyid dynasty (1414–1451), there were four rulers, none of them distinguished except for the claim of the founder, Khizr Khan, that he was a descendant of the Prophet. Ethnically, he came from a family from Arabia to Multan, where the ruler had adopted his father as a son. Khizr Khan became the governor of Multan during the time of Firuz Shah Tughluq. He had no ethnic support base in Delhi, where the Turkish and Afghan nobles predominated. It was for this reason that after he became the sultan in 1414, he acted as the nominee of Timur.

Much before the birth of the Sayyid dynasty, the Sultanate of Delhi's domains had shrunk so badly that when

Khizr Khan ascended the throne, he had control of Delhi and some portion of the Doab region between the Ganges and Jumna rivers. The Tughluqs had lost control over those territories by the middle of the fourteenth century, and the sultan's territories were quite limited even by the time of Timur's invasion. The whole country had split into several sultanates—Gujarat, Bengal, Malwa, Khandesh, Jaunpur, the Bahmanis in the Deccan, and Vijayanagar farther south, to mention only the most important polities. During Khizr Khan's seven years (1414–1421) and the thirteen years of his successor, Mubarak Shah (1421–1434), the Sayyid rulers had reestablished Delhi's control over the Punjab, the Doab, and parts of Rajasthan.

The Sayyid dynasty lasted until 1451, its last two rulers, Muhammad Shah (1434–1445) and Ala-ud-din Alam Shah (1445–1451), managing to hang on to diminished territory and administrative control. During their regimes, Buhlul Lodi, an Afghan chief of Sirhind, commanded a force of more than 20,000 cavalry and a much larger infantry force. He extended his authority over all of the Punjab. Multan and Jaunpur became completely independent kingdoms under Muhammad Shah. During the last Sayyid's rule, the sultan's authority was barely limited to Delhi and its immediate environs. The sultan himself retired to Badaun for personal safety, whereas his *wazir* (minister) Hamid Khan invited Buhlul Lodi to take over. That marked the beginning of the Lodi dynasty; Buh-lul allowed the last Sayyid ruler to remain at Badaun.

The Lodis

The ascension to the throne of Buhlul Lodi (1451–1489) as the sultan of Delhi marked the dominance of an Afghan tribal family over the long-term primacy of the Turks. Buhlul once again restored the Sultanate of Delhi's authority to Jaunpur, the entire Doab, Malwa, and portions of Rajasthan. Like the Sayyids before him, he was not intolerant of the Hindu majority community. As a tribal Afghan, he behaved as the chief of all the nobles rather than as the sultan. The same tribal considerations were seen in the division of his territory just before his death among his relatives and fellow emirs for administration and use of revenues. Consequently, his son and successor, Nizam Khan, who would take the title of Sultan Sikandar Shah (1489–1517), had direct control over only Delhi, the Punjab, and the Doab.

The Lodi dynasty, which lasted seventy-five years (1451–1526), had the merit of having only three rulers, the first two having long reigns, covering sixty-six years. Whereas the founder, Buhlul, had little time for administration, Sikandar Shah was a talented administrator who broke the tribal ways of his Afghan nobility and raised the authority of the sultan's office in their eyes and in the provincial establishments. He had a regular system of receiving not only reports from the provinces on the crops and prices but also intelligence on the political relationships among the nobility. Consequently, his long reign saw the further consolidation and stability that were already the hallmarks of Buhlul's regime.

Contrary to the Sayyid rule, which did not have any ethnic support, Turk or Afghan, and was more of a holding operation of territories that had not recovered from the crippling economic devastation of Timur's invasion, the first two Lodis showed more self-assurance and, in Sikandar's case, attention to culture and learning in the land. The cultural renaissance that Sikandar fostered was irrespective of communal affiliation, Hindu or Muslim. In fact, a joint Indo-Saracenic style in architecture developed during this period, whereas in literature there was an efflorescence, which included translations of many Sanskrit works into Persian. The sultan also promoted the collection of all kinds of manuscripts—Arabic, Persian, and Sanskrit—attracting scholars, Muslims and Hindus, from all parts of his domain to his court, where he himself presented some poems he composed. In the generally liberal atmosphere all such efforts produced, there was a bonhomie among the scholars, writers, artists, and musicians, setting a good stage

for the Mughal period during which far more conscious efforts would be made to bring the two communities closer together for the betterment of both.

The last of the Lodis, Ibrahim (1517–1526), was no match for his father, Sikandar. Ibrahim was weak, diffident, vacillating, and deficient of interactive skills, all of which promoted a series of rebellions not only in the distant provinces but also in the family patrimony of Punjab, which was ruled by Daulat Khan Lodi as governor. Both Daulat Khan and Ibrahim's uncle Alam Khan, who had been sent to the distant Gujarat as governor, independently approached the Mughal Babar in Kabul, asking him to attack India, remove Ibrahim, and bolster their own authority over the sultanate. But Babar had his own agenda. In a conclusive confrontation with Ibrahim's forces and without the aid of the undependable Daulat Khan or Alam Khan's forces, in what history records as the First Battle of Panipat, on April 20, 1526, Babar's much smaller force, estimated at 10,000, trounced his fellow-Muslim adversary's force of more than 100,000 to make a successful bid for the establishment of Mughal power in India. Ibrahim lost his life on the battlefield.

———

NOTES

1. Jalaluddin Rumi Balkh, *Mathnavi*, edited by Reynold A. Nicholson (London: Luzac, 1925–1940), story 17.

2. "Chachnama," in vol. 2 of *History of India as Told by Its Own Historians*, edited by H. M. Elliot and John Dawson.

3. Quoted in Romila Thapar, *A History of India*, 233–34.

4. E. A. Sachau, trans. and ed., *Alberuni's India* (London: Kegan Paul, Trench, Trubner, 1910), 22.

5. Ibid, 46.

6. S. A. A. Rizvi, "Islamization in the Indian Sub-continent," in *Religious Change and Cultural Domination*, edited by D. N. Lorenzen (Mexico City: El Colegio de Mexico, 1981).

7. Ibid, 46.

8. Vincent Smith, *The Oxford History of India*, 238.

9. Quoted in K. A. Nilakanta Sastri, *Advanced History of India* (Bombay: Allied Publishers, 1970), 352.

10. M. Hussain, *The Rise and Fall of Muhammad bin Tughluq* (London: Luzac, 1938), 108.

11. Elliot and Dawson, *History of India*, 3:239; M. Hussain, trans., *The Rehla of Ibn Battutah*, Gaekwad's Oriental Series, vol. 122 (Baroda: Oriental Institute, 1953), 94.

12. Elliot and Dawson, *History of India*, 3:239.

13. Ishwari Prasad, *History of the Qaranuah Turks in India* (Allahabad: University of Allahabad, 1936), 101.

14. Elliot and Dawson, *History of India*, 389–477.

15. Ibid., 445–46.

The Vijayanagar rulers, without exception, were tolerant of all religions and of the different sects within the Hindu fold. There is no mention in any of the Muslim, Jewish, or Christian records of the desecration or demolition of a single place of worship or prayer of those religions by any Vijayanagar ruler. An occasion of a religious dispute between the Jains and the Vaishnavas was used by Bukka I to issue an edict, copies of which were displayed in important places, "proclaiming that from the standpoint of the State, all religions were equal and entitled to protection and patronage. The policy of religious concord indicated in this edict, was followed by all his successors." (page 151)

8

PENINSULAR KINGDOMS
Vijayanagar and Bahmani

THE VIJAYANAGAR EMPIRE

The Founders:
Harihara and Bukka

The founders of the Vijayanagar Empire were two brothers, Harihara and Bukka, who had an unusual personal history. They were in the employ of the kingdom of Warangal when Muhammad Tughluq annexed it. They managed to flee in time to the neighboring smaller kingdom of Kampili (Anantpur, Shimoga, and Chitaldurg districts). When Kampili was annexed by Muhammad Tughluq in 1326, the two brothers were taken as prisoners to Delhi, where they were forcibly converted to Islam. The sultan liked the two brothers, Harihara and Bukka, and sent them back as governor and deputy governor, respectively, to Kampili, where a revolt was in progress.

Back in Kampili, the two brothers found themselves in the midst of a very strong reaction among the Hindu rulers, nobility, and learned men of eastern and southern parts of peninsular India. The invasions by Ala-uddin Khalji and Malik Kafur in peninsular India had shocked the Hindus of the South, who had traditionally been untouched by Muslims, except as traders in the Malabar region and never as a political or military power. There were at least three centers of a coordinated resistance movement, which coalesced in the mid-1330s to restore Hindu rule in those areas of Andhra Pradesh, Tamil Nadu, and the Malabar Coast, which had recently come under Muslim rule. These centers were led by Prolaya Nayak, the ruler of a small Reddi kingdom based on Addanki and Kondavidu, and after his death, his nephew, Kapaya Nayak; Chalukya Somadeva, the founder of the Aravidu kingdom in Kurnool district; and Vira Ballala III, the only Hindu king whose lands had survived the Khalji and Tughluq invasions. They were successful in restoring Hindu rule in Warangal, Madura, and Tondaimandalam, the last reestablished as a kingdom based on Kanchi. And in

Kampili, there was an active resistance movement led by some of the nobles who had managed to flee when the kingdom had been attacked and annexed by Malik Kafur.

Hindu Resurgence in the South

Harihara's and Bukka's arrival as the Tughluq sultan's governor and deputy governor of Kampili must be seen in this context of Hindu resistance to extension of Muslim rule in peninsular India. Finding themselves encircled by what was virtually a Hindu confederacy of some seventy-five rulers, big and small, Harihara and Bukka reconverted to Hinduism, became the leaders of the resistance movement, and founded the Vijayanagar (the City of Victory) Empire (also known as Vidyaranya) in 1336. In this, the chroniclers of the time attribute a major role to Vidyaranya, a Hindu sage of the region who acted as a mentor to the first three rulers of Vijayanagar and whose name may have inspired the alternate name by which the empire is known. In order to overcome the opposition of the orthodox Brahmans who were adamantly opposed to converting to Islam, they declared that the new empire belonged to the god Virupaksha and that Harihara would act as his vice regent on earth. In fact, Harihara signed all documents in the god's name.

The Vijayanagar Empire lasted for two centuries as a strong and stable entity, from 1336 until its defeat at the hands of an alliance of four Bahmani kingdoms in 1565 at the famous but wrongly named Battle of Talicota. It was the only empire in Indian history that extended to both coasts, Malabar and Coromandel. The founders came from a Telugu-speaking region but made their empire a bilingual kingdom, the two languages being Kannada and Tamil. The empire stood guard against Islamization of South India, helping to preserve the Hindu heritage there, a task continued after a gap by the Marathas under Shivaji and the Peshwas.

The Vijayanagar Empire had three dynasties: Sangama, named after the father of the founders (1336–1485), Saluva (1485–1505), and Tuluva and Aravidu (1505–1646). Its heydays were marked by its greatest rulers: the founders, Harihara I (1336–1356) and Bukka I (1356–1377), Harihara II (1377–1404), and Krishnadeva Raya (1509–1529). Its rulers styled themselves as the *raya* (king or emperor) and prided themselves on being the protectors of the Hindu dharma. Some of its successions to the throne, at least three of them, were not smooth but did not involve any patricide or fratricide, or killing of all possible claimants to the throne, the kind of brutalities that marked such a process in the Delhi sultanate. Its record for promotion of art and architecture, literature, and music was worthy of the best contemporaries anywhere in the world.

Besides the local records, the Vijayanagar history is found in the accounts of several European travelers: Nicolo Conti, an Italian in around 1420; Domingos Paes and Fernao Nunez, Portuguese visitors to the court of Krishnadeva Raya; and Edoardo Barbosa, during the same period. And there was a noted Persian traveler, Abdur Razzaq, who left the account of his visit in 1442–1443.

The Vijayanagar rulers, without exception, were tolerant of all religions and of the different sects within the Hindu fold. There is no mention in any of the Muslim, Jewish, or Christian records of the desecration or demolition of a single place of worship or prayer of those religions by any Vijayanagar ruler. An occasion of a religious dispute between the Jains and the Vaishnavas was used by Bukka I to issue an edict, copies of which were displayed in important places, "proclaiming that from the standpoint of the State, all religions were equal and entitled to protection and patronage. The policy of religious concord, indicated in this edict, was followed by all his successors."[1]

Historical Highlights

A cofounder of the empire, Harihara I, extended his small polity of Vijayanagar on the southern bank of the Tungabhadra River, comprising just a few Kannada and Telugu districts, westward and southward by absorbing the much larger Hoysala kingdom, eastward by annexing the Reddi kingdom of Addanki and Kondavidu, and southeastward, vanquishing Tondaimandalam in the Tamil country where he made Nellore and its fort of Udaygiri his eastern headquarters under his brother Kampana. Under the command of one of his brothers (he had four), Marapa, the western kingdom of Kadamba, extending over the Konkan coast and its harbors, was annexed in 1347, whereas the sultan of Madura was defeated and taken prisoner in 1352–1353 and Sambuvaraya, Vijayanagar's feudatory in Kanchi, placed on his throne. However, he was overthrown in 1359–1360 by local elements, and the Sultanate of Madura revived. Under Harihara I's successor, Bukka I, Madura was besieged, defeated, and annexed in 1370, thereby ending the -decade-old only Muslim kingdom in the deep south. By the end of Bukka I's reign, the small polity of Vijayanagar that he had helped found with his brother Harihara I had become an empire, covering South India from coast to coast.

The only major extensions of the Vijayanagar Empire occurred during the reigns of Harihara II, who acquired the important harbors of Goa, Dabhol, and Chaul on the west coast, and Krishnadeva Raya. Beginning in 1513, Krishnadeva Raya led his forces against Prataprudra Gajapati of Orissa, whose predecessors had captured the fort at Udaygiri and some of the Vijayanagar territory in the Tamil country on the east coast. As a result of Krishnadeva Raya's three campaigns against Orissa, the Vijayanagar Empire was extended to include the east coast territory up to the Vizagapatam district. On the other hand, there were losses. During the time of Devaraya II (1424–1446), the ports of Goa, Dabhol, and Chaul were lost to the Bahmani kingdom.

Notable about the Vijayanagar Empire was the time and effort expended by some of its monarchs on the economic development and cultivation of arts and literature. Both domestic and overseas trade expanded during the period, and South India's ports, known for their commercial and cultural contacts with Southeast Asia, bustled with activity, as traders and mariners from China, Southeast Asia, the Arabian and Persian gulfs, Morocco, and Portugal exchanged goods. Portuguese sources indicate that *rayas* had ships constructed in the Maldive Islands, though they depended for the supply of horses on the Portuguese bringing them from the Gulf region. Devaraya I (1406–1422) deserves credit for building a dam in the Tungabhadra River with a fifteen-mile-long aqueduct, bringing a water supply to the teeming capital city. Extensive irrigation helped the farmers raise two to three crops to tide over the vagaries of the monsoon seasons.

Most important, women occupied a high and useful role in the society, economy, educational system, and bureaucracy. This is not surprising, considering the place of women in South Indian society throughout the ages. To quote the Portuguese travel companion of Paes, Fernao Nunez, who has been quoted before: "[The king of Vijayanagar] has women who write all the accounts of expenses that are incurred inside the gates, and whose duty it is to write all the affairs of the kingdom and compare their books with those of the writers outside; . . . even the wives of the king are well-versed in music. . . . It is said that he has judges, bailiffs and watchmen who every night guard the palace, and these are women."[2]

Noted for their patronage to scholars, some of the rulers were scholars in their own right. The most notable of these was Krishnadeva Raya, who wrote his famous *Amuktamalyada* in Telugu and five other works in Sanskrit. At his court there were the *astadiggajas* (literally, "eight elephants"), eight great men of literature, including his Telugu poet laureate, Peddana. The noble example of the rulers was emulated by lesser rulers, viceroys, and nobility all over the empire, thus making the Vijayanagar era known for its cultural efflorescence. Music flourished, some of the emperors themselves, including the versatile Krishnadeva Raya, being proficient in classical music.

Vijayanagar Administration

Krishnadeva Raya's *Amuktamalyada* gives the prevailing philosophy of administration, the king's role in upholding dharma, and his relationship with his subjects. The king, or *raya*, ruled with the help of a council of ministers, which included influential persons from the Brahmans, Kshatriyas, and Vaishyas, nominated on principles of both heredity and merit. Besides the important ministers such as for defense, finance, and external affairs, there was a minister specifically dealing with complaints from villages and for the improvement of villages, called a *mahanayakacharya*, who reported directly to the emperor.

The empire was divided into six provinces, further divided into *mandalas* and *chavadi*. The subdivisions in the two principal parts of the empire were *venthe*, *nadu*, and *sima* in the Kannada part and *kottam*, *parru*, and *nadu* in the Tamil part. Each of the provinces was headed by a *nayak* or *naik*, a very high office, often held by a member of the imperial family. He was responsible for raising revenue and sending one-third of it, which was quite high, to the imperial treasury, along with accounts of the income and expenditure of the province. A *nayak* could consequently be very harsh in his administration; if he was excessively so, he could be liable for punishment by the emperor himself. The *nayaks* maintained a military force and contributed to the imperial forces, when needed. A *nayak* was also a regional holder of the dharma and a dispenser of justice in accordance with the Hindu *shastras*. Apart from these obligations, a *nayak* was a law unto himself, fairly autonomous, almost a king in the area

under him. At the lowest level of administration was the village assembly of elders with some hereditary officials: the *senateova* (accountant), *talara* (watchman), and *begara* (superintendent of labor for public works).

The Defeat and Sack of Vijayanagar

The Bahmani kingdom in the Deccan, founded contemporaneously with Vijayanagar in 1347, proved to be a thorn in the latter's side throughout its existence, even after the Bahmani kingdom was split into its five components toward the end of the fifteenth century. A major bone of contention was the Raichur *doab* region between the Krishna and the Tungabhadra, but sometimes it was plain religious zeal on the part of some of the Bahmani rulers, particularly that of Bijapur, to extend the domain under Islam. The recurrence of the feud was a drain on the economy of both the Bahmani kingdom and the Vijayanagar Empire. It also helped the Portuguese, who played the two rivals against each other and in the process acquired territories on the west coast in the sixteenth century. The running feud ended with the practical liquidation of Vijayanagar as a major power in the South in 1565 by the combined effort of four of the five Bahmani kingdoms at the Battle of Talikota.

The city of Vijayanagar was sacked. According to Nicolo Conti, an Italian traveler in 1420, the circumference of the city was sixty miles, its seven-mile walls extending up to the mountains and enclosing "the valleys at their foot." Domingos Paes, a Portuguese visitor, recorded the following: "In this city you will find men belonging to every nation and people, because of the great trade which it has and the many precious stones there principally diamonds. . . . This is the best provided city in the world." Its riches were phenomenal. Abdur Razak, a Persian traveler in 1442–1443, wrote of the emperor's treasury having "chambers with excavations in them, filled with molten gold, forming one mass." Apparently, the wealth had trickled down to common people, because Razak adds, "All the inhabitants of the country, whether high or low, even down to the artificers of the bazaar, wear jewels and gilt ornaments in their ears and around their necks, arms, wrists and fingers." The sack was described by Robert Sewell in his work *A Forgotten Empire: Vijayanagar* in these unforgettable words:

> The third day saw the beginning of the end. . . . The enemy had come to destroy and they carried out their object relentlessly. They slaughtered the people without mercy; broke down the temples and palaces; and wreaked such savage vengeance on the abode of the kings that, with the exception of a few great stone-built temples and walls, nothing more remains but a heap of ruins to mark the spot where once the stately buildings stood. . . .

With fire and sword, with crowbars and axes, they carried on day after day their work of destruction. Never perhaps in the history of the world has such havoc been wrought and wrought so suddenly, on so splendid a city, teeming with a wealthy and industrious population in the full plenitude of prosperity one day, and on the next seized, pillaged, and reduced to ruins, amid scenes of savage massacre and horror beggaring description.[3]

THE BAHMANI KINGDOM

The Bahmani kingdom was one of the states born as a result of the protests of the nobility over the excesses of Muhammad bin Tughluq. After an abortive attempt at Daulatabad, the nobles raised one of them, Zafar Khan, with the title of Ala-uddin Bahman Shah to the throne at Gulbarga in 1347. There are two different stories of the origin of the name Bahmani by which the kingdom and the dynasty came to be known. One linked the name to the Persian hero Bahman; the other, put forth by the historian Ferishta (1560–1620), whose real name was Muhammad Kasim Hindu Shah, referred to the ruler's humble origins as Hassan, working as a servant of a prominent Brahman by the name Gangu in Delhi. Gangu had tremendous influence at the royal court because of his abilities as an astrologer. One day, Hassan, who was known for his honesty and loyalty, found a copper pot full of gold in Gangu's field and took it to his master. Gangu was grateful and introduced him to the sultan, who appointed him to the command of 100 cavalrymen with the title Zafar Khan. Gangu prophesied that someday Hassan would rise up to become a ruler somewhere. When Hassan or Zafar Khan was the sultan at Gulbarga, out of his gratitude for his old master, he included the name Bahman standing for Brahman in his official title. The kingdom came to be known as Bahmani.

If Ferishta's point of Hassan's loyalty to a Hindu Brahman is to be underlined, it was far from matched by Hassan's or most of his successors' (both in the Bahmani kingdom and in the successor states) treatment of Hindus in their kingdom. Except for two most notable examples in the Bijapur sultanate, the founder Yusuf Adil Khan and Ibrahim Adil Shah II, all others were iconoclasts. The major rationale for the Bahmani kingdom and its offshoots seemed to be their annual jihad against the Hindu Vijayanagar Empire to their south, and their moment of greatest religious triumph was a massacre of Hindus, including the inhabitants of the populous city of Vijayanagar after the humiliating defeat of the Vijayanagar Empire at the combined hands of Bahmani sultanates in 1565. The sack of Vijayanagar, indeed, was a time of gloating glory, as the victors methodically destroyed the temples and each piece of their decorated exteriors because of their Hinduness.

Despite the Bahmani kingdom being a new sultanate, the process of succession witnessed the same macabre pattern of killings, blinding, or mutilation of the opponents as in the northern sultanates. Of the fourteen sultans of the Bahmani kingdom in roughly 150 years, five were murdered, including an infant king; three died of excessive drinking; three were deposed; and two were blinded. Only three died of natural causes. Preoccupation with capturing the throne and the wars with Vijayanagar seemed to have engaged the energies of the royalty and the nobility, leaving little time or attention for the redeeming qualities of a state such as sustained striving for the well-being of the people or for cultural pursuits. One major exception at least for part of its history was the Sultanate of Bijapur.

The Conquests

Within a decade of his accession and death in 1358, Ala-uddin Bahman Shah had extended his kingdom much beyond the old Daulatabad to include territory from the Wainganga in the North to the Krishna River in the South and from Daulatabad in the West to Bhongir in the East. The kingdom importantly included the west coast ports of Dabhol and Goa and the strategic passes from the south Deccan across the Western Ghats to the Konkan. For administrative convenience, he divided the territory into four *tarafs*, each in the charge of one of four prominent nobles who had supported the establishment of the kingdom. The tradition of political autonomy continued, in time, crystallizing into altogether independent kingdoms or sultanates. The second sultan, Muhammad Shah I (1358–1377), established the practice, which remained throughout the history of the Bahmani sultanate, of a sultan's council of eight ministers, with a *peshwa,* a title that would become prominent during the Marathas. The eighth sultan, Firuz Shah (1387–1422), annexed the old Hindu kingdom of Rajahmundry of Telangana in 1417. His successor, Ahmad Shah (1422–1435), enlarged the Bahmani kingdom substantially with the conquest of the Hindu kingdom of Warangal. He shifted the capital in 1429 to Bidar, where he built a new city named after himself. Later in the century, an extremely capable minister, Mohammad Gawan, was able to annex parts of Konkan on the west coast, including the retaking of the important ports of Chaul, Dabhol, and Goa, which strengthened the kingdom's ties with Persia, which was predominantly Shia, and augmented the overseas trade with the Gulf states and made possible the direct import of Arab horses. Like its much later successor state of Hyderabad under the Nizams, the Bahmani kingdom encompassed three different populations: speakers of Marathi, Kannada, and Telugu.

Toward the end of the next century, the Bahmani sultanate fell apart, in a period of three decades, to become the five sultanates of the Deccan, each one named after the person who established his independence. Thus, the Imad Shahi of Berar was the first to do so in 1484, Adil Shahi of Bijapur the second in 1489, and Nizam Shahi of Ahmednagar third in 1490. When Golkonda's Qutb Shahi was established in 1518, the residue of the Bahmani kingdom after the separation of the four became the Barid Shahi of Bidar. Two of these were absorbed by the others. Berar was absorbed by Ahmednagar in 1574 and Bidar by Bijapur.

There were two aspects of the Bahmani sultanates that were different from those in the North. First was its orientation away from Delhi, establishing its own separate links with the Middle East, notably Persia, which was predominantly of the Shia faith, whereas the North Indian Muslim sultanates were principally Sunni. Second, the politics of the Deccan were different, being between the Afghan-Turk-Persian nobility, also called *pardesis* or foreigners, mostly Shias, and the so-called Deccan nobility or *desis,* mostly Sunni. Many of the *pardesis* were adventurers from the Middle East whom the sultans encouraged to immigrate. There were racial and religious differences between the two groups, the Deccani Muslims being, in large part, the progeny of African, principally Abyssinian (known as *Habshi*), fathers and Indian low-caste convert mothers. The sultans of Bijapur and Golkonda were examples of the latter; the founders of Bidar and Ahmednagar were Sunni converts from Hinduism.

Some of the notable figures who deserve notice, apart from the Bahmani founder, are Mohammad Gawan, one of the greatest generals and administrators of Indian history; Ibrahim Adil Shah II, the foremost liberal sultan of Bijapur; and the valiant Chand Bibi of Ahmednagar who defended the state against the Mughals.

Mohammad Gawan

Mohammad Gawan (1466–1481) was a Persian belonging to the *pardesi* party at the court of Sultan Mohammad Shah III (1463–1482), appointed as *vakil-us-sultanat* (deputy of the kingdom) in 1466; he held that supreme position, next only to the sultan, until he was assassinated in 1481. He was a great warrior and an astute and able administrator. He extended the sultanate's boundaries all the way from Orissa to Rajahmundry in the East and to Konkan and Goa in the West, also adding Hubli, Belgaum, and Bagalkot in the South. Gawan divided the extensive Bahmani kingdom into units, increasing the four old *tarafs* to eight, held by important nobles, some of whom simultaneously held a minister's position at the royal court. Each *taraf* was subdivided into *sarkars* and the latter into *parganas* and the *parganas* into villages, which were the primary administrative units. The *tarafdars* were revenue collectors as well as army commanders, usually of 2,000 cavalrymen, and had all the civilian and military appointments in the territory under their control. In order to curb the *tarafdars'* tendency to become independent, a progression that could not be halted for too long, Mohammad Gawan made their posts transferable. Gawan was himself the *tarafdar* of Bijapur and the *vakil-us-sultanat,* or chief minister, at the same time.

The rival Deccani, or Desi, party at the court plotted against Gawan, producing before the sultan a forged letter with Gawan's seal, inviting the king of Orissa to invade the Bahmani kingdom. Accused of treachery, Gawan was ordered to be executed by the sultan on April 5, 1481. When the sultan later learned the truth, he was in much pain and began drinking excessively to drown his regret. He died soon after his honest, loyal, and able minister's death, in 1482.

Ibrahim Adil Shah II

Ibrahim Adil Shah II (1556–1627) was only nine years old when he succeeded his uncle to the throne of the Sultanate of Bijapur. His early training was under the direction of Chand Bibi, the dowager queen, and his aunt. A contemporary of the Mughal emperor Akbar, he had a lot in common with him, particularly in his regard for all religions. In this, he was perhaps the only Bahmani sultan to be not only tolerant of other faiths but a respecter of them as well.

Ibrahim worked to bring about harmony between the two principal rival sects of Islam—Shias and Sunnis—as well as between the Muslims and the Hindus through the medium of music. He himself played several musical instruments and knew Indian classical music and its nuances well. His book *Kitab-e-Navras* (Book of Nine Rasas), in Dakhani, a variant of Urdu, was a collection of fifty-nine poems and seventeen couplets, opened with a prayer to Saraswati, the Hindu goddess of learning. He also sang in praise of Saraswati and the Hindu god of education and general well-being, Ganapati.

Ibrahim loved music so much that he built a new township dedicated to the study of music and named it Navraspur ("the city of New Raga"). During his reign, Bijapur became a great center of Indian classical music, attracting the best proponents of music and dance from all over India.

Ibrahim was a great devotee of Hazrat Banda Mawaj, the well-known Sufi saint of the first capital of the Bahmani dynasty and a flourishing city by that time, Gulbarga.

Ibrahim was a man of the masses, fluent in the languages of the region—Marathi, Kannada, Dakhani, and Urdu. The masses called him Jagadguru Badshah, or "the sultan who was teacher of the world."

Chand Bibi

Notable in the annals of Bijapur and Ahmednagar was a valiant female figure. Chand Bibi became prominent for her heroic defense of the Ahmednagar state in 1595 when Emperor Akbar sent forces under his own son, Murad, to bring it under Mughal rule. Chand Bibi has ever since remained in Indian history a great woman warrior of medieval times.

Chand Bibi was the sister of the sultan of Ahmednagar and married to the sultan of Bijapur. On her husband's death, she served as the dowager queen and regent to her nephew, the successor as the sultan of Bijapur, Ibrahim Adil Shah II. Tired of the court intrigue and expecting to be assassinated, she left Bijapur for good and returned to Ahmednagar to serve as regent to her late brother's son, Bahadur.

Prince Murad's siege of the Ahmednagar fort lasted three months. The heroic resistance against the mighty Mughal army was led by Chand Bibi, who also organized attacking parties against the Mughals. Finally, both sides agreed to a truce, whereby Akbar recognized Bahadur as his nominee in the Deccan under the Mughal's nominal suzerainty. Chand Bibi was, however, constrained to cede Berar, which had been annexed by Ahmednagar only two decades earlier. She lost Berar to the Mughals but not the core of the Ahmednagar kingdom. She was not successful in repelling the second such attack by the Mughals in 1600. There are conflicting reports as to how she died during that attack, whether by murder or poisoning.

NOTES

1. N. Venkataramanayya, "The Kingdom of Vijayanagara," in *The History and Culture of the Indian People*, edited by R. C. Majumdar (Bombay: Bharatiya Vidya Bhavan, 1960), 6:280.

2. "Chronicle of Fernao Nunez," quoted in Robert Sewell, *A Forgotten Empire: Vijayanagar,* 382–83.

3. Sewell, *Forgotten Empire,* 207–8.

The Mughal rule is not regarded by most historians as an alien rule because, barring the exception of its founder, Babar, they had become Indianized and worked for the good of the people. Unlike some of the previous Muslim predators and the British rulers who came from outside the Indian borders and were ill-regarded for their massive drain on the country's wealth, the Mughals invested their earnings in India, allowing it to be used as capital for India's manufactures and boosting indigenous employment. A lot of their Indianization had to do with the partial Hinduizing of the imperial household through marriages with Rajput princesses and the consequent regard to their feelings, likes, and dislikes. This extended not only to the celebrations of Hindu festivals in the palace precincts but also to the tastes in dance and music, culinary preferences and fasting observances, and dress and deportment. Mughal art and architecture were considerably influenced by Hindu concepts in those fields.　(pages 161–62)

9

THE GREAT MUGHALS
Babar to Aurangzeb

The fourth period of India's major contact with Muslim rule was the period of the Mughals. It was different from the sultanate in many respects. First, it was one single dynasty that ruled effectively from 1526 to 1707 (with a short break of 15 years, from 1540 to 1555) as contrasted with the period of multiple dynasties and centers of power during the sultanate (1206–1526). In effect, there were five great Mughal emperors: Babar (1526–1530), the founder; Akbar (1556–1605), meaning the Great, who lived up to his name; Jahangir (1605–1627), basically continuing the policies of his father; Shah Jahan (1627–1658), who was among the human race's great builders; and Aurangzeb (1658–1707), who reversed Akbar's policies of tolerance and trust and destroyed the empire. The lesser Mughals who followed Aurangzeb presided over a diminishing and far less regarded empire until the last of them, Bahadur Shah Zafar II, barely ruled the grounds of the Red Fort in Delhi. He was symbolic, however, of an ever growing feeling among the Mughal emperors, that of being Indian. He became the symbol of India's nationalism as the rebels opposing the British rule in the Great Uprising of 1857–1859 marched on to Delhi and to their leader, *bahadur* (brave) only in name. Bahadur Shah (1837–1858; deposed) was too old and fragile to lift a sword yet wielded his pen gracefully as he continued his vocation of composing beautiful verse in his exile in Burma (Myanmar). He died there in undeserved obscurity.

The Mughal rule is not regarded by most historians as an alien rule because, barring the exception of its founder, Babar, they had become Indianized and worked for the good of the people. Unlike some of the previous Muslim predators and the British rulers who came from outside the Indian borders and were ill-regarded for their massive drain on the country's wealth, the Mughals invested their earnings in India, allowing it to be used as capital for India's manufactures and boosting indigenous employment. A lot of their Indianization had to do with the partial Hinduizing of the imperial household through marriages with Rajput princesses and the consequent regard to their feelings, likes, and dislikes. This extended not only to the celebration of Hindu festivals in the palace precincts but also to the tastes in dance and music, culinary preferences and fasting observances, and dress and deportment. Mughal art and architecture were considerably influenced by Hindu concepts in those fields.

BABAR

The founder of the Mughal dynasty was Babar (born February 14, 1483; r. 1526–1530) who inherited at age eleven his father's small principality of Ferghana, in Uzbekistan. Most of his biographers have attributed his valor, bravery, courage, and ambition to his descent from Timur Lane on his father's side and from Chingis Khan on his mother's. However, unlike those infamous barbarians who did not have any redeeming qualities of heart and mind, Babar had an emotional and cultural side to his personality. In the midst of military and political turbulence, he kept a journal, *Babarnama*, which reflects abundantly his sensitive nature and great powers of perception as well as his observations on the fragmented polity of North India that was truly his object of rule.

Babar's military skills were impressive, but they had failed to acquire for him his ancestor Timur's capital of Samarkand.

Twice he lost his patrimony of Ferghana to the Uzbeg chief, Shaibani Khan, and was compelled to give his eldest sister to his foe in matrimony. By 1501, he was a "throneless wanderer," taking refuge at Tashkent with his maternal uncle. It was around that time of desperation that a desire to carve out a future for himself away from Ferghana and Samarkand gripped him. In October 1504, he conquered Kabul, which became his staging ground for ambitions into the fertile plains of India, to which so many adventurers before him had repaired.

Babar led his troops in seven expeditions between 1505 and 1526, five of them after 1519, into India. His initial forays into India were possibly for laying hands on enough plunder to finance his attack on his native Ferghana and Samarkand. He briefly reconquered Samarkand in 1511 but could not hold it for more than a few months. The dream of holding Timur's capital remained with him even after his spectacular success and establishment of power in Delhi.

The ambition to establish power involved dislodging Sultan Ibrahim Khan Lodi, a fellow Sunni Muslim, whose dynasty had held authority there since 1451. Babar's march into India, therefore, was not a jihad or religious war but a fight with a coreligionist for power. The Lodis had been an agglomeration of several semi-independent polities, where the governors ruled autonomously like sultans themselves. Thus, sultans ruled in Gujarat, Malwa, Khandesh, Sind, Multan, and Bengal. Outside of the loose confederacy these states could possibly put together in the North was the group of five Shia Muslim states in the Deccan that would not countenance any alliance with the northern Sunni rulers.

Additionally, Ibrahim Khan Lodi lacked the qualities of leadership. Vain, rude, and insufferably arrogant, he had discord within his family and among the coterie of nobles at the court. The Lodis had remained in power so far by balancing the recalcitrant Afghan nobles at the court against their non-Afghan rivals, a game at which Ibrahim Khan was most inept. Ibrahim's own uncle Alam Khan, who had been forced to take refuge at the court of the sultan of Gujarat, fled to Kabul to plead with Babar to defeat Ibrahim Khan Lodi and place him (Alam Khan) on the throne of Delhi. In 1524, Ibrahim's governor of the strategic state of the Punjab, Daulat Khan, fearing deposition at Ibrahim's hands, wrote to Babar, pledging his allegiance and offering help in dislodging Ibrahim. Babar's sixth invasion in that year was to open the eyes of the intriguers, who were surprised that their ally had his own plans to establish Mughal power in India. They moved away from Babar but attacked Ibrahim's forces, only to weaken them against Babar, who was then planning his seventh and last expedition. All this would indicate the divided state that was India, in which a variety of Muslim rulers were fighting each other and unable to put up joint opposition to another Muslim adventurer from beyond the northwestern borders.

Babar had only 24,000 men when he faced Ibrahim Khan Lodi's army of 100,000 men and 1,000 elephants. But he had the benefit of artillery, only a few pieces, but enough to create fear and confusion among Ibrahim's troops, who were experiencing artillery for the first time on an Indian battlefield. The result was completely in Babar's favor, as Ibrahim was killed along with at least 20,000 troops. Babar made his intentions of staying clear on April 27, 1526, as the *Khutba* was read on that day proclaiming him the emperor. Perhaps to please the *qazis*, the religious leaders in his entourage, he also announced he had become a *ghazi*, slayer of the infidels.

Babar met a real challenge in the following February, as the Rajput states joined forces under the capable leadership of Rana Sangram Simha of Mewar, a legendary warrior who had lost an arm and an eye and was known to have eighty scars on his body. Babar suffered successive defeats at Rajput hands. At this point, he declared a jihad against his Hindu opponents. Desperate, Babar dramatically renounced drinking, breaking all bottles and goblets before his soldiers, vowing not to touch liquor until all his enemies were vanquished. This boosted his troops' morale when they met the Rajput forces at Khandwa, about thirty-five miles west of Agra on March 17, 1527. Once again, the artillery gave Babar an unprecedented advantage, as the Rajput fighters were routed, the rout becoming worse with the retreating elephants. Although Babar had to continue his fight against several Afghan rulers, notably the coalition arranged under the leadership of Ibrahim Khan Lodi's brother Sultan Mahmud, in Bihar, as well as some Rajput states such as the Malwa ruler Medini Rai at the Chanderi fort that still held out, historians aver that the Battle of Khandwa was far more consequential than any other conflict, making Babar the undisputed master of the Jumna and central Ganges region.

Babar's early death, only four years later, in 1530, left behind to his son Humayun his possessions extending all the way from Oxus in Afghanistan in the West to Bihar in the East and south to Rajasthan and Malwa. He had neither the time nor the aptitude for administration. He basically adopted the corrupt administration of the Lodis. He did not have much hold over considerable parts of his kingdom that were still left to be ruled, for all purposes, under autonomous emirs and descendants of the former sultans. Moreover, as he repeatedly states in his well-written memoirs, he did not like India and longed for the landscape, greenery, and fruits (particularly melons) of his homeland. He had no time to appreciate India, its arts, music, literature, or architecture. His forte was his mastery over military strategy and ability to inspire men and to lead them to victory. In his limited legacy, he was closer to his ancestors Chingiz Khan and Timur Lane, far from his illustrious grandson Akbar. By his own admission, he ordered wanton killing of the population of Bajaur and Saiyyadpur and taking women as prisoners during his fifth and sixth invasions, which was more in the style of Chingiz Khan and Timur than the cultured person that Babar was.

HUMAYUN AND SHER SHAH

Babar's son, Humayun, is known more for the remarkable tomb built over his grave than any heroic exploits or administrative or artistic achievements. In 1540, ten years into his reign, he was easily defeated by Sher Shah Suri and his son, Islam. Humayun spent the next decade and a half fleeing Delhi and living in exile in Kabul.

Sher Shah, son of a modest middle-ranking holder of a *jagir* in the present Jharkhand state, was born in 1486 as Farid. His early reputation as an innovative administrator of his father's *jagir* brought him to the attention of the sultan of a principality in South Bihar. It is from him that he received the title of Sher Khan for killing a tiger (*sher* means tiger) single-handedly in a hunting expedition. Because of the death of the sultan and the infancy of his son, Sher Khan soon came to be put in charge of the small state's administration. In time, he assumed the leadership of Afghan nobles opposed to the Mughals and built a base of power around the important fort of Chunar. In 1539, while Humayun was in Bengal, Sher Khan cut off his supplies and return route to Agra. In two major engagements between the forces of Humayun and Sher Khan in 1539–1540, Sher Khan prevailed, and Humayun's troops were routed. In a matter of a few months, Sher Shah, as he called himself now, quickly brought all the Mughal possessions under his own control, leaving Humayun no choice except to go into exile in 1540, eventually to reach Persia in 1544 and seek the help of his host, Shah Tahmasp, to regain his throne. In exchange for the shah's military assistance, Humayun had to make some very important concessions. He agreed to become a Shia and to spread the faith in India. Once in India, he would renege on those undertakings.

It was during these travels in exile that Humayun's wife, Hamida Begum, gave birth in Umarkot, Sind, to a son, the future emperor Akbar, on October 15, 1542. The proud father is alleged to have opened a bottle of the best musk in his possession and announced that his son's fame, when he grew up, would spread like the perfume all over the world. Indeed, the child was to be the greatest ruler of the Mughal line and arguably one of the two greatest monarchs in the Indian annals, the other being Asoka.

In 1545, during the siege of the fort at Kalinjar, Sher Shah died, the victim of an accidental explosion. His son and successor, Islam, was not a capable leader. The intrigues among the Afghan nobles at the court and in the distant provinces weakened the state. Islam dragged on for

a little less than ten years and died in November 1554.

In the following year, after several turns of fortune, good and bad, Humayun was able to overcome his enemy and reenter Delhi on July 23, 1555, after adversity and exile lasting fifteen years. That was his moment of great triumph, but the glory was not to last long. Always associated with bad luck, Humayun died within months of his victory. On the evening of January 14, 1556, as he was hurrying down the stairs of his library, in response to the call for prayer, he fell and died.

The short interregnum of fifteen years during which Sher Shah ruled is known for several accomplishments, the most notable being the construction of a major highway from the Punjab to Bengal, which was made famous by the British writer Rudyard Kipling in the late nineteenth century as the Grand Trunk Road. Sher Shah also helped the trading and manufacturing community by encouraging and aiding the establishment of new towns all along the Grand Trunk Road.

AKBAR

Akbar succeeded to the throne at the young age of thirteen and was initially guided by his regent, Bairam Khan. Through extensive campaigning, he had made himself master of northern India, including Gujarat in 1572, but he realized that peace in the subcontinent could come about only by keeping harmonious relations between its two principal communities: the Hindus and the Muslims. In 1562, Akbar married a Rajput princess, Jodhabai, the daughter of the powerful Raja Bihari Mal of Amber. He did not convert her to Islam. In fact, he built a temple for her in his new capital city of Fatehpur Sikri, the construction of which began in 1571. He had alliances with a number of Rajput kings, some of them holding positions of authority at his court and in the army. They became the pillars of his empire. One of them was Raja Todar Mall, his revenue minister, who instituted a land-revenue system whose merits were such that the British adopted it for large parts of their Indian empire.

Akbar and Rana Pratap of Mewar

Akbar wanted Chitor to submit to his sovereignty because he knew that it would lead to the other Rajput rulers, who had so far stayed away from him, also agreeing to be part of his empire. Such was the prestige of the house of Chitor in all of Rajasthan.

In 1572, the proud ruler of Mewar, Uday Singh, died. Soon after, Akbar sent several missions to Uday Singh's son and successor, Rana Pratap, led by fellow Rajputs such as Man Singh; his father, Bhagwan Das; and Raja Todar Mall, inviting him to present himself at the Mughal court. The proud Rana refused, regarding his fellow Rajputs as traitors to India, having submitted to an alien ruler. Rana Pratap treated Akbar's diplomatic missions with courtesy but did not yield an inch that would compromise his freedom or sovereignty.

Finally, Akbar sent a huge army, mostly cavalry supported by elephants and artillery, led by his brave Hindu general Man Singh, whose pride had been hurt by the indifferent treatment he had received at Chitor. Aware of the likely Mughal military response, Rana Pratap had prepared for the confrontation by putting together a defense that would match the enemy's. During the celebrated Battle of Haldighati on June 21, 1576, he had a direct confrontation with Man Singh, who ducked in time to avoid a javelin thrown by Rana Pratap, as the latter's famous companion of many battles, his horse Chetak, stood with his forelegs on Man Singh's massive elephant. Chetak was wounded in the leg by a sword blade fixed to the pachyderm's trunk. He died of the wounds but not before he had carried Rana Pratap to safety. Mewar's bards have lauded Chetak's loyalty. He has been immortalized in literature. His name has come to be identified with valor and service, and statues have been raised in his honor, even in recent times.

By a timely withdrawal from the battleground, Rana Pratap saved his men and mounts. The loss in manpower was just a couple hundred men, and no prisoners of war were taken. For Akbar, it was no victory; for Rana Pratap, it was no inglorious defeat, although his kingdom had fallen. Aware of the possibility of failure on the battlefield, Rana Pratap had planned for long-term low-level warfare through guerrilla tactics. He had enlisted the help of the local Bhils, the tribals who knew the terrain well. In the aftermath of Haldighati, their help would be most critical in the years of harassment he caused the Mughal forces. It is because of such plans that he left the Battle of Haldighati before complete military defeat. The Rajput annals are filled with a mixture of pride and compassion for their hero, who moved with his family from place to place, subsisting on poor fare and living in great discomfort, vowing never to give up his freedom. Rana Pratap remained a hero to many, including the seventeenth-century Maratha leader Shivaji and his successors, who employed guerrilla tactics and brought Akbar's great-grandson Aurangzeb to his knees. Significantly, Rana Pratap's heroism was invoked in the nationalist movement in the twentieth century all over India, notably in Bengal and Maharashtra.

Akbar disgraced Man Singh for some time. A few months after Haldighati, Akbar himself came to Mewar to capture the elusive Rana Pratap but in vain. Two years later, he sent another huge force under the command of Mir Bakshi (the defense chief) Shahbaz Khan, who could take Rana Pratap's principal fort of Kumbalgarh but not Rana himself. Akbar was exasperated. Here was the most powerful emperor of the subcontinent bent on destroying one individual, who was saved not only by his personal

heroism and bravery but also because the people regarded him as their own and shared his love of freedom and refusal to surrender it. By the time of his accidental death on January 29, 1597, he had regained most of his territories except his beloved Chitor fort. British historian Vincent A. Smith concludes:

> The emperor desired the death of the Rana and the absorption of his territory in the imperial dominions. The Rana, while fully prepared to sacrifice his life if necessary, was resolved that his blood should never be contaminated by intermixture with that of the foreigner, and that his country should remain a land of freemen. After much tribulation, he succeeded, and Akbar failed.[1]

Akbar and Religion

Akbar was a ruler in the true Indian tradition, allowing the right of religious freedom to all his subjects. He had grown up in liberal, tolerant traditions. His ancestors, though they were Sunnis, had, out of a liberal disposition or political pragmatism, befriended the Shias. Thus, Akbar's grandfather Babar had obtained, in the pursuit of his territorial ambitions, the assistance of the Safavid rulers of Persia, who were Shias. As a child, Akbar had witnessed how hospitable and helpful his father Humayun's Persian hosts were, although they were Shias. Humayun himself had come under the religious influence of Sheikh

Muhammad Gawth, a Persian Shia of great spiritual standing. After Humayun's early death, Akbar was brought up by his guardian, Bairam Khan, who was not only a Shia but also the leader of the Shia community in Delhi. Those who point out that Akbar's broadmindedness in religion was a natural outcome of such a liberal family tradition cannot explain his intolerant and bigoted great-grandson Aurangzeb, the last powerful Mughal, who was Akbar's exact antithesis in matters of religion.

Although born a Sunni, Akbar had been exposed favorably to Shiism while he was growing up in Persia. After ascending the throne in Delhi, he found his Sunni religious officials, the *Sadr*, violently ill-treating the Shias. Matters reached an intolerable point in 1570 when Akbar openly took the Sunni *ulamas* to task.

In his personal life, he was concerned that his queen had not borne him a son. He approached Sheikh Salim Chisti, a revered Sufi mystic. When a son was born in 1569, he named him Salim in honor of Chisti, whom he visited annually thereafter. When the latter died, he built a tomb for him at a prominent location within his fort-capital at Fatehpur Sikri, eighteen miles from Agra.

Apart from his Rajput Hindu wife, Jodhabai, Akbar was influenced by two great scholars who were extremely well read in Hinduism and other religions: the historian and his closest confidant, Abul Fazl, and the latter's brother, Faizi.

Akbar went beyond merely tolerating other religions in his empire; he created a new one: Din-I-Ilahi, which was a syncretic faith drawing from a number of religions then practiced in India. The emperor invited leaders of several faiths—Islam, Hinduism, Judaism, Christianity, and Zoroastrianism—and held elaborate discussions with them: Sunni *ulamas*, Sufi sheikhs, Hindu *pandits*, Zoroastrian (Parsi) *dasturs*, Jain *munis*, and Catholic priests from Goa. He invited them to his new capital, Fatehpur Sikri, where he had built the Ibadat Khana, the Hall of Worship. Badauni, the well-known historian at Akbar's court, who was not very happy with the emperor's deviation from Sunni Islam, describes the meetings:

> The Emperor came to Fathpur. There he used to spend much time in the Hall of Worship in the company of learned men and shaikhs and especially on Friday nights, when he would sit up there the whole night continually occupied in discussing questions of religion, whether fundamental or collateral. The learned men used to draw the sword of tongue on the battlefield of mutual contradiction and opposition, and the antagonism of the sects reached such a pitch that they would call one another fools and heretics.[2]

In these supposedly frank discussions, the severity of the criticism of the Shias by the orthodox among the

Sunni *ulamas* did not impress him. Nor was he impressed with the exertions of the Catholic priests, who openly expressed their hope that the emperor would convert to their faith. On the other hand, he was impressed with the Hindu Upanishadic spirit: God could be reached in a variety of ways, including through pantheism and agnosticism. Badauni, however, believed that the emperor's purpose in these discussions was political.

The result was Akbar's issue of a *mahzar*, or declaration, in 1579 that stipulated that thereafter he would act as the final arbiter in all religious disputes. Three years later, he proclaimed his new eclectic faith, the Din-I-Ilahi, or Divine Faith. There is no document extant detailing the beliefs and practices of the new faith. Drawing from diverse sources, one scholar commented, "The Divine Faith was Sufi in conception, with ceremonial expressions borrowed from Zoroastrianism. It was strictly monotheistic and incorporated Shi'ite ideas of the role of the *mujtahid* or interpreter of the faith. In brief, it appears to owe more to Islam than to Hinduism."[3]

Although the Din-I-Ilahi included the principal tenets of Islam, Akbar was partial toward Hinduism. He asked that the Atharva Veda and the two epics the *Ramayana* and the *Mahabharata* be translated into Persian. In deference to the Hindus, he banned the slaughter of cows in the capital and personally gave up eating meat of any kind on two days

of the week as well as during certain major Hindu festivals.

Religious Policy after Akbar

Akbar's "secular" policy was not followed to the same degree by his successors. And though after his marriage Jahangir came increasingly under the influence of his Muslim wife, the dynamic Nur Jahan, he did not disturb the political and religious balance his father had established. The Mughal dependence on their Rajput allies continued as before. So did it during the reign of Shah Jahan, although the influence of the Muslim divines at his court increased visibly.

Another person in the imperial family who was spiritually influenced was Akbar's great-grandson Dara Shikoh (1615–1659). He was well read in philosophy and mysticism in both Hinduism and Sufism. He wanted to embrace Hindu beliefs without abandoning the Muslim faith. In his work *The Confluence of the Two Seas*, he tried to find a common ground between the two religions. He translated fifty-two of the Upanishads into Persian because he regarded them as a "treasure of monotheism and there are few thoroughly conversant with them even among the Indians." Following his great-grandfather's quest for truth, he assembled a number of Hindu scholars and ascetics in Benares to discuss "every sublime topic which he had desired or thought and had looked for and not found." Those who would read his translation of the Upanishads, he asserted, "shall become imperishable, fearless, . . . and eternally liberated." Many at the court and in the Sunni community feared he would become an apostate and convert to Hinduism. In 1659, after losing in the battle for succession, Dara was seized by Aurangzeb, who had him tried by orthodox Sunni court theologians, found guilty of apostasy, and executed.

JAHANGIR

Akbar's son and successor, Jahangir (1605–1627), was born Muhammad Salim to a Hindu Rajput mother. Salim was married at the age of fifteen to Man Bai, from the same Rajput family as his mother, Amber. Well educated and fluent in a number of languages including Persian, Turkish, Hindi, and Urdu, Jahangir (Holder of the World) retained his interest in the finest literature of the time. His *Memoirs* are not merely a historical source but also a mirror into his sensitive mind.[4]

Jahangir's own accomplishments have been unjustly downgraded by his later complete dedication to drink and an almost complete delegation of authority to his wife, Nur Jahan. Very early in his reign, he had a thirty-*gaz*-long Gold Chain of Justice, with sixty bells attached to it, extending from the wall of the Agra Fort to a stone column in the public square. Anyone who felt justice had not been done to him or her could draw the emperor's attention by pulling the chain. It symbolized easy access to the emperor and the latter's desire to be just and fair to all his subjects.

That he intended to continue the benevolent and liberal policies of his father is attested by his issue of the Twelve Ordinances, most of which ensured his subjects, regardless of their creed, security of life and property whether inherited or acquired, shelter for the travelers and the homeless, and fair conditions for traders and artisans. He forbade making wines and spirits in his dominions, regretting his own habit(!). Acknowledging his father's practice, he prohibited the slaughter of animals on two days a week and annually for a number of days "corresponding to the years of my life." He treated Hindus, Jews, Zoroastrians, Christians, and Muslims alike and continued with the official celebrations of Hindu festivals in his palace, a practice started by his father.

In the second part of his reign, he came increasingly under the influence of Nur Jahan, her father, and her brother, who formed a coterie at the court and practically excluded Jahangir from all decisions, major and minor. Born Mihr-un-nisa in 1577, daughter of a former Persian nobleman who had risen to the high position of *diwan* of the household during Akbar's time, Nur Jahan was first married to Ali Quli Beg, also known as Sher Afghan, who had a *jagir* in Bengal. Historians disagree on Jahangir's role in the death of Sher Afghan two years after he became emperor. Four years later in 1611, Jahangir married Mihr-un-nisa and gave her the title of Nur Mahal

(Light of the Palace) and later Nur Jahan (Light of the World). The accounts of the time, Indian and European, attest to her extraordinary beauty and administrative ability. In a few years, she built a powerful clique consisting of her father, Itimad-ud-daulah, and brother, Asaf Khan, who showed his abilities as much on the battlefield as in the behind-the-scenes intrigues at the court. Increasingly, Jahangir withdrew from his duties, declaring in the words that would remind one of Omar Khayyam that he required nothing "but a *sir* of wine and half a *sir* of meat."

Jahangir officially granted Nur Jahan the right to rule and issued new gold coins in her name whose obverse read: "By Order of the King Jahangir, gold has a hundred splendours added to it by receiving the impression of the name of Nur Jahan, the Queen Begam." Her seal was added to his own on all imperial orders.

An event of much significance for the later history of India was the arrival in August 1608 at Jahangir's court of an English captain, William Hawkins, with a letter from his monarch, James I, and a present of 25,000 gold coins requesting permission for the newly established East India Company (EIC) to open a "factory" at Surat on the west coast of India in Gujarat. Hawkins was well treated, receiving the gift of a slave girl from the emperor's harem but not permission to open the factory because the court was pressured both by the Portuguese as well as by the Surat merchants not to yield. Two more similar visits by Englishmen failed as well until in 1615, Sir Thomas Roe, an official envoy and accomplished diplomat who stayed at the court for more than three years, was able to get the official permission to open a factory at Surat with control over other factories in three cities: Agra, Ahmadabad, and Broach. The factories consisted of an office and warehouses, enabling the purchase and sale of goods at the right time. The Agra factory was known for its purchase of the best indigo and sale of English broadcloth.

SHAH JAHAN

The place in history of Shah Jahan (1627–1658) is as the builder of the fabulous Mughal monuments, including, indeed, the most beautiful building in the world, the Taj Mahal, a memorial for his wife, Arjumand Banu Begam, better known by her title, Mumtaz. The daughter of Empress Nur Jahan's brother Asaf Khan, she married Shah Jahan in 1612.

Basically a mausoleum to house the body of Mumtaz (and, later, Shah Jahan), the Taj stands on the right bank of the Jumna River at Agra, visible for miles, including from the Agra Fort, another of Shah Jahan's creations, where the emperor spent the last decade of his life under "house arrest" and from which he was able to see the marbled memorial for his beloved wife but was unable any longer to pay his daily visit. The massive yet elegant tomb rises to a height of 208 feet from the garden level, with four

four-level minarets on its sides forming a square and rising to 162 feet. The square marble platform on which the entire mausoleum stands measures 313 feet on each side with a height of 22 feet. Though massive, the architects and artists who built the Taj managed superbly to give an overwhelming impression of delicate elegance and subtle beauty. The monument took an estimated 20,000 artisans twenty years to build, begun two years after Mumtaz's death during childbirth (her fourteenth delivery) in 1631 and completed in 1653.

The monument, which can be seen for miles from its north side, is not seen at all from the southern side, where the entrance portal, 100 feet high, brings the main edifice of the Taj into view with perfect proportion as one advances. The inside of the portal frame carries on its three sides inscriptions from the Koran in black marble inlay over a white marble background so deftly carved that all the lettering, from the height of the frame to a little over the garden level, appears to the human eye to be of the same size. The same is true of the four facades of the main tomb where the black marble lettering of the Koranic inscriptions brings out the calligraphic skills of the time, the emperor himself known as a brilliant calligrapher, a skill much prized in the Islamic tradition.

The Mughals were famous for their love of gardens. The Taj garden and the courtyard are different from the other Mughal monuments in that the monument is not built in the center, and the courtyard is rectangular and not square. The monument is placed at the far end of the courtyard, leaving the unrestricted sky to form the monument's background, evoking the American novelist Bayard Taylor to say, "Did you ever build a castle in the air? Here is one brought down to earth and fixed for the Wonder of Ages" or the Nobel laureate poet of India, Rabindranath Tagore, to exclaim, "Let this one tear drop, this Taj Mahal, glisten spotlessly bright on the cheek of time, forever and ever." And then there have been women who wished something like the Taj were built for them. The wife of a well-known British officer, Colonel W. H. Sleeman, said in the mid-nineteenth century, "I cannot tell what I think . . . but I can tell what I feel. I would die tomorrow to have such another over me."[5]

The Indo-Muslim Arts and Architecture

Who built the Taj and, for that matter, the string of Mughal monuments from the time of Akbar to that of Aurangzeb? Fortunately for the historian, there are detailed records of the artisans and what many of them were paid, notably for the Taj. As noted before, by the end of the sultanate, many schools of Indo-Saracenic or Indo-Muslim arts were developing not only around Delhi-Agra but also in the sultanates of Bengal, Gujarat, Jaunpur, Malwa, and the Deccan. Additionally, many Rajput rulers who had joined hands with the Muslim rulers, particularly the Mughals, combined Islamic concepts of architecture in the building of their new palaces and forts. The evolution of a mixed Indian and Islamic art culture, however, was not as pronounced among the Marathas.

The design of the Taj was a logical evolution from that of Humayun's tomb, which had been built by Humayun's widow, Hamida Banu Begum, in Delhi by 1570. The desire on the part of the Mughals to spend huge amounts on monuments developed the arts of construction, using a variety of materials, notably sandstone, plentifully available in the region around Agra, and white marble, whose main source was and still is Makrana in Rajasthan. Armies of auxiliary artisans grew up in the countryside working on these materials and on precious stones, which would be used for decorative purposes. The design of the Taj itself was the work of Shah Jahan, who labored for two years with the architects. Once finished, the design could not be altered, in keeping with contemporary beliefs. The chief of the entire Taj project was Ustad Isa of Agra. The garden, along with its water turrets, was designed by a Hindu, Ranmal, from Kashmir. Hindu craftsmen from Multan and Kanauj carried out the extensive work of ornamentation. Only two areas were handled by non-Indians: the calligraphy and the construction of the dome, particularly the double dome of the main structure. Ismail Khan Rumi from Turkey was the architect for the domes,

and Amanat Khan Shirazi from Kandahar supplied his calligraphic skills on black marble.

The Taj was, by and large, an Indian monument, worked jointly by Muslims and Hindus, a product of their cooperation and partnership in the continuing evolution of Indo-Muslim architecture.

The Red Fort and Jama Masjid

There were several less acclaimed monuments deserving of high acclaim that the great builder-emperor completed during his three-decade reign. Among them were the Red Fort (so-called because it was built of red sandstone) in Delhi, with extensive red citadel walls. It became his new capital, called Shahjahanabad, destined to be called Old Delhi after the British moved their capital from Kolkata to their newly built city of New Delhi in 1912. Located on the south bank of the Jumna River, the spacious palace-fortress took ten years (1638–1648) to build; it would be a residence of the Mughal emperors for 210 years. It would also be the seat of its tremendous power, though on a declining curve after 1707. One of its two main gates, the Lahore Gate, would face the Chandni Chowk, the space between the two, with its arcaded passages, north to south, forming the richest boutique, jewelry mart, and crafts corner where traders from all over the known world with a lust for lucre came to exchange their choicest wares.

Close to the Red Fort is the Jama Masjid, possibly the grandest and largest mosque of the subcontinent, also built by Shah Jahan between 1644 and 1658, the last being the year of his incarceration in the Agra Fort, which makes it unlikely that he ever visited that mosque. Though it was much smaller, a mosque was also built next to the Agra Fort, allegedly for Shah Jahan's affectionate and pious daughter, Jahanara, who stayed with her father until his death in the Agra Fort. Of the two, the Delhi mosque is far larger and must have taken a lot more expense and labor to build. Its flight of steps leading to the top of a terraced platform, the three gateways with cloistered rooms on the sides enclosing an immense courtyard with a reservoir in the middle, made the whole structure the most imposing of all in Shahjahanabad.

Shah Jahan also built the Agra Fort and the Peacock Throne. They were reflective of the emperor's fine taste and a desire to leave an artistic legacy of a very high order. They were also evidence of a finely tuned administration, a sound revenue base, and a full treasury. But even the wealthiest have their limits. Toward the end of his reign, the emperor had to leave some projects unfinished for want of funds, the most notable being a replica of the Taj, in black marble, opposite the Taj across the river.

An Estimation of Shah Jahan

Shah Jahan did not distinguish himself as a conqueror. On the contrary—he lost the province of Kandahar in Afghanistan. His campaign, in the middle of his reign, to recapture his family's ancestral homeland of Samark and ended in disastrous failure. Yet he managed to keep the core of the empire in northern India that he had inherited intact. And though he continued his father's and grandfather's policy of using generals of both faiths, Hindu (mostly Rajputs) and Muslims, the number of Hindu generals declined from 38 percent under Akbar to 16 percent. Moreover, the majority faith failed to receive the liberal treatment it had in the previous two reigns. The celebration of Hindu festivals was stopped and the tax on pilgrimage to Hindu holy places revived. For the first time in nearly three-quarters of a century, many Hindu temples were demolished, and new ones were disallowed to be built. Conversions of Muslims to Hinduism and Christianity were punishable on grounds that they affected the security of the empire. The emperor became a favorite of the Sunni *ulamas* because of his orthodoxy and opposition to other faiths, including Shiism.

There are contradictory estimations of Shah Jahan as a man and as a ruler. Muslim contemporary writers extol him for his religiosity and sense of justice. Two British historians of India contradict each other. Mountstuart Elphinstone, an eminent civil servant under the Raj, wrote in his *History of India* that Shah Jahan's age was "the most prosperous ever known to India . . . together with a larger share of good government than often falls to the lot of Asiatic nations." In the early part of the twentieth century, Vincent A. Smith wrote, "In affairs of state, Shah Jahan was cruel, treacherous and unscrupulous. He had little skill as a military leader. . . . His justice was merely the savage, unfeeling ferocity of the ordinary Asiatic despot, exercised without respect for persons and without the slightest tincture of compassion." Two eminent Indian historians, K. A. Nilakanta Sastri and G. Srinivasachari, writing later in the twentieth century, observed:

> Shah Jahan's character has often been estimated more favourably than it deserves, perhaps because historians are dazzled by the magnificence of his court, the extent and wealth of his empire, the comparative peace that prevailed for the best part of his reign, and the glory of his monuments, particularly the Taj. As a son, Shah Jahan revolted against his father and got the throne by merciless slaughter of all possible rivals. . . . The best feature of Shah Jahan's character was his intense love for Mumtaz Mahal. Indeed she was a good check on his passion, but after her death he disgraced himself by gross licentiousness.[6]

Battle for Succession

The last decade of Shah Jahan's life was spent in misery. It began in September 1657 when he fell ill with strangury, a disease in which urine is discharged slowly and painfully drop by drop. His eldest son, Dara, and daughter, Jahanara (Ornament of the World), were solicitous; the latter was to remain with him until his death in 1666 as a prisoner in the Agra Fort. In his young days, as Prince Khurram, Shah Jahan had rebelled against his father, Jahangir. And to make sure he had no rivals to the throne left, he had killed all potential candidates. Now it was his turn to be at the receiving end of the common curse, that of revolt and bloodshed for the throne.

Of his four sons—Dara, Shuja, Aurangzeb, and Murad—Shah Jahan named in his last will his eldest son, Dara, his successor. Dara was Shah Jahan's favorite and had long been bestowed a military command of 60,000, larger than the three other brothers' forces combined, and unlike the other sons, he was given the title of viceroy for the territories placed under his administration. Dara was spiritually oriented, well read in Hindu thought and philosophy, and a writer of great merit. But his charming ways overcame the distress his appreciation of Hinduism caused the emperor, who was a follower of orthodox Islam.

Hearing the news of the emperor's illness, the second son, Shuja, who was in charge of Bengal, crowned himself emperor before marching on to Delhi. Murad, who was known for his vices, was in Gujarat. He joined Aurangzeb, who promised him the border provinces of Afghanistan, Sind, the Punjab, and Kashmir in addition to one-third of the spoils of war. By the summer of 1658, the combined forces of the two brothers inflicted two major defeats on the imperial forces sent against them. Reaching Agra, Aurangzeb took over the fort, imprisoned his father there, and proceeded to Delhi, where he proclaimed himself emperor on July 21, 1658.

Among Aurangzeb's first tasks was to pursue Dara, who was moving from pillar to post for military and political support to the Punjab, Multan, Sind, and Gujarat. Finally, as he was attempting to cross through the Bolan Pass into Kandahar, he and his son were captured by a local chief and handed over to Aurangzeb's general Bahadur Khan. Brought in chains and paraded through the streets of the imperial capital, Delhi, Dara was tried for his Hindu beliefs and possible conversion to that religion. He was executed on August 30, 1659.

In the month before he became emperor, Aurangzeb had broken his alliance with Murad and imprisoned him in the Gwalior fort, where after three years, he was tried for an old crime and beheaded in December 1661. As for Shuja, Aurangzeb hated him for his adherence to the Shia faith. Aurangzeb's forces hounded him from place to place until he fled for refuge to Magh Raja of Arakan. There he tried to take over his host's kingdom, was found out, and was killed.

AURANGZEB

The reign of Aurangzeb of a half century (1658–1707) is divided into two halves, the first in the North and the second, from 1682, in the Deccan. After the death of his father in Agra Fort prison in 1666, Aurangzeb (Ornament of the Throne) tried to overcome the charge of usurpation of the throne in 1658 by holding a second coronation for himself.

The last among the mighty but not great Mughal emperors, Aurangzeb was a very capable general who had proved his superior strategy and valor during the lifetime of his father in different campaigns, then during the three-pronged war of succession and, indeed, in the wars of expansion during his entire reign. There was constant warfare during his long reign against diverse enemies of the state, from the Afghans in the Northwest to the Ahoms and Arakanese in the East, from the Marathas in peninsular India to the Sikhs and Jats in the North. The extension of empire and the additional revenue it brought far outweighed the cost in men, matériel, and money. Much before the end of Aurangzeb's reign, the imperial war machine was breaking under the tremendous strain of the constant campaigns; the army was exhausted, their ranks diminished in numbers, and their morale sunk to an unacceptably low level. The only territorial gains made were Cooch Behar and Chittagong in the East and Bijapur and Golkonda in the Deccan. The costs were high.

Aurangzeb proved to be the exact antithesis of his grandfather. He completely abandoned secularism, which was the basis of Akbar's spectacular success in bringing about a harmonious relationship between the government and the diverse religious communities of the empire. Instead, beginning in the year following his first coronation, Aurangzeb issued ordinances openly promoting Islamic orthodoxy at his court, vowing to rule strictly as a Muslim king. He appointed censors of public morals, *muhtasibs,* in all urban centers throughout his empire to enforce morality as prescribed by the Koran. Consumption of wine was forbidden; the cultivation of *bhang* was banned. Gambling, prostitution, and trafficking in women attracted severe punishment. All Muslims, Sunnis and Shias, were asked to observe strictly the requirement of prayers five times a day and fasting during the month of Ramadan.

The orthodox Muslim emperor continued to employ Hindus at high levels of bureaucracy and in leadership of military campaigns, but his purpose was to use them against their Muslim colleagues. He was suspicious of everyone working under him. He generally appointed two generals in charge of a campaign, one Muslim and one Hindu, depending on their religious differences to prevail in reporting each other's activities to the emperor.

During his long rule of a half century, Aurangzeb openly declared war against the Hindus, reversing his great-grandfather's policy of tolerance and regard for all faiths. Aurangzeb's reign was marred by the destruction of temples and a general intolerance toward people

of non-Muslim, non-Sunni faiths. For the first time in a century, since it was abolished by Akbar in 1564, the hated *zizya* tax on non-Muslims was reimposed. All such regressive measures antagonized the Hindu majority and grievously affected the hundred-year-old Mughal-Rajput partnership, giving rise to inveterate enmity among the Sikhs, the Jats, and the Marathas. Aurangzeb failed to realize that the secular basis of Akbar's polity was not just a matter of political tact; it was, and is, a basic requirement for a peaceful and progressive polity in a plural society such as India.

The result of such a major reversal of policies toward the non-Muslim majority population was seething discontent spiraling into dissension and posing challenges to the imperial authority in different parts of the subcontinent. Among such major challenges were those by the Sikhs in the Punjab; Jats in East Punjab, Rajasthan, and around Delhi; and the Marathas in Maharashtra.

MUGHAL ADMINISTRATION

The Mughal empire was divided into provinces: during Akbar's time, the number of provinces, initially twelve, was raised toward the end of his reign to fifteen, two of the additions being new conquests. The number rose to seventeen in Jahangir's time and to twenty-one by the end of Aurangzeb's. Each province, or *subha,* was headed by a *subhedar* or *sahib subha*, usually a nobleman or general of the highest rank or sometimes a prince who was conveniently kept at a distance from the imperial capital. He had the command of a force of 2,000 to 7,000 depending on his personal status as a *mansabdar* of the empire. His administrative setup mirrored to a certain extent that at the emperor's court.

The *subhas* were divided into *sarkars* and *parganas*, the latter being a group of villages. Each village was regarded as a semiautonomous unit with its own staff of a *muqaddum* (headman) and a *patwari*, who was the primary official who would record the area under various crops. At the *pargana* level, there were a number of state officials, among the most important being the *qanungo* (keeper of revenue records), *bitikchi* (accountant), and *potdar* (treasurer). There also were, depending on the needs, a number of *karkuns* (clerks) and measurers of land and assessors of crops. At a higher level of the *sarkar* was the *malguzar* (revenue collector).

The Mughal emperor took the affairs of state very seriously except during Jahangir's time, when he delegated his authority almost completely to his wife, Nur Jahan. The emperor had a certain official routine except when he was on military campaign. The morning prayers were followed by a *jharokha*, or a *darshan*, when he appeared on a balcony. At that point, any person, from any part of the empire, could petition with a grievance. Daily there was an open session in which a variety of important matters would be transacted: receiving ambassadors, commanders successfully returning from campaigns, or commanders taking leave and receiving final instructions before proceeding on campaigns. All important appointments, awards of *jagirs*, and other major rewards and gifts would be announced there. For discussion of very confidential matters, there were special sessions at the Ghusalkhana, where particular officials were allowed entry with a pass and where amid relatively lax protocol the emperor would seek advice or just confabulate.

Although the Mughal emperors could be described as absolute monarchs or despots with peremptory decisionmaking authority over the most sensitive and consequential matters including life and death, they usually conducted business with the help of ministers. The chief of these were the *diwan* or the *wazir*, the highest official, in charge of the revenue and treasury departments, who would be present at all important meetings and shared the highest confidence of the emperor. Next came the *bakshi*, in charge of the military, keeping the rolls of both the recruits as well as the commanders, or *mansabdars*, of all levels, to be presented to the emperor at the start of each campaign. He was responsible for anything related to military supplies and was also in charge of payments of all salaries. The other ministers were the *khan-i-saman*, in charge of the imperial household; the chief *qazi*, heading the judiciary; and the chief *sadr*, in charge of ecclesiastical affairs as well as charities. Various other officials attended the open session, standing at a distance from the throne, ready to be of assistance on any question related to their responsibilities, such as the superintendent of imperial *karkhanas* (workshops), chief of the artillery, chief of the elephants and boats, chief of the navy (not very important), chief of the mint, and others. Also important were the *muhtasibs*, particularly under Aurangzeb. They were principally in charge of the morals of the people, including whether they attended regular prayers. With Aurangzeb, these functions assumed extraordinary importance in trying to get all Muslims to be in good standing. Under Aurangzeb, they were expected to enforce strictly all regulations prohibiting the sale and consumption of all intoxicants, wine, and opium; banning gambling; and restricting prostitution to certain quarters. The *muhtasibs* were also expected not to allow Hindus to worship in a public place or to repair and build temples. At times they exceeded their power and also ordered the demolition of temples.

Revenue System

The revenue system of the Mughals underwent major reorganization under Akbar and, with some minor variations, was continued throughout that dynasty. Akbar found that there were several different systems prevalent in the different parts of his empire. The crops were different, the agricultural inputs varied, and the climatic conditions determined the

effort of the cultivator. Akbar wanted a uniform and equitable system of assessment that would bring in a steady amount of revenue yet not be a burden on the peasantry. It should be easy to collect, and there should be less scope for fraud. The architect of the new revenue system was Raja Todar Mall, who was associated from 1570 with a rational reassessment of the land. Akbar was so impressed with his assessment methods, particularly in the newly conquered Gujarat, and their favorable impact on the peasantry as well as on the treasury that he appointed him *diwan-i-ashraf* in 1582 with full responsibility for revising the land-revenue system throughout the empire. The wise Rajput minister had the weal of the state and of the millions of peasants in mind as he devised an equitable system. He ordered a measurement survey of all lands, for which purpose he standardized a measuring rod of tight rope held by two bamboo rods on either end. The lands were divided into four categories depending on whether they were regularly cultivated or left fallow for recovery of the land's productivity and for how long. The categories were *polaj*, land that was regularly cultivated; *parauti*, land kept fallow for a while for the restoration of its productivity; *chachar*, land kept fallow for three or four years; and *banjar*, land kept fallow for five or more years. In order to encourage the farmer to bring his fallow lands back to cultivation, the assessment would be brought to a normal level only in the fifth year so that the cultivator would be able to recover the additional expenses involved in the transition. In the *zabti* system only the lands actually cultivated were taken into account and an average of the three classes of land used for determining the standard production. The price was fixed by averaging the prices prevailing in the previous decade. For this purpose, the empire was divided into 172 assessment circles. The state share was fixed at one-third.

During Aurangzeb's time, this share was raised to one-half, resulting in much peasant discontent. The peasants were given the option of paying in cash or kind. This system, known as the *ray-atwari*, came down to British colonial times and had been used since Akbar's times in North India and Gujarat. Its basis was the *rayat*, the peasant, whose stake in the land and the produce was thus regarded as the primary factor in arriving at the state share.

Crucial to the system were the two village officials, the *patwari* and the *muqaddum*, the former being the primary official who would maintain a record of the areas under different crops. Based on his report, the village *muqaddum*, or headman, issued demand slips well in advance of the harvest and sent the demand register to his higher official. All such demand registers were consolidated for the benefit of the *diwan* of the state and of the imperial government. At the end of the season, another register was prepared of those who had defaulted on payment. Based on their explanations for the lapse and if the

lapses were widespread because of general factors such as the failure of the crop and prevalence of famine, the *diwan*, with the consent of the *subhedar* at the state level and the imperial *diwan* with the approval of the emperor, announced a partial or whole remission of the land tax for that season or year.

THE LATER MUGHALS— EMPIRE ONLY IN NAME

Like the Roman Empire, the Mughal empire involved a long period of decline before its formal fall. And again like the Roman Empire, the causes of the decline have been ascribed by historians to a period when the empire was at its physical zenith, during Aurangzeb's reign. The nonagenarian emperor himself was apprehensive of the empire's ability to survive. A little before his death, he prepared a will dividing the vast empire from Kabul to Assam and Kashmir to the Deccan among his three sons, the fourth having fled to Persia for refuge.

The emperor was blessed with a good memory but had obviously forgotten the history of his own bloodstained succession, which had involved imprisonment of his own father, a reigning emperor, but also elimination of his own brothers and other lesser rivals to the throne. In fact, a violently contested succession to the throne had been the bane of all Muslim dynasties on the subcontinent. This was largely due to the absence of rules of succession that left room for the right to be determined by might and fostered the growth of factional infighting at the court both during the lifetime of the reigning monarch and on his death. As for the nobility, they were divided among three main factions, where loyalties were not necessarily constant: the Hindustani Party, consisting of Indian Muslims, including those whose ancestors came from Afghanistan; the Turani Party, who descended from immigrants from beyond the Oxus and central Asia; and the Irani Party, mostly from Persia or territories under Persia, and mostly of the Shia faith. Rival leaders of these parties joined their candidates in the imperial household for fictional authority and honors.

From the death of Aurangzeb to the accession of the last Mughal "emperor," Bahadur Shah Zafar II in 1837, there was less and less territory to rule until the Mughal emperor's writ was limited to the fort and its environs in Delhi. Yet there were such contests for succession that there were six reigning emperors killed and one blinded, the "power" being usurped by interlopers and rival kingmakers. There were three coronations held in 1713, four in 1719. Imperial *firmans* continued to be issued to distant governors, who habitually ignored or used them for unintended purposes. Consequently, many provinces and smaller kingdoms became virtually independent, reading the *Khutba* in their own names, a decreasing number approaching the imperial court for the formal robes of authority. Another de-

velopment was the rise of non-Muslim centers of power: the Peshwas, prime ministers of the kings of Shivaji's line; the Sikhs; the Jats; and the Rajputs.

By the time of a major invasion by Nadir Shah of Persia in 1739, the empire of the Mughals resembled the political mosaic of the late sultanate, when a number of independent sultanates held power in different parts of the subcontinent. Among them, a new and principal center was Hyderabad, the seat of the *nizam-ul-mulk,* the viceroy of the Deccan.

PERSIAN AND AFGHAN INVASIONS

The political vacuum and anarchy in the historic city of imperial power, Delhi, were most inviting to external invaders, tempted to take the fabulous wealth of the Mughals for their own benefit. Such foreign invasions came from two sources in the period from 1739 to 1767, first from Persia and then a series of invasions from the Durranis in Afghanistan. Toward the end of that period, the extreme weakness of the emperor's forces was bared at Buxar in 1764 against the British-Indian forces.

Nadir Shah

The Persian invasion was led by Nadir Quli (later called Nadir Shah), a person of humble origins who first recovered Persia from the Afghans, who had captured it in 1722 and restored the Persian throne to the Safavi dynasty. Ten years later, he deposed the Safavi ruler and became the real power in the country. His ambition was to bring to his native Persia the glory of the old times, meaning the conquest of Kandahar, which he would use as a staging post for conquests in the region. With the acquisition of that strategic city, he became aware, more than ever before, of how open India lay to an invader. He wanted its immense wealth, which he could use for his plans of aggrandizement in central Asia. This was no different in motivation than Muhammad of Ghazni centuries earlier. With the excuse that his envoys had not been treated well in Delhi, he invaded India in 1738, capturing the Punjab; after defeating a force led by Emperor Muhammad Shah in February 1739, he entered Delhi. The murder of some of his officers and an attempt on his own life became his excuse to blockade the city and order a general massacre of the male population and enslavement of the women, looting and burning the houses for several weeks. When peace was finally restored in response to an appeal from Muhammad Shah, the invader agreed to return to his country. The loot taken to Persia included Shah Jahan's Peacock Throne (which is still in Iran), large amounts of bullion (estimated to cost 150 million rupees) and jewelry, precious stones, furniture, and apparel, besides an estimated 300 elephants, 10,000 horses, and camels. Nadir Shah has remained a personification of wanton death and destruction in India ever since.

Nadir Shah's invasion dealt the decrepit Mughal empire a blow from which it never recovered. It marked the nadir of Mughal power and its ability to muster a force to defend itself. Its intelligence about Nadir's strength and his intentions totally failed. So did its defenses in the Punjab and the Northwest. What is more, Nadir Shah's invasion vetted the appetite of greedy invaders such as Ahmed Shah Abdali, who nailed shut the coffin of the Mughal empire.

Ahmed Shah Abdali

One of Nadir Shah's officers in his invading force to Delhi was Ahmed Shah, an Afghan of the Abdali clan. In the wake of Nadir Shah's assassination in 1747, Ahmed Shah Abdali became the ruler of Afghanistan and assumed the title of *durr-i-durran* (the pearl of the age). The Durranis, as his followers would thereafter be known, invaded India seven times between 1748 and 1767, the sixth raid in 1761 being the worst and the most consequential. Unlike Nadir Shah, Ahmed Shah Abdali had plans for establishing an Afghan empire extending at least over the Northwest, the Punjab, and the Doab region between the Jumna and Ganges. He had witnessed during Nadir's invasion the wealth of North India and particularly of the Mughal capital. He had also been a witness to the helplessness of the Mughal emperor and the infighting among the nobles that made a concerted military effort impossible. The Mughal empire lay prostrate; it was open to anyone with the guts and ambition to bleed it white.

Ahmed Shah Abdali's second invasion in 1750 led to his conquest and annexation of the Punjab, whereas the third invasion, in December 1751, added Kashmir and the territory up to Sirhind. The fourth invasion in January 1757 brought him to Delhi, which he systematically looted, making the emperor agree to a truce by which he formally ceded the Punjab, Kashmir, Sind, and Sirhind to the invader. On that occasion, he left his son, Timur Shah, as his viceroy in Lahore, Punjab.

Timur Shah was an extremely incompetent administrator who brought chaos and anarchy to the fair city of Lahore. Thereupon, the governor of Jullunder, Adina Beg Khan, requested the help of the Marathas to expel the Afghans. The Marathas did expel the Afghans but did not want to occupy Lahore for more than six months. They left Adina Khan

as their governor there. Infuriated, Ahmed Shah Abdali invaded Punjab in October 1759 and conquered it. It would be the base for the next raid, which marked the most ferocious contest between several parties for supremacy over North India.

The sixth raid is known more for the Third Battle of Panipat on January 14, 1761, between two major contestants to fill the vacuum of power in Delhi, the two being the Afghans and the Marathas. The contest humbled the Maratha power, which suffered the worst losses in men, matériel, and wealth. The Mughal empire was crushed; Abdali regarded Shah Alam II as his nominee for the Mughal throne. Its unintended contribution to Indian history was the rise of the Sikhs as the major power west of Delhi. In fact, when Abdali came on his seventh raid in 1767, it was the Sikhs who turned him back.

NOTES

1. Vincent A. Smith, *Akbar the Great Mogul* (Oxford: Clarendon Press, 1917), 151.

2. Badauni, *Muntakhab ut-Tawarikh*, translated by W. H. Low (1884; reprint, Delhi, Low Price Publications, 1986), 2:200–201.

3. William Theodore de Bary, ed., *Sources of Indian Tradition* (New York: Columbia University Press, 1958), 1:443.

4. *Tuzuk-i-Jahangiri,* translated by Alexander Rogers, edited by Henry Beveridge, 2 vols. (London: Royal Asiatic Society, 1909–1914).

5. "The Story of the Taj Mahal," http://www.tajmahalagra.com/story-of-taj-mahal-agra.html, n.p.

6. Mountstuart Elphinstone, *History of Hindu and Muhammadan India*; Vincent A. Smith, *Akbar the Great Mogul;* K. A. Nilakanta Sastri and G. Srinivasachari, *An Advanced History of India* (Bombay: Allied Publishers, 1970), 503.

Shivaji's religious policy underlined respect toward all religions, including Islam. None of his wars were religious or *jihadi* conflicts. Paralleling the best practices under the Mughals and the Bahmanis of employing Hindus in high positions of trust, Shivaji correspondingly employed Muslims in high positions and made grants to mosques and *pirs*. Thus, he regarded Baba Yakut of Kelsi, a Muslim divine, as one of his gurus. His personal secretary and confidant was Mulla Haidar, a Muslim. His most noted naval commanders were Muslim: Ibrahim Khan, Daulat Khan, and Siddi Misri. Khafi Khan, a contemporary chronicler, generally hostile to Shivaji, noted that he did not desecrate or demolish any mosques or ill-treat women of any community. Whenever a copy of the sacred Koran came into his hands, he treated it with respect and gave it to some of his Muslim followers. When the women of any Hindu or Muhammadan were taken prisoners by his men and they had no friends to protect them, he watched over them until they were restored to their relatives.   (pages 189–90)

10

THE RISE OF THE MARATHAS AND THE SIKHS

Two major challenges to Aurangzeb's ambition to extend the Mughal domination all over the subcontinent came from the Marathas in peninsular India, specifically western Maharashtra, and the Sikhs in the Punjab and the Northwest. While his father, Shah Jahan, was still in control of the empire, Aurangzeb had himself appointed viceroy of the Deccan, first in 1636 and again in 1653. He was not the eldest of Shah Jahan's four sons and wanted to distinguish himself on the battlefield and create an independent base of power so that when the right time came, he could make a bid for the imperial throne over the claims of his elder siblings.

Aurangzeb's goal in peninsular India was to replace the Shia Muslim domination of the Deccan with the Mughal Sunni rule. The Bahmani kingdom established in 1336 had, by the end of the fifteenth century, broken into four: Bijapur, Ahmednagar, Golkonda, and Bidar. Together, they had defeated and dismantled the Hindu Vijayanagar Empire

to the south in 1565. In 1636, Mughal forces had defeated Ahmednagar, but the other Bahmani kingdoms had proved intractable. During his second viceroyalty of the Deccan beginning in 1653, Aurangzeb was determined to bring the remaining Bahmani kingdoms into the Mughal empire.

Aurangzeb's grand plan met resistance from some unexpected quarters. The news of the rise of Shivaji as the leader of a motley group of Mavlas, in the twenty-mile-wide mountainous region east of the Sahyadri Mountains west of Pune, was at first only an annoyance. Aurangzeb grossly underestimated its potential, calling Shivaji a "mountain rat."[1]

THE RISE OF THE MARATHAS: SHIVAJI

Shivaji (1630–1680) was the second son of Shahaji Bhonsle, who had held important positions successively at several Muslim courts in the Deccan. At the time of Shivaji's birth on February 19,

1630, at Shivner Fort, forty miles north of Pune, Shahaji served the ruler of Ahmednagar, holding a prosperous *jagir* (fief) covering Pune and Chakan. Shahaji himself had inherited the fief from his father, Maloji, who was given the title of "Raja" by the Ahmednagar ruler in 1595. In those days, there were a number of such capable Maratha military adventurers who served different courts and switched masters for short-term benefits. Thus, Shahaji had served the Mughals after the fall of Ahmednagar in 1636, when the Mughal stars seemed to be ascending. When Shivaji was a growing teenager with lofty political ambitions, his father was in the employ of the Bijapur ruler, who rewarded him an extensive *jagir* in Bangalore with responsibility for acquiring territories in Karnataka and Tamil Nadu.

Always on the march and concerned for the safety of his family, Shahaji kept his wife, Jijabai, and Shivaji on his estate in Pune in care of his trusted lieutenant, Dadoji Konddev. Apart from administrative duties, Dadoji was responsible for educating his young ward in martial arts. Jijabai nourished Shivaji spiritually and instilled in him heroism and ambition based on a sound moral character by recounting stories from the epics *Ramayana* and *Mahabharata*. Later, he made reading the sections in the *Ramayana* dealing with the conduct of war mandatory at all his fort garrisons.[2] At sixteen, Shivaji was placed in full charge of the *jagir*. In the same year, he had conquered the fortress at Torna. By that

time, he had rallied the youth of the neighboring Maval region, roughly extending from Wai to Junnar, holding before them the ideal of an independent kingdom, free of Muslim control.

Several seventeenth-century accounts —Mughal, Maratha, Portuguese, English, French, Dutch, and Jesuit— establish Shivaji's astuteness, personal valor, military prowess, and tolerance toward people of other religions. Shivaji began his military exploits on a small scale in the neighboring areas, which were formerly under Ahmednagar but had recently been annexed by Bijapur, his father's current employer. His pretext for taking over those territories was consolidation in Bijapur's behalf; in reality, it was the foundation for his own kingdom or, as he called it, the *swarajya* (literally, "self-rule").

Beginning in 1657 (by which time Aurangzeb had been reappointed viceroy of the Deccan), Shivaji came out into the open and attacked and conquered several Bijapur forts. In September 1659, the Bijapur court resolved to deal with him once and for all and sent a powerful general, Afzalkhan, to destroy him. On his way, the khan detoured to Tuljapur to desecrate and damage the temple of Bhavani to whom Shivaji was deeply devoted. There, the khan audaciously slaughtered a holy cow in the temple compound and challenged the goddess to save Shivaji. Afzalkhan also detoured to Pandharpur and damaged the famous temple of Vithoba, the focal point for centuries of an annual pilgrimage by hundreds of thousands of Maharashtrians.

The two acts added to the ire of Shivaji and his young followers, who were now determined to avenge the atrocities. Aware that his own small force would be no match for Afzalkhan's well-equipped army of 15,000 in a conventional battle, Shivaji suggested a meeting in the thickly wooded region at the foot of Pratapgad Fort, where his own knowledge of the terrain and the use of guerrilla warfare would offer a distinct advantage. Both leaders came to the meeting of November 10, 1659, armed. As Stewart Gordon writes, "Shivaji had every reason to be suspicious. In a parallel situation, a decade earlier, Afzal Khan had used just such a truce ceremony to imprison a Hindu general."[3] When the tall khan rushed to embrace the diminutive Maratha leader with his left hand and stab him with his right hand, Shivaji used his own left hand armed with *wagh-nakhs* (tiger claws) to dig out the khan's entrails while his Bhavani sword concealed under his right-hand sleeve deftly decapitated his head from his torso. He sent the head to the Bhavani temple, previously desecrated by the khan. Shivaji signaled his own forces hiding in the jungle to attack the khan's troops, killing or scattering them.

That was the year Aurangzeb threw his father, Emperor Shah Jahan, into captivity, usurped the throne, and eliminated his brothers, one by one. When he learned of Shivaji's success against Bijapur, Aurangzeb sent his own maternal uncle Shayista Khan to deal with the "mountain rat" once and for all. In a surprise nocturnal raid on April 15, 1663, on Shayista Khan's residence in Pune's Rang Mahal, Shivaji cut off the forefinger of the khan's left hand while he was trying to escape by jumping out of his bedroom window. In the ensuing fracas, the khan also lost his son and many of his large retinue. Shivaji proceeded to conquer several Mughal fortresses and raided and looted the well-guarded Mughal port of Surat in 1664. Enraged, Aurangzeb sent a huge army against Shivaji under the renowned Rajput *mansabdar* Jaisingh, assisted by Dilir Khan, a Muslim general following his usual strategy of using generals from the two religious communities, so that one could watch and report on the other.

Realizing that he would be fighting a losing battle against such a powerful force, Shivaji surrendered several important forts to Jaisingh, who offered him peace provided he appeared in person at the emperor's court and either he or his son Sambhaji accept the position of a Mughal *mansabdar*. Shivaji received Jaisingh's personal guarantee that he would be treated like a *shahjada*, which Shivaji thought would be a position only slightly lower than that of the emperor, maybe equivalent to a king. Shivaji's loud and indecorous remonstrations on May 12, 1666, at the Mughal court against the humiliating treatment (he was made to stand in the third row of nobles) led to his house imprisonment. Undeterred, he planned a ruse to escape. He began sending daily presents of baskets laden with sweets and carried by his personal guard to different Mughal dignitaries, including the security force. Both the father and the son escaped one day hiding in two such baskets; adopting various guises, they returned to their homeland in a matter of twenty-five days, on September 12, 1666.

Shivaji's Military Strategy

Shivaji's spectacular successes were owed to two principal elements in his military strategy: guerrilla warfare and a wide array of about one hundred forts to which his forces could withdraw for security. Ninety percent of his fortresses were located in the mountain fastnesses of the Sahyadri (Western Ghats) range, one of them, Raigad, serving as his capital.

Shivaji's strength lay in the swift movement of his cavalry contrasting with the unwieldy, slow-moving Mughal armies. The components of his guerrilla strategy were an intimate knowledge of the terrain in western Maharashtra: its mountains and rivers, during the torrential monsoon as well as in the dry season; his close relations with the local youth and their families, who were, to use the imagery used in much later times by Mao Tse-tung, like fish in water drawing their sustenance from it; and his ability to starve the enemy's troops of food supplies. Shivaji's leadership of his men was at a personal level. They were not mercenaries but "nationalists" who shared his dream of establishing a polity

that would not be subservient to an alien power and would be based on equity and fairness, irrespective of creed or caste. Shivaji and his men were capable of quick movement in difficult terrain and surprising their foes. His guerrilla strategy was to catch the enemy off guard and appear in several places in swift succession. In such a situation, not only would the enemy need the cooperation of local people, but the enemy would also need a force ten to twenty times his to overwhelm him.

Alone among the Indian rulers since the time of Rajendra Chola in the eleventh century, Shivaji realized the importance of maritime defenses, the lack of which under the land-oriented Delhi Sultans, the Mughals, and the Deccan rulers had enabled the minuscule Portuguese navy to control the coastal commerce all the way from Bassein to Cochin. Shivaji's navy commanded by the redoubtable Angria family not only ended the Portuguese monopolistic control of western India's coastal traffic and commerce but also actively stopped the early moves of the English East India Company in Bombay to step into the Portuguese role.

Coronation and Administration

In 1674, Shivaji held his own coronation as *chhatrapati* (lord of the umbrella), or king, at the fortress of Raigad, which he made his capital. Consecrated by pandits led by Varanasi's Gaga Bhatt, Shivaji proclaimed a new era, becoming the *shaka-karta* (founder of an era) and issued a new gold unit, the *shivarai hon.* Unfortunately for his *swarajya*, the illustrious founder did not live long; he died in 1680.

The coronation was also marked by Shivaji's proclamation of the *Kanujabata*, containing basic principles of government, and *Rajyavyavaharkosh*, detailing instructions for the routine guidance of administrators. His administration was far ahead of the times, at least in India. The *Kanujabata* provided for the *astapradhana*, the council of eight ministers, among whom the work was well divided: *mukhya pradhan* or *peshwa* (prime minister); *amatya* (in charge of the land revenues); *surnis* or *sachiv* (finance and records); *waqenavis* or *mantri* (home minister); *sarnaubat* or *senapati* (commander in chief); *dabir* or *sumant* (foreign minister); *panditrao* (religion); and *nyayadhish* (chief judge). All ministers were paid cash salaries. Shivaji was against the practice of giving *jagirs*, or grants of land, as a reward of military or civil service of note.

Shivaji's *swarajya* consisted of three large divisions (each under a *sarsubhedar*), subdivided into *subhas* (each under a *subhedar* called a *deshpande* or *deshmukh*), and further subdivided into *parganas*, *mahals*, and *tarfas*. At each level, there were central government nominees such as a *muzumdar* (accountant), *chitnis* (writer), or *daftardar* (recorder). Each village had a self-governing *gota*, or council, with representatives of the community and twelve kinds of *balutedars* (craftsmen) who were entitled, by tradition, to a portion of the village's agricultural produce in return for their services to the community. With their primary jurisdiction in settling land disputes, the *gotas* were respected by the central administration under Shivaji, his successors in the Bhosle line, as well as by the Peshwas.

Shivaji had separate regulations for his armed forces: army, navy, and forts. He had more than one hundred forts, whose administration was separate from the administration of civilian lands. Each fort was deemed self-sufficient in terms of its food and water supplies so that when besieged by the enemy, the garrison could hold on for an appreciable amount of time. For the armed forces on the move, he had specific regulations, particularly how to treat the civilian population and restrictions on plunder. There were also separate regulations on the collection of *chauthai* (one-fourth of the revenue) in lands that were not directly under Shivaji's administration but whose rulers had accepted Shivaji's suzerainty. This was an innovation that was continued by his successors, including the Peshwas in the eighteenth century.

Shivaji's Policy Toward the Muslims

Shivaji's religious policy underlined respect toward all religions, including Islam. None of his wars were religious or *jihadi* conflicts. Paralleling the best practices under the Mughals and the

Bahmanis of employing Hindus in high positions of trust, Shivaji correspondingly employed Muslims in high positions and made grants to mosques and *pirs*. Thus, he regarded Baba Yakut of Kelsi, a Muslim divine, as one of his gurus. His personal secretary and confidant was Mulla Haidar, a Muslim. His most noted naval commanders were Muslim: Ibrahim Khan, Daulat Khan, and Siddi Misri. Khafi Khan, a contemporary chronicler, generally hostile to Shivaji, noted that he did not desecrate or demolish any mosques or ill-treat women of any community. Whenever a copy of the sacred Koran came into his hands, he treated it with respect and gave it to some of his Muslim followers. When the women of any Hindu or Muhammadan were taken prisoners by his men and they had no friends to protect them, he watched over them until they were restored to their relatives. The Mughal emperor Akbar was certainly his model. As Stewart Gordon points out in the volume on the Marathas in the *Cambridge History of India*, Shivaji wrote to Aurangzeb "to act like Akbar in according respect to Hindu beliefs and places."[4]

Jadunath Sarkar, perhaps the greatest Indian historian of India's preindependence era, an acknowledged authority on the Mughals, and a biographer of Shivaji, sums up Shivaji's contribution:

> [Shivaji] called the Maratha race to a new life. He raised the Marathas into an independent self-reliant people, conscious of their oneness and high destiny, and his most precious legacy was the spirit he breathed into his race. He has proved by his example that the Hindu race can build a nation, found a state, defeat enemies. . . . He taught the modern Hindus to rise to the full stature of their growth. Shivaji has shown that the tree of Hinduism is not really dead, that it can rise from beneath the seemingly crushing load of centuries of political bondage; that it can put forth new leaves and branches. It can again lift up its head to the skies.[5]

Sambhaji

Shivaji's elder son, Sambhaji (1680–1689), succeeded his father and was crowned *chhatrapati* at Raigad in 1680. In the following year, Aurangzeb came to the Deccan at the head of a huge force with a determination to liquidate the Maratha kingdom, which he expected to be in chaotic condition in the wake of Shivaji's death. Instead, he found in Sambhaji a valiant defender of *swarajya*, able to deal with not only the Mughals but also the Siddis of Janjira and the Portuguese in Goa. However, thanks to treachery, Aurangzeb's forces were able to capture Sambhaji in 1689. Brought into the emperor's presence, he was asked if he would agree to convert to Islam. When he refused, the angry Aurangzeb ordered him blinded, tortured, and killed. Aurangzeb sent Sambhaji's widow, Yesubai, and son, Shahu, to the imperial harem, where Shahu would be brought up as a Hindu until after Aurangzeb's death in 1707, when his successor released him to provoke a civil war of succession in Maharashtra.

Rajaram

Before the Maratha capital fell, however, Sambhaji's younger stepbrother, Rajaram (1689–1700), was quickly crowned the *chhatrapati* and whisked away to the safety of far-off Jinji in Karnataka. The Mughal forces followed him and besieged the Jinji fort for seven long years, ably defended by loyal Maratha generals. Rajaram eluded the Mughals, left Jinji secretly, and was back in Maharashtra. The entire ordeal produced tension and fatigue in Rajaram, who died on March 2, 1700, at the Sinhagad fort.

Tarabai

The leadership of the Maratha "war of independence" was now assumed by Rajaram's widow, the intrepid Tarabai, who crowned her infant son, also named Shivaji, as *chhatrapati* at Panhala (near Kolhapur). The aged and tired Aurangzeb, by then in Deccan for twenty years, was harassed by her guerrilla forces until his death in 1707. It was at this point that Aurangzeb's successor, Azam Shah, released Shahu on the con-

dition that he would help the Mughal cause. Tarabai died in 1761.

Shahu

Whether Shahu (1707–1749) ever intended to assist the Mughals or not, the Maratha generals and civilian advisers who defected from Tarabai's side to join him did not appear to have any such plans. They helped Shahu reach Satara, where on January 2, 1708, he crowned himself *chhatrapati*. The two rival claimants to Shivaji's throne at Satara and Kolhapur began an internecine war that lasted a quarter century and ended with the Treaty of Warna on April 13, 1731, whereby Shahu and his able *peshwa* recognized the "minor" branch of the Bhonsle family as Karweer *chhatrapatis* of Kolhapur. It remained after the final defeat of the Marathas in 1818 as a princely state under British protection until 1948 when it was merged into the Indian Union. Meanwhile, Shahu's state of Satara "lapsed" to the East India Company in 1848 for lack of a biological heir and Governor-General Dalhousie's refusal to recognize an adopted son as heir to the throne.

THE PESHWAS

The power and polity that Shivaji established flourished far beyond the limits of his *swarajya* into North India under the brilliant Peshwas, whose office was invested with tremendous authority and made hereditary by Shivaji's grandson Shahu. The period of the expansion of Maratha power under successive Peshwas with Pune as the seat of their power for nearly a century (1713–1818) is often called the Peshwai. There were two important political "arrangements" that helped such a large extension of Maratha polity, which exercised tremendous authority over the ruins of the fast-declining Mughal empire. During that period, the Peshwas encouraged and supported some of their *sardars,* notably Shindes centered in Gwalior, Holkars in Indore, Gaikwads in Baroda, and Bhosles in Nagpur, to establish and maintain their own extensive semiautonomous fiefdoms, constituting together with the Peshwa a pentarchy under the overall control of the Peshwas. The second "arrangement" was between the Peshwas and the *chhatrapatis,* or kings, in Shivaji's line in Satara—Shahu and successors. It resembled the position of the hereditary shogun vis-à-vis the Japanese emperor with separate capitals for the Maratha king and the Peshwa, with the latter receiving the robes of investiture from the king. Although the Peshwas lived virtually like kings in Pune with most of the royal accoutrements, they kept the respect owed to their royal masters when visiting Satara. There, much before entering the capital, the Peshwa stopped the marching strains of his troops, dismounted from his elephant, and walked up to the *chhatrapati*'s palace and sat on an ordinary low *baithak* (seat) in his presence. All grants of titles, honors, and lands to the *sardars* were made on the recommendation of the Peshwa but with the knowledge and seal of the *chhatrapati.* All treaties and important documents were explained, in most cases, personally by the Peshwa to the *chhatrapati* before the latter's seal was affixed to make them final legal documents.

Balaji Viswanath

The founder of the line of the Peshwas was Balaji Vishwanath (1713–1720), a Brahman who came from the Bhat family of Shrivardhan in Konkan. The crucial help he gave Shahu in rallying important *sardars* and administrators from Tarabai's camp dramatically strengthened Shahu's position, who showed his appreciation by appointing him his *peshwa* (prime minister). Balaji went far beyond the territorial limits of Shivaji's kingdom or that of his successors, in any case far beyond Maharashtra, the home of the Marathas, to the capital of the Mughal empire in Delhi, where the instability and weakness among Aurangzeb's successors afforded tremendous opportunities for someone with the ambition and ability to match it. In 1719, Peshwa Balaji Viswanath marched on Delhi and secured not only Shahu's family from Mughal captivity but also, importantly for the future of the aratha polity, the Mughal court's recognition for the Maratha *swarajya* and additional *sanads* (deeds)—*chauthai* and *sardeshmukh* (the right respectively to collect and keep 25 percent and 10 percent of the revenues)—over six *subhas* (provinces) of the Deccan.

The origin of the *peshwa*'s authority lay in two *yadya* (plural for *yadi*), or lists, drawn up in a handwritten document by Shahu himself in 1714, stipulating the duties and obligations of the *peshwa* and making that office hereditary in the family of Balaji Viswanath. After the childless Shahu's death in 1749, Ramaraja, twenty-five, from the Kolhapur branch of the Bhosle family, was adopted and crowned as *chhatrapati* in the following year. Not trained to be a king and having little or no administrative abilities, he readily signed a second *yadi*, most likely drawn up by Peshwa Balaji Bajirao, giving the Peshwas additional authority to act on behalf of the *chhatrapati* in all matters. The new *yadi* also validated the total authority of the *peshwa* over all Maratha domains.

Bajirao I

Balaji Viswanath's elder son, Bajirao I (1720–1740), broke the traditional limits of the Bhosle kingdom, as he adopted a forward policy that would extend the Maratha dominion into the North. In 1734, he captured the Malwa territory, and in 1739, his brother Chimnaji drove out the Portuguese from almost all their possessions in the northern Konkan, notably Salsette and Bassein. Bajirao himself attacked the Nizam of Hyderabad four times because he would not let the Peshwas collect the *chauthai* and *sardeshmukhi* that were their due in terms of

the *sanads* (deeds) from the Mughal emperor. At the time of Bajirao's early death on April 27, 1740, the *peshwa* writ ran over directly in Maharashtra and over large chunks of territory in central and North India through the new Maratha *sardars* loyal to the *peshwa*. Later, they would develop into a pentarchy— Gujarat under Gaikwads of Baroda, Shindes in Gwalior, Holkars in Indore, and Bhosles in Nagpur—all under the overall authority of the *peshwa* or his council in Pune.

Balaji Bajirao

The elder son of Bajirao I, Balaji Bajirao (1740–1761), known as Nanasaheb Peshwa, succeeded his father. He had two brothers, Raghunathrao, who later betrayed the Marathas and joined hands with the British, and Janardan, who died in his early youth. Nanasaheb was talented in the arts of war, diplomacy, and administration. Soon after assuming the position of the *peshwa*, he spent a year improving the civil administration of Pune. The period 1741 to 1745 was of comparative calm in the Deccan, which enabled Nanasaheb to reorganize agriculture and introduce effective measures for protecting the villagers and their produce. There was an all-around improvement in Maharashtra in terms of revenue collection, services, and law and order. Thereafter, he resumed military campaigns for consolidation and fresh acquisitions, leading the forces himself to Karnataka and sending his ambitious and able uncle Raghunathrao to Gujarat and the North.

A major flaw in Nanasaheb's policies was the destruction in 1756 of the Maratha navy so farsightedly built by Shivaji under the Angres. Because Tulaji Angre would not toe his line, Nanasaheb took the help of the British East India Company in Bombay to attack the Angre navy and destroy it, thus leaving the field open for the English to establish their maritime supremacy on the west coast.

The Third Battle of Panipat

In 1761, the Marathas were dismally defeated at the Third Battle of Panipat against Ahmad Shah Abdali, an invader from Afghanistan. He raided the Mughal capital, Delhi, several times in the 1750s. To save his capital, the effete Mughal emperor asked his vizier, Safdarjung, to sign an agreement (called the *Ahmadnama*) with the Marathas, whereby the *peshwa* agreed to defend the Mughal emperor against his domestic and foreign foes. The Nizam of Hyderabad, not too happy with the *Ahmadnama* and the prominence it gave the Marathas, attacked them. The *peshwa* defeated the Nizam's forces at Sindkhed in 1757 and Udgir in 1760. The Marathas also successfully drove out Abdali's forces from the Punjab, raising their own flag at Attock in 1756. When Abdali heard the news, he led a major force that would end in challenging the very large force sent by Peshwa Nanasaheb under his own brother Sadashivrao and son Vishwasrao.

On January 14, 1761, the Third Battle of Panipat took place, which dealt a major setback to the Marathas in the North. They lost more than 100,000 men and dozens of important *sardars* in the battle in addition to elephants and countless horses, heavy equipment, and treasure. Both Sadashivrao and Vishwasrao died in the battle. The news shattered Nanasaheb, who died shortly afterward, on June 23, 1761. Panipat drew a dividing line in the fortunes of the Marathas; Nanasaheb's reign marked the highest and the lowest points of Maratha power up to that time.

Madhavrao I

Madhavrao (1761–1772), the second son of Nanasaheb and his wife, Gopikabai, became the *peshwa* because his elder brother, Vishwasrao, lost his life at Panipat. This fourth *peshwa* was only sixteen and held office for only eleven years but was notable for reestablishing the Maratha authority on almost all the lands that had been theirs before 1761.

Historians give a lot of credit for the childhood education of Madhavrao to his mother, Gopikabai, who continued to guide him, particularly in handling his uncle Ragunathrao. When Madhavrao assumed the reins of power, he was besieged by many enemies who wanted to take advantage of the post-Panipat dire weakness of the Maratha polity, whose props of power in the North had been devastated by losses of important members of the prestigious *sardar* families.

Nearer home, the Nizam took advantage of the dissensions within the *peshwa* household, the *peshwa*'s warrior-uncle Raghunathrao, in the early years of Madhavrao's rule, who did not hesitate to use the Nizam's assistance to buttress his own ambitions. Very soon, Madhavrao divided the work of dealing with the regime's external enemies: he took up those like Nizam and Hyder Ali nearer at home, choosing to send his recalcitrant uncle Raghunathrao to the distant North to deal with the Bundelas, Jats, and Rohillas who had challenged the Maratha positions there. When the Nizam, with the help of some Maratha dissenters, attacked Pune in 1763, the young Madhavrao led his regular as well as guerrilla forces against Hyderabad, looted the treasury there, and faced the divided forces of the Nizam at Rakshasbhuvan on the banks of the Godavari and inflicted a defeat of such magnitude on August 10, 1763, that the Nizam did not seriously attack the Marathas for the next twenty-two years. Madhavrao maintained the new initiative by marching south in the following year against Hyder Ali, defeating his forces at three different locations in Karnataka and compelling him to return all Maratha territories north of the Tungabhadra River in addition to a large cash of 3.2 million rupees.

As for the North, Madhavrao reestablished Maratha authority there through the exertions of Raghunathrao, Tukoji Holkar, and Mahadji Shinde, who not only defeated the rebellious Bundelas, Jats, and the Rohillas but also wrested control over Delhi from Najib Khan's son, Zabit Khan, and brought back emperor Shah Alam from his refuge with the British in Allahabad and restored him to the throne on January 6, 1772. They also recovered considerable portions of the loot Abdali's forces had hidden. The Maratha ascendancy in Delhi continued for the remainder of the century thanks to the leadership of Mahadji Shinde and Tukoji Holkar.

By 1772, Madhavrao had largely made up for the defeat and losses suffered at Panipat. Additionally, he had shown impressive gains in administration, steady collection of revenues, introduction of a number of schemes for the welfare of the common man, and, above all, the establishment of respect for the Maratha judicial system. Just when stability had returned to Pune as the center of power and administration, the young *peshwa* died of tuberculosis on November 18, 1772. His untimely death proved a great destabilizer of Maratha power, which led the noted British administrator-historian Grant Duff to comment, "The plains of Panipat were not more fatal to the Maratha empire than the early end of this excellent prince."[6]

Ineffective Peshwai and the Rise of the Pentarchy, 1772–1800

Dissensions in the Peshwa family largely arising from the ambitions of Raghunathrao led to the assassination of Narayanrao Peshwa (1772–1773) and

Raghunathrao's usurpation of the position of *peshwa*. This was not only opposed by the elite of Pune but also declared illegal by an upright judge, Ramashastri Prabhune, whose name has been ever since the personification of integrity, courage, and justice in Maharashtra. When Narayanrao's widow gave birth on April 18, 1774, to a son, Sawai Madhavrao (1774–1795), he was recognized as the new *peshwa* by a council of twelve (*barbhai*, or twelve brothers), which included Nana Phadnavis, Holkar, Phadke, and Shinde. The arrangement lasted more than a quarter century, until Nana's death in 1800. Appealing to the Maratha "destiny" and the importance of unity in the context of the fast-disappearing nominal Mughal "empire" and the rapidly rising empire on its ruins of the East India Company (EIC), the frail but tenacious Nana virtually presided over the Maratha polity by judiciously giving adequate prominence and credit to the pentarchy's constituents.

Early in this new phase of the Peshwai, Raghunathrao sought refuge with the East India Company in Bombay whose forces joined his in a march toward Pune in 1774. The *barbhai* defeated them in what is known as the First Anglo-Maratha War (1775–1782). Very soon, the EIC's disgruntled Bombay council took up Raghunathrao's cause again. Once again, the Marathas defeated the EIC's forces; the *barbhais* demanded the EIC hand over Raghunathrao. Instead, Governor-General Warren Hastings asked General Goddard to attack

the Maratha positions in Konkan and Gujarat. For the third time in a decade, the Marathas prevailed, and the EIC was forced to sign the Treaty of Salbai in May 1782, by which they handed over Raghunathrao to the *barbhais*. He was confined thereafter at Kopargaon, where he died on December 11, 1786.

The Maratha triumphs in the North by the pentarchy and nearer home against the EIC were all carried out in the name of Peshwa Sawai Madhavrao. On October 25, 1795, in a delirious state induced by high fever, the young *peshwa* jumped down from his quarters and died two days later. By that time, the aging Nana was finding it increasingly harder to keep the pentarchy together, particularly in the face of the aggressive EIC. The pentarchy practically dissolved itself with Nana's death in 1800.

Bajirao II

When Sawai Madhavrao died in 1795, Raghunathrao's incompetent but ambitious son, Bajirao II, became the *peshwa*. Following his father's example, he took the EIC's help to strengthen his own position and signed with the company the Treaty of Bassein in 1802. This essentially ended the *Peshwai* as a power. When in 1804 General Wellesley proclaimed the Deccan to be in a state of chaos and on those grounds established military rule there, the Peshwas remained rulers only in name. In 1818, Bajirao II was removed from his nominal position as the *peshwa* and exiled to far-off Bithur in Uttar Pradesh, where the last of his line, the adopted son, Nanasaheb, was not recognized by Governor-General Dalhousie. Nanasaheb became a crucial leader of the 1857 uprising. He eluded capture and possibly disappeared in the wilds of Nepal.

Conclusion

The role of the Marathas, particularly the Peshwai, as the major predecessor power before the British conquest of the subcontinent has been aptly summed up by the eminent historian of the Mughals and the Marathas, Jadunath Sarkar:

> Marathas attained unparalleled historical importance in India. . . . They attained control over the Mughal rulers in Delhi and kept the control until 1802. The Marathas were the last major power the English had to contend with. . . . [The Marathas] showed tremendous intellectual ability, capacity for hard work, simple living, high thinking and ability to attain their dreams and plans. What they lacked were discipline, organizing ability, acquaintance with modern technology and science, ability to comprehend the power of the navy.[7]

THE SIKHS AND THEIR RELATIONS WITH THE MUGHALS

The relations between the Sikhs and the Mughals, which had been excellent under Emperor Akbar, turned sour under Jahangir and came to a confrontation under the last great Mughal emperor, Aurangzeb. In the process, their religion became a militant faith.

Guru Nanak

The Sikh religion was originally founded by Guru Nanak in the fifteenth century, partly in response to the then Muslim oppression of the Hindus. Born in 1469 at Talwandi (modern Nankana), thirty-five miles from Lahore, Nanak, like the other saints of the *bhakti* movement, aimed at removing the irritants between the Hindus and Muslims by preaching the unity of God and the brotherhood of man. Also like the *bhakti* preachers, he sought to reform the Hindu fold by advocating the abolition of the caste system and treating all human beings as equals regardless of their creed. Like most of them, he used not Sanskrit but the language of the common masses for the propagation of his beliefs. There was a lack of emphasis on rituals, only on devotion and, as in Nanak's case, repetition of the *Sat Nam* (the True Name), which would signify devotion to God and lead to the attainment of salvation. In order to enforce his casteless society of followers and to bring about a solidarity among them, he introduced the Sikh practices (which are continued to this day) of *sangat* (meeting each other, socializing) and *pangat* (sitting together for meals, interdining) at the community kitchen, or *langar*, which was a hospitality provided to all by his wife.

Yet Nanak was different from the other *bhakti* preachers in some respects, including in his conception of God. For him and his followers, God was without body, form, or time; there was to be no idolatry. And although he quoted from some thirty-four Hindu saints in his writings, he did not believe in the appearance of God's incarnations on earth, as Hinduism did. Moreover, he denounced a life of renunciation, instead insisting that all Sikhs, including the gurus, lead their lives as householders. They should live an ethical life, help the poor, and protect the weak against oppression and cruelty.

Nanak's model was Kabir, who too preached to Hindus and Muslims alike. All *bhakti* preachers traveled; Nanak traveled the most, some of it not for preaching. Thus, he went on four separate journeys, two of them in the subcontinent, the third to Sri Lanka, and the fourth to the Middle East, including Mecca. The last met his intention to study Islam in all its aspects. He gave new meaning to the Muslim practice of praying five times a day and then adapted the practice differently for his followers, asking them to observe five things: *nam,* singing the praise of God; *san,* giving of alms; *ashnan,* keeping the body clean through a daily bath; *seva,* the service of all human beings without regard to their caste, creed, or status; and *simran,* praying for the deliverance of the soul.

Guru Nanak died in 1539. He nominated as his successor Guru Angad, a devoted disciple, who was not related to him. He was so close to him, Nanak called him a limb of his own body. He was, therefore, named Guru Angad (*angad* means body). Guru Angad's (1539–1552) major contribution was to put Nanak's hymns into a refined version of the prevalent Lande script to a new script called Gurmukhi (literally, "Guru's mouth"), in which all the holy writings of Sikhism appear to this date.

Emperor Akbar, curious to know the teachings of every religion, visited the third guru, Amar Das. Impressed with the faith and the Sikh practice of *langar,* Akbar donated some neighboring villages, free of land tax, to meet the expenses. Guru Amar Das is known to have removed the practice of *purdah* (covering the face), then prevalent among Hindus and Muslims alike in the Punjab. He also began the practice of holding a general assembly of his followers twice a year, almost six months apart, on Baisakhi Day (generally April) and *Diwali* (generally in October–November). The same guru is known to have started a practice that remained valid through to the tenth guru, that of making the office of guru hereditary. To start with, he nominated his son-in-law Ramdas as the fourth Guru.

Guru Ramdas (1574–1581) too was visited by Emperor Akbar. On that occasion, Akbar gave Guru Ramdas some land at Amritsar. There Guru Ramdas built a beautiful tank and named it Amritsar (the tank of *Amrit,* or nectar).

The fifth guru, Arjan (1581–1606), was an excellent organizer who spread the faith among large numbers of people all over the Punjab. His great contribution as a spiritual and intellectual leader was to compile the *Adi Granth* (The First Sacred Book) by selecting verses from the works of his four predecessors but also from those of Hindu and Muslim saints. In order to put the finances of his organization on a sound and regular footing, he offered to appoint *masands*, a class of nobility who would agree to give 10 percent of their income to the Sikh *panth*. In practice, the *masands* collected the funds from people in their "jurisdiction" and appropriated, with the consent of the guru, some judicial and administrative functions to themselves that elevated their social status and financial standing. With the ensured funds, Guru Arjan not only constructed some impressive buildings but also gave his court a royal look. Hereafter, the gurus would have gallant horses, caparisoned elephants, and liveried retainers.

Thus far, the gurus had strictly stayed away from politics, believing in the separation of religion and politics, church and state. Guru Arjan broke that tradition and interfered with the Mughal imperial politics. It so happened that in the year of Akbar's death, his grandson Prince Khusrav rebelled against his own father, Jahangir. When pursued by the imperial forces led by his own father, he fled to Taran Taran in the Punjab to seek help from Guru Arjan, whom he had met previously at his grandfather Akbar's court. Khusrav begged the guru for some financial assistance to meet his travel expenses (he had a number of armed followers with him). The guru complied.

A furious Jahangir captured Guru Arjan, fined him 200,000 rupees, a very large sum in those days, and ordered him at the instance of his Muslim advisers to strike off certain verses from the Sikh holy book, the *Adi Granth*. The guru refused, whereupon the emperor ordered his sons arrested and his assets confiscated. He was charged with treason and ordered to be tortured to death. Thus, the forty-two-year-old guru was made to stand on the hot desert sands in the summer heat; he died of hunger and exhaustion there on May 30, 1606. The Sikhs were angered, but as it was their practice until then, they did not challenge the emperor. Yet the martyrdom of their guru became the turning point in the Sikh attitude toward the Mughal rulers. According to the Sikh tradition, the dying guru said that his son, the next guru, Har Govind, would "sit fully armed on his throne and maintain an army to the best of his ability."

Guru Har Govind (1606–1644) was then eleven years old. Whether he understood the meaning of such a complete departure from the Sikh traditions is debatable. At the time of his consecration, he had two swords hanging by his side, *piri* and *miri*, representing his spiritual and temporal authority. He changed the ways a Sikh should live, encouraging them to give up vegetarianism and take up hunting and body-building exercises. As he grew up, he raised a small army of foot soldiers, three hundred cavalry, and six gunners. He built a fort, Lohgarh, at Amritsar and the *Akal Takht* (God's Throne) in front of the temple Hari Mandir.

For all intents and purposes, Guru Har Govind behaved as head of religion and state, sitting on the throne and rendering justice to his people. During his time, the Sikh society of believers was transformed into a militarist state, headed by its guru with the traditional umbrella, signifying sovereignty, over his head. He established an administration independent of the Mughal government and asked his people not to obey its orders or pay taxes. When the Mughal government asked him for the fine that had been imposed on his late father, he refused to pay. Thereupon, he was sentenced to twelve years' imprisonment (later commuted to a three-year sentence) in the Gwalior Fort. It appears that sometime later he mended his relations with Emperor Jahangir, who may have offered him a *mansabdari* in the Punjab. It is not known whether he accepted it, but he did accept a supervisory position of some sort, which involved the command of a Mughal force of several hundred cavalry and seven guns. The relationship with the Mughals continued several years into the next reign, that of Shah Jahan, but then began to sour even over petty matters. In the end, the Mughals sent forces to eliminate him. The Sikh annals are replete with Guru Har Govind's heroic exploits, his small force proving its mettle against the much larger force of his adversary. Finally, tired of the continuing conflict, the Sikh guru moved the seat of his government to Kiratpur, a site between the Sutlej River and Siwalik Hills. There he died on March 3, 1644. Just before his death, he nominated his grandson Guru Har Rai as his successor.

Guru Har Rai (1644–1661) and his son Guru Har Kishan (1661–1664) were not warlike, as the two previous gurus were. However, the institutions and policies created by their predecessors, including the creation of an army, became consolidated during that period.

The next guru, Tegh Bahadur (1664–1675), was capable of military leadership, as was proved during his participation in the Assam War in 1668. However, he preferred to be nearer home to take care of the problems created by Emperor Aurangzeb's religious fanaticism. There were repeated reports of the demolition of *gurudwaras* (Sikh places of worship) and their conversion into mosques. He could not ignore the appeals of Kashmiri Brahmins, who were being forced to convert to Islam in large numbers. The emperor received reports of the guru's leadership and that both the Sikhs and the Hindus looked up to him for redress. From his base in Anandpur, the guru offered them comfort and encouragement. The emperor received reports of the guru performing miracles, which were contrary to the Islamic faith. Aurangzeb ordered the guru to be arrested and produced before him. There he ordered the guru and his five followers to perform the miracles or convert to Islam. The guru denied any special powers to perform miracles but refused to convert to Islam. At that point, the emperor's men killed two of his disciples through torture, including boiling alive. The guru himself was chained and then beheaded on November 11, 1675. In his dying days, he repeatedly and proudly said, *"Sar dia par sir na dia,"* a message to his disciples to give up their lives but never to give up their faith.

Guru Govind Singh

The die was cast. The Sikh patience had been sorely tried. Things would never be the same again between the Sikhs and the Mughal government. Guru Tegh Bahadur's son Guru Govind (1675–1708; born in Patna in 1666) realized the need for a complete change in the Sikh attitude toward the Mughal government, which had cost the lives of his father and grandfather. He decided to take advantage of the problems Aurangzeb's government faced in the Punjab, which was virtually under the control of the rebel Prince Muazzam, who had taken refuge in Kabul. The emperor himself had moved to the Deccan, where he was engaged in crushing the Shia kingdoms there. The emperor was also involved in what appeared to be an unwinnable conflict against the Marathas.

On Baisakhi Day 1756 of the Hindu Vikrama Samvat era (March 30, 1699), Guru Govind completely transformed the Sikh community, making it a militant nation of the Khalsa (the Pure). At a special congregation, he spoke of saving Sikhism and Hinduism from the grave perils it faced. "A brick has to be returned with a stone," he said. In a dramatic moment, he asked the assembly for someone who would be willing to offer his head to the cause. After two such calls, five ordinary persons, including a barber and a water carrier, came up to the dais, one by one, and each was asked to accompany the guru to the adjoining tent. The audience presumed that each one of them had given his life to the cause, because each time the guru returned, his sword was dripping with blood. The guru had dipped it in a cauldron of goat's blood. After all five had thus "offered" themselves as a "sacrifice," the guru returned with all of them, this time dressed in finery. They had symbolically committed their lives thereafter to the guru's mission. The guru gave them *pahul*, a form of baptism, which included stirring the water with a double-edged dagger. He declared them his *Panja Pyare* (Five Beloved Ones) and announced they were the *Khalsa* (the Pure). Those who opted for the *Khalsa* were required to wear five *K*s, or five jewels, as the guru called them: *kesh* (long hair), never to be cut; a *kangha* (comb); a *kripan* (sword, in practice, a short dagger); *kachcha* (short drawers); and a *kara* (steel bracelet). Each of these *K*s had a religious or military significance or both and was intended to enhance the fighting ability of the new militant nation. Their creed would be never to show their backs to their foes on the battlefield and at all times to act to help the poor, protect the weak, and fight to the death against oppression of any kind. Further, the *Khalsa* eschewed the caste system and the oppression of the Sudras and the untouchables.

In an internal reform, the guru abolished the system of tithe collection by *masands*, appointed since the time of Guru Arjan. Though originally appointed to ensure the faith of finances, the *masands* had become corrupt, oppressive, and a power unto themselves. Instead, the guru asked the followers to make offerings in person to the guru on major occasions such as Baisakhi Day and the *Diwali*.

Guru Govind was a great scholar, proficient in several languages. He created a supplementary holy book, *Daswen Padshah ka Granth* (The Book of the Tenth Sovereign), which included voluminous materials in Persian, Hindi, and Punjabi, all in the Gurmukhi script.

The position of the guru in the Sikh religion for quite some time had been hereditary. All of Guru Govind's sons had been killed. Guru Govind did not want a contest among his distant relatives or among imposters who would like to become the next guru for the office. He, therefore, declared that he was entrusting the *Khalsa* to the care of Akal Purkh (God) and that in all spiritual matters, the *Granth* would be their guide. If disputes arose on spiritual matters, a Sikh congregation should be called and five of them elected to resolve the question. Their opinion, called the *gurumata* (lit-

erally, "opinion of the guru"), should be submitted to the entire assembly for ratification. It would then carry the force of "law" for the Sikh *panth* (following). On the other hand, all temporal matters would be looked after by the holy *panchayats* meeting before the *Granth*.

In 1708, Guru Govind Singh was stabbed by an Afghan whose identity is not well known. Sensing his own end was near, the guru entered an enclosure, forbidding anyone else to enter it, and took *samadhi* in the style of the Hindu sages. He died at the age of forty-two on October 7, 1708.

The Emergence of Banda as a Leader

The premature death of the last guru left the Sikh community in a quandary. The gap in leadership was for the time being filled by Banda, who established his power based on the fort of Lohgarh at Mukhlispur. There he assumed a regal position for himself and even issued new coins in his own name signifying a Sikh revolt for independence. The Mughal emperor, Bahadur Shah, quickly marched against him and laid siege to Lohgarh, which made Banda flee to the safety of the hills north of the Mughal city of Lahore. It was not long before he reasserted himself in the Sirhind region. Bahadur Shah again led his forces against Banda and besieged him in the fortress of Gurdaspur. This time, Banda was captured and taken to Delhi, where his son was tortured and killed in his presence; later, in 1716, Banda himself was crushed under the feet of an elephant.

The period from 1716 to 1799 is known in Sikh history as the era of the confederacy of small states of Sikhs, loosely linked by common ties of religion and culture. The chiefs who were often hostile to each other had the common practice of issuing coins in the name of Guru Govind Singh or the Sikh religion. Disputes between any two chiefs were brought to the *Sarbat Khalsa*, which met biennially in the holy city of Amritsar. In case of any joint military action, the common strategy of the *Dal Khalsa* (Sikh army) was worked out by the military head of the confederacy, who was elected by the council of all the chiefs of the states meeting at Amritsar. Because of mutual rivalries and jealousies among the small Sikh states, a common military action was not easily possible, hence the inability of the Sikhs of that period, at least until 1767, to make conquests outside Punjab and carve out a kingdom.

After 1716, the Mughal efforts to crush the Sikh spirit continued but failed to eliminate the Sikh military ardor and spiritual strength. Another leader, Kapur Singh of Fyzullapur, emerged to establish *Dal Khalsa*, the army of the Khalsa. The Sikhs took advantage of the chaotic situation created in the Punjab by the disastrous invasions against India by the Persian Nadir Shah in 1739 and the Afghan Ahmed Shah Abdali from 1748 to 1752 and again from 1757 to 1767, to build up their own finances and military strength. Kapur Singh built a fortress at Dalewal and built his treasury by looting the region around the rich city of Lahore. All this had the effect of the dilution of the Mughal authority in the Punjab almost to the point of extinction.

With Abdali's retreat to Afghanistan in 1767, the Sikh power grew remarkably all over the Punjab, the Kangra Valley, and northward all the way up to Jammu. The Sikh "nation" was organized as a coalition of twelve semiautonomous *misls*, or federations. The Sikhs found it hard to remain united, questioning the leadership of the other *misls*. Finally, one leader emerged, the greatest temporal head of all in the history of the Sikhs, Ranjit Singh.

Ranjit Singh Establishes a Sikh Empire

Ranjit Singh was born a son of the chief of the *misl* of Sukerchakia (not the strongest of the twelve *misls*) on November 13, 1780. He was hardly twelve when his father, Maha Singh, died. Ranjit showed his qualities of valor and leadership very early during the invasion of the Afghan Zaman Shah in 1793–1798. The invader was so impressed that he placed Ranjit, then nineteen, as raja of Lahore. Yet in a few years' time, Ranjit was able to use the sharp differences among the Afghans to incorporate the *misls* west of the Sutlej into his growing domains. In 1799, he made Lahore his capital, and two years later, on April 12, 1801, Baisakhi Day, he assumed the title of maharaja.

Ranjit Singh's aim was now to bring all the Sikhs, between the Sutlej and the Jumna, under one banner. He first checked the incursions of the Maratha *sardars*, notably Holkar and Scindia, through the Treaty of Lahore with the British on New Year's Day 1806. Then he turned to the Sikh chiefs who were quarreling among themselves. Some of them joined him; others despised his ambitions and appealed to the British for help. But the British did not want an additional problem on their hands, particularly with the intelligence that the French had struck an alliance with the Turks and the Persians and planned to attack India through the northwest passages.

With the French threat receding in 1809, the British signed, on April 25, 1809, the Treaty of Amritsar, which recognized Ranjit Singh's kingdom up to the right side of the Sutlej, taking the British control up to Ludhiana. Ranjit's dream of bringing all the Sikhs under his control had been thwarted, at least for the time being, by the British, who were trying to bring the entire subcontinent under their domination.

Checked in the East, Ranjit Singh expanded his domains in the west, north, and northeast. Within the next decade, he had incorporated the entire territory from Multan and Kabul to Jammu and Kashmir into his kingdom.

For the first time in a millennium, large parts of Afghanistan and the northwest territory of the Pathans came under non-Muslim control. The Afghan king, Shah Shuja, became Ranjit Singh's captive in Lahore, surrendering the world-famous Kohinoor diamond to the Sikh monarch in 1814.

Ranjit Singh, who died at the age of fifty-nine in 1839, had an impressive personality despite the loss of his left eye to smallpox. Unlike most rulers of his time, he was not a cruel man. He did not resort to violence as his first choice but preferred patient negotiations. He realized fairly early in his dealings with the British the immense difference in the rival strengths between them and himself. He knew that one day the British would be the power on the subcontinent, saying in his well-known words, *"Ek din sab lal ho jayega"* (One day, it will all be red), meaning the map of India would be colored red, the color of the British Empire.

Maharaja Ranjit Singh was a benevolent ruler. Although he was personally religious, as a ruler he was secular, treating Hindus and Muslims well. He made tax-free endowments for the Jawala-mukhi temple of the Hindus and Baba Farid Shrine at Pak Pattan for the Muslims. The majority of his subjects were Muslims, who were appreciative of his rule and were loyal to him. He employed Muslims in high places; his foreign minister, Fakir Azizuddin, was a Muslim.

After Ranjit Singh

Ranjit Singh was followed by several weak rulers until in 1843, a minor, Duleep Singh, was recognized as the king with his mother, Rani Jhindan, as regent. The real control passed on to the army, which was the only organized center of power. In their overestimation of their own strength, they believed the British were out to destroy them, and, therefore, they needed to defend their positions.

Two Anglo-Sikh wars followed, in 1845–1846 and 1849. The British records testify to the valor of the "Sikh nation," the bravery of its soldiers, but also the paucity of its military leadership. The losses on both sides were heavy. The Sikhs paid a heavy price after each of the wars. The first war concluded with the British occupation of Ranjit Singh's capital of Lahore on February 20, 1846; the victors imposed a very harsh treaty. The Sikhs were compelled to surrender the territories south of the Sutlej and the large fertile territory between the Sutlej and the Beas. A penalty of 15 million rupees was imposed, one-third of it in hard cash and the balance by giving away to the British the territory between the Beas and the Indus, including Kashmir. The Sikhs were allowed a limited force on the condition that they not have any European military advisers. The minor Duleep Singh and his regent, Rani Jhindan, were to be protected by a force commanded by the British resident, Henry Lawrence, but paid for by the Sikh state. Kashmir was sold to Gulab Singh, a *sardar* of the Sikh monarch, for 10 million pounds sterling by a separate treaty with him at Amritsar on March 16, 1846. At the end of the Second Anglo-Sikh War, primarily over an uprising in Multan, the British governor-general annexed all of Punjab, extinguishing the Sikh empire. Maharaja Duleep Singh was pensioned off to England where he converted to Christianity and married another convert, Victoria Gouramma. His mother, Rani Jhindan, died in England. Duleep Singh later returned to India and reconverted to Sikhism.

———

NOTES _____

1. Stewart Gordon, *The Marathas, 1600–1818*, 84.

2. G. S. Sardesai, "Shivaji," in *The History and Culture of the Indian People: The Mughuls*, edited by R. C. Majumdar (Bombay: Bharatiya Vidya Bhavan, 1974), 7:249.

3. Gordon, *The Marathas, 1600–1818*, 67.

4. Ibid., 81.

5. Jadunath Sarkar, *Shivaji and His Times*, chap. 16, section M9.

6. Grant Duff, *A History of the Marathas* (1818; reprint, Jaipur, 1986).

7. Jadunath Sarkar, on the Marathas' conclusion.

Most notable was his [Hastings's] encouragement and support of Sir William Jones (1746–1794), a judge of the Supreme Court in the latter's foundation of the Asiatic Society of Bengal (later the Bengal Branch of the Royal Asiatic Society of Great Britain and Northern Ireland, which itself was established in 1823), whose chief aim was to promote and publish research in Sanskrit. Jones had learned Arabic and Persian while at Harrow, and he would know Hebrew and Greek before coming to India. He was also a talented jurist and came to India in that capacity to be a judge. Master of many languages, he now studied Sanskrit. In his first address to the society, he showered praise on Sanskrit, which he lauded for its "wonderful structure; more perfect than the Greek, more copious than the Latin and more exquisitely refined than either." (page 226)

11

THE EUROPEAN
POWERS IN INDIA

THE AGE OF COMMERCE, 1498–1757

The initial period of European contact with India was not, except in the case of the few Portuguese possessions, marked by any significant clash of cultures. The contacts were chiefly coastal and commercial. Europeans—the Portuguese, French, Dutch, Danes, and the English—bought spices, textiles, and luxury goods; in return, they had little to sell. In the early period, the Europeans could not claim any technological superiority either, except in the casting of cannon and use of fast-moving ships. A marked disparity in military capabilities and in manufacturing between the Europeans and Indians came in the wake of the outbreak of the Industrial Revolution in the second half of the eighteenth century in England and its spread thereafter over the continent of Europe. The demands of the new industrial society in terms of cheap raw materials and guaranteed sheltered markets for European manufactures partly led to the change in the policy: from commerce to conquest, from trade to territorial acquisition.

The Portuguese in India

The Portuguese were the first Europeans to arrive in India by sea and secure a monopoly of Asia-Europe maritime trade for a century until the advent of the Dutch, English, and the French in the region. Vasco da Gama's "discovery" of the sea route inaugurated the Age of Colonialism, which brought revolutionary changes, pleasant and unpleasant, in economic, political, and cultural spheres in most of Asia, justifying the subtitle "The Vasco da Gama Epoch of Asian History" for K. M. Panikkar's monumental work, *Asia and Western Dominance*.[1]

The Portuguese exploratory enterprise vigorously supported by Prince Henry the Navigator in the mid-fifteenth century may be seen in the context of a major event that affected both trade and religion. Thus, after the fall of Constantinople to the Turks in 1453, the Italian city-states trading in spices, sugar, and other Eastern goods demanded astronomical prices from their European customers on the pretext that it was much harder to get such goods through the Arab- and Persian-controlled Middle East. There was much profit in bypassing the traditional route and reaching the source of these products directly by sea. Second, concerned with the threat of Muslims advancing toward Europe, Pope Alexander VI encouraged finding a route to India, which was then, albeit erroneously, believed to be Christian, thanks to the exertions of the apostle Thomas in the first century CE. He hoped that with the help of "Christian" India, it would be possible to attack the Muslims in a pincer movement.

The Papal Bull of 1492 specifically authorized the Portuguese with such a mission, which brought Vasco da Gama and his four ships to Calicut in the present-day Kerala on May 18, 1498. Asked by two Muslim merchants of Tunis who happened to be in Calicut, "What the devil has brought you here? In search of what have you come from such a long distance?" a man in Vasco da Gama's party promptly replied, "We have come in search of Christians and Spices." The Portuguese thought the people of Calicut were Christians and their temples were chapels. Vasco da Gama and his men offered prayers in a "chapel" before the image of "Mary" in what was, in fact, a Hindu temple in Calicut. The mistake was not discovered until the second Portuguese visit led by Cabral in 1500, which led the king of Portugal to order conversions of as many Indians as possible to the Catholic faith. Profits from the spice trade and the spread of Christianity remained the twin Portuguese goals, though relatively modest success crowned their prodigious efforts over the 450 years of their presence in the East.

The event's importance was recognized by the Portuguese king Manuel I, who made Vasco da Gama "admiral of the Indian Ocean" and assumed for himself, in 1499, the pompous title, which reflected more a hope than any reality, "lord of the conquest, navigation, and commerce of Ethiopia, Arabia, Persia, and of India." Conquest, commerce, and Christianity were closely intertwined as the intrepid Portuguese worked for God, gold, and glory for their king.

The Portuguese were very fortunate in the timing of their arrival in South India. The Bahmani kingdom in the Deccan had split into five entities, none of which had a significant navy. Historically, although India had distinguished itself in maritime trade, no Indian ruler (with the exception of Rajendra Chola in the eleventh century) had built a navy, for offense or defense, because no enemy had ever attacked India from across the seas. The rulers of Calicut, Cochin, and Cannanore, to mention only a few coastal states dependent on the substantial revenues coming from coastal and oceanic trade, were accustomed to large numbers of merchants from China, Malacca, Java, Arabia, and North Africa who came as peaceful traders, exchanged merchandise, and some even leaving their representatives behind to look after their trading interests, including warehouses.

Initially, the *samudri* (*zamorin* in Portuguese parlance) of Calicut was friendly and hospitable to the Portuguese. His attitude changed with pressures both from the anti-Portuguese Arab merchants as well as from Vasco da Gama himself, who demanded that the *samudri* abandon all trade with the Muslims and, in addition, grant the Portuguese exemption from customs duties.

In the first decade of contact with the Portuguese, the horrendous atrocities of both da Gama and Albuquerque, including burning Arab ships carrying cargo and pilgrims—men, women, and children—to hajj, wanton bombarding of port cities in Malabar and the Persian Gulf, chopping off noses and ears of unarmed fishermen, forcing conversion of widows and daughters of the defeated to Catholicism, and converting temples and mosques into churches—affected the attitude of the Hindu rulers of these coastal kingdoms. They approached the sultan of Gujarat, who in turn took the help of Egypt and Ottoman Turkey to launch a combined naval attack on the Portuguese at Chaul in 1507–1508. To avenge the defeat, the Portuguese viceroy, d'Almeida, mobilized a large fleet and wrested a spectacular victory in 1509 by defeating the combined Mus-

lim fleets at Diu, a strategic location at the entrance to the Gulf of Cambay.

The Portuguese were not the best examples of Christianity or of European culture. Their lack of personal hygiene, going without bathing for months, and their wild behavior under the influence of alcohol at all times of the day left an unsavory impression, to put it mildly, of the first major contact between Europe and India. And if the religion they professed was given by the "Prince of Peace," there was no hint of it in the Portuguese propensity to violence even against unarmed people, women and children not excepted. Far from being the harbingers of a respectable civilization, the Portuguese left an impression of unmitigated and wanton barbarism, no different from the uncivilized marauders who had destroyed civilizations in the past. Indeed, the Portuguese were, by and large, still medieval in their thinking, their religious fanaticism typical of new converts from Islam to Catholicism. The European Renaissance had not yet touched Portugal to any significant degree.

The vision and foundation of the Portuguese thalassocracy in the East are appropriately attributed to Afonso de Albuquerque. With a view toward securing and enforcing a monopoly in Asia-Europe trade, Albuquerque envisioned an empire of ports and forts at key points on the trade routes between South and Southeast Asia and the Persian Gulf. His conquest of Goa in 1510 (and making it the headquarters of the

Portuguese possessions in the East), and of Malacca, the major mart for spice trade in Southeast Asia in 1511, and of Ormuz, the key port in the Persian Gulf in 1515, provided the beginnings of an empire, which would, by the middle of the sixteenth century, extend from So-fala in Southeast Africa, to numerous islands and ports in the Indonesian Archipelago and Macao off the China coast.

In India, the Portuguese held almost complete maritime supremacy over the west coast and some limited control over the east coast and the Bay of Bengal. It was based on three props of policy. First, they had control over the high seas, disallowing Arab shipping, seizing it, and confiscating the cargo and at times the ship itself or setting it on fire. Such piratical acts were, indeed, aimed at dissuading non-Portuguese shipping in what had been for centuries, true to its name, the Arabian Sea. Second, the Portuguese built forts and equipped them with powerful cannons at all major ports on the west coast from Cochin to Diu for the protection of the traffic and goods there. The Portuguese centered their trade on three great *feitorias* (factories) at Malacca, Calicut, and Ormuz, which made it possible for them to purchase and store spices and other products at low prices during the season until ships arrived to take the goods to Portugal. And, third, and most important, the Portuguese controlled trade traffic in and around India by requiring all non-Portuguese seacraft, large or small, to carry a *cartaz* (pass), issued by the Portuguese, for a fee. The system was enforced by a fleet of two squadrons supported in an emergency by naval units under the governor-general of Goa and seven fortresses in other principal ports. Of the two squadrons, one was used to block the Red Sea and the other to go up and down the west coast of India, stopping the non-Portuguese craft and demanding to inspect them. In tune with the rise of religious bigotry in Europe and the establishment by the middle of the sixteenth century of the Jesuits and the Inquisition, the Portuguese banned in their colonies, including those in India, the exercise of all religions other than Catholicism. They destroyed Hindu and Buddhist temples in western India and Sri Lanka, respectively, burned their sacred books, and banned the public observance of non-Catholic religious rites associated with birth, marriage, and death. In the void thus created, large-scale conversions were carried out by the official use of force and direct threats to life and property. In the eyes of the Jesuits, "God's purpose" in assisting the Portuguese in their seaborne trade with India was to increase "the harvest of souls." The Portuguese monarchs were active partners in this religious enterprise by dint of their *Padroado Real* (Crown Patronage of the Church).

The period between the arrival of Vasco da Gama in 1498, the Dutch in 1595, and the English and the French in the next two decades is aptly called "the Portuguese century" in Asia. The Portuguese fortunes in the East first suffered from neglect when the crowns of Portugal and Spain were combined from 1580 to 1640. Their enterprise was, in any case, too overextended for a nation with a meager population of less than 1 million. In contrast to the Portuguese enterprise, the English East India Company and the Dutch Vereenigde Ostandische Compagnie (VOC, or Dutch East Indies Company) focused on trade and profit and stayed away from propagation of religion. Their success in India and Indonesia was at the cost of the Portuguese, whose once extensive empire shrank by the end of the seventeenth century to a few far-flung, poorly administered, hardly profitable "territorial niches." By that time, they had lost their monopoly of Asia-Europe maritime trade and the supremacy of the sea to their English, French, and Dutch competitors. After the loss of the relatively valuable Bassein in North Konkan to the Marathas in 1739, the Portuguese in India were limited to Goa, Daman, and Diu.

The Portuguese in Goa

After its conquest by Afonso de Albuquerque in 1510, Goa was made the capital of the *Estado da India* (State of India) for the most part under a governor-general with authority over all the Portuguese possessions in Asia and Africa. Goa was also dubbed "Rome of the Orient," because it was the headquarters of the papal ecclesiastical enterprise in the East, where the archbishop lived and where the "incorrupt body" of Saint Francis Xavier has been kept since 1553. Goa saw new peaks of prosperity under the Portuguese, at least until 1580, as a substantial slice of the profits from their extensive spice trade poured into the city of Old Goa, enabling the government to build impressive office buildings and churches, mostly following the Iberian patterns of architecture. The lavish lifestyle of the *fidalgos* did not please the austere Saint Francis Xavier but certainly made the Portuguese say, "Quem vio Goa, excusa de ver Lisboa" (One who has seen Goa need not see Lisbon).

The Portuguese possessions in India, minuscule in comparison to the vast British Indian Empire, remained with them because of their special relationship with Britain as its "oldest ally." This was by virtue of the marriage in the seventeenth century of the Portuguese princess Catherine of Braganza to the British monarch Charles II.

The Portuguese acquired Goa in two stages: *Velhas Conquistas* (Old Conquests), consisting of Tiswadi, Bardez, Mormugao, and Salsette in the sixteenth century, between 1510 and 1543, and the *Novas Conquistas* (New Conquests), comprising Pernem, Sanguem, Quepem, Ponda, Sattari, Bicholim, and Canacona in two phases in the eighteenth century, between 1763 and 1788. The rigors of the Inquisition in the Old Conquests account for the overwhelming majority there of Catholic converts, whereas the later tolerance is reflected in the overwhelming majority of Hindus and their temples there.

Goa's prosperity declined along with the erosion of Portuguese power in the East during the period of Spanish rule over Portugal from 1580 to 1640. As the well-kept Portuguese archives repeatedly attest, after paying the salaries, there was hardly anything left for public services. Beginning in the nineteenth century, large numbers of Goans, particularly Catholics from poor families, sought employment as butlers in affluent British households, waiters and cooks in expensive restaurants in metropolitan cities and hill stations, and in diverse capacities on oceangoing ships. Both Hindus and Catholics, about 150,000, or more than one-fourth of the entire Goan population, migrated to British India, more than 100,000 to Mumbai (Bombay) for educational and employment opportunities, with several thousand more in Portuguese and British East Africa. The economy was linked to British India; the colony used the British Indian rupees as the currency for all purposes, except for payment of official taxes and fees.

The Portuguese in Goa had several instances of clashing with the Marathas. On occasion, their hold over their territories was precariously threatened. In 1739, they lost the "Northern Province" of Bassein to the Peshwas. As the British soon after became the dominant power on the subcontinent, they provided protection to the Portuguese.

The Dutch and the English in India

The defeat and destruction of the Spanish Armada in 1588 gave the English and the Dutch a big boost in their dreams of trading with the East. The Dutch decided to challenge the lucrative Portuguese monopoly of trade in the East. They established a private company, although with some state support, in 1595 called the *Vereenigde Ostandische Compagnie.* The VOC established many factories in India, the oldest being Masulipatam in 1605, Pulicat in 1610, and Surat in 1616, a year after the English had received the Mughal emperor's permission to establish a factory, which included warehouses and offices. The Dutch also established factories in Karikal, Chinsura, Cossimbazar, Patna, Negapatam on the Coromandel, and Cochin in Kerala. In fact, the Dutch had more trade and political connections with the local powers than the English all through the seventeenth century.

Additionally, the Dutch had established firm trading connections in the East Indies (Indonesia) where the Portuguese had a virtual monopoly of spice trade bound for Europe. The interisland trade and maritime passenger traffic was very much in local hands. The overextended Portuguese power, already weakened by their subservience to Spain (1580 to 1640), was unable to match the Dutch fleets and ferocity. The Dutch had patched up their hostile relations with Catholic Spain in 1609 with a twenty-one-year truce pact, which gave them additional strength in dealing with the local Portuguese in the East. By the 1640s, the Dutch had, in effect, broken the Portuguese monopoly in the Indonesian Archipelago and replaced it with their own.

The two non-Catholic countries, the English and the Dutch, sought mutual cooperation in the Eastern trade. That was at least the thinking of the two governments but not necessarily that of the officials of the two rival trading companies in the East. Thus, despite two major Anglo-Dutch conferences in 1611 and 1613–1615 in London and at The Hague, respectively, and a friendly agreement that was signed between the two countries in 1619, the VOC's headstrong representative in the East Indies, Governor-General Jan Pieterscoon Coen (1619–1623 and 1627–1629), was not prepared to give up the Dutch drive toward monopoly. He ordered the massacre of the English on the island of Amboyna (now Ambon) in 1623. Ten Englishmen and ten Japanese were killed. The incident is regarded by most historians as the incident that directly resulted in the EIC's decision to abandon most of its positions and trade in the archipelago to the Dutch and to concentrate instead on Indian coastal areas. The Dutch thereafter focused on the Portuguese outposts, which fell fairly rapidly. In 1641, the main Portuguese bastion, Malacca, was captured by the Dutch, who thereby secured control of both of the strategic straits in Southeast Asian waters: Malacca and Sunda.

The prime objective of both the Protestant powers—the Dutch and the English—was trade, not territory or religion, unlike the Portuguese and the French, both Catholic powers, who mixed trade with religion and did not do well in either. Neither proselytization nor the material welfare of the indigenous people was among their concerns. Direct administrative responsibility was to be avoided at all costs unless the territory was of an obvious economic or strategic significance and was likely to fall under rival European domination. Both the Dutch and the English trading companies would avoid direct administrative responsibility until past the middle of the eighteenth century, and both would lose profits on company account.

The French in India

The French trading efforts began in 1601 but were jeopardized by the Dutch. Their missionary efforts were, however, relatively successful in Vietnam but failed miserably in Thailand. In India, their activity was not significant until the establishment of the Compagnie des Indes Orientales (French East Indies Company) in 1664. Like the Catholic countries Portugal and Spain, the French enterprise was sponsored and financially supported by the state. The first French factory was established just like those of the English and the Dutch, in the Mughal port of Surat, in 1668 by François Caron. In the following year, the

French obtained the permission of the sultan of Golkonda for a factory in Masulipatam, where the Dutch had an establishment. The French capture of San Thome near Madras (now Chennai) in 1672 ended in a disaster, as the sultan of Golkonda, with the help of rival Dutch, drove the French out. But in the following year, two enterprising Frenchmen, François Martin and Bellanger de Lespinay, secured a village from a Muslim potentate, which was to be known as Pondicherry, formally established in 1674. In the same year, the French obtained from the Nawab of Bengal permission to build a factory, which they built at Chandernagore in 1690.

François Martin's name is indelibly associated with Pondicherry, which was lost to the Dutch in 1693 and restored to the French four years later by the Treaty of Ryswick. Martin, who became its governor in 1697, worked for its growth, bringing the population to 40,000 by 1706, the year of his death. As for the fortunes of the French company, they fluctuated with the politics at the French court. Finally in 1720, the company was reconstituted as the French Company of the Indies or the Compagnie Française des Indes (1720–1789). Thereafter, the French initiative was seen in their capture of Mahe and Karikal, two tiny outposts on the west coast in 1721 and 1739, respectively. The French also took Mauritius in the Indian Ocean in 1721. The French objectives in this new phase were strictly trade, not religion or territory for the sake of aggrandizement. That would happen when an ambitious Frenchman, Joseph Dupleix, would arrive in 1742 and think like Robert Clive of the EIC of building empires in the East.

Establishment of the East India Company

Within five years, on December 31, 1600, 125 English shareholders, mostly merchants, invested 72,000 pounds in what they called the East India Company. That must have been one of the best investments ever in history; in time, the EIC became the greatest trading and empire-building corporation in the history of the world. It operated under a charter issued by Queen Elizabeth I.

In 1609, the EIC sent William Hawkins to Emperor Jahangir's court, requesting that he allow the EIC's ships to use the Mughal western Indian port of Surat. Hawkins was given an Armenian girl from Jahangir's harem but no trading rights. He soon fell into disfavor with Jahangir; in 1612, he left for England empty-handed. The informal approach had failed. In 1615, the EIC successfully persuaded King James I to send an official embassy headed by Sir Thomas Roe. He was successful in obtaining permission for the EIC to open a "factory" in Surat in that year. The term *factory* signified a group of residences, offices, and warehouses of the "factor," or agent. Two more "factories" were opened: Fort St. George in Madras (now Chennai) in 1640 and Fort William in Calcutta (now Kolkata) in 1690. In 1669, the EIC obtained a lease from King Charles II on the "manor of East Greenwich," a group of islands known to the Portuguese as "Bombaim" (later christened Bombay by the English and now called by its local name, Mumbai) "on payment of the annual rent of 10 pounds in gold on the 10th of September each year." That short-sighted English monarch had received the islands as part of the dowry in 1661 when he married the Portuguese princess Catherine of Braganza and had not known what to do with the distant fishing communities. The three factory towns—Bombay, Madras, and Calcutta—came later to be known as the headquarters of the three "presidencies," so-called because they were the headquarters of the president of the council of merchants at each of those places. Their primary function was trading, with the object of raking profits and declaring better dividends year after year for the EIC's stockholders. They brought metals such as lead, zinc, silver, and copper to the three Indian ports and exchanged them for textiles and silk, pepper and spices, sugar and opium, the last destined mainly for the markets of China.

The first half of the seventeenth century was not very profitable for the English enterprise. They had first to deal with the Portuguese dominance in coastal, particularly western, India as well as their hold over Ormuz, the gateway to the Middle East. The English wrested Ormuz from the Portuguese in 1622 with the help of the shah of Persia. Portugal had been quite subordinate to Spain, as the crowns of the two countries were united from 1580 to 1640. This was the period when the Portuguese interests were neglected by the Spaniards. The Portuguese saw the wisdom of a rapprochement with the English; in 1634, the president of the EIC at Surat and the Portuguese viceroy at Goa signed a convention that would ensure increasing cooperation between the English and the Portuguese. This relationship improved further with Portugal's independence from Spain in 1640, and a few years later, in 1654, the Portuguese, who always claimed to have the monopoly on trade in the East on the strength of the Papal Bull of the late fifteenth century, now officially conceded the right of the EIC to trade in the East. The Anglo-Portuguese relations were then cemented in 1661 by the well-known cession of Bombay by Portugal to King Charles II as part of the dowry mentioned above. It is this set of agreements that Portugal evoked in the eighteenth to twentieth centuries to claim that it was the oldest ally of Great Britain and therefore entitled to protection of their minuscule possessions in western India. In return for all the benefits the EIC received from the Portuguese, it agreed to protect the Portuguese possessions and trade from the growing power of the Dutch in the East.

For quite some time, the EIC's policy was noninterference in politics, whether in England or India. In 1688, the EIC's directors backed the wrong horse, James II, during the Glorious Revolution. Unrelated to that event, two years later, Sir Josiah Child, a company director, advocated the "establishment of British dominion in India and not over it." The EIC tried it and suffered grievously at the hands of the Mughal emperor, Aurangzeb.

But as the Mughal power declined after Aurangzeb's death in 1707, the EIC became increasingly concerned with security. Fortunately for the EIC, the Mughal emperor Farrukhsiyar was restored to health from a serious ailment in 1715 by the EIC's physician, William Hamilton. The grateful monarch issued a *firman* (executive order) allowing the EIC to rent additional territory around Fort William in Calcutta, duty-free trade up to 3,000 rupees in Calcutta and up to 10,000 rupees in Madras, Hyderabad, and Surat. More significantly, the EIC was allowed to mint coins in Bombay that could be circulated throughout the Mughal Empire. The *firman* was regarded as the Magna Carta of the company. It contributed to the rapid growth of the company's activities and responsibilities in all three presidencies, particularly in Calcutta and Madras. For their self-defense, they built or strengthened the outer walls, turning the factories into forts; they also raised a native militia.

In order to meet the rising expenses, they raised local customs duties, coined money, and acquired additional territory to grow food for the garrison. Within the fort and its environs, the company "ruled," exercising sovereignty within a sovereignty. By 1735, Calcutta's population rose to more than 100,000.

The development from factory to fort, from trade to territory, in the second quarter of the eighteenth century was not limited to the English. Their worldwide rivals—in Europe, in North America, and in the East—the French, did likewise. It was no coincidence that some of the French factories were located not too far from those of the EIC: French Chandernagore near the English Calcutta, both lying in the jurisdiction of the Nawab of Bengal; French Pondicherry near the English Madras, both located in the kingdom of the Nawab of Arcot. In Bengal, the English were better located than the French and the Dutch at Chinsura. Their Calcutta (Fort William) settlement was further down the river; the French and the Dutch ships had to pass it before getting to their own factories.

The first to think of India in the wake of Mughal decline as a weak polity capable of acquisition by an ambitious power as a huge colonial enterprise for political domination and economic exploitation was a Frenchman, Joseph Dupleix, governor-general at Pondicherry in 1742. He wanted to outwit the English and establish France as the dominant power in India and the East.

European Position in the Middle of the Eighteenth Century

What was the European position in India in the middle of the eighteenth century? The mode of address by the EIC's president of the Bengal council to the Nawab of Bengal in 1748 would show their relative status: "I, the smallest particle of sand, John Russel, President of the East India Company, with his forehand at command rubbed on the ground."[2] Nor was the British naval or military position paramount. In 1738, the British naval authorities on the west coast reported that the naval strength of Sambhaji Angria, the Maratha naval commander, was far greater than their own. Angria had defeated both the Portuguese and the British in 1738. The Marathas (Peshwas) had wrested the extensive Portuguese "Northern Province" of Bassein in 1739. In the middle of the eighteenth century, the Peshwas were the dominant power in most of northern India including a kingmaker's position at the Mughal court.

The English and the French were ranged in three European conflicts on rival sides: the War of the Austrian Succession (1740–1748), the Seven Years' War (1756–1763), and the French Revolution and Napoleonic Wars (1789–1814). In all three conflicts, there was an Indian dimension in which the French and the English would face each other for territorial and power prizes in a seemingly autonomous theater yet, in reality, not so obviously competing for colonies that would serve the rival needs of the incipient Industrial Revolution in the two European countries.

India's then fractious and weak political situation would yield the two European powers an opportunity to resolve the question of ascendancy, not so much for commercial gains but for political power in Bengal and on the Coromandel Coast. The Seven Years' War coincided with succession struggles both in Bengal and in Arcot, where the French and English had important factories.

THE AGE OF CONQUEST, 1757–1848

Bengal and the English

The English and French intervention in the succession disputes in Arcot and especially in Bengal represented their first major political intervention, resulting in the so-called Battle of Plassey in 1757, with the English emerging as the European power that would be dominant in India. The details of that intervention also showed the English morality of the time, which was not shy of corruption, double-dealing, and forgery and emphasized the ends, whatever the means.

Bengal at that time, only nominally subservient to the Mughal emperor, was, for all purposes, independent. In 1756, the Nawab of Bengal, Alivardi Khan, died, and his youngest daughter's husband, Siraj-ud-Daula, succeeded him. Alivardi Khan had no sons, only three daughters, and two sons-in-law died soon after. That should have ended palace intrigues but for the fact that Siraj, like his father-in-law, was not at all conversant with world affairs and had no appreciation of the military strength of the Europeans, whom he tended to regard like most others in India did, as traders. Realizing the potential for conflict as part of the Seven Years' War, the English and the French had begun to fortify their respective settlements. Siraj-ud-Daula was piqued that the English had approached the rival faction at his court for cooperation. The nawab ordered both the European parties to stop the efforts to strengthen their defenses.

The French replied with a friendly note; the English refused to comply. Thereupon, the nawab sent a large force to capture the English factory at Cossimbazar and attack Calcutta. Going by the European accounts, the nawab had no military strength. His forces, however, quickly overwhelmed Calcutta on June 16, 1756, forcing the white population to flee to the security of Fort William. Soon, the Englishmen, after sending their families down the river to Fulta, chose to remain in the fort, now led by a former surgeon, Commander John Zephaniah Holwell. The nawab's army took over the fort and confined the English to a room for one night. This was the infamous Black Hole of Calcutta. Holwell's account stated that there were 146 persons in a small room he called the Black Hole, eighteen feet

long by fourteen feet. Of the number, 123 died of suffocation, leaving only 23 survivors. The story, still being reproduced in many English history books, has been exhaustively researched and analyzed by Brijen K. Gupta in the *Journal of Asian Studies*.[3] His figure of persons involved was 64, of whom 43 died. Even that kind of inhuman act would be inexcusable. There is no proof that Siraj-ud-Daula was personally involved in the sordid event.

The English, now based in Fulta, conspired with Siraj's enemies and other important persons at his court and in his army. Thus, they befriended Manikchand, the officer Siraj left in charge of Calcutta; Jagat Sheth, a most important banker; and Omichand, a rich merchant of Calcutta. The English appealed to the nawab for the restoration of their trading privileges, and the nawab agreed.

The Emergence of Robert Clive as the "Hero" of Plassey

The Bengal Council received the most valuable assistance from its counterpart in Madras, which decided to send a large expedition under the command of Robert Clive and Admiral Charles Watson. By now, the Englishmen at Fulta were not in favor of a military attack against the nawab, who had already agreed to restore the East India Company's trading privileges in Bengal. This was not satisfactory to the ambitious Clive, who asked for reparations for the losses incurred as a result of the nawab's attack against Calcutta and Cossimbazar, as well as the restoration of all the privileges ever granted to the EIC. Clive retook Calcutta in January 1757 and plundered Hooghly. In a conciliatory mood, Siraj-ud-Daula himself went to Calcutta and signed with the English the Treaty of Alinagar on February 9, 1757, by which all the privileges and immunities that Clive had requested were granted. Siraj presumed that there would be no reason for any belligerence on the part of the English.

By November 1756, the two European parties had received news that the Seven Years' War had broken out. Thereupon, the English occupied the French factories at Chandernagore despite Siraj-ud-Daula's objections on the grounds that he was obliged to protect the French interests as well. The nawab did not want to abandon the French, because he thought of the circumstances in which they could be of help in a conflict with the English. In fact, much to the chagrin of the English, he gave the French refuge at his court.

Clive now sought to replace Siraj-ud-Daula with his own candidate, Mir Jafar. He hatched a conspiracy with the help of Mir Jafar and another general, Rai Durlabh, as well as the banker Jagat Seth. An official treaty was drawn up in June that stipulated the rewards the new nawab, Mir Jafar, would give to the various officials of the EIC in Calcutta. The proceedings were momentarily

held by the avaricious Omichand, the prosperous merchant, who had brokered the treaty and who wanted a large share of the amount coming from Mir Jafar. Admiral Watson refused to sign any such agreement. Thereupon, Clive forged Watson's signature and handed the paper over to Omichand.

The nawab still trusted Mir Jafar, the chief commander of his forces. He sent him at the head of his forces to meet the English forces under Clive marching from Calcutta. The two forces "clashed" at Plassey, the mango grove on the banks of the Bhagirathi River on June 23, 1757. Mir Jafar and Rai Durlabh stayed out of the battle, which from the nawab's side was waged by a small force under Mir Madan and his adviser, a French officer. Madan lost his life on the battlefield. When the news reached the nawab, he consulted with Mir Jafar, who advised closing the campaign and negotiating with the English. As the historian K. M. Panikkar puts it, the Battle of Plassey was hardly a battle; it was a transaction in which the nawab's commanders had agreed for personal gain to betray their master.[4]

THE BLACKEST CHAPTER IN BRITISH INDIAN HISTORY

The quarter century from Plassey in 1757 to the passing of the Pitt's India Act in 1784, which monitored the EIC's rule in its new Indian possessions, is rightly called the "blackest chapter in British Indian history."

The Battle of Plassey and Clive's Plunder of Bengal

Following the success of the conspiracy at Plassey, Mir Jafar, the protégé of the English, became the Nawab of Bengal, with an English "resident" stationed at his court, thereby setting a pattern for the future arrangements between the English and the Indian princely states. For all intents and purposes, the new nawab was a puppet ruler, all major decisions being made by Clive, whose position was anomalous, until he would be declared the governor of the company's affairs in Bengal in 1758. Significantly, the Nawab of Bengal bestowed sovereignty of the EIC over Calcutta.

Based on company records, details of the financial "benefits" the EIC officials received or appropriated are available. Clive received in cash 234,000 English pounds, a *jagir* (fief) worth 30,000 English pounds annually, and a title of nobility. The English officers received a sum of 1,238,575 pounds. By 1760, EIC officials would accuse the nawab, Mir Jafar, of failure to give them additional presents. The "permanent" governor, Henry Vansittart, took steps to replace Mir Jafar with his son-in-law Mir Kasim. That accomplished, company officials extorted a further 200,269 pounds; Governor Vansittart pocketed 58,333 pounds. Three years later, in 1763, the English officers received further "presents" worth 500,165 pounds. In eight years, the English army officers took as forced presents 2,169,665 pounds in addition to claims of 3,770,833 pounds.[5] Clive's first term in India ended in 1760. He returned to England a great hero.

Three years later, Mir Kasim fell out of favor with the English, who had insisted that they have preferential duties. Kasim's proposal to abolish the duties altogether would not serve their purpose, which was not to allow any other traders, Indian or European, to compete with them. In the middle of 1764, the English forces clashed with Kasim's, and the latter suffered reverses. Nawab Mir Kasim fled to Oudh, where the nawab there and the Mughal emperor, Shah Alam II, agreed to help Mir Kasim to recover Bengal from the English. In what was a real confrontation between Indian and English forces and a battle far more consequential than that at Plassey, the Mughal forces were defeated at Buxar on October 22, 1764.

Clive's corrupt practices opened the floodgates of corruption for the company's European officials of all ranks. The Nawab of Bengal was forcibly made to issue a *firman*, giving the EIC the right to trade throughout Bengal without the payment of toll taxes. This had originally been granted in 1717 by the Mughal emperor Farrukhsiyar but was strictly applicable only to external trade and not domestic trade within Bengal. Such authorizations, called *dastaks*, had for quite some time, been abused by applying the privilege to domestic trade and, worse, by selling the *dastaks* to Indian merchants who misused them for claiming similar exemptions. The EIC had, from the beginning of its operations in the East, allowed its officials of all ranks the privilege of private trade. They now claimed the same privilege as the company in regard to transit dues and tolls. In the post-Plassey period, company officials quickly used these exemptions and others to monopolize the entire internal trade in Bengal and made fabulous profits not for the company but for themselves. Mir Jafar and later Mir Kasim protested the enormous loss in revenue, but company officials had become a law unto themselves.

Clive and the Diwani of Bengal

To put an end to such practices, the EIC in England sent Robert Clive to India in 1765 for the second time as governor of Bengal. Critics have called him a poacher turned gamekeeper. Clive could only marginally remedy the situation, but he could not clean up the administration that had become thoroughly corrupt and callous. His most important achievement was to make a settlement with the Mughal emperor following the debacle of the latter's forces in 1764. By the Treaty of Allahabad of August 12, 1765, Clive restored the Nawab of Oudh to his throne on payment to the EIC of 50 lakhs of rupees. His territories of Allahabad and the neighboring areas were detached from his state and given to the Mughal emperor, Shah Alam II. In return, the latter gave the EIC the *Diwani* (the right to collect the revenues) of Bengal, which then included Bihar and Orissa. This created a "dual government" in Bengal. The EIC, as *Diwan*, would collect the revenue; its excesses in doing so and its adverse impact on the population would not be the EIC's responsibility but that of the nawab's officials, who would still be in charge of administration and justice.

With the *Diwani*, the rape of Bengal was official. The EIC officials now lived like "nabobs," complete with their own little courts and the dancing girls and armies of domestics whose jobs ranged from massaging and bathing the *sahibs* (bosses) to making noises on their hunting expeditions so as to confuse the animals, making them easy prey. As for profits, they would do anything to push them to their benefit.

The plunder was not limited to the nawab's treasures. The EIC's officials looted the wealth of the landlords and feudal potentates in the interior. It is estimated that the draining of capital ruined trade and industry in Bengal. "From 1765 when the Company received the *Diwani*, the surplus revenues of Bengal was invested in purchasing the articles exported from India by the East India Company. By 1780, when this drain of wealth finally ceased, its amount exceeded ten million [pounds]."[6]

The news of the ruin of Bengal's manufactures and trade, the series of famines, and the miserable condition of peasants reached England, where the conscience of some persons was stirred. The famine of 1769–1770 killed one-third of the population of Bengal. Writes Ramsay Muir, professor of modern European history at the University of Manchester: "One-third of the population is said to have died and there is reason to believe that the sufferings of the population were increased both by the severity with which the land revenue was collected and by the unscrupulous profits which some of the Company's servants made out of the needs of the people."[7]

The famine was created by the EIC servants' monopoly of provisions. Referring to it, Horace Walpole, a noted contemporary politician and author, said, "We have outdone the Spaniards in Peru. They were at least butchers on a religious principle, however diabolical their zeal. We have murdered, deposed, plundered, usurped—nay, what think you of the famine in Bengal, in which three millions perished, being caused by a monopoly of the provisions by the servants of the East India Company?"[8]

The higher classes in Britain, however, were more concerned with the effect of the new money flowing from India on British politics. One of those concerned was Robert Clive, who had returned to England at the age of thirty-five and in a bid to rise through the ranks of the fairly corrupt politics of Britain, already tainted by pocket boroughs and rotten boroughs,

purchased 200 shares of the East India Company at 500 pounds each and distributed them to members of Parliament. Other EIC returnees imitated Clive. The new nabobs bought their way into the upper reaches of English society and politics, which was what bothered the establishment. In decrying the newcomers, the Earl of Chatham, the Elder Pitt, said, "The riches of Asia have not only Asiatic luxuries but also Asiatic principles of government. Importers of foreign gold have entered the Parliament. . . . India teems with inequities so rank as to smell to earth and heaven."[9]

Parliament took up a motion to discuss Clive's actions in India. Clive defined himself thus:

In a country where money was plentiful, where fear was the principle of government, and where arms were ever so victorious, it was no wonder that the lust of riches should readily embrace the professed means of gratification or that corruption and extortion should prevail among men who were the uncontrolled depositories of irresistible force.

Clive said when he moved between piles of gold and precious stones, he did not take so much as would make the nawab poor. He was astounded at his own moderation. In judging his honor, he said he hoped that the members of Parliament would remember their own. Was he referring to the stock he had distributed among them? After a whole night's debate, Parliament exonerated Robert Clive of any wrongdoing.

All this had not prevented the British Parliament from demanding in 1767 from the EIC an annual payment of 400,000 pounds in order for the company to keep its monopoly on trade. Thereby, the state claimed a share in the Indian spoils. The government was not aware that the company's expenses had mounted from 700,000 pounds in 1765 to 1.7 million pounds in 1772. The surplus revenue from Bengal had been transported to England in the form of raw materials, and it was not the EIC so much as its servants who were lining their pockets. The EIC was bankrupt; it applied in 1772 for a government subsidy of 1 million pounds.

The Regulating Act of 1773

On examining the EIC's financial conditions, the Parliament's Select Committee recommended a subsidy of 1.4 million pounds, which was approved in 1773 by the Parliament along with an act to regulate the company's affairs. It was a hurried action. More careful study was made preceding the Pitt's India Act of 1784.

The act of 1773 was the first attempt in the EIC's 173-year history that Great Britain was regulating its affairs. Its provisions were briefly to centralize the EIC's affairs in India. Accordingly, the Bombay and Madras presidencies were placed under Calcutta, which would be the headquarters of the EIC's operations in India with a governor-

general (GG) and a council, which had all the powers except to declare or settle a war. In reality, it did not prevent the GG-in-Council from leading into war.

British Expansion in India

Despite the repeated assertion of the EIC in England that further territorial acquisitions were detrimental to the company's interests, expansion continued. Historians have wondered what made the British proconsuls such as Hastings, Cornwallis, and Wellesley go on an unrelenting spree of conquest. Then there is the question of why and how the indigenous powers fell one after another to the British military juggernaut until by 1818, the major post-Mughal indigenous powers such as the Marathas, the Nizam of Hyderabad, and Tipu Sultan of Mysore were all vanquished, leaving the Sikhs as the last major power to be overwhelmed by 1848.

How did so much territorial expansion take place despite express instructions not to do so? Could it all be ascribed to the aggressive personality of the men-on-the-spot who claimed, justifiably enough, that they knew the ground realities better and had to take action without waiting for orders from home? The tyranny of distance worked in favor of the governors-general; the sailing ships that plied in the pre-Suez and pretelegraph days took two and a half to three months each way. Meanwhile, the after-the-event reports from the governors-general rationalized their actions on the grounds of security of the company's territories. There was "turbulence" across the frontier whether it was the Marathas or Tipu Sultan, threatening the Pax Britannica in the British-ruled domains. The situation brooked no delay and could not await reporting to London and getting its orders. Besides, as the company's directors and later (after 1784) the government-appointed Board of Control observed, most, if not all, of the acquisitions were made with the use of Indian British-trained *sepoys* (soldiers) and without expenditure to the British, who always recovered the costs from the fallen foe. The argument of the "turbulent frontier," which was a variation of the Turner thesis on western expansion in the United States, was advanced by an eminent British Empire historian of the second half of the twentieth century, John S. Galbraith, to explain a lot of expansion in the world.[10]

Expansion Continues with the Subsidiary System

Expansion went apace on those lines, especially during the Napoleonic Wars when Marquis of Wellesley, the brother of Arthur Wellesley, the Duke of Wellington, became the GG of India (1797–1805). The GG was helped by yet another brother, Henry, in his Indian campaigns. His arrival coincided with Napoléon's expedition into Egypt. Intercepted messages had revealed the agreement between Napoléon and Tipu Sultan of Mysore to attack their common en-

emy, the British. It was Napoléon's feeling that if the British were dislodged from India, it would be easier for him to defeat them in Europe as well.

Wellesley used a system called the Subsidiary System that had been employed by Napoléon in seeking the support of eastern European states in which he subsidized them to raise troops for him. Wellesley turned the concept around, called it the Subsidiary System but achieving his aims of forging alliances without giving any subsidy. In the process, he enlarged the British possessions. He first experimented with his plan in Oudh by asking the ruler to disband all his troops, including foreign advisers, and instead accept British-trained troops. In order to facilitate payment of their expenses, he should cede to the British a certain portion of his state. The ruler, such as Oudh, would be required to accept a British resident at his court, who should be consulted on all matters. Such a stratagem guaranteed the security of the state for the ruler, while the British, at no cost to themselves, divested him of his sovereignty. In a short half-dozen years, Wellesley had cajoled or coerced several important rulers, including the Peshwa Bajirao II, the Nizam of Hyderabad, Bhosle of Nagpur, Holkar of Indore, and Scindia of Gwalior. Wellesley had usurped the role of the *peshwa* in settling the disputes among the former Maratha subsidiary states of Nagpur, Indore, and Gwalior. In some cases, Wellesley played on their rivalries, in some others mutual fear and jealousies. By the Treaty of Bassein in 1802, Peshwa Bajirao II had accepted the overlordship of the British. That marked the virtual end of the Maratha power; the formal end came in 1818 when the Maratha state was confiscated and the *peshwa* exiled to distant Bithur in Uttar Pradesh.

There was one opponent the British were left with, and that was the intrepid Tipu Sultan of Mysore. He was among the few Indian rulers of his time who realized that the real enemy from a long point of view was the British and that all efforts should be made to thwart their ambition. He was educated and spoke several languages. Tipu found himself tricked by Wellesley, who had gotten the Nawab of Seringapatam to sign a subsidiary alliance; the same was repeated in the Karnataka as well as in Tanjore. Tipu found that half of his allies had been whittled away. He responded most favorably to Napoléon's proposals of an alliance. On his own, Tipu sent emissaries to Arabia, Afghanistan, Turkey, Mauritius, and the French court at Versailles. Some Frenchmen arrived in the port at Mangalore in April 1799 to join Tipu's army as advisers.

With evidence of Tipu's alliance with Napoléon, Wellesley offered Tipu a Subsidiary Alliance. The proud Tipu refused. Two forces were sent against his state of Mysore. Tipu took refuge in nearby Seringapatam. He died fighting in May 1799. His sons were de-clared disqualified to succeed him on the grounds that Tipu's father, Hyder Ali, had usurped the kingdom. A scion of the old Hindu ruler was installed, and a subsidiary treaty was forced on him after he agreed to cede large tracts of territory surrounding Mysore to the British.

By 1818, more than two-thirds of the subcontinent was under the British, under direct control or under indirect influence. The territories directly administered would be called British India, painted red on the map. The territories indirectly governed with the prince on the throne, completely under the influence of the British resident, were called the princely states, painted yellow on the map, the British "informal empire." The princely states were, in most cases, at least in the case of large states, separated by British India. The princes, isolated from each other, had to get the approval of the resident for any correspondence, including marriage "alliances" with another princely family. The internal administration of the state was left to the prince and his court. If he defaulted on his payment to the British troops, there would be a further demand to alienate some of his territory to British India.

Warren Hastings and Orientalism

Thinking Indians were not as concerned about the trial and impeachment of Warren Hastings, who had flouted the EIC directors' wishes, as they were about his deliberate steps to promote Orientalism. Throughout his long term as governor-general (1774–1785), he encouraged the EIC's employees, such as Charles Wilkins (1749–1836), to study and publish his research in Sanskrit studies. He asked Nathaniel Brassey Halhed, the first serious student of Bengali, to translate a Bengali law digest into English, in order for the company's judges to know the existing laws of Bengal and reduce their dependence on local translators, who may be prejudiced for or against the litigants. Hastings officially established a *madrasa*, a school in Calcutta for the study of Arabic and Muslim law. His successor, Cornwallis, approved the Sanskrit College at Benares (now Varanasi) for the study of Sanskrit and Hindu law.

Most notable was his encouragement and support of Sir William Jones (1746–1794), a judge of the Supreme Court in the latter's foundation of the Asiatic Society of Bengal (later the Bengal Branch of the Royal Asiatic Society of Great Britain and Northern Ireland, which itself was established in 1823), whose chief aim was to promote and publish research in Sanskrit. Jones had learned Arabic and Persian while at Harrow, and he would know Hebrew and Greek before coming to India. He was also a talented jurist and came to India in that capacity to be a judge. Master of many languages, he now studied Sanskrit. In his first address to the society, he showered praise on Sanskrit,

which he lauded for its "wonderful structure; more perfect than the Greek, more copious than the Latin and more exquisitely refined than either."[11]

Hastings was not interested in Indian culture per se, but he believed the information he learned could be useful for administering a country so different from Britain. In fact, but for a handful of genuine Orientalists such as Jones and Wilkins and later Elphinstone and Munro, Eastern learning was regarded as something fundamentally different from Western, and it was believed that there was very little for the West to learn and benefit from Eastern learning. Hastings's real motivation is brought out in a letter he wrote in 1784:

> It is not very long since the inhabitants of India were considered by many, as creatures scarce elevated above the degree of savage life; nor, I fear, is that prejudice yet wholly eradicated, though surely abated. Every instance which brings their real character home to observation will impress us with a more generous sense of feeling for their natural rights, and teach us to estimate them by the measure of our own. But such instances can only be obtained in their writings; and these will survive when the British dominion in India shall have long ceased to exist.[12]

In the period of the EIC's history before the territorial conquests, the company had relied overwhelmingly on Indian translators of materials in the local languages or Persian when dealing with the Muslim governments. The company's officials had primarily confined themselves to the presidency cities of Bombay, Madras, and Calcutta. The need for learning the local languages was further obviated by the Indian merchants bringing business to the EIC, which enjoyed the extraterritorial status of the company and its exemption from payment of transit and toll taxes at least since 1717. With the responsibility for administration and justice, the relevance of the languages as well as of ancient learning became patent to the company's officials.

The first generation of Orientalists, as they were now called, produced an array of translations, including Wilkins's *Bhagavad Gita* in 1784 and *Hitopadesa* three years later. Jones translated Kalidasa's *Sakuntala* in 1789 (three editions within twenty years) and *Gita Govinda* three years later. *Sakuntala* created a great commotion in Europe's intellectual circles, as Goethe, who held it on his head and danced, and Herder introduced it to others with superlative praise. Important was the posthumous publication of Jones's translation and editing of Manu's laws under the title *Institutes of Hindoo Law* in 1794. The society had an extraordinary array of scholars of Indology such as Henry Colebrooke (1765–1837) and Horace H. Wilson (1789–1860), who published in the society's *Asiatick Researches*. Most notable were the researches of James Prinsep (1799–1840),

who deciphered the Brahmi script in 1837 that helped reading Asokan inscriptions, and the work of Alexander Cunningham (1814–1893), who is called the father of Indian archaeology, who labored in India from 1831 to 1885. His methods were not satisfactory by later standards, but his work was critical and of great value to generations of later archaeologists. Similar work was done by the Asiatic Society of Bombay and of Madras.

Interest in ancient Indian studies spread rapidly to the continent of Europe. In 1795, the government of the French Republic, despite the turbulent conditions, established the École des Langues Orientales Vivantes; the first chair in Sanskrit was established at the College de France in 1814. A French scholar, Abraham-Hyacinthe Anquetil-Duperron (1731–1805), first translated four Upanishads from Persian and later translated and published fifty Upanishads directly from Sanskrit in 1801. It was from Alexander Hamilton, on parole in France, that the German Friedrich von Schlegel (1772–1829), learned Sanskrit.[13] The Schlegel brothers' enthusiasm was responsible for establishing a number of Sanskrit professorships in German universities. In England, Sanskrit was taught at the EIC's training college at Hertford. The first chair was at Oxford in 1832 to which Horace H. Wilson of the Asiatic Society of Bengal was appointed. Other British universities followed suit in establishing chairs in Sanskrit studies. As mentioned before, the Royal Asiatic Society of Great Britain and Northern Ireland, which would become the parent of the three societies in India and of numerous others in Malaya, Singapore, and Hong Kong, was established in 1823. The most well-known of English scholars in ancient Indian studies was the German-born Max Müller (1823–1900), professor at Oxford, who edited the massive Rig-Veda and the series Sacred Books of the East in fifty-one volumes, published, partly posthumously, by Oxford between 1879 and 1910. Among his other notable works were *History of Ancient Sanskrit Literature* (1859–1860) and *India: What It Can Teach Us* (1883).

Britain Establishes a Board of Control for India

The reports of Warren Hastings's aggressive war policy made the government and Parliament in Great Britain take a fresh look at Indian affairs and take measures to establish some statutory control. The result was the more well-conceived Pitt's India Act of 1784, which established a Board of Control whose members would be appointed by the government. Hereafter, all correspondence from the EIC's Board of Directors to the governor-general in India and vice versa would be routed through the Board of Control. So would all major appointments be made with the knowledge and "approval" of the Board of Control. The new arrangement virtually brought the substance of power into the government's hands, leaving the shadow of authority with the company. In fact, the act established a government-corporate partnership, with government having the better hand.

The Regulating Act of 1773 had provided for a review and renewal of the EIC's charter every twenty years. Accordingly, the charter came up for renewal in 1793. There was no major change except that missionaries would be allowed into India with a license. In 1813, the company's monopoly on Eastern trade, except for the China portion, was abolished because of the clamor among business circles in England, whose trade had suffered because of Napoléon's continental blockade. In 1833, the act said that the Indian empire existed for the Indian people, who would hereafter be recruited into service without discrimination in regard to race. The company's remaining monopoly on trade to China was ended.

In 1853, the EIC's charter was renewed without a definite date of expiration. There was a growing feeling that the Board of Control was practically in charge of India without any responsibility for its action to Parliament. The act, therefore, made the EIC administrator in trust for the Crown until Parliament established a "responsible" mechanism. That opportunity came within five years with the Great Uprising of 1857 and Parliament's decision to dissolve the company and authorize the "Crown" to take over the direct administration of India.

NOTES

1. K. M. Panikkar, *Asia and Western Dominance* (London: George Allen and Unwin, 1953).

2. Ibid., 94.

3. Brijen K. Gupta, "The Black Hole of Calcutta," *Journal of Asian Studies* 19, no. 1 (November 1959): 53–63.

4. Panikkar, *Asia and Western Dominance*, 100.

5. R. C. Majumdar et al., *An Advanced History of India*, 3d ed. (London: Macmillan, 1967), 800.

6. Ibid., 800.

7. Ramsay Muir, *The Making of British India* (Manchester: University of Manchester Press, 1923), 81.

8. A. Mervyn Davis, *Strange Destiny: A Biography of Warren Hastings* (New York: G. P. Putnam's, 1935), 76.

9. *The Cambridge History of India* (Cambridge: Cambridge University Press, 1934), 5:187. Chatham was himself nouveau riche—his grandfather bought the Old Sarum diamond from India and was known as "Diamond Pitt."

10. John S. Galbraith, "The 'Turbulent Frontier' as a Factor in British Expansion," *Comparative Studies in Society and History* 2, no. 2 (January 1960): 157–62.

11. Lord Teignmouth, ed., *The Works of Sir William Jones*, 13 vols. (London: John Stockdale and John Walker, 1867), 3:34.

12. Warren Hastings to Nathaniel Smith, October 4, 1784, in *The Bhagavat-Geeta; or, Dialogues of Kreeshna and Arjoon*, translated by Charles Wilkins (London: C. Nourse, 1785), 12–13.

13. Douglas T. McGetchin, Peter K. J. Park, and D. R. SarDesai, eds., *Sanskrit and "Orientalism": Indology and Comparative Linguistics in Germany, 1750–1958*, 106–30.

The Great Uprising was called the "Sepoy Mutiny" by most British officials and writers. It was called the "First War of Independence" by some Indians and by at least one British official, Sir James Outram, who helped Havelock in the recovery of Lucknow. Using the same archival and library materials that the British scholars had a half century earlier, an Indian revolutionary, Vinayak D. Savarkar, wrote a book in 1906, calling it the First War of Indian Independence. The book was, as one would expect, banned in India and was clandestinely and widely circulated and translated. (page 240)

12

REACTION TO
BRITISH RULE

AGENTS OF CHANGE

At the end of the eighteenth century when the East India Company's domains were fast increasing and the British government was getting officially, though indirectly, involved in the governance of the EIC's territories in India, there were three major movements in Britain that had potential for international outgrowths. All three had an inevitable effect on the policy in India. These were the Evangelical Revival; the Enlightenment or Liberalism, as it was called in Britain; and the Industrial Revolution. The first two shared the belief that they were justified in imposing their morality on an alien people. It hardly bothered them that their standards of good and morality may not be universal or that it would be morally wrong to impose such standards on other societies.

The rise of evangelism was signified in the birth of missionary societies in 1795 such as the London Missionary Society and the Church Missionary Society, which believed that it was their sacred duty to spread the word of the Gospel to non-Christians around the globe. It did not bother them that such an activity could offend others who believed equally fervently in their own faith or that it was immoral to use one's political superiority to impose one's spirituality on others less militarily endowed. For them, the expansion in "heathen" India by the EIC was a blessing and an opportunity to work toward the Indian people's conversion to Christianity. The major hurdle was the EIC's two hundred–year-old policy of not mixing religion with trade or politics. The EIC did not officially permit any missionary on board its ships. If one sneaked through, the company officials sent him back to England on the next available ship.

The missionaries at least had their own supporters in Parliament, the government, and the bureaucracy. Several humanitarian societies that were not missionary but were sympathetic to them included the Aborigines Protection Society and the Anti-Slavery Society. The first opportunity for the missionaries came up when the Pitt's India Act was approved by Parliament in 1784. The act empowered the newly created Board of Control to reverse the EIC's decision and give a license to a missionary to go to India. The missionaries could not advance any further when the act of 1793 considered the renewal of the EIC's charter. On the contrary, the act stressed that the company's officials respect Hinduism and Islam, the two major religions being practiced by the bulk of its subjects. The EIC disallowed William Wilberforce's specific request to allow missionaries to go to India without a license. The company made it clear it would deport a missionary if found in the company's territories; its god still remained money, by trade or any other means. It was not until the act of 1833 renewing the EIC's charter that the requirement for a missionary to obtain a license to go to India was totally removed. The missionary societies were decidedly arrogant, fanatically holding that they were on a divinely ordained mission to eliminate heathenism, in this case Hinduism, from the face of India.

The missionaries had at least a grudging respect for Islam, being an Abrahamic and monotheistic religion. These were Protestant missionaries who, for the time being, ignored the Catholic practice of worshiping images, just as the Hindus did. The Protestant missionaries also abhorred the EIC's practice of giving financial assistance to Hindu temples, which was, in fact, continuance of the grants made under their previous regimes, both Hindu and sometimes Muslim.

The second movement was led by the Liberals, who influenced and were, in turn, influenced by the Enlightenment movement. The Liberals were secular missionaries who felt responsibility for the ruled and for their transmission of a "higher" culture, better administration, rule of law, sophisticated academic institutions, and better health care. By the second quarter of the nineteenth century, the Liberals would be dominated by the Utilitarians, led by Jeremy Bentham and including John Stuart Mill, Thomas Babington Macaulay, David Ricardo, and Thomas Malthus. The Benthamites specialized in writing constitutions, administrative frameworks and procedures, civil service rules, drafting laws, establishing a judicial system, and devising academic structures. They fervently believed that such advances were for the benefit of not just the "mother country" but the whole world. Their disciples were spread throughout the academic establishment, including the major English and Scottish universities. Young university graduates, who would take and pass the civil service examination before going to India, were overwhelmingly influenced by the philosophy of Bentham and Mills. Macaulay and James Mill (father of John Stuart Mill) worked at the India Office. Macaulay would proceed to India in the 1830s to join the Governor-General's Council and be responsible for the adoption of English as the medium of instruction in Indian schools. James Mill's *History of India* would be made mandatory reading for all members of the Indian Civil Service.

Both the Christian evangelicals and the Liberals were, in a sense, "missionaries." They fervently believed in the superiority of British institutions and in their divine or moral mission to spread the benefits of Western culture to the "benighted" subjects in India and elsewhere in the growing empire. They would be the principal agents of change in the increasingly growing British India.

Two Schools of Thought in India

The British officials in India were divided into two major schools of thought. Yet they had a common goal that was articulated by William Bentinck, a former governor of Madras and governor-general of India (1828–1835): "British greatness must be founded upon India's happiness," but not necessarily on Indian tradition or institutions.

Thus, on the one hand, there were in the 1820s a number of young scholar-administrators in India, all of them products of British universities. They were mostly Liberals who believed that the administration should be based on whatever had worked well in India in the past, including Thomas Munro, governor of Madras; Mountstuart Elphin-stone, governor of Bombay; and Charles Metcalfe, in charge of the District of Delhi and, for some time, a member of the Governor-General's Council. They studied Indian law and customs and had respect and appreciation for them. They would not blindly introduce English ideas and institutions, particularly in the fields of land tenure and law. Thus, Metcalfe plainly stated that the Permanent Settlement introduced by Lord Cornwallis in Bengal in 1793 inflicted a grave injustice on the peasants.[1] The same was true in Maharashtra, where Elphinstone applied the old laws in the former Peshwa territories. He also supported the self-governing activities of the age-old village communities, lauding them as "the first and most important feature of the Indian system."[2] He went further than most in pointing out defects in the British system of law and judiciary as it was applied to India following the Regulating Act of 1773. In the Madras presidency, Munro confirmed the traditional *ryotwari* system. Each one of these civil service officials had carefully studied the varying practices in the territory under his charge and found them to be feasible and, above all, beneficial to the common peasants. They even contemplated a time when the English would quit India, though they were in no hurry to do so. Representative of such thinking was Munro's note of 1824:

> It ought undoubtedly to be our aim
> to raise the minds of the natives and to

take care that whenever our connection with India might cease, it did not appear that the only fruit of our dominion there had been to leave the people more abject and less able to govern themselves than when we found them. . . . [N]o one [measure] appears to me so well calculated to insure success as that of endeavouring to give them a higher opinion of themselves, by placing more confidence in them, by employing them in important situations . . . without danger to the preservation of our own ascendancy.[3]

On the other hand, some powerful Liberals, mostly middle-aged, led by Bentinck, held the belief that it was the duty of the British to introduce into India what had been tried and tested in the West. The Eurocentric attitude was based not only in their innate faith in the superiority of Western ideas and institutions but also on a contempt of their Oriental counterparts. In doing so, the Europeanists argued that it would be a great dereliction of duty if the opportunity presented by British rule were not used to India's benefit and to "exalt the character of our nation."[4]

These two approaches sometimes came into conflict with each other. In their well-founded zeal, the Europeanists often demonstrated their callousness and insensitivity toward Indians. Two major decisions during Bentinck's governor-generalship demonstrate the British desire to reform India and the Indian reaction to them.

Sati

In 1829, Bentinck and his council made a Hindu practice, then prevalent among very few families, illegal. This was sati (literally, "true" wife), or suttee, cremation or self-immolation of widows on the funeral pyres of their husbands. Absent during Vedic times, it is not known when the evil practice started. It held that marriage ties were sacred and the couple would be reborn in the next life as husband and wife. It was irreconcilable with the practice of polygyny. Lord Shiva's spouse was supposed to have cremated herself because of her father's slight on her husband. She was reincarnated as Uma, again as Shiva's wife. In India, Rajputs gloried in the practice of *jauhar*, when women leaped into a sacrificial fire before men, ceremonially attired with a sacred *tilak* on their foreheads, and rode out of the gates of the fort to meet their foe in a "do or die" situation. They did not want their wives and daughters to fall into the enemy's hands.

Bentinck's minutes of November 8, 1829, on the subject of sati outlines the dilemma facing the two schools of thought in his administration:

Whether the question be to continue or to discontinue the practice of sati, the decision is equally surrounded by an awful responsibility. To consent to the consignment year after year of hundreds of innocent victims to a cruel and untimely end when the power exists of preventing it is a predicament which no conscience can contemplate without horror. But on the other hand, if heretofore received opinions are to be considered of any value, to put to a hazard by a contrary course the very safety of the British Empire in India to extinguish at once all hopes of those great improvements affecting the condition, not of hundreds and thousands, but of millions, which can only be expected from the continuance of our supremacy, is an alternative which even in the light of humanity itself, may be considered as a still greater evil.

Bentinck consulted British officials in India and at least one Indian, a great Indian, Raja Ram Mohun Roy, regarded as the father of Indian renaissance or the father of modern India. He opposed sati but advised caution, adding that the practice should be suppressed "quietly and unobservedly" by increasing the difficulties and by the indirect agency of the police. He apprehended that any public enactment would give rise to a general anxiety, that the reasoning would be "while the English were contending for power, they deemed it politic to allow universal toleration and to respect our religion, but having obtained the supremacy their first act is a violation of their profession, and the next will probably be, like the Mohammedan conquerors, to force upon us their own religion."

Bentinck concluded:

Prudence and self-interest would counsel me to tread in the footsteps of my predecessors. But in a case of such momentous importance to humanity and civilization, that man must be reckless of all his present and future happiness who would listen to the dictates of so wicked and selfish a policy. . . .

I may be permitted to feel deeply anxious that our course shall be in accordance with the noble example set us by the British Government at home, and that the adaptation, when practicable to the circumstances of this vast Indian population, of the same enlightened principles, may promote here as well as there the general prosperity, and may exalt the character of our nation.[5]

Sati was abolished in 1829, with Bentinck disavowing any intention "to conversion to our own faith. I write and feel as a legislator for the Hindus, and as I believe many enlightened Hindus think and feel."

Education: Medium of Instruction

The British had assumed some responsibility for public education in India in 1813 with an allotment of less than 100,000 rupees. The act of 1813 approving it said that it was "for revival and improvement of literature, encouragement of the learned natives of India and for introduction and promotion of a knowledge of the sciences among the inhabitants of the British territory in India." It was an ambitious goal with very little funding or will. A decade later, Mountstuart Elphinstone, who had always favored support for the traditional Indian learning, wrote:

> It may be alleged with . . . justice that we have dried up the fountain of native talent, and that from the nature of our conquest not only all encouragement to the advancement of knowledge is withdrawn, but even the actual learning of the nation is likely to be lost, and the production of former genius to be forgotten. Something should surely be done to remove this reproach.

The government's direction of education took a quantum leap with the arrival in 1833 of the well-known Liberal and writer Thomas Babington Macaulay, as a member for law on the Governor-General's Council. Soon after, he was appointed chair of a special committee to decide on the medium of instruction in public schools in India. In February 1835, the committee was divided fifty-fifty, and Macaulay used his casting vote as its chair to approve English as the medium of instruction. It was, indeed, a momentous decision. Apart from producing an English-educated elite, well versed in English law and literature, it brought the knowledge of revolutionary movements in Europe and the United States to Indians, who would, over the next century, gather in "all-India" conventions, deliberate in English, and negotiate with

their colonial masters in their own language how best and how soon to liquidate their hold over the Indian empire!

Macaulay himself was aware of the short-term and long-term consequences of the decision. In the short run, the adoption of English would produce an army of Indian *babus*, clerks to run the burgeoning administration at lower levels. In the long run, it would produce individuals, who, English in education and taste, would, he rightly predicted, demand English institutions. Indeed, they would give themselves a Western-style constitution and practice the largest parliamentary democracy in human history.

Consequences of the decision apart, the manner in which Macaulay made his "jaunty and cocksure argument" indicated the "official mind" of those who mattered in India. Macaulay admitted he had no knowledge of either Sanskrit or Arabic, the two languages in which the pre-British elite wrote and conversed. He said he had read translations and that he had consulted scholars in both those languages. He wrote in his minutes endorsing the decision of February 1835, "I have never found one among in them [Orientalists] who could deny that a single shelf of a good European library was worth the whole native literature of India and Arabia." He chose Sanskrit for an additional thrashing: "It is I believe no exaggeration to say that all the historical information which has been collected from all the books written in the Sanscrit language is less valuable than what may be found in the most paltry abridgments used at preparatory schools in England."[6]

For those who might question his choice of English over any other language, he added,

> Whoever knows that language [English] has ready access to all the vast intellectual wealth which all the wisest nations of the earth have created and hoarded in the course of ninety generations. It may safely be said that the literature now extant in that language is of far greater value than all the literature which three hundred years ago was extant in all the languages of the world together.[7]

Macaulay's statistics had no basis in fact. It was clearly an attempt to use the advantage of his reputation as a scholar to forge his way. His far less erudite committee colleagues had no means of refuting his argument. He had made an overwhelming case but without any intellectual qualms. After all, the colonial masters of India did not have to apologize to anyone. As Macaulay himself observed, "I think it clear that we are not fettered by any pledge expressed or implied; that we are free to employ our funds as we choose." He was right in his conclusion: "It is possible to make natives of this country thoroughly good English scholars, and that to this end our efforts must be directed."[8]

Measures of this kind were essentially progressive and for India's good. But the arrogance of the rulers did not allow for patience, sensitivity, or taking the subjects adequately into confidence in an effort to convince them that the reforms were essentially for their own good. Sati was an abhorrent custom but not widely practiced. As Ram Mohun Roy, an extremely enlightened man, had warned, a precipitate and peremptory official ban would be widely misunderstood by millions of people who would be apprehensive about the government's future intentions. As it was, the missionary activities were being watched with deserving suspicion. Was the government in collusion with the missionaries to turn the whole country to Christianity? The adoption of English as a medium of instruction brought its corollary that only those who knew how to read and write in English would find employment in government offices. It was an act that at once devalued Sanskrit and Arabic learning. Men who had traditionally held positions at the royal courts or in the Mughal or Maratha bureaucracy found it necessary to learn a new language in order to retain their jobs under the new dispensation. It was hard or too late for the middle aged to retool themselves. As society's leaders, they became increasingly critical of the alien rulers and their religion.

Bentinck and Macaulay left no doubt that the reforms, whether administrative, social, or economic, would conform to Western patterns. What slowed the pace of such ideologically aggressive changes was the government's preoccupation with a number of wars—in

Punjab, Afghanistan, and Burma (now Myanmar). This was to change with the end of the conflict in the Punjab in 1848.

Lord Dalhousie and the Princes

A crisis of confidence was reached by the middle of the century. By then, the British sway had enveloped the whole subcontinent. All indigenous rulers had been subdued, their territories either absorbed into "British India" directly under British administration or indirectly governed through British "residents" or political agents appointed at their courts. The territory under the latter system was called "princely India," accounting for one-third of the subcontinent. A notable fact in 1848 was the dissolution of the Sikh monarchy and the government's direct takeover of the Punjab. In fact, the Punjab was to become a laboratory of modernization under John Lawrence's "kindergarten."

The almost six hundred princely states, large and small, were interspersed by territory directly ruled by the British. The relationship with the princes was then governed by individual agreements between them and the EIC. These required the appointment of a British resident in the case of larger states such as Baroda, Gwalior, Hyderabad, or Mysore, and a political agent for a single small state or a group of small states to advise the ruler on all matters concerning the administration. All relations between princely states, including marriages, would have to be approved by the British representatives and the Office of the Governor-General. Most important, the succession to the princely throne needed to be recognized by the EIC each time it fell vacant, mostly through the death of the incumbent. There would be a new policy in regard to recognition of adopted sons as successors to the throne during the governor-generalship of Lord Dalhousie (1848–1856), which would be a cause of major apprehension and dissent among the princes and the participation of some of them in the Great Uprising commencing in 1857.

In that atmosphere of victory and glory, overconfidence and arrogance came the Marquis of Dalhousie as governor-general, arguably among the most gifted governors-general sent by Great Britain to a colony that would soon be called "the brightest jewel in the Crown." Dalhousie was truly a hardworking man, who put in sixteen to eighteen hours a day, traveling extensively on horseback despite a bad back. He penned the most detailed and thoughtful minutes, a delight for the historians of the period, and maintained a voluminous correspondence with his superiors in London as well as with his subordinates on the subcontinent.

Seemingly a man in a hurry, Dalhousie set himself to bringing the maximum territory under direct British rule and modernizing, which for him and many British rulers then and later meant Westernization. To these ends, he wanted to end the anomalies of pompous titles and misgoverned princely states. Among the anomalies was that although the British government had progressively and closely controlled the EIC's Indian affairs since 1784, the legal responsibility for whatever was happening in India was entirely that of the company. An unintended consequence of Dalhousie's actions would swiftly bring the EIC to a close. Another legal anomaly was that the British technically drew their authority in India from the Mughal emperor, whose writ, by 1848, barely extended to the limits of his palace in the Red Fort in Delhi. Therefore, Dalhousie, the governor-general of India, would have to bow down before the Mughal emperor, as a subordinate. Moreover, the British head of state was merely a queen, whereas the would-be last Mughal, Bahadur Shah, was an emperor!

During his tenure, Dalhousie introduced a number of measures for India's modernization. He had drawn up a railroad plan for the country and made beginnings in Bombay (now Mumbai) in 1853 with a rail track from Fort to Thane. He laid 4,000 miles of telegraph wires, which would help the British move troops during the Great Uprising of 1857. He inaugurated a cheap (one-half anna or one-thirty-second of a rupee) and uniform postal system throughout the country. He used Sir Charles Wood's Education Dispatch of 1854 to make the beginnings of a grants-in-aid system for schools and colleges. It was the implementation of his plan that led in 1857, the year after his departure, to the establishment of the first three Western-style universities in Bombay, Madras, and Calcutta. His administration marked the beginnings of technical education in India with the opening of the Engineering College at Roorkee.

Dalhousie reorganized the entire administration, establishing in 1852 a new Department of Public Works with a staff of civil engineers to plan and implement master projects. One of these was the Ganges (Ganga) Canal, 500 miles of navigable stream with hundreds of canals, inaugurated in 1854. Punjab, acquired in 1848, received Dalhousie's special attention.

Dalhousie was an example of a man who was at once a colossal success and an even more colossal failure, an illustration of the adage that the path to hell may be paved with the best of intentions. His departure from the subcontinent was followed by the worst crisis the British had faced up to that point in time in India. The dam burst in 1857 with the Great Uprising.

THE GREAT UPRISING

In the annals of British association with India, the Great Uprising or Mutiny of 1857–1859 stands out at the chronological midpoint, marking a watershed. In point of fact, that was not the first rebellion or violent resistance to British rule. There were several serious revolts before in different parts of the country: the Bareilly Revolt in 1816, uprisings in Chota Nagpur, Muslim movements such as the Moplah outbreaks on the Malabar Coast from 1849 to 1855, and the Santal tribal rebellion in 1855–1857. These faded in importance compared to the losses in life and property, the number of locations and area covered by the Great Uprising of 1857–1859, and its impact on the psyche of the rulers and the ruled.

The Great Uprising was called the "Sepoy Mutiny" by most British officials and writers. It was called the "First War of Independence" by some Indians and by at least one British official, Sir James Outram, who helped Havelock in the recovery of Lucknow. Using the same archival and library materials that the British scholars had a half century earlier, an Indian revolutionary, Vinayak D. Savarkar, wrote a book in 1906, calling it the First War of Indian Independence. The book was, as one would expect, banned in India and was clandestinely and widely circulated and translated.

The uprising was a violent event that continues to stir emotions among Indians and could not be ignored even by the Indian National Congress, which won India's "war" of independence with Gandhi's weapons of nonviolence and truth and may not have wanted to glorify an event marked by so much violence. During World War II when a great Indian nationalist hero, Subhash Chandra Bose, raised an army, mostly consisting of defectors from the British Indian army in Southeast Asia, the women's brigade was named after one of the principal figures of the 1857 event, Rani Laxmibai, and the slogan he chose in 1942 was the same as in 1857: *Chalo Delhi* (Onward to Delhi). In 2005, two years before the scheduled 150-year celebrations marking the Great Uprising, Bollywood made a movie, *Mangal Pandey*, based on the rebel leader of the *sepoys* at Meerut who was ordered to be executed by the colonial rulers. The movie drew one of the largest crowds, weeping and cheering, reflecting the kind of hold the uprising continues to have on the Indian mind.

To commemorate the 100th anniversary of the event, the government of independent India sponsored the writing of a book by an eminent Indian historian, R. C. Majumdar, and made all the archival documentation available to him. When he presented his book draft to the government, a joint education secretary "in charge" of the "project" refused to accept Majumdar's conclusions that the events of 1857 were far more than an army mutiny because of the nonarmy participation, though not from all over the country, and said they certainly did not amount to a war of independence. Majumdar refused to make any changes in his conclusions just to make them politically appropriate. Thereupon, the government entrusted the "project" to another eminent historian, S. N. Sen, who came basically to the same conclusions. The government published his work under the neutral title *1857,* whereas Majumdar's work was published by a commercial publisher in the same centenary year of the event. It would be safe to call it a Great Uprising.

Causes

There were both distant and immediate causes for the Great Uprising of 1857. The distant causes stemmed from the reforms initiated and implemented by the agents of change: the Occidentals and the Orientals. In general, the Occidentals dominated and were able to overcome the objections of their opponents. The adoption of English as the medium of instruction antagonized the Brahmans as a class, and the abolition of sati, although practiced by only a handful, was seen by the bulk of the Hindus as a major interference in their religion and as the work of the missionaries.

A major immediate cause of the Great Uprising was the series of actions by Governor-General Dalhousie. His well-intentioned measures to bring India in line with the modernization in England created a tide of misunderstanding without any effort to conciliate the influential indigenous sections of people. Dalhousie wanted the reforms to be applied to the whole country but felt hamstrung by the existence of the six hundred–plus princely states. Dalhousie was not alone,

nor was he the first one to yearn for total control of India by liquidating the princes. Sir Charles Napier, the conqueror of Sind in 1843, said, "Were I emperor of India for 12 years, she should be traversed by railways and have her rivers bridged. . . . No Indian Prince should exist. The nizam should no more be heard of. . . . Nepal would be ours."[9] Dalhousie decided by whatever "legal" means to lapse some states to direct British control. There were three different grounds he used for the "lapse" of a state. First was maladministration. One such state was Avadh, a large state under a Shia nawab, particularly notorious for his extravagance, dissolute habits, and incompetence. The ruler had been warned previously by William Bentinck in 1831 and Henry Hardinge in 1847 that his state would be annexed if he did not mend his ways; the threat had gone largely unheeded. Avadh was too important for any peremptory action on the part of the British, one-third of whose Bengal army recruits were from Avadh. When Dalhousie proposed to take over the administration of the state, leaving the prince with titular sovereignty, the EIC's Board of Directors authorized a full annexation without specifying what should be the prince's fate. As such, it would appear that at least in this one case, Dalhousie had not exceeded his authority.

The second kind of action taken by Dalhousie against the princes was abolition of titles such as that of the Mughal emperor Bahadur Shah in Delhi. Legally, the East India Company's authority stemmed from the grant of powers, beginning with the Diwani of Bengal in 1765, by the Mughal emperor, who sat on the throne in the Red Fort of Delhi but whose territorial control by 1848 did not extend much beyond the fort's rampart walls. Protocol required the powerful British governor-general to stand in his presence and take a much less distinguished seat in his court. Great Britain and the empire were headed by a queen, whereas the Mughal descendant in Delhi carried the title of emperor! Not willing to countenance the "indignity," and in spite of the fact that the Board of Directors balked at the idea, Dalhousie decided to abolish Bahadur Shah's title of emperor and move the defunct emperor and his family to unpretentious living conditions in nearby Meherauli. There were a couple of cases of abolition of titles, such as that of the rulers of Tanjore and Carnatic (Arcot), on the grounds that the title was personal, not hereditary. However, the action against Emperor Bahadur Shah was unique in that it marked the unceremonious formal dissolution of the Mughal empire. It shocked the princely order throughout the country; their titles too could come under Dalhousie's hammer before long.

The third measure for bringing a half-dozen princely states under direct British rule was the application of the Doctrine of Lapse, which meant that if a prince died without a biological or natural son, the state would lapse to the East India Company. The Indian tradition, particularly Hindu, was for the princes and their consorts to adopt, through an elaborate, publicly held religious ceremony, a son in case there was no biological heir. The Hindu tradition gave such an adopted son the same rights and duties that a biologically conceived son would have—most important, the right to light the funeral pyre of his adopted parents, which would ensure the salvation of their souls to a future birth. The states affected by adoption and the Doctrine of Lapse included Satara in Maharashtra, whose ruler was a scion of the almost deified Shivaji, and Jhansi in central India, where the young prince had died and his young widow had adopted an infant son. The Rani of Jhansi would be one of the principal leaders of the Great Uprising; she placed her child on her back and led her troops on horseback against the mighty British. A third important case was that of Nanasahib, adopted son of the last *peshwa,* who after his defeat in 1818 had been sent into exile to Bithur, in Uttar Pradesh, where he died in 1853. He had no territories, only a palace, courtiers, a title, and a sumptuous pension. Nanasahib and one of his retainers with the ability to lead thousands of fighting men, Tatya Tope, would be the principal leaders of the uprising.

The last straw and immediate cause of the army's mutiny centered around the issue of the greased cartridges. More than 90 percent of the troops were Hindu or Muslim. A newly introduced rifle required the user to bite the pouch containing gunpowder before emptying the powder into the barrel. The pouch was coated with grease made from the fat of either pigs, anathema to the Muslims, or cows, sacred to the Hindus. The British first denied the use of such fat; denial strengthened suspicion of a deliberate conspiracy to have the Indian soldiers, Hindus and Muslims, lose their religious affiliation and then convert them to the Christian faith. Even though the British stopped using the grease immediately, the damage had been done, and the Indians saw it as another conspiracy by the missionaries and the rulers to convert the troops (and consequently their families) to Christianity. They also believed the withdrawal of the greased cartridges was a sign of weakness and alarm on the part of the British. Many soldiers felt betrayed; they lost respect for their commanders. The effect was more distrust of the rulers on the part of the ruled; every official decision thereafter would be looked upon by the multitudes with palpable suspicion.

The princes and peasants, soldiers and Brahmans now thought that the British had made pledges for the protection of their states, property, and religion "in an hour of weakness"; they were now being revoked "in an hour of strength." Where would the British stop?

Principal Events

The Great Uprising began with the Mutiny at Meerut on May 10, 1857, when the *sepoys* stormed the British officers' premises, killed several, and burned their homes. They marched on to Delhi and took over that historic capital and proclaimed the venerable old emperor, Bahadur Shah II, the emperor of Hindustan (India). It was a very important action, because it symbolized the restoration of national authority in the eyes of those who declared their determination to oust the British from Indian soil.

The revolt spread rapidly. Within a month, the rebel troops and their supporters (hereafter referred to as the Indian side) had captured several important locations, such as Bareilly in Rohilkhand, Nasirabad in Rajasthan, Kanpur (Cawnpore), Lucknow, and Benares. The siege in Kanpur was led by Nanasahib, whose title had been withdrawn by Dalhousie, but he now proclaimed himself the *peshwa*. The siege lasted from June 8 to June 26, at which point the seventy-five-year-old commander, Sir Hugh Wheeler, surrendered on the condition of safe passage to Allahabad for himself, about four hundred men, and some women and children. Two atrocities took place on the Indian side. As the men were getting into the boats, they were killed; only four survived. Second was the incident at Bibigarh, in which a large number of women and children, who were confined there, were killed and their bodies thrown into a well. The atrocities, unforgivable as they were, aroused tremendous feelings of revenge among the British in India and in England.

Kanpur was not recovered by the British until December 6.

The British came down brutally on the "mutineers" as well as on others, notably in Delhi. As Percival Spear, a Cambridge historian puts it, "The treatment of the aged Bahadur Shah was a disgrace to a civilized nation; also, the whole population of Delhi was driven out into the open, and thousands were killed after perfunctory trials or no trials at all. . . . Ferocity led to grave excesses on both sides, distinguishing this war in horror from other wars of the 19th century."[10]

The Mughal emperor, the eighty-three-year-old Bahadur Shah II, who never wielded a weapon except the pen he used for writing beautiful poetry, was arrested at Humayun's tomb along with his sons and a grandson as prisoners of war. The arresting officer was a particularly uncouth cavalry officer, Lieutenant Hodson, who shot and killed all the Mughal princes on the specious reasoning that they were implicated in the killing of many Englishmen and women. There was, indeed, no trial, nor was there a court-martial for Hodson. The former Mughal emperor was unceremoniously bundled away to Burma, where he died at the age of eighty-seven in 1862.

The Indians attacked Lucknow but could not completely defeat the British troops, who took refuge in the residency from July 1 until November 16, when they were freed. Early in the siege, on July 4, Henry Lawrence lost his life; Henry Havelock did not arrive until

September 25 but was in turn besieged. Lucknow itself was not recaptured by the British until March 1, 1858, by Colin Campbell, who had come from England to become commander in chief of the Indian Army. Before the retaking of Lucknow, Campbell had been able to restore control over all of Avadh and Rohilkhand. In this, he received substantial assistance from Jang Bahadur of Nepal and his Gurkha regiment.

The principal leaders on the Indian side were Nanasahib Peshwa, Tatya Tope, Rani Laxmibai of Jhansi, Kunwar Singh and his brother Amar Singh (both of Jagdishpur), and Mangal Pandey, who started it all at Meerut.

The major battles against the British in central India were fought by the young Rani of Jhansi, who was joined later, in December 1857, by Tatya Tope. Leading the troops on horseback, with her infant son tied to her back, the Rani stormed out of her fort on the night of April 4, 1858. The British followed her everywhere, to Kalpi and then to Gwalior, which she had occupied with Tatya Tope and made the pro-British Scindia flee to Agra. Hugh Rose, who was in charge of the campaign against her, recaptured Gwalior. In one of the battles against him, the Rani, dressed in male attire and on horseback, died a *sowar*'s (horseman's) death on June 17, 1858, giving India the greatest female icon ever.

Tatya Tope was chased from place to place by the British for the next ten months until April 1859 when he was captured by a feudatory of the Scindias. He was hanged. As for Nanasahib Peshwa, he was known to be moving in the forests of Nepal for years, given refuge by numerous families. Some reports appeared of his death in Nepal in September 1859, marking the end of the Great Uprising.

The British had several advantages, among them the newly installed telegraph line. Thus, when the *sepoys* took over Delhi, two telegraph signalers sent a message to the Punjab government, which sent an immediate relief force to recapture Delhi. The Indian side lacked trained leaders, particularly in the field, whereas the British troops not only were well led but also had the advantage of unlimited supplies of superior guns and ammunition. The rebel leaders did not have an all-India plan, nor did they know what would ensue if they were able to push the British out of the country. The British benefited also because the uprising did not spread everywhere; large chunks of the subcontinent were quiet. Thus, the region south of the Narmada River was, on the whole, quiet. And though one regiment mutinied at Kolhapur, the Bombay Presidency remained undisturbed. Punjab, which had just seen a war with the British and had been subjugated, remained quiet; in fact, some of the Sikh chiefs helped the British in their hour of crisis; so did Gulab Singh of Kashmir, Sir Jang Bahadur of Nepal, Sir Salar Jang of Hyderabad, the Begam of Bhopal, and the Scindia of Gwalior and his minister, Sir Dinkar Rao.

Consequences

Some of the major consequences of the Great Uprising included a radical change in the formal structure of the British control over India. Thus, the era of the EIC was coming to a close, and the affairs of India were taken over by the Crown. Parliament passed the Act for the Better Government of India in 1858 by which the East India Company was officially dissolved and the affairs of India taken over by the Crown, that is, the British government. The Board of Control established under the Pitt's India Act of 1784 was replaced by the appointment of a secretary of state for India, who would be a member of the cabinet and, therefore, responsible to Parliament. Unlike any other member of the cabinet, he would have a council of fifteen (eight of them with Indian experience) to assist him in his onerous responsibilities. In practice, it was an "advisory" body whose advice was hardly sought, a body without any initiative. The secretary of state for India had a casting vote and a veto over the council. He was required annually to submit to Parliament a "Report on Moral and Material Progress in India" as well as accounts. In practice, Parliament was content to leave the Indian affairs to the governor-general and the extensive bureaucracy under the remote supervision of the secretary of state for India.

As long as their actions did nothing to foment another uprising, Parliament would be uninterested in even a debate on India.

Did the move from the company to the Crown substantially alter the colonial relationship with India or the British government's responsibility for India? In the view of most observers, the change was more of form than of substance. As the first secretary of state for India, Lord Derby, pointed out, except for the right to recall a governor-general and certain powers of "obstruction and delay," the EIC had had no ability to influence decisions in India for a long time, all powers being exercised by the government-appointed Board of Control.

The second major consequence of the Great Uprising was that there would be no future British official interference in religious matters. On November 1, 1858, the British government issued a proclamation in the name of Queen Victoria. Designed to "quiet the fears of the Indian people and Indian princes," it assured the Indian public on at least three counts: the official policy from then on would be one of religious tolerance; "ancient rights, usages and customs of India" were to be respected; and there was to be "due regard" with respect to "rights in land." Additionally, the queen disapproved of "differentiation on grounds of race or creed in the public service."[11]

Third, the Doctrine of Lapse lapsed. The princes were assured that "all treaties and engagements made with them by or under the authority of the East India Company" would be honored thereafter by the British Crown. There were to be no more annexations of princely territories. The government said in the name of the queen, "We shall respect the rights, dignity, and honour of native princes as our own."[12] To enforce this part of the proclamation, a viceroy would be sent to India. In practice, all governors-general from 1858 to 1947 doubled as viceroys. All correspondence with the princes was carried out in the name of the viceroy; all matters regarding territories directly under the British were under the jurisdiction of the governor-general.

Fourth, a general amnesty was declared. There would be no recriminations against the participants in the Great Uprising except those who were charged with directly taking part in the murder of British subjects.

Fifth, there were some significant changes made in the military administration. Thus, the armies of Bombay, Madras, and Calcutta were separated and remained so until 1893 when they were amalgamated. The ratio of Europeans to Indians was improved from one to five to one to two. Care was taken to see that no station would be without British troops. Except for a few mountain batteries, the *sepoys* were no longer in charge of artillery; in effect, it became a European monopoly.

———

NOTES

1. See Ralph B. Price, "The 'New Political Economy' and British Economic Policy for India," 411–13.

2. Mountstuart Elphinstone, *History of India* (London: John Murray, 1841), 126–27.

3. Ramsay Muir, *The Making of British India* (Manchester: Manchester University Press, 1915), 284–85.

4. Ibid., 279.

5. Ibid., 293–96.

6. G. M. Young, ed., *Macaulay's Prose and Poetry* (Cambridge: Harvard University Press, 1952), 721.

7. Ibid.

8. Ibid., 723.

9. http://acharya.iitm.ac.in/in/mirrors/vv/vvc/history_eng_html.

10. "India," in *Encyclopaedia Britannica's Guide to Normandy, 1944,* http://www.school.eb.com/dday/article–47031, p. 2.

11. "The Queen in Council to the Princes, Chiefs, and People of India," proclamation of November 1, 1858, in *Making of British India,* by Muir, 381.

12. Ibid., 383.

Naoroji wrote not only about a stifling of growth but also about a "drain" of wealth from India to Britain. This outflow, the profits of empire (what later economists would call "invisible") derived form payments to British civil and military officials, who carried their wealth back to Britain; military expenses paid by India for operations outside the country; profits from British businesses sent to Britain; a trading relationship between India and Britain, distorted by British-imposed tariffs at both ends, in which Britain reaped the largest share of the profits; and miscellaneous hidden flows of wealth out of India for insurance premiums, interest payments, and so forth.   (page 265)

13

THE INDIAN NATIONALIST
MOVEMENT, 1850–1919

NATIONALISM IN EUROPE
AND ASIA COMPARED

Nationalism was undoubtedly the single most potent, dynamic, emotive element that altered the political configuration of Asia and Africa in the twentieth century. That nationalism was, in most cases, a response to imperialism and the political and economic exploitation of the governed.

It would be difficult to provide a definition of nationalism that would be acceptable to all. Boyd C. Shafer lists ten "beliefs and conditions" present in most cases of nationalism: (1) a certain defined unit of territory; (2) some common cultural characteristics such as language; (3) some common dominant social and economic institutions; (4) a common independent or sovereign government or the desire for one; (5) a belief in a common history and in a common origin; (6) love or esteem for fellow nationals; (7) a devotion to the entity called the nation, which embodies the common territory, culture, social and economic institutions, government, and fellow nationals and is at the same time more than their sum; (8) common pride in the achievements of the nation and a common sorrow in its tragedies; (9) disregard for or hostility to other like groups, especially if they present or seem to threaten the separate national existence; and (10) a hope that the nation will have a great and glorious future.[1]

It may generally be agreed that a conscious sentiment of kinship is the bedrock of nationalism, fostered by common characteristics such as language, territory, religion, race, and heritage. Beyond this, sociologists have stressed common cultural and psychological traits or the group consciousness engendered by literature, arts, and institutions.

Modern nationalism based on a commonality of some or all of such characteristics was, by most Western accounts, bred in Europe beginning in the late eighteenth century, flowering in the nineteenth, and "degenerating" in the twentieth with European fascism and Nazism. Some scholars have, therefore, held that nationalism has been the most dynamic of all of Europe's exports to the colonial world; some others have simply described it as a "gift" of the West to the peoples of Asia and Africa. Writing about nationalism in France's Southeast Asian colonies, Virginia Thompson, just before World War II, stated: "Nationalism is undeniably the Occident's gift to Indochina. It is the most creative indigenous movement to which contact with a Western nation has given birth." A little later, Philippe Devillers regarded Vietnamese nationalism with its social and ideological underpinnings, paradoxically enough, as "the most beautiful fruit of France to Viet Nam."[2] "Export" should imply an order placed by a willing and needy importer in the colonial world; a "gift" should connote a deliberate act of kindness and generosity on the donor's part. The use of either word becomes debatable, semantically speaking, to describe the interaction between the East and the West in the area of nationalism.

Does fulfillment of nationalism among a people necessarily lead to imperialistic expansion, often provoking latent nationalist sentiment among the subjugated people? Scholars of modern European history have often described the development of nation-states in Europe as unique to the West. Was imperialism a product of such nationalism and monopoly capitalism? The race for colonies in the period from 1850 to 1914 among Western powers leading to the partition of Africa and the division of China into rival spheres of influence and Southeast Asia into colonial parcels demonstrates a nexus of nationalism and economic imperialism. A Westernized, industrialized, nationalistic Japan was infected by the bug of imperialism; so was another nation, the United States, itself born of a successful revolution against colonial rule and in the late nineteenth century, in a fairly advanced state of industrial revolution, believing in its "manifest destiny," and ready as a nation to embrace imperialism by suppressing the nascent Republic of the Philippines, making that nation of islands an American colony in 1902.

Nationalism may be neither an export nor a gift from the West to the East. But could it be that the subject peoples were overcome by a colonial power concerned because they lacked nationalism? That logic was advanced progressively in the post–World War I era as a "compensatory rationalization" of the colonial rule because imperialism had, by then, begun to be regarded as unsavory by a number of Western intellectuals. Frederick L. Schuman, a spokesman of such a point of view, writes, "All successful rebellions of colonial peoples against their masters were products of a new sense of nationhood among those hitherto innocent of any such sense of collective identity but moved by the impact of the West to initiate the dominant cult of the West and use it to achieve emancipation from the West."[3]

SPECIAL CHARACTERISTICS OF ASIAN AND INDIAN NATIONALISM

In the eyes of the anticolonial freedom fighters in Asia and Africa, nationalism was neither an export nor a gift of the West. It was partly the result of the fact and impact of imperialism, a reaction to the repressive, racial, and economically exploitative policies of their colonial masters. In most cases, paradoxically enough, those who received Western education from the colonial rulers were the ones who led the movement against those rulers. To quote Rupert Emerson: "The general conclusion is . . . unavoidable, that the groups and classes which have been most susceptible to infection by the nationalist germ are those who have been most sharply divorced from their old worlds by the impact of the new."[4]

Many of these educated elites in diverse colonial settings became collaborators, logs in the colonial service, alienated from the masses of illiterate and impoverished people whom they only grudgingly accepted as fellow subjects. Such elites were also alienated from the country's traditions and customs and, at times, its ethos and values. The leaders of the nationalist movements were not created by Western rule; they became so despite the lures of a better life that could be theirs if they had completely collaborated with the masters and become complacent with the crumbs offered them. At most, the colonial rule served as a catalyst, its negative policies triggering a patriotic upsurge among nationalists who became more articulate because of their study of their heritage. These history lessons, at times, included the efforts of their ancestors in overthrowing alien rule. The new knowledge of successful revolutions elsewhere, particularly in the Western world, helped them to devise strategies that were likely to yield dividends.

The leadership that succeeded the most was not one that adopted Western techniques completely but one that blended with the country's spiritual beliefs and practices, the economic needs of the masses, identification with their aspirations, all galvanized to participate in a "people's war," whether violent or nonviolent. Gandhi inspired thousands of other Western-educated (whether in India or in Europe) "elites" to shed their elitism and join hands with the masses in a common endeavor to overthrow the colonial rule and establish a nation-state. Gandhi's nationalism followed his abandonment of a semicollaborator role and awareness of the offensive, racial, dehumanizing British role in the Jalianwala Bagh park massacre and the loss of faith in the British form of justice.

The racially and culturally different colonial rule against which Asian and African nineteenth- and twentieth-century nationalist movements were directed was one major difference between European and Afro-Asian nationalism. The latter was at times a struggle against European imperialism, which was partly the outgrowth of European nationalism.

Afro-Asian nationalism was fueled by a commonly felt hostility toward a colonial rule imposed by a distant discriminating and economically dominant people. Above all, nationalism divided the peoples of Europe; on the other hand, nationalism united the people in India. In that sense, the British rule may be regarded as a catalyst for Indian unity and nationalism.

Another major variant in Afro-Asian nationalism absent in European experience was the nexus between communism and nationalism. This was partly a chronological consequence. Nationalist movements predated the success of Marxist philosophy in the overthrow of existing governments in favor of the dictatorship of the proletariat. The success of the Russian Revolution in 1917 and, even more significantly, the role of Lenin, author of the well-known tract *Imperialism, the Highest Stage of Monopoly Capitalism* (1917), set the stage for definition of the communist role in the nationalist movements in the colonial world. Lenin's "Theses" of 1923 further elaborated the communist countries' role vis-à-vis the nationalist movements in the colonies, with, most significantly, bold modifications by the then Indian communist thinker M. N. Roy.

Asian-African nationalism marked an advance over European or Western nationalism. The French Revolution and the American War of Independence are often regarded as marking the first great escalation of the process of nation-building. They successfully challenged the traditional institutions of monarchy (British and French) and the feudal nobility in France. More significantly, they underlined the rights and responsibilities of each citizen, who was given the "natural" right to participate in the governmental process through the right of representation. This made the nation-state more broadly based in its political sanctions than ever before.

The essence of modern nationalist movements in Asia and Africa is the quest for freedom—political, social, and economic—for all people. In most cases of the new nation-states, decolonization and achievement of independent status were almost coterminous with granting of political rights—to all members of the nation-state above the age of eighteen, irrespective of sex, color, or religious persuasion. What is notable was the universal promise during the nationalist movement of granting of political rights, pulling down of social barriers, and freedom from want and hunger following the overthrow of colonial rule. In other words, the most significant difference between modern nationalism and its parallels in the premodern period is this broad-based sanction of the masses of the people, whose political, social, and economic aspirations were raised by leaders who found such a policy essential for securing the participation of the people and their sanction for the new nation-state. It was not a movement of the elite or the aristocracy but of the people that made continuation of the colonial rule untenable. It created, in the words of Hans Kohn, one of the first students of nationalism, "a state of mind in which supreme loyalty of the few is felt to be due to the nation-state."[5]

INDIA'S UNITY AND BEGINNINGS OF NATIONALISM

The factors helping the growth of Indian nationalism in the nineteenth century were diverse. Some were the result of British innovations in administration and modernization policies, and some came in the form of reaction to the Christian missionary challenge.

British Innovations Help Unification of India

The railroad network beginning in 1853 but extensively widened in the wake of the Great Uprising made for easier transportation throughout the country. It helped the British investor, who was guaranteed a return of 5 percent from the day the project began. It helped tighten the British grip on India by easing the movement of troops, making sure that the various army cantonments were linked to each other. Railroads helped the British economy to transport raw materials to the port cities for export to Britain and to distribute the British manufactures in India. On the other hand, the easy transportation helped Indian unity, making it possible for the delegates of the Indian National Con-

gress (INC) to meet annually to express themselves. The railroad network progressively helped the Indian economy as well.

The introduction of a cheap and uniform postal system and telegraphs after 1853, widened with the use of the railroad network, also had similar results in terms of better communications and the means to establish and maintain contacts among nationalist leaders and workers throughout the country.

Until the British employment of the policy of divide and rule by encouraging the birth of the Indian Muslim League (IML) in 1906, the official policy was to promote secularization in the educational system, legal institutions, civil service, and the armed forces. Additionally, the uniting element was the common use of English not only as a medium of instruction but also as a language of administration and the courts. Above all, there was the growing implementation of the rule of law, although the British government respected and retained the marriage and inheritance laws of the different communities, so as not to provoke rebellions of the 1857 kind.

Agitations Against Government Policies

Some of the British policies and administrative decisions from 1870 were marked by crass racism and discrimination, which engendered Indian resentment and fostered unity, nationalism, and anticolonialism. First came the agitation against the new restrictions on Indians entering the Indian Civil Service, in contravention of the assurances given in the queen's proclamation of 1858 and the provisions of the Indian Civil Service Act of 1861. In the 1870s, there was a growing alarm among the British rulers that the number of Indians passing the civil service examination, which was held only in Britain, was rising. This was despite the fact that they had to invest considerable sums of money, face the severe climate of England, stay away from their families, and ignore the humiliation of the discriminatory treatment in England fostered by social Darwinism, disallowing Indians to eat in certain restaurants, which put up signs such as "Indians and Dogs Not Allowed."

Already there were indications that the government would go to any extent to deny Indians from entering the civil service. Surendranath Banerjea, who had passed the civil service examination, learned that his name was removed from the roster of successful candidates. He filed a writ of mandamus in the Queen's Bench and got the name restored. He joined the civil service but was soon dismissed on a minor charge. Banerjea then joined the Indian Association of Calcutta in 1876. He used the organization to agitate against the government's announcement lowering the maximum age limit from twenty-one to nineteen, thereby gravely affecting the chances of Indians getting into the service. Banerjea took the issue to audiences in ten cities of North India. As Banerjea wrote

in his book *A Nation in Making,* "The agitation was the means; the raising of the maximum limit of age for the open competitive examination and the holding of simultaneous examinations [in England and India] were among the ends; but the underlying conception, and the true aim and purpose of the civil service agitation was the awakening of a spirit of unity and solidarity among the people of India."[6]

A major irritant to Indians was the administration of Viceroy Lord Lytton (1875–1880). Alarmed at the growth of Indian vernacular newspapers, which criticized the government policies more freely than the European-owned English newspapers, and whose numbers had increased dramatically to 644 by 1878, the viceroy issued what came to be called "the Gagging Act." The act, officially the Vernacular Press Act, empowered the magistrates to close down newspapers that promoted "disaffection against the government" or hatred between different races. No appeal was permitted. There was an uproar in India, and some of the newspapers appealed to the House of Commons for justice. Lytton's successor, Lord Ripon, eventually repealed the hated measure in 1882.

Lytton also passed the Indian Arms Act, limiting the possession of arms by Indians, while imposing no restrictions on the Europeans. The measure was widely criticized as an act aimed at "emasculating Indian manhood" besides being racist. The agitations against such measures promoted a new kind of activism in India, creating among the new leaders not only an amount of distrust of the British but also self-confidence in the agitational approach to politics.

Another official measure that brought a severe Indian reaction was the Ilbert Bill in 1883. Ilbert, the law member of the Viceroy's Council, had in response to the demands from the Indian members of the Indian Civil Service introduced a bill to stop the practice that required that Europeans outside the presidency towns of Bombay, Madras, and Calcutta be tried only by the magistrates and judges of their own race. This not only humiliated the Indian officers but also weakened their authority. In an atmosphere reeking with social Darwinism, the European community in India and Britain protested Ilbert's initiative and demanded the withdrawal of the bill. They established the Defence Association and a fund to help their agitation all over India. Ultimately, the government withdrew the Ilbert Bill and instead settled on a compromise that Indians of the rank of sessions judges and district magistrates could try the Europeans, who would further have the right to ask a high court to transfer the case from one court to another and to ask for a jury. The entire episode left a bitter taste in the mouths of educated Indians.

British Scholarship and Pride in Indian Culture

British scholarship both among the officials of the East India Company and among scholars in Britain extolled Indian scholarship and culture in ancient India. Some of it was extremely high praise that had the effect of instilling pride among Indians, who mused if the past could be so glorious for all Indians, it would be great if they could unite to make for the future glory of India. Foremost among the British first generation of scholars was Sir William Jones, judge of the Supreme Court in India and founder of the Asiatic Society of Bengal. As a philologist, he saw great affinity among Sanskrit, Latin, and Greek. In his inaugural address to the society, he said, "Sanskrit is more perfect than the Greek, more copious than the Latin and more exquisitely refined than either."[7] Jones translated Kalidasa's *Shakuntala* and several other works, including the *Manu Samhita*.

The labors of others such as Henry Colebrooke, Charles Wilkins, James Princep, and Alexander Cunningham brought numerous notable works in Sanskrit to light for the benefit of European scholars. Soon after, Professor Monier Williams established the famous center of learning on India at Oxford. Sir Edwin Arnold's work *The Light of Asia*, which went into sixty English and eighty American editions in twenty years played a substantial role in introducing India's ancient glory and religious traditions to the West.

The foremost scholar on ancient India in Britain in the second half of the nineteenth century was Max Müller, a German immigrant who was often assisted financially by the East India Company and, later, by the India Office (1823–1900).

The Role of Western Education

The most important single factor that helped the growth of nationalism was education, which blossomed in the grant-in-aid schools and after the birth of three universities—Bombay, Madras, and Calcutta—in 1857. The liberal education they provided included the study of revolutions, French and American, and the steady growth of democratic institutions and the triumph of Parliament over monarchy in Britain itself. Education helped to look beyond the intellectual cloister created by the Brahmans' narrow-mindedness born out of their vested interest. The knowledge of English opened a window on the world. With the combination of the knowledge of the greatness of ancient Indian culture, which was common to all Indians, and the study of revolutions and democratic institutions, it was no wonder that bright young Indian minds thought of application of some of those ideas to the Indian scene, to arrest the exploitation by the British rule and the unjustified subordination of the Indian intellect to that of the colonial master.

Such knowledge helped tremendously also in the Indian renaissance, the urge to revive the old, not to perpetuate those elements of the old culture that divided the Hindus or promoted the caste system, untouchability, or the low place of women in contemporary Indian society. The syncretic process between the East and the West in the religiocultural field through an assimilative educational process changed India. It marked a cultural revolution with an impact on nationalism and the urge to improve their lot in the political field. Pride in the past and hope in the future went hand in hand. The expression of new ideas often came through the vernacular press; by 1875, there were 475 vernacular newspapers.

INDIAN REACTION TO THE CHRISTIAN MISSIONARY CHALLENGE

The initial Indian reaction of those who were influenced by the Western learning and study of Christianity was to propose removing some of the "evil" practices from Hindu society. Such was the reaction of the leaders of the Brahmo Samaj, which was established by Raja Ram Mohun Roy in 1828. The second type of reaction took some Hindus to the Vedic teachings and to the advocacy of eliminating some evil practices that had been allowed in society. The Arya Samaj founded by Swami Dayanand Saraswati in 1875 represented such a reaction. The Ramakrishna Mission and the Theosophical Society, founded toward the end of the nineteenth century, would fall in a different category. Both favored eclecticism in religion, but with an emphasis on the superiority of the Indian spiritual heritage.

In this, one can see that the Hindu response to the Christian challenge came full circle from resistance, through defense by imitation, to the proud self-confidence under the Ramakrishna Mission. The Theosophical Society was a clear flattery of the Indian spiritual heritage.

The Brahmo Samaj

The Brahmo Samaj (Divine Society) was founded in 1828 by Raja Ram Mohun Roy, who was very highly esteemed by the East India Company's highest officials, who often consulted him on sensitive matters regarding Hindu society and laws. He was proficient in many languages: Persian, Arabic, Greek, Hebrew, and Sanskrit besides Bengali and English. He had spent several years in Tibet studying Buddhism. There was probably no one among contemporary Indians who could be compared to him for such versatility and scholarship. He founded several secondary schools and edited newspapers in English, Bengali, and Persian.

Roy aspired to make his Brahmo Samaj a universal house of prayer. His liberal mind saw wisdom and spiritual solace in all the great religions of the world. The missionaries misunderstood him and suggested he was an apostate, making him offers of material prosperity. When he published his book *Precepts of Jesus* with the subtitle "Being a Vindication of the Hindoo Religion against the Attacks of Christian Missionaries,"

there was an uproar among the missionaries. For three years thereafter, he was involved in a theological controversy with the scholarly Joshua Marshman. In defense, Roy published *Three Appeals to the Christian Public,* the last of which ran 303 pages and was full of citations in Greek and Hebrew. The controversy embittered Roy, who then began writing under a pseudonym, the Brahmanical Magazine or the Missionary and the Brahmin. So forceful were his arguments against the Holy Trinity that he converted to Unitarianism the Scottish missionary with whom he was translating the New Testament into Bengali. He rejected Christianity's doctrinal shell but warmly welcomed its humanitarian message. At the same time, he singled out those classic Hindu scriptures that came closest in content to an ethical monotheism, thereby offering to fellow Hindus a means of reforming corrupt beliefs without losing their self-respect.

Because of his progressive views, Roy has been called the father of modern India. His mission was not to decry the Indian heritage but to modify it, weed out the curses, or accretions, as he called them, such as idolatry, suttee, child marriage, and caste, with a plea to enlarge and enrich it by accepting all that was good and great in all other civilizations. In publicizing those portions of the Hindu scriptures that stress faith in one supreme being, Roy attempted to demonstrate that idol worship was an excrescence, not an essential part of his ancestral religion.

For two generations after Roy, Brahmo Samaj remained dominant among the Hindu elite of Bengal. During part of the time, Debendranath Tagore (the great poet's father) strengthened the Samaj, particularly in its corporate worship, through his book combining the Upanishadic and Christian spirit, emphasizing monotheism. In 1865, the Samaj split into two: the Brahmos insisted that the members discontinue wearing the sacred thread. Debendranath Tagore left and went on a pilgrimage into the Himalayas, and the Samaj came under the leadership of Keshub Chunder Sen. His period saw the peak and decline of the Samaj, as in 1878 he flouted the Samaj's known opposition to child marriage and allowed his thirteen-year-old daughter to marry a Hindu prince.

Sen defended his action, saying it was the will of God. That broke the Brahmo Samaj, as Sen's critics formed the Sadharan (General) Brahmo Samaj. He used revivalist sermons and Brahmo missionaries to spread a gospel, the New Dispensation, in 1879 that came so close to Christianity in its content that his conversion to Christianity was thought imminent.

Prarthana Samaj

The Brahmo Samaj influenced the new elite in different parts of the country, most notably in the state that has often paralleled developments in Bengal, Maharashtra, where the founders of the Prarthana Samaj (Prayer Society) held two ideals before its members: the rational worship of one god and social reform for the benefit of the disadvantaged. Unlike the followers of Brahmo Samaj, particularly under Keshub Chunder Sen, those of the Prarthana Samaj did not feel that they were establishing a new faith, but were simply a movement within the Hindu fold. They adopted the devotional, *bhakti* approach, which had remained a part of the Maratha tradition of saints: Namdeo, Tukaram, and Ramdas.

Instead of religious discourses, they focused on social reform: interdining and intermarriage among castes, remarriage of widows, and improvement of the lot of women and depressed classes. The Prarthana Samaj established a Foundling Asylum and Orphanage at Pandharpur, and opened night schools, widows' homes, and the Depressed Classes Mission. Their leader was Justice Mahadev Govind Ranade, who had a string of achievements in the fields of education and social reform. Thus, he founded the Widow Remarriage Association in 1861 and the Deccan Education Society in 1884. The latter inspired a particularly bright band of workers whose mission was the service of the country for twenty years for a monthly salary of seventy-five rupees, much less than what they could have earned elsewhere. They were called "life-workers," among them Gopal Krishna Gokhale, who would become a national figure and Gandhi's mentor, as the latter claimed. Ranade himself believed that social work must take priority over political work. He held annually his social conferences alongside the annual Congress sessions.

The Arya Samaj

The establishment of the Arya Samaj in Bombay in 1875 by Swami Dayanand Saraswati (1824–1883) took the reform movement from Brahmo Samaj's passive stance to an aggressive stance in meeting the challenge of Christian missionaries.

The swami lived his early life in Gujarat, where the Western influence was not as pronounced as in presidency cities such as Bombay and Calcutta. By fourteen, young Dayanand spoke against idol worship. At nineteen, he ran away from home because he was asked to marry. He spent the next fifteen years as a wandering ascetic. During that time, he also acquired proficiency and scholarship in Sanskrit. He regarded the four Vedas as the founts of ancient wisdom and a supreme repository of human knowledge and concluded that the social evils among the Hindus were not present in the Vedas. He saw the intellectual and religious degeneration of Indians and condemned their outdated beliefs. He was conversant with Western thinking, including in the scientific field, but held at the same time that all those ideas were already present in the Vedas, which for Dayanand Saraswati contained "all the truth."

In the process, Dayanand Saraswati antagonized both the Christian missionaries and orthodox Hindus. Like Raja Ram Mohun Roy but with altogether different arguments, he condemned the Hindu evil practices of child marriage, suttee, untouchability, and the rigid caste system on the simple grounds that they were not present in the Vedic times. He held debates with Brahman scholars in that citadel of orthodoxy, Varanasi, and humbled them. He "proved" to them that the caste system, with its unjust social gradations, the worship of idols, child marriages, and many other practices, was an accretion wholly alien to the simple and benign religion of the Vedic Aryans. He pleaded with them to work for social equality, removal of untouchability, revival of Vedic studies, and the diffusion of true knowledge. At the same time, he condemned the Christian missionaries for their conversion of Hindus to Christianity.

The swami was a practical social activist. He was most successful in his socioreligious activities in Punjab, where he established schools and colleges, which continue to flourish to this day. He gave the Indians of his time the much needed faith and pride in their culture and a hope of better days by rooting out the social evils and reestablishing a life based on the teaching of the Vedas.

The swami was physically strong and defended himself ably against swordsmen, thugs, and cobras, set against him by the orthodox Hindu groups. However, an attempt to poison him succeeded. He had accused a princely ruler of loose living; the woman who was involved managed to have ground glass added to his glass of milk. The Arya Samaj has a very large following in Punjab, Haryana, and parts of Maharashtra and Gujarat.

Ramakrishna Mission

The fourth major reform movement in the Hindu fold came from a saintly, poor priest, Ramakrishna (1836–1886), in a temple not far from Calcutta and his disciple, Narendranath Datta (1863–1902), who assumed the name of Swami Vivekanand. The latter established the Ramakrishna Mission, a monastic order dedicated to religious and social reform, with no mission to convert people. The mission has remained the most effective of all the reform movements to date.

Ramakrishna was known in Calcutta and the surroundings to have had mystical and spiritual experiences. He saw God in a variety of manifestations—as a divine mother, as Sita, as Rama, as Krishna, as Muhammad, as Jesus. He worshiped them turn by turn, suiting his dress, food, and meditation to the particular religious tradition. He found solace after twelve years of such mystical experiences. Unlike the Brahmo Samaj leaders, Ramakrishna was uneducated. He knew neither Sanskrit nor English, only his native Bengali. He was completely a child of the soil, lived the life of a traditional *rishi* (sage) with only the most essential personal pos-

sessions. Like Dayanand Saraswati, he stood for the rebirth of the ancient Indian tradition in the midst of the tide of Westernization and modernization, but unlike Dayanand, he was not militant; rather, his was a gentle voice preaching a gentle faith of selfless devotion to God and of ultimate absorption in him.

Ramakrishna's approach to God was more in the style of the *Bhakti marg*, the path of devotion, which suited everyone, educated and the illiterate, poor and the rich alike. He believed that the worship of images need not be scoffed at as idolatry; the images may be used as an excellent means of focusing one's spiritual growth. However, he condemned the external rituals without the essential spirit, replacing the real with the symbols.

Among his disciples was Swami Vivekanand, who came to him a little before his day for travel to England for higher studies. Ironically, a Christian missionary told him about Ramakrishna. After meeting the sage, he was so impressed that he canceled his plans for the Western-style education and instead lived with Ramakrishna for nonformal spiritual education for the next twelve years.

In 1893, Swami Vivekanand went to Chicago to attend the First World Parliament of Religions. His personality—serene and confident—his learning and eloquence, spiritual fervor, and the desire to reach the hearts and minds of his listeners, as well as the content of his message, were impressive. He addressed the audience as "my brothers and sisters," something unusual in the Western world. His message was that there was truth in all religions: "All the different religious views are but different ways leading to the same goal." God is both one and many, with and without forms, and may be conceived as a great universal spirit or through different symbols. That was the Upanishadic thought—that there are different paths of reaching the Ultimate Truth. Additionally, his message was that each person was potentially divine and that he or she should both work to unleash the infinite power within himself or herself and should help other persons do the same. Instead of returning home, the swami spent the next four years delivering lectures in the United States and United Kingdom. He had successfully carried the age-old Indian approach to Western Christian and Jewish audiences.

On his return to India, he received a hero's welcome. His confidence in the Upanishadic approach as an all-encompassing approach applicable and available to everyone in the world transferred to his compatriots. He had, after all, preached to the world the greatness of Hinduism, a far cry from the Christian missionaries and the bureaucrats who read Mill's *History of India*, which unreservedly looked down on the Hindus. With swami's work, the challenge posed by the missionaries had been met.

In addition to his religious and spiritual work, Swami Vivekanand took up the task of regenerating his countrymen through social service to improve their lot and minimize their suffering. Through his fiery speeches, he urged the youth to devote themselves to uplifting the poor and starving millions of India. His Ramakrishna Mission made social service an essential discipline for spiritual life. His zeal to serve the downtrodden masses opened up a new dimension of activity to Indian nationalist leaders, whose Western outlook and constitutional approach had confined their activities to the salons and debating rooms, petitions, and memoranda in the name of the people, whom they hardly met. Gandhi acknowledged his debt to Swami Vivekanand in this regard by making the uplift of the poor and the voiceless illiterate the focus of his work. He wanted them to be as eloquent as the swami.

The brilliant swami died at thirty-nine in 1902. In addition to giving the world a message of hope, he had restored to Indians a sense of dignity and pride in Indian culture.

The Theosophical Society

In the same year as the founding of the Arya Samaj, in far-away New York, two individuals, the Russian Helena Petrovna (1831–1891), known as Madame Blavatsky, and the American colonel H. S. Olcott (1832–1907), founded the Theosophical Society in 1875. The society's members were increasingly those who rejected Western civilization and became open enthusiasts of Indian thought and culture. Their core belief was syncretism, that the ultimate reality can be reached through a variety of religious beliefs, an Upanishadic approach. The society held reincarnation, the Gita's message of karma, and other Hindu or Buddhist conceptions as central doctrines.

In 1879, Madame Blavatsky and Colonel Olcott came to India and in 1886 established their headquarters in Adyar, near Madras (Chennai). A decade later, in 1889, Annie Besant, then forty-two, the society's next leader, made India her home. Her Irish background led her to identify herself with the Indian nationalist movement. She became prominent in Indian politics; in 1917, she became the president of the INC (fifth and last British to receive the honor).

Annie Besant identified herself completely with Indian causes. She was much impressed with the work of Swami Vivekanand and saw the cultural and religious regeneration in India as a prelude to the large-scale nationalist movement. She started the Central High School in Benares as a chief means of achieving her object; it developed gradually into Hindu College and later, with Pandit Madan Mohan Malaviya's leadership, into the Benares Hindu University.

She wrote in her autobiography in 1893, "The Indian work is first of all, the revival, strengthening and uplifting of the ancient religions. This has brought with it a new self-respect, a pride in the past, a belief in the future and, as an inevitable result, a great wave of patriotic life, the beginning of the rebirth of a nation."[8]

ESTABLISHMENT OF THE INDIAN NATIONAL CONGRESS

The major political organization that led India to its independence from Great Britain was the Indian National Congress, founded in 1885. Though India's marathon battle for freedom is identified in the global public mind with Mohandas Karamchand Gandhi (better known as Mahatma Gandhi), and for his insistence on truth and nonviolence as the twin essential and unshakable principles guiding the movement, certain mileage had been registered by the INC before Gandhi's leadership began after his return from South Africa in 1915, but more effectively from 1920.

Ironically, the INC was founded by a British bureaucrat, Allan Octavian Hume (1829–1912), who was helped in its initial years by another Britisher in India, William Wedderburn, and at least for the first two years enjoyed the official support of the viceroy himself. As a member of the Indian Civil Service, Hume wrote to his superiors that the Indian peasantry was oppressed by "certain notorious political grievances, which led to complaints not loud but deep" with regard to the "costly and unsuitable" legal system, the "corrupt and oppressive" police, the "rigid" revenue system, and the "galling administration" of the Arms Act and the Forests Act beginning in Governor-General Lytton's regime. People "despaired of getting justice, cheap, sure and speedy," a police they could look up to as "friends and protectors," a land revenue system "more elastic and sympathetic," and a less harsh administration of the Forests Act. Wedderburn joined Hume in condemning the Lytton regime, pointing out that the government had taken away some of the privileges inherited from a former generation of liberal British administrators, such as the liberty of the press, the right of public meeting, municipal self-government, and the independence of the universities.

Hume had "unimpeachable evidence" that there was a lot of political discontent underground. He came into possession of seven volumes containing reports of the "seething revolt" incubating in various districts based upon the communications of the disciples of various gurus to their religious heads. The reports were arranged according to districts, subdistricts, subdivisions, and cities. Hume did not think that an organized mutiny was ahead but did believe that the people, pervaded with a sense of hopelessness, might indulge in "a sudden violent outbreak of sporadic crime, murders of obnoxious persons, robbery of bankers and looting of bazaars, acts really of lawlessness, which by a due coalescence of forces might develop into a National Revolt." Hume thereupon resolved to open a "safety valve" for this unrest; the Congress would be such an outlet. He conceived of an idea of bringing into existence a national gathering of Indians.

In a letter of March 1, 1883, addressed to the Calcutta University graduates, he appealed: "If only 50 men, good and true, can be found to join as founders, the thing can be established and the further development will be comparatively easy." The ideals he placed before them were "a democratic constitution, freedom from personal ambitions and the dictum that 'he that is greatest among you, let him be your servant.'"9

Hume's idea was originally to allow the existing provincial organizations such as the Indian Association of Calcutta, the Presidency Association of Bombay, and the Mahajan Sabha to take up political questions and the "All-India National Union" to concentrate more or less on social questions. He wanted the governor of the province to preside and promote cordiality between the officials and nonofficials. The viceroy, Lord Dufferin (1884–1888), wanted to go further than Hume. He said there was no body of persons in India performing the functions that Her Majesty's Opposition did in England. Besides, the newspapers were not reliable as indicators of public sentiment. He preferred that the Indian politicians meet once a year to comment on the administration, point out defects, and suggest measures for improvement. The local governor should not preside, for in his presence, the people may not like to speak their minds. Dufferin did not, however, want his association to be divulged until the end of his viceroyalty. The first conference of leaders from all over India was planned to meet in Pune on December 25–30, 1885; it was, in the end, held in Bombay.

The direct objects of the conference were simply to enable "the most earnest laborers in the cause of national progress to become personally known to each other." But indirectly, it was hoped that the conference would form the "germ of a National Parliament" that would give an "unanswerable reply to the assertion that India is wholly unfit for any form of representative institutions."[10]

Hume went to England armed with Dufferin's support. Among those he consulted were former governors-general Ripon and Dalhousie and political leaders such as James Caird and John Bright. He organized the Indian Parliamentary Committee in England to speak on behalf of India. He also made arrangements for periodic telegraphic dispatch of funds for the planned Indian National Congress, and, very important, he made arrangements for publicity in English newspapers.

The Early Leadership of the Congress

Although the seeds of nationalism could thus be seen, the people who led the movement for the first decade and a half were essentially moderates who appeared to be Empire loyalists. They shared a great many assumptions with those liberal Englishmen who advised and encouraged them. They expressed a belief, although this could be a matter of strategy and tact, in the "providential character" of British rule and in the gradual evolution of India toward enlightenment and self-government under that rule. W. C. Bonerjee, president of the INC's first session in 1885, asked the delegates whether such an assembly of his countrymen, speaking one language, could have been possible in the past, and proceeded to answer that question: "Such a thing is possible under British rule and under British rule only." Even a person who had been patently wronged by the British government such as Surendranath (nicknamed "Surrender Not") Banerjea said in his presidential address at the INC in 1902 that Indians had "no higher an aspiration than that we should be admitted into the great confederacy of self-governing states, of which England is the august mother."[11] Another major leader, Gopal Krishna Gokhale had no doubt in his mind that "whatever advance we seek must be within the Empire itself." And Dadabhai Naoroji, Grand Old Man of India, who wrote and spoke fearlessly in defense of India's demands, was equally forthright in expressing his faith in British justice: "We are British subjects," he said and on that ground claimed "a right to all British institutions." Thomas Babington Macaulay's statement in 1835 had come nearly true in the case of the Indian moderates: "Having become instructed in European knowledge, they may in some future age demand European institutions."[12]

Dadabhai Naoroji and the "Drain" Theory

Naoroji went far beyond the moderates, though, who were at least outwardly enthusiasts of the British rule in India. In 1892, Naoroji had become the first Indian member of the House of Commons in Britain. Nine years later, he published *Poverty and Un-British Rule in India*, which has remained a classic indictment of the British rule in India. Although later economists challenged some of Naoroji's interpretations and facts, few of them would deny one of his contentions that British policies toward India in the nineteenth century had direct relevance to its impoverishment.

Naoroji wrote not only about a stifling of growth but also about a "drain" of wealth from India to Britain. This outflow, the profits of empire (what later economists would call "invisible") derived from payments to British civil and military officials, who carried their wealth back to Britain; military expenses paid by India for operations outside the country; profits from British businesses sent to Britain; a trading relationship between India and Britain, distorted by British-imposed tariffs at both ends, in which Britain reaped the largest share of the profits; and miscellaneous hidden flows of wealth out of India for insurance premiums, interest payments, and so forth.

The same source that produced the alleged "drain" from India, Naoroji argued, also brought the country a moral loss "no less sad and lamentable." To quote him:

> With material wealth go also the wisdom and experience of the country. Europeans occupy almost all the higher places in every department of Government directly or indirectly under its control. While in India, they acquire India's money, experience and wisdom; and when they go, they carry both away with them, leaving India so much poorer in material and moral wealth. Thus, India is left without, and cannot have those elders in wisdom and experience who in every country are the natural guides of the rising generations in their national and social conduct, and of the destinies of their country; and a sad, sad loss this is![13]

Moderates and Extremists: Gopal Krishna Gokhale and Bal Gangadhar Tilak

Two of the principal leaders of the INC in the first two decades hailed from Pune, a well-known intellectual center as well as the pride of the Peshwa power in the eighteenth century. Both came from similar social, economic, and intellectual backgrounds and worked together in educational enterprises but later held divergent views of what needed to be done about colonial rule. Whereas Gopal Krishna Gokhale was the model of grace and gentility, a believer in politics by memoranda and petitions who regarded a place in government councils as a sufficient measure of progress, his rival, soon to be branded a radical and a revolutionary, was Bal Gangadhar Tilak, called by the admiring masses *"Lokmanya"* (hailed by the people), believed in the message of the Bhagavad Gita, the role of a *karmayogi*. He founded two periodicals in Marathi, *Kesari* (Lion) and the *Maratha*, in which the editorials increasingly became indirectly critical of the British rule. Tilak was also the first to take the politics out of the salons and to the masses. His innovations were to hold the festival of Shivaji, the seventeenth-century Maratha king who was practically deified by the Maharashtrians. The occasion would be used for lectures and symposia extolling Shivaji's exploits and opposition to the mighty Mughal rule, with a subtle message substituting the British rule for the Mughal. The second innovation was the holding of the community Ganesh festival, which he organized for ten days, in which the evenings would provide entertainment as well as discourses where seemingly socioreligious themes were used for passing on to the large audiences subtle messages on the ills of alien rule.

Maharashtra, particularly Pune, also became the center of violent opposition to British rule. Although the incidents were few and far between, the government kept an eye on "extremists" such as Tilak, whose writings aroused religious sentiments as a factor in the growth of nationalism. He never openly goaded his audience to violence; he was aware the alien rulers were far too strong to be vanquished with arms. As he saw the strength of the movement against the partition of Bengal, he advocated the use of boycotts as a weapon. He ridiculed moderates, such as Gokhale, who were prepared to wait "another 80 years" for a dose of reform at the hands of the British. Presaging Gandhi's Non-Cooperation Movement, he told an audience at the Calcutta University on January 3, 1907:

> We are not armed, and there is no necessity for arms either. We have a stronger weapon, a political weapon, in boycott. . . . We have perceived . . . that the whole of this administration, which is carried on by a handful of Englishmen, is carried on with our assistance. We are all in subordinate service. . . . We shall not give them assistance to collect revenue and keep peace. We shall not assist them in fighting beyond the frontiers or outside India with Indian blood and money. We shall not assist them in carrying on the administration of justice . . . and when time comes we shall not pay taxes. Can you do that by your united efforts? If you can, you are free from to-morrow.[14]

Tilak and Gokhale came to a confrontation at the annual session of the INC at Surat in 1907. The INC split into two factions, moderate and extremist. The government decided to go after the extremists. Tilak was arrested, tried, sentenced to six years, and sent to Mandalay in Burma from 1908 until 1914. The moderates had won, at least for the time being.

The Partition of Bengal, 1905

The passive character of the INC's deliberations and activities changed dramatically during the viceroyalty of Lord Curzon and his decision to partition Bengal in 1905. Curzon was a rabid imperialist, thoroughly opposed to the rise of nationalism. In a deliberate misreading of the tide, he wrote in 1900, "My own belief is that the Congress is tottering to its fall, and one of my great ambitions while in India is to assist it to a peaceful demise."[15]

Historically, Bengal had become the responsibility of the East India Company in 1765, when it received the formal *Diwani* rights from the Mughal emperor. The Bengal Presidency, as a province, included the present-day Bangladesh, West Bengal, Orissa, Assam, and Bihar. In February 1901, a new scheme to partition Bengal originated in a letter of Sir Andrew Fraser, chief administrator of Central Provinces (CP), suggesting that Orissa be made a separate province, with the inclusion of the linguistically similar Sambhalpur in the CP. Two years later when Sir Andrew became the lieutenant governor of Bengal, he proposed a plan that would lead to the controversial partition of Bengal.

At that time, Bengal, with a population of 80 million and an area of 189,000 square miles, was under a mere lieutenant governor. It included millions of non-Bengalis from Bihar and Orissa. Although Bengal's outlook was prosperous and progressive, that of Biharis and the Oriya people was not. While the bureaucrats begged for relief from their excessive burden, the outlying districts in non-Bengali regions of the vast province complained of inefficient administration.

Curzon proposed the partition of Bengal into two provinces. The "divisions" of Dacca, Chittagong, and Rajshahi were joined to Assam to make the new province of East Bengal. West Bengal would then have a population of 54 million. The partition was defended by the British with the argument that it would give the two religious communities—Hindus and Muslims—scope for their separate development. In February 1904, Curzon toured East Bengal to feel the popular pulse and found opposition to the idea among the Bengali population. Even so, Curzon went ahead with his scheme and announced it would be effective on October 16, 1905.

Just a little before, the educated elite of Calcutta had protested the government's adoption of the Universities Act of 1904, which had curtailed the elite's influence over higher education. The partition was seen not so much as an administrative convenience but more as a means to curtail the nationalist sentiment among the Bengalis.

The partition received the support of the Muslim population in the eastern province, where they had a clear majority.

They looked for a larger number of important administrative positions for their community. The move would make the Hindus, among whom the numbers of the educated, particularly lawyers, were increasing, a minority. Those who loved the Bengali culture (and which Bengali does not?) believed this was a grave attack on the uniting reality of the Bengali language, literature, and culture, irrespective of religion. The movement brought even the moderates such as Surendranath Banerjea among the ranks of the activists, making him the first political prisoner in India. An inflammatory statement came from the lieutenant governor, Fuller, who said that he had two wives, Hindu and Muslim, and that he preferred the latter. Most historians agree that the real motive behind the partition of Bengal was to divide the people on the basis of religion and to create disunion and enmity between the Hindus and Muslims in pursuit of the imperial policy of *divide et impera*, divide and curb the nationalism, an effort to strangle the renascent Bengal.

The official decision to partition Bengal on religious lines motivated protests all over the country, not just Bengal, among Hindus and Muslims against the partition. The antipartition movement dramatically transformed the Indian National Congress from a relatively sedate movement, with a membership of mostly educated middle-class men, to a mass movement in which the common man participated vociferously. It also produced certain new forms of agitation that would become the kernel of the nationalist movement all through the remainder of the colonial rule. In the meetings immediately following the government's decision to partition the province, the moderate Surendranath Banerjea toured the province, East and West, asking the people to sign a pledge to boycott British goods and use Indian-made ones. "Boycott and *swadeshi*" (use indigenous goods) became the new slogan and a potent means to attack the colonial masters where it would hurt them most. Public bonfires were held as a manifestation of nationalism at which British textiles were burned with a pledge to use only indigenously manufactured substitutes. The agitation spread throughout the country and was seen positively as a means to support indigenous industries.

The day of the partition, October 16, 1905, was observed as a day of mourning. The day was also observed as *rakhibandhan* (tying of the *rakhi*, or band, around the wrist), symbolic of the union between the two halves of the former province, and a *hartal* (closure of all establishments) and fast were observed. On that day was laid the foundation stone of a "Federation Hall," to borrow the analogy of the Hotel des Invalides in Paris, wherein statues of all the districts of Bengal, those of the sundered districts (on the analogy of Alsace-Lorraine) being shrouded until the day of the reunion. The vernacular press in the entire country lauded these efforts, and the INC itself passed strongly worded resolutions in 1905 and 1906 to undo the partition.

As tools of the movement, the boycott and *swadeshi* went far beyond being merely economic measures; they provided the emotional core of the nationalist movement in which a very large number of students and youth participated. *Swadeshi* now came to be equated with patriotism. At the antipartition meetings, a new national song, not just a song for Bengal, "Bande Mataram" (Salute to My Motherland), composed by Bankim Chandra Chatterji, was sung all over the country. It was to become one of the two national songs (the other being "Jana Gana Mana," composed by the Nobel laureate Rabindranath Tagore) of the nationalist movement throughout the country. After the country's independence, "Bande Mataram," a product of the movement against the partition of Bengal, was given the status of a national song, while "Jana Gana Mana" became the national anthem.

The newly awakened national spirit spread far and wide, as the government responded through violent repression. Meetings and demonstrations in support of their Bengali brethren were held throughout the country and were met with similar police brutalities, which only resulted in fanning the flames of nationalism. Official action was taken against students for participation in the boycott and *hartal,* and the school and college administrators were warned that government grants to those institutions would be stopped. Thousands of people were fined or imprisoned or both. Singing "Bande Mataram" was declared illegal.

A by-product of the antipartition movement was the establishment of twenty-four "nationalist" schools under the Society for the Promotion of National Education in Bengal (Banga Jateeya Vidya Parishad). The INC resolved in 1906 to support the running of such schools "on National lines and under National control" directed toward "the realization of the National destiny." The government under Fuller continued to divide the people along religious lines, favoring the Muslims through appointments to government posts and sending Gurkha battalions against the protesting Hindus. But in the end, the agitators won, although it took several years. The British rulers were compelled by the continued public discontent to annul the partition of Bengal in 1911.

Morley–Minto Reforms; or, The Indian Councils Act of 1909

The Bengal agitation and the support for it all over the country made the colonial government aware that some positive response to the demands of the INC would be necessary. Because the viceroy, Lord Minto, was a Conservative and the secretary of state, John Morley, a prominent Liberal, the resultant measure of reform in 1909 was tinged with what was styled Conservative Liberalism. Minto's policy was essentially to divide and rule: to divide the entire Indian community all over the country into Hindus and Muslims, by encouraging the establishment of the Muslim League in 1906 and encouraging the demand for separate electorates. And as observed before, the government decided to support the moderates in the Congress led by Gokhale and repress the extremists in that organization led by Tilak. Under Minto's administration, reform and repression would go hand in hand.

The Indian Councils Act of 1909 extended the elective principle from the Governor-General's Legislative Council to the provincial Governor's Councils; it also extended a limited suffrage in the election of members to the GG's Council, consisting of very high property-tax payers and those holding high educational qualifications. The act enlarged the GG's Legislative Council to sixty, exclusive of ex-officio members. The councils in Bombay, Bengal, and Madras presidencies and provincial councils in United Provinces (UP) (more or less the Uttar Pradesh of today), Bihar, and Orissa were to have fifty members, whereas those of Punjab, Burma, and Assam were to have smaller ones of thirty. Their composition was to be a mix of officials and nonofficials, of which the former were to be ex-officio and nominated members, whereas the nonofficial members were to be drawn from the public, some of them nominated by the government and the others elected by a limited number of qualified voters. The "imperial interests" were guaranteed by providing for a majority of officials in the GG's Council, which was not done at the provincial level, where certain "safeguards" were provided, such as exclusion of a large number of important matters from the council's jurisdiction, through powers reserved for the governor, including the right to withhold consent to any piece of legislation and the right reserved to the GG's Council to legislate even on provincial matters. In any case, the nonofficial majority did not mean a majority of elected members. As mentioned above, a number of nonofficial members were nominated and could be depended on for their "unflinching loyalty and steadfast support" to the colonial government.

Although the reform was deemed "a gradual increase in the democratization and indigenization of responsible rule" in India, the elections themselves were not held on the basis of geographical constituencies, as would be the natural method. That was deemed unsuitable to India because of its division into castes and religious sects with their diverse interests. Would this be a disabling factor in the country's constitutional development toward a democratic setup? Such philosophical questions were best left unanswered by the "Liberal" secretary of state, Morley. In 1909, all that was granted in the name of constitutional reform was indirect representation in the councils, by classes and interests such as landholders, chambers of commerce, universities, municipalities, and district local boards.

An advance was, however, marked in the functions of the councils. The GG's

Legislative Council would now have a "financial statement," or budget estimates, presented to it on a certain day in March, and although each member would be given a copy of it only a day before the general discussion, they had a right to suggest changes in taxation, new loans, or additional grants. The council was, however, forbidden to discuss matters regarding military, foreign, and political affairs (including relations with the princely states). Beyond the realm of discussion were the "imperial interests" such as interest on public debt and expenses on ecclesiastical establishment and state-owned railroads.

Indian Reaction

The British thought that they had given India a liberal dose of reform much in keeping with India's ability to digest and implement. In reality, then as in the case of future doses of reform, it was a case of "too little, too late." Indian politics had undergone some radical changes in the years immediately preceding the Indian Councils Act of 1909. The agitation following the partition of Bengal in 1905 was followed by the birth of the Muslim League in 1906 and acts of repression of Indian nationalism in the following two years, including the trial of Tilak on groundless and unsubstantiated charges of sedition in 1908 and the six-year prison sentence given to him. From 1908 till 1914, Tilak was banished to a jail in distant Mandalay in Burma. At

his trial, Tilak bravely told the judge he could award him the maximum sentence, adding, "*Swaraj* [self-rule] is my birthright and I shall have it."

Although the moderates attempted to praise the reforms as "the first step leading up to the ultimate grant of *Swaraj*," the British supporters of the Indian cause were dismayed by Lord Morley's statement in the House of Lords in December 1908: "If I were attempting to set up a Parliamentary system in India," said the so-called Liberal leader, "if it could be said that this chapter of reforms led directly or necessarily up to the establishment of a Parliamentary system in India, I for one would have nothing at all to do with it." To illustrate his point, he said, in what was perhaps an unintended racial slur, that the "fur coats of Canada would have no use on the plains of the Deccan." In fact, the act had removed any semblance with parliamentary franchise, had provided only for the constitution of the councils on the basis of classes and interests, not geographical or demographic constituencies. Moreover, the franchise granted was very limited and provided for indirect elections: only about 650 voters, mostly taxpaying subjects, elected a man to the district local boards; they, in turn, elected representatives to the provincial council and the provincial councils to the central council. The worst criticism came from the greatest moderate on the Indian political scene, Gopal Krishna Gokhale, who criticized the limitations on the council's powers to influence matters as follows: "Once the government had made up their mind to adopt a particular course, nothing that the non-official members may say in that Council is practically of any avail in bringing about a change in that course." And, a decade later, when the Joint Committee of the British Parliament reviewed the Montagu-Chelmsford reform proposals in 1918, it commented that the act of 1909 provided "no connection between the supposed primary voter and the man who sits as his representative in the Legislative Council." It added that the existence of a "strong official bloc" gave no opportunity for the political education of the so-called representatives of the people. It concluded: "We have at present in India neither the best of the old system nor the best of the new. Responsibility is the savior of popular government and that savior the present Councils wholly lack."[16]

The Congress—Muslim League "Pact"

Although there was dissatisfaction with the working of the council, there was a growing appreciation by the INC of the needs of the Muslim community. In 1914, Tilak returned from his imprisonment in Burma and rejoined the Congress in 1916 at the Lucknow session, thereby bridging the moderates-extremists breach in the Congress caused in 1907. That meeting became even more momentous when the two major political bodies—the INC and the Muslim League—signed what came to be called the Lucknow Pact. Notable for the later history of the subcontinent was the crucial role played by one leader who made the pact possible. That "ambassador of Hindu-Muslim unity," as Sarojini Naidu called him, was Mohammed Ali Jinnah.

Both the INC and IML agreed on the vital issue of the nationalist movement being "self-government within the British Empire as an equal partner . . . with the self-governing Dominions." The Lucknow Pact guaranteed to Muslims certain proportions of the seats in central and state legislatures. The preamble to the pact stated:

> That having regard to the fact that the great communities of India are the inheritors of ancient civilizations and have shown great capacity for government and administration, and to the progress in education and public spirit made by them during a century of British rule . . . the time has come when His Majesty the King-Emperor should be pleased to issue a Proclamation announcing that it is the aim and intention of British policy to confer self-government on India at an early date.[17]

MONTAGU-CHELMSFORD REFORMS

In the crucial year of World War I, 1917, when the United States entered it, the British government brought in a

Liberal, Edwin Montagu, as secretary of state for India (1917–1922). He was a known disciple of John Morley, who was responsible for the previous measure of reform in 1909, prided on calling himself an "Oriental." He was the first secretary of state for India to go personally to India. Touring with the viceroy, Lord Chelmsford, he saw the Indian leaders, including Gandhi, who had cooperated in the war effort by working for the Red Cross and taking care of the wounded soldiers.

The British government appreciated India's cooperation in the form of more than 1 million soldiers in the war effort, including in the famous Mesopotamian campaign. It also noted the Lucknow Pact of 1916 between the Indian National Congress and the Muslim League and its demands for "self-government" as a dominion. Montagu's statement of August 20, 1917, in Parliament on the constitutional reform in India was seen by the INC and the IML as Britain's appreciation and reward for India's cooperation: "The policy of His Majesty's Government . . . is that of the increasing association of Indians in every branch of the administration and the gradual development of self-governing institutions with a view to the progressive realization of responsible government in India as an integral part of the British Empire."[18]

The last part of that statement was in diametrical contrast to what Montagu's mentor, Morley, had said in 1909. In fact, it was the first time since 1854 when the first steps were taken to give Indians representation in the Indian Legislative Council that an official British representative would make a pronouncement that would lead India's constitutional development toward full responsible government on the British pattern, paving the way for the Indian leadership to make it the cornerstone of free India's constitution itself in 1950. Called the Montagu-Chelmsford (MC) reforms, the Government of India Act of 1919 was Montagu's creation.

Principal Features of the Act of 1919

The main features of the Montagu-Chelmsford report of July 1918 were: the introduction of "dyarchy" at the provincial level, whereby the functions of the government would be divided between "transferred" and "reserved" subjects. The Indian Legislative Council at the center would be enlarged and made more representative and its "opportunities of influencing government" increased. Correspondingly, the control of Parliament and of the secretary of state for India over the government of India and provincial governments would be "relaxed."

The changes at the provincial level were the most crucial. To avoid conflict and to ensure continuing central protection of the "imperial interests," the functions of the government of India and of the provincial governments were "listed." The central "subjects" included defense, foreign and political relations, public debt, tariffs and customs, posts and telegraphs, patents and copyright, currency and coinage, communications, civil and criminal law, and all matters not specifically listed as provincial subjects. The latter included such subjects as would not hurt the "imperial interests" or the colonial benefits to Great Britain. The "transferred" subjects would thus include local self-government, public health and sanitation, education, public works, irrigation and land revenue administration, forests, law and order, and so on, and "any matter ordered by the Governor-General-in-Council as provincial." In case of doubt as to whether a subject is "reserved" or "transferred," the governor's decision was final.

The Central Legislature

Thus far, the GG-in-Council was in charge of making laws. In 1861, 1892, and 1909, some additional members were added to the council, at first wholly by nomination and then by both election (with a limited franchise) and nomination. The act of 1919 made a radical change by creating a legislature distinct from the council. The new legislature would have two chambers: the Council of State as an upper chamber and the Legislative Assembly as the lower chamber. Members of the Executive Council were to be members of the legislature on nomination by the governor-general.

The Council of State would have 60 members of whom 26 would be nominated and a slightly larger number, 34,

elected. Nineteen of the 26 were to be officials; of the 34 elected, 20 would be non-Muslim, 10 would be Muslim, 3 would come from the European Chamber of Commerce, and 1 would be Sikh. The Legislative Assembly, the popular chamber, would have 145 members, of whom 105 would be elected and 40 nominated, 25 being officials. Of 105 elected members, 32 would be Muslims and Sikhs, and 20 would be elected by landholders, Europeans, and Chambers of Commerce. The rest would be seats open to all. Unlike in 1909, the communal electorates were not frowned upon by nationalists because the two principal political organizations, namely, the Indian National Congress and the Muslim League, had, through the Lucknow Pact of 1916, accepted the communal electorates.

Again, unlike the previous constitutional measures in 1892 and 1909, which had provided for indirect elections, the method of election in 1919 was direct. The suffrage, however, was still limited to high property-tax payers, landholders, and men with high educational qualifications, which together accounted for less than 4 percent of the population and about 14 percent of the urban population.

There were enough exceptions and caveats that put brakes on the power of the legislatures both at the central and the provincial levels. Thus, there were grave restrictions in legislating on vital matters such as public debt, public revenue, religion of British nationals, defense, and foreign relations, in the name of "the safety, or tranquility of British India." In regard to any bill passed by both houses and submitted to the governor-general for his assent, he had four alternatives: to assent; to return it back to the legislature for fresh discussion and amendment; to reserve it for the "signification of His Majesty's pleasure," which meant referring it to London; or to veto it outright. Additionally, London had the right to disallow any bill signed by the governor-general. Thus, although the act of 1919 was a step in the direction of India's eventual attainment of a "responsible" democratic government, the imperial grip on India's political and economic life, not to mention its defense and foreign relations, was as before.

Gandhi Emerges as the Leader of the Nationalist Movement

Once again, the suggested reforms were a case of "too little, too late." The INC, at its annual session of 1918, expressed its disappointment. India, in its view, was ripe for democracy, and the proposed reforms fell far short of what was needed. As before, the British succeeded in rallying the support of the moderates in the INC, who now formed a separate party called the Liberal Party. It declared that the reforms marked a "substantial step in the right direction" and that "reform was a better path to their common goal than revolution." It implored that the government put the scheme into effect without delay.

In the years from 1919 to 1921, the INC's dissatisfaction with the act of 1919 increased. The deliberations of the Congress of Versailles, where President Wilson included the right to self-determinations of nations among his famous Fourteen Points, had raised the hopes of most colonial societies that their misery was at an end and that imperialism would give way to self-determination. There was frustration when it became clear that Wilson's offer was limited to nationalities included in the former Austro-Hungarian empire and not to European colonies in Asia or Africa.

Jalianwala Bagh Massacre in Amritsar. A worse shock was administered by the government's random use of force at Jalianwala Bagh in Amritsar, on April 13, 1919, when Brigadier-General Reginald Dyer opened fire on a civilian unarmed gathering of men, women, and children, which, according to the official count, killed 379 persons and injured 200 and which, according to unofficial surveys and the estimate of civil surgeon Dr. Smith, took more than 1,000 lives and injured 1,800. The event shook the nation and the INC and changed Gandhi's attitude toward British rule.

For some days prior to the ghastly event, there was tension in Amritsar and in several parts of Punjab. In response to government orders to deport two political leaders, Satyapal and Saifuddin Kitchlew, a crowd had marched peacefully on April 10 toward the residence of the deputy police commissioner of Amritsar and had been fired upon by the military. That incited the crowd, who burned several government buildings and banks and attacked several white men. The military fired on the crowds and killed 20 persons. Violence begot more violence, as the crowds in several Punjabi cities and towns cut down telegraph posts, damaged railroad lines, and burned more government buildings. The government banned gatherings of five or more persons in the city.

April 13 was the Baisakhi Day for the Sikh people, when followers of the faith customarily converged on the holy city of Amritsar. Most of the people who gathered in the city's Jalianwala Bagh came from villages, unaware of the proclamation banning meetings.

A little past five in the afternoon, Reginald Dyer, at the head of two armored cars mounted with machine guns (the cars were not able to enter the *bagh* because the entrance was not wide enough), and a force of 90 Gurkhas ordered firing at the crowd, without any advance warning to disperse. The venue was surrounded by brick walls, with six entrances besides the one used by the military. Five of them were locked, leaving only one narrow exit for the crowd, many of whom attempted to climb the walls and were mercilessly shot. Some 120 of the crowd jumped into a well in the *bagh* to escape the firing; a monument to them commemorates their deaths.

What was perhaps equally bad was the government's response. Punjab's lieutenant governor, Sir Michael O'Dwyer, telegraphically approved General Dyer's action. The action was defended by the British press as well as many British civilians in India and England, the *Morning Post* opening a fund for General Dyer. The viceroy, Lord Chelmsford, approved O'Dwyer's recommendation that a martial law be proclaimed in Amritsar and all cities and towns of Punjab. Noting the outcry all over the country, the secretary of state, the Liberal Montagu, appointed Lord Hunter as the chair of the Parliamentary Commission of Enquiry. Appearing before that commission, Dyer admitted: "I think it quite possible that I could have dispersed the crowd without firing but they would have come back again and laughed, and I would have made, what I consider, a fool of myself."[19]

The Hunter Report of 1920 condemned Dyer, who was demoted. He returned to Britain, where the reaction was mixed. Thus, while the House of Lords, in a resolution, commended his action, the House of Commons censured him. The *Morning Post*'s collection for him amounted to 26,000 pounds, a substantial sum for those days; worse, it showed a section of the people believed he was a hero. A jeweled sword and a memorial book, signed by his admirers, was presented to the "saviour of Punjab."

The Indian Reaction.   The Indian reaction was of profound sadness as well as anger, a loss of trust in the British sense of fairness and justice, and a disdain for their cruelty and inhumanity. The Nobel laureate Rabindranath Tagore, who had been knighted, returned the honor to the king-emperor in protest. The INC, under Gandhi's leadership, now decided to launch its Non-Cooperation Movement; it resolved not to cooperate in the implementation of the act of 1919. It charged the British rulers with an unacceptable level of variance between their profession and practice. In 1920, the INC declared that its object was "the attainment of *swarajya* [self-rule, independence] by the people of India by all legitimate and peaceful means."

The Jalianwala Bagh massacre marked a great watershed in the nationalist movement. Gandhi lost faith in the British ability to deliver India's destiny. He and Jawaharlal Nehru, whom he would later name his political "heir," would lead the nationalist movement all the way to the country's freedom.

NOTES

1. Boyd C. Shafer, *Nationalism: Myth and Reality* (New York: Harcourt Brace, 1955), 7–8.

2. Virginia Thompson, *French Indochina* (London: Allen and Unwin, 1937), 493–94; Philippe Devillers, *Histoire de Viet Nam de 1940 à 1952* (Paris: Éditions du Seuil, 1952), 54.

3. Frederick L. Schuman, *International Politics* (New York: McGraw-Hill, 1965), 414.

4. Rupert Emerson, "Paradoxes of Asian Nationalism," *Far Eastern Quarterly* 1 (February 1954): 136. See also his *Empire to Nation* (Boston: Beacon Press, 1960), 45.

5. Hans Kohn, *The Idea of Nationalism: A Study in Its Origin and Background* (New York: Macmillan, 1943), 3.

6. Surendranath Banerjea, *A Nation in Making* (1925; reprint, Bombay: Oxford University Press, 1963), 41.

7. William Jones, Discourse at the Asiatic Society, February 2, 1786, in John Marriott, Bhaskar Mukhopadhyay, and Partha Chatterjee, eds., *Britain in India, 1765–1905*, III (London: Pickering and Chatto, 2006), 28.

8. Annie Besant, *How India Wrought for Her Freedom* (Adyar, Madras: Theosophical Publishing House, 1915), 52.

9. William Wedderburn, *Allan Octavian Hume* (London: T. Fisher Unwin, 1913), 50–53.

10. Indian National Congress report, 1885, 1:39.

11. Surendranath Banerjea.

12. Quoted in Percival Griffiths, *The British Impact on India* (Hamden, Conn.: Archon Books, 1965), 247.

13. Dadabhai Naoroji, *Poverty and Un-British Rule in India* (1901; reprint, Delhi: Government of India, Publications Division, 1962), 180.

14. Bal Gangadhar Tilak, *Speeches and Writings* (Madras, Ganesh, 1919), 64–65.

15. V. B. Kulkarni, *Princely India and Lapse of British Paramountcy*, 113.

16. Government of India, *Montagu-Chelmsford Report* (New Delhi: Government of India, 1918), 227.

17. Pattabhi Sitaramayya, The *History of the Indian National Congress* (Bombay: Padma, 1946), appx. 2.

18. Quoted in A. C. Banerjee, ed., *Indian Constitutional Documents, 1757–1939* (Calcutta: A. Mukherjee, 1946), 3:2.

19. Government of India, Home Department, Disorder Inquiry Committee Report (New Delhi: Government Central Press, 1921), 2:197.

_____

In a letter of September 1944 from Mohammad Ali Jinnah to Mahatma Gandhi:

"We maintain and hold that Muslims and Hindus are two major nations by any definitions or tests of a nation. We are a nation of a hundred million, and what is more, we are a nation with our own distinctive culture and civilization, language and literature, art and architecture, names and nomenclature, sense of values and proportion, legal laws and moral codes, customs and calendar, history and traditions, aptitudes and ambitions—in short, we have our own distinctive outlook on life and of life. By all canons of international law we are a nation." (page 300)

Did Jinnah really believe in the two-nation theory? Did he believe the new country of Pakistan was the homeland for all the Muslims of the subcontinent? Mohammad C. Chagla, a staunch nationalist who had in his early days worked as Jinnah's junior attorney and later rose to be a judge of the International Court of Justice at The Hague, asked him a question that must have been on the lips of millions of Indian Muslims for whom moving to Pakistan was not possible. Chagla writes, "I will never forget the answer he gave me. He looked at me for a while and said: "They will look after themselves. I am not interested in their fate."   (pages 311–12)

14

THE ROAD TO FREEDOM THROUGH PARTITION

No one in the early 1930s could have imagined that the British withdrawal from the subcontinent would take place within the space of a decade and a half and that two nations—India and Pakistan—would be born out of the ashes of the British Indian Empire. This included even the founder of Pakistan, Mohammed Ali Jinnah, who had been in England for several years, immensely frustrated over not getting as important a political role as he would have liked in the Indian National Congress of which he had been a leader for fifteen years, until 1929. After the electoral politics of the Montagu-Chelmsford reforms, he was particularly unhappy with the leadership of Gandhi and the latter's resort to what Jinnah said were "illegal" measures such as *satyagraha* (insistence on truth, willingness to take any punishment), protest fasts, noncooperation with the government, and, capping them all, willful and openly proclaimed refusal to obey laws—Gandhi's Civil Disobedience Movement of 1930.

During his long stay in Britain, Jinnah was met by a small group of Indian Muslim students at Cambridge. Much significance has been attached to this meeting, because, according to some, the idea of Pakistan was born there. Two of the students, Chaudhury Rahmat Ali and Aslam Khattak, had co-authored *Now or Never: Are We to Live or Perish Forever?* In that booklet, they presented a scheme "more contrived than remarkable":[1] they had asked for several homelands for India's Muslims, one of them being Pakistan, the others being Bang-I-Islam (or Bangistan) for Muslims in Bengal and Assam and Usmanistan for the Muslims of Hyderabad (Deccan). The name Pakistan was to cover *P* for Punjab, *A* for Afghani border, *K* for Kashmir, *S* for Sind, and *TAN* for Baluchistan—or was it for the ending of the name, Pakistan? The 243 principalities, or *Rajwaras*, as they called them, were to be divided among caste Hindus and grouped together as "Hanoodias." Sikhs were to be put together in an enclave called "Sikhia." Every non-Muslim was to remain subservient to the master race he called "the Paks," and the subcontinent itself was to be renamed Dinia. Rahmat Ali's scheme envisaged a Pakistan Commonwealth of Nations for his eight Muslim homelands to be integrated with an Islamic string of states from central Asia to the Bosporus, which he called "the original Pakistan"![2]

Rahmat Ali's collaborator, Aslam Khattak, subsequently held many positions, first under the British government in India and then under the government of Pakistan as governor of the NWFP, as a member of Nawaz Sharif's cabinet and as Pakistan's ambassador to Iran. In an article written on the fiftieth anniversary of Pakistan, Khwaja Salahuddin Ahmad stated that it was his own father, Khwaja Abdul Rahim, who was a contemporary of Rahmat Ali at Cambridge, who was the first to suggest the name of Pakistan at the third meeting of the Woking Muslim Mission in England in mid-1932. According to him, "the name was not chosen because it contained the first letters of names of areas that were to be in Pakistan, the name was accepted because *pak*, meaning *pakessgi* or purity, was deemed a first necessity before 'our approach to God.' In Islam, *pak* is cleanliness in its purest form."[3]

The scheme dismissed out of hand by the Muslim League leaders as a "student scheme" was, however, inspired by the famous poet Muhammad Iqbal, whose song, "Saare Jahanse Achcha, Hindostam Hamara" (Of All the Lands in the World, Hindustan or India Is the Best), a song still sung with continued emotion in India, was sung at the midnight golden jubilee celebration of the country's independence on August 14, 1997, in the Central Hall of India's Parliament, without the Indians' awareness that the poet had provided the inspiration for the "student scheme." Iqbal himself had advocated special cultural enforcement of Islam in specific areas of the subcontinent in provinces, which exactly form Pakistan today: Sind, Punjab, NWFP, and Baluchistan. However, he did not ask for the partition of his *Hindostam*; on the contrary, he said that the "North-West Indian Muslims will prove the best defenders of India against foreign invasion, be that invasion one of ideas or bayonets." After all, the land had been vulnerable to invasions by marauders in that quarter for centuries.[4]

Jinnah returned to India in 1934, became the president of the Muslim League, and actively campaigned in 1937 in the provincial elections envisaged in the Government of India Act of 1935. If a single factor were to be regarded as responsible for the sudden and successful rise of separatist politics among the Muslims that would, in the short span of a decade, lead to the birth of Pakistan, it would have to be the Muslim leaders' frustration over their dismal failure to win seats in the provincial legislatures, even in the Muslim-majority provinces in 1937. Events quickly followed the outbreak of World War II: the INC's refusal to cooperate with the war effort except as an independent state, the Muslim League's Lahore Resolution in 1940 demanding the creation of Pakistan as a separate state, Gandhi's "Quit India" call in 1942, and the subsequent arrest and imprisonment of all Congress leaders for the remainder of the war. The Muslim League's cooperation during the war was amply rewarded by the retreating British during the postwar negotiations on the future of the subcontinent. The experience of the failure of a joint interim government of the Congress and the Muslim League in 1946–1947 convinced the Congress's leaders to concede the partition of the country into the two dominions of India and Pakistan.

THE TWO NATIONALISMS

The idea that the two principal communities of British India—the Hindus and the Muslims—would not be able to work together in a democratic, electoral polity was Sir Sayyid Ahmed Khan's (1817–1898). Initially, Sir Sayyid strove for the common interest of all communities in the context of both the British rule and the intellectual and scientific domination of the West. In 1884, during the agitation in Aligarh in favor of the Ilbert Bill, he appealed to the Hindus and Muslims to become "one heart and act in unison" because the alternative would be "the destruction and downfall of both." Ironically, the dramatic change

transforming him into a communal leader, interested in the welfare of his coreligionists alone, occurred in the same year when he thought of the consequences of the elections to be held to the local self-governing institutions introduced in 1883 by Lord Ripon. Sir Sayyid said: "Elections pure and simple were quite unsuited to diversified India where the religious institutions have kept even neighbours apart." In the following years, as the newly established Indian National Congress demanded representative government of the British kind, Sir Sayyid clarified to his coreligionists that a "majority rule" would mean "the Hindus in greater part of India in power and the Muslims never."

Already, Sir Sayyid had been advocating that the Muslims take to Western-style education and improve their economic and intellectual status. In 1877, he had founded the Anglo-Oriental College in Aligarh. He had progressively become a collaborator with the British and desired for the Muslims a favored position in the services, civil and military. Beginning in 1886, he held the Muslim Educational Conference simultaneously with the sessions of the INC at which he advocated not only that Muslims go for higher education but also that they actively display their support and loyalty to the British Crown, characterizing criticism of government action as disloyalty. He also wanted the government attitude, which had become anti-Muslim in the aftermath of the 1857–1859 Great Uprising, to become pro-Muslim.

The reforms of 1892 showed the disadvantages of the principle of electoral representation for the Muslims. Sir Sayyid asked successive viceroys to give Muslims special treatment because of their relative educational and economic backwardness and to redress the inequality by giving the Muslims more posts in the higher ranks of the civil service. No viceroy until Lord Minto (1905–1910) was willing to make any special arrangements or exemptions in favor of any particular community. Although the official policy remained unchanged, the English faculty and administration at the Aligarh college took upon themselves the task of advising the Muslim leadership to establish a separate political organization and challenge the INC's claim that it represented all communities, including the Muslims. This would additionally and effectively blunt the ongoing movement against the partition of Bengal and enable the Muslims to benefit from the impending measure of constitutional reforms.

The result was the birth of the Indian Muslim League on December 30, 1906, in Dacca (Bangladesh). Principal Archibald of the Aligarh college suggested that Muslim leadership collect signatures of representative Muslims of all provinces on an important memorandum. The memorandum itself began with an expression of loyalty to the Crown and appreciation of the steps taken in the direction of self-government. It suggested that nomination or representation or both be given by religion, giving due weight to the *zamindars* (large landlords) and the feudal class. On October 1, 1906, a deputation of seventy Muslims, which included a large number of prominent feudal landholders, merchants, and lawyers from all over India, met the viceroy under the leadership of the religious leader of the Shii Ismailia community, the prestigious Aga Khan (1877–1957), and presented the memorandum to him. The core of the memorandum stated that the representative institutions of the Western kind would not succeed in India because of the plural nature of its society and urged that the interests of the Muslims be protected by giving them separate representation, either by nomination or election or both. Interestingly, it pleaded that such representation be "commensurate not merely with the numerical strength but also with their political importance and the value of the contribution which they make to the defence of the Empire." The last part was rather disputable since Sir Sayyid and other Muslim leaders were complaining of a lack of Muslim recruitment in the armed forces after 1857. The memorandum requested additional representation of the Muslims in the services, protection of Muslim interests in case an Indian was appointed to the viceroy's Executive Council, and specific help in founding a Muslim university. Lord Minto's oft-quoted reply stated: "I am entirely in accord with you. . . . I am as firmly convinced as I believe you to be, that any electoral representation in India would be doomed to mischievous failure which aimed at granting a personal enfranchisement regardless of the beliefs and traditions of the communities comprising the population of this continent."[5]

The official hand in the whole affair was grossly suspect. Lady Minto noted in her diary that the meeting of the Muslim delegation with the viceroy on October 1, 1906, was hailed by the British bureaucracy as "nothing less than the pulling back of 62 millions of people [the Muslims] from joining the ranks of seditious opposition."

Regarded as the Charter of Muslim Rights, the memorandum and the government's response to it in the form of the Act of 1909, paved the way for Muslim separatism and the eventual partition of the subcontinent and the creation, within four decades, of an Islamic state. The Muslim League, thereafter, usually held its sessions at the end of the All India Muslim Educational Conference. The IML did not meet regularly (there were no meetings, for example, between 1916 and 1922). Its political importance, however, could not be underestimated. It represented the Muslim side in the negotiations with the government immediately preceding the reforms of 1909, and the principle of separate representation it advocated was included in the Act of 1909. The Aga Khan, who remained the president of the IML until 1912, commented in his memoirs a half century later about the significance of the events of 1906: "Lord Minto's acceptance of our demands was the *foundation of all future constitutional proposals for India* by successive British Governments and its final, inevitable consequence was the Partition of India and the emergence of Pakistan."[6] [Emphasis added.]

A lot has been written about the possible collusion between the Indian Muslims and the colonial government. Although there is no evidence that the government pursued a policy of divide and rule, by favoring the Muslims against the Hindus, the bureaucracy used every opportunity to undermine the Indian nationalist movement in which both communities marched together by injecting the virus of communalism and separatism into it. There were large meetings of Muslims in India and Britain in favor of the communal electorates. A deputation of Muslims met the secretary of state, Lord Morley, whose personal adherence to Liberal philosophy would not allow him at first to permit "invidious distinctions" between Hindus and Muslims, because it would mark a flagrant breach of democratic principles. However, Minto's efforts succeeded in changing Morley's mind, and the principle of separate electorates and the devil of communalism were incorporated in the so-called Morley-Minto reforms.

THE KHILAFAT OR CALIPHATE MOVEMENT

Some political events in the international arena involving the caliphate in Turkey weakened the trend of close relations between the colonial government and the Muslims on the subcontinent. In the war between Italy and Turkey over Tripoli, Britain had chosen to remain neutral. In the Balkan War of 1912–1913, the Muslims, in general, suspected a conspiracy of Christian powers against their coreligionists. The Indian Muslims sent a medical mission to help the Muslims wounded in the war effort. In World War I, Turkey had sided with Germany, which made the Indian Muslims also side with the Germans. The Indian Muslims regarded the sultan of Turkey as the caliph and, therefore, the spiritual leader of all Muslims all the world over. The Indian Muslims together with other Muslims met the Germans in Afghanistan and went as far as inviting the emir of Afghanistan to invade India. The postwar dismemberment of the Turkish Empire and the abolition of the caliphate angered the Indian Muslims. The British supported a move by some Arabs to make the sheriff of Mecca, a descendant of the Prophet, responsible thereafter for protecting the Holy Shrine of Kaaba. This was not acceptable to the Indian Muslims, who strongly supported an international movement for the restoration of the Turkish caliphate.

The war between Turkey and Britain stirred antagonistic feelings against the British rulers in India. It brought the INC and the IML together, resulting in the important "Lucknow Pact," named after the city where the two political organizations held their 1916 annual session. It was a major agreement that would have grave consequences for the future course of Indian constitutional development and eventually for the creation of a separate Muslim state. The two parties agreed to a common "scheme" for constitutional reform, which incidentally supported the presidential, not the British-type parliamentary, system for India. However, the most notable feature of the Lucknow Pact was an INC-IML agreement that there should be separate electorates in any future constitution for the Hindus and the Muslims.

Two brothers, Maulana Muhammad Ali and Shaukat Ali, led a movement in favor of the caliphate, known in India as the Khilafat movement. It was supported by Gandhi, who saw in it a great opportunity for the Hindus to show their solidarity with their Muslim brethren. Hindus, he said, must be prepared to "perish" with their Muslim brethren in order to vindicate "the honor of Islam." The INC unanimously endorsed Gandhi's sentiments. In opposing the British, Muhammad Ali went to the extent of formally inviting the emir of Afghanistan to invade India. This led to his arrest by the government. In 1921, Muhammad Ali said to the British in those memorable words: "We divide and You rule."

However, the INC-IML bonhomie did not last long. Many Muslims had questioned Gandhi's leadership of the

Khilafat movement, since he was not a believer in their religion. The Khilafat movement itself collapsed, as the internal situation in Turkey changed dramatically, with the country becoming a republic. The new government abolished the sultanate and the caliphate. In fact, Turkey's new leader, Ataturk Kemal Pasha, who stood for modernization and Westernization, declared Turkey a secular state. Interestingly, Mohammed Ali Jinnah, the future founder of a Muslim state, Pakistan, regarded the caliphate of Turkey as a "discredited cause."

Apart from the Khilafat movement, the Jalianwala Bagh massacre at Amritsar by General Dyer brought the Hindus and Muslims together.

THE SIMON COMMISSION AND THE MUSLIMS

The Act of 1919 provided for the appointment of a commission a decade later to review the constitutional progress, particularly the working of the provincial dyarchy and recommend further measures to augment the responsible government in India both at the center and in the provinces. It should also consider the relations between British India and the Indian states (princely) and explore the possibility of bringing them into a common constitutional entity. In 1927, a commission under Sir John Simon was announced; it was an all-white commission with

no Indian representatives on it. The INC rejected it outright. Throughout the commission's stay in India, it was greeted with banners saying, "Simon, Go Back." The INC contended that Indians should have been asked to collect evidence and contribute toward making the recommendations.

With the prospect of the appointment of a statutory commission, the diehard separatists among the Muslims appointed a committee and on March 20, 1927, published the "Muslim Proposals." They demanded that Muslims be given one-third of the seats in the central legislature, far beyond their numbers—25 percent—in the country would warrant. Alternatively, they wanted a "constitutional guarantee" that the majority of the representatives from Punjab and Bengal to the Central Assembly would be Muslims. They wanted also an additional "guarantee" that representatives to the Central Assembly from the rest of the country would include Muslims at least in proportion to their numbers in the general population. The British threw up their hands that they could not guarantee definite levels of representation where free elections were involved. The situation helped the British secretary of state for India, Lord Birkenhead, who declared that the Indians would not be able to come up with an agreed upon and practical solution. In fact, he challenged them to do so.

The Indian response was to appoint the All Parties Conference, which in turn

appointed the Motilal Nehru Committee, consisting of seven members, of
whom three were Muslims. Its report
of 1928 recommended what would be a
virtual transfer of power to Indian hands
on the lines of a government, fully responsible to a fully elected legislature as
envisaged in Montagu's statement of August 1917. The report endorsed the Muslim demand for separate electorates in
central as well as provincial legislatures
in proportion to the total Muslim population. The Muslims would additionally
be allowed to contest the "general" seats
for a period of ten years. However, it was
opposed by the aging Aga Khan, then
president of the All Muslim Parties Conference, which prepared its own alternative set of proposals. Of note was the
resolution passed by that conference on
January 1, 1929, stating that "no constitution by whomsoever proposed or devised,
will be acceptable to Indian Mussalmans
[Muslims] unless it conforms with the
principles embodied in this resolution." It
is notable that Jinnah endorsed that resolution. From that time on, the Muslims
would ask for that kind of a veto on any
constitution proposed for the country.

Three months later, on March 28, Jinnah published his own Fourteen Points.
He contended that any future constitution of the country should not affect
the Muslim majority of Punjab, Bengal,
the Northwest Frontier Province, and
Sind, the last of which should be separated from the Bombay Presidency
forthwith. Any future constitution must
be federal with residuary powers vested
in the provinces. All the minorities
should have separate electorates; however, it should be open for individual
communities to opt for joint electorates.
All legislatures and other elective bodies
must provide for adequate and guaranteed communal representation. As for
the central legislature, he endorsed the
demand of the All Muslim Parties Conference that the Muslims be given at
least one-third of the seats. So should the
cabinets at the central and provincial
levels have at least one-third of its members as Muslims. Finally, the constitution
should be changed only with the consent
of all the federal units, thereby giving a
veto to the Muslim majority provinces.

Some of the demands in Jinnah's
Fourteen Points were clearly impractical
in the parliamentary system of government that required joint responsibility on
the part of the cabinet. How could this be
secured in a situation where one-third of
the ministers would belong to a particular
religious community most likely with affiliation to a different party, such as the
Muslim League? As the future would
bear out, it was on this point of Muslim
League representation in the ministry of
the United Provinces in 1937–1939, regardless of whether they were elected or
not, that there was the hue and cry that
led finally to the demand for a fully separate state. Again, it was a similar situation
of a divided responsibility of the Cabinet
that the Interim Government broke
down in 1946–1947.

IRWIN'S DECLARATION AND CALL FOR A ROUNDTABLE CONFERENCE

There was a major political change in 1929 in England, bringing the Labor Party leader, Ramsay MacDonald, into power. He was sympathetic to the Indian demands and called the viceroy, Lord Irwin, for immediate consultations. The INC had given the deadline of December 31, 1929, to accept the Motilal Nehru report. Britain asked Irwin to make a major statement on October 31, 1929, that "it is implicit in the Declaration of 1917 that the natural issue of India's constitutional progress . . . is the attainment of the Dominion Status."[7] The statement completely eclipsed the remaining deliberations of the Simon Commission.

The statement, which was far-reaching in its consequences, proposed to put India on a footing of equality with the dominions such as Canada, South Africa, Australia, and New Zealand. The government announced that before the Simon Commission's recommendations were examined, it would like to call for a Round Table Conference (RTC) at which the representatives of the British government would meet those of British India and the princely states for securing "the greatest possible measure of agreement."[8]

There were vital differences between Britain and the INC in the parties to be invited to join that roundtable. Also, whereas Viceroy Irwin wanted a commission to work on the details, the INC wanted the immediate convening of a constituent assembly to draft a constitution of the proposed dominion. Irwin and Gandhi met. Their differences were irreconcilable because of the differing approaches to these talks. Meanwhile, the INC with Jawaharlal Nehru as its president brooked no further patience. It resolved dramatically on the banks of the Ravi River that India's goal was to attain *Poorna Swaraj* (Complete Independence). The INC resolved to boycott the proposed RTC and instead launch a civil disobedience movement.

The British government called three Round Table Conferences (1930, 1931, and 1932) in London to which they invited representatives of the INC, IML, "Depressed Classes," and the princes to meet the representatives of the British political spectrum. Whether Britain was truly interested in evolving a constitution leading India to the promised dominion status or the conference was simply an opportunity to present to all assembled the hurdles—real, imagined, or freshly created—and sabotage any settlement that would take the British closer to giving Indians a chance to rule themselves is anybody's guess. Apart from the representatives of the princely states, who were representing the princes and not the population or the political parties (if any) in those states, there was one individual, "a prince without a principality," "Prince" Aga Khan, who was officially recognized as the leader of the Indian delegation. In the words of Sir Samuel Hoare (later Lord Templewood), a participant at the RTC: "Pope, Prince, accomplished man of two worlds, eastern and western, equally well-known on the race course, in the casinos of Europe, and the mosques of Africa and India, a consummate diplomat and an untiring peace-maker, the Aga at once took a foremost place at the Round Table."[9] He was singly able to stall the progress at the RTC by declaring time and again that recognition of Muslim communal claims would have to take precedence over any serious consideration of a constitution for India.

The INC boycotted the first RTC. When civil disobedience spread all over the country, the viceroy was alarmed, because it was ruining the trade of the towns, pressed heavily on government revenues, and strained the police and the jails to the utmost. He sought accommodation with Gandhi. Irwin and Gandhi reached an agreement. Gandhi agreed to call off the movement after securing a formal agreement with the government as to its political conduct, and the Congress agreed to participate in the second RTC, with Gandhi as its sole representative.

The second RTC ended in failure to reach any accord primarily because of a lack of consensus on the minorities and the communal problem, in general. There was a change in government in Britain, which was also in the grip of the Great Depression. From this hostile environment, Gandhi returned disappointed and was quickly arrested by the government. There were wide-scale arrests of political activists, and the Congress itself was declared an illegal organization. With the leaders behind prison bars, none from the Congress could attend the third RTC.

GANDHI BREAKS THE SALT LAWS

When the INC resolved to launch the Civil Disobedience Movement, it left the details to Gandhi. He decided to break the Salt Laws that had established salt as a government monopoly; the people on the coast who used to get their salt free found that the essential commodity had to be bought at the prices fixed by the government.

In the late eighteenth century, as Cheshire increased its salt production, Britain looked for markets overseas. In India, it could not compete in price and quality with the salt produced in Assam. At first, the East India Company banned salt in Bengal, yet the Bengalis preferred the Orissa variety, which encouraged traders to smuggle from Orissa. In 1803, the EIC annexed Orissa, and in the next decade, salt was declared a government monopoly. It is notable that salt was one of the three state monopolies the French colonial masters established in their Southeast Asian possessions.

It took a long time for the public protests against the costly salt sold from government depots. The first such meeting was held in Cuttack, Orissa, in 1888, protesting the tax on salt, which was several times the amount of tax in Britain. In 1929, Nilakantha Das, a member of the Central Legislative Assembly from Orissa, asked the government to allow salt production in Orissa and repeal the salt tax.

The British used large ships for transporting the bulky raw cotton bales from India to feed the textile plants in Lancashire and Manchester. On the outward journey from Britain, the cargo of finished textiles and other manufactures was supplemented by Cheshire salt to provide ballast.

Gandhi chose salt as the commodity to protest the laws that affected the lives of millions in India, mostly the poor people. Not that he found it hard to pay for the commodity, which he had stopped using in his diet since his incarceration in South African prisons. One wonders if he was aware of the dramatic impact the salt campaign would make, as he and his companions would walk the 240-mile distance from Ahmedabad to the coastal village of Dandi, 12 miles a day, every day, from morn to sunset, the campaign gathering momentum as more and more people joined this old Pied Piper who held not a pipe but a unrefined peasant's walking stick, attracting newspaper headlines for twenty-five days, getting on the nerves of British officials in India, if not in Britain itself. The world media found it fascinating, as they reported the British unjust laws in India being defied by a "frail little man marching against a mighty empire."[10]

On April 5, 1930, Gandhi and his swollen entourage of several thousands, rich and poor, men and women, intellectuals and illiterates, reached Dandi. The next day, as the sun rose, the Mahatma and the huge mass bent down on the beach where a crust of salt was cracking and picked up a piece of it. Those unarmed *satyagrahis* were beaten mercilessly and arrested. That was the sure beginning of the not too distant attrition of the British Empire over which the British boasted the sun never set, shrinking to a size over which it would hardly rise! Gandhi had broken the laws and dared the mightiest empire in history.

THE COMMUNAL AWARD AND GANDHI'S REACTION

After the failure of the second RTC, acting like King Solomon dividing a baby between two contesting mothers, Prime Minister Ramsay MacDonald gave his own Communal Award on August 4, 1932, prescribing formulas for the composition of new provincial legislatures in which the principal religious communities and the Depressed Classes would have neatly designated separate electorates. The policy of divide and rule had once again scored a victory for the British. In keeping with the separatists' demand, the award ensured the Muslims of their majority status in the Punjab and Bengal. Additionally, it recognized two more Muslim-majority provinces in

Sind (officially separated from Bombay Presidency on April 1, 1936) and the NWFP. In addition to such religious and caste groupings, the Communal Award recognized the European commercial and industrial interests in India, as well as the British residents of Bengal, giving them separate representation in the legislatures far beyond what their small numbers warranted.

One aspect of the Communal Award hurt Gandhi most: the award's recognition and allocation of separate electorates to the Depressed Classes, who were part of the Hindu fold, even though historically they had received grossly unfair treatment at the hands of the upper castes. Gandhi had personally labored in the cause of their uplift, from the shame of their centuries-old positions in the Hindu fold. He saw it as an unconscionable effort on the part of rulers who had no understanding whatsoever of the country's ethos to sunder from its parent a significant section of the Hindu community for which the government had done precious little. Gandhi undertook a fast unto death demanding the abrogation of the separate electorates for the Depressed Classes, who numbered about 10 percent of the population. It is notable that it was not the British rulers but the leader of the *Harijans*, the learned Dr. B. R. Ambedkar, who saved Gandhi's life and the Hindu community from dismemberment, by concluding with Gandhi what is known as the Poona Pact on September 25, 1932, by which the Depressed Classes were, in fact, ensured of a larger representation than in the award by their exercising a franchise in "double constituencies" as part of the general electorates. In the double constituencies, one seat would be guaranteed to the Depressed Classes, whom Gandhi and with him, most of his country, called *Harijans*. Unlike Prime Minister MacDonald, Ambedkar and Gandhi had, like King Solomon, saved the baby without amputating it.

Apart from the Depressed Classes, the Communal Award remained the basis for all the negotiations from that time until the British left India fifteen years later. Within two years of it, in July 1934, the government announced that 25 percent of all new positions in the civilian and armed services would be reserved for the Muslims. And a year later, on July 2, 1935, the government assured the Muslims that the Communal Award would not be allowed to be modified "without the express consent of the communities concerned," thus giving the IML a veto over India's constitutional future and freedom.

Were the British rulers genuinely interested in leading India to dominion status? Was it sincere in the 1930s in translating its undertaking of 1917 to lead to "a progressive realization of responsible government in India"? The latter phrase involved the progression toward a constitution of the British type wherein the executive would be drawn from the majority political party in the legislature. How would that be possible if they willfully encouraged the division of the citizenry into Hindus, Muslims, Sikhs, Depressed Classes, Anglo-Indians, the European (British) community, the European (British) commercial interests, and women, to add to the classes and groupings already recognized such as landlords and property holders and university graduates? If all these were to be reconciled with ideological and party interests and combined with guarantees for the Muslim majority provinces, was there any polity in the Western world or any conceivable democratic tapestry that could be held up as an example of the possible for India? The conclusion is inescapable that the British would not be moved by any lofty principles of spreading democracy and freedom to a large, competent, and deserving part of humanity and were manipulating to the best of their ability to stir baser feelings of hatred and distrust among two communities that had coexisted for centuries before the advent of Western colonial rule. Far from uniting India into one country and promoting the nationalist spirit there, as some British claimed, in those last decades of their rule, the British were ignominiously involved in dividing the Indian citizenry into religious groupings in an effort to perpetuate an alien autocracy.

What were the weighty reasons behind all this skullduggery and dishonesty in the "cause" of continued colonial rule? Nehru was later, in 1946, to write in his work *The Discovery of India* that there was an inevitable conflict between British and Indian interests that was, for example, not conducive to the functioning of autonomous governments in India:

> The major obstruction to progress in India was the political and economic structure imposed by the British. . . . The inherent tendency of the Indian economy to expand was not restricted so much by these forms and habits as by the political and economic stranglehold of the British. But for that steel framework, expansion was inevitable, bringing in its wake many social changes and the ending of outworn customs and ceremonial patterns. Hence attention had to be concentrated on the removal of that framework. . . . That framework was itself based on and protected the semifeudal land tenure system and many other relics of the past. Any kind of democracy in India was incompatible with the British political and economic structure, and conflict between the two was inevitable. Hence the partial democracy of 1937–39 was always on the verge of conflict. Hence also the official British view that democracy in India had not been successful, because they could only consider it in terms of maintaining the structure and values and vested interests they had built up.[11]

THE PROBLEM OF THE PRINCELY STATES

The invitation to the princely states to send their representatives to the RTC marked the injection of a new element that could be used by the colonial masters indefinitely to postpone any major constitution for India at the central level. Their loyalties to the "paramount power" would insert a wedge in the political discussions.

Historical Background

The agreements between the East India Company and the princes were endorsed by the Crown after the Great Uprising of 1857 and the dissolution of the EIC in the following year. A few years before the uprising, in 1853, the *Times* of London commended: "We have emancipated these pale and ineffectual pageants of royalty from the ordinary fate that awaits an oriental despotism." Ironically, as the British rulers would from stage to stage over the next ninety years progressively move toward freedom in British India, they fervently protected the feudal rights and privileges of the princely order, leaving the tens of millions under them away from the democratic winds sweeping the subcontinent.

Along with the Simon Commission, Britain had appointed a committee of three with Sir Harcourt Butler as president in December 1927 "to review the relations between the British Crown and the Indian princely rulers." The Butler Committee had listed 562 states covering an area of 716,000 square miles with an estimated population of 93 million. Some of them, notably Hyderabad, Kashmir, Mysore, Gwalior, and Baroda, were as large as some European states; some were no larger than a good-size tea plantation, with many rulers living in a large mansion rather than a palace but entitled to certain privileges, which were measured in terms of the number of volleys in a "gun salute" on their birthdays or coronation anniversaries. Saurashtra alone in Northwest Gujarat had 225 states. The rulers were entitled to be addressed as "His Highness," and only one of them, the Nizam of Hyderabad, arguably the richest of them and one of the richest individuals in the world, styled "His Exalted Highness." Many of them printed their own postal stamps (favorites of the philatelists), had their own flags flying alongside the Union Jack, maintained armies mostly commanded by the British, and had harems controlled by eunuchs for the pleasure of the princes. Ordinarily, they held powers over the life and death of their subjects, but even the greatest of them shivered in the presence of the British representative at their court. As K. M. Panikkar, prime minister to at least three princely states, including Kashmir and Bikaner, said dramatically, "A whisper in the residency echoed like thunder in the palace."

Whereas British India, covering two-thirds of the subcontinent, had come alive with the massive Civil Disobedience Movement under Gandhi in 1930, the princely states were islands of relative, but not complete, political quietude. They were largely playing the role they were designed to, namely, to act as buffers between territories directly under British rule. They thereby hampered, though not very effectively, the raging nationalist movement in British India.

A few princes themselves were, however, touched by the Gandhian movement, and their subjects had, in the same manner as the INC, established the All India States People's Congress (AISPC). Although not as powerful as the INC, the AISPC had made certain demands, such as limiting the ruler's privy purse to a reasonable percentage of the revenues instead of the practice of some of them to use up to 50 percent for their personal use, starving the public works and education in their states except for the capital city. The AISPC had also demanded the rule of law with adoption, as far as possible, of the laws prevalent in British India. And they had pushed for a more efficient administration by rulers who tended to spend time on vices, laziness, and eccentricities.

What would be the role and attitude of the princes in the steps the British government took after the publication of the Motilal Nehru and the Simon Commission reports? The British government and the numerous commissions it appointed seemed to vacillate between the strictly legal interpretation of the treaties with the princes and the need

for substantial revision so as to produce a progressive constitution for the whole subcontinent. Thus, the Indian States Committee, or Butler Committee as it was known, took, on the one hand, the strictly legal position that the princes' relations were with the British Crown and not with the government of India. Britain, as a paramount power, should deal only with the princes and not their subjects in suggesting constitutional reform. On the other hand, the same Butler Committee stated that time and usage had "naturally" justified changes and "lighted up the dark places of the treaties."[12] The matter would become further complicated, as the Butler Committee referred the entire question of the legality of the treaties to the government's legal counsel, Sir Leslie Scott. He was legalistic, as could only be expected. He was also retrograde in his approach, because his opinion did not match with the changing times and the need to bring people in the princely states in line with the democratic aspirations of their counterparts in the rest of the subcontinent. Scott insisted that the princes were originally independent sovereigns who had transferred to the EIC and then to the Crown only the conduct of foreign relations in exchange for unconditional protection against the "dangers, external and internal." Such a doctrine of the primacy of direct and treaty relationship, wrote V. B. Kulkarni, an expert on princely states, was "an adroit invention in order to use the states as one more counterpoise to the Indian demand for national independence. . . . It was as though all the mighty labour that had gone into the production of its Report was intended for the sole purpose of making a gift of one more veto to the British Government against the demand for Indian freedom."[13]

THE ACT OF 1935

The Act of 1935 was the most important constitutional document in the entire British-Indian relationship before the British Parliament approved the measure in 1947, agreeing to transfer the power to India and Pakistan. Although the part in the 1935 measure that proposed the federal structure was not implemented, it became, by and large, the model for the Indian Constitution of 1950, making it a linear and logical progression of the democratic process that had begun in 1853 by adding a half-dozen members to the then Governor-General's Council and making it a legislative body. The main features of the Act of 1935 were a federation consisting of the provinces of British India and the princely states and full autonomy to the provinces, with the federation exercising only such powers as were defined by the constitution. Most important, both the federal as well as the provincial governments would be responsible to their elected legislatures except for the "safeguards" provided in the act. There were to be no "reserved" subjects at the federal or provincial levels. Instead, certain powers were given to the governors to be exercised by them in their "discretion and individual judgment."

From Britain's point of view, the act marked a clear step in the direction of dominion status in the same manner as the other dominions had evolved. Britain took steps also to reduce the Indian government's accountability to Britain. Thus, the Council of India, established in 1858, was abolished, and the governor-general of India and the provincial governors were held accountable to the secretary of state for India only when they acted "according to their discretion and individual judgment." Otherwise, they would be completely responsible to the Indian legislatures. Such "safeguards" were to be considered "transitional" by India, which would have the same freedom, internal and external, as the other members of the British Commonwealth of Nations.

The British argued that the few "safeguards" were essentially to protect the imperial interests of defense not only of the Indian Empire but also of British possessions around it in East Africa, the Gulf region, and Southeast Asia. The Indian legislatures, federal and provincial, were forbidden to amend or modify the Act of 1935 or affect any of the discretionary powers given to the governor-general or the governors by that act. Importantly for the nation that had found its way to India for trading in the seventeenth century, the Indian legislatures were forbidden to legislate to discriminate against the British commercial and other economic interests.

There was much criticism of the act by Congress leaders, Nehru leading them and characterizing the reform as "a slave constitution." An eminent constitutional lawyer and Congress leader, Bhulabhai Desai, criticized the act as falling terribly short of what was needed for complete freedom. He listed some essential functions of a truly independent government: external and internal defense; the right to control foreign relations, including currency and exchange; fiscal policy; and day-to-day administration of the land. There were too many matters reserved for the governor-general, whose discretionary power and "special responsibilities" amounted to a veto. Moreover, he had the "positive power of individual legislation," which could make him an "absolute and sole dictator." Bhulabhai asked: "With what sense of honor and self-respect and hope could we look forward to the future under such a constitution?"[14]

Taking another perspective but essentially condemning the Act of 1935, Abdur Rahim, president of the Central Assembly, found the proposed federal scheme "devoid of all basic and essential elements . . . necessary to form any Federation." This was because the consent of the princes had not been obtained as to whether they were willing to federate as federating units on the terms laid down by the princes or by the British

government. As it was, the terms that the princes laid down as antecedent to their joining the federation would make it impossible to "construct any kind of Federation worth its name." Therefore, Abdur Rahim concluded that the proposed federation was not workable. Besides, he queried, what was the use of power when "there are 98% of the safeguards and only 2% of responsibility?" His conclusion was that the "idea of an All-India Federation was started as a device in order to withhold responsibility at the Center and thus . . . we were put on the wrong track."

Rahim was right. A major hurdle that would not make the federal part operative was that it was left to the princely states whether and when to join the federation. The act pointed out their special legal status and the varied internal political structure of the diverse princely states, which were at different stages of political development. There was also a lack of any participatory government in most of them, unlike the British Indian provinces, which had benefited from the various constitutional measures, notably under the Act of 1919.

As for the federal legislature, its members from the princely states were to be nominated by the princes, whereas those from the provinces were to be elected by the people on a fairly wide franchise. The federal part of the constitution of 1935 could be implemented only if and when a sufficient number of princely states agreed to join so as to occupy 52 of the

104 seats allotted to them in the Council of States, as they represented at least 50 percent of the total population of all princely states. The federal part of the Act of 1935 was never implemented because the princes did not agree to join the proposed federation.

Provincial Governments

The Act of 1935 granted almost complete provincial autonomy to the provinces, which were now deemed free from the "superintendence, direction and control" of the central government and the secretary of state for India except for "certain specific purposes." For this, the provincial governors were given "special responsibilities": the good government of backward areas (mostly tribal areas) designated "partially excluded areas"; the prevention of "any grave menace to the peace and tranquility of the province"; and implementation of all areas falling in the governor-general's "discretion or individual judgment" regarding that province. For this, the governors were given special powers of legislation, including the right to promulgate an ordinance, valid for six months. In all other matters, the provincial governors were to act according to the advice of the ministers, who would be responsible to the legislature.

A question raised by constitutional experts was how much closer did the Act of 1935 bring India to its goal of dominion status? The answer would be that at least in three main respects, India would be short of equality with Britain or other dominions. The act did not state how long it would take for India to make the next grade. In defense of this lacuna, it was stated that all colonies in their march toward dominion status had allowed Britain to be in charge of their defense and foreign affairs until 1914. But the critics said there was no constitutional device such as the "safeguards" in the constitution of other dominions. This was countered by two points: first, that they were needed for "peace and tranquility" and for "the protection of the minorities" and, second, that such safeguards appeared more formidable on paper than in practice. For example, the "power of certification" provided under the Act of 1919 was used only ten times between 1921 and 1937. In practice, it would be most difficult for the governor-general or the governor to misuse the power of intervention over the wishes of the elected legislature. The elected ministers could, in that case, resign or rally public opinion in favor of the particular matter. A reelection on the controversial issue or issues might return the same party to power with an increased majority. In the long run, the ministers would "either get their way or the constitution would break down." Only in one constitutional aspect was India not on equal footing with the dominions, and that was the primacy of the British Parliament over the Indian Federation. However, the Statute of

Westminster of 1931 precluded the British Parliament from legislating for dominions except at their request or with their consent. When that disability was removed in the case of India, it was argued, the Indian Parliament would be truly supreme and independent.

Working of Provincial Autonomy

Historians dealing with the last decade of British rule and the partition of the subcontinent have emphasized the Muslim League's electoral frustration in the provincial-level elections in 1937 as being directly responsible for its aggressive demand for a separate state. The Congress had done extremely well in the Muslim-majority provinces, winning outright in eight of the eleven provinces and forming governments in July 1937 in Bombay, Madras, the Central Provinces, the United Provinces, Bihar, and Orissa and a little later in the Northwest Frontier Province and in Assam, in October 1938. The Muslim League failed to win a majority even in the Muslim-majority provinces and not a single seat in two of them—Sind and the NWFP. They could not, therefore, form a government in any of those Muslim-majority provinces. It had not won a single seat in Bihar, the CP, Orissa, Sind, or the NWFP. It won only one seat in the Punjab. In Bengal, the league won only 39 out of the 117 Muslim seats. Despite the separate electorates, the Muslim League won only

109 seats out of a total of 482 Muslim seats, getting only 4.8 percent of the total Muslim vote. The explanation of the IML debacle lay in the fact that it was an urban-based party with hardly any support in rural India, where more than 80 percent of the people—Hindus and Muslims—lived. The elections proved that the league was, at that point of time, not a vital force in Indian politics and that it did not have support even in the Muslim-majority provinces. This should have exploded forever the "two nationalisms" theory and shown how strongly the Indian electorate—Hindu and Muslim—endorsed the nationalist spirit, Hindu-Muslim harmony, and secularism.

The IML's position in the Muslim-majority provinces was the least promising. Thus, in Punjab, the National Unionist Party, which won the majority and formed the government, was headed by Sir Sikandar Hayat. He believed in Punjabi nationalism regardless of religion; his cabinet had three Muslims, two Hindus, and one Sikh. He did not agree with Jinnah and his separatist philosophy. When the Muslim League met in Lahore in 1940 and passed the famous resolution demanding the creation of Pakistan, Sir Sikander and members of his party were opposed to the partition of India.[15] In Bengal, the ministry led by A. K. Fazul-al-Huq was a Hindu-Muslim coalition. In Sind, where there were numerous parties and none held a majority of seats, Sir Ghulam Hussain

Hidayatullah, who called himself a nationalist, had one Hindu in his three-man cabinet. His successor as chief minister, Khan Bahadur Allah Baksh, was asked by Jinnah to convert his ministry into a Muslim League Ministry, but Jinnah was rebuffed.

As the IML's frustration built, Jinnah's determination for a separate state increased. In this, some historians have blamed the Congress leaders, particularly Nehru, for their insensitivity in not accommodating the Muslim League's political ambitions in a crucial state, namely, the United Provinces, even though that province was not a Muslim-majority province. They have argued that it was an important factor in the league's subsequent demand for Pakistan. In the UP election, as elsewhere, the league's performance had not been promising; it had won only 27 out of 64 Muslim seats, the rest being won by other Muslim groups. In the non-Muslim general seats, the Congress had won an overwhelming victory and, therefore, was called upon by the British governor to form the government.

Maulana Abul Kalam Azad, a prominent Congress leader, had proposed, despite the fact that the Congress had a clear majority in the UP legislature, that it form a coalition government with two members of the UP Muslim League. According to him, such a concession would have completely satisfied the local IML politicians' ambitions. In his memoirs, *India Wins Freedom*, Azad says that this would have met the wishes of the UP Muslim League president, Choudhury Khaliquzzaman. Azad accuses Nehru of "reversing the decision" and proposing only one seat for the IML in the UP cabinet, in which case either Khaliquzzaman or Nawab Ismail Khan would have to stay out.[16] The league had agreed informally to Azad's offer, because it fitted into its long-term demand that one-third of the cabinet seats (assuming that it would have six members) in any province, regardless of the electoral results, should go to Muslims. As Khaliquzzaman wrote about the incident later: "Pandit Pant [the head of the ministry in the UP] asked me how many seats in the Cabinet I would demand in case of a coalition between the Congress and the League. I replied: three in nine and two in six, that is, one-third of the total strength of the Cabinet whatever it may be."[17]

When the cabinet was formed, it did have two Muslim ministers, one of them a congressman who had been elected from a general constituency and the other a non-IML person elected with a large majority over a league candidate. The two Muslim members, in fact, represented the Muslims but did not belong to the Muslim League, which believed that only it could represent Muslims, a contention that even the British had not accepted because it was patently undemocratic. There was no democratic logic in the vehement criticism of the Congress that the league now launched. This was even true of Jinnah, who was known for his razor-edge analytical abilities and who was critical of any argument based on emotion.

Jinnah now accused the UP Congress-led government of following a Hindu policy to the exclusion of Muslim sentiments. His list of atrocities of the UP Congress-led government was trivial. It included: singing of the national song, "Bande Mataram," and the use of the tricolor flag, this despite the fact that there is not one word offensive to Islam or the Indian Muslims in the song and that the Congress's tricolor flag was used during the Khilafat movement as the flag of that movement. The IML said that the Congress had no right to "make common cause" with the Muslim masses, which was the sole privilege of the Muslim League. In particular, the league also opposed the provincial government's support of the Wardha education scheme, drawn up by Dr. Zakir Hussain, an eminent educationist and future president of India.

Alluding to Jinnah's accusations, Maulana Azad, who was in charge of the working of the Congress Party in the UP, Punjab, Sind, and the NWFP, wrote:

Every incident which involved communal issues came up before me. From personal knowledge and with a full sense of responsibility, I can, therefore, say that the charges leveled by Mr. Jinnah and the Muslim League with regard to injustice to Muslims and other minorities were absolutely false. If there had been an iota of truth in any of these charges, I would have seen to it that the injustice was rectified.[18]

Although denying any charges, Nehru wrote to Jinnah offering to refer the specific instances, if any, of the kind alleged by Jinnah to the chief justice of the federal court in India, Sir Maurice Gwyer.

Jinnah did not take up the challenge. He was no longer interested in the electoral politics or Western-style democracy. On March 3, 1938, he wrote to Gandhi demanding that the Muslim League be recognized as "the sole representative of the Muslims of India" and Gandhi as the sole representative of the Congress and the Hindus. Did he expect this to be a permanent political arrangement for the subcontinent's future? In September 1939, following the outbreak of World War II, the Muslim League's Working Committee, under Jinnah's leadership, resolved that it was "irrevocably opposed" to any federal constitution that "must necessarily result in a majority-community rule [Hindu] under the guise of democracy and a parliamentary system of government." The IML also resolved that "such a constitution is totally unsuited to the genius of the peoples of this *country which is composed of various nationalities and does not constitute a national state.*"[19] [Emphasis added.]

Jinnah presented his two-nationalism thesis most explicitly in a letter of September 1944 to Gandhi, who was in prison at that time:

We maintain and hold that Muslims and Hindus are two major nations by any definitions or tests of a nation. We are a nation of a hundred million, and what is more, we are a nation with our own distinctive culture and civilization, language and literature, art and architecture, names and nomenclature, sense of values and proportion, legal laws and moral codes, customs and calendar, history and traditions, aptitudes and ambitions—in short, we have our own distinctive outlook on life and of life. By all canons of international law we are a nation.

CONGRESS, THE MUSLIM LEAGUE, AND WORLD WAR II

As the clouds of war were gathering, Nehru, who was virtually in charge of Congress's foreign affairs, had, a year before World War II broke out, in a letter of September 8, 1938, to the *Manchester Guardian,* urged Britain to grant India its independence so that it would decide in freedom to oppose fascism and Nazism. As he stated:

We in India want no fascism or imperialism and we are more convinced

than ever that both are closely akin and dangers to world peace and freedom. India resents British foreign policy and will be no party to it. . . . [T]he British Government has given us an additional and unanswerable argument for complete independence. . . . The people of India have no intention of submitting to any foreign decision on war. They alone can decide and certainly they will not accept the dictation of the British Government, which they distrust utterly. I would willingly throw the entire weight on the side of democracy and freedom. . . . If Britain is on the side of democracy, then its first task is to eliminate empire from India. That is the sequence of events in Indian eyes and to that sequence the people of India will adhere.[20]

In other words, Nehru and the Congress were demanding immediate independence and the right of an independent country to declare war.

The Congress was shocked that Great Britain and in India its viceroy, Lord Linlithgow, unilaterally declared war on India's behalf without consulting its wishes. The Congress Resolution on September 14, 1939, made its resentment clear to the British:

The British Government had unilaterally, without consulting the Indian leaders or the provincial governments declared the war against Nazism and

Fascism on India's behalf and to help the war effort, promulgated ordinances and other far-reaching measures by which to circumscribe the powers of provincial governments.

The Congress felt this was neither fair nor proper. It may be legal under the "safeguards" of the Act of 1935 by which the Governor-General and the Governors could take decisions in defense and foreign affairs including declaring a war. The Congress itself including Jawaharlal Nehru and Gandhi were against Nazism and Fascism but in the view of the Congress, the "Issue of War and Peace for India" must be decided by the Indian people.

The resolution said that if cooperation was desired for a worthy cause, it could not be obtained by compulsion and imposition. Above all, India could not associate itself "in a war said to be for democratic freedom when that freedom is denied to her and such limited freedom as she possesses taken away from her."[21] It invited the British government to declare its war aims particularly in regard to democracy and imperialism and what treatment India would get. The Congress called for the resignation from the provincial ministries by October 10, 1939. By November 15, 1939, the Congress Party ministries in eight provinces had resigned.

In order to appease public opinion in India, the viceroy, Lord Linlithgow, declared in January 1940 that dominion status of the Westminster variety, "as soon as possible after the war," would be the goal of British policy in India.

August 1940 Offer

The British government needed India's cooperation in the expanding war. To assuage the feelings of the Congress and obtain its support, Viceroy Linlithgow made an offer in August 1940. Contrary to its previous pronouncements, the government conceded that the framing of a new constitution would be "primarily the responsibility of the Indians themselves and should originate from the Indian conceptions of the social, economic and political structure of Indian life." However, because of the exigencies of the war, this would have to be done after the war, at which point Britain would appoint a constitution-drafting committee for India.

In the meantime, "the enemy must be kept away." Therefore, Britain asked for India's and the Congress's cooperation in the war effort, paving "the way for the attainment of free and equal partnership in the British Commonwealth of Nations." In other words, Britain did not commit to granting complete independence to India but promised only dominion status. The caveat to this offer, however, said that no power would be transferred to an Indian government "whose authority is directly denied by large and powerful elements in India's national life." If a clear signal was needed for the Muslim League to push its demand for Pakistan, the August 1940 "offer" did it![22]

Predictably, the Congress rejected the August 1940 "offer." It was again a case of "too little, too late." Nehru declared that the "whole conception of Dominion Status for India was as dead as a door nail" and that the country wanted complete independence and would fight Nazism and fascism as a free country. The Muslim League neither accepted nor rejected the offer. It was satisfied that the offer had given it the right to veto any constitution. It, therefore, appreciated "the clear assurance . . . that no future constitution, interim or final," would be adopted "without its approval and consent." The August offer became a dead letter.

Meanwhile, realizing the strained relationship between the viceroy, Lord Linlithgow, and the Congress leaders, Jinnah played his cards most adroitly by offering the viceroy all support, although he did nothing concretely to help the war effort either in manpower recruitment or in raising funds. In a letter of November 5, 1939, Jinnah offered to the viceroy that during the course of the war, the Muslim League would not make any political demands on the government and that in return the government should give an assurance that the country's constitution would not be framed without the approval of the two major communities, the Hindus and the Muslims. After consulting with London, the viceroy replied on December 23 that the British government was "fully aware of the importance of the Muslim community whose views would never be underrated." The secretary of state for India in Churchill's War Cabinet, Lord Zetland, also assured Jinnah in his letter of April 18, 1940, that "the British Government will not attempt to impose a constitution that would not be acceptable to eighty million Muslim subjects of His Majesty."[23] Jinnah interpreted that to mean that the colonial masters had accepted his role thereafter as the "sole spokesman" of Indian Muslims, giving him the right of veto on all constitutional proposals for all of India!

The Muslim League Calls for Pakistan

Such was the background of the momentous Muslim League Resolution of March 23, 1940, at Lahore demanding the creation of the separate state of Pakistan, a "homeland" for the Indian Muslims. The resolution read:

> Resolved that it is the considered view of this Session of the All-India Muslim League that no constitutional Plan would be workable in this country or acceptable to Muslims unless it is designed on the following basic principle, namely, that geographically contiguous units are demarcated into

regions which should be so constituted, with such territorial readjustments as may be necessary, that the areas in which the Muslims are numerically in a majority as in the Northwestern and Eastern Zones of India should be grouped to constitute "Independent States" in which the constituent units shall be autonomous and sovereign.[24]

The resolution had spoken of "independent states" in the plural and of them being "autonomous and sovereign," indicating that there could be more than one Pakistan. In fact, this was inserted because of A. K. Fazul-al-Huq, who spoke of Bengal as a separate state and may, in that sense, be regarded as the progenitor of Bangladesh. The ambiguity in the resolution was reflective of divisions within the IML's leadership, many of whom, including Jinnah, were far from clear about the details of the proposed state or states.

After the Lahore Resolution, in his correspondence with the viceroy, Jinnah spoke of a "Muslim India" and demanded parity for Muslims with the Hindus, in other words moving from the pre-1927 demand for one-quarter representation for the Muslims, stepped up subsequently to one-third, and in the post–Lahore Resolution phase to 50 percent, or parity with the Hindus. He suggested that the viceroy enlarge his Executive Council to help the war effort by the addition of a few members,

provided the Muslim numbers in that body are "equal to that of the Hindus" if the Congress came in; otherwise the Muslims should have the majority of the additional members. He was bluntly asking for parity for the two "nations" of Hindus and Muslims! He further added that all the Muslims to be chosen for the "various bodies must be the Muslim League's nominees."[25]

The Cripps Mission

Meanwhile, with the Japanese attack on Pearl Harbor in December 1941, the war was not going well for the Allies, who now had to fight on an additional front. The Allies, particularly the United States, pressed that Indian cooperation be obtained. In Britain, the Labor Party members of the national coalition government were urging a dialogue with the Indian leaders. Therefore, Sir Stafford Cripps, a Labor leader known for his liberal views and his personal friendship with Jawaharlal Nehru and sympathy for the Indian nationalist cause, was sent to India to secure cooperation from the leaders of both the INC and the IML. Cripps was aware that he had to reconcile his differences with the viceroy, Lord Linlithgow, whose coldness to Gandhi was well known and appreciated by his prime minister, Churchill.

As it was, the Cripps offer was not very conducive to India's emergence as a free country. It promised dominion status after the end of the war and allowed any province to opt out of that dominion, if it liked, which virtually conceded the Muslim League's demand for a separate state. Gandhi rejected it outright, calling it "a post-dated cheque on a crashing bank"! And Linlithgow, who least appreciated Cripps's meetings with Gandhi and Nehru as well as with President Roosevelt's "Special Representative," Louis Johnson, in New Delhi, corresponded directly with Churchill, undermining Cripps's connections with the Indian leaders.

"Quit India" Resolution

On August 9, 1942, under Gandhi's leadership, the All India Congress Committee meeting at the historic Gowalia Tank (literally a stone's throw away from the birthplace of the Congress in 1885) passed a resolution demanding "the withdrawal of the British Power from India." Known as the "Quit India" resolution, it made it clear that "the immediate ending of British rule in India is an urgent necessity both for the sake of India and for the success of the cause of the United Nations. The continuation of that rule is degrading and enfeebling India and making her progressively less capable of defending herself and of contributing to the cause of world freedom." It added that on declaration of India's independence, it would establish a "provisional government," and as "free India, it will become an ally of the United Nations, sharing with them in the trials and tribulations of the joint enterprise of the struggle for freedom." India thus made it clear to Britain that it would not fight for its imperialistic ambitions—on the contrary, it would fight for the freedom of other Asian colonies under Western powers. "The freedom of India must be the symbol of and prelude to the freedom of all other Asiatic nations under foreign domination. Burma, Malaya, Indo-China, the Dutch Indies [Indonesia], Iran and Iraq must also attain their complete freedom." Apprehensive of the Western power returning to their former colonies including those occupied by Japan in Southeast Asia, the resolution said that those lands "must not subsequently be placed under the rule or control of any colonial power."[26]

Britain was headed at this time by a historic personality, Winston Churchill, who could be totally blind when it came to Britain's imperialistic possessions. Millions around the globe appreciated his dedication and fighting spirit in taking up the Nazi and Fascist challenge to democracy and freedom. However, although he was a champion of democracy at home, asking his compatriots for "blood, sweat, and tears" in defense of their freedom, he had no sense of shame or compunction in denying such freedoms to several hundred millions of Indians, who counted among themselves men and women who had sacrificed their careers and lives at the altar of human freedom. In response to Gandhi's call for freedom of 400 million of the human race, the "British Bulldog" barked: "Let there be no mistake about it. We mean to hold our own. I have not become the King's First Minister in order to preside over the liquidation of the British Empire."[27]

Linlithgow ordered the entire Congress leadership from all over the country arrested and jailed without the benefit of a trial. They were to languish in British jails for the rest of the war, leaving Jinnah and the Muslim League an unfettered scope to confabulate with the British hierarchy in India.

Gandhi's "Quit India" call was taken up by millions of people throughout the country, not only in the major cities but even in the smallest towns and villages. The news that all the Congress leaders had been thrown behind bars spread like wildfire, and although Gandhi had advised to hold the demonstration peacefully, the crowds in many places became violent and destroyed a lot of government installations, including government-owned buses and trains, telegraph wires, and telephone connections. The Socialist wing of the Congress Party went underground; most of them eluded the police and indulged in violent activity from their secret hideouts. Jaiprakash Narayan, Achyutrao Patwardhan, Asoka Mehta, and Aruna Asaf Ali became household heroes with their pictures in millions of homes.

Linlithgow retired on October 20, 1943, and was succeeded by Lord Wavell, who had been commander in chief in India, including during the Cripps visit. He liked neither Gandhi nor Jinnah.

From his house imprisonment in the Aga Khan's palace in Pune, Gandhi remained in correspondence with the viceroy. Finding Wavell cold, he turned to Jinnah, only colder and nastier. The Gandhi–Jinnah talks of September 1944 ended in an anticipated failure.

British Pyrrhic Victory and Decision to Quit

The war ended in Europe with Germany's defeat; in Asia, the Japanese withdrawal began in March 1945 from Indochina and Indonesia. At the Potsdam Conference, the British were authorized to occupy Southeast Asia south of the fourteenth parallel. Britain asked the Southeast Asia Command under Lord Louis Mountbatten (the future last viceroy of India) to do so. Britain itself returned to its former colonies of Burma (Myanmar), Malaya, and Singapore. In contrast to France and the Netherlands, Britain as a colonial power realized that it was not welcome in its colonies.

According to some British accounts, Britain realized that the costs of administering the colonies had become prohibitive, meaning that they could not make enough profits for the mother country. Some historians such as D. K. Fieldhouse would later state that empires never paid and that the colonies were "white elephants."[28] In truth, the white masters, paid far beyond the natives and well above what they would have been at home, were the "white elephants"—a brown man's burden.

The real truth was that the victory over Germany and Japan was a Pyrrhic one that was achieved at an excessive cost. Moreover, there had been two major rebellions in the British Indian armed forces, which undermined British confidence in its ability to hold the empire for long. The first was a major defection of some 40,000 British Indian troops in Singapore who joined the newly created Indian National Army under a former Indian National Congress president (1938 and 1939), Subhash Chandra Bose (1897–1945), the event considered by large numbers of Indian masses to be of great importance for the Indian nationalist movement, though it did not fit into Gandhi's nonviolent lines. Bose had fallen out with Gandhi and the Congress and proceeded to found his own Forward Bloc in 1939, with sympathy for Hitler. In the following year, the British placed him under house arrest in Calcutta, from which he escaped in disguise, and traveled to Germany through Afghanistan. He met Hitler, who thought he would be of greater help to Japan, an Axis power, and, therefore, sent him by submarine to Japan in 1943. The Japa-

nese helped him to establish the Azad Hind Fouj (literally, "Free India Army") although in most accounts it is referred to as the Indian National Army (INA) primarily made up of freed Indian prisoners of war who had been captured by Japan when Singapore fell. The following year, Bose established the government of Free India in exile, with himself as president and having his own cabinet, flag, and army. The INA marched westward with the slogan "Chalo Delhi" (Onward to Delhi) but was halted at the Indian border.

On August 18, 1945, Bose reportedly died in a plane crash on the island of Taiwan. His government and army were taken prisoners by the returning British forces under the Southeast Asia Command. In the latter half of 1945, while talks for handing over power in India were going on, there was a deafening nationwide excitement created by the trial the British staged of the top INA leaders as criminals of war in Delhi's Red Fort, where for only the second time in his life, Nehru donned the robes of a lawyer to defend them. The war criminals became heroes overnight all over the country, their pictures adorning the walls of innumerable homes. People did not believe that Bose was dead; they believed he was keeping away from the British and would return triumphantly home once the country became free.

A second revolt that jolted the British confidence in the loyalty of its troops was in its navy in Bombay in 1943. Indian armed forces had formed an overwhelming part of the famed Indian Army, which had distinguished itself in the battlefields of Europe, North Africa, and the Middle East during the two world wars. The question was whether the British could depend anymore on the Indian Army, particularly when India had demonstrated its opposition to imperialism on such a large scale during the "Quit India" movement in 1942.

Simla Conference

None perhaps understood the significance of this Pyrrhic victory better than the viceroy, Lord Wavell, former commander in chief of the Indian Army. On June 14, 1945, he announced his plans to expand and reorganize his Executive Council, which would be fully Indian but for the commander in chief and the viceroy himself. The provincial administration would be restored to Indian hands and would operate under the Act of 1935.

On June 25, a conference of all political parties, notably the Congress and the Muslim League, was called to meet at the summer capital of Simla to discuss the details. The conference was practically sabotaged by two missives dated June 8 and June 18 from Jinnah to the viceroy. In the first letter, he referred to his correspondence with the previous viceroy, Lord Linlithgow

in which he was "promised" that the Muslim League and the Congress would be given an equal number of seats in an expanded Executive Council and that the most important portfolios such as home, defense, external affairs, and finance would be equally shared by the two parties. The second letter specifically objected to the possible inclusion of Dr. Zakir Hussain in the Congress list, because only the Muslim League was entitled, in his view, to nominate Muslims. If the Congress were allowed to do so, Jinnah threatened the viceroy, "the reaction of Muslim India would be deadly." At Simla, he insisted that the Congress represented only the Hindus; the viceroy coolly countered that the Congress represented its myriad members. The Simla talks failed because of Jinnah's intransigence, though. As Bertrans Glancy, the then governor of Punjab wrote, Jinnah emerged as "a champion of Islam" in the eyes of "a large section of the Muslim population."[29]

The Indian political scene changed dramatically the following day as in far-off Britain Churchill was thrown out of power, as the electorate roundly defeated his party in the elections and gave the majority to the Labor Party, whose leader, Clement Attlee, assumed the office of prime minister.

With Japan's formal surrender on August 8 following the U.S. dropping atomic bombs on Hiroshima and Nagasaki, the British government decided it was time to wind up its affairs in India by giving India full self-government. To that end, it was announced on September 19 that general elections would be held in India, after which a constitution-making body would be established.

Those elections were contested by the Muslim League with a total determination to win, no matter what it took. Jinnah abandoned his constitutionalist and legal ways. He wanted to gain whatever electoral mileage he could even by crudely appealing to religious extremism, something completely contrary to his lifelong behavior. He openly asked the masses: "Are you a true believer or an infidel and a traitor?" Muslims were posed the question whether they would like to live in a united India under "Hindu domination" or as Muslims in their own autonomous state.[30] There was a dramatic change in the fortunes of the Muslim League, in stark contrast with the electoral results of 1937. The Muslim League won all the seats reserved for Muslims in the Central Assembly and 427 of the 507 Muslim seats in the provincial legislatures.

Keen on transferring power, the Labor government sent a new three-man mission to India in May 1946. Because all the three members held the rank of cabinet ministers, it came to be called the Cabinet Mission. Headed by Lord Pethick-Lawrence, the secretary of state for India, the other two members were: Sir Stafford Cripps, who had already visited India in 1942, well known specially to the Congress leaders and now the president of the Board of Trade, and A. V. Alexander, First Lord of the Admiralty. On May 16, it proposed a weak federal government with complete autonomy to the provinces, any of which, after an initial stipulated period, could leave the federation. The princely states were urged to join the federation. The IML, which was at first somewhat inclined to accept the proposal because it saw in it "the germ of Pakistan," rejected it after the Congress, with Nehru as its president (effective July 1946), considered it unworkable.

INTERIM INDIAN GOVERNMENT FORMED

The earnestness of the British government to give up power was seen in two moves. First, Viceroy Wavell invited the Congress and the Muslim League to join his Executive Council and form an interim government in the hope that the princes too would join it. The Executive Council would be all-Indian with the viceroy being the only foreigner in it, with, however, emergency powers that he expected he would have no occasion to use. He wanted the council to have fourteen members, six to be nominated by the Congress including one from the Scheduled Castes, five from the IML, and three to represent the minorities, to be nominated by the viceroy himself. As soon as Jinnah learned that there was a Muslim among the Congress nominees, he refused to send IML representatives.

Therefore, the interim government, which was inaugurated on September 2, 1946, under Nehru's leadership did not have IML representatives. It was not until October 15 that the Muslim League, after reconsideration of the issue, agreed to send its representatives to Nehru's cabinet. Among the conditions was that Liaquat Ali, a prominent IML leader and future prime minister of Pakistan, be given the finance portfolio.

Transfer of Power: Mountbatten Arrives

Meanwhile, not happy with the pace of decolonization, the Attlee government announced on February 20, 1947, a change in its representative in India, replacing Wavell with Admiral Louis Mountbatten with a mandate that the transfer of power be completed by June 1948. The dashing Mountbatten with his regal wife, Edwina, had a tremendous presence. He had been in the East as the supreme commander of the Southeast Asia Command during World War II and was conversant with the postwar scenario in which he had seen firsthand the impatience of the leaders and the people to close the colonial chapter in their country's history. He asked for and was given plenipotentiary powers, to handle the situation the best he could and commit Britain to a new

order. Arriving on March 24 with an excellent team of experts, he quickly realized that if Britain were to retain some goodwill in India, the transfer of power would have to be precipitate; he announced he would like it by August 1947.

Mountbatten wasted no time in getting to know the principal leaders—Gandhi, Nehru, Jinnah, and Sardar Vallabhbhai Patel. He realized that Gandhi had charisma and immense popularity but would be kept out by Nehru, Patel, and others in settling the thorny questions of the transfer of power. He had known Nehru briefly and was overwhelmed by his liberal views and vision for the country. He and his wife became very close friends, and he used that relationship to hasten the process of decolonization in the best way possible. After his first meeting with Jinnah, he exclaimed: "My God, he was cold!" Even three decades after the events, in his interview with authors of the widely read *Freedom at Midnight*, Larry Collins and Dominique Lapierre, the once affable Mountbatten used strong language in describing Jinnah, epithets such as "a bastard" and "an evil genius." He was aware, however, of Jinnah's crucial role in any peaceful process of transfer of power. "If it could be said that any single man held the future of India in the palm of his hand in 1947," said the viceroy, "that man was Mohammed Ali Jinnah."[31] Mountbatten was shocked that the man who would not accept anything less than a separate state—Pakistan—was devoid of administrative knowledge or sense of responsibility. He had not formulated any details of what his homeland of the Muslims would look like. As Alan Campbell-Johnson wrote in his eyewitness account:

> Jinnah has dropped a carefully timed and placed bombshell. He demanded an eight-hundred mile corridor to link West and East Pakistan. When the Viceroy told Jinnah that the non-Muslim districts of Punjab and Bengal would not be allowed to be annexed to Pakistan, the latter protested saying, "Punjabi unity and Bengali unity are much more important than Hindu-Muslim differences." Mountbatten countered: "in that case, surely, Indian unity is much more important than Hindu-Muslim differences."

Commenting later on this confrontation, Mountbatten said, "I never met anybody, who could say 'no' so persistently and so effectively."[32]

Every passing day, Nehru found his administration of the country blocked by lack of cooperation from his Muslim League colleagues, most notably the finance minister, Liaquat Ali (the future prime minister of Pakistan), who as Maulana Abul Kalam Azad, the education minister, regretted in his memoirs, *India Wins Freedom*, would not approve even a rupee or the appointment of even a *chaprasi* (peon).[33] There were communal riots in Bengal and Punjab as refugees began moving across what they thought would mark the border between India and Pakistan. Gandhi moved to the worst-affected district of Noakhali in Bengal. He walked in its villages every day from dawn to dusk wiping tears and offering solace to the suffering. Bengal's Muslim chief minister, H. S. Suhrawardy, who was known to have instigated the riots in the first place, in time was so moved as to join Gandhi in his walking tours. Mountbatten ordered 50,000 border troops to be sent to the Punjab to quell the riots there. He paid tribute to Gandhi, calling him his one-man boundary force in Bengal. Peace had been restored to the province through his efforts and without, of course, any troops.

Mountbatten's top adviser, Lord Ismay, had a paper block on the wall. As a page was torn off it each passing day, the block would show the number of days remaining until D-Day, India's Deliverance Day from the colonial yoke of a century and a half. There were deadlines for a myriad details affecting army bases, ordnance factories, army personnel, nonmilitary official real estate, liquid assets, division of personnel, protection of refugee property, maps, charts, and demographic data to help determine what villages and towns would go to which side. To determine the last and most contentious item, Mountbatten appointed a Boundary Commission with Sir Cyril Radcliffe as chairman. His award would be published on August 17, a couple of days *after* the partition of the subcontinent and the birth of the two dominions. Despite his two-nation theory, Jinnah wanted to leave the non-Muslim population of Punjab and Bengal as subjects of the new dominion of Pakistan. In the end, the Radcliffe Commission divided the two large provinces along a line that resulted in human history's largest exodus. Some 10 million people—men, women, children, old and young, sick, and even pregnant women, belonging to three faiths, Hindus, Muslims, and Sikhs—crossed the border in Punjab's summer heat, trying to remain alive. Some 10 percent of the total did not make it, leaving deep scars on the minds that have lasted decades and generations despite the passage of more than a half century since the cataclysmic event of partition of the country.

FREE AT LAST BUT THROUGH PARTITION

Pakistan was born on August 14, 1947, with Jinnah himself as its first governor-general or head of state. He was also president of its Constituent Assembly, which also served as the new country's highest legislature. In India, Nehru and his colleagues approved Mountbatten as independent India's first governor-general, favoring continuity that would help smooth many a thorny issue with the British. The act of (the British) Parliament creating the two dominions of India and Pakistan had made India the

successor state to the British Raj. It had also, in a legal sense, allowed the 562 princely states the option to join either dominion or remain independent, theoretically permitting the birth of 564 dominions! Mountbatten's aristocratic status and bearing would be most useful in persuading these feudal relics to listen to his advice to join the geographically contiguous dominion and not even think of an independent status for themselves that would have jeopardized their security and the unity and integrity of a resurgent India.

Who was responsible for the partition of the subcontinent that had held an image of Mother India for millions of both Hindus and Muslims? In the opinion of Ayesha Jalal, who researched deeply in all the relevant papers, private and public, for her excellent biography of Jinnah, the founder of Pakistan strove hard almost to the end to avoid an outright division of India. He would have, in her opinion, been satisfied if "some form of union government," based on complete autonomy for the provinces, was conceded by the British. A member of the House of Commons blamed the partition on the British: "I do not accept the statement that the people of India were responsible for the partition any more than the people of Ireland were responsible for the partition of Ireland. . . . [T]he ruling class here with their kindred in India must take responsibility."[34]

Did Jinnah really believe in the two-nation theory? Did he believe the new country of Pakistan was the homeland for all the Muslims of the subcontinent? Mohammad C. Chagla, a staunch nationalist who had in his early days worked as Jinnah's junior attorney and later rose to be a judge of the International Court of Justice at The Hague, asked him a question that must have been on the lips of millions of Indian Muslims for whom moving to Pakistan was not possible. Chagla writes, "I will never forget the answer he gave me. He looked at me for a while and said: 'They will look after themselves. I am not interested in their fate.'" What about the two-nation theory? Would the Muslims, one-third of the total number Jinnah was leaving behind in India, be able to live under the Hindus he had demonized? As Choudhury Khaliquzzaman writes, the two-nation theory had not only driven "an ideological wedge between the Muslims and the Hindus of India" but had also "raised a natural barrier even between the Muslims of the majority and the minority provinces."[35]

Once he got his wish, Jinnah acted sober. In his inaugural address to the new nation's Constituent Assembly on August 11, 1947, he delivered a speech that could have been delivered by a secularist such as Nehru:

> You are free; you are free to go to your temples, you are free to go to your mosques or to any other place of worship in this State of Pakistan. . . . You may belong to any religion or caste or creed—that has nothing to do with

the business of the State. . . . We are starting in the days when there is no discrimination, no distinction between one community and another, no discrimination between one caste or creed and another. We are starting with this fundamental principle that we are all citizens and equal citizens of one State.[36]

If that is what he wanted, why did he ask for a separate country based on an undemocratic tenet such as religion?

Did the creation of Pakistan automatically mean harmony among all the Muslims in their alleged homeland? Barely a quarter century later, the Bengalis of East Pakistan had suffered from enough discrimination from their West Pakistani, mostly Punjabi, compatriots, in civilian and military forces, as well as in the economic development of East Pakistan vis-à-vis its western counterpart. On a personal level, the tall and light-skinned Punjabis looked down on the short, dark-skinned East Pakistani Bengalis. The West Pakistani army men clamped down on the educated Bengalis; mowed down the academics of the Dacca University, throwing them in mass graves; and brutalized and raped hundreds of thousands of Bengali women, all for voting a Bengali majority into the national assembly and demanding that a Bengali head the country's government. The two-nation theory exploded, as the East Pakistanis fought a war with their West Pakistani masters, which ended with their own liberation and emergence as the free country of Bangladesh. Obviously, all the points that Jinnah had raised in his letter to Gandhi in 1944 about the common bonds of Islam and a Muslim way of life had proved ineffectual in providing a glue capable of keeping the two wings of Pakistan as one nation.

As for India, the dream of its several hundred million people of whom so many hundreds of thousands had been sent to jails for long periods of time or executed in their prime was being fulfilled on that midnight of August 14 when the country's independence was ushered in. On that occasion, standing in the Central Hall of the Indian Parliament, Jawaharlal Nehru, the first prime minister, Gandhi's chosen heir who liked to describe himself as a child of the Indian Revolution, delivered extemporaneous remarks, which have been included in several anthologies of the world's best speeches:

> Long years ago we made a tryst with destiny, and now the time comes when we shall redeem our pledge, not

wholly or in full measure, but very substantially. At the stroke of the midnight hour, when the world sleeps, India will awake to life and freedom. A moment comes, which comes but rarely in history, when we step out from the old to the new, when an age ends, and when the soul of a nation, long suppressed, finds utterance. It is fitting that at this solemn moment we take the pledge of dedication to the service of India and her people and to the still larger cause of humanity.

He referred to Gandhi, who was not there to celebrate the moment he had labored all his life to arrive. Nehru said: "The ambition of the greatest man of our generation has been to wipe every tear from every eye. That may be beyond us, but so long as there are tears and suffering, so long our work will not be over."[37] Gandhi was then in Noakhali, in distant Bengal, walking from village to village, wiping the tears and offering solace to the suffering. They too had made sacrifices for India's freedom.

————

NOTES

1. Ayesha Jalal, *The Sole Spokesman: Jinnah, the Muslim League, and the Demand for Pakistan*, 12n.

2. Chaudhuri Rahmat Ali, *Pakistan: The Fatherland of the Pak Nation* (1946; reprint, Lahore: Book Traders, 1978).

3. Khwaja Salahuddin Ahmad, "Woking Muslim Mission's Role in the Creation of Pakistan," *Light of Islamic Review* 74, no. 4 (July–August 1997): 6. The article was first published in the *Light*, January 16, 1966. Also see Khalid Hasan, "Let Chaudhry Rehmat Ali

Lie in Peace," *Friday Times*, October 15, 2004, http://www.khalidhasan.net/fridaytimes/ 2004–10–15.htm.

4. Text of Iqbal's speech in Jamil-ud-Din Ahmad, ed., *Historic Documents of the Muslim Freedom Movement* (Lahore: Publishers United, 1970), 126–27.

5. John Buchan, *Lord Minto: A Memoir* (London: Nelson, 1924), 244.

6. Aga Khan, *The Memoirs of Aga Khan* (London: Simon and Schuster, 1954), 94; emphasis added.

7. A. C. Banerjee, ed., *Indian Constitutional Documents, 1757–1939* (Calcutta: A. Mukherjee, 1946), 3:177.

8. Ibid., 179.

9. Viscount Templewood, *Nine Troubled Years* (London: Collins, 1954), 51.

10. Mohinder Singh, "The Story of Salt," *Gandhi Marg* 2214, no. 3 (October–December 2002), 3.

11. Jawaharlal Nehru, *The Discovery of India* (London: John Day, 1946), 383–84.

12. Indian States Committee, *Report of Indian States Committee, 1928–1929* (London: His Majesty's Stationery Office, 1929), paras. 40, 52.

13. V. B. Kulkarni, *British Dominion in India and After* (Bombay: Bharatiya Vidya Bhavan, 1964), 166.

14. Banerjee, *Indian Constitutional Documents*, 3:228.

15. Penderel Moon, *Divide and Quit* (London: Chatto and Windus, 1961), 21–22.

16. Maulana Azad, *India Wins Freedom* (Bombay: Orient Longmans, 1957), 161.

17. Chaudhury Khaliquzzaman, *Pathway to Pakistan* (Karachi: Longmans, 1961), 160.

18. Azad, *India Wins Freedom*, 22.

19. Pattabhi Sitaramayya, *The History of the Indian Congress* (Bombay: Padma Publications, 1947), 2:147; emphasis added.

20. Quoted in Frank Moraes, *Jawaharlal Nehru* (Bombay: Asia Publishing House, 1956), 271–72.

21. Ibid.

22. For the text of the August offer, see Government of India, *Speeches by the Marquess of Linlithgow* (Simla: Government of India, 1944), 2:238–42.

23. For details of Linlithgow's role during this critical period, see Gowher Rizvi, *Linlithgow and India: A Study of British Policy and the Political Impasse in India, 1936–43*, (London: Royal Historical Society, 1978).

24. Text of the resolution in Syed Sharifuddin Pirzada, ed., *Foundations of Pakistan: All India Muslim League Documents, 1906–1947* (Karachi: National Publishing House, 1970), 2:340.

25. Marquess of Linlithgow, *Speeches and Documents by Marquess of Linlithgow, 1936–43* (New Delhi: Government of India, 1945), 401–5.

26. http://www.aicc.org.in/the_congress_ and_the_freedom_movement.htm.

27. Winston Churchill, speech at the Mansion House, November 10, 1942, quoted in *The Times* (London), November 11, 1942.

28. D. K. Fieldhouse, "Imperialism: An Historiographical Revision," *Economic History Review*, 2d ser., 45 (1961): 207.

29. Nicholas Mansergh and Penderel Moon, eds., *The Transfer of Power, 1942–47: Constitutional Relations Between Britain and India* (London: Her Majesty's Stationery Office, 1977), 7:972, 71.

30. Michael Brecher, *Nehru: A Political Biography*.

31. John Terraine, *Life and Times of Lord Mountbatten* (London: Hutchinson, 1968), 151; Dominique Lapierre and Larry Collins, *Mountbatten and the Partition of India* (New Delhi: Vikas Publishing, 1982), 1:44–47.

32. Alan Campbell-Johnson, *Mission with Mountbatten* (London: Robert Hale, 1951), 232; Terraine, *Life and Times of Lord Mountbatten*, 153.

33. Azad, *India Wins Freedom.*

34. Jalal, *Sole Spokesman*, 179; Pyarelal, *Matahma Gandhi: The Last Phase* (Ahmadabad: Navajivan Publishing House, 1958), 2:301.

35. Mohammad C. Chagla, *Roses in December: An Autobiography* (Bombay: Bharatiya Vidya Bhavan, 1973), 80; Khaliquzzaman, *Pathway to Pakistan*, 17.

36. Mohammad Ali Jinnah, *Quaid-e-Azam Speaks: Speeches of Quaid-e-Azam Mohammad Ali Jinnah* (Karachi: Ministry of Information and Broadcasting, 1950), 133–36.

37. Nehru. Full text of this speech on Guardian Unlimited, www.guardian.co.uk, May 1, 2007.

———

Indira's last name was Gandhi but that was because she married a Zoroastrian Parsi whose family name was Gandhi, not related at all to the Mahatma. She was in an essential way not related to the Mahatma, who stood for the primacy of means over ends; with Indira, it was exactly the opposite. [Inder] Malhotra correctly says:

> If the list of Indira's faults and flaws is long, that of her achievements, some of them dazzling, is even longer and more impressive. . . . It was in Indira's time that India became the third largest reservoir of skilled scientific and technical manpower, the fifth military power, the sixth member of the nuclear club, seventh in the race for space, and the tenth industrial power.

> In December 1999, on the eve of the new millennium, a British Broadcasting Corporation poll rated India's first and only woman prime minister the "greatest woman of the past 1,000 years"! (page 351)

15

THE MARCH OF INDIAN DEMOCRACY, PART I

At the stroke of the midnight hour, when the world sleeps, India will awake to life and freedom. A moment comes, which comes but rarely in history, when we step out from the old into the new; when an age ends, and when the soul of a nation long suppressed finds utterance.

—Nehru ringing in India's Independence
at midnight, August 14–15, 1947

JAWAHARLAL NEHRU, PRIME MINISTER

Nehru led India for an uninterrupted seventeen years (1947–1964) as prime minister, for several years holding the position of the president of the ruling Congress Party. There was full democracy in the country; all parties were free to pursue their political ambitions, including the Communist Party of India. The press was free, people were free to express themselves in whatever way they liked, and they did. During that entire period, only one party, the Congress Party, won a majority of seats in the Parliament, with the elections being free and fair. The Congress Party also held power in all the states. Nehru's leadership was unchallenged within the party; there was no rival in the entire political spectrum who thought he or she matched his attraction for the masses. His public meetings in any metropolitan city in the country attracted audiences in the hundreds of thousands, at times around a million; people who attended such conclaves came on their own, neither coerced nor enticed, mostly to see their beloved leader. He moved around in a sedan with a single police patrol in the capital and, most often, in a convertible with a couple of outriders in other cities, receiving flowers from the crowds and tossing them back to them. Such adulation had hardly been any other leader's fortune throughout the world of his time, maybe very few in human history. His charisma was not new to the Indian political scene. He had received love and admiration, confidence and trust from large throngs of people throughout the country for at least a couple of decades before he became prime minister.

Nehru could easily have been a dictator. In fact, he feared he could be one. He hated fascism and Nazism and had participated in the anti-Franco movement in 1938. In an article he authored for Calcutta's *Modern Review*, under a pseudonym, "Chanakya," he had warned his fellow Indians in 1937 of the dangers of the charismatic Nehru becoming a "Caesar":

> [Nehru] calls himself a democrat and a socialist, and no doubt he does so in all earnestness . . . but a little twist and he might turn into a dictator. . . . [H]e has all the makings of a dictator in him—vast popularity, a strong will, energy and pride . . . and with all his love of the crowd, an intolerance of others and a certain contempt for the weak and inefficient. . . . His overwhelming desire to get things done . . . will hardly brook for long the slow processes of democracy.[1]

Yet throughout the period he was the prime minister, he was scrupulous in his respect for the democratic norms. Bar-

ring emergencies, he and his successor, Lal Bahadur Shastri, did not leave the capital when the parliament was in session, being present there for most of its deliberations, particularly the "Question Hour." Such could not be said of all the succeeding prime ministers. For the electoral campaigns in their constituencies, Nehru and Shastri did not use the official vehicles or any government personnel or machinery.

Historical Compulsions

As the first prime minister of a country that had just emerged from a long freedom struggle, Nehru had to take into consideration the hopes and aspirations of millions of people, who had been promised during the movement that there would be not just political freedom but also economic and social freedom. In that sense, India's postindependence development—social, economic, and political—was conditioned by the history of its nationalist movement, its leaders, the variety of forces that contributed to unity among its people, and, overwhelming them all, the life and thought of one great personality, Mohandas Karamchand Gandhi, whom the people called the Mahatma (the Great-Souled One) or affectionately and respectfully, Bapu (Father). During the movement, Gandhi involved substantial numbers of women, who came out of their kitchens on the streets and, along with men, courted prison, wore hand-spun *khadi* cloth, and adopted Gandhian values, among them the simple life, non-violence, and concern and empathy for fellow human beings in India as well as in the rest of the world. Gandhi carried all levels of people with him, regardless of their caste, color, or creed; therefore, the postindependence programs, be they constitution making or economic planning, including education, had to take into consideration the promotion and protection of all, creating a plural and secular society and ensuring them all individual rights. It was Nehru's role to serve as a link between Gandhi's traditionalism and the urge of the new intellectuals and youth to have the country change with a modern outlook. India's constitution had to accommodate the historical pledges made during the freedom struggle as well as the modern aspirations of change and progress.

To keep together the diverse Indian society, which appeared physically more like Europe with its dozen nations rather than the melting pot the United States proudly projected, Nehru's India had to adopt various measures to integrate its similar plural society along secular lines. It would also have to look for historical antecedents of pluralism and secularism to India's long past to make them the people's preference: the policies of the Mughal emperor Akbar and the Maratha king Shivaji toward people of diverse religions, the philosophy and social practices of the *bhakti* movement, and the emphasis of Vivekanand on the multipronged Vedantic approach to human salvation and his advocacy of the socio-economic uplift of the underprivileged. Western humanistic liberalism and socialistic leveling of society, represented by a whole generation of which Jawaharlal Nehru was the prototype, and Gandhi's unique approach for the all-around social transformation of India all provided precedent and inspiration in the first decade after India's independence to create an intellectual and social infrastructure for Nehru to use for the integration, unity, and uplift of the Indian society.

In this massive effort, there was a choice before Nehru and his deputy prime minister, Vallabhbhai Patel (known to the people as *Sardar* [Warrior], a sobriquet Gandhi had bestowed on him after the Bardoli *satyagraha* under Patel's leadership), of whether to scrap the colonial institutions including the Indian Civil Service, which had not hesitated in carrying out the Raj's orders to throw the freedom fighters into jail. However, Nehru and Patel preferred continuity rather than abrupt change in the interests of stability, which was at stake, what with roughly 10 million refugees from across the borders with Pakistan, the presence of 562 princely states, which had the legal option not to join India, the need for a right atmosphere in which to draft a constitution, and a dozen other "teething" problems of an infant state. They, therefore, continued with those of the institutions created by the British rule that ensured integration of the country and the unity of its plural society along secular lines: the all-India civil services, the armed forces, the judiciary and rule of law, communications, and the higher-education apparatus. Most Indians and scholars of the postcolonial societies have, by and large, lauded Nehru and Patel's decision in favor of continuity, an option almost unanimously endorsed by the nation's founding fathers in the Constituent Assembly, which also served as the nation's legislature.

The legal position at the dawn of Indian independence too favored continuity. Thus, legally, in terms of the Dominion Act of 1947 adopted by the British Parliament, India was a "successor state," with all the assets and liabilities that went along with that status. Pakistan was created as a new dominion, with no obligations internationally to observe the various treaties and agreements that Great Britain had entered into with other countries and the United Nations on behalf of an undivided India. This was a significant factor favoring continuity. Second, prior to its independence, India had gone through a series of constitutional reforms beginning in 1861 as Britain took hesitant and, sometimes, reluctant steps introducing parliamentary institutions, painfully slowly widening the suffrage, extending people's representation from local to state and national levels, deepening the power-sharing arrangements between elected representatives and appointed officials until, finally, a British-style parliamentary and cabinet type of government became the reality. From the time this was done in a major way in October 1946 for undivided India and from mid-August 1947 for the newly independent

India (and Pakistan), the Indian government under Jawaharlal Nehru continued with the same political institutional framework and parliamentary procedures as before. There was some criticism, notably by the Socialist Ram Manohar Lohia and the Communists, in general, who followed the Moscow line of calling Nehru and his associates "the lackeys" or "running dogs" of imperialism, forgetting that such descriptions fitted their own subservience to their Soviet masters until the latter changed the "party line." They were particularly critical of the option given to the Indian members of the Indian Civil Service to continue to serve the new government and of the new government leaders moving into the residences formerly occupied by the colonial masters and, in fact, continuing with similar pomp and panoply that had marked the preindependence official life. Did the Indian leadership and notably the Congress Party have a choice? Gandhi, for one, proposed the formal dissolution of the Congress Party, which, in his view, had served as a national platform for bringing everyone together for the dominant purpose of bringing freedom to the country and need not be involved in the divisive electoral politics after independence.

Nehru's Leadership

As prime minister, Nehru was full of ideas and innovations in every field—education, economy, science, transportation, and foreign policy. Most of the crowds did not understand him but trusted him to do the right thing. His speeches in the parliament, before his party's conventions, and addresses to the annual sessions of the Indian Science Congress (which he attended with regularity) and of the dozens of inaugurals whether of dams and canals, hydroelectric projects, or fertilizer factories—"temples of New India," he called them—were evidence of a bubbling mind, an impatient individual, of a man in a hurry who wanted to make up for the time lost by the country being under alien rule. He was regarded by the masses as being thoroughly honest, a man of integrity, who had throughout his life sacrificed his personal interests for the nation's good.

The first two Indian parliaments of 1952 and 1957 had an extraordinary array of eminent individuals, many of them with law education in India and England, many with a record of years of prison terms as political offenders in the same manner as Nehru himself. Their numbers included writers and poets, philosophers and thinkers of exemplary merit, who commanded respect. The parliamentary debates, in the same manner as the Constituent Assembly debates, were consequently presentations of a very high level and were couched in polite language even while being critical of their opponents. The proceedings then were in distinct contrast to the proceedings of later parliaments.[2]

Likewise, the chief ministers of states were men and women of eminence who could not be trifled with by the central government. They were also party leaders in their provinces and often called the shots in naming candidates for the parliamentary elections and campaigning for them. Nehru was aware of the central leadership's dependence on political support from the chief ministers and politely wrote fortnightly letters to them, apprising them of his plans and informing them of the progress made in taking the nation further. Their feedback was, at least seemingly, given high consideration.

Nehru may be credited with establishing a string of scientific and technological institutions, which created in time the third-largest scientific manpower pool in the world. Thus came the national physical and chemical laboratories, institutes of science, and the three Indian Institutes of Technology, the famous IITs, which later grew to seven and produced world-class engineers. He established the Atomic Energy Commission with Homi Bhabha as its prime mover and with Nehru himself as the minister in charge. The University Grants Commission oversaw the growth of existing universities, the establishment of new ones, and the regulation of standards in higher education, including professional education in medicine, engineering, and architecture. These steps have continued to yield dividends to this date. Above all, he established the Planning Commission in 1951, to propose and monitor an orderly socialistic development, in which his main adviser was P. C. Mahalonobis, a renowned statistician-cum-economist.

Nehru's leadership in economic matters and in world affairs is discussed in Chapters 18 and 19, "Toward Economic Freedom" and "India's Foreign Policy." Likewise, the issue of Jammu and Kashmir is dealt with in Chapter 17, along with the larger question of integration of the 562 princely states into the Indian Union.

Gandhi's Assassination

Within months of India's independence, the country lost its greatest son of modern times, Mahatma Gandhi, father of the nation, at the hands of a Hindu communalist, a member of the Rashtriya Swayamsevak Sangh (RSS), Nathuram Vinayak Godse, editor of a newspaper in Pune, who had been writing most critically of what he and his associates regarded as Gandhi's perfidy and pro-Muslim acts. Thus, he was agitated about Gandhi's insistence that the homes of the Muslims who migrated to Pakistan should be protected by the government, even if the Pakistani government did not do so in regard to the Hindus and Sikhs who had migrated to India. A Hindu refugee, Madanlal, had hurled a bomb at Gandhi's prayer meeting a few days before the assassination. Sardar Patel, who immediately took steps to strengthen the security around Gandhi, was rebuffed by the latter, who did not want any such protection. Godse was particularly critical of Gandhi's fast "unto death," protesting the Indian government's deliberate delay in giving Pakistan its share of the sterling balances, which India had received as a successor state. The amount of five hundred and fifty million rupees was held up by the government because it would likely be used by its adversary to buy arms to use against India in the Kashmir conflict. Gandhi would not brook any such unethical moves. The government relented and paid the amount.

The entire nation was shocked. It was a sigh of relief to many that the assassin was a Hindu and not a Muslim. Had that been the case, there would have been a bloodbath, as the communities, already enveloped by tension, could have gone at each other's throats. The government immediately banned the RSS. Nehru best expressed the nation's loss and grief in an extemporaneous radio address:

> Friends and comrades, the light has gone out of our lives and there is darkness everywhere. . . . Our beloved leader, Bapu as we called him, the Father of the Nation, is no more. The light has gone out, I said, and yet I was wrong. For the light that shone in this country was no ordinary light . . . that light represented something more than the immediate present; it represented the living, the eternal truths, reminding us of the right path, drawing us from error, taking this ancient country to freedom.[3]

Problems and Shortcomings of the Nehru Era

Nehru did not have smooth sailing in everything he desired in terms of the country's direction. From early on, he was opposed for his overzealousness in taking the country along a socialist path. The right-wing faction of his own party, which had the tacit support of Sardar Patel (he died in 1950) and the Congress president, Purshottamdas Tandon, was tentatively suppressed with Tandon's removal and the assumption of the party's presidency by Nehru himself. In 1955, under a pliant party president, U. N. Dhebar, the Congress adopted the "Socialistic Pattern of Society" as its creed. The right-wing opposition continued, albeit clandestinely, at times raising its head, but finding itself ineffective in the face of Nehru's ability to attract the mass vote, which kept all of them in power.

Another major challenge came in the form of a demand to reorganize the states along linguistic lines. To be sure, Gandhi had been in favor of it because it would facilitate better access to the millions who knew only their "mother tongue." The linguistic enthusiasts dug up the old resolution favoring such an administrative reorganization, adopted by the Congress in 1921. Nehru chose to ignore such demands until in December 1952, Potti Sriramulu fasted "unto death" on the issue of creation of a Telugu-speaking state. Nehru con-

ceded, against his own wishes, in the fall of 1953, giving birth to the first linguistic state, Andhra Pradesh. The government also agreed to appoint a three-man commission, the States Reorganization Commission (SRC) under K. M. Panikkar, a noted scholar-diplomat-administrator, as chair. Its brief was to propose changes, keeping in mind "the preservation and strengthening of the unity and security of India."

The SRC's report of 1955 became the basis of the States Reorganization Act of 1956, which created fourteen states based on language, leaving Maharashtra and Gujarat as a combined bilingual state, with Bombay as its capital. The other state affected was the Punjab. The reaction of the Marathi-speaking people was one of outrage. A Samyukta Maharashtra Samiti (SMS) (United Maharashtra Committee) was launched by the non-Congress Maharashtrian political organizations, which demanded a separate state of Maharashtra, with Vidarbha, at the northeast extremity, which the SRC had suggested be a separate state, and with portions of the Karnataka state, notably Belgaum and Nipani, on the grounds that the majority population there were Marathi speakers. Although many Gujaratis, unquestionably those living in Bombay, had no quarrel with a bilingual state, there were those who wanted a separate state of Gujarat. They formed the Mahagujarat Janata Parishad (Greater Gujarat People's Conference).

In the elections of 1957, a sizable number of candidates put up by these two organizations were elected, defeating their Congress rivals. The Congress was shocked that it had lost heavily in its stronghold of Bombay. There were three years of disquiet and occasional riots in the city of Bombay, where the popular SMS would declare a *hartal* and stop all activity. On one of those occasions, the government of Maharashtra, with Morarji Desai as chief minister, ordered the police to fire on unarmed SMS demonstrators at the busy Flora Fountain in the heart of the business district, killing 105. Those martyrs, now memorialized at that locale, brought untold amounts of anger and frustration among the general public who felt the central government under Nehru had been unduly unmindful and unjust. Nehru's finance minister, the erudite and capable C. D. Deshmukh, resigned. In 1959, when Indira Gandhi was the president of the Congress Party, she reopened the issue; she found in President Radhakrishnan an influential supporter and secured an agreement by the government to allow the bifurcation of the bilingual state into Maharashtra and Gujarat on May 1, 1960.

Punjab, created as a trilingual state after the merger with it of the princely states comprising the Patiala and East Punjab States Union (PEPSU) in 1956, had speakers of three languages—Punjabi, Hindi, and Pahari. There was a strong demand by the Punjabi speakers for a Punjabi *suba* (state). Quickly, the issue became embroiled with religious politics, the Akali Dal demanding a separate Sikh state with Punjabi language and Gurmukhi script. This was opposed by the right-wing Jan Sangh, who encouraged the Hindus to deny that Punjabi was their language and instead favor Hindi. In New Delhi, the Nehru government identified the demand for a Punjabi-speaking state not as linguistic agitation but as a communal or religious issue. The question remained unresolved during the Nehru administration. In 1966, Indira Gandhi divided the Punjab into two states, Punjab and Haryana. The former would be a Punjabi-speaking state, whereas the latter would consist of primarily Hindi-speaking people. The two states would have a common capital in the new city of Chandigarh, which would become a union territory. Then the Pahari-speaking region of Kangra and a portion of the Hoshiarpur district were merged with Himachal Pradesh.

The states' reorganization on a linguistic basis and the later bifurcation of the Bombay State were issues that were not to Nehru's liking. In fact, it made for a better India, more coherent, where the government and the courts were more accessible to the public. As a well-known Indian political scientist, Rajni Kothari, wrote:

> in spite of the leadership's earlier reservations and ominous forebodings by sympathetic observers, the reorganization resulted in rationalizing

the political map of India without seriously weakening its unity. If anything, its result has been functional, in
as much as it removed what had been
a major source of discord, and created
homogeneous political units which
could be administered through a
medium that the vast majority of the
population understood. Indeed it can
be said with the benefit of hindsight
that language, rather than being a
force for division has proved a ce-
menting and integrating influence.[4]

Nehru was often a dreamer and a vi-
sionary, never short of ideas, but he was
not a great day-to-day administrator.
He wrote long minutes and letters, a
delight to future historians probing his
mind, but a drag on decisionmaking.
This was the exact opposite of Sardar
Patel, whose brevity with words, written
and spoken, carried a firm message of
Nehru's unshakable determination. One
of his biographers, Michael Brecher,
writes that he was "completely lacking
in ruthlessness. Ever the quintessential
democrat. He had a compulsion for
universal consent."[5] He was completely
above corruption but would not act
against some of his corrupt colleagues,
particularly if they had served long
prison terms during the nation's fight
for freedom. He was again a true democrat in the sense that he would not
nominate a successor. After he suffered
a stroke, he brought back Lal Bahadur
Sastri as minister without portfolio, in
an act that was seen as indicating his

preference. When Nehru died on May
27, 1964, the group of party managers
known as the Syndicate chose Lal
Bahadur Sastri as the country's next
prime minister.

THE QUESTION OF PORTUGUESE COLONIES IN INDIA

Nehru was much concerned that several
years after India's independence, there
were still some small pockets of territory under European colonial rule. For
him and millions of Indians, India's
independence was not complete until
France and Portugal gave up the colonies, just as the British had done.

The Indian Government experienced
unexpected inflexibility on the part of
not only Portugal but also France in
their reluctance to release their hold over
three pockets of Portuguese and five
pockets of French territory on Indian
soil. In both cases, these specks of territory had remained thanks to the British
protective umbrella, which dispensed
with even the need for travel documents
between them and the rest of India. In
the month of India's independence in
August 1947, the French government
agreed to study with the government of
India "ways and means of friendly regulation of the problem," taking into account "the historical and cultural links of
those people with France and . . . the
evolution of India."[6] The outbreak of
the First Indochina War (December
1946–May 1954) created for France the

need to retain their colonies in India, particularly Pondicherry (near Madras, now Chennai), whose airport facilities were used by France to refuel the aircraft, civilian and military, from France to Vietnam. The French procrastinated in the negotiations, dragging their feet until October 21, 1954, three months after the Geneva Agreements on Indochina were concluded, to hand over their Indian possessions to the Indian government.[7]

The Portuguese Rule in Goa

Unlike in the Portuguese colonies in Africa, such as Angola and Mozambique, there were no Portuguese settlers in the Portuguese Indian possessions of Goa, Daman, and Diu, despite a long rule of four and one-half centuries. At the sunset of the Portuguese rule, according to the Portuguese government's statistics, 98.7 percent of the total population of 626,667 in 1960 was of Indian stock, 61 percent Hindus, 37 percent Christians, and 2 percent Muslims. There were only 1,384 whites, mostly officials and businessmen, temporarily resident in Goa; there were no Portuguese settlers with permanent homes in Goa, Daman, or Diu.[8]

The tiny Portuguese possessions totaled 1,662 square miles, Goa being the largest, with 1,429 square miles. As the Indians, free from British colonial rule, repeatedly averred, the continued colonialism in Goa, Daman, and Diu constituted a blemish on the fair face of independent India with its population of 359 million in 1947 and a land area of more than 1.2 million square miles.

One factor in the Portuguese intransigence was the sudden discovery of iron and manganese ore in Goa in 1946, which not only made that colony fiscally solvent but also provided Portugal with valuable foreign exchange earned from the exportation of the mineral ore to Japan, Germany, and the United States. Only a small portion of the foreign exchange was made available to Goa, but it was enough to import luxury items—each Goan "could wear a hundred watches on each arm and more"— not only for the use of the inhabitants but also for prolific smuggling across the porous border to the rest of India.

Goa's Freedom Movement. The Portuguese rule of 450 years was punctuated by at least sixty revolts, some of which were led by Catholic priests, who were discriminated against on the grounds of race. In the second quarter of the twentieth century, an erudite Goan Catholic scholar, Tristao Braganza da Cunha, on his return from higher studies in Europe, founded the National Congress (Goa) in 1928 in Bombay. In his well-circulated *Decolonization of Goans*, he condemned the suppression of liberties and personal freedoms under Salazar's dictatorial regime. In 1946, the Indian Socialist leader, Ram Manohar Lohia, who was in Goa on a personal visit to his contemporary at the University of Berlin,

Juliao Menezes, witnessed firsthand the intolerably repressive conditions while the rest of India was poised to usher in an era of independence. On June 18, 1946, he held a *satyagraha* in the public square of Margao, Goa's most populous city. Lohia and Menezes were quickly arrested along with about 150 others. The event was followed on the eighteenth of the succeeding months in numerous cities and towns of Goa. Large-scale arrests and detentions without trial followed. Some protesters were formally charged and tried and awarded long sentences to be served in Goa's Aguada Fort prison, whereas the leaders were sent off to jails in distant Portugal, Angola, and Mozambique. In the decade and a half that followed, an estimated 2,500 persons, men and women, Hindus and Catholics, were arrested in Goa.

The arrest of a prominent leader such as Ram Manohar Lohia captured headlines in all Indian newspapers and drew the attention of India's millions to the plight of their fellow Indians under Portuguese rule. It produced a reaction from Mahatma Gandhi, who wrote the following in his weekly *Harijan* on June 30, 1946:

In Free India, Goa cannot be allowed to exist as a separate entity in opposition to the laws of the free State. Without a shot being fired, the people of Goa will be able to claim and receive the rights of citizenship of the free State. The present Portuguese

Government will no longer be able to rely upon the protection of British arms to isolate and keep under subjection the inhabitants of Goa against their will. . . . I would venture to advise the Portuguese Government of Goa to recognize the signs of the times and come to honourable terms with its inhabitants rather than function on any treaty that might exist between them and the British Government.[9]

Gandhi's expectation that the Goans would attain freedom "without a shot being fired" ultimately proved wrong. It was, however, in tune with the general expectation all over India that after the British left the subcontinent, a telephone call to the Portuguese authorities from India's prime minister was all that would be needed for the Portuguese to quit as well.

The Portuguese "official" response to Gandhi's article and "advice" was a letter from the head of the Goan government's Information Bureau to the editor of *Harijan:*

There is nothing more out of place as a comparison between French India and Portuguese India. The objects, administrative methods and the goal are absolutely dissimilar in their essence. . . .

If the inhabitants of French India wish to identify their destinies with Free India (what has yet to be ascertained), the same does not happen in Portuguese India where the totality of inhabitants wish to continue under the beneficial action of Portuguese Administration which has been the cause of its material and moral progress to the point of being the pride of the Portuguese colonizing effort and part and parcel of the Motherland.[10]

Gandhi chose to respond by writing on August 2 a "dear friend" letter directly to Jose Bossa, governor-general of Portuguese India, stating inter alia, "It is ridiculous for the Head of the Government Information Bureau to write of Portugal as the Motherland of the Indians of Goa. Their mother country is as much India as mine. Goa is outside British India, but it is within geographical India as a whole. And there is very little in common between the Portuguese and the Indians of Goa." Therefore, he advised the Portuguese to "withdraw all the African police, declare yourself whole-heartedly for civil liberty and if possible, even let the inhabitants of Goa frame their own Government."[11]

Salazar's Reaction to the Goan Freedom Movement

The Portuguese reaction since the 1930s to the Goan demands for civil liberties must be seen in the context of lack of liberties in Portugal itself. There, in the aftermath of the military takeover in 1926, Oliveira Salazar, a professor of economics at the University of Coimbra, had become increasingly the civilian face of the dictatorship. In June 1932, he was named the prime minister, a post he held until his death. In reality, he appropriated for himself full powers in executive and legislative spheres. As in Spain, Italy, and Germany, he created a fascist organization, the Uniao Nacional, and its youth wing, the Mocidade Portuguesa. All political parties, except the Uniao Nacional, were banned.

The key themes of the Uniao Nacional were patriotism, Catholic morality, and personal loyalty to Oliveira Salazar. As long as the people indulged in "fado, Fatima, and football" (music, religion, and sports), they would stay out of trouble. The press was completely under the government's control; all kinds of meetings, political or social, other than those sponsored by the Uniao Nacional, required the prior permission of police.

The Salazar regime's reaction to the freedom movement in Goa was totally predictable. Salazar's approach toward the colonies was entirely different from that of the other colonial powers such as Great Britain or the United States. It was more akin to the Dutch reaction to the Indonesian freedom movement or later of the Belgians to that of Congo. In 1949, Portugal made itself valuable to the North Atlantic Treaty Organization (NATO), of which it was a charter member, by allowing its off-shore Azores islands for a NATO military base in the Atlantic. Two years later, in 1951, Salazar decreed that Goa and all other Portuguese colonies were "overseas provinces" and an integral part of Portugal and, therefore, entitled to NATO's protection.

India's Policy Toward the Goa Question

In 1951, Nehru enunciated his policy on Goa as follows: "India cannot tolerate any footholds of foreign powers in this country. . . . There are only two ways of bringing this about—either through war or through diplomatic means. In pursuance of our ideals, we have ruled out war as a means of redress, unless we are forced into one. The only alternative we are left with is the diplomatic method and we are pursuing it."[12]

As years of Portuguese intransigence rolled on without any progress on the Goa question, numerous prominent politicians, media writers, and others accused Nehru of needlessly internationalizing the Goa issue. They openly said that it was his "blunder" in 1947 not to have served an ultimatum to the Portuguese to leave Goa. After all, it would have been regarded as a part of the larger anticolonial struggle in tune with the ultimatum five years previously in 1942 when Gandhi had asked the British to "Quit India." A month before India's march into Goa in December 1961, a prominent writer and member of India's parliament, Joachim Alva, said regretfully, "Our blunder was that in 1947, we did not occupy Goa without any notice or without ultimatum." Arthur Rubinoff, whose doctoral dissertation is titled "In-

dia's Use of Force in Goa," observes: "Since neither France nor Portugal could possibly have maintained their enclaves in India without British support, India should have attempted to press for a general agreement that would have brought independence to all foreign possessions at the same time." In 1961, India's ambassador to the United States, B. K. Nehru, lamented, "We, in our naivete, did not know then, as the world knows now, that the regime in Portugal was, and apparently still is, completely oblivious of the pace and purpose of the 20th century."[13]

Although the government of India was frustrated but was still handling the matter with diplomatic delicacy, all the political parties including the ruling Congress Party were losing their patience. To millions of Indians, Indian independence was not complete until the 600,000 Indian souls in Goa had been freed from foreign domination. The megalopolis of Bombay had been home to nearly 150,000 Goans; to these were added the "undesirables" thrown out of Goa by the Portuguese government whose oppressive rule they had the courage to protest. The National Congress (Goa) operating from Bombay and several other cities was aware of the diplomatic impasse between Portugal and the Indian government. Its members, growing impatient but still wedded to Gandhian methods, were joined by other Indians in entering Goa as *satyagrahis*, on Indian Independence Day, August 15, 1955. They were peacefully and nonviolently demanding freedom for Goa. Twenty-two of these unarmed demonstrators were shot dead by the Portuguese army; another 225 were wounded. The incident triggered huge demonstrations in Indian cities, legislative assemblies, and the national parliament, asking New Delhi to take punitive action and send its troops for a military takeover. Nehru resisted all pressures, twice offering to resign his high office. There was an impasse, as the irresistible force of the spirit of free India met the irremovable object in the form of Oliveira Salazar, who refused to acknowledge the "winds of change" that were then swiftly sweeping the European empires of yore from the face of Africa and Asia.

The question of continuation of colonial rule in Goa that was always at the top of the Indian political consciousness surfaced every year in August when the Indian nation and the Goans attempted to celebrate the country's Independence Day. After the ruthless mowing down of the unarmed and peaceful *satyagrahis* by the Portuguese police and military personnel in 1954 and 1955, there had been no further attempts of the Gandhian kind. There was a general understanding that the peaceful methods that had appealed to the British conscience and resulted in the attainment of freedom for India would not make any impression on the cold sovereignty-oriented logic of Salazar and his government. India had failed in its diplomatic efforts with the Western countries and the United States

in persuading a fellow NATO member, Portugal, to negotiate the transfer of its colonies on Indian soil. Utterly frustrated, Prime Minister Nehru finally conceded in August 1961 that the use of force in Goa could no longer be ruled out.

Africa, the United Nations, and the Goa Question

Certain other factors also operated on the Indian public opinion, Parliament, and the government in the second half of 1961. Among these was the news of the brutal Portuguese repression of the freedom movement in Angola. In June, Nehru had observed that "the most horrible thing in the world today is what is happening in Angola. It is horrible beyond belief."[14] At the urging of the embassies in New Delhi of numerous African states, the Indian Council of World Affairs held a major seminar in October 1961. Many African delegates openly criticized India's inability to end Portuguese rule in Goa. Underlying their criticism was the inadequacy of peaceful means and the failure of quiet diplomacy on the part of India as the leader of the nonaligned world to end colonialism in Asia and Africa. Kenneth Kaunda pointedly stated that India's inaction in Goa had helped Portugal in Africa.[15] The importance of the seminar's deliberations is underlined by Arthur Rubinoff:

As the seminar progressed, it became apparent that what had begun as a condemnation of Portuguese colonialism had become an attack upon India's Goa policy. . . . What the Africans wanted from India was more positive action. They maintained the occupation of Goa by Indian forces would not be a small step in aiding their revolution. Rather they regarded such an event as the key, for it was alleged that the Portuguese Empire in Africa would collapse once Goa fell. Moreover, Africans acknowledged India was provided with the opportunity to give the anti-colonial movement direction and indicated their willingness to follow if only Nehru would reassert his leadership.[16]

In Rubinoff's view, "what the Delhi sessions accomplished was to inform India that a substantial body of world opinion would support her if she resorted to force in Goa."[17]

In November 1961, a month before taking up the military option, Nehru made a last-ditch effort to bring U.S. diplomatic pressure on Portugal. Present at the Kennedy-Nehru meeting was the U.S. ambassador to India, John Kenneth Galbraith, who had a close personal relationship with both leaders. In mid-December, Galbraith would play an important role in persuading the U.S. State Department to put its weight on the Indian side in regard to ending Portuguese colonial rule in Goa and in dissuading the Indian prime minister from sending troops into Goa. On both counts, he failed.

The recently released papers on India-U.S. relations during the Kennedy administration unravel Galbraith's efforts to urge upon the Indian government the postponement of any drastic action in regard to Goa by six months. Revelatory of the futility of such efforts was Galbraith's telegram of December 14 asking the State Department if he had "a card to play." A strong card would be the knowledge of a U.S. approach to Portugal in support of India's position on Goa. The State Department's reply was both frustrating and indicative of Salazar's unbending position. The department regretted it had no cards for Galbraith. In the telegrams to Galbraith, the State Department was careful to point out that "Goa is a colonial issue, and recognizes that the colonial age is passing and has and will continue to urge Portugal to recognize the fact."[18]

On December 18, the Indian military action dubbed "Operation Goa" began with the bombing and disabling of the only Portuguese frigate, SS *Afonso de Albuquerque,* named after the conqueror of Goa in 1510. In an action lasting a mere twenty-six hours, Indian troops entered Goa from three directions—north, south, and east—and took over the territory with hardly any resistance from the small Portuguese force. Representatives of the international press present in Goa reported that the Indian troops were welcomed by the Goans, who offered them not only flowers but also food and drinks along the way to the capital, Panaji. With that, the four and a half centuries of Portuguese colonial rule ended; to the teeming millions of India, their country's freedom from Western colonial rule was finally complete.

At the United Nations, India's then defense minister, V. K. Krishna Menon, categorically denied Portugal's charge of aggression, countering that India and other former colonial peoples regarded colonialism itself as "permanent aggression." He repeated India's charge that it was Portugal that had committed aggression some four centuries earlier and that the Indian military action just taken had "vacated" that aggression.[19]

Looked at from a postcolonial perspective, there were three European states—Great Britain, France, and Portugal—exercising colonial authority over an ethnic Indian population. There were hardly any white settlers in India except for some few hundred British tea- and coffee-plantation owners. This was true of Goa as well. There was not a single Portuguese who had settled down in more than 450 years of rule. All three colonial powers were, by and large, simply economic exploiters.

To conclude, colonialism and imperialism were among the "arrangements" that the stronger states made to overpower and rule weaker people and weaker states. Just as slavery and the inferior status of women would be things of the past, so also would it be for colonialism and imperialism. As C. Wilfred Jenks, a noted authority on international law, observes in his *Common Law*

of Mankind, widely used in the Western world in the middle decades of the twentieth century: "It is futile to take refuge in the dogma of sovereignty which no longer commands the respect of those who challenge the existing order. . . . It is idle to disregard these forces; they are vital; they are growing in strength; and the civilization of West Europe must come to terms with them on a basis of mutual respect and cooperation or it will be overwhelmed by them."[20] In other words, colonialism was an anomaly that had to go, if not by nonviolent means, then by violent ones.

THE MAKING OF THE CONSTITUTION AND HOW IT WORKS

A major achievement of the Nehru era was the adoption of India's constitution. The Constituent Assembly had been convened before India's independence based on the provincial elections of 1946. It was, therefore, dominated by the Congress Party, which had won the most seats and had been foremost in the struggle for independence. Most of the members of the Constituent Assembly (and some belonging to the other parties as well) were dressed in white *khadi* with Gandhi caps, which had become the badge of freedom fighters, adorning their heads. The learned Rajendra Prasad, a Congress stalwart, presided over the Constituent Assembly. The deliberation lasted nearly three years, until the constitution, which was adopted on November

26, 1949, and became effective on January 26, 1950, would make India a republic. With that, Rajendra Prasad would become the first president and Nehru would continue as the prime minister.

The Constituent Assembly had been established to approve a system of government for a people about to become free, a system that would enable a social transformation of the country through economic development within a democratic structure. Its goal was to hammer a constitution into shape, striking a balance between governmental authority and individual rights. The chair of the Constitution Drafting Committee was the erudite B. R. Ambedkar, a jurist who had been trained in India, the United Kingdom, and the United States and had authored several tomes on politics, economics, and jurisprudence. The debates in the Constituent Assembly offer a rich mine of information on the thinking and philosophy of India's leadership of the time and reflect the fears and hopes underlying the people's aspirations.

Consisting of 395 articles and 8 schedules, the Indian Constitution is one of the longest such documents in the world. It has an eloquent preamble and, unusual except perhaps for the constitution of the Irish Free State, a chapter on "Directive Principles of State Policy," which lacks legal validity. The preamble declared India to be a sovereign, democratic republic.

The later amendments made socialism and secularism a part of the constitution and its philosophy. The secularism is owed to the Congress Party's and in particular Gandhi's absolute rejection of the two-nation theory, and Gandhi's insistence, throughout his participation in the long struggle for freedom that India must be governed without discrimination on the basis of caste, creed, color, or gender. Therefore, as a fundamental law of the land, the Indian state is democratic, secular, federal, and republican.

Critics have dismissed the chapter on "Directive Principles" as a "revised edition" of the manifesto of the ruling party, namely, the Congress Party. In fact, it was more like an agenda of the young republic set forth by the founding fathers of the new nation. Another criticism was on the length of the chapter on fundamental rights, which the critics pointed out were limited by the provisions of Article 19, which vaguely spelled out the circumstances in which the government might suspend the use of those rights.

The Indian Constitution borrowed some ideas from its U.K. and U.S. counterparts. First, unlike the British Constitution, it is a written document and is enforceable in courts. Unlike the U.S. Constitution, it provides not for the separation of powers but for a separation of functions. The U.S. influence on the constitution is evident in the judiciary, which includes the creation of the Supreme Court and the principle of judicial review.

However, in one of the most important aspects, it was different from the U.S. Constitution, and that was in

---

PREAMBLE OF THE INDIAN CONSTITUTION

We, the people of India, having solemnly resolved to constitute India into a Sovereign, Socialist, Secular, Democratic Republic and to secure to all its citizens:

Justice, social, economic and political;

Liberty of thought, expression, belief, faith and worship;

Equality of Status and of opportunity; and to promote among them all.

Fraternity assuring the dignity of the individual and the unity and integrity of the Nation; in our constituent assembly this twenty-sixth of November, 1949, do hereby adopt, enact and give to ourselves this constitution.

---

the deliberate choice of the Westminster type of government, in which the executive is responsible to the legislature, making the parliament supreme. It is different from the British Constitution in having a federal constitution like that of the United States, Canada, and Australia, but with a unitary bias. India's founding fathers were keen on strengthening the "Indian Union," and the constitution encouraged integration by downplaying diversity. A large number of the constitution's articles spell out center-state relations, which has been the subject of much discussion in the parliament and special commissions over the decades. The strong basis for the centralized federation, almost a contradiction in terms, was made possible by the drawing up of three lists—central, state, and concurrent—and stipulating that, unlike in Canada and the United States where, in case of doubt, the states are assumed to have the power, in the Indian case, in a conflict over jurisdiction between the center and the states, the center prevails.

Another difference between the British and Indian constitutions is that the attorney general in India is appointed by the president and charged with giving a legal opinion to the government without being influenced by the political party in power; in Britain, the attorney general is a member of the cabinet and often supports the ruling party. Again, the Election Commission in India is an autonomous and independent body, a creature of neither the parliament nor the executive. Its responsibility is to conduct the elections in a fair and free manner, in an impartial manner; in Britain, the responsibility for elections rests with Parliament.

A third major governmental agency enjoying independence is the comptroller and auditor-general of India, whose task is to maintain and audit government revenues and expenditures and to see that the latter conform with the budget approved by the legislatures at central and state levels. The terms and conditions of service of these officers are not subject to revision during the tenure of the individuals holding the positions. They can be removed only by a two-thirds majority voting on a resolution in both the houses and approved by the president.

The Lok Sabha and the Rajya Sabha

In India, when the term *parliament* is used, it usually refers to the Lok Sabha, which is truly the nation's fully directly elected legislature. It was named House of the People in the constitution; its name was later altered to Lok Sabha, which literally means "House of the People." Elected on an adult franchise, the Lok Sabha is the real representative of the people, a forum for the free expression of the people's representatives without fear or favor. It had provided on many occasions a dignified debate on some of the major issues affecting India and the world. Sometimes, it has presented a chaos and a cacophony, as the people's representatives reflected the heat of the protests in the metropolitan streets or in some situation where the churlish and impolite ones, having run out of reasoning, have resorted to

throwing the microphones or furniture at their opponents in the hope of making a point.

The Indian parliament is bicameral, with the lower house called the Lok Sabha and the upper house called the Rajya Sabha. Although both houses have similar powers, it is generally acknowledged that the Lok Sabha has a broader sanction than the indirectly elected Rajya Sabha. In a very significant aspect, it is superior to the Rajya Sabha: No "money" bill, that is, a bill with financial implications, can be introduced in the Rajya Sabha. Therefore, all budgets or estimates of revenue and expenditure are first presented to the Lok Sabha, and if they are not approved by that house, the government falls and the cabinet has to resign forthwith. The finance minister usually submits the annual budget on the last day of February; for a long time now, the railroad budget, because of its size and national importance, is submitted separately a few days in advance of the general budget.

The mode of election and constitution of the Rajya Sabha is entirely different from that of the Lok Sabha. It has 250 members (roughly one-half the size of the Lok Sabha), of whom 12 are nominated by the president for excellence in arts and sciences. This furnishes opportunities for the nation to use the unusual talents and experience of individuals (who may feel too shy or reluctant to face an election) to participate in national life through the expression of their views in the upper house. The Rajya Sabha, like the U.S. Senate, represents the states *(rajya)*, and its members are elected by members of the state legislatures and of the Lok Sabha through a proportional representation system. It is expected to conform to tradition and to restrain the popular house from any hurried or impulsive legislation. Again like the U.S. Senate, the Rajya Sabha as well as the upper houses in state legislatures are permanent bodies in the sense that one-third of its members are elected every two years. As in the United States, the vice president is the presiding officer of the Rajya Sabha. The nation's experience so far vindicates the rationale to have a Rajya Sabha, a second deliberative chamber, which has at many times applied the brakes to the excessive enthusiasm and emotion that may have led the lower house to approve a measure. The second such brake is the president, who has the right to send a piece of legislation approved by both houses and submitted for his signature back to the legislature for reconsideration.

The number of seats in the Lok Sabha may vary slightly from one election to the next. In the Lok Sabha elected in May 2004 for five years, there were 545 seats (413 in the general category, 81 reserved for Scheduled Castes, 49 for the Scheduled Tribes, and 2 for Anglo-Indians). The candidate with the highest vote among all candidates wins, even though he or she may earn fewer than 50 percent of the total votes cast. The government of the day may have a substantial majority in the Lok Sabha without winning a majority of votes in the country. Thus, the Congress Party that was in power from 1947 to 1977, even during Nehru's time, had a majority of seats but not a majority of votes.

The Speaker, on the British pattern, is elected by members of the Lok Sabha and like the president is expected, after election, to be above partisan politics. After assuming the position of the Speaker, he or she no longer attends his or her former political party's meetings.

Generally speaking, the Indian elections at the central and state levels have been fair and free. Not that they are completely corruption free. Numerous incidents of tampering with voting booths, running away with ballot boxes, stuffing ballot boxes with premarked voting papers, and using money or muscle power have been reported both by the Election Commission and the police. But these have been few and far between considering the enormity of the task. Such incidents are no worse compared with the experience in the Western democracies and on the whole are not known to vitiate the electoral results. The voters, though so many of them are poor, illiterate, and live in remote areas, have shown that they regard voting as a precious and priceless privilege. Interestingly, a considerable numbers of voters have shown that although they are not allergic to receiving favors in kind—the practice of distribution of saris, *dhotis*, and blankets to a large number of constituents on the eve of the election is neither uncommon nor limited to any one political party—they vote according to their conscience and wits. Politically educated though not formally schooled, the voters have time and again changed their representatives and their government to the shock and surprise of the politicians. The most dramatic example of this was in 1977, when Indira Gandhi employed every ploy to influence the voter, who dished her Congress Party the worst defeat ever, breaking the record of 1967, when the Congress had lost in eight states. Such reverses have been fairly frequent, showing the importance of the anti-incumbency factor in Indian elections.

The Lok Sabha's life is five years, according to the constitution, extendable for one year at a time. Only once in the life of the constitution, mid-1970s, during the "emergency," has the Lok Sabha's life been extended, by one year. India follows the British practice of allowing the prime minister to call for elections before they are due, at an opportune moment when his or her party is likely to get the maximum number of seats. It is amazing how often such an estimation has been proved wrong by the Indian electorate.

Supremacy of the Parliament

There is an axiom in the British political parlance that Parliament is supreme; it can make and unmake anything except making a man a woman and vice versa. Theoretically, the Indian Constitution bestows similar immense powers on the Indian parliament in finance and legislation, including amending the Constitution. In practice, it is the executive that holds and exercises the substance of power. This is typical of the Westminster British type of government. It is the majority party in the lower house that holds power, both legislative and executive. The prime minister and the members of his cabinet are mostly drawn from the majority, which sets the parliamentary legislative agenda. In case of doubt as to how its members might vote, all parties, including the majority party, frequently issue a "whip"; a three-line whip requires all parliament members belonging to the party issuing the whip to attend the parliament, to vote on a given issue, and to vote in favor of it. When the majority party in the parliament does not agree with the cabinet, the latter's days are numbered. In those circumstances, the cabinet or the government of the day would not be able to have its measures, including the money bills, approved by the parliament. The prime minister and the cabinet might as well reconcile with the majority of their party in the parliament or resign and call for fresh elections. If there is a matter in which the majority in the nation apparently does not agree with the government, any member or party in the parliament may introduce a "vote of no confidence" in the government. On a designated day, a debate, which may last a few hours or days, is held, and a vote is taken on the motion. If it passes, the government has to resign. It has two choices before it resigns. Its leader, the prime minister, may recommend that the majority party designate some other person as the leader and form a government that can win a vote of confidence of the house, or the prime minister may recommend to the president that fresh elections be held. Until then, he or she continues to lead the government as a caretaker prime minister.

The Tilt Toward Unitary Government

The constitution gives the central government an absolute control over the defense, foreign affairs, and communications. Subject to the parliament's powers of legislation, approval, and overview, and the judiciary's powers of review, the executive has a total jurisdiction over declaration of war and peace, citizenship and extradition, foreign exchange, currency and coinage, customs tariffs, and central excise duties. The states do have their own taxation options, but often they fail to yield the amounts needed. In practice, therefore, the states have depended on the largesse from the central government, which has substantial powers of taxation and distribution to the states in the form of loans and grants. Periodically, the central government appoints a Taxation Commission that reviews the flow of receipts and expenditures and declares a formula for the equitable distribution to the states. An organization that has led to the tremendous accumulation of authority and power to change the country's dynamics

has been the Planning Commission, established in 1951. With the prime minister as its chairman, it has appropriated and exercised a tremendous extraconstitutional authority, in some respects running a parallel administration. Consulting with diverse ministries at the central and state levels in the preparation of the Soviet-style five-year plans (the country is at present in the Tenth Plan, 2002–2007), the Planning Commission influences their policies and has, in the process, evolved as a very vital mechanism for the unitary government in the country. Helping in the same direction was the institution of the National Development Council in 1952, consisting of the chief ministers of all the states under the chairmanship of the prime minister, to discuss critical issues regarding development. Examples of such common action during Nehru's time was the proposed adoption of land reforms, including legislation on establishing a ceiling on landholdings in all the states. Such moves have further institutionally strengthened the central government.

The Reservations: India's Affirmative Action

In a conscious effort to remedy the social and economic injustices of the long past, the founding fathers provided for reservations to the Scheduled Castes and Scheduled Tribes. They intended such provisions for a limited period of ten years after the promulgation of the Constitution. Accordingly, 10 percent of the seats of the central and state legis-latures, in educational institutions, and in government employment were to be reserved. B. R. Ambedkar, the eminent chairman of the Constitution Drafting Committee and himself the chief spokesman and leader of the Scheduled Castes, wanted that time limit for vari-ous reasons, including that the prolon-gation of the practice or its permanence would ossify the identity of the members of the Depressed Classes and also affect their integration with the nation.

Yet when the time came to end the reservation at the end of the first ten years, on the grounds of both the need of the Depressed Classes and, perhaps more important, the reluctance of the politicians not to alienate a substantial section of the voting bloc, they were not only renewed time and again but be-came a rallying point for the "Other Backward Classes" (OBC) to demand and secure similar concessions. The reservation quota was extended also to promotions in service. Nehru saw the effect of this on the quality of adminis-tration. In one of his periodic letters to the chief ministers, he focused on the issue on June 27, 1961:

I dislike any kind of reservation, more particularly in service. I react strongly against anything which leads to inef-ficiency and second-rate standards. . . . The only real way to help a back-ward group is to give opportunities for a good education. But if we go in for reservations on communal and caste basis, we swamp the bright and able people and remain second-rate or third-rate. It has amazed me to learn that even promotions are based some-times on communal and caste consid-erations. This way lies not only folly, but disaster. Let us help the backward groups by all means, but never at the cost of efficiency.[21]

NEHRU'S DEATH

What crushed Nehru was the Chinese invasion of India in October 1962, the details of which will be found in the chapter on India's foreign policy. He admitted that India (meaning he) had lived in a world of "delusion" in regard to China. He aged suddenly. Only three years before, he had spurned the assis-tance he was offered and climbed 3,000 feet to the Pratapgad fort to unveil a statue of Shivaji. Past seventy then, he had the energy of a youth, putting in seventeen hours of work every day since the country's independence. He suf-fered a stroke, and then his aorta burst, and he died on May 27, 1964.

LAL BAHADUR SASTRI

Sastri (May 1964–January 1966) was, to all appearances, a contrast to Nehru. Born and raised in very humble circum-stances, educated in India, clad in *dhoti*, of short stature, he did not have a com-manding personality. He was known to be scrupulously honest and capable. When he was a minister for railroads, he tendered his resignation at once when there was a particularly bad accident, assuming complete responsibility as the minister in charge. He and his family had always lived simply. He had proved himself an excellent administrator and had enjoyed Nehru's complete confidence. But he was such a contrast to Nehru that people did not easily accept him as the nation's leader. In cinema halls, when he appeared in the news documentaries, people mimicked his somewhat squeaky voice and laughed at his lack of personality.

The second war with Pakistan in 1965 (details in the chapter on foreign policy) brought out his true leadership qualities. Firm and decisive, he was the architect of a victory that Pakistani generals had been sure would be theirs. The country—people and the media—showered immense praise on his abilities and leadership. On the evening of the day he successfully negotiated a peace agreement with Pakistan that Soviet Premier Aleksei Kosygin brokered in the central Asian city of Tashkent, Sastri suffered a heart attack and died, in January 1966.

IMPERIOUS INDIRA

The selection of Indira Gandhi in January 1966 as prime minister over the seasoned politician and administrator Morarji Desai by the Congress bosses known as the "Syndicate" was done primarily because she was perceived as a pliable, inexperienced young person who would be heavily dependent on the party stalwarts. The Syndicate consisted primarily of regional bosses such as Kamraj Nadar, president of the Congress and former Chief Minister of Tamil Nadu; Sanjeeva Reddy, former chief minister of Andhra Pradesh; and S. K. Patil, a long-time member of the cabinet, until 1963, and dubbed the "king of Bombay," whereas the Congress boss he could sponge at will off the Bombay business community for funds. Indira's image was still of a docile daughter; prominent opposition parliamentarian Madhu Limaye would publicly describe her as a *gungi gudiya* (dumb doll) who would depend heavily on the Syndicate for major decisions. That image lasted only a couple of years, until 1969 when she broke the Congress and established domination over her own faction of the Congress Party.

The electoral defeat of the Congress in February 1967, reducing its Lok Sabha majority to 54 percent and, even more important, in the following month losing six states—Bihar, Madras, Kerala, Orissa, Punjab, and West Bengal—exposed the weakness of the Syndicate as an electoral machine. Very soon after, the Congress-led coalition government in Uttar Pradesh collapsed, and a constitutional breakdown ushered in presidential rule to Rajasthan. The party's defeat was indicative of people's frustration with economic failure. There had been three successive years of famines and large-scale imports of rice and wheat from abroad, particularly the United States under the Public Law 480 scheme. It was humiliating to have the U.S. Senate hearings and American media describing India as living from "ship to mouth." This was deeply offensive to the sensitive Indira, who summoned the very able C. Subramaniam, the minister for food and agriculture, and offered him all the assistance needed to turn the country's food position around. Thanks to the Green Revolution made possible by Norman Borlaugh (he later received the Nobel Prize for Peace in 1970), new wheat strains and Subramaniam's immense administrative and financial management abilities, self-sufficiency in food was achieved in a few years, and the country was able to export grain for the first time. Since the late sixties, despite the growth in population, India has been completely self-sufficient in food and able to export some in some years.

Meanwhile, Indira had created her own coterie of advisers, mostly leftists, some of them former, disillusioned, members of the Communist Party: Inder Kumar Gujral, D. P. Dhar, Mohan Kumarmangalam, and Dinesh Singh. These individuals constituted the "Kitchen Cabinet," meeting regularly at her home and serving her loyally to counteract the dominance of the Syndicate. They were committed, loyal, hardworking, and determined to wean Indira away from the rightist, capitalist orientation of the Syndicate. They emphasized reduction of poverty through land reform and a ceiling on personal income, private property,

and the profits of large companies. In a bid to create a new populist electoral support base for their policies, they pushed for nationalization of banks, which brought Indira directly into conflict with the Syndicate. On November 8, Indira outlined the ideological contours of the confrontation. "What we witness today is not a mere clash of personalities and certainly not a fight for power. . . . It is a conflict between those who are for socialism, for change and for the fullest internal democracy and debate in the organization . . . and those who are for the status quo, for conformism."[22] When she refused to back down, the Syndicate expelled her on November 12, 1969, from the Congress Party, for which three generations of the Nehru family, including Indira, had done so much.

Undeterred, Indira split the Congress Party in two: the Syndicate and most of the rightist and older leaders of the Congress would remain with the organization. Their Congress would be called "Congress (O)," whereas as "requisitioners," the Indira-led Congress would be called "Congress (R)." To have enough support in the Lok Sabha for her new "radical" policies, she came to depend increasingly on the Communists.

The Congress (R) was, in reality, not a completely leftist party. It could be more appropriately described as left of center, just as the Congress (O) was right of center. But in order to bolster her populist image, Indira announced the nationalization of banks and went ahead with the abolition of privy purses for the erstwhile princes.

The justification for the nationalization of banks was that they had thus far catered to the rich and had been most unwilling to take risks in lending to the underprivileged. In reality, the nationalization of banks brought under government control vast resources, which could be used, within limits, to win the support of the common people. The party leaders held loan *melas* (festivals) on different occasions in rural areas, giving loans to small farmers and peasants and any promising individuals who would like to start a small business. In the urban centers, many taxi drivers were given loans and enabled to become owners of vehicles. Indira came through such measures as the savior of the poor and the underprivileged.

In March 1971, Indira went to the polls in India's fifth general election, held a year before the term of the Lok Sabha would be due to expire. Whereas the Congress (O) centered on the slogan *Indira Hatao* (Remove Indira), Indira's slogan was *Garibi Hatao* (Remove Poverty). It was not, however, her domestic successes that would raise her to a pinnacle of power and popularity. Events in India's neighborhood, in East Pakistan, in the same month as her reelection would engage her mind and would by the end of the year make her a world figure of great consequence. Indira's greatest moment of triumph was the birth of Bangladesh and the partition of Pakistan. When she met Pakistan's new pres-

ident, the once haughty, arrogant India hater Zulfikar Ali Bhutto, at Simla in 1972, the visitor pleading for the release of the 93,000 members of the Pakistani Armed Forces in Indian captivity and for the return of the Pakistani territory under Indian occupation, she walked with great confidence but also with an air of statesmanlike modesty that she could well afford. The Simla Agreement could have been harsh on Pakistan but for the gracious host, Indira, who was in a forgiving mood.

Although the Bangladesh war left the Indian treasury depleted and the economy in a highly inflationary state, the public adoration of Indira, equating her with Goddess Kali and Durga, destroyer of enemies, continued unabated for at least a year. Consequently, the state assembly elections of 1972 gave her a resounding public endorsement of her personal leadership, not of the party as such. Her style of government became increasingly personal. She now chose the chief ministers of the states, removing that selection from the hands of the elected Congress Party members of the state legislatures and out of the influence of the state party bosses. It now became customary for the state leaders to fly to Delhi and wait for a chance to see and impress the prime minister, who would keep a rival candidate for chief minister in the wings; her assistants and advisers would let the visiting chief minister discreetly know about it and ensure his or her complete loyalty and commitment to the supreme leader. Indira systematically eliminated challenges to her leadership from within the party at all levels. The federal setup of the government provided by the constitution and of the party structure established since the party's reorganization in 1920 by Gandhi himself was deliberately and systematically undermined. The Indian democracy was increasingly made to function on near-fascist lines. The state chief ministers ensured that their "quotas" for the party's election fund were met in time and that the visits of the prime minister to the states would be successful demonstrations of public enthusiasm and support, the crowds lining the roads from the airport to the official residence and the venues of public meetings. It was no longer uncommon for the party minions to hire buses to bring thousands of audience members to such conclaves and shout slogans endorsing Indira's leadership and policies. A very important appointment in her own cabinet was of the minister for information and broadcasting to make sure that there was positive and adequate publicity for herself and her policies. On the government-owned national television network, the Doordarshan, and in the government-made short documentaries mandatorily shown just before the main feature movie, the information minister made sure to promote, in effect, a personality cult, indeed, at state expense. A new level of sycophancy was attained by a Congress Party president, D. K. Barooah, who coined a new slogan, "India is Indira, Indira is India." The prime minister did not discourage the slogan or the equation. In fact, she promoted what a journalist called the "courtier culture" of sycophancy.

In addition to the "Kitchen Cabinet," Indira instituted a new agency, the Prime Minister's Office (PMO), paralleling the various ministries, the setup looking more like a presidential type of government. A number of decisions were made at the prime minister's residence before and after office hours, often helped or enforced by a new center of power, her son, the ambitious, thoughtless hater of institutions Sanjay. Indira's "personalized" rule was helped by a new intelligence agency, the Research and Analysis Wing (RAW). The PMO, with the help of RAW, began maintaining files on all major political figures belonging to the Congress and the opposition parties alike. Together, all these factors ensured politics of loyalty at the party level and at the institutional level by a "committed" bureaucracy and judiciary that was ready to flout tradition, to bend if not break the rules in order to make the leader's policies work. Not all bureaucrats or judges complied. It is to their credit that most did not. Those who did prospered or wallowed in the glow of power.

The Emergency

The huge costs of maintaining an estimated 10 million refugees from East Pakistan, who crossed the border into India's West Bengal, and the costs of the Bangladesh war and for maintaining the 93,000 prisoners of war as prescribed by the relevant Geneva Conventions grossly affected India's economic situation. Additionally, the two years following that war were marked by crop failures affecting the price levels of essential commodities. Internationally, the world oil prices tripled following the Egypt-Israel War in 1973, affecting the costs of industrial products, again adversely affecting the cost of living. For the masses, the pride and glory of winning the Bangladesh war and partitioning Pakistan gave way to the frustration of balancing the pocketbook in trying to meet the family's expenses. There were numerous strikes, the worst being that of the railroad employees.

Discontent and J. P.'s Total Revolution

The public discontent over the spiraling inflation, unemployment, and mounting corruption was channeled in two states—Bihar and Gujarat—into mass movements. In the latter state, students led the agitation and forced the Congress-led government to resign in 1974. In the following year, the Congress Party was trounced at the polls in Gujarat in June, and the opposition parties came together to form a government there. In both the states, the activists took inspiration and guidance from Jaiprakash Narayan, popularly known as J. P., the nationally known Gandhian Sarvodaya leader who led the public discontent and advocated a civil disobedience movement, reminding

people of the Gandhian movement by that name against the alien, colonial British regime four decades before.[23] If the Bangladesh war had raised Indira's personal stature to unprecedented levels, J. P.'s movement, called the Total Revolution, made Indira and her acolytes run for succor. The movement influenced the defeat of her party in the Gujarat elections in June 1975 as a multiparty coalition, the Janata Morcha (People's March) Party, won the majority of seats in the state assembly.

Allahabad Court Judgment Against Indira's Electoral Violations

The final straw that broke the proverbial camel's back came in the form of a writ issued by Justice J. M. L. Sinha of the Allahabad High Court on June 12, 1975, declaring Indira's election to the parliament in 1971 invalid on the grounds that she had violated the election rules. She had appointed as her election agent one Yashpal Kapoor, who was during part of that period on the government payroll in the PMO. She had also benefited from the UP state government's free construction of a speakers' rostrum and free electricity supply to her public address system during her election campaign. The judgment concerned a case filed by her opponent in that election, Raj Narain of the Samajwadi Socialist Party.

Indira's infractions were petty, but the Representation of the People Act demanded that all violations, small or large, not only rendered the offender's election invalid but would also make the individual ineligible to hold public office for six years. Two chief ministers of states and a member of Indira's cabinet had previously been sanctioned in the same manner. Justice Sinha gave the Congress Parliamentary Party twenty days to elect a new leader for the position of the country's prime minister.

It was the first bad news for Indira and her party on June 12. That evening came the news of the Congress Party's defeat in the Gujarat state elections, where out of 182 seats, her party had won only 75.

The Congress Party appealed to the Supreme Court of India for an "absolute and unconditional" stay order against the Allahabad High Court judgment. It was a tribute to the Indian judicial system that on June 24, 1975, Justice V. R. Krishna Iyer of the Supreme Court, going strictly by the letter of the law, denied a stay order, thereby closing all legal options for Indira, who was then expected to resign. On the same day, at a massive rally in Delhi, the opposition parties under J. P.'s leadership announced that they would launch a civil disobedience movement throughout the country if Indira continued as prime minister. J. P. went further and appealed to the army and the police not to obey any illegal orders even if they were issued by the prime minister.

Proclamation of "Emergency"

Should Indira have resigned? If she had, it was most likely that the Congress Party would have picked as her successor a weak and pliable person, who in his or her capacity as prime minister, could be depended on to recommend to the president that he set aside the Allahabad High Court judgment and pardon her. But feeling insecure, the Indira Gandhi government issued an ordinance in the early hours of the fateful June 26, 1975 (after waking up President Fakhruddin Ahmed to obtain his signature), declaring a national emergency under the provisions of Part 18 of the Constitution. The ordinance said that "a grave emergency exists whereby the security of India is threatened by internal disturbances," justifying the suspension of fundamental rights. Using her majority in the parliament, Indira proceeded to amend the constitution, exonerating her from all culpability. In predawn raids across the country, some 676 members of the opposition parties, including 59 members of the parliament and including the venerable J. P. and political leaders of stature who had rendered long-term public service such as Morarji Desai, were arrested under the hated Maintenance of Internal Security Act (MISA), without the benefit of habeas corpus or a court trial. Women leaders such as the Maharani of Jaipur, Rajmata of Gwalior, and Mrinal Gore were closeted in the same wards as some mentally deranged criminals, whose shrieks and cries would not allow them to sleep. As for J. P., he contracted renal disease while in detention and had no access to dialysis. Most of the right-wing Rashtriya Swayamsevak Sangh and Jan Sangh (later Bharatiya Janata Party [BJP]) members, including the future prime minister Atal Bihari Vajpayee, were jailed. Within a week of the ordinance, on July 4, twenty-six political organizations, including the RSS, were declared illegal.

Indira's Emergency Government also imposed a strict censorship of the press and the media. On the day of the massive arrests of opposition leaders, the supply of electricity to all major newspapers in the capital was cut off so that they would not be able to publish the news of the arrests. The press protested for days by leaving the editorial space blank, sometimes bordered black. Even the mildest criticism was not permitted by the censors. Newspapers that even subtly criticized government actions were denied government advertising, which was and is an important revenue source for Indian newspapers. Several journalists managed to smuggle bits of information to the foreign press, which regularly reported Indira's excesses and the constitutional amendments that had lent legality to her ignoble actions.

Indira then proceeded to "legalize" her own position in the context of the Allahabad High Court judgment. Thus, at her behest, the parliament adopted the Thirty-ninth Amendment to the constitution in August 1975, placing elections to certain positions—president, vice president, prime minister, and speaker of the Lok Sabha—beyond challenge in a court of law and also beyond the pale of judicial review. The amendment, retroactive in its application, nullified the Allahabad High Court judgment. As if this was not enough, the Allahabad judgment was submitted to the Supreme Court, which ruled on November 7, 1975, that the judgment be "set aside."

It was widely reported that in imposing a national emergency, Indira acted on the advice of her younger son, Sanjay. He was also her principal adviser throughout the period of the emergency, which lasted nineteen months, from June 25, 1975, to January 18, 1977. Even while Nehru was the country's prime minister, Indira had to approach him if something could be done to help Sanjay, who had been arrested by the police for reportedly being involved with an automobile-stealing gang in Delhi. While in Great Britain as an apprentice at Roll-Royce, he was arrested for fast driving and other demeanors; he had to be bailed out by the Indian High Commission. Over the years, he had built a reputation for behaving as if he was above the law. During the emergency, he came to be known for "getting things done" in the public interest and also for personal favors to well-placed businessmen and industrialists, securing them permits and additional quotas in return for funds for the party. There was no knowing whether he drew a line between the funds meant for the party and for his own expenses. He had expensive habits, including flying, which, according to parliamentary records, cost fuel charges of 3,600 rupees a day. Both sons, Sanjay and Rajiv, lived with their wives and children (Sanjay had one son, Rajiv had two children—a son and a daughter) with the prime minister. There were wide rumors that Sanjay's financial affairs were carried out with his mother's knowledge, and perhaps some substantial amounts were transferred to Swiss bank accounts.

Sanjay's most notorious campaigns during the emergency rule included forcible vasectomies as a means of family planning on those who lived in Delhi slums and the eviction of an estimated 700,000 squatters and slum dwellers from their huts, which were summarily destroyed. Some of those who resisted near the Turkman Gate were shot dead. Incidents of this kind were repeated elsewhere, particularly in Indira Gandhi's home state of Uttar Pradesh, where, according to the *Economist* of London on December 4, 1976, in twenty-one such incidents, police opened fire and killed 467 people to make room for some beautification projects. Vasectomy was forced on men even in their seventies and eighties. Riders in buses were ordered to come out and were sterilized in makeshift tents. There was tremendous panic created by these drives not just among the people immediately affected. Others wondered, "When will this reign of terror stop?"

Sanjay soon became a law unto himself. He made and unmade chief ministers and announced major policy decisions in the name of his mother, without consulting with the cabinet minister concerned. A feeling spread among members of the Congress that Indira was preparing for a dynastic succession of her son Sanjay, who had used the emergency period to organize the Youth Congress on a large scale with himself as its supreme leader. The government-owned radio and television gave Sanjay tremendous exposure, lauding his various campaigns, subtly hailing him as the future leader. A wisecrack was, after the end of the emergency, to describe the emergency period as "one and a half person's rule." He did not specify whether Indira was the one or the half!

Indira, however, was not happy with the emergency and the criticism, particularly in the foreign media, leveled at her. One such criticism concerned the extension of the life of the Lok Sabha by one year, which the constitution allowed but had never been done before and has not been done since. A number of Western leaders and their ambassadors in New Delhi used every opportunity to convey to Indira most tactfully that it would be best to restore democracy. Perhaps bowing to such pressures and possibly because she herself believed she could not rule indefinitely without a public mandate, on January 18, 1977, Indira surprised everyone in India and abroad with her announcement that the next elections would be held in two months, in March 1977; she also ordered all political prisoners released. She was confident that the opposition leaders, with very little time to reorganize their lives and campaigns after nineteen months in prison, would be defeated in the elections and that she would emerge with a substantial majority in the new parliament.

THE JANATA INTERLUDE

While in prison, the opposition leaders had had plenty of time to think about all kinds of political strategies. They realized that their ideological and pro-grammatic differences would be inconse-quential if democracy itself were to be allowed to be emasculated by Indira and her Congress Party. They decided to form an anti-Congress coalition through the merger of four major parties: Con-gress (O), the Jan Sangh, the Socialist Party and the Bharatiya Lok Dal. Thus was born the Janata (People's) Party in January 1977, within a week of the end of the emergency and announcement of elections. J. P., who midwifed the birth of the Janata Party, himself chose to stay outside it to act as its adviser. Indira was alarmed at the popular reaction to Janata's emergence as a viable coalition. To her annoyance, the senior-most member of her cabinet, Jagjivan Ram, the Congress leader of the Harijans, sud-denly announced his resignation from the government on February 2, 1977. He created a new party, Congress for De-mocracy, pledging complete cooperation with the Janata Party and agreeing to merge with it after the elections. An-other major "defection" from the Con-gress was Nehru's sister and Indira's aunt, Madame Vijayalakshmi Pandit, former president of the United Nations General Assembly and India's ambassador to the United States, United Kingdom, and Soviet Union, who had remained a quiet opponent of her niece's abridgment of democracy.

The brief election campaign brought millions of people to meetings, showing their resentment of the emergency nightmare. V. B. Kulkarni describes the mood of the time:

> The imposition of the emergency, the arbitrary arrest of tens of thousands of people, the detention of a large number of leaders, many of them aged and infirm, the perpetration of leonine violence on a defenceless population in the name of social re-form, and the non-fulfillment of even the most solemn pledges to the de-prived classes caused countrywide resentment against the ruling party. These facts, his epic sacrifice for the country and his grave physical mal-adies helped lift Jaiprakash Narayan to legendary fame and popularity.[24]

Janata defeated Indira's Congress handily, winning 271 seats out of 542 in the Lok Sabha. Its electoral allies, the Congress for Democracy, won 28, and the Communist Party of India (Marxist) won 22. The Congress won only 153 seats. Its rout was complete in most of the Hindi Belt states of Uttar Pradesh, Bihar, Punjab, Haryana, and Himachal Pradesh and the capital city of Delhi. Madhya Pradesh and Rajasthan, also parts of the Hindi Belt, gave Congress (R) 1 seat each. Of the 299 seats in ten states of northern India (including West Bengal and Orissa), the Congress (R) won only 9. Above all, Indira Gandhi herself was defeated by the voters in her Rae Bareilly constituency. Many Congress stalwarts, including several cabinet ministers, met their electoral nemesis. The Indian masses, despite millions of illiterates, had shown their political maturity, and shown the door to those who had briefly tried to subvert the democracy.

A veteran of the old Congress (O) and now the Janata leader, Morarji Desai, became the new prime minister. For the first time since the country's independence, a non-Congress government had come to power in Delhi. His government immediately reversed all the curbs on personal freedoms of the Emergency Rule and restored India's democratic norms as they existed before the emergency. The Janata rule was, however, plagued with programmatic inconsistencies, personal feuds among leaders, and worse, a fierce competition among Morarji Desai and his two deputy prime ministers: Charan Singh and Jagjivan Ram. A cartoon of the time summed up the triangular rivalry, each one of the trio

wanting the other two dead so he could be or remain the prime minister! Desai resigned in July 1979, not wanting to face a no-confidence motion. Charan Singh succeeded him but could not get enough support from his Janata colleagues. He resigned and announced new elections to be held in January 1980.

INDIRA'S RULE AGAIN

The Congress (R) was now renamed Congress (I), the *I*, of course, for *Indira*, who was the sole dominant center of the party. Indira's campaign slogan in the 1980 elections was "Elect a government that works!" The people were disgusted with memories of Janata leaders' infighting and a government that had failed to work on anything mentionable except, as a wisecrack said later in mid-1980, that it had successfully cleared Sanjay's gift plane through customs!

A major setback for Indira's new government was a personal tragedy for the prime minister. Her son Sanjay, who liked to perform stunt flying, died when his private plane crashed. The aircraft itself had been a gift of the International Harvesters and had been cleared through all the formalities by the Janata government, one of its few favors to the Gandhi family. After Sanjay's untimely death, Indira felt lonesome in politics; she had lost her confidant, although she had not always liked his ways. She now persuaded her older son, Rajiv, an airline pilot and a very private person in matters of probity, exactly the opposite of his dead brother, to help her in public life. Very soon, she gave him the role of general secretary of the Congress Party.

The Punjab Crisis

During her second and briefer spell in power, Indira gave considerable attention to Punjab politics. In the late seventies, Indira's lieutenant Giani Zail Singh, the chief minister of Punjab, had thought it prudent to boost one Sant Jarnail Singh Bhindranwale, an orthodox Sikh with some following, to challenge the Akali leadership. But Bhindranwale had his own religious and political agenda, namely, to create an independent Sikh state. In May 1984, reports reached New Delhi that Bhindranwale and several hundred Sikh extremists had occupied the Golden Temple at Amritsar and that he had amassed a large cache of arms and ammunition in the sacred precincts of the temple. Indira responded in early June by launching Operation Blue Star. On October 31, 1984, she paid a heavy price for her operation in Amritsar: her two Sikh bodyguards opened fire on her that morning as she was on her way from her residence to another building within her residential compound.

As the nation mourned Indira's shocking death, New Delhi was enveloped in anti-Sikh riots for three days before her son and successor, Rajiv, called in the troops. Thousands of innocent Sikhs, men, women, and children, who had no hand whatsoever in the dastardly assassination, were killed by angry mobs, who as the later inquiries revealed were hired by local Congress leaders.

Indira's legacy has been a mixed one. People remember her as Nehru's daughter who broke the Congress, which at one time was led by Mahatma Gandhi and Jawaharlal Nehru, and his father, Motilal Nehru, and had led the nation to freedom. They remember her even more as the "invincible goddess," for her determination and courage during the Bangladesh war that sundered the enemy nation Pakistan, undeterred as she was by the U.S. threat to enter the war on the opposite side. The people equally remember her for being the only person in independent India's history to deal a body blow to democracy in the country by clamping down an Emergency Rule for nineteen scary months, when she was all but a dictator. Almost a quarter century after her assassination, the masses still revere her, whereas the intelligentsia reviles her. They are not willing to forgive her for the centralization of power and the personalization of a government that rewarded those committed to her personally and, in the process, undermined the fine structure that was built by her father not only by the continuation of the British traditions of the rule of law and the integrity of the civil service and the judiciary but also by his own steadfast adherence to parliamentary norms and ethical ways in public life based on personal honesty,

integrity, and probity. As Inder Malhotra wrote two decades after her death of
the residual impact of the emergency:
"It clouds some of the brighter elements
she bequeathed to her country. This is
so because the poison that the emergency introduced into the Indian system has not yet been fully flushed out of
the body politic."[25]

Indira's last name was Gandhi but
that was because she married a Zoroastrian Parsi whose family name was
Gandhi, not related at all to the Mahatma. She was in an essential way not
related to the Mahatma, who stood for
the primacy of means over ends; with
Indira, it was exactly the opposite. Malhotra correctly says:

If the list of Indira's faults and flaws is
long, that of her achievements, some
of them dazzling, is even longer and
more impressive. . . . It was in Indira's
time that India became the third
largest reservoir of skilled scientific
and technical manpower, the fifth
military power, the sixth member of
the nuclear club, seventh in the race
for space and the tenth industrial
power.[26]

In December 1999, on the eve of the
new millennium, a British Broadcasting
Corporation poll rated India's first and
only woman prime minister the "greatest woman of the past 1,000 years"!

———

NOTES

1. Chanakya, "The Rashtrapati," *Modern Review* 62 (November 1937): 546–47.

2. For details, see Subhash Kashyap, *The Ten Lok Sabhas: From the First to the Tenth, 1952–91* (Delhi: Shipra Publications, 1992).

3. http://encarta.msn.com/media_461550590, n.p.

4. Quoted in Bipan Chandra, Aditya Mukherjee, and Mridula Mukherjee, *India after Independence* (New Delhi: Penguin Books, 1999), 102–3.

5. Michael Brecher, "Nehru's Place in History," in *The Legacy of Nehru: A Centennial Assessment*, edited by D. R. SarDesai and Anand Mohan, 54.

6. Joint French-Indian Declaration of August 27, 1947, in India, Lok Sabha Secretariat, *Foreign Policy of India* (New Delhi: Lok Sabha Secretariat, 1959), 135–42.

7. For the links between the Indian government's policy toward the French possessions in India and the First Indochina War, see D. R. SarDesai, *Indian Foreign Policy in Cambodia, Laos, and Vietnam, 1947–1964*, 15–22.

8. Government of Goa, Daman, and Diu, *General Information* (Panaji: Central Press, 1962), 3.

9. Mohandas K. Gandhi, "Goan Struggle for Freedom," *Harijan*, June 30, 1946.

10. Letter to the editor, *Harijan*, August 11, 1946.

11. *Harijan*, September 8, 1946, reproduced in M. K. Gandhi, *Goan Struggle for Freedom* (Ahmadabad: Navijivan Publishing House, 1954), 7–8.

12. Jawaharlal Nehru, *Speeches, 1949–1953* (New Delhi: Ministry of Information and Broadcasting, 1967), 19.

13. India, Lok Sabha, *Debates*, 2d ser., 59, no. 4 (November 24, 1961), n.p; Arthur Rubinoff, *India's Use of Force in Goa* (Bombay: Popular, 1971), 37; *India News*, December 27, 1961, n.p.

14. *New York Times*, July 1, 1961, 4.

15. *Times of India*, October 23, 1961.

16. Rubinoff, India's Use of Force in Goa, 81–82.

17. Ibid., 82.

18. John Kenneth Galbraith to Department of State, telegram 1754, December 14, 1961, in Department of State, Central Files, 753 D.00/12-1561, secret; Department of State to Galbraith, December 14, 1961, telegram 1461, in ibid.

19. Menon at the UN Security Council, Official Records, Meetings 987–988, December 18, 1961. See also C. S. Jha to the UN Security Council, December 20, 1961, in *UN Weekly Newsletter* 9, no. 53 (December 26, 1961).

20. C. Wilfred Jenks, *The Common Law of Mankind* (London: Stevens, 1958), 85.

21. Quoted in Nani Palkhiwala, *The Nation: The Lost Decades* (New Delhi: UBS, 1994), 182.

22. Quoted in Zareer Masani, *Indira Gandhi: A Biography*, 209.

23. Sarvodaya was Gandhi's program for the total uplift of the villages, promoting social equality and economic self-sufficiency and preferring village handicrafts to industrial manufactures.

24. Kulkarni.

25. "Indira Gandhi's Legacy," BBC News, October 28, 2004, news.bbc.co.uk/2/hi/south _asai/3960877/stm.

26. Ibid.

TABLE 15.1

PRIME MINISTERS, GOVERNORS-GENERAL, AND PRESIDENTS OF INDIA, 1947–2006

Prime Minister	Party	Period in Office
Jawaharlal Nehru	Congress	August 1947–May 1964
Lal Bahadur Shastri	Congress	June 1964–January 1966
Indira Gandhi	Congress	January 1966–March 1977
Morarji Desai	Janata	March 1977–July 1979
Charan Singh	Janata	July 1979–January 1980
Indira Gandhi	Congress (I)	January 1980–October 1984
Rajiv Gandhi	Congress (I)	October 1984–December 1989
V. P. Singh	Janata	December 1989–November 1990

Prime Minister	*Party*	*Period in Office*
Chandra Sekhar	Janata	November 1990–January 1991
P. V. Narasimha Rao	Congress	January 1991–June 1996
H. V. Dewe Gowda	United Front	June 1996–April 1997
Inder Kumar Gujral	United Front	April 1997–December 1997
Atal Bihari Vajpayee	BJP	March 1998–April 1999
Atal Bihari Vajpayee	BJP (NDA)	October 1999–May 2004
Manmohan Singh	Congress	May 2004–

Governors-General (GG) or President (P)	*Office*	*Period in Office*
Lord Mountbatten	GG	August 1947–1948
C. Rajagopalachari	GG	1948–January 1950
Rajendra Prasad	P	January 1950–1962
Sarvepalli Radhakrishnan	P	1962–1967
Zakir Hussain	P	1967–1969
V. V.Giri	P	1969–1974
Fakhruddin Ali Ahmed	P	1974–1977
N. Sanjeeva Reddy	P	1977–1982
Giani Zail Singh	P	1982–1987
R. Venkataraman	P	1987–1992
Shankar Dayal Sharma	P	1992–1997
K. R. Narayanan	P	1997–2002
A. P. J. Abdul Kalam	P	2002–

Who was responsible for the act of demolition on December 6, 1992? Was it planned by the BJP? By the RSS? By the VHP? To this date, there are no definite answers, only denials and accusations. Advani, who was present on the scene, seated on the speakers' platform nearby, was reported by independent media to have asked the *kar sevaks* not to climb the domes. Following the demolition, he resigned his position as leader of the opposition in the Lok Sabha; so did Kalyan Singh (BJP) as the chief minister of Uttar Pradesh for his government's failure to stop the demolition. Vajpayee, who was not present at the demolition, commented on the following day that it was the BJP's worst miscalculation; he could see that it would damage his party.   (page 375)

16

THE MARCH OF INDIAN DEMOCRACY, PART II

RAJIV GANDHI, PRIME MINISTER

In October 1984, Rajiv Gandhi became the prime minister. He was drafted to that high position in the wake of the assassination of his mother, Indira Gandhi. At the time of her sudden death, Rajiv was some miles away from Calcutta; the president of India, Giani Zail Singh, was out of the country, in Aden. Both returned to the Indian capital immediately. On the previous two occasions when the prime minister died in office, the seniormost member of the cabinet, Gulzarilal Nanda, had been temporarily sworn in as prime minister, pending a formal meeting of the majority party in the Lok Sabha to elect their leader, who was then sworn in as prime minister. Going by that practice, it should have been Pranab Mukherjee as the seniormost member of the cabinet to be temporarily holding the office of the prime minister until the majority party, namely, the Congress, had for-

mally elected its leader, who would then be called by the president to become the prime minister. Instead, on instructions from President Zail Singh, Rajiv was brought directly from the Delhi airport to the Rashtrapati Bhawan (Presidential Palace) and sworn in as prime minister. A shocked nation hailed the appointment on the grounds of stability and continuity.

Rajiv was the least-experienced Indian individual to hold such a high office. At forty, he also was the youngest prime minister in independent India's history. Until 1980, when his brother, Sanjay, died in a flying accident, and their mother asked Rajiv to help her, he had been working as a pilot in the state-owned Indian Airlines. Married to the Italian-born Sonia Maino, whom he met at Cambridge during his student days, on return to India, Rajiv and his own immediate family lived with his mother, Indira Gandhi. However, he stayed away completely from politics. The very few newspaper or magazine references to him pointed to his penchant for privacy, socializing only with a few nonpolitical friends. Unlike his brother, Sanjay, Rajiv was known for being scrupulous about money matters, some reports indicating that he contributed his share to the prime minister's household expenses from his salary. Stray references also indicated that whereas Sanjay was politically close to his mother, his wife, Maneka, daughter of an army officer and a strong-willed lady, was not; on the other hand, Rajiv's wife, Sonia, shared Indira's confidences in politics and finances.

Rajiv's cool and dignified demeanor at his mother's funeral and in the first few months of his taking over as prime minister was most impressive. In his new garb, he reminded television news viewers of his great-grandfather Motilal Nehru. He was youthful and handsome and looked determined to build a new India based on honesty, integrity, and incorruptibility, earning him the sobriquet "Mr. Clean." His penchant for the latest technology and large-scale use of computers in administration, rare before his time, earned him another sobriquet, Mr. Computerjee (*jee* being a Hindi honorific). He gathered around him a team of young technocrats, who had been his contemporaries in the famed Doon School and who had earned their success in the private sector. They included the two Aruns—Arun Nehru and Arun Singh. He also attracted a very successful nonresident Indian entrepreneur, Sam Pitroda, from Chicago

to head the Department of Telecommunications. The nation held high hopes for him and gave the Congress Party the highest vote ever in independent India's history, winning in the elections of December 1984 a comfortable majority in the Lok Sabha. It was not just a "sympathy vote"; it was a vote of confidence in Rajiv personally.

Rajiv began well, although the problems he faced were truly staggering: the Sikh agitation in the Punjab for an independent Khalistan; separatist movements in the Northeast; bringing honesty and efficiency into the government and his own party; modernization of the economy to make it more efficient and productive, possibly with technical and financial assistance from the United States and Indian Americans; and improving relations with neighbors Pakistan, China, and Sri Lanka.

As Mr. Clean, Rajiv began his administration with a clear understanding that it was not going to be "business as usual" for the businessmen who were accustomed to greasing the palms of bureaucrats and Congress Party middlemen to get licenses and quotas. In his first Independence Day Address, soon after he became prime minister, he castigated his own party members for forgetting their role in the freedom movement and succumbing to a life of dishonesty and corruption. He warned the industrialists that India had for too long tolerated a poor quality of manufactures and that the consumer had been shortchanged. He spoke of new initiatives, particularly in electronics and telecommunications, and attracting foreign investment and competition that would compel the improvement in the quality of domestic products. He encouraged the Finance Ministry and the Income Tax Department to investigate gross cases of tax evasion and punish the guilty. He assured them of protection and noninterference in their work. There was much in his program that made several sectors of the society look forward to a new India, reminding them of the atmosphere that had prevailed in the early 1950s, full of promise for the country's future. They gave Rajiv a new mandate in the elections of December 1984, with the largest plurality ever since independence.

Within a year of that momentous election, it was getting clear that Rajiv was not able to break the nexus among the bureaucrats, industry, and politicians, which had since the breakup of the Congress Party in 1969 and Indira's drive to raise large amounts for elections thereafter introduced large-scale corruption in Indian politics. In the mid-1980s, the Congress Party managers, who had been lying low since Rajiv became prime minister, clarified to him that the election he had just won had been financed from the funds left by his mother; it would be necessary to begin to replenish the kitty to prepare for the next election in 1989. Hence the Bofors scandal.

Until the Bofors scandal, discussed later, Rajiv Gandhi had scored a number of policy successes, the major ones being an accord with the Punjab leader, Longowal, and his initiatives on the conflict between Sri Lanka and the Liberation Tigers of Tamil Eelam (LTTE).

Rajiv's Sri Lanka Policy

At the time of Rajiv's assumption of authority as India's prime minister, the Sri Lankan effort through the All Party Conference had failed. Rajiv himself was in favor of giving up the Indian stance, which was thus far tilting somewhat toward the Tamils in the island nation, an approach partly dictated by India's domestic politics needing the support of the Tamil Nadu government. Rajiv's change in favor of neutrality between the two warring sides in Sri Lanka may have been occasioned by the Indian need not to encourage any ethnic separatist movements because of their likely impact on different movements in India itself, including a potential demand for a separate and wider Tamil Nadu. India now urged upon the Sri Lankan Tamil separatists to accept a compromise formula by which they could have autonomy in the Tamil districts within the political framework of a united Sri Lanka. On the other hand, the Indian government would weigh in with the Sri Lankan government to soften its stance toward the Liberation Tigers of Tamil Eelam.

Though seemingly cooperative in talks with India, Sri Lanka followed a two-pronged policy. In January 1987, it suddenly blockaded the Jaffna Peninsula and launched an aggressive military campaign against the Tamils. From that time on, the Tamils insisted on the Indian government's continuing role as a mediator and urged it to become a guarantor of any agreement signed between the LTTE and the Sri Lankan government. Meanwhile, the Sri Lankan military campaign against the Jaffna area had caused tremendous hardships on the population of nearly a quarter million there in terms of access to food, kerosene, and medicine. Indian appeals to the government seated in Colombo failed to make such supplies possible. On June 4, 1987, India acted unilaterally and airdropped supplies on humanitarian grounds, an action that was denounced at that time by many countries including, indeed, Sri Lanka as a breach of international law and violating that country's sovereignty. New Delhi had perhaps no choice because the government of Tamil Nadu appeared ready to help the fellow Tamils across the straits. The Indian assistance proved crucial, as the Colombo government climbed down and signed a peace accord with India.

The Indo–Sri Lanka Peace Accord of 1987, signed by Rajiv Gandhi and President J. R. Jayewardene, in Colombo, on July 29, 1987, was not to the liking of many Sri Lankans, including Prime Minister Ranasinghe Premadasa. The Indian government agreed to send the Indian Peace-Keeping Forces (IPKF) to make sure that the LTTE was "neutralized." The agreement as well as the IPKF eventually failed because India had misjudged Jayawardene's commitment and the "reasonableness" of the LTTE leaders.

In January 1989, there was a changing of the guard in Sri Lanka, as Premadasa, who had opposed the Indo–Sri Lanka Peace Accord, was elected president of the country. Two parties—the Sri Lanka Freedom Party and the United National Party—in Sri Lanka, who had opposed the Indian intervention, had received 95 percent of the popular vote. Premadasa immediately demanded that the IPKF be withdrawn. The Indian intervention was, at that point of time, unpopular in India as well, because the IPKF operations had involved the deaths of more than 1,000 Indian soldiers and more than 5,000 Sri Lankan Tamils. The operation had cost the Indian treasury in excess of 2,000 crores of rupees and had attracted considerable criticism of the IPKF's violation of human rights. Rajiv refused to withdraw the IPKF because he did not want to admit the failure of his Sri Lanka policy. One of the early decisions of V. P. Singh, his successor as prime minister in December 1989, was to withdraw the IPKF in March 1990.

Rajiv-Longowal Accord over the Punjab Question

On the other hand, Rajiv succeeded in arriving at an agreement with the then president of the Akali Dal, Harchand Singh Longowal. Rajiv successfully overcame his initial reluctance to deal with the Sikhs, remembering that his mother was a casualty of the Khalistan movement.

Within weeks of the December 1984 elections, Rajiv revealed his conciliatory approach to the Punjab problem. In January 1985, he released all the important Sikh leaders, including the Akali Dal's president, Longowal. In the following month, he formally established an independent judicial inquiry into the controversial November Hindu-Sikh riots in Delhi, following his mother's assassination. These measures mollified the Akali Dal, who withdrew their support of the militant tactics and instead came to believe that negotiations would be a fruitful course of action.

It is in such a conciliatory atmosphere on both sides that the Rajiv-Longowal Accord was signed in August 1985. The major points of the accord were that all political detainees would be released, and there would be a special enactment of an All-India Gurdwara Act.

Chandigarh would be transferred to Punjab by January 1986. Since this was a capital for both Punjab and Haryana, the State of Punjab would compensate Haryana with equivalent territory for a new capital. A tribunal, headed by a Supreme Court judge, would adjudicate the sharing of the waters of the Ravi and the Beas by nonriparian states. It would take consumption of water in July 1985 as the baseline.

As for those responsible for the Delhi riots in November 1984, the prosecutions would be referred to the Mishra Commission. Army desertions, as a reaction to Operation Blue Star, would be condoned, and the deserters concerned would be rehabilitated and given gainful employment.

There was a mixed reaction to the accord in Punjab and among the Sikhs in Delhi. Longowal himself was killed by extremists who were strongly opposed to the accord, which they regarded as a "sellout." All the provisions of the accord were not carried out. Thus, despite three commissions considering the question of transfer of Chandigarh and the refusal of the Punjab government to part with any of the state's territory to Haryana to enable the latter to build a new capital, the central government decided in mid-1986 to postpone the issue indefinitely. In February 1987, the Congress was absolved of direct responsibility for the Delhi riots. The responsibility was blamed on the delayed deployment and action of the Delhi police. In May 1987, the Eradi Tribunal reduced Punjab's July 1985 level and doubled Haryana's share.

Following the accord, elections for the Punjab State Assembly as well as for Punjab's parliamentary seats were announced for September 1985. Despite the mixed reaction to the accord and the assassination of Longowal, the elections were held with an impressive turnout of 66 percent in which the Akalis won a majority for the first time and formed a government.

Neither the Rajiv-Longowal Accord nor the formation of the Akali government under the weak Surjit Singh Barnala solved the Punjab problem. In fact, Barnala's soft and ill-conceived measures, including the release of all the terrorists, strengthened the ranks of the militant movement. The Akalis could not completely dissociate themselves from the militant movement. In May 1987, within less than a year of the elections, the Barnala ministry was dismissed by New Delhi, which proclaimed "president's rule" over Punjab.

During Rajiv Gandhi's time, there was no appreciable progress in containing terrorism in the state. The Khalistan movement fizzled because the common people were tired of militancy and terrorism, which had grossly affected their livelihood and profits from trade and manufacturing. The people were also increasingly irked by the Taliban-style restrictions imposed by the Khalistani purists on their lifestyle: the ban on meat, liquor, and tobacco; no wearing of saris, and insistence on *salwar-kameez* (the loose, pajama-like trousers and long shirt or tunic widely worn by men and women in Pakistan and Afghanistan) as the only dress; school uniforms to conform to the Khalistani code; and a code for marriage rites. The financial support to the movement from abroad declined substantially as reports circulated of the lavish style of living of some of the terrorists. By 1992, the strong police action taken by two police

commissioners, K. P. S. Gill and Julio Ribeiro, was most effective in rooting out terrorism in Punjab.

The Bofors Scandal

In the post-Nehru period, there have been numerous corruption scandals but none with as much public interest or political damage to the ruling party as the Bofors scandal during the administration of Rajiv Gandhi. The Bofors affair broke out in 1987 and was one of the main factors leading to the defeat of the Congress in the elections of 1989. During the government of his successor, V. P. Singh, the investigation still occupied a central place in the headlines. The amount of kickbacks or commission, whatever one chooses to call it, was all a matter of rupees 64 crores (about 16 million dollars), at that time a small amount compared to the magnitude of corruption cases in later times. Yet Bofors does not die away; it keeps cropping up again and again, even two decades later.

In the decadelong search for a good howitzer for the Indian army, two weapons were selected by the army brass as the top competitors in the mid-1980s. One was the French gun Sofma and the other the Swedish 155-mm howitzer from the A. B. Bofors Company. The final agreement signed with the Swedish manufacturer was for US$1.3 billion. The kickbacks, or commissions, were estimated at rupees 64 crores. There were rival proponents in the army for the two guns. General Sunderji's group advocated the Bofors gun because it had shoot-and-scoot capability, the ability to move it after it was fired, which was lacking in the Sofma gun. Sunderji's opponents privately accused him of "non-professional motivation" in advocating for the Bofors gun. In keeping with his reputation as "Mr. Clean," the prime minister, Rajiv Gandhi, declared that there would be no agents involved in the purchase of arms; the Defense Ministry offices had signs to indicate that the ministry's officials would not see any agents.

In retrospect, it appears that Rajiv Gandhi was only massaging his own clean image and was assured by his two closest advisers, the Doon buddies, Arun Nehru and Arun Singh (the latter the minister of state for defense, who was in charge of army purchases), that they had devised a "system" by which nobody would ever point a finger at the prime minister or his advisers. At the time, Rajiv Gandhi was under considerable pressure from his party managers to find ways of raising funds for the ensuing elections. Rajiv had already denounced the "license and permit *raj*," which gave industrial licenses in exchange for huge monetary favors. His advisers now recommended that instead of asking all manner of businessmen for contributions to the party, mostly in unaccounted funds and then repaying the favors, it would be best to monitor the huge purchases on the government account by the Ministry of Defense and the numerous public-sector undertakings and strike a deal with the suppliers. This would not influence the process of selection of the supplier and the quality of the supplies. The commissions that such large suppliers would have, in any case, given to the middlemen could be harvested for the Congress Party's election fund. The seller would secretly deposit the commissions in a secret account overseas, which would be accessible to the money handlers of the Congress Party. The country would not be a loser, since there would be no compromise on the quality of goods. As for the sellers, they would have paid the amount anyway to some selling agent in keeping with the global practice!

Everything would have perhaps worked according to the plan and Rajiv Gandhi's image would have then remained untarnished but for Swedish Radio revealing in the spring of 1987 that the A. B. Bofors Company had paid a bribe to secure the Indian contract. It appears that the Bofors company had, for some time, been in financial trouble, and the Swedish government had been scrutinizing the company's affairs, perhaps for some tax liability. The multi-million-dollar question raised in India was: Who had received the bribe? The A. B. Bofors Company had, like all others, at first pleaded that they had fired their agents in India to meet the government's requirement. Later, it admitted that it had "forgotten" to do so; still later, it said that it had rehired its former agent, Win Chaddha, as a consultant. Win had a loose tongue. When Bofors won the contract, he threw a party at which numerous large signs announced that "Win had Won!" As time rolled on, the opposition as well as the media unraveled additional names, including that of the brother of Rajiv's then close friend, the Bollywood megastar, Amitabh Bachchan. He lived in Switzerland, and his brother-in-law was employed by one Inlaks Group, which was alleged to have received the bribe on Rajiv's behalf. The prestigious newspaper *Hindu* published some documents showing that the Bofors' checks were made out to a company called Pitco and mailed to an Indian company, the well-known Hindujas in London.

In order to appease the critics, Rajiv Gandhi appointed a Joint Parliamentary Committee (JPC); the opposition refused to serve on it. The JPC report, however, pointed out that the Bofors Company had two agents in India: Pitco (read: Hindujas) and Svenska (read: Win Chaddha). The company pleaded that it had dismissed both in keeping with the government's directive not to have agents and that its payments to them were merely "winding-up charges for terminating the contract."[1] By the time the electorate handed out to Rajiv and the Congress Party an inglorious electoral defeat in 1989, the image of Mr. Clean had become that of "Mr.

Cover-up." After Rajiv Gandhi's assassination in 1991, the Bofors Scandal seemed to have died.

Not so, thanks to the Swedish government, which came into possession of a diary meticulously maintained by the Bofors president, Martin Ardbo, who used the most obvious code names for individuals involved. Veer Sanghvi writes, "Where Ardbo did not use code, he employed bad spelling. Thus, one entry read: 'GPH's [G. P. Hinduja] enemies are Serge Paul and Nero.' As the Hinduja battle with Arun Nehru and Swaraj Paul was well-known, the implications were obvious." Ardbo said elsewhere in the diary that he would be meeting "a Gandhi trustee lawyer" to finalize details but "Q's involvement could be a problem because of closeness to R." *R* was, indeed, for Rajiv. The Indian newspapers wondered whether *Q* stood for Ottavio Quattrochi, the Indian representative of the Italian multinational corporation Snamprogetti who was known to be close to Rajiv Gandhi's family. Could Rajiv's wife, the Italian-born Sonia Gandhi, be involved? Quattrochi immediately fled the country and has ever since been issuing statements pleading his innocence from his refuge in Kuala Lumpur, Malaysia.

On May 31, 2005, after eighteen long years of legal battle, the Delhi High Court gave its verdict on the Bofors kickback case. Three of the accused—Win Chaddha, former defense secretary S. K. Bhatnagar, and former Bofors company president Martin Ardbo—had died during the protracted investigation leading up to the trial. The Delhi High Court acquitted the three Hinduja brothers—Gopichand, Prakashchand, and Srichand—because the prosecution had failed to prove that they were linked to the kickbacks. Previously, on February 5, 2004, the court had exonerated Rajiv Gandhi of any involvement in the scandal. The court blamed India's Central Bureau of Investigation (CBI), the country's top intelligence agency, for its failure to produce enough evidence to charge the accused. With that, the only person charged with accepting bribes or kickbacks from Bofors would be Ottavio Quattrochi, whom the CBI has tried to extradite back to India, in vain. In 2003, the Vajpayee government had requested the British banks in which Quattrochi held accounts to freeze those accounts. In what appears to be the closing action on the whole case, on January 11, 2006, the High Court in London ordered the "defreezing" of the two accounts in British banks of Ottavio Quattrochi on the grounds that there was insufficient evidence to link those accounts with the Bofors case.

Rajiv Loses the 1989 Elections

The Bofors scandal was not the only reason for losing the nation's confidence. Increasing reports of Rajiv's personal style in administration showed his preference for his mother's ways—

demanding unquestioning loyalty and summarily transferring bureaucrats who did not do his bidding. He gave little time to public affairs and administration, preferring to be with his family and friends. He came to be known for his short attention span. Lengthy reports or minutes were anathema to him; everything had to be reduced to a page or one and a half pages with bullet points. That was not so with his mother, who was very studious and hardworking. If the elections in 1984 gave Rajiv the victory because of his personal qualities, the defeat in the elections five years later in 1989 was an equal measure of the public disenchantment with him.

In the elections of 1989, called by Rajiv Gandhi two months ahead of schedule, the opposition parties coalesced, making the rampant corruption, notably the Bofors affair, the focus of the campaign. Rajiv's Congress (I) Party won more seats than any other party, but not enough to form a government on its own. The opposition parties had formed an alliance, the National Front (NF), which formed the government with Viswanath Pratap (V. P.) Singh as the prime minister.

VISWANATH PRATAP SINGH, PRIME MINISTER

Viswanath Pratap Singh's victory was almost completely owed to his anticorruption drive, which had, in the first place, brought about the rift between himself and Rajiv Gandhi and led to his expulsion from the Congress Party in 1987. The people deduced that the corruption at the highest levels had the effect of sanctioning it at the various levels of bureaucracy and the ruling party's ranks. V. P. had been able to rope in two young ministers who were close to Rajiv and had fallen out with him: Arif Mohammad, a young, dynamic, and secular Muslim who had opposed Rajiv's retrograde stance on the Shah Bano case, and Arun Nehru, Rajiv's cousin and "minister of state for home" (the CBI was under him) whom Rajiv found to be beyond his control, inquiring too closely in the Bofors scandal.[2] V. P. also recruited some other Congress dissidents, notably the powerful V. C. Shukla, to join the newly created Jan Morcha (JM), or People's Forum. Amazingly, he also established a covert understanding with the leftist parties and the Bharatiya Janata Party on "seat adjustments," which meant a mutual agreement with the newly created National Front on August 6, 1988, with the merger of several splinter parties. It is the NF and the BJP that agreed not to oppose each other in 85 percent of the seats.

Apart from the pullout of troops from Sri Lanka, the government achieved little. Many mistakes were made, among them the appointment of Jag Mohan as governor of Kashmir, which immediately brought in the resignation of the chief minister, Farook Abdullah, and political turmoil in that state.

Unfortunately, V. P. Singh's coalition government, which was the first of its kind in the history of independent India, was fractious. There were too many disputes among the leaders of the constituent parties: Ajit Singh (Charan Singh's son) against Devi Lal, Chandra Sekhar against V. P. Singh, and everyone against Devi Lal. The latter had his own son, Om Prakash Chautala, an unruly and scandalous politician, as the chief minister of Haryana. He had to be formally elected from a constituency. He chose Meham, where he created a mayhem, what with his scandalous rigging of the elections and intimidating the voters. In the face of nationwide criticism, Chautala resigned but was reinstated two months later. The action cost V. P. the support of two extremely able ministers: Arif Mohammad and Arun Nehru. Then the old, crafty Devi Lal produced a letter written by V. P. to the president in 1987 pointing out Arun Nehru's involvement in the Bofors scandal. V. P. retaliated, accusing Devi Lal of forgery and dismissing him on August 1, 1990.

What resulted from the V. P.–Devi Lal confrontation was the only thing for which the V. P. Singh regime is known. In order to show his political clout among the masses, Devi Lal called for a peasants' rally to be held at the Boat Club grounds in Delhi on August 9. To divert the public attention from the rally and to please the masses, V. P. pulled out an old report, the Mandal Commission Report, and announced on

August 7 in the parliament that it would be implemented at once.

The Mandal Commission Report

The Mandal Commission, so named after its chair, B. P. Mandal, had been appointed by the Janata government a decade earlier, in 1978, to decide the criteria for defining the socially and economically backward classes and recommend measures for their advancement and amelioration. The commission had submitted its report in 1980, by which time Indira was back in power and had not felt bound to consider its recommendations. A principal recommendation was to reserve 27 percent of the positions in the central administration and the state-owned enterprises (SOEs) for Other Backward Classes. Given the quota of 22.5 percent already allocated to the Scheduled Castes and Scheduled Tribes, the total of reservations would now amount to 49.5 percent. The same formula would also apply to educational institutions, including in the coveted medical and engineering colleges, as well as in the promotions of employees in central service, SOEs, and academic institutions. Although V. P. has always denied it, his populist measure was obviously calculated to blunt Devi Lal's populist rally to play the peasant card. It would also help divert the attention from the BJP's rally of 5,000 holy men assembled at Vrindavan who announced on August 1 that huge numbers of *kar sevaks* (volunteers; literally, "manual workers") would march on Ayodhya and the Babri Mosque in September.

V. P.'s decision and announcement were made without consulting the cabinet or perhaps any of his colleagues in the government or in his own party. He gave no indication of it to the leftist parties or the BJP who were supporting the government from outside the formal National Front. There was a nationwide uproar, particularly from the middle classes, whose children had been preparing for the tough examinations for the small number of seats in the professional colleges. As it was, they were hoping that the reservations for the SCs and STs would end at some early date. Their parents now became aware that the extension of reservations to the OBCs would ossify the concessions to SCs and STs forever. There had been no prior discussion of the Mandal Commission's recommendations in the parliament, nor on the criteria for identification of the backward castes or its impact on the integrative policies of the government after independence. The BJP was furious, because the measure would divide Hindu society. Its mouthpiece, the *Organiser*, attacked the entire reservations approach: "The havoc the politics of reservation is playing with the social fabric is unimaginable. It provides a premium for mediocrity, encourages brain drain and sharpens caste-divide."[3] In the same issue, it accused V. P. of undoing "the great task of uniting Hindu society from the days of Vivekananda, Dayanand Saraswati, Mahatma Gandhi. . . . What V. P.

Singh . . . intends to achieve is a division of Hindus on forward, backward and Harijan lines." V. P.'s policy completely countered the BJP's policies, right or wrong, of coalescing all layers of Hindu society, regardless of caste, on the Ayodhya temple issue.

The nationwide protests, meetings, and riots ended with the Supreme Court's decision on October 1, 1990, to stay the implementation of the government's decision to implement the Mandal recommendations. The anti-Mandal agitation and the government's action against the Rath Yatra (pilgrimage or procession on a chariot) led by the BJP's Lal Krishna Advani (described later) led to the fall of the government. With Advani's arrest on October 23, the BJP withdrew its support of the National Front government. On November 5, the main constituent of the NF split, and the government fell two days later. The government that succeeded was a "four-month wonder," under Chandra Shekhar, with, incredibly enough, the Congress's support, which was withdrawn on March 5, 1991. The national elections were announced for May 19.

RISE OF THE BHARATIYA JANATA PARTY

Although the Congress won the 1991 elections, what was most notable was the progress the BJP had made on the national scene. The right-wing party had moved from just 2 seats out of 543

in the Lok Sabha in 1984 to 88 in 1989 and 120 in 1991, making it the largest opposition party, having more seats than the Congress Party. From then on, it came to be regarded as a serious national alternative to the Congress Party, and in 1999, it became the largest element in a coalition, Atal Bihari Vajpayee becoming the prime minister for the following six years.

Historical Background

After the dismal defeat at the polls of the Janata Party in 1980, the Bharatiya Janata Party was launched on April 5, 1980, as a separate party. Was it the heir of the Janata Party or of the former Jan Sangh Party, which was openly a communalist Hindu organization? Vajpayee, the BJP's first president, urged his party's members to regard themselves as heirs of the Jayaprakash Narayan People's Revolution and, therefore, of the Janata Party rather than that of the Jan Sangh, so as to have a broader appeal to the masses. In fact, the BJP adopted the Janata Party's program for its election manifesto and stressed that its guiding principles would be "Gandhian socialism," "positive secularism," nationalism, national integration, democracy, and value-based politics. It emphasized that its creed of secularism differed from that of the Congress by qualifying the latter's approach as being opportunistic, designed to appease the minorities, particularly Muslims, for electoral purposes. To underline its secular credentials, the BJP elected a Muslim, Sikandar Bakht, as a vice president of the party. There were others such as Hamid Qureshi and Hasnat Siddiqui as the BJP's candidates in Madhya Pradesh. It actively supported Muslim politicians such as Mukhtar Abbas Naqvi and Najma Heptulla, and when it would get into power in 1998, its candidate for president of the country would be the current president, A. P. J. Abdul Kalam. The late Sikandar Bakht allowed that "Hinduism epitomizes the values of tolerance" and that true secularism should not recognize special rights for the religious minorities. The BJP's constitution did not have the word *Hindu* anywhere, and the BJP focused on socioeconomic themes, staying away from Hindu nationalism.

There has always been an ambivalence in regard to projecting Gandhi's name in the right-wing communalist party's principal programs. In fact, it has been so ever since Gandhi's assassination and the banning by the government of the RSS. In 1985, the party's adherence to "Gandhian socialism" came under fire and was temporarily replaced at the urging of the party's doctrinaire, K. Upadhyaya, by "integral humanism." The latter now became the BJP's fundamental philosophy and was included in 1986 in the party's constitution. As for Gandhism, the party adopted a "Gandhian approach" to economic development; a year later, Gandhian socialism

was restored as one of the party's doctrines, indicating the lip service necessary for any party professing secularism to swear allegiance to Gandhi.

On the other hand, the Congress had, since the early 1980s, begun to invoke the Hindu vote. At a personal level, Indira, during her days of political adversity, 1977–1980, had turned to Hindu swamis, Tantric gurus, and astrologers for her "mental peace" and even participated in numerous orthodox religious rituals. She continued the practice even more after the death of her son Sanjay. In the 1982 elections in Jammu and Kashmir, she had solicited the Hindu vote in Jammu. The secularist Romesh Thapar frowned on Indira's new stance: "The vibrations of Indira Gandhi's recent posturings in Assam, Punjab and Jammu (including Kashmir) have sparked speculation about the possibility that the Congress (I) is to be fashioned into a tribute of Hindu assertion. . . . She is obsessed with the business of retaining power at all costs, and whatever the consequences to the nation."[4] The BJP thought Indira was treading on the BJP's alleged turf and openly accused the Congress Party of acting like a Hindu party in the 1984 elections.

Meanwhile, Hindu diehards in the old Rashtriya Swayamsevak Sangh and Hindu Mahasabha were displeased with the BJP's new approach to politics. Such right-wing politicians and workers coalesced to help build "Hindu vote banks." Among these organizations was the Vishwa Hindu Parishad (VHP), World Hindu Conclave, founded in 1964 but dormant for a long time. In May 1984, the VHP established the Bajrang Dal, under the former student leader of the right-wing Akhil Bharatiya Vidyarthi Prishad, Vinay Katiar. Together, all these right-wing communal organizations came to be grouped as Sangh Parivar (Family of Associations). The right-wing politics from 1984 would be a balancing act for the BJP, which could not afford publicly to embrace them, nor to alienate them, for fear of losing the Hindu vote. Within the BJP, Vajpayee stood more for the secularist and integration politics of the old Janata Party, whereas Lal Krishna Advani saw more common ground in the Sangh Parivar's brazenly enunciated Hindu aspirations and interests. It is again in that context that the BJP's campaign for the rebuilding of the Ram temple at Ayodhya must be viewed, as will be discussed later.

Although the Congress won the 1991 elections, what was most notable was the progress the BJP had made on the national scene. The BJP had moved from 85 in 1989 to 120 seats in the Lok Sabha, from 11.36 percent to 20.08 percent of the votes. The analysts said that the BJP had the support of the youth: since 1989 alone, 40 million voters, ages eighteen to twenty-one, had been added to the voters' list. The BJP performance had demonstrated that its stronghold was the Hindu or Cow Belt states of Rajasthan Madhya Pradesh, Uttar Pradesh, and Bihar. Outside of that belt, the states of Gujarat and Karnataka were supporters of the BJP, the weakest areas for that party being most of the South, East, and Northeast.

NARASIMHA RAO, PRIME MINISTER

(P. V.) Narasimha Rao, India's "sphinx" politician, who held a number of important cabinet positions and that of the chief minister of his native state, Andhra Pradesh (1971–1973), became prime minister most unexpectedly. The election campaign for the Sriperimbudur (Tamil Nadu) Lok Sabha seat took Rajiv Gandhi there in support of the Congress candidate, Maragatham Chandrasekhar. There, on May 24, 1991, a LTTE suicide bomber, Dhanu, killed him. The unexpected removal of Rajiv Gandhi from the electoral scene brought in Narasimha Rao as the candidate for the prime ministership. Rao had actually retired from politics and had not offered himself as a candidate for the Lok Sabha in the elections. It appears he had fallen out of favor with Rajiv and had even packed his household and prepared to return to his native Andhra Pradesh when the call came to serve the party in the exalted position of prime minister.

The elections of 1991 failed to give any party an absolute majority in the

Lok Sabha. Rao led the Congress as the largest single party but did not hold a majority. Thus, he became the first to lead a minority government in India at the federal level, although unlike the later coalition governments, his dependence on his coalition partners was marginal. Although he continued to be popular in Andhra Pradesh as "Telugu *bidda*," the Telugu son who had done the Andhraites proud, he was nationally known as a linguist, scholar, and, after his retirement, novelist, the last not of great merit. Among politicians, he was regarded as man of wisdom, a "Chanakya" similar to the third-century BCE scholar and royal adviser.

The two most far-reaching events during his full term of five years as prime minister were the demolition of the Babri Masjid in December 1992 and the economic liberalization that, in the words of the architect of those reforms, Manmohan Singh, made Rao "the father of India's economic reforms." When Rao became prime minister, the country was facing its worst balance-of-payments crisis. According to P. C. Alexander, India's former top bureaucrat as cabinet secretary, Rao called him and asked him who would be the best candidate for the position of finance minister, capable of pulling the country out of the foreign-exchange crisis and also take measures to see it did not happen again. Alexander suggested two names, both with firsthand experience as governor of the Reserve Bank of India, India's central bank: I. G. Patel and Manmohan Singh. The first excused himself, and the latter accepted on certain conditions, those being that Rao should give him a free hand and that in case of a political controversy would give his reforms unstinting support. Rao accepted, and the Indian economy was opened up, leading it within years to the position of the second-fastest-growing economy globally, averaging 7–8 percent annually, far from the "Hindu" rate of growth of the previous four decades and holding in 2006 a foreign-exchange reserve of more than $160 billion. That could be considered Rao's great success. The economic liberalization is dealt with at length in the chapter "Toward Economic Freedom."

THE BABRI MASJID–RAM MANDIR DISPUTE

The Babri Masjid/Ramajanmabhoomi (Birthplace of Rama) is one of the most important controversies in the history and politics of independent India. It is as much a politically charged issue as it is a religious one. Both the Congress Party and the Bharatiya Janata Party and its *pariwar* organizations have handled the issue politically with an eye on the votes. It is an issue that concerns the core of the Indian state, questioning its secular credentials. It has ranged intellectuals, notably historians and archaeologists, on rival sides of the question.

The uncontested facts of the question are that Babri Masjid was built at Ayodhya in 1528, two years after the founder of the Mughal power, Babar, invaded India. On December 6, 1992, the edifice of three domes was razed to the ground by a crowd of Hindus estimated to range from 75,000 to 200,000. It was the day following the conclusion of the Rath Yatra of the BJP leader, L. K. Advani. The ruling party in New Delhi at the time was the Congress Party, with P. V. Narasimha Rao as the prime minister; the ruling party at the Uttar Pradesh state level where Ayodhya is located was under BJP's Kalyan Singh as chief minister.

Barring these facts and a few others, mostly appeals to the judicial authorities and the diverse judgments of the courts, almost everything else has been mired in controversies in which the politicians, lawyers, historians, and archaeologists have participated.

Historical Background

Ram, the hero of the epic *Ramayana*, was, according to that text, born in Ayodhya, which was the capital of his kingdom and before him that of his father. An Austrian Jesuit, Joseph Tieffenthaler, after visiting Ayodhya, wrote in 1767, that it was the common belief of the people of Ayodhya and the pilgrims who came to it that Ram's birthplace was marked by a small *chabootra* (platform) next to the Babri Mosque

and that the latter was built forcibly on the site of the temple dedicated to Ram's birthplace. He added that innumerable Hindu pilgrims came to the site to worship Ram.

Almost immediately after the British annexation of Oudh (Ayodhya) in 1856, the first time a Muslim government there had been ended since Babar's time, some Hindu ascetics claimed the site on the grounds that a mosque had been built on Ram's birthplace. In the 1850s, the British said that Hindus could offer their *puja* at this *chabootra*, as the birthplace of Ram. The practice continued without incident until 1883. A Hindu *pandit* (priest or learned man) applied for permission to build a temple to Ram on that site. The British turned down the request on the grounds that it would be too close to the Babri Masjid.

More than a half century later, two years after the country's partition on the basis of religion, on the night of December 22–23, 1949, the police reported that someone had broken into the mosque and placed the idols of Ram Lalla (the infant form of Ram). The matter was considered important enough to be brought to the attention of Jawaharlal Nehru, India's prime minister, by the chief minister of Uttar Pradesh, Gobind Vallabh Pant, a politically towering figure. The incident was preceded by the recitation of the Ramcharitamanas continuously for nine days at the site. After the placement of the idols, crowds estimated in the thousands came from far and near to offer their prayers to the idols. Nehru asked Pant to restore the situation as it was before December 23, and on December 26, Pant asked the district magistrate, K. K. Nair, to remove the idols. Nair pleaded his inability to carry out the orders on the grounds that there would be riots. It appears that the Muslims did not bother much at that time, because the mosque had not been used by them since 1936.

This is when the Hindu Mahasabha, the twice-removed precursor of the BJP, stepped in, issuing a circular to its party officials, high and low, to observe March 27, 1950, as the birthday of Lord Ram (Ramanavmi) and also as Ram Janmabhoomi (Place of Birth) Day. The circular mentioned that the mosque was standing on top of fourteen original pillars of the temple that had been demolished. At this point, the secretary of the Hindu Mahasabha of Ayodhya, Gopal Singh Visharad, applied and obtained a restraining order from the Civil Court of Faizabad against anyone removing the idols and interfering with the *puja* (worship). Someone, it is not clear who, decided that the inner courtyard gates of the disputed site be locked and the keys kept in the custody of the receiver of property, the chairman of the Ayodhya Municipal Board. In practice, a sentry posted at the site opened the lock and the gate, allowing devotees to give their food offerings to the *pujari* (priest), who was generally present at prayer time beyond the gate at the site. The devotees sang *bhajans* (devotional songs) and said their prayers through a lateral grille.

On January 25, 1986, U. M. Pandey, an Ayodhya lawyer, applied to the local magistrate, requesting the gates of Babri Masjid be unlocked so as to give access to all devotees to worship the idols without any restrictions.

On January 31, a similar appeal was made to the district and sessions judge of Faizabad, who ordered on February 1 that the gates to the mosque be unlocked. This was a political decision. As Arun Nehru, a close adviser to Rajiv Gandhi, wrote in 1989 about the events of 1986: "In early 1986, the Muslim Women's Bill was passed to play the Muslim card; and then came the decision on Ayodhya to play the Hindu card. It was supposed to be a package deal."[5] The reference to the "Muslim card" in Arun Nehru's statement was to the Rajiv Gandhi government's Muslim (Protection of Rights on Divorce) Bill, appeasing the orthodox Muslim leaders who were opposed to the Supreme Court's judgment in the Shah Bano case. The Hindus were now free to enter the *masjid* (mosque) at any time and worship the idols.

The new development was appreciated by the RSS, Vishwa Hindu Parishad, and other rightist groups as the central government's effort to appease the Hindus. The BJP had clearly, perhaps with Vajpayee's reluctant agreement, shifted from the politics of secularism to overt pro-Hindu position.

Two days after the unlocking of the gates to the Masjid/Ramjanmabhoomi temple, the Ram Janmabhoomi Mukti Yagna Samiti established a Ram Janmabhoomi Trust. It now raised its ante of demands, asking the government to transfer the *masjid*/temple site to the trust so that a temple to Ram could be built there. On the same day, a Muslim from Ayodhya, Mohammed Hashim, filed a writ in the Lucknow branch of the Allahabad High Court against the unlocking of the gates. Two days later, on February 5, the Babri Masjid Action Committee (BMAC) was established by some Muslims, who included Syed Shahabuddin and Imam Bukhari of the Jama Masjid, on Republic Day (January 26) if the government failed to hold "serious negotiations" with the VHP. Syed Shahabuddin disagreed on the question of boycotting the Republic Day, which made him a "moderate" among the BMAC and eventually led to his moving out of the BMAC and establishing the Babri Masjid Coordination Committee.

The radical members of the BMAC continued their activities under the leadership of Imam Bukhari. They announced a march on Ayodhya on October 14, 1988, to coincide with the VHP's call for a five-day Shri Ram Maha Yagna (Great Sacrifice for Lord Rama) from October 11.

The rival plans led to riots in several cities with large Muslim populations

such as Muzaffarnagar, Aligarh, and close to Ayodhya, Faizabad. The central government's home minister, Buta Singh, talked to both sides, asking for the postponement of the march and the *Yagna* and for the entire question to be placed before the Allahabad High Court.

Mobilization for a New Ram Temple at Ayodhya

The Ram Janmabhoomi issue gave the BJP and its *pariwar* a tremendous opportunity to create cohesion among the Hindus across the country and, in the process, enlarge its electoral potential. This was done through religious conclaves called *dharma sansad/shilanyas* and the Rath Yatra.

The third *dharma sansad* (conclave) in Allahabad in February 1989 attracted more than 50,000 people. The crowd applauded the *sansad*'s resolution to "Hinduize" public life by electing only those who would be favorable to Hinduism and to build a temple for Ram at the Babri Masjid site. It resolved to raise the funds for the temple construction from as large a number of Hindus as possible, each family's donation to be rupee 1.25, which would not hurt anybody's family budget, at the same time giving every donor a spiritual feeling of contributing to the sacred cause. While the amount was being collected in cities and villages across the length and breadth of the country, there would be communal *puja* (worship) of bricks on which the name of Ram would be inscribed. Such Ram *shilas* would be carried in processions that would converge on Ayodhya, where the *shilas* would be used in the construction of the temple beginning November 9, on which day all the donors all over the country would offer a special prayer to Ram.

On the appointed day, chosen in consultation with noted astrologers, November 9, 1989, the *shilanyas,* or foundation-stone, laying ceremony was held with 167,063 Ram *shilas* sent from the collection centers from all over the country (the place-names were inscribed on the *shilas*). Christophe Jaffrelot explains the significance: "The bricks were used to signify the huge dimensions of the collectivity which, although consisting not of a concentrated mass but of a myriad of towns and small village communities, had acted in the same way at the same time to produce these concrete manifestations of its common will."[6] The groundbreaking ceremony underlined the geographical unity of all Hindus, as jars of water brought from all the sacred rivers from all over India were emptied on the site. The first five bricks were mixed with materials brought from the four *dhamas* at the four geographical points—east, west, north, and south—designated by Sankaracharya-Puri, Dwarka, Badrinath, and Rameswaram. The first layer of bricks serving as the foundation stone used soil from all the sacred sites from all over the country. The soil from the site was used to mark a *tilak* on the forehead of the pilgrims, who also carried a part of the soil to their homes. Simultaneously, all over India, *mahayagyas* (great sacrifice ceremonies) were held enabling spiritually to connect with the *shilanyas* in Ayodhya, all participants facing Ayodhya and offering *pushpanjali* (flower offerings) to Ram at the moment when the foundation stone was being laid at 1.35 PM on Friday, November 10. The elaborate *shilanyas* and the synchronous *mahayagyas* sought to make Ayodhya and the future Ram temple the point of convergence of all Hindus everywhere. It is hard to imagine that all this symbolism and points of convergence were planned without political benefit in mind. A religiopolitical leader would, after the demolition of the Babri Masjid, call Ayodhya the Vatican of the Hindus.

A third major effort to promote the social and geographical cohesion of the Hindus focusing on the Ayodhya issue and, indeed, drawing considerable political capital was the Rath Yatra. Beginning on September 25, 1992, and led by BJP's Lal Krishna Advani, the Rath Yatra started from the Somnath Temple, known to the Hindus all over as the temple looted by Mahmud of Ghazni repeatedly at the turn of the first millennium CE. It logged more than 6,000 miles as the *yatra* wended its way to Ayodhya, not directly but wending its way circuitously and crossing eight states before reaching there on October 30 where it would inaugurate the *kar seva* (manual service). The *rath* (chariot) itself was decorated with the Hindu sacred symbol of lotus (coincidentally, also the BJP's electoral symbol) and the letter *Om* sacred to the Hindus. Equipped with a public address system, the *yatra* paused to hold public meetings on the way—passing through Ahmadabad, Mumbai, Nasik, Hyderabad, Jabalpur, Indore, Udaipur, Ajmer, Jaipur, and Delhi and countless villages and small towns, involving millions of people.

For the 1991 elections, the BJP included a commitment to build "a grand temple, for the great national hero, Shri Rama." The BJP's manifesto was aware of its implications for Hindu-Muslim relations, which it believed the erection of the temple would improve:

> [The BJP] seeks the restoration of the Ramjanmabhoomi in Ayodhya only by way of symbolic righting of historic wrongs so that the old unhappy chapter of acrimony would be ended and a grand national reconciliation be effected. Hindus and Muslims are blood brothers, but on account of historical reasons, their relationship has not been harmonious. It shall be the endeavour [*sic*] of the BJP to make all Indians fraternal and friendly once again.[7]

D–Day, December 6, 1992

On December 6, 1992, the day of the symbolic *kar seva*, at 11 AM, a large number of *kar sevaks* crossed the line formed by RSS volunteers and quickly climbed the domes of the mosque with the help of ropes. Some of them carried iron rods, which they used for dismantling the domes. The idols were safely removed from the site. While the police stationed there did not stop the act, the Central Reserve Police Force withdrew from the site. By 3 PM one dome had collapsed; ninety minutes later, the second fell, whereas the main large dome came down at about 4:45 PM. The *kar sevaks* then proceeded to clear the debris of the mosque and erected a small temple on the site in which the idols were placed.

The event shocked the nation, to put it mildly. On the other hand, many millions who had participated in the run-up to the event, planned or not, celebrated the success of the *kar sevaks*. The Babri Masjid/Ram Janmabhoomi issue has engaged the hearts and minds of millions of Hindus and Muslims, intellectuals, professionals, media persons, and others. All political parties have been affected by it, and most have tried to benefit from it. Several inquiry reports, court judgments, and white papers have been issued over the past two decades. Piles of pamphlet literature and books, overwhelmingly partisan, have been produced.

As could only be expected, many questions are still left unanswered, some of them basic about the site and the construction of the *masjid* and its use by the Muslim worshipers. Another basic question is about the wisdom and justice of the restoration of temple sites several centuries after the temples were demolished and *masjids* built on their ruins.

Who was responsible for the act of demolition on December 6, 1992? Was it planned by the BJP? By the RSS? By the VHP? To this date, there are no definite answers, only denials and accusations. Advani, who was present on the scene, seated on the speakers' platform nearby, was reported by independent media to have asked the *kar sevaks* not to climb the domes. Following the demolition, he resigned his position as leader of the opposition in the Lok Sabha; so did Kalyan Singh (BJP) as the chief minister of Uttar Pradesh for his government's failure to stop the demolition. Vajpayee, who was not present at the demolition, commented on the following day that it was the BJP's worst miscalculation; he could see that it would damage his party. The "Citizens Tribunal" on Ayodhya held that it was a preplanned event, known to the BJP leaders assembled in Ayodhya, but whose details may not have been known to them in advance of it.

The Babri Masjid was built in 1528 by Mughal Emperor Babar's general, Mir Baqi. An inscription there said so, but the fact is not found in another primary source, the *Babarnama*, the memoirs left by Babar, not because he did or did not write about it but because the

memoir's pages surrounding that event are missing. Was it just an accidental loss or deliberate loss? Was the mosque built after the demolition of a Ram temple there? If the *Babarnama* pages were available, perhaps they would have shed some light. There is no eyewitness account of the demolition of a temple there in the sixteenth century, though some accounts of demolition of other temples exist. In August 2003, the Archaeological Survey published its investigatory report ordered by the Lucknow court. According to this report, there was a tenth-century Hindu temple below the Babri Masjid.[8]

There is ample writing—Indian and non-Indian[9]—confirming that several thousand temples in North and South India were razed to the ground by Muslim rulers or their subordinates or converted, after proper alterations, into mosques. That was the practice of Muslim invaders of India, whether it was Mahmud of Ghazni, Babar, a ruler like Aurangzeb, or some overzealous sultans of Bijapur. One did not have to be a *jihadi* to indulge in such activities, which were not limited to India or to the Hindus. The Hindu activists had averred, time and again, that they would stop demanding the restoration of other temple sites if the Muslims, in a cooperative spirit as fellow citizens, would agree to the surrender of three sites, most sacred to the Hindus: the Gyanvapi Mosque in Varanasi, where a visible part of the mosque constitutes the former Kashi Visvanath Temple; the Babri Masjid site in Ayodhya; and the temple at Mathura. An important question: If there was hard incontrovertible evidence that the Babri Masjid was built on the site of an existing temple, would that justify demolishing the *masjid* and restoring the site for building a temple to Ram? There is no doubt, however that the demolition of the Babri Masjid has affected, very grievously, the delicate edifice of pluralism and secularism carefully built during the nationalist movement by leaders such as Gandhi and Nehru and after independence by those liberal and broad-minded founding fathers of the Indian republic who wrote India's constitution.

THE BJP IN POWER—THREE TIMES

In 1996, the BJP was the single largest party in the Lok Sabha, and in keeping with Westminster conventions, the president, Shankar Dayal Sharma, promptly called the BJP's leader, Atal Bihari Vajpayee, to form a government. Although the BJP had consistently insisted that it was a secularist party, hardly anyone in India's political spectrum had taken it seriously. For almost all of them, a communal Hindu party had come into power. They rallied to form the United Front (UF) and created a parliamentary majority. After only thirteen days as prime minister,

Vajpayee resigned, and with that the first BJP government fell.

The two UF governments that followed, the first with the small-town, unkempt H. K. Deve Gowda and the second with the urbane and engaging, experienced and competent, endowed with wit and humor Inder Kumar Gujral lasted less than one year each. The United Front was a motley organization of some sixteen to eighteen parties, some of them without a coherent ideology or program, bickering for a berth in the cabinet or chairmanship of any of the numerous state-owned enterprises "with a cabinet rank," which brought in a lot of perquisites of power—a house, cars, staff, unlimited domestic air travel, and an unstated opportunity to feather one's nest. Gujral, a most happily married man to a poetess of proven merit, complained of his political polygamy with sixteen consorts, quarrelsome and demanding, leaving hardly any time or space to make creative decisions. Except for extremely well-managed Fiftieth Independence Day Celebrations and Mother Teresa's funeral, there were no achievements. None was possible; none was expected. Fresh elections were announced.

In the elections of 1998, the BJP became a constituent of the National Democratic Alliance (NDA), which won a slim majority in the Lok Sabha. The NDA's by far largest constituent was the BJP, so therefore, Vajpayee became the prime minister. The coalition lasted only months because one of the NDA partners, the All-India Anna Dravida Munetra Khazagam under Jayalalitha, withdrew its support. The government was short of just one vote to prove its majority on the floor of the Lok Sabha. The government fell. Another electoral test with all the attendant expenses for a nonaffluent democracy was announced.

In the 1999 elections, the NDA won a clear majority, with 303 seats, the BJP with its largest tally ever of 183 seats. For the third time, Atal Bihari Vajpayee was sworn in as prime minister. By now, the country was familiar with his liberal, coolheaded, and, incredibly enough, secularist credentials. He would lead the country for a full term of five years.

In joining the NDA, the BJP had, just as its previous incarnation, the Bharatiya Jan Sangh, had done in 1977 vis-à-vis the Janata coalition, abandoned its own manifesto and adopted that of the NDA. In doing so, it had given up its basic demands such as the promulgation of the Universal Common Civil Code, the construction of the Ram Janmabhoomi Temple, and the repeal of Article 370 of the Indian Constitution inhibiting non-Kashmiris from owning property in that state.

During Vajpayee's second and third administrations, the governments scored several notable achievements both in domestic and in foreign policy. In the latter field, the government conducted five nuclear tests in 1998, making India a nuclear power and earning the ire of the Western powers, notably the friendly Clinton administration, and facing the U.S. Congress–mandated sanctions. The second was the military and diplomatic effort that compelled Pakistan to withdraw its troops from Kargil in Kashmir in the following year. (Details of both these events are given in the chapter on foreign policy.)

On the economic front, the liberal policies launched since 1991 were continued, only with greater vigor. A major campaign was the privatization of several SOEs, under Arun Shourie, as minister. The finance minister, Yashwant Sinha, further liberalized trade to the satisfaction of the World Trade Organization (WTO), opened the skies to commercial airlines, and announced the establishment of "special economic zones," with specific facilities and concessions to industries. During the period, the information-technology (IT) industry prospered the most, Bangalore emerging as India's Silicon Valley. In fact, many U.S. companies from Silicon Valley opened extensive offices in Bangalore, Hyderabad, Pune, Delhi, and Mumbai. Outsourcing and back-office operations for principals in many countries, notably, the United States, boosted the software industry. New Indian giants in the IT industry Wipro, Infosys, and Satyam made their debut at the global level. The number of jobs created and foreign exchange earned was most impressive. In 2004, India signed the South Asia Free Trade Agreement with all the South Asian Association for Regional Co-operation countries.

Among the major initiatives that would engage the governments of the future were the Golden Quadrilateral Project, building roads capable of bearing heavy industrial traffic, linked to the four corners of the country. Another would link all the major rivers in a grid.

On the negative side was the terrorist attack on India's parliament on December 13 (India's 12/13) three months after the 9/11 attack on the United States. There have been some more attacks of note thereafter but none of the magnitude of 12/13. The nation paid a price in curbs on individual freedoms in the government's adoption of the Prevention of Terrorist Activities Act (POTA) in 2002, making it easier for the police and intelligence agencies to nab suspected terrorists.

Elections of 2004

With all such pluses, it was a shock to the BJP that it lost in the elections of 2004. There were several possible reasons. One was that the BJP itself was so satisfied with its performance in the previous five years that it thought the elections could only increase its strength in the parliament. The party workers took the victory for granted and did not work hard enough among the electorate. Second, when the BJP made "In-

dia Shining" their election slogan, it ignored the vast rural population that had not benefited significantly from economic liberalization. An ally of the BJP was Chandra Babu, the chief minister of Andhra Pradesh, a truly shining example of the IT revolution and its benefits. However, he and his party, the Telugu Desam, were thrown out of power by the rural electorate, which had nursed a grievance, presumably not reported to the boss by the intelligence agencies, that the government had almost completely ignored their interests in the previous five years. To campaign in the name of "India Shining" was like rubbing salt in the wound. Third, the BJP did not think much of the Sangh Parivar and their concerns that the BJP had done little to get the Ram Temple built at Ayodhya or to apply the universal code to all citizens, including minorities. The party leaders, particularly Vajpayee, did not want to risk the secularist image he and his supporters were carefully building in the country. The Sangh Parivar may not have gone so far as to canvass against the BJP, but its component organizations did nothing to help the BJP's prospects at the polls either.

The most important single factor that may have worked against the BJP were the Gujarat riots of 2002 and the central government's inability to rein in Gujarat's BJP chief minister, Narendra Modi. The riots had followed a ghastly incident when a railroad compartment full of chanting devotees returning from Ayodhya was burned after the train pulled out of the Godhra station and was forcibly stopped a half mile away. One hundred and eight pilgrims, which included men, women, and children, were scorched to death by the flames. The locale of the incident was a part of Godhra in Gujarat where the Muslim population was close to 100 percent. The reaction to the incident was ghastly too, not just in Godhra but several cities in Gujarat, where the Hindus and Muslims clashed and the superior numbers of the Hindu community prevailed.

There was an uproar all over India, not just among Muslims, that the riots in which more than 1,000 lives, 70 percent Muslim, were lost could have been averted if the BJP government had taken timely action. It was widely held by the media that the Gujarat police had looked away and that the BJP members may have participated in the mayhem. The popular reaction to the initial incident of igniting the railroad compartment and the loss of human lives was no longer the issue. Whatever the public reaction, "How could the government be so callous?" the people asked all over the country. BJP's leadership did not condemn the Gujarat government for fear the overwhelmingly prorevenge electorate would have dumped the BJP. It was widely held that had elections been held at that point in Gujarat, Narendra Modi would have been riding a wave of public approbation. The BJP's image

now was unquestionably Hindu, not the secular image leaders like Vajpayee had sedulously cultivated.

THE CONGRESS PARTY IN POWER AGAIN

The elections of 2004 were a direct contest between the BJP and allies (the National Democratic Alliance) and the Congress Party and its allies. The NDA secured only 185 seats against the BJP with 138. The Congress Party secured 145 seats, close to the BJP's score, but it could ally with others and claim a coalition strength of 217 with outside support of the Left and some other parties, which would ensure it a majority in the Lok Sabha. On May 13, Vajpayee conceded defeat, which opened the way to the Congress to put together a coalition. There was every indication at that point that the Congress Party would elect its president, Sonia Gandhi, as its party leader in the Lok Sabha and that she would be the prime minister. There were, however, large protests in the country against her foreign origins; she was an Italian by birth and had taken Indian citizenship only after her husband, Rajiv Gandhi, became prime minister. The BJP announced it would keep protesting also because she was not comfortable with any Indian language. The media also speculated some opposition from Sonia's two children, Rahul and Priyanka, who feared a risk to their mother's life. Sonia Gandhi surprised everyone from within and without her party when she announced on May 19 that she would not accept the position and, instead, nominated Manmohan Singh for the office.

Manmohan Singh was a most widely respected economist holding a doctorate from Oxford University, the architect of India's economic liberalization, and finance minister under Prime Minister P. V. Narasimha Rao from 1991 to 1996. He had held numerous positions in the government, including governor of the Reserve Bank of India (India's central bank) and deputy chairman of the Planning Commission, and had experience working with the International Monetary Fund (IMF). Modest and soft-spoken, he is highly regarded both in India and the world. While the BJP was in office, he was conferred the Outstanding Parliamentarian Award in

2002. He became the first Sikh prime minister in India's history.

His most outstanding achievement in the first two years has been bringing India closer to the United States, paying an official visit to the States in July 2005, and hosting a reciprocal visit by President Bush in March 2006. A series of agreements were signed by the two countries, including the most critical agreement on the U.S. sale of nuclear technology to India, despite the fact that it is one of the three countries that has not signed the Nuclear Non-Proliferation Treaty (NPT). (Details and analysis will be found in Chapter 19, on India's foreign policy.) The nuclear deal is for civilian purposes of producing energy, which should enable India to make progress in industrial production without power interruptions.

————

NOTES _____

1. Vir Singhvi, "Bofor's Ghosts," *Redrift on the Net,* September 23, 1999.

2. The Shah Bano case was an infamous divorce suit concerning a sixty-two-year-old woman with five children, divorced by her husband in 1978 by simply uttering the word *Talaq* (I divorce you) three times. The Supreme Court rewarded her maintenance money (akin to alimony) in 1985. This was contrary to Muslim Personal Law and was considered judicial interference in the rights of Muslims. To appease the strident fundamentalist Islamic opposition to the judgment, Rajiv Gandhi used his party's parliamentary majority to approve Muslim women (known as the Protection of Rights on Divorce Act, 1986), thereby diluting the rigor of the Supreme Court's decision. The measure was regarded as appeasement of fundamentalist Muslims and a step backward in Muslim women's rights.

3. *Organiser,* August 26, 1990, 15.

4. Romesh Thapar, "Communalising Our Politics," *Economic and Political Weekly,* July 2, 1983, 1163.

5. Arun Nehru, "A Package Deal," *Statesman* (Delhi), August 17, 1989, p. 9.

6. Christophe Jaffrelot, *The Hindu Nationalist Movement and Indian Politics* (London: Hurst, 1996), 403.

7. BJP, *White Paper on Ayodhya* (New Delhi: BJP, 1993), 8.

8. *Tribune* (Chandigarh), August 23, 2003, 1.

9. See H. M. Elliot and John Dawson, eds., *The History of India as Told by Its Own Historians;* and Richard M. Eaton, *Sufis of Bijapur, 1300–1700: Social Roles of Sufis in Medieval India.*

————

The Indian Independence Act of 1947 passed by the British Parliament, creating the two dominions of India and Pakistan, stipulated that "an Indian State shall be deemed to have acceded to the Dominion if the Governor-General has signified his acceptance of the Instrument of Accession executed by the Ruler thereof." (pages 394–95)

Mohammad Ali Jinnah, the founder of Pakistan, known for his thorough knowledge of law and constitutionality, understood the position. Barely a month before he would become the governor-general of the new state of Pakistan, he said on July 11, 1947, "I have already made it clear more than once that the Indian States are free to join either the Pakistan Constituent Assembly or the Hindustan Constituent Assembly or remain independent . . . We have made it clear that we are not going to coerce, intimidate, or put any pressure on any State regarding its choice." (page 395)

17

THE PRINCELY STATES AND
THE KASHMIR QUESTION

When independence came to India, it came with some heavy legal shackles. The Indian Independence Act of 1947 that the British Parliament, with its Labor Party majority, approved in fact created a medley of 562 political entities in addition to India and Pakistan. The act simply stated, "The suzerainty of His Majesty over the Indian States lapses, and with it, all treaties and agreements in force at the date of the passing of this Act between His Majesty and the rulers of Indian States." These Indian native states, which were supposedly "ruled" by Indian princes, whose rights and privileges originally contracted with the East India Company, were endorsed by the British "Crown" when the EIC was dissolved in the wake of the Great Uprising of 1857–1859 and Britain took over the treaty responsibilities. Thereafter, the British governor-general of India was given an additional title of viceroy, to represent the British royalty while

dealing with the Indian princes. To regard the princes as independent and declare that with the British withdrawal from the subcontinent the treaties with the princes lapsed and, therefore, they were legally independent and free to choose to join either dominion, India or Pakistan, or not to join any was a mischievous move, intended, according to some observers of the time, to weaken the new Indian state. Whatever the unstated wishes of the top Labor Party leaders, the head of the Political Department in New Delhi, Conrad Corfield, told the princes not to join the Indian Union. He said that his interpretation of the act of 1947 had the support of the secretary of state for India, a British cabinet member, Lord Listowell. On the positive side of the states' integration with India was Lord Mountbatten, who in his capacity as viceroy plainly advised the princes to join either dominion, preferably on the basis of geographical contiguity.

LEGAL BASIS FOR THE INDEPENDENT STATUS OF THE PRINCELY STATES

Were the princely states independent entities during the British Raj? Britain had retained these oddities after the uprising of 1857 and into the modern world out of deference for tradition, which arguably has been the reason for retaining the British monarchy in a country, which, for all intents and purposes, is a republic. As the decades rolled on after 1858, Britain came to understand the economic argument of an "informal empire" over the formal one, as, for example, in Britain's role in China, and saw wisdom in continuation of the princely states because it was less expensive to do so and was far less of a headache administratively. What was important was the promotion and protection of British economic interests on par with the territories directly under the Crown. And, very important, the princely states, dispersed as they were all over the country, and except in a few cases, topographically not contiguous to each other, served as strategic buffers for the defense of the Raj. This advantage for the rulers extended also during the nationalist movement when the Indian National Congress operations were limited to the territories under the Raj. The All-India States People's Congress, the INC's counterpart, established in 1927, found it hard to work as a homogenous organization having to deal with so many princely potentates of dif-

ferent backgrounds, education, and political orientation. In the British Indian annals, the closest the foreign rulers of the subcontinent came to argue in favor of wiping out the princely entities and paint India's map in one color, the imperial red, was during the governor-generalship of Lord Dalhousie (1848–1856). Supporting such a policy, the influential *Times* (London) wrote in 1853:

> We have emancipated these pale and ineffectual pageants of royalty from the ordinary fate that awaits an oriental despotism. . . . It has been well said that we give these Princes power without responsibility. Our hand of iron maintains them on the throne despite their inability, their vices, and their crimes. The result is in most of the States, there is a chronic anarchy, under which the revenues of the States are dissipated. . . . The heavy and arbitrary taxes levied on the miserable *raiyats* [peasants] serve only to feed only the meanest and the most degraded of mankind. The theory seems in fact admitted that the government is not for the people but the people for the king.[1]

The Great Uprising was directly blamed on Dalhousie's annexation policies and, therefore, thereafter, despite the liberal voices periodically raised against this gross feudal ruler, the British continued the princely order in India.

Britain had indirectly and less expensively ruled the princely states, measuring some 716,000 square miles, with (in 1947) an estimated 93 million people, a little more than one-fourth of the subcontinent's population. Most of the princely states were separated from each other by swaths of British Indian territory, which was legally the only territory that under the act of 1947 was partitioned into independent India and Pakistan. Britain had controlled these states, small and large, by posting at each prince's capital a British representative, who would "advise" the prince in all administrative, commercial, and investment matters. Very significant in this respect was the Viceroy Lord Reading's (1921–1926) reply to the greatest of all these princes, the Nizam of Hyderabad (the only one who was entitled to be addressed as His Exalted Highness as against all the rest being called "His Highness"), when he claimed to be a sovereign ruler. Reading wrote on March 27, 1926, "The sovereignty of the British Crown is supreme in India and therefore no ruler of an Indian State can justifiably claim to negotiate with the British Government on an equal footing."[2]

THE PRINCES AND THE NATIONALIST MOVEMENT

Although the problems and aspirations of the people in British India and the princely states were the same, the Indian National Congress had until the late 1930s, by and large, stayed away from a direct role in the states. The INC tended to regard the princely states as a separate entity and sometimes tended to treat the princes with kid gloves. In 1920, following the Montagu-Chelmsford reforms for British India, the INC approved a resolution appealing to the princes to grant responsible government to their subjects. A part of the reticence to attack the Indian princes may have been Gandhi's belief that they would behave like the trustees and would, at the opportune hour, fall in line with the people's urge for freedom. Nehru had consistently opposed the princes' autocratic rule in the states. He did not endorse Gandhi's view that the princes were like trustees. Nehru wrote, "If there is anything in this idea of trusteeship, why should we object to the claim of the British Government that they are trustees for the Government of India. Except for the fact that there are foreigners in India, I see no difference."[3]

It was a remarkable common feeling that caused some leading people of the princely states to come together to establish the All-India States People's Congress (AISPC) in 1927, with the goal of attaining "responsible government for the people in the Indian States through representative institutions under the aegis of the rulers." By 1939, they had progressed to the adoption of a constitution for the AISPC that stated the objective as "the attainment by peaceful and legitimate means of full responsible government by the people of the States as integral parts of a freed and federal India." This was in line with the INC's resolution in the previous year that the INC's work was "for the same political, social and economic freedom in the States as in the rest of India and considers the States as integral parts of India, which cannot be separated."[4]

BRITISH DEALINGS WITH THE PRINCES JUST BEFORE INDIA'S INDEPENDENCE

However, Britain used the princes to obstruct the establishment of an Indian federation under the act of 1935. In August 1939, Viceroy Linlithgow, addressing the Standing Committee of the Chamber of Princes, stated, "This has always seemed to me a block which, if the Princely Order are wise, and hold together, no political party can possibly afford to ignore."[5]

There were quite a few princes who lived up to what Linlithgow had said in spoiling the joy of independence by attempting to raise a banner of their own independence. The Congress Party had always insisted that the decision in regard to the states' future should be left to the people; instead, the Indian Independence Act of 1947 left it to the rulers. The Nawab of Bhopal, a medium size among the princely states, who was then the chancellor of the Chamber of Princes, told Lord Mountbatten that he "abhorred Congress" and that he would have nothing to do with a Congress-dominated India.[6] He proposed the par-

tition of the subcontinent into three: Pakistan, Rajasthan (consisting of the princely states, which he called the "third force"), and residual India. Alan Campbell-Johnson, Mountbatten's able aide, wrote, "As the ablest Moslem Prince, I would guess he is not averse to playing an important role in the higher politics of Pakistan. He has for some time been Jinnah's closest adviser. Unhappily for him, his State is predominantly Hindu and in the heart of Indian territory."[7] Then there was C. P. Ramaswami Aiyar, the very able and erudite *diwan* of the state of Travancore in Kerala, who proclaimed his ruler's independent status, and the Nizam of Hyderabad, right in the heart of peninsular India, who contemplated joining the United Nations as an independent state! He had a large military force, which along with most princely states, had augmented its numbers during World War II.

At first, Mohammed Ali Jinnah, the founder of Pakistan, declared, rather precipitately, that, not far in the future, he would regret the question of Kashmir's accession coming up. On June 17, 1947, barely two months before the birth of Pakistan, he endorsed the British legal position in regard to the princely states:

Constitutionally and legally, the Indian States will be independent sovereign States on the termination of [British] paramountcy and they will be free to decide for themselves to adopt any course they like; it is open

to them to join the Hindustan Constituent Assembly or the Pakistan
Constituent Assembly, or decide to
remain independent. In the last case,
they enter into such agreement or relationship with Hindustan or Pakistan as they may choose. The policy of
the All-India Muslim League has
been clear from the very beginning;
we do not wish to interfere with the
internal affairs of any States, for that
is a matter primarily to be resolved
between the rulers and the peoples of
the States.[8]

He had, just on the basis of the doctrine
of princely sovereignty, offered a blank
sheet of paper to each of the Hindu
rulers of the overwhelmingly Hindu border states of Jodhpur and Jaisalmer, and
said, "Write your terms on that, Your
Highness, and I will sign them."[9]

Following the same legal logic, he offered full protection to Mahabatkhan
Rasulkhanji, the Muslim ruler of a predominantly Hindu state of Junagadh, far
inside the Indian territory, if he acceded
to Pakistan. Within weeks, when the
Hindu maharaja of the predominantly
Muslim state of Jammu and Kashmir
prevaricated, Jinnah shifted his position
completely and would not accept the
ruler's constitutional right to join either
dominion or remain independent. He
even armed irregular forces and sent
them across the border into Kashmir,
wanting the maharaja to sign the document acceding to Pakistan at gunpoint.

SARDAR PATEL HEADS THE MINISTRY OF STATES

In July 1947, Sardar Vallabhbhai Patel
took over the Ministry of (Princely)
States. He was also the minister of
home affairs and deputy prime minister
in Nehru's cabinet. He was held as a
member of the nation's triumvirate
along with Gandhi and Nehru and was
regarded very highly by the rank and
file of the Congress Party. Only in the
previous year, all the provincial committees of the Congress had nominated
him to be the prime minister of the
country. Gandhi had preferred Nehru
because of the latter's popularity with
the masses, for his far better international recognition, and for his relative
youth and good health as against Sardar
Patel, who was more like a younger
brother to Gandhi, already past seventy
and had had a heart attack. Sardar's administrative acumen balanced Nehru's
grand vision; Nehru was leftist, whereas
Patel veered toward the right. Both
were intensely nationalist and had sacrificed immensely for the cause of India's
freedom. Both had spent years of their
lives in British prisons. They would
work together as a team, Patel's charge
being domestic affairs, including the
princely states, and Nehru's international affairs.

Even before he took over the Ministry of States, Sardar Patel appealed to
the nobler sentiments of the princes and
asked them to make sacrifices in the

cause of the freedom of their country. He asked them to send their representatives without delay to the Constituent Assembly that was then engaged in the historic task of creating a democratic constitution for the newly independent country. In response to Sardar's call, on April 18, 1947, numerous states—Baroda, Bikaner, Cochin, Jaipur, Jodhpur, Patiala, and Rewa—joined the Constituent Assembly. On July 5, as minister of states, he formally appealed to the princes to see the "compulsive logic of mutual interests" and accede to the Indian Union. Sardar urged that it was "far better for us to make laws sitting together as friends than to make treaties as aliens." He appealed to their patriotism, asking for cooperation in a joint endeavor, "inspired by common allegiance to our motherland for the common good of us all." He asked them to keep in mind the "ultimate paramountcy of popular interests and welfare" of their subjects.[10]

The Sardar's appeal was endorsed on July 25 by Lord Mountbatten at a meeting of the Chamber of Princes, advising them that the best security for their states and themselves lay in their quick accession to the right dominion, which should be decided on the basis of geographical contiguity. There was no question of proclaiming their independence. Meanwhile, the Sardar had been in touch with the States' People's Congress, whose chapters had already begun to put pressure on the princes to join

the Indian Union. Only legal barriers had so far kept them apart from the rest of India and the Indian National Congress. The people there had the same regard for the leaders of the Indian national movement as those from British India and now wanted to join the mainstream to celebrate the joy of independence. The princes realized that if they insisted on their feudal right to rule, they might be going against history and be swept off by the strong democratic tide that had enveloped the country.

Patel sent his ministry's officials to special conclaves of princes in different parts of the country. The officials were armed with draft "Instruments of Accession." His instructions to these officials were to be generous to the princes in the amount of privy purses, personal guard, and personal property, including estates, palaces, and jewelry. His message to them was that he was aware that this was a matter of "life and death," and he would like them to have all the time in the world but would appreciate their response by the end of the day. The Sardar's reputation as an "iron man," a man of few words, written or spoken, was being put to the test. Some princes were genuinely happy to sign on the dotted line; others did not want to incur the Sardar's wrath. India's Bismarck had acted. All but three of the 562 states fell in line. A country had been created out of the tattered patchwork left behind by the colonial British. If Gandhi was the father of the nation and Nehru the creator of modern India, then Patel, the third member of the triumvirate, had used his tact and temper, sagacity and shrewdness, in integrating the country, a true architect of the Indian state. It was a bloodless revolution.

Hyderabad

Only three states refused to sign. These were Hyderabad, Junagadh, and Jammu and Kashmir. Of these, Hyderabad State was located right in the center of the peninsula. Its ruler, Mir Usman Ali Khan, who carried the title of Nizam and was the only one entitled, since 1918, to be addressed as His Exalted Highness because of the substantial monetary contributions his father had made to the British effort during World War I, held grandiose notions of sovereignty, although his father had been snubbed in this regard by Viceroy Reading in 1927. The Indian government's pleas to him to join the Indian Union fell on deaf ears. On November 29, 1947, he signed a Standstill Agreement for one year, under which the Nizam could maintain an army and a police force and the Indian government would have to withdraw its troops that had been stationed in the state since the British days.

Unfortunately for the Nizam, he had bad advisers, including an adventurer, Kasim Rizvi, who raised a second army consisting of marauders, called the Razakars, who exercised an extralegal jurisdiction on the civil population. The Razakars created anarchy not only in the Hyderabad State but also in the Indian territories that surrounded it on all sides, creating a grave law-and-order situation for the adjoining Indian provinces of Bombay and Madras. The Nizam now sought an independent outlet to the sea and began negotiations with the Portuguese in Goa. He engaged the services of an intrepid international adventurer, Sydney Cotton, an Australian pilot who smuggled arms and ammunitions supplies worth twenty-two crores of rupees from Europe secretly through Goa airport to Hyderabad. The international legal status of Hyderabad would be affected if its application to the United Nations for membership was approved. As it was, one member of that body, Pakistan, declared on June 1, 1948, that the Nizam's dominion was an independent state and that "not only Muslims of Pakistan but the Muslims the world over fully sympathize with Hyderabad in its struggle." The Nizam had given Pakistan a loan of twenty crores. All these moves by the Nizam, Usman Ali Khan, were in his capacity as a feudal ruler, without the benefit of expression of public opinion in his state.

Patel's representative in Hyderabad State was a major Congress leader, the highly successful lawyer and writer K. M. Munshi. He found that neither the Nizam nor his advisers would be amenable to negotiations. Feeling that matters were getting out of hand, Sardar Patel, with the consent of the full cabinet, authorized a military action. On September 13, 1948, Indian troops marched into the Hyderabad State, under the command of Major General J. N. Chaudhuri. It took only four days for the Nizam's forces and the irregular Razakars to surrender. Kasim Rizvi fled, was later captured, and was sentenced to a long term of imprisonment. Released early, he went to Pakistan to live in obscurity in Karachi.

Hyderabad was integrated into the Indian Union. As for the Nizam, as a wag put it, His Exalted Highness had been suddenly reduced to His Exhausted Highness!

Junagadh

Compared to Hyderabad, Junagadh had no major resources or wealth. It was a small principality in Northwest Gujarat, not contiguous to Pakistan, about 250 miles from its border. Just as in the Hyderabad State, Junagadh's ruler, Mahabatkhan Rasulkhanji, was a Muslim with a predominantly Hindu population of more than 85 percent. He was known among the princely order for his large harem and a larger number of eight hundred dogs. He spent enormous sums of money and attention on both. He would periodically celebrate a canine wedding royally with much pomp, lavish expenditure, and a proclamation of a state holiday. Left to himself, he would have likely acted in concert with his princely colleagues in Kathiawar, part of Gujarat, but in May 1947, a Muslim League leader from Karachi, Sir Shah Nawaz Khan Bhutto (father of Pakistan's future president Zulfikar Ali Bhutto and grandfather of Pakistan's future prime minister Benazir Bhutto), arrived in Junagadh to become the state's *diwan*. Jinnah had advised Shah Nawaz and through him the ruler to "keep out under any circumstances until August 15" and then announce the state's accession to Pakistan. The lack of geographical contiguity did not bother him.

Junagadh's accession to Pakistan did not go well with either the people of the state or with the Kathiawar princes. The States' People's Congress under Samaldas Gandhi (no relation to the Mahatma) compelled the *diwan* of Junagadh to hold negotiations. There was a complete breakdown of law and order throughout the small state. Sensing the popular mood, the nawab fled to Karachi by air in late October 1947, taking with him in addition to gold as many of his dogs and wives as the small aircraft could hold. On November 1, Indian troops entered the state to restore law and order. The *diwan* of the state, Shah Nawaz Khan Bhutto, fled to Pakistan on November 8. The nawab's council declared the state to have joined the Indian Union on November 9. Two months later, the elected representatives of the Junagadh State requested that the state be made an integral part of the Indian Union.

India was now organized as Part A, Part B, and Part C states. Part A states consisted of the former provinces of British India; Part B states included the larger of the princely states such as Mysore, Travancore-Cochin, Hyderabad, Jammu and Kashmir, and groupings of small and medium-size states into "unions" such as Madhya Bharat, Rajasthan, Saurashtra, and the Patiala and East Punjab States Union (PEPSU). Part C states were those territories, for example, Delhi, that were centrally administered. Whereas the Part A states had governors, Part B states had *rajpramukhs*, who were appointed from among the former princes.

THE KASHMIR QUESTION

Of the princely states, Jammu and Kashmir was the largest in area, about 84,258 square miles, with a relatively small population of 4,021,160, of which 78 percent were Muslims, 21 percent Hindus, and the others Buddhists and Sikhs. The state had three distinct units in terms of religious affiliation: the Vale of Kashmir is predominantly Muslim, Jammu has a large Hindu population, and Ladakh is predominantly Buddhist.

Jammu and Kashmir is strategically extremely important, touching China, the former Soviet Union, Tibet, and Afghanistan. In the era of cold war politics, it was undeniably an extremely strategic location. Besides which, whoever controls Kashmir controls the headwaters of many rivers.

Historical and Cultural Background

We know about the early history of Kashmir from its own historian, Kalhana, who wrote his *Rajatarangini* in Sanskrit verse in 1148–1149 CE. His work was continued by Jonaraja, who brought the historical account down to the reign of one of Kashmir's greatest rulers, Sultan Zain-ul-Abidin (1420–1470 CE). Three scholars—Srivara, Prajyabhatta, and Suka—continued the work until the conquest of Kashmir by Emperor Akbar in 1586. Thereafter, the tradition of history writing was maintained by numerous writers, Hindu and Muslim, mostly in the Persian language.

According to tradition, Emperor Ashoka introduced Buddhism to Kashmir in the third century BCE. It was further reinforced by Emperor Kanishka in the first century CE. However, with the decline of the Kushanas, Buddhism declined in the valley of Kashmir, Hinduism becoming the more dominant religion of the people. In the sixth century, Kashmir came under the Vikramaditya dynasty of Ujjain in central India, marking Kashmir's golden age. It is from that time on that Kashmir came to be known as a great center for the study of Sanskrit. The arts of music, architecture, sculpture, and scholarship flourished during the reign of the greatest of Kashmir's Hindu kings, Lalitaditya (697–738), a great warrior whose political sway was recognized by rulers as far northeast as Tibet, east as Bengal, and south up to Konkan in western India. He was known for his public and charitable works. He built the famous temple of Martand and the beautiful city of Parihaspura, whose ruins are extant. Another major ruler in the same dynasty was Avantivarman (853–883 CE), who with the help of an engineering genius, Suyya, constructed a drainage system in the Kashmir Valley. Walter Lawrence, who perhaps wrote the best account during the British times, summarized the Hindu period of Kashmir's history as follows:

> The Hindu period must from certain points of view have been of great magnificence. With the plunder of conquest, splendid temples and fine public works were constructed, and their ruins show that Kashmir in those days was endowed with noble buildings while the potsherds of ancient cities . . . suggest that the Valley must have been very thickly populated. About the condition of the people little is known, but as Hindus living under Hindu kings their lot must have been fairly happy, and irrigation canals testify that the Rajahs did not spend all their wealth on temples, but had some thought for the cultivators.[11]

The traditional date when Kashmir came for the first time under Muslim rule was 1339 when Shah Mirza or Shah Mir occupied Srinagar. But for some zealots such as Sikandar in the fifteenth century, who ordered all sacred books of Hinduism to be thrown in the Dal Lake and who gave the non-Muslims three choices—death, conversion, or exile—and ordered a general destruction of temples and idols, Kashmir's Muslim rulers, such as Sultan Qutb-uddin and Zain-ul-Abidin in the pre-Mughal period, established a tradition of religious toleration. Both these rulers observed the practices of Hinduism as well as of Islam. They encouraged Sanskrit learning and funded Hindu theological institutions as well as students proceeding to Benares (Varanasi) for advanced studies. Zain-ul-Abidin, popularly known as Badshah, or Great King, himself was a student of Sanskrit who committed to memory the text of Yoga Vashista, reciting it in his old age for the spiritual solace it provided him. For the first two centuries of Muslim rule, Sanskrit was used as the court language, and the administration was led by Brahmans. Such traditions of Muslim-Hindu harmony were the heritage of the Kashmiris until only a few years ago when the seeds of hatred and suspicion were sown and became responsible for the ethnic cleansing of Kashmir's 400,000 Hindu *pandits*, who were forced to leave the valley for the first time in several centuries.

The Mughal rule in Kashmir was notable for laying out spacious and gorgeous gardens. Emperor Jahangir and Empress Nur Jahan, who spent long stretches of time in Kashmir, built the terrace gardens of Achibal, Nasim, and

Shalimar. Akbar's able minister, Todar Mall, introduced his well-known land tenure system, which continued down to recent times. The institution of village officers in Kashmir dates from the Mughal times. The only grouse that Kashmiris had about the Mughal rule was that they were not allowed to enlist in the imperial army, nor were they given higher positions in the civil service.

Unfortunately, the last days of the Mughal rule were marked by anarchy, loot, rape, and plunder, which brought in the tribal Pathans from India's Northwest as marauders. Their "rule," beginning in 1752, was remembered for a very long time as "the cruelest and the worst" in Kashmir's entire history.[12] The tyranny was mercifully ended when a nobleman from the valley, Birbal Dar, invited the Sikh monarch, Ranjit Singh, in 1819 to invade Kashmir to save it from the Pathan rule. After the conquest, Ranjit Singh rewarded one of his principal ministers, Gulab Singh, with the rulership of Jammu. By that time, the British had become the principal power all over India. They did not want to conquer Kashmir and to administer it. Instead, they were happy to allow Gulab Singh to have it on payment of rupees 7.5 million, perhaps because they badly needed the money, and in any case, they were "selling" something that was not theirs. The British Treaty of Lahore of March 8, 1846, stipulated that Gulab Singh would become an independent sovereign of some territories that the British would give him. These were

named in the Treaty of Amritsar the British signed the following week, on March 16, transferring to Gulab Singh the territories "east of the River Indus and Westward of the River Ravi including Chamba and excluding Lahul."[13] That marked the beginning of the last family of rulers of Jammu and Kashmir, the Dogra dynasty.

It was not until the last two decades of the nineteenth century that the British, for strategic reasons, became interested in Kashmir. The Great Game was now being played, and the fear of expanding Russia was the reason for the British forward policy in the Northwest and Tibet. In 1889, the British created the Gilgit Agency and placed it under a British political agent beyond the jurisdiction of the rulers of Kashmir. The Dogra maharaja at that time was Pratab Singh, who died in 1925, leaving the throne to the last ruler of the dynasty, Maharaja Hari Singh, who was the one who signed the Instrument of Accession and invited the Indian government at the end of October 1947 to send its troops to push the invading forces from his state.

Popular Movement

In the early 1930s, a popular movement began in Kashmir under the leadership of Sheikh Abdullah. Born and raised in Kashmir, he was educated at Aligarh Muslim University in Uttar Pradesh. In 1932, he founded the Muslim Conference, whose name was changed by him to the Kashmir National Conference (NC) in 1939 because the progressive and modern-minded sheikh did not want the organization to appear communal. The NC had large numbers of Hindus and Sikhs as its members.

The organization's aims were political and economic. Sheikh Abdullah was concerned that the land system was outdated and the government favored only the dominant classes. The NC agitated for political reforms and a responsible government. It was no different from what the Indian National Congress was demanding under Gandhi and Nehru. The NC joined the All-India States People's Conference. Sheikh Abdullah was its vice president before he was thrown in jail by the maharaja; while in prison, he was elected president of the AISPC. The Kashmir movement was thus in line with the movement in the rest of the country.

Maharaja Hari Singh, who was at first opposed to any kind of political reforms that would share the power with the people, relented. In 1934, he allowed the creation of a Legislative Assembly, with seventy-five members, of whom thirty-five would be nominated and forty elected. However, the franchise was limited to only 8 percent of the population, based as it was on literacy and property qualifications. The assembly had no powers; it was merely a deliberative body. In 1939, a Council of Ministers was allowed but without impairing the final authority in the state, namely, the maharaja himself.

The NC was, to a certain extent, happy with the gains it had made in the thirties. It contested the elections for the state assembly and won many seats. One of its leaders became a member of the Council of Ministers. The NC's policy was to cooperate with the maharaja and secure a responsible government with the maharaja as the constitutional head like the monarch in Britain. The maharaja too managed a good relationship with the NC until the end of World War II, when he brought in one of his favorites, a very narrow-minded person, Ramachandra Kak, as prime minister. His communal and divisive policies angered and frustrated the NC; its lone member in the Council of Ministers resigned in 1946. When the Cabinet Mission, headed by Sir Pethick Lawrence, arrived in 1946, the NC tried to approach it; the NC was in favor of sending Kashmir's representatives to the Indian Constituent Assembly. In retaliation, Kak arrested Sheikh Abdullah, only helping the NC, which through mass demonstrations showed its popularity and that of its leader, Sheikh Abdullah. The sheikh's wife, Begum Abdullah, for the first time, gave up her *purdah* and led the people.

Kashmir's Accession to India

The Indian Independence Act of 1947 passed by the British Parliament, creating the two dominions of India and Pakistan, stipulated that "an Indian State shall be deemed to have acceded to the

Dominion if the Governor-General has signified his acceptance of the Instrument of Accession executed by the Ruler thereof." Article 7 of that act stated that the "suzerainty of His Majesty over the Indian States lapses, and with it, all treaties and agreements in force at the date of the passing of this Act between His Majesty and the rulers of the Indian States." Although undemocratic, the legal position was that the ruler and the ruler alone became entitled to decide which of the two dominions his state should join, the other alternative being to remain aloof from both and, if he felt like it, sign a Standstill Agreement with either or both the dominions, namely, India and Pakistan.

Mohammed Ali Jinnah, the founder of Pakistan, known for his thorough knowledge of law and constitutionality, understood the position. Barely a month before he would become the governor-general of the new state of Pakistan, he said on July 11, 1947, "I have already made it clear more than once that the Indian States are free to join either the Pakistan Constituent Assembly or the Hindustan Constituent Assembly or remain independent. . . . We have made it clear that we are not going to coerce, intimidate, or put any pressure on any State regarding its choice."[14]

On that basis, Pakistan recognized the independent entity of the state of Jammu and Kashmir and the legality of its ruler, Maharaja Hari Singh, when he signed a Standstill Agreement with Pakistan on August 12, 1947 (Pakistan signed it on August 16). Neither party made the Standstill Agreement subject to the wishes of the people of Jammu and Kashmir because the legal position did not require it; the maharaja's assent and signature made the Standstill Agreement legally valid.

What was India's stance in regard to Kashmir's status at that point of time? During his visit to Kashmir in July 1947, Lord Mountbatten, still the viceroy of India and the direct legal link between the king-emperor of Britain and the Indian princes, advised Maharaja Hari Singh to opt for either dominion before August 15. He added that should he decide to accede to Pakistan before that date, "the future Government of India had allowed me to give His Highness an assurance that no objection would be raised by them."[15]

The maharaja did not want to exercise his options immediately. He would not accede to Pakistan because it would have gone against the wishes of his people, as represented by the NC, led by the "Lion of Kashmir," Sheikh Abdullah, the principal secular-minded leader. The maharaja could not contemplate with equanimity the political unrest that would necessarily erupt if he decided to accede to Pakistan. On the other hand, accession to India would put his arch-enemy, Sheikh Abdullah, in power. The latter's close relationship with the Congress Party and especially with Nehru would have made him too dominant for his liking. The maharaja, therefore, proposed on August 12, 1947—only three days before the subcontinent's partition—to enter into Standstill Agreements with India and Pakistan, as provided by the Cabinet Mission to cover the transitional period. Pakistan accepted it on August 16, thereby agreeing to keep communication and supply lines to Kashmir open as before.

History would have been different if Pakistan, particularly Jinnah, had been patient. However, he decided to force the issue through a military operation ill-disguised as tribal raids. He was personally in a hurry because he alone and his doctor knew that he did not have much time to live.

By August 31, however, Major General Scott, who commanded the maharaja's army, complained to his government of tribal raids from Pakistan. On October 13, Norman Cliff of the *London News Chronicle* reported that Pakistan had cut off from Kashmir supplies of petrol, sugar, salt, and kerosene oil, "although a Standstill Agreement between them has been signed." Two days later, the maharaja complained to the British prime minister, Clement Attlee, about the economic blockade and the invasion of his state. As Stanley Wolpert wrote of the situation in October 1947,

> On October 23, British trucks and jeeps of the Pakistani army loaded with some 5,000 armed Pathan Afridi, Waziri, and Mahsud tribesmen of the North-West Frontier crossed the Kashmir border and headed east along the Muzaffrabad-Baramula road that led to Srinagar itself. That "invasion" of Kashmir from Pakistan would long be called by Pakistan a purely "volunteer" action undertaken "spontaneously" by irate "tribals" rushing to the aid of oppressed Muslim brothers. But the trucks, petrol, and drivers were hardly standard tribal equipment, and British officers as well as Pakistani officials all along the northern Pakistan route they traversed knew and supported, even if they did not actually organize or instigate, that violent October operation by which Pakistan seems to have hoped to trigger the integration of Kashmir into the nation.[16]

The maharaja wrote to Attlee, "As a result of obvious connivance of the Pakistan Government, the whole of the border from Gurdaspur side up to Gilgit is threatened with invasion which has actually begun from Poonch."[17] By October 22, the invaders had captured several towns, massacred large numbers of civilians, particularly in Baramula, and reached Uri, only fifty miles from Srinagar. Two days later, the maharaja appealed to India for protection. His formal letter dated October 26 requested immediate military help. On the same day, he signed the Instrument of Accession.

The maharaja's letter addressed to the governor-general of India, Lord

Mountbatten, informed him of the grave emergency that had arisen in Kashmir as a result of the invasion by Pakistan. The latter had made no attempt to stop the invasion in spite of repeated appeals. He was, therefore, asking for aid from India. Since such aid could come only after the accession of the state, he was signing the Instrument of Accession. The maharaja's letter also stated that it was his intention to set up an interim government and ask Sheikh Abdullah to carry out the responsibilities along with the prime minister of the state.

In accepting the accession, Lord Mountbatten wrote to the maharaja on October 27,

> In the special circumstances mentioned by Your Highness, my Government has decided to accept the Accession of Kashmir State to the Dominion of India. Consistently with their policy that, in the case of any State where the issue of accession has been the subject of dispute, the question of accession should be decided in accordance with the wishes of the people of the State. It is my Government's wish that as soon as law and order have been restored in Kashmir and its soil cleared of the invader, the question of the State's accession should be settled by a reference to the people.[18]

The Instrument of Accession was the usual document signed by the states, as stipulated in the Government of India Act of 1935 as amended and in force on August 15, 1947. According to this act, "An Indian State shall be deemed to have acceded to the dominion if the Governor-General has signified his acceptance of an Instrument of Accession executed by the Ruler whereby the ruler on behalf of the State declares that he accedes to the Dominion."[19]

Regarding the legality of accession, in the narrow juridical sense of the term, there is no doubt that with the acceptance by Mountbatten (as governor-general of India) of the Instrument of Accession signed by the maharaja Kashmir became an integral part of India. Such a procedure for accession was in accordance with the Partition Agreements. Moreover, it had the sanction of the Muslim League, as evidenced by Jinnah's statements of June 17 and July 31, 1947, on the constitutional position of the Indian princes after the transfer of power.[20]

The international legal status of Kashmir and the Indian government's responsibility to defend it was at first accepted by the United States, whose representative to the United Nations, Warren Austin, stated on February 4, 1948, "The external sovereignty of Kashmir is no longer under the control of Maharaja. . . . With the accession of Jammu and Kashmir to India, this foreign sovereignty went over to India and is exercised by India, and that is how India happens to be here as a petitioner."[21]

In regard to the argument that the acceptance of accession was conditional, Michael Brecher says that the statement made by Lord Mountbatten about the ascertainment of the wishes of the people did not in any way affect the legality of this act that was sealed by India's official acceptance of the Instrument of Accession. Furthermore, Mountbatten specifically indicated that this Indian offer to seek the will of the Kashmiri people on the accession issue would be implemented "*after* law and order have been restored in Kashmir and the invaders expelled from the State."[22]

India, Kashmir, and the United Nations

It was to get the invaders out of Kashmir that India approached the Security Council of the United Nations on January 1, 1948. Kashmir had legally acceded to India, and an attack on any part of Kashmir, therefore, became an aggression against Indian territory. Invoking Article 35 of the UN Charter, India complained that raiders from Pakistan had invaded Kashmir, that they were allowed transit across Pakistan and were permitted to use Pakistani territory as their base of operations, that they included Pakistani nationals, and that they drew their military equipment, transportation, and supplies, including petrol, from Pakistan. It added that Pakistani officers were training, guiding, and otherwise actively helping the raiders. India, therefore, requested that the Security Council "prevent Pakistan Government personnel, military and civil, from participating or assisting in the invasion of Jammu and Kashmir state; to deny to the invaders (a) access to and use of its territory for operations against Kashmir, (b) military and other supplies, (c) all other kinds of aid that might lend to prolong the present struggle." India also indicated to the council that if Pakistan did not put an end to the raid, India would reserve for itself the freedom to take, at any time it became necessary, such military action as it might deem the situation required.

A long diplomatic battle then ensued in the UN, with Pakistan's rejoinder completely denying any role in the tribal invasion of Kashmir. Pakistan charged India with obtaining the accession of the state of Jammu and Kashmir "by fraud and violence." It further alleged that "large-scale massacre and looting and atrocities on the Muslims of Jammu and Kashmir State have been perpetrated by the armed forces of the Maharaja of Jammu and Kashmir and the Indian Union and by the non-Muslim subjects of the Maharaja and the Indian Union."

The Pakistan government, therefore, requested that the Security Council

> appoint a Commission or Commissions, . . . to arrange for the cessation of fighting in the State of Jammu and Kashmir, the withdrawal of all out-

siders whether belonging to Pakistan or the Indian Union including members of the armed forces of the Indian Union . . . and thereafter to hold a plebiscite to ascertain the free and unfettered will of the people of Jammu and Kashmir State as to whether the State shall accede to Pakistan or India.

Pakistan also set out her own version of the events: "It is not surprising if independent tribesmen and persons from Pakistan, in particular, the Muslim refugees (who it must be remembered are nationals of the Indian Union) from East Punjab are taking part in the struggle for the liberation of Kashmir as part of the forces of the Azad Kashmir government."

Thus, Pakistan introduced a new party into the dispute, namely, the "Azad Kashmir" government, which was being established in the territory occupied by the invaders. Officially, Pakistan disclaimed any part in the invasion, or in training or arming the invaders. This contradicted an account of a meeting between Mountbatten and Jinnah immediately after the invasion began. According to the account, Jinnah told Mountbatten, the first governor-general of independent India, that "both sides should withdraw at once and simultaneously." When Mountbatten asked him to explain how the tribesmen could be induced to remove themselves, his reply was, "If you do this, I will call the whole thing off."[23]

The Security Council appointed the United Nations Commission for India and Pakistan (UNCIP) to review the situation in Kashmir and recommend suitable action to resolve the conflict. It collected considerable testimony and passed numerous resolutions, three of which are important to the understanding of the Kashmir impasse: those on January 17, 1948 (by the Security Council), August 13, 1948, and January 5, 1949 (both by the UNCIP). The first of these, which asked both parties to refrain from the use of force and to "inform the council immediately of any material change in the situation," was based on Pakistan's denial that any of its troops were in Kashmir. However, before the crucial resolution of August 13 was passed, the UNCIP received some surprisingly contradictory testimony from the foreign minister of Pakistan, Sir Zafrullah Khan. According to the UN records, Sir Zafrullah Khan told the UNCIP in the course of an interview on July 7, 1948, that "the Pakistan Army had at the time three brigades of regular troops in Kashmir and that the troops had been sent into the State during the first half of May." A member of the UNCIP, Josef Korbel, described such a flagrant, contradictory admission by Pakistan's foreign minister as a "bombshell," because it completely vitiated the basis of the UNCIP's thinking up to that point. After Sir Zafrullah's interview, a confounded UNCIP noted, "The situation that confronted the Commission upon its arrival was different from that which had been envisaged by the Security Council during the deliberations which preceded the formulation of the resolutions, inasmuch regular Pakistani troops were within the frontiers of the state of Jammu and Kashmir participating in the fighting."[24]

The UNCIP's August 13 resolution therefore made any further action conditional on Pakistan's complete withdrawal of its regular troops as well as of the invader tribesmen. The August resolution consisted of three parts, of which Part II contains two subparts. Implementation of each part and subpart was conditional on the implementation of the previous one. Part I (A) and (B) proposed that the two countries issue cease-fire orders to their respective forces. Part II (A) and (B), titled "Truce Agreement," deserves to be quoted in extenso.

Part II-A stated:

1. As the presence of troops of Pakistan in the territory of the State of Jammu and Kashmir constitutes a material change in the situation since it was represented by the Government of Pakistan before the Security Council, the Government of Pakistan agrees to withdraw its troops from the State.
2. The Government of Pakistan will use its best endeavor to secure the withdrawal from the State of Jammu and Kashmir of tribesmen and Pakistani nationals not normally resident therein who have

entered the State for the purpose of fighting.
3. Pending a final solution, the territory evacuated by the Pakistani troops will be administered by the local authorities under the surveillance of the Commission.

Part II-B stated:

1. When the Commission shall have notified the Government of India that the tribesmen and Pakistan nationals referred to in Part II-A2 have withdrawn thereby terminating the situation which was represented by the Government of India to the Security Council on having occasioned the presence of Indian forces in the State of Jammu and Kashmir, and further that the Pakistan forces are being withdrawn from the State of Jammu and Kashmir, the Government of India agrees to begin to withdraw the *bulk* of their forces from that in *stages* to be agreed upon with the Commission. [Emphasis added.]

And, finally, Part III stated:

The Government of India and the Government of Pakistan reaffirm their wish that the future status of the State of Jammu and Kashmir shall be determined in accordance with the will of the people and to that end, upon acceptance of the Truce Agreement both governments agree to enter into consultations with the Commission to determine fair and equitable conditions whereby such free expressions will be assured.

It took the two governments four months to communicate their acceptance of the UNCIP Resolution of August 13, 1948. According to the Indian spokesman, V. K. Krishna Menon, the delay was caused by his government's seeking and securing certain clarifications. Among these were:

1. Responsibility for the security of the State of Jammu and Kashmir rests with the Government of India.
2. There shall be no recognition of the so-called Azad Kashmir government.
3. The administration of the evacuated areas in the north shall revert to the Government of India who will, if necessary, maintain garrisons for preventing the incursions of tribesmen and for guarding the main trade routes.
4. If a plebiscite is found to be impossible for technical or practical reasons, the Commission will consider other methods of determining fair and equitable conditions for ensuring a free expression of the people's will.
5. Plebiscite proposals shall not be binding upon India if Pakistan does not implement Parts I and II

of the Resolution of August 13, 1948.[25]

Thanks to the persistent efforts of the UNCIP, the two sides ordered a cease-fire effective "one minute before midnight of first January, 1949." That, in effect, implemented Part I of the resolution of August 13, 1948. Part II regarding withdrawal of forces was not then, and has not since, been implemented. But assuming it would, the UNCIP approved an important resolution on January 5, 1949, on the question of plebiscite that was included in Part III of the August 13 resolution. It stated, inter alia:

1. The question of the accession of the State of Jammu and Kashmir to India or Pakistan will be decided through the democratic method of a free and impartial plebiscite.
2. A plebiscite will be held when it shall be found by the Commission that the cease-fire and truce agreements set forth in Parts I and II of the Commission's Resolution of August 13, 1948, have been carried.[26]

Despite attempts made by several UN representatives and plebiscite administrators—notably, General A. G. L. McNaughton, Sir Owen Dixon, Admiral Chester W. Nimitz, and Dr. Frank Graham—between 1949 and 1953, no plebiscite could be held in Kashmir. Pakistan had still not withdrawn its forces.

There were major disagreements between the two sides on the procedure for, and extent of, demilitarization of the state preparatory to the holding of a plebiscite and the degree of government control necessary in the state to ensure a free and fair plebiscite. Pakistan refused to withdraw its troops as required under Part I (A) of the UNCIP Resolution of August 13, 1948.

From that time to this date, Pakistan has not complied with Part I (A) of the August 13, 1948, resolution requiring it to withdraw its troops. Since the plebiscite was conditional on such a compliance, it has not been possible for the United Nations to move any further in the matter. As the years rolled on and Pakistan had still not complied, the Indian government pleaded it could not be held accountable for its promise to hold the plebiscite. In any case, it said, it was not legally obliged to hold a plebiscite or a referendum under the provisions of the Indian Independence Act of 1947. The Indian government held that its offer to ascertain the wishes of the people of Jammu and Kashmir on that question was an "extralegal offer" that could not be held valid for all times and under all situations. The offer was made to the people of Kashmir, not to the government of Pakistan.

By late 1953, India was concerned with the impact of the impending Mutual Security Pact between the United States and Pakistan not only on the defense of India but also on that of Kashmir because of its strategic location closer to the Chinese and Soviet borders and the use that might be made of it by the United States. India alleged pressures from the United States on some of the leaders of the National Conference in Kashmir to demand completely independent status for that state. India now held that apart from the fact that Pakistan had still not withdrawn its troops from Kashmir, the political and military circumstances in which the offer of plebiscite had been agreed upon in the UNCIP had altered drastically since 1954, and Pakistan's membership in U.S.-led military alliances such as the Middle East Defense Organization, the Central Treaty Organization (CENTO), and the Southeast Asia Treaty Organization (SEATO) entitled Pakistan to military assistance from those organizations. India argued that the U.S.-Pakistan military relationship had altered the military balance on the subcontinent. The Indian prime minister wrote to his Pakistan counterpart on December 21, 1953, "Military aid to Pakistan . . . produces a qualitative change in the existing situation and, therefore, it affects Indo-Pakistan relations, and, more especially, the Kashmir problem."[27]

India Refuses to Hold a Plebiscite

Critics of Indian foreign policy have vociferously condemned India for allegedly reneging on its commitment to hold a plebiscite on Kashmir without, at the same time, condemning Pakistan for its failure to comply with the UNCIP resolution of August 13, 1948, that made such a plebiscite conditional upon Pakistan's withdrawal of its troops from a part of Kashmir. Such a partisan, prejudiced attitude could be explained only by the interplay of international cold war politics in which Pakistan had chosen to align itself with the Western powers, while India in its international leadership role of the nonaligned movement was accused of pro-Soviet leanings by the same Western powers. Kashmir became an issue in the cold war rivalry between the superpowers that was reflected in the voting pattern in the Security Council whenever the question came up for a vote. The political context of the time of the partition of the Indian subcontinent in which the matter had been referred to the world body vanished into thin air. A number of proposals on Kashmir supported by the Anglo-American bloc were vetoed by the Soviet Union. Interestingly, the same cold war had created an impasse in Vietnam where, under the terms of the Geneva Agreements on Indochina of 1954, an election was due to be held in July 1956 to facilitate the reunification of that country. The Geneva Agreements had been signed by nine countries, with Great Britain and the Soviet Union as cochairs charged with the responsibility of implementation of the agreements. Neither Great Britain

nor the United States, which was an ally of the government of South Vietnam, would allow the elections to take place on the grounds that circumstances in the two Vietnams were not conducive to holding such elections. To Indians, it seemed that the Western powers were applying different standards to the Kashmir question, where Pakistan had so altered the population balance in the part of Kashmir it controlled that a plebiscite in all of Jammu and Kashmir would have a vitiated result.

In this changed context, India's stance on the plebiscite question remained more and more legalistic. In the late fifties, Indian spokesman V. K. Krishna Menon told the Security Council that Kashmir's accession to India was complete and final, because legally "the assent of the people was not necessary for the validity and the perpetual character of the state's accession. Accessions are not revocable. The Indian Constitution contains no provision for 'de-accessions' or partial or temporary accessions." Menon added that the Indian Union "was created by the people of India in the Constituent Assembly in which the representatives of Kashmir participated." If the accession of Jammu and Kashmir is to be reopened, "the same will apply to hundreds of States which have acceded to India." Menon pointed out that it was "the established international law and practice that acceded territories cannot withdraw from accession. The Supreme Court of the United States, the High

Court of Parliament in Britain, have both so decided in the case of Texas and Western Australia respectively."[28]

Finally, India argued that if its promise is regarded as an international commitment, it would be perfectly entitled to rely on the principle of *rebus sic stantibus* in denying the performance of the promise. This doctrine, which is somewhat akin to the doctrine of frustration in contract law, provides that a state is exonerated from its obligation to an international undertaking if there is a vital

change in the circumstances existing at the time the obligation was undertaken. In the words of Justice P. B. Gajendragadkar of India, "There have been such vital changes in the material circumstances since 1947 that it would be impossible to claim performance of the undertaking now. . . . It is, I think, naïve for any country to suggest that even after the passage of such a long time, and even after several events have radically altered the situation, India should agree to hold the plebiscite."[29]

NOTES

1. Quoted in Sisir Gupta, *Kashmir: A Study of India-Pakistan Relations* (London: Asia Publishing House, 1966), 33.

2. Government of India, *White Paper on Hyderabad* (New Delhi: Government of India, 1948), 19.

3. Jawaharlal Nehru, *Towards Freedom: An Autobiography*, 532–33.

4. Quoted in A. C. Banerjee, ed., *Indian Constitutional Documents, 1757–1939* (Calcutta: A. Mukherjee, 1946), 3:465–66.

5. Lord Linlithgow, *Speeches and Statements by the Marquess of Linlithgow* (New Delhi: Government of India, 1945), 195–98.

6. Leonard Mosely, *Last Days of the British Raj* (London: Weidenfield and Nicholson, 1961), 159.

7. Alan Campbell-Johnson, *Mission with Mountbatten* (London: Robert Hale, 1951), 147.

8. Quoted in Gupta, *Kashmir*, 48.

9. V. B. Kulkarni, *Princely India and the Lapse of Paramountcy* (Bombay: Jaico, 1985), 222.

10. Ibid., 226.

11. Walter W. Lawrence, *The Valley of Kashmir* (Oxford: Oxford University Press, 1895), 197.

12. Ibid., 190.

13. K. M. Panikkar, *The Founding of the Kashmir State* (London: Allen and Unwin, 1953), 112.

14. Z. H. Zaidi, *Quaid-I-Azam Mohammad Ali Jinnah Papers: Pakistan in the Making*, First Series (Islamabad: National Archives of Pakistan, 1994), document 108, 2:298–99.

15. Quoted in Lord Birdwood, *Two Nations and Kashmir* (London: Robert Hale, 1956), 42. See also Geoffrey Tyson, *Nehru: The Years of Power* (London: Pall Mall Press, 1966), 81.

16. Stanley Wolpert, *Jinnah of Pakistan*, 348.

17. Quoted in V. K. Krishna Menon, "What Is at Stake?" in "Kashmir: A Symposium on the Sub-continental Implications of a Critical Question," special issue, *Seminar* (June 1964): 33.

18. Mosely, *Last Days of the British Raj*, 159.

19. S. L. Poplai, ed., *Select Documents on Asian Affairs: India, 1947–50* (Bombay: Oxford University Press, 1959), 1:75.

20. See Michael Brecher, *The Struggle for Kashmir* (New York: Oxford University Press, 1953).

21. Quoted in "Kashmir: A Symposium," 39.

22. Brecher, *The Struggle for Kashmir*, 65.

23. Campbell-Johnson, *Mission with Mountbatten*, 229.

24. UN Security Council, document 651, January 17, 1948; UN Security Council, Official Records, *Interim Report of UNCIP: Supplement to November 1948*, 25; Josef Korbel, "The Kashmir Dispute and the United Nations," *International Organization* 3, no. 2 (May 1949): 280; UN Security Council, document S/1000, November 9, 1948.

25. Menon, "What Is at Stake?" 38–39.

26. UN Security Council, document S/1196, January 5, 1949.

27. *White Paper on Kashmir: Meetings and Correspondence between Prime Ministers of India and Pakistan, July 1953–October 1954* (New Delhi: Ministry of External Affairs, 1954), 22.

28. Menon, "What Is at Stake?" 40.

29. P. B. Gajendragadkar, *Kashmir: Retrospect and Prospect* (Bombay: Bombay University Press, 1967), 115–16.

For almost a half century since its independence in 1947, India's image abroad and reality at home had been the same, namely, of stark poverty afflicting its half-million villages, sending droves of peasants to live on the pavements and in the slums of its bursting metropolitan cities. That image has altered dramatically since the late 1990s and more so in the twenty-first century. India and China, two demographic billionaires and sleeping giants, have emerged as the world's fastest growing economies. . . . If India's socialist-oriented economy of the first period had failed to help nearly one-half of its burgeoning population make ends meet, the second period holds a hope that the billion-plus population will achieve an economic standard beyond the wildest dreams of its people. Will that really happen? That is the question not only for economists and politicians but, more important, for "the revolution of rising expectations" among India's population that accounts for one-sixth of the human race.   (page 407)

18

TOWARD
ECONOMIC FREEDOM

For almost a half century since its in-dependence in 1947, India's image abroad and reality at home had been the same, namely, of stark poverty afflicting its half-million villages, sending droves of peasants to live on the pavements and in the slums of its bursting metropolitan cities. That image has altered dramatically since the late 1990s and more so in the twenty-first century. India and China, two demographic billionaires and sleeping giants, have emerged as the world's fastest-growing economies. India has been consistently growing at a gross domestic product (GDP) rate of 7–8 percent annually for more than a decade and is expected to become the world's third-largest economy by 2015. If its first period, 1947–1990, was marked by excessive state planning and strangu-lating economic controls, the second period beginning with the economic lib-eralization in 1991 has led to rapid sale of state economic enterprises (SEEs), gradual but assured lifting of state con-trols over the private sector, lowering of

trade tariffs, an active role in the World Trade Organization, and allowing mul-tinational corporations (MNCs) fairly easy entry into the Indian market. If India's socialist-oriented economy of the first period had failed to help nearly one-half of its burgeoning population make ends meet, the second period holds a hope that the billion-plus population will achieve an economic standard be-yond the wildest dreams of its people. Will that really happen? That is the question not only for economists and politicians but, more important, for "the revolution of rising expectations" among India's population that accounts for one-sixth of the human race.

POLITICAL AND ECONOMIC BACKGROUND OF INDIA'S ECONOMIC DEVELOPMENT

At the dawn of India's independence, the country's leaders were divided in terms of the economic orientation that should guide and govern the new state

407

in its policies. The Congress Party had been at the vanguard of the country's struggle for independence and had been funded by the houses of Birla and Bajaj, Thackersey and Dalmia, to name only a few. Leaders such as Sardar Vallabhbhai Patel (deputy prime minister) and Rajendra Prasad (first president) were among many in the top echelons who were not just grateful but truly believed in the nationalist spirit among the country's industrialists who would now be ready to help in its economic development. On the other hand, there was the towering Jawaharlal Nehru (first prime minister), whose personal affluent background had not stood in the way of his fascination for Soviet planning, which had pulled that huge country out of its backwardness and turned it into a superpower. There were other leaders, too, who thought of the economic development of the country but did not know or did not want to decide how to go about it. In order to find a consensus, in October 1938, the Congress president, Subhash Chandra Bose, convened the industry ministers of the Congress-ruled provinces to discuss the plans for the economic development of the country. They were of the view that large-scale industrialization alone would make it possible for the country to make adequate progress. Bose appointed a National Planning Committee (NPC) with Nehru as chair and an economist, K. T. Shah, as secretary. Despite the intervening war and subsequent imprisonment

of the Congress leaders, the NPC had produced a number of studies on various aspects of planned development of the country. These studies were influenced by "democratic socialism," which denounced Soviet totalitarianism but lauded socialist planning in a democratic environment. Both were regarded as crucial for the nascent India. Within the Congress fold, a number of leaders supported Nehru's thinking that if the economy were left to the country's capitalists, they would continue to fatten only themselves at the expense of the poor. On the periphery of the Congress was a band of young socialist but anticommunist leaders such as Jaiprakash Narayan, Asoka Mehta, Achyutrao Patwardhan, and others who were formerly members of the Congress Socialist Party but had moved out and formed the Socialist Party in 1947. Indeed, they believed in the transformation of the society along socialist but democratic lines, much like the Labor Party in Britain or the Scandinavian states, which increasingly adopted social welfare programs for the benefit of its people. In the global postcolonial phase, there was considerable hope and enthusiasm all over the developing world. Nehru held out such a hope.

Three other plans were prepared in anticipation of India's independence. Thus, several industrialists presented the so-called Bombay Plan in 1944. Its emphasis, predictably enough, was on heavy industry as an essential step toward the people's progress. It projected an outlay of rupees 10,000 crore (1 crore equals 2 million dollars), over a period of fifteen years. Second, Shriman Narayan, a Gandhian, prepared a plan emphasizing village development as the basis of economic development. The third plan was prepared by the noted humanist thinker M. N. Roy at the behest of the Post-War Reconstruction Committee of the Indian Federation of Labour. It projected an outlay of rupees 15,000 crores over ten years. Its emphasis was on a dramatic development of agriculture that would not only augment the gross national income but also create substantial employment.

In the end, the socialist approach was helped by a perception that India had limited capital, which even after it was augmented by various means would still be grossly inadequate for its vast population. It was, therefore, argued in what was called "Nehruvian socialism" that in a capital-scarce and labor-surplus economy, the available capital must be used to its optimum best in order to maximize employment. No attention was given to the increase in wealth through maximizing production as well. This approach further demanded that the capital so employed needed strict scrutiny and control, not necessarily according to market needs but as demanded by social needs that would include creating jobs for a maximum number of people. The socialist approach required that the jobs so created must be protected even if

the industry concerned did not make a profit.

The development strategy of new India emerged in an atmosphere of extremely high expectations by the masses who had participated in the long nationalist movement that had promised them a millennium of prosperity. It was no surprise that Nehru succeeded in adopting the socialist approach, which also appealed to intellectuals of the time because it was anticolonial. He had no difficulty persuading the Constituent Assembly, which also served as the nation's central legislature, to adopt the first Resolution on Industrial Policy on April 6, 1948:

> The nation has now set itself to establish a social order where justice and equality of opportunity shall be secured to all the people. . . . For this purpose, careful planning and integrated effort over the whole field of national activity are necessary; . . . the Government of India proposes to establish a National Planning Commission to formulate programs of development.

Very soon after, the same assembly adopted the Directive Principles of State Policy as part of the Indian Constitution:

> The State shall strive to promote . . . a social order in which justice, social and economic and political, shall inform all the institutions of the national life, and in particular, shall

secure that the citizens, men and women equally, have the right to an adequate means of livelihood, and that the operation of the economic system does not result in the concentration of wealth and means of production to the common detriment.

In December 1954, the Indian parliament accepted "the socialist pattern of society" as the objective of the country's social and economic policy.

The "intellectual infrastructure" for planned economic development in the decade of the nation's birth came from numerous Indian economists trained in the country's two foremost economics departments (later schools) of the Universities of Bombay and Delhi. Many others had trained in the prestigious London School of Economics and been influenced by the Fabian socialist thinking of many of its faculty. They had also read the works of liberal economists on the primacy of state action and planning from liberal economic theorists such as Paul Rosenstein-Rodan, Ragnar Nurske, and Tibor Scitovsky, founders of New Development Economics, who had argued why free enterprise and a free market could not be the governing engine of the process of rapid industrial progress in backward economies. As Mrinal Dutta-Chaudhuri, in a seminal article, stated, a substantial body of literature around the theories of "market failure" formed the intellectual core of the development strategies advocated by the dominant group of economists in

the 1950s. Dutta-Chaudhuri adds, "The social-democratic political ethos surrounding India's independence movement provided a fertile ground for the cross-fertilization of ideas, domestic and foreign."[1]

In 1950, the Planning Commission was established directly under Prime Minister Nehru, who vowed to combine the centralized developmental planning for the country along Soviet lines but, importantly, within a democratic framework. The country has had ten plans, beginning with the First Five Year Plan (1951–1956), with only one break, a "plan holiday" from 1966 to 1969. In that bleak period, because of a major recession and famine in the country, the Planning Commission believed the country could not sensibly plan for a half decade and, instead, adopted three annual plans.

In 1951, the commission declared in the First Five Year Plan its social and economic objectives:

> Maximum production, full employment, the attainment of economic equality and social justice which constitute the accepted objectives of planning under the present-day conditions are not really so many different ideas but a series of related aims. . . . None of these objectives can be pursued to the exclusion of others; a plan of development must place a balanced emphasis on all of these.[2]

The plan's outlay was modest. Unlike its sequels, it gave pride of place to agriculture, in which more than 75 percent of the country's working population was engaged, allocating 31 percent of the total outlay. It proudly declared at the end of the plan that it had overshot its target by 50 percent.

The Second Five Year Plan, in which Nehru's statistical adviser, P. C. Mahalonabis, played a crucial role, favored industry over agriculture, which remained the focus of planning thereafter for the next nearly three decades. The allocation to industries and minerals was raised from 4 percent to 20 percent. Even the modest targeted increase of national income by 25 percent in five years failed to materialize.

In the first decade of its planning (up to December 31, 1962), India received a modest amount of external assistance of rupees 2,332 crores (US$1 equaled 4.75 Indian rupees) as loans and only 302 crores as grants. This did not include nondevelopmental aid but crucial U.S. credits. Under Public Law, 480 of rupees 1,156.33 crores enabled imports of wheat to tide over the food deficit. The U.S. aid was the largest among all donors, who together loaned 724.08 crores and gave grants worth rupees 140.62 crores.

Some non-U.S. donor countries, however, stole the thunder. The Soviet Union, the United Kingdom, and West Germany each gave a steel plant to Bhilai, Durgapur, and Rourkela, respectively, to add to the only two other smaller plants in the private sector. The production thereby of steel ingots went up from 1.4 million tons in 1951 to 3.5 million tons a decade later. Again, three countries—the United States, the USSR, and West Germany—and the United Nations Educational, Scientific, and Cultural Organization (better known as UNESCO) helped India develop four of the seven Indian Institutes of Technology, in chronological order, at Kharagpur, Powai in Mumbai (formerly Bombay), Chennai, Kanpur, Delhi, Guwahati, and Roorkee.

India, on its own, launched some major river valley projects, "temples of New India," as Nehru called them, at Bhakra-Nangal, Hirakud, Nagarjunasagar, and the Damodar Valley Corporation. These would serve the twin purposes of helping agriculture through increased irrigation and industry through the generation of power. Although the power generated fell short of the target, the land acreage under cultivation increased from 51.5 million acres in 1950 to 70 million in 1960. The country took pride in these achievements under Nehru's planning and leadership. Meanwhile, the Planning Commission developed into a large body with an army of advisers in different disciplines, matching each ministry and activity of the government at the central and state levels. The commission would operate in two main divisions: the Perspective Planning Division and the Economic and Resources Division. Some of the best economists and statisticians in the country were employed or consulted as they worked with the Ministry of Finance and the Reserve Bank of India

(India's central bank) both in putting the five-year plans together and in monitoring the plans' implementation, from year to year. The Planning Commission also discussed with each state its plans for development and coordinated them with the central government plans.

After a few years of its operation, it was apparent to all that the commission had, in effect, become a parallel government and a very powerful body in the country, although it did not have any statutory existence in the sense that neither the Indian Constitution nor the parliament had ever formally created it or given it the authority for its actions that in reality affected millions of people.

INDUSTRIAL POLICY AND SOCIALIST PATTERN OF SOCIETY

By the mid-fifties, Nehru wanted the critics within his own party officially to drop their opposition to planning. The Avadi session of the Congress in 1955 adopted the "Socialistic Pattern of Society" as the country's and the party's goal. It was to be the official philosophical underpinning of the Second Five Year Plan, then being formulated. (At the next session of the party's annual concourse, the resolution amended "socialistic" to "socialist.") Nehru espoused "democratic socialism," the middle position by which he would steer adroitly between the rightists who believed in full economic laissez-faire and the ultraleftists who would be happy only

with full nationalization. Just as Nehru chose the middle path between capitalism and communism in foreign policy, so did he in economic policy, bridling the scope of the private sector by not letting it stand in the way of the "common good"; if it did, the state would step in in favor of nationalization or establish a cooperative enterprise.

Even before the planning began formally, India announced its industrial policy on April 6, 1948, which was to remain in force until the major policy enunciation of October 30, 1956. The latter prevailed, in essence, until the economic liberalization of 1991.

The 1948 policy statement was deemed essential in view of the insecurity in the minds of some major industrialists, who were not sure how the postindependence government would treat them and what role they should have in the building of new India. The policy statement would clear the atmosphere and indicate the roles of the public and private sectors in a mixed economy. Pending clearer thinking, the industries were divided into four broad groups: (1) those that would be completely under the central government—arms and ammunition, atomic energy, and railroad industries; (2) new units that could be started only by the government—coal, iron and steel, petroleum, aircraft and ships, telephone, telegraph, and wireless apparatus but excluding radios; the existing units owned by the private sector could be acquired by the state in the public interest; (3) industries that were categorized as being of basic importance (some of them hardly fit the description), which may be regulated by the central government in the national interest: textiles, sugar, rubber, industrial alcohol, newsprint, salt, automobiles, tractors and mechanical movers, electrical engineering, machine tools, heavy chemicals and fertilizers, electrochemical industries, nonferrous metals, air and sea transportation; and (4) the "remaining" industries were left to the private sector.

As a sop to Gandhian economists and those who favored rural development, the policy emphasized the role of cottage and small-scale industries in economic development. Fearful of the return of colonialism through the back door, the statement welcomed foreign capital but on terms that would hardly encourage it. An important condition was that "the major interest in ownership, and effective control should always be in Indian hands. . . . In all cases . . . the training of suitable Indian personnel for the purpose of eventually replacing the foreign experts will be insisted upon."[3]

The 1956 Industrial Policy Resolution was a sequel to the official acceptance of the "Socialist Pattern of Society" as the goal of economic development. The classification of industries in force since 1948 was modified, further enlarging the state's role. There were to be only three categories corresponding to the concept of a mixed economy of public, private, and public-private sectors. The first category was broadened to cover manufacture of all communications—rail, shipping and air, telephone, telegraph, and radio; electricity; iron and steel; mining in copper, lead, and zinc; heavy machinery and heavy electrical industries; and, important, all defense-related industries. The second category included those industries in which the state would have a leading role but expected the private sector to supplement the effort. These would include transportation by road and sea, mining in aluminum and other nonferrous metals, machine tools, chemicals and pharmaceuticals, and fertilizers. The third category was left to the private sector on the condition that it must conform to state policy for social and economic regeneration of the country and be subject to state regulation. In the words of one critic, the private sector became a "sort of residuary legatee. Economic development was more explicitly equated with state enterprise."[4]

Once again, the government supported the notion of village and small-scale industries by differential taxation and the offer of state subsidies. The state would also help in the improvement and modernization of the nonindustrial sector through the organization of co-operatives.

From the Second Five Year Plan, the government was clearly committed to a socialist direction for the economy. Progressively, the public sector would attain dominance, the private sector being placed at the mercy of the politicians and the rapidly growing bureaucracy that had the power to issue licenses and monitor economic performance to see that it met the predetermined targets.

All sectors taken together, the share of the public sector in the GDP increased from 9.99 percent in 1960–1961 to 27.12 percent in 1988–1989. The large majority of public-sector enterprises, particularly the nondepartmental nonfinancial enterprises, were sustaining losses and had to be subsidized year after year. In 1970–1971, such subsidy amounted to 3.05 percent of their GDP (at factor cost). By 1975–1976, it rose to 10.61 percent and in 1979–1980 to 19.47 percent. In 1980–1981, the subsidy was extraordinarily high, constituting 25.67 percent of the GDP.

The industries left to the private sector were regulated by the Indian (Development and Regulation) Act of 1951, vesting the government with the necessary powers for regulation and control of existing and future "undertakings" in a number of specified industries. A license was necessary for establishing a new undertaking, taking up the manufacture of a new article in an existing undertaking, and changing the location of an existing unit. All units using power and employing at least forty-nine persons and those not using power and employing more than one hundred persons needed a license to operate and became subject to regulation by the Ministry of Commerce and Industry. Furthermore, to prevent private monopolies and the concentration of economic power, the gov-

ernment enacted, in 1969, the Monopolies and Restrictive Trade Policies Act. All such regulations and controls inevitably led to a growth of bureaucracy, inhibited enterprise and industry, and spawned patronage and corruption.

FAILURE OF SOCIALIST PLANNING

The First Five Year Plan was a "successful failure." It achieved its target, but the target was very low, both in itself and in relation to the actual rate of growth of population, which was far higher than the assumed growth. The latter, at an annual rate of 1.25 percent, was based on the figures for the decade of 1941–1951, part of which was covered by World War II, during which a large number of people died of famine and shortages of food partly created by the government's improper management. Again, based on that estimate, it was assumed that the population would increase by only 1.4 times in twenty-seven years, which in turn became the basis for the GDP growth projection at 2.13 percent, expected to double in twenty-seven years! The rate of investment for the Second Five Year Plan (1956–1961), targeted at 7 percent, was achieved but not so with the next six plans whose goal was between 5 and 5.5 percent, whereas the actual achievement was so low that the average annual growth rate for the period from 1950–1951 to 1989–1990 was only 3.71 percent, dubbed by critics as "the Hindu rate of growth." Yet the government's official publication did not pronounce it a failure because, after all, it had met the projected doubling of the GDP in twenty-seven years.

Calculated differently, the growth picture was even more dismal. Taking into consideration the increase in population, the per capita GDP rose by an annual rate of merely 1.37 percent, that is, 50.98 percent in thirty years from 1951–1980. The situation improved in the next decade, 1981–1990; the GDP grew at 5.13 percent, whereas the population grew by 2.13 percent, marking a net per capita GDP increase in the annual rate to 3.09 percent.

POPULATION AND PLANNING

The estimates of population growth also went completely awry: The population increased from 359 million in 1950–1951 to 679 million in 1980–1981 at an annual average growth rate of 2.15 percent, far above the estimates. By the launching of the Third Five Year Plan, the Planning Commission was alarmed by the figures of population increase. Its perspective declared that "the objective of stabilizing the growth of population over a reasonable period must . . . be at the very center of planned development." The commission realized that mortality would decrease with advancements in health measures, and, therefore,

the plan should focus on reducing fertility rates to stabilize the population. The 1960s saw further effort in the direction of promoting family planning with a much wider outreach program than before and an emphasis on implanting intrauterine devices and sterilization. Unfortunately for family planning efforts, a major handicap was the U.S. Congress's legislation banning the use of U.S. funds for family planning. The government's Family Planning Ministry revealed that the population had grown alarmingly fast since 1951, with a birthrate of 41.1 and death rate of 18.9 per thousand, giving a "natural" increase in population at 22.2 per thousand people. In 1968, the Indian government promoted a "cafeteria" approach to family planning devices and allowed a commercial and more public distribution of condoms.

In the following decade, the birthrate declined from 36.9 per thousand in 1971 to 33 in 1977, thanks to the rather outrageous measures taken by Sanjay, Indira Gandhi's son, during the emergency (1975–1977). Legislation in 1972 lowered the legal obstacles to abortion. A qualified setback to family planning came during the Janata Party regime following Indira Gandhi's defeat in the elections of 1977. Condemning Sanjay Gandhi's hated measures of forced sterilization, the new government went to the other extreme and declared that family planning, including sterilization, would be entirely voluntary. However, the Janata Party government introduced improvements in women's health and women's education as the more positive measures that would impact family planning. However, thanks to the sustained and energetic measures of the Family Planning and Family Welfare Ministries and Departments of the central and state governments, the "number of births averted," as the official report stated, brought down the birthrate.[5] Thus, in 1987–1988 alone, it "averted" 9.9 million births, 12.68 births per thousand. In 1991, the census showed a decline in the rate of growth of population from 2.2 in 1981 to 2.14 in 1991. It declined further in 2001 to 1.93, though in that year the news that India had reached the 1 billion population mark made global headlines!

As with most indicators, the South and most of the western parts of the country had registered impressive progress in the decline of fertility rates, paralleling their improvements in education and health. The glowing examples of this phenomenon were Kerala and Goa; the trends in Maharashtra and Gujarat were also very promising. In 1992–1993, a major national survey brought out what was already well known to workers in the family planning field globally: that the fertility rates varied inversely with the educational attainment of people, more particularly females. It was pointed out that whereas, nationally, the figures for education for persons above the age of fourteen were 55 percent for men and 26 percent for women, in Kerala, where

family planning had succeeded dramatically, the corresponding figures were 86 percent for men and 71 percent for women. By contrast, the dismal performance in economic development and education sectors in four states, which are dubbed the Hindi Belt, the Cow Belt, and BIMARU (the Hindi word for sickness is *bimari*), the acronym standing for Bihar, Madhya Pradesh, Rajasthan, and Uttar Pradesh, affected the national image and averages in family planning and growth in population.

FAILURE OF PLANNING

As the decade of the 1980s ended, it was clear after four decades of a planned economy that the country was facing a critical situation on both the domestic and the external fronts. On the domestic front, there was a persistent and growing fiscal deficit in the central budget that was being financed by borrowing both from the public and from the Reserve Bank of India. The state governments followed the central government's example in profligacy and borrowing— in short, living beyond their means. The borrowing from the Reserve Bank of India, crudely put, meant printing extra currency; it contributed directly to inflationary pressures on the economy. On the external front, the country had been showing a deficit on the current account for years, though in all fairness it could be said that the country had never defaulted on its international debt obligations. The external debt had now reached the limits of India's repaying capacity. New international loans were unavailable.

India could not or did not take advantage of the phenomenal *world* trade expansion in the 1960s. By contrast, small countries of East Asia such as South Korea, Taiwan, and Hong Kong and countries of Latin America took advantage of these trade opportunities and expanded those industries whose products could be exported profitably to the world. Some of these countries that started their development efforts much later than India were ahead of the latter in improving their GDPs.

The primary handicap of the Indian industry *was* the government control and a regime of licensing and granting permits that were costly and time-consuming and encouraged corruption at different levels of bureaucracy. With the passage of time, government procedures became more and more rigid and inflexible. Bureaucrats ruled the roost. One could see this class of facilitators on the Delhi-bound morning flights from the industrial-financial capital of Bombay (now Mumbai) and the return flights in the evenings, developed to grease the appropriate palms in the capital. They were the Indian version of the lobbyists in some Western countries. A new triangular nexus of businessman, politician, and bureaucrat developed, as business not only lined the pockets of the other two but also helped the uninitiated two into investing ill-gotten "black money" into profitable domestic channels such as hotels and restaurants, construction and real estate purchase and management, and the entertainment industry, particularly the huge movie industry in India's Bollywood. They also introduced them to overseas opportunities, not necessarily limited to Swiss bank accounts. Corruption became rampant, considered by business as a "necessary" expense, and helped inflation. A country that once prided itself on the ethical quality of its political leaders and thronged to have their *darshan*, an opportunity to see and hear them, found it hard to believe that their successors in office had sunk so low. As for the civil service, it had ceased to be civil or a service.

While industry was complaining of the lack of proper atmosphere for innovation and competition in the world market, most were also taking advantage of a guaranteed home market. Consumers had to register on a waiting list for several years—five to six for a small Fiat car, nine to ten years for a Godrej nondefrost refrigerator, thirteen to fourteen years for a Bajaj scooter. It was not unusual for one to come across a television commercial for some of these products proudly proclaiming that they had not changed their product for two whole decades! Moreover, the controlled economy was stifling and did not generate adequate purchasing power, and, therefore, the production of such manufactured goods was modest. From the mid-1960s, many of the industries had substantial excess capacity.

Helping the moribund state of the industry were the unions, mostly controlled by leftist parties, mostly the Communist parties, which led to legislation guaranteeing jobs whether an industry made a profit or not. This applied to all industries, none of which could be closed down or its employees dismissed. If the industrial units were successively unprofitable, the management applied for a state subsidy, which brought in state supervision and control under a state agency run by bureaucrats. The number of such "sick" units increased.

NEW ECONOMIC POLICY

Beginnings Under Indira and Rajiv

Soon after Indira Gandhi returned to power in 1980, she took some steps to reduce restrictions on the private sector, but she was far from opening the country to the outside world for economic investment as her much older contemporary, Chinese vice premier Deng Hsiao-Ping, had done for his country's closed Maoist economy in the previous year. Her son and successor, Rajiv Gandhi (1984–1989), however, opened up some areas of the economy, which may be regarded as preliminary or tentative measures, precursors to the major economic liberalization beginning in 1991. He had been a pilot in the Indian Airlines, had traveled frequently overseas, and had seen the power of computers in the technologically oriented New World. Because of his fascination with computers and his desire to introduce them in a large way, he was dubbed "Mr. Computerjee" (*jee* is an honorific). He had a band of young business executives such as Arun Nehru and Arun Singh who had been his fellow students at the prestigious Doon School and Arun Singh at Cambridge University as well. Through them and some younger Indian industrialists, Rajiv Gandhi turned the cabinet and the Planning Commission in the direction of changing the Indian developmental trajectory toward newer technology in every sector of the economy. In one major case, he went beyond the "Doon Goons" and put Sam Pitroda, an Indian American entrepreneur, in charge of the modernization of telecommunications.[6] In 1987, Pitroda became an official advisor to Rajiv. He founded the Center and later Department of Telematics (C-DOT) and was given complete autonomy in his task of shaping India's telecommunications policy—internal and external. In a short time, Pitroda's presence was felt all over the country, as the yellow-striped "public call offices" appeared even in remote villages and along the nation's highways, revolutionizing domestic communications and India's link to the rest of the world. As Montek Ahluwalia, deputy chairman of the Planning Commission, asserted, "These policy initiatives paid rich dividends ten years later, when India emerged as the most globally competitive emerging market country in software and IT services."[7]

Pitroda's revolution in telecommunications can be appreciated by the simple fact that instant and secured communications between the outsourcing countries and the operating offices in India on a 24/7 basis would have been unthinkable in the pre-Rajiv and pre-Pitroda revolution. The closeness to the prime minister helped Pitroda overcome the bureaucratic obstacles to change. India's Planning Commission calls these changes under Indira and Rajiv in the 1980s the "internal liberalization" to distinguish it from the "external liberalization" of the following decade.

Rajiv was not able to bring about a real revolution in overturning the Nehruvian socialism and the "Permit Raj," but he did widen the cracks his mother had hesitantly made in the planned economic regime of more than three decades that had clearly kept India in a cocoon and behind some of the advancing Asian countries.

Liberalization at Last

Although Rajiv Gandhi started with a note encouraging the private sector in the mid-1980s, the real liberalization was to come after his assassination and the advent of government led by P. V. Narasimha Rao (1991–1996). What triggered the major change and its acceptance across all sections of the Congress Party and the state governments was the worst balance-of-payments crisis India had ever faced. India was compelled to seek a loan from the International Monetary Fund, which presented India with a "Structural Adjustment Package" as a condition to the loan grant. Instead of just implementing the IMF's suggestions, India went much beyond in using this "window of opportunity" to dismantle the "Permit License Raj" and open the economy to the world. Globalization had begun.

Despite several changes in government, the "liberalization" policy, as it has been called, has had the sustained support of all the Indian governments since 1992 to the present. At times, the pace of reforms and further opening of the country's economy domestically to the private sector and internationally to the forces of globalization has generated less enthusiasm than at other times, but no political party, including the Communists, has been able to question the general thrust of liberalization.

Politically, Rao and his finance minister, Manmohan Singh, who piloted the liberalization, had the advantage that Indira and Rajiv Gandhi had initiated some reforms in the early and mid-1980s. From a political point of view, the Congress Party had thus been prepared for some major economic changes. Yet improvement in the economic rate of growth in the 1980s from the long-term "Hindu rate of growth" of 3–3.5 percent annually to 5–5.5 percent had been achieved without any fundamental alterations such as scrapping the Industrial (Development and Regulation) Act of 1951.

Thus, the atmosphere was in favor of a major change in the direction of the economy. The country was facing a balance-of-payments crisis; there was just enough foreign exchange to meet the country's needs for a month. For the first time in a common man's memory, the country's stock of gold had been physically shipped to the Bank of London as collateral. To an average householder in India, gold has traditionally served as a final hedge, something a housewife gave to her husband to save him from going to jail for nonpayment of a debt or to make possible the marriage of a daughter or to get food in a persisting famine. The country's psyche had been touched. Rao called Manmohan Singh, a most respected economist, holding a doctorate from Oxford, who had served his country most ably in diverse capacities, including as governor of the Reserve Bank of India, and had represented India at the International Monetary Fund. When Rao personally offered him the position of finance minister, Singh said with all the modesty that comes so naturally to him that he would if the prime minister would consider two conditions: that Singh be given carte blanche, or full freedom, to introduce innovations in policy and that the prime minister should support him publicly. Politicians normally agree to

anything in times of distress. If the results are good, they take the credit, but whoever heard of one willing to take the blame publicly? Rao agreed on both counts; fortunately, the moment of testing his pledged word never came. The new policy became a resounding success. Singh brought back the country's gold from London, a sure sign of success to a large segment of the electorate!

On July 4, 1991, within a month of coming to power, Prime Minister P. V. Narasimha Rao announced major changes in the trade policy, and, after extensive consultation with industry, a more comprehensive Statement on Trade Policy was issued on August 13, 1991. It was preceded by an official indictment of the official policy, a rare phenomenon most of the previous four decades. Meanwhile, the Statement on Industrial Policy of July 24 criticized the official policy in no uncertain terms. It was the first indictment of the public sector since the country's independence. The statement provided the best Maoist-style self-review and critique of India's dismal economic performance in the four decades of socialism-guided planned development programs.

Noting the country's initial exuberance over the public sector entering new areas of industrial management, the review pointed out that serious problems had developed in many areas: productivity, poor project management, overstaffing, lack of continuous technological upgrades, and inadequate attention to research and development and human resources development. The review was very critical that public enterprises had shown a very low rate of return on the capital invested. It had inhibited their ability to regenerate themselves in terms of new investments as well as in technological development. The result was that many of the public enterprises became a burden rather than an asset to the government.

The review recommended that instead of closely monitoring the private sector, it would be necessary to let the entrepreneurs make investment decisions on the basis of their commercial judgment. The attainment of technological dynamism and international competition requires that enterprises be enabled to swiftly respond to fast-changing international conditions that have become characteristic of today's industrial world. This can be done only if the role played by the government were to be changed from that of control to one of help and guidance by making the management procedures fully transparent and eliminating delays! The government announced a new policy on August 13, 1991, to "unshackle the Indian industrial economy from the cobwebs of unnecessary bureaucratic control." In doing so, it noted that the world economy was changing rapidly, and most countries, including developing countries and the former socialist countries of Eastern Europe, were gearing up to the challenges of competing in an increasingly integrated, highly

global marketplace. It added that India could not afford to ignore these global challenges. It concluded that India could grow faster only as part of the world economy and not in isolation.

The results of the new policy marked a sea-change from the policy of state planning, which had produced isolation in the name of self-reliance, leading to a stagnant economy, a "Hindu rate of growth," which was only marginally higher than the rate of growth of the population. The changes, officially called "external liberalization," encompassed substantial lowering of import duties, removal of quantitative limits on imports, and a major liberalization of foreign direct investment (FDI). Fortunately, India already had the necessary "soft infrastructure" in the form of commercial and legal institutions: the rule of law, an independent judiciary, accounting standards, a stock exchange, and acceptable corporate practices. What was not adequate by world standards was the "hard infrastructure"—roads, railroads, ports, and airports.

Why was this not done yet? Since the late eighties, increasing reports appeared in the Indian press of the economic miracles in some Southeast Asian and East Asian states such as Singapore, Taiwan, Hong Kong, South Korea, Thailand, and Malaysia. Their admirers were the growing numbers of Indian politicians, including members of the ruling Congress Party. On the other hand, diehard leftists in the Congress and leftist parties scorned the "new tigers," calling them cubs, not to be compared to India. They were derided as pro-West, pro-U.S. appendages manipulated by London's and New York's financiers. At the same time, a growing number of economists and policymakers had become aware of the sea-change in the communist world itself. The failure of communism, the replacement of the Communist Parties in government, and the elimination of socialist economies in the Kremlin, the Mecca of the faith, and the echoes of that phenomenon all over Eastern Europe made the politicians sit back and think. These were countries with which India had had economic ties for four decades, partly because of easier terms of payment. Even those countries such as China and Vietnam that retained the political dominance of the Communist Party in a one-party government, the economic orientation had changed to a "market-based" economy, in China in 1979 and in Vietnam in 1986. The results had been spectacular for economic growth through removal of trade barriers, facilitating the influx of FDI, welcoming MNCs to produce consumer goods with cheap and controlled labor, and dramatically improving the balance of trade. All those socialist economies were, in the 1990s, in the process of becoming members of the WTO. Could India remain behind? The people, politicians, economists, and media all asked that question.

Even after the liberalization of the Indian economy, its domestic leftist critics were quick to point out the drawbacks of the policy, among them the lack of proportionate benefits to the lower classes. They drew some satisfaction from the fact that during the currency crisis of 1997, several Southeast Asian economies that were tied to MNCs had shrunk by about 5 percent, with Indonesia's economy the worst affected, at 12 percent. Both the critics and the enthusiasts of the Indian liberalization expressed satisfaction that India was not affected by the crisis because of the far greater economic depth of the Indian economy and the buffer provided by foreign exchange and other controls to the currency. It was pointed out that China had also weathered the currency crisis largely because of such state controls.

The Results of Globalization or Liberalization

There has been a distinct improvement in the Indian economy since the liberalization began. Economic growth accelerated to an annual 6.5–7 percent in the late 1990s and to 7.5–8 percent by 2006, with higher projections by 2010. Economists and planners in India, the IMF, and the World Bank hold that these projections would be more realistic if further steps were taken to improve the soft and hard infrastructures. According to a Goldman Sachs study, adopted by the U.S. National Intelligence Council's *2020 Report,* India, China, Russia, and Brazil will be the four economies that are expected to grow rapidly over the next three decades, and by 2040 India will be the third-largest economy in the world, behind the United States and China. India's Planning Commission currently works on these assumptions.

Its own review, however, adds to the criticism of the new economic policy. The major question asked is whether the reforms of the 1990s were "appropriate or even necessary." Were the reforms under Indira and Rajiv not adequate? Did India buckle under the pressure of the IMF, other international agencies, and Western investors and the governments supporting them? How useful and relevant have the reforms been to the Indian masses, particularly in reducing poverty?

The criticism of the "new" economic policy has been varied. Some charge that India has focused on "issues that were of little concern to the masses," that they affect mostly the financial sector and foreign trade. Some allege a conspiracy by international institutions such as the IMF, WB, and Asian Development Bank, allegedly with the assistance of their high-level former employees of Indian origin, now in the employ of the Indian Ministry of Finance, Planning Commission, and other relevant agencies. These latter hope that the experience of such employees, with their knowledge of how the international agencies work and their international contacts, will ease approval of India's applications for international loans. Indeed, many of them

proved "deft" in representing India's case in Washington, D.C., and New York. Rob Jenkins, one of the foremost commentators, calls the new economic policy "reforming by stealth" in which the governing elites endeavor to keep the regional leadership and those involved in agriculture in the dark. Furthermore, he alleges that the key actors have deliberately refrained from highlighting the long-term implications of the reform decisions on the various sectors of the economy, particularly the rural sector.[8]

Montek Ahluwalia, deputy chairman and de facto chief of India's Planning Commission, defends the reforms, pointing out, first, that the reforms of the 1980s during Indira's and Rajiv's administrations had not addressed the question of international competition, which needed an extensive liberalization of trade policy and liberalization of foreign investment. He points out that in the absence of action in this area, there was not enough improvement in export competitiveness. He adds that India's share of world exports improved only marginally in 1980 from 0.4 percent to 0.5 percent a decade later. The balance of payments had remained under pressure, and the country had resorted to additional external borrowing, leading inevitably to a deterioration in external debt ratios. The IMF's conditional approval of a loan in the foreign exchange crisis of 1990 was a temporary solution; a substantial increase in exports was needed to earn the needed foreign exchange.

The most important question, how-ever, has to be: How much has the liber-alization helped the common man, and has it reduced poverty in India? Critics charge that the reforms have not affected poverty at all and have helped only the upper and middle classes. According to them, the number of middle-class con-sumers who could buy appliances and telecommunications gadgets had risen progressively, to well over 150 million people in 2006, more than the figures for middle-class consumers in any of the European countries except Russia. Ahluwalia repudiates the charge of a lack of impact on poverty by pointing out that the percentage of people below the poverty level has declined from 40 per-cent in 1987 to around 23 percent in 2003. He does admit that the perfor-mance in this regard has been below the targets. After all, that still leaves an unac-ceptably large number of about 250 mil-lion below the poverty line.

CONCLUSION

It is nearly a half century since "We, the people of India" promised in the solemnly worded preamble to the In-dian Constitution "to secure to all its citizens" a number of goals, including economic justice. Has the state's social-ist role at the commanding heights of the economy for four decades followed by economic liberalization and the dilu-tion of the state's role since 1991 taken India's teeming millions closer to that promise in the preamble? The father of the Indian nation, Gandhi, wanted to wipe every tear from every eye on the globe. Humanity is still far from that goal. The question for the politicians and economic planners in India in the new millennium is whether their stew-ardship of affairs is at least headed in the right direction.

————

NOTES

1. Mrinal Dutta-Chaudhuri, "Mistakes of an Early Starter," *Seminar* 329 (January 1987): 47.

2. Government of India, Planning Com-mission, *The First Five Year Plan* (New Delhi: Government of India, 1950), 28.

3. Government of India, *Report of the Fiscal Commission, 1949–50* (New Delhi: Govern-ment of India, 1950), 14.

4. H. Venkatsubbiah, *Indian Economy since Independence* (New York: Institute of Pacific Relations, 1959), 94.

5. Each of the divisions of the central gov-ernment is called a ministry. At the state level, they are called departments.

6. Sam Pitroda, whose real name is Satya-narayan Gangaram Pitroda, was born in Orissa and educated at M. S. University of Vadodara in Gujarat. He founded a number of corpora-tions in Chicago, where he lives. Among his in-novations was "One Wallet," an M-commerce application, and "Compucards," a computer-themed card game using binary numbers

instead of decimals. In the deck of cards, the "Programmer" closely resembled Sam Pitroda. During the government of V. P. Singh, Pitroda did not enjoy the same autonomy as before. Facing bureaucratic jealousies and the reluctance of the minister of telecommunications, K. P. Unnikrishnan, to support him, Pitroda resigned and returned to Chicago. In 2005, Prime Minister Manmohan Singh invited Pitroda to chair the newly created National Knowledge Commission.

7. Montek Ahluwalia, "India in a Globalising World" (Twenty-seventh Jawaharlal Nehru Memorial Lecture, London, April 20, 2005), 4.

8. Rob Jenkins, *Democratic Politics and Economic Reform in India* (Cambridge: Cambridge University Press, 1999). See also his article "How Federalism Influences India's Domestic Politics of WTO Engagement and Is Itself Affected in the Process," *Asian Survey* 43, no. 4 (2003): 598–621; and Jenkins and Sunil Khilnani, eds., "The Politics of India's Next Generation of Economic Reforms," special issue, *India Review* 3, no. 2 (November 2004). For a critique of Jenkins's argument elaborated in his book, *Democratic Politics and Economic Reform in India,* see C. T. Kurien, "Reform by Stealth?" *Frontline,* 17, 17 (August 19–September 1, 2000).

————

As India entered the second half of its first century of independence, its foreign policy imperatives changed drastically, one of them being very close cooperation with the United States. The issues were no longer anticolonialism and antiracism from the Indian side and anticommunism from the United States as they were in the middle of the last century. The new issues are centered around global trade and investment opportunities, which can help India overcome poverty and disease for millions of its people. On the U.S. side, the strategic issues of nuclear nonproliferation, war against terrorism, securing the oil supplies of the Middle East, and reining in the historical expansionist urges of China hold the greatest priority.   (pages 446–47)

19

INDIA'S
FOREIGN POLICY

THE NEHRU ERA

No single aspect of the Indian political experiment in the first quarter century of its independence in 1947 evoked so much world attention as its role in international affairs, which was certainly disproportionately large when compared with India's then economic and military strength. The major reason was Jawaharlal Nehru, who as prime minister steered the infant ship of state for the first seventeen years of independence and presided over the formulation and direction of his government's foreign policy. Preoccupation with world events had always been a matter of passion for the Indian leader since the early days of his life, when he jumped into the country's fight for political freedom. After India's emergence as an independent nation, the imprint of his views was evident on every aspect of governmental activity but on none so clearly and exclusively as in the field of external relations. Not only were the philosophy and

style of foreign policy molded by Nehru, but even the daily direction of it became the prime minister's preoccupation.

Politics, domestic or international, is hardly a field where one should look for consistencies. The history of international relations is full of shifting alliances, where yesterday's bedfellows are today's enemies. Yet many countries covetously claim consistency in their foreign policies, conveniently placing their pragmatic policies on the high pedestal of immutable principles. India was one such country, boasting a lack of variations in its basic approach to world affairs. With the solitary exception of October 1962, when Nehru confessed his Himalayan blunder in trusting China and "living in an artificial atmosphere of our own creation," the principal aims of Indian foreign policy were consistently stated as nonalignment, peaceful coexistence, anticolonialism, and antiracism.

The first two years after independence, 1947–1949, were noted for their anticolonial emphasis. Indian initiative led to the convening of the Asian Relations Conference in March 1947, where Nehru defined India's new role vis-à-vis colonial rule:

> All countries of Asia have to meet together on an equal basis in a common task and endeavour. It is fitting that India should play her part in this new phase of Asian development. Apart from the fact that India herself is emerging into freedom and independence, she is the natural center [sic] and focal point of the many forces at work in Asia. Geography is a compelling factor, and geographically she is situated as to be the meeting point of Western and Northern and Eastern Asia and Southeast Asia.[1]

As if to prove that this was not just empty rhetoric, he called a Conference on Indonesia in January 1949 in New Delhi, to which he invited nineteen Asian nations to consider the question of Indonesia's freedom, which had been threatened by Dutch "police action." Nehru's concluding statement at the momentous meeting included a warning to the colonial powers: "If this gathering is significant today, it is still more significant in the perspective of tomorrow. Asia, too long submissive and dependent and a plaything of other countries, will no longer brook any interference with her freedom."[2] Yet there were some limiting factors to India's enthusiasm. Thus, India's attitude toward Vietnam's fight against France for independence was cautious and circumspect because of the continued presence of five small French colonies in India. There was also the problem of domestic communist-led insurgency in a part of India and the conflict with Pakistan over Kashmir. Such factors may have led to the need for a friendly attitude toward the West, particularly Great Britain. In 1949, India agreed to become a member of the Commonwealth of Nations. Indicative of Great Britain's anxiety to accommodate its former nonwhite colonies into a hitherto all-white British Commonwealth of Nations was its action to amend the constitution of that body, making it possible for the Indian republic to be a part of an organization whose head was the British monarch. First, it dropped the word *British* from the name of the organization and, second, it made the British monarch not the commonwealth's sovereign but its nominal head.

Most newly independent countries of Asia and Africa followed India's lead in steering an independent course in the cold war between the two superpowers, which began in 1949 with the establishment of the North Atlantic Treaty Organization and the Warsaw Pact among the communist states. Such an independent policy, adopted by most states emerging from colonialism, was first called neutralism, soon to be designated nonalignment. India would be a principal leader of the group of nonaligned nations, which did not want to take sides and as a mark of its hard-earned independence insisted on taking a position on international issues based on their merits and not as predetermined by their alliance with a superpower. Nehru called an alliance with a superpower as one between a giant and a pigmy and, in a sense, a "return of colonialism by the back door." Among the few exceptions that would not join India in this "exercise in freedom" would be its neighbor Pakistan. Their estrangement began within months of their independence from Britain, in October 1947, in the first of the four inconclusive armed conflicts over Jammu and Kashmir.

INDIA'S NEIGHBORS AND THE SUPERPOWERS

India and the U.S. Policy of Containment of Communism

It was an altogether different case with India's giant neighbor to the north, where a communist revolution had culminated in the establishment of the People's Republic of China in October 1949. In an act that could be interpreted as ingratiating itself with Beijing, India rushed to recognize the new government. It would have been the first in the world to do so, except for Nehru's deference to neighboring Burma's government, which wanted to be the first. Many Western governments too recognized China, the major exception being the United States, which would not recognize such a major change on the international horizon until three decades later.

At the same time, in late 1949, the cold war had set in with its concomitant, the U.S. and Western Europe's policy of containment of communism and the creation of NATO. The advent of the communists to power in China and the recognition of the Democratic Republic of Vietnam by China and the Soviet Union had extended the communist parameters all the way from East Germany to North Vietnam. For India, the change was real, not necessarily welcome. The new China was hardly friendly to India. It followed the monolithic global communist policy and branded the Indian leaders, including the anti-imperialist Nehru, along with other nationalist leaders of the new Asia such as U Nu and Sukarno, as "lackeys of imperialism." Caution marked India's relations with communist China, particularly after the latter's march into Tibet in 1950, thereby establishing a common border with India. During the period from 1949 to 1953, until the death of Stalin and the emergence of a new leadership and a new policy in Moscow, India followed a policy of circumspection, an attitude of cautious neutrality, "a plague on both houses" in the cold war dispute.

In the fifties, the U.S. containment policy promoted a new international architecture under the U.S. secretary of state John Foster Dulles, as he went around signing clusters of countries into alphabet-soup alliances: SEATO, CENTO, and MEDO. To lure states into such groupings, the United States also offered bilateral "mutual security" treaties such as with Pakistan. India would not join such alliances between unequal powers, in which the weaker signatory would, in reality, lose the freedom to act independently. It was painful for the newly independent countries, emerging from the dark night of colonial rule, once again to slip under neocolonialism, to be taken for granted by the powerful superpower ally. Dulles regarded communism as the immediate global enemy, just as dangerous as the recently defeated scourge of fascism and Nazism, and believed that any country not joining his crusade of containment of communism was being immoral, even if it did not join hands with the communist bloc. Under his direction, the U.S. Department of State retaliated, according to some because of the desire "to cut India to size" for providing nonalignment as an alternative to an alliance-based policy.[3] Another interesting analysis speaks of the U.S. role as an "off-shore balancing power," helping the obliging Pakistan to "realize its goal of 'parity' with its much bigger neighbor."[4] Dulles saw communist skeletons in every cupboard and branded neutralism and nonalignment as "immoral," an unacceptable path in world affairs, when there was a "clear danger" that Southeast Asian states and later India could fall like dominoes to the communist tide.

While India sought its fulfillment as an independent nation in nonalignment, Pakistan's quest for security against a much larger, much better-equipped neighbor, India, obliged it to look for an alliance with a powerful country so as to match its military capabilities with India—hence its insistence that it be treated, aided, and armed on a parity with India. Historically, Pakistan's demand for parity harks back to most of the first half of the twentieth century, when the Muslim League asked for an electoral system that would include reservations and give extra weight to Muslim votes, making the Muslims the political equal of the much larger Hindu population. Despite India's argument in the postindependence period that its much longer borders and coastline warranted larger numbers of defense personnel and weaponry than Pakistan, the latter insisted on parity, which became and has ever since remained the principal pursuit of its defense and foreign policy. Therefore, it joined the U.S.-sponsored CENTO and MEDO, and although it was not geographically part of Southeast Asia, it joined the Southeast Asia Treaty Organization in August 1954. Not feeling secure enough, it also signed a Mutual Security Pact with the United States. These pacts made available to Pakistan an array of weaponry and provided it with a protective umbrella against its enemies, particularly India.

Pakistan's membership of such alliances spelled an alienation from India and the large number of countries that had recently emerged from colonialism and domination by outside powers. Moreover, the superior array of arms Pakistan received because of such pacts compelled India to acquire similar weapons systems and divert much needed funds from development to defense. President Eisenhower assured Prime Minister Nehru that the arms given to Pakistan would not be allowed to be used against India. They were meant as defense against expanding communism. But as President Ayub Khan, a military man, said later, he did not know of any gun that could not be used in more than one direction.

India and the Soviet Union After Stalin's Death

From 1947 until Stalin's death in 1953, Nehru tried to maintain a "correct" relationship with the leader of the communist world, although Moscow described him as the "running dog of imperialism" or "an Anglo-American satellite."[5] Neither Nehru's sister, the famous Madame Vijayalakshmi Pandit, nor the erudite philosopher, and future president of India, Sarvepalli Radhakrishnan, both of them India's ambassadors to the Kremlin, was successful in having any meaningful interaction with Stalin.

In the post-Stalin period, particularly after the rise of Nikita Khrushchev to the all-important position of secretary general of the Communist Party of the So-

viet Union, Moscow decided to include the numerous new states emerging out of the ashes of crumbling empires into its international orbit through a policy of friendship with the nonaligned states of Asia and Africa. Obviously, wooing India, the leader of the nonaligned group of states, would open the doors to others. India's role at Geneva and Bandung crystallized the Soviet perception of India's crucial role in the new world. Whereas the United States while Dulles was at the Department of State refused to recognize the "third path" of nonalignment, the Soviet Union and China resolved from 1954 to give India major recognition. When India pushed itself in international negotiations such as at the Geneva Conference on Indochina in 1954 (in the words of French premier Mendes-France, "these nine powers at the table—and India"), the Soviet Union and China lauded India's contribution. India helped so much to shape the settlement that the conference made India its guarantor by appointing it the chairman of a three-nation—India, Canada, and Poland—International Control Commission in Cambodia, Laos, and Vietnam, believing India's nonaligned role would help to keep the East and West in balance there.[6] And just before the Indochina part of the conference (May 8–July 21, 1954), Premier Chou En-lai and Nehru met in April 1954 and signed an agreement over Tibet that carried, for the first time, the *panchasheel,* or the five principles of peaceful coexistence. The Asian and

African nations applauded India's international leadership of a new postcolonial world at the twenty-nine-nation Asian-African Conference at Bandung in 1955, where Nehru introduced China's Chou En-lai to the newly independent nations. Most of these new states joined the non-aligned movement, signing with each other *panchasheel* agreements. Nehru's approach to world affairs received a tremendous boost when the concept of peaceful coexistence was adopted (after Dulles's death) at the Camp David talks in 1959 between Khrushchev and Eisenhower, promising an era of peace between the two superpowers.

Nehru's visit to the Soviet Union in June 1955 was followed six months later by that of Premier Bulganin and Secretary-General Khrushchev to India. That set the basis of a close India-USSR relationship that lasted until a little before the collapse of the Soviet Union in the late 1980s and has continued, though on a much less exclusive basis, since. Khrushchev entirely endorsed Nehru's foreign policy, including India's position on Kashmir and on the Portuguese Indian enclaves of Goa, Daman, and Diu. It was Khrushchev who suggested to Nehru that in view of the radically changed power equation on the subcontinent caused by the Pakistan-U.S. Mutual Security Pact of 1954 that Nehru was not obliged to stand by his commitment to hold a plebiscite in Kashmir. Over the next decade, India had reason to appreciate the Soviet veto in the Security Council in

India's favor; it was also grateful to the Soviet Union for its veto on the resolution condemning India's action in Goa in December 1961.

There were early signs in the late fifties of cracks in the Sino-Soviet relationship when China, in the aftermath of the Soviet launch of a satellite in 1958, insisted that the USSR should use its enhanced strategic capabilities to force the supremacy of the East over the West, by which was meant the superiority of the communist world over its rival world headed by the United States. Mao Tse-tung told visiting Edgar Snow that a thermonuclear war between the superpowers would not be so bad for China; even if one half of the world's population were killed, it would still leave China with 350 million people (China's population was, at that time, estimated at 700 million).

The Sino-Soviet rift paralleled the serious differences between India and China over India's grant of asylum to the Dalai Lama and about 35,000 of his followers fleeing from China's oppressive policies in Tibet. In order to strengthen its control over Tibet, China began constructing an all-weather road connecting its Xinjiang Province with Tibet. The road passed through the Aksai Chin Plateau, a part of Ladakh in Indian Kashmir. India also protested several Chinese incursions across their common frontier. Several rounds of border negotiations extending over two years between the two sides failed. Hostilities between the two Asian giants began on a major scale as China marched into Northeast India in October 1962 coinciding with U.S.-USSR confrontation over the Cuba missile crisis. The Chinese withdrew unilaterally and declared a cease-fire but not before laying claim to some additional territory in India's Arunachal Pradesh. The real intention most likely was, as Deng Hsiao-ping would say later, that the Chinese wanted to teach India a "lesson." Faced with military reverses in India's Northeast, Nehru wrote to heads of state of all member states of the United Nations, except Portugal and South Africa, the two regimes with which India had cut off diplomatic relations, with Portugal because of the Goa question and with South Africa because of its apartheid policies, asking for assistance to enable India to defend its sovereignty.

The India-China War brought India closer to both of the superpowers. Even before that brief war, U.S.-India relations had already improved significantly during the brief Kennedy administration. His ambassador, the economist John Kenneth Galbraith, had a personal intellectual rapport with Prime Minister Nehru. The relationship accentuated the distress felt in the White House over the Chinese invasion of India in October 1962 at a time when the United States itself had a confrontation with the Soviet Union over the missile crisis in Cuba. Nevertheless, Kennedy ordered large consignments of equipment, weaponry, and ammunition useful in mountain warfare. The United States rushed

its nuclear-powered USS *Enterprise* to the Bay of Bengal to warn the Chinese that "there could be effective military support for India if the conflict crossed certain thresholds which could threaten India's territorial integrity."[7] Although China had ended the warfare before the U.S. supplies made it to India's northeastern frontier, the government and the people were most appreciative of the U.S. assistance. However, Pakistan protested to the United States against its delivery of arms to India; they could be used against Pakistan, perhaps leading the United States to withdraw to the prewar level in its relations with India.

As for the Soviet Union, Nehru had secured Moscow's neutrality on the India-China border skirmishes since 1959 and the asylum given to the Dalai Lama. Khrushchev again remained neutral in the 1962 India-China conflict. By that time, the Soviet Union had chosen between India and China; in fact, by 1960, the quantum of Soviet military assistance to India had surpassed that given to China, a communist ally. In 1962, before India's conflict with China, the Soviet Union had agreed to allow India to manufacture MiG-21 fighter planes in India under license. The India-China war delayed the implementation for two years.

Following that war, Pakistan and China moved closer to each other, despite Pakistan's anticommunist alliance with the United States and the West. In the following year, Pakistan signed an agreement with China ceding a portion of Kashmir, about 2,700 square miles under its occupation, to enable China to build the "China-Pakistan Friendship Highway" in the mid-1960s, linking Pakistan-held Kashmir with China's Xinjiang Province. The alliance with China had the potential of creating a China-Pakistan nexus in case of an outbreak of hostilities between India and China. In return, China verbally supported Pakistan's claim to Kashmir. During the 1965 India-Pakistan war, China threatened to attack India's northeastern borders if India did not immediately dismantle its military posts along the Sikkim-China border.

For the next two decades, India-China relations remained frozen. There were no border negotiations, no exchange of high-level visits, no commercial or economic exchanges of note. Nehru's *Hindi Chini Bhai Bhai* (Indians and Chinese Are Brothers) policy, based on the five principles of peaceful coexistence, was totally in ruins. In 1962, the Indian parliament passed a resolution forbidding alienation of any portion of India's "sacred soil" to any other country, which made border negotiations impossible, as neither party would legalize any alienation of territory.

All through the 1960s and until 1987, the Soviet Union continued to be the dominant external influence in India. During most of that period, there was a corresponding growing axis between the United States and Pakistan and between Pakistan and China, leading to a triangular axis—the United States, Pakistan, and China—during the Nixon administrations. That axis vis-à-vis India's foreign policy needs drove India even further into Soviet arms. The peak of that relationship was during the period 1971–1976.

The Second War with Pakistan, 1965

Pakistan wanted to take advantage of India's debacle at China's hands in 1962 and attack India. According to Ayub Khan, President Kennedy compelled him to remain neutral in the conflict. As a soldier, Ayub expressed his frustration to Kennedy in his reply of November 5, 1962: "How can we in a situation like this be expected to show our friendship to them?"[8] Pakistan's army continued to be upbeat and believed that Nehru's death in May 1964 gave Pakistan an opportunity to take advantage of an ill-perceived leadership gap in India. The Pakistani army's morale was high, as its army chief of staff boasted that it would be an "easy walk" to march into India and take over Delhi. In his view, the Indian military had not recovered from the sound beating it had received from China in 1962. Moreover, Pakistan believed it had more than an edge of superiority in weaponry, with its F-104 fighter planes and the Patton and Sherman tanks.

The first test came in January 1965, when Pakistan attacked India in the Rann of Kutch, a marshy land, 320 miles long and 50 miles wide, on Pakistan's southeastern border. There was a stalemate, as the Rann was not suited to any kind of warfare. A truce on July 1 referred the matter to an international tribunal. Its award, given almost three years later, in February 1968, gave 90 percent of the area to India.

Pakistan's real objective was acquiring the Indian part of Kashmir. In a much more sophisticated version of the raids of 1947, Pakistan sent across the border into Indian Kashmir thousands of its soldiers in civilian clothes in what was termed "Operation Infiltration." At an opportune moment, there was to be a conventional war, in which 50,000 regulars, for some unknown reason called the "Gibraltar Forces," would be sent in. The expectation was that the Kashmiris, being Muslim, would welcome them and join in the effort to end Indian control. Instead, the local residents captured the infiltrators and handed them over to the Indian army and police. Not to be outdone, Ayub Khan launched an attack on September 1 in the Chhamb sector, with the aim of cutting India's access to Jammu. The operation was named "Operation Grand Slam."

The Second India-Pakistan war lasted only three weeks. In addition to frustrating Pakistan's plans in the Chhamb sector, Indian forces marched on Lahore, Pakistan's second-largest city, and halted outside its ramparts. The Indian home-made Vaijayanta knocked out the Sherman and Patton tanks, and the Indian Gnats, built under license, proved more than a match for the F-86 Sabre Jets.

The Indian army could take over and occupy the historic city of Lahore, but the Shastri government refrained from doing so, being aware of the perils of administering an alien population, even if briefly. On September 15, Ayub Khan appealed to President Lyndon Johnson to intervene to save his troops in Chhamb and Lahore. On the following day, Pakistan's ally, China, served an ultimatum to India, moving its troops on the Sikkim border. Although India had done better than Pakistan, the results of the brief war were inconclusive. Moreover, both sides ran out of spares and thanks to an understanding between both superpowers, none were made readily available. Instead, both superpowers acted in concert in the United Nations Security Council and brought about a cease-fire on September 23.

The Soviet premier offered his good offices as a peace broker and invited Ayub Khan and Shastri to Tashkent in then Soviet central Asia for talks. An agreement was signed on January 10, 1966, whereby both parties agreed to withdraw to the positions they held before the hostilities. They also agreed to restore diplomatic relations, and the Soviet Union promised evenhandedness in its relations with both South Asian nations.

The Third India-Pakistan War and the Emergence of Bangladesh

India-Pakistan relations reached their nadir during the civil war between the two halves of Pakistan in 1971, resulting in the birth of Bangladesh. The immediate cause of the conflict was the elections of December 1970, which gave an overwhelming majority in East Pakistan to the Bengali nationalist Awami League (AL), led by Sheikh Mujibur Rahman. Though the AL did not win a single seat in West Pakistan, the larger population of East Pakistan gave it enough seats to claim a clear majority in the National Assembly and by virtue of that the position of prime minister for its leader, Mujibur Rahman. The Pakistan People's Party (PPP) of Zulfikar Ali Bhutto won a majority in West Pakistan but not a single seat in East Pakistan. The electoral tally was as follows: the AL, 160 seats; the PPP, 86 seats. The two halves of Pakistan showed they did not trust each other. Yet the electoral results were not acceptable to the West Pakistanis, including President Yahya Khan and the PPP's leader, Bhutto, who did not want to give the entire country's government to a Bengali. In their view, Mujibur Rahman had committed treason, demanding autonomy (in the view of his critics, secession) for East Pakistan.

The East Pakistanis, who spoke and shared their beloved Bengali language and culture with West Bengalis, were not willing to adopt Urdu as their language. That is what President Ayub Khan (until 1969) had urged them to do. Over the years, they had developed a resentment against the Punjabis dominating the federal government, the civil service, and the armed forces. The federal government, they charged, appropriated the bulk of the foreign exchange earned by the country's principal exports of tea and jute, both grown in East Pakistan. They resented the superior airs and arrogance of the tall and fair-skinned Punjabis, reminding them of British colonialism. On the other hand, as Bengalis, the East Pakistanis regarded the West Pakistanis as culturally uncouth and no match for Bengal's standards in art and music, literature and philosophy. They shared with West Bengal their love for the Indian Nobel laureate Rabindranath Tagore's works and enjoyed *Robindra Sangeet*, Tagore's songs set to music by the poet himself. In material terms, the per capita income of an East Pakistani was only 40 percent of his counterpart in West Pakistan. Whereas 90 percent of the central government personnel, including those posted to East Pakistan, came from West Pakistan, the armed forces had hardly any Bengalis in it. Sheikh Mujibur Rahman best expressed the East Pakistani resentment of West Pakistan's "colonialism" in the phrase *swadhin deshe paradhin nagarik* (dependent citizens of an independent country.) In 1964, Maulana Bhashani had warned the authorities that "a lava was boiling up" in the hearts of his people. Two years later, on February 12, 1966, Mujibur Rahman presented at an all-party convention at Lahore a six-point program that would make Pakistan a truly federal polity with provincial autonomy for East Pakistan with the full rights to collect revenue and parting with only a small portion to the federal government, with the federal government holding authority over defense and foreign affairs for the whole country.

When the talks between the PPP and the AL, mediated by President Yahya Khan's nominees, broke down, Yahya Khan ordered the new governor of East Pakistan, General Tikka Khan, to launch an operation that could be regarded only as genocide. A particular target was the intellectual faction—lawyers, doctors, engineers, artists, and writers. His tanks rolled on the campus of the Dacca University, razing buildings to the ground and killing thousands of professors and students and unceremoniously throwing them in mass graves. The acts were repeated on all other university campuses and in all other cities and towns against the "intellectuals." It was estimated that some 3 million people were killed, some 200,000 women raped (large numbers committed suicide). All the leaders of the Awami League, including Mujibur Rahman, were arrested. The senseless pogrom, intended to teach the rebellious Bengalis a lesson, was regardless of the fact that they were fellow Muslims, a part of the same nation, created on the basis of Mohammed Ali Jinnah's theory that only the cement of a common religion could weld them into a strong state. The Awami League leaders went into hiding. They created a militant force, the Mukti Bahini (Liberation Force),

which spread its activities throughout East Pakistan with substantial clandestine assistance it received from India.

The West Pakistani army's excesses led an estimated 10 million people to flee across the western border into India, imposing an incalculable burden on its already strained economic resources. India appealed to the United Nations within days of the atrocities on March 31. In the following weeks, as the number of refugees crossing into India exceeded the 1 million mark, India had to spend a monthly $200 million for their maintenance. In the last week of October, Prime Minister Indira Gandhi went to Western Europe and the United States to apprise the governments there of genocide in East Pakistan, the plight of the refugees, the economic burden on India, and, above all, the conditions of anarchy in East Pakistan. She appealed to the world community, in particular to the United States, to do something to restore peace and order in East Pakistan.

India was not the only country to be astonished by America's silence and inaction, despite the atrocities and bloodbath in East Pakistan. At that point of time, the United States was moving fast toward a policy of détente with China that would help the United States withdraw from its quagmire in Vietnam and the return of the American troops home. The U.S. dollar was under attack, as the United States had to buy enormous amounts of perishable supplies from Southeast Asian countries against promises to pay in dollars. The architect of the new policy of bringing the boys home and reducing the financial drain was Henry Kissinger, who did not want anything to disturb, if not sabotage, his larger plan. In July 1971, the world was stunned with the news of Kissinger's dramatic visit to China through the good offices of Pakistan's president, Yahya Khan. Another visit, this time without the drama, by Kissinger to Beijing in October would be followed by President Richard Nixon's visit to China in February of the following year. The events in Bangladesh, ordinarily demanding U.S. intervention on the side of humanitarianism, did not fit into Kissinger's political landscape. Thus, when the U.S. consul general in Dacca, Archer K. Blood, reported the Pakistani army's excesses to the State Department, Kissinger was furious. He reprimanded Blood and ordered that his report be kept under wraps. He was keen on a U.S.-China-Pakistan triangular relationship, which would have to include containment of India and turning a blind eye to the happenings in East Pakistan.

Before his secret visit to Beijing in July, Kissinger visited New Delhi and met the prime minister, Indira Gandhi. Kissinger wanted her support in allowing Yahya Khan to solve the East Pakistan problem on his own. He did not want India to support the liberation struggle launched by the Mukti Bahini in East Pakistan. In return for such support, he assured Gandhi that the refugees from East Pakistan would be sent back. The Indian prime minister found his attitude to be "morally unjustifiable and politically unacceptable."[9] Kissinger flew from Delhi to Islamabad and from there to Beijing on July 9 in a Pakistani plane. The world was told that he was resting in the hill resort of Murrie recovering from a bout of "Delhi belly." In fact, his stomach was fit enough to consume Peking duck and add five pounds of weight in three days!

Following his visit to Beijing, Kissinger called the Indian ambassador to the United States, C. S. Jha, to meet him at the western White House in San Clemente, where the secretary of state would be reporting to Nixon on his recent furtive diplomacy that would lead to the opening of China. Jha was told plainly that in the event of a war between India and China, the former should not expect any help from the United States.

It is Jha's report to Indira Gandhi that led swiftly to the twenty-year Treaty of Peace, Friendship, and Cooperation of August 1971 between India and the Soviet Union. The treaty committed the two parties to "abstain[ing] from providing any assistance to any third party that engages in armed conflict with the other." If China or the United States or both were to help Pakistan in a war with India, the Soviet Union could be expected to be on India's side. In the last quarter of 1971, India received urgent supplies of armaments from the Soviet Union.

Meanwhile, with the dramatic increase in Mukti Bahini numbers and its ability to fight a guerrilla war, Yahya Khan sent additional troops to Bengal. He expected that his alliance with the United States and China would deter India's military involvement in his plans to "fight to the finish with the Bengalis." As for military preparedness, Yahya Khan's and foreign minister Zulfikar Bhutto's pronouncements both at home and at the United Nations were full of bravado about how the Indian forces would be mauled if they interfered in the situation in East Pakistan. Besides the help provided by the United States in the past, China had been a principal supplier of advanced weaponry, such as F-5A and F-7A fighter planes and T-59 tanks to match India's MiGs and Mirage fighters. Since the late 1960s, as the U.S. intelligence sources revealed in the late 1980s, China had also been the provider of all kinds of equipment and weapons-grade uranium to Pakistan's main nuclear facility at Kahuta. To deter India from giving any assistance to the Bengali "rebels," Yahya Khan ordered a preemptive strike on December 3, 1971, on several Indian airfields, including Agra and Amritsar, hoping to immobilize India's air force. He also opened the western front, focusing on the Chamb sector, southeast of Jammu, hoping to cut off the Indian access to Kashmir, which could then be easily captured.

Following Pakistan's strike on India's airfields on December 3, the two countries went to war, which ended in a complete defeat for the Pakistani forces. On December 16, the war ended with General Niazi's official surrender to India's General Jagjit Singh Arora on December 16. Some 93,000 Pakistani soldiers were taken prisoner. India unilaterally declared a cease-fire on the western front, under joint pressure from the superpowers. It was a disaster for the Pakistani military, as it lost one-third of its army, one-half of its navy, and one-third of its air force. The Pakistani army had lost face, and General Yahya Khan was compelled to step down. The turbulent week ended with Zulfikar Bhutto becoming president and chief martial law administrator of a truncated and dispirited country. He was aware of the 93,000 Pakistani troops still in Indian captivity as prisoners of war as well as some 5,000 square miles of Pakistani territory under Indian occupation.

There was a low point reached, arguably the lowest in India-U.S. relations, during the Bangladesh war. In the third week of December 1971, President Nixon, advised by Kissinger (who wanted to return Yahya's favor), ordered the Seventh Fleet and nuclear-powered USS *Enterprise* into the Bay of Bengal, on the pretext of evacuating Americans and Westerners from East Pakistan. It had no military effect, if it was intended to bring pressure on Indian forces to withdraw. Prime Minister Indira Gandhi declared in the parliament that India's efforts in behalf of the Mukti Bahini would not be restrained by the appearance of a nuclear-powered aircraft carrier. The U.S. action did not help to improve its image already clouded by its siding with a military dictator who had stained his hands with the blood of a genocide in what would soon be the independent country of Bangladesh.

On December 16, 1971, the Awami League and the Mukti Bahini declared the birth of independent Bangladesh, with Mujibur Rahman, still in a West Pakistani prison, as the country's first president. He would be released from prison by Bhutto on January 7, 1972. Both he and the Mukti Bahini invited the refugees in India back to their homes and their country. Despite Mujibur Rahman's request for the Indian troops to remain in his country for six to eight months, the bulk of the Indian troops were withdrawn from Bangladesh in two weeks and all of them by March 17, 1972.

The Simla Agreement

Six months after the end of the Bangladesh war, Prime Minister Indira Gandhi and President Zulfikar Ali Bhutto met from June 28 to July 2, 1972, in Simla, the summer capital of the British Raj. It was possible for India to dictate the terms as a victor. In the Indian government, there were two different points of view: one supported by the foreign minister, Swaran Singh, and the prime minister's chief adviser, known as her "brains trust," P. N. Haksar, who cited

that a treaty imposed on Germany after World War I had produced a Hitler, favored magnanimity and a peace treaty that would once and for all bring friendship and cooperation between the two estranged "brothers." The rival point of view was held by defense minister Jagjivan Ram, foreign secretary T. N. Kaul, and P. N. Dhar, chairman of the Policy Planning Committee, who favored harsher terms. Both sides agreed that instead of a mere war settlement in terms of the prisoners of war and such issues, the agreement should aim at a comprehensive settlement, most important on Kashmir as well.

Bhutto came to Simla with weak cards, and he pleaded leniency. One witness to the talks, the former Indian foreign secretary J. N. Dixit, reports Bhutto's words: "Look, I am in a weak position. I have just taken over. If you make very harsh demands and if I concede them I may not survive back home. Already there is a lot of anger and frustration in Pakistan. We don't want an extremist Muslim or military government to come back. So please help me stabilize myself in my office."[10] On July 2, 1972, Indira Gandhi and Zulfikar Bhutto signed the Simla Agreement, which remained the basis of India-Pakistan relations in regard to Kashmir for at least a decade and a half. Under the agreement, both nations undertook "to abjure conflict and confrontation which had marred relations in the past, and to work towards the establishment of durable peace, friendship and cooperation." India agreed to return all 93,000 prisoners of war as well as the 5,000 square miles of Pakistani territory, settling for Pakistan the two major concerns that the prisoners of war would not be tried as war criminals, which was the demand of the Mukti Bahini in Bangladesh.[11] The maintenance of the large number of prisoners of war, on the lines laid down by the Geneva Convention, had been a drain on Indian resources.

The Simla Agreement was described at the time as a landmark agreement and a "comprehensive blueprint" for good-neighborly relations between India and Pakistan. It is still quoted as the basis for a settlement of the Kashmir question because it established a line of control (LOC) in Jammu and Kashmir instead of the old 1949 cease-fire line, which was temporary. The agreement would honor the status quo in Kashmir as of December 17, 1971. The agreement did elevate India's stature in the global community as one working for peace. The short duration of the military intervention and the withdrawal of its troops within a short time of the birth of Bangladesh are contrasted with subsequent examples of armed intervention and long-term occupation of countries.

There were a number of personal agreements and assurances reportedly given by Bhutto that were not incorporated into the agreement because Bhutto astutely pleaded their inclusion would undermine his political position back home. He managed to get Indira Gandhi to acknowledge Jammu and Kashmir as "an issue at dispute" that would be resolved bilaterally. As for the LOC being regarded as an international border, Bhutto requested it be kept out of the agreement; he would make it a reality in four years' time. This was rightly regarded in later years as a failure of Indian diplomacy because Bhutto reneged on most oral assurances as soon as he had stabilized his political position in Pakistan. Such critics of the Simla Agreement hold that Indira Gandhi had missed a golden opportunity to resolve the Kashmir question once and for all.

India-Soviet Relations

Even before the August 1971 India-Soviet Treaty, the Soviet Union had developed a special economic relationship with India, contributing to India's plans for the state to hold the economy's commanding heights. Thus, the new post-treaty bilateral agreements made Soviet long-term, low-interest loans available to build state-owned plants to produce electricity, steel, heavy machinery, machine tools and precision instruments, and oil refineries. The agreements also provided for extensive technical training for Indian personnel both in the Soviet Union and on the site in India. The repayments were allowed in Indian rupees or by barter in the form of Indian raw materials or cheaply manufactured consumables, which was a tremendous help to a country starved of foreign exchange.

Since the early 1960s, India had been a large-scale purchaser of weaponry from the Soviet Union, against deferred low-interest rupee payments. The Soviet Union also allowed India to manufacture highly sophisticated weaponry, including MiG-21 fighter planes. By the end of the 1970s, the Soviet Union became India's number-one trading partner. The arrangement of rupee-ruble payment in trade continued until May 1992, beyond the date of the collapse of the Soviet Union, when Russia would insist that India pay in hard currency.

Significantly for the healthy relationship between a democracy such as India and the largest and the oldest communist state, the Soviet Union, none of the agreements with India including the August 1971 twenty-year Treaty of Peace, Friendship, and Co-operation compelled India to make any foreign policy compromises such as naval-base rights, acceptance of Soviet military advisers, or compulsory membership in the Soviet alliance system. This was extraordinarily tactful because none of the India-Soviet agreements ever became a subject of serious criticism or opposition in the Indian parliament, where successive Indian prime ministers were able to declare that India's foreign policy based on nonalignment had not been compromised by any of the agreements.

Even before the collapse of the Soviet Union and its communist system, Mikhail Gorbachev had called for a "China First" policy, marking Russia's soon-to-be new foreign policy orienta-tion toward the East. There was a clear difference between what Mikhail Gorbachev sought during his visit to New Delhi in 1986 as compared to his visit two years later. During the first visit, following the two-decade-old Brezhnev initiative, Gorbachev was seeking active cooperation from Rajiv Gandhi in building an Asian collective security system for what China had been protesting for long, calling it a mechanism to "encircle" it. By the time of Gorbachev's second visit to New Delhi, such strategic imperatives were no longer needed in view of his "China First" policy; the need for India's friendship because of its position in the developing world was still there but not for its assistance in containing China.

This became evident when in 1991 the renewal of the twenty-year Treaty of Peace, Friendship, and Co-operation came up. Clauses 8, 9, and 10 providing security to India implicitly from the United States and China were dropped. The new Russia would still continue with military sales, supply of arms and spare parts, and the joint manufacture in India of certain defense equipment as before, but these would be payable in hard currency only. Indian dependence on Russian strategic equipment and supplies of certain kinds of materials continued, as the visiting Russian president Boris Yeltsin in 1993 signed a $350 million package to deliver cryogenic engines and space technology to relevant Indian agencies. Yeltsin tried to delay the deliveries but agreed to restore them during the visit of Prime Minister P. V. Narasimha Rao to Russia in July 1994.

Rajiv's Sri Lanka Initiative

At the time of Rajiv's assumption of authority as India's prime minister, the Sri Lankan effort through the All Party Conference had failed. Rajiv himself was in favor of giving up the Indian stance thus far, which was tilting somewhat toward the Tamils in the island nation, an approach partly dictated by India's domestic politics needing the support of the Tamil Nadu government. Rajiv's change in favor of neutrality between the two warring sides in Sri Lanka may have been occasioned by the Indian need not to encourage any ethnic separatist movements because of their likely impact on different movements in India itself, including a potential demand for a separate and wider Tamil Nadu. India now urged the Sri Lankan Tamil separatists to accept a compromise formula by which they could have autonomy in the Tamil districts within the political framework of a united Sri Lanka. On the other hand, the Indian government would weigh in with the Sri Lankan government to soften its stance toward the Liberation Tigers of Tamil Eelam.

Though seemingly cooperative in talks with India, Sri Lanka followed a two-pronged policy. In January 1987, it suddenly blockaded the Jaffna Peninsula and launched an aggressive military campaign against the Tamils. From that time on, the Tamils insisted on the Indian government's continuing role as a mediator and urged it to become a guarantor of any agreement signed between the LTTE and the Sri Lankan government. Meanwhile, the Sri Lankan military campaign against the Jaffna area had caused tremendous hardships on the population of nearly a quarter million there in terms of access to food, kerosene, and medicine. Indian appeals to the government seated in Colombo failed to make such supplies possible. On June 4, 1987, India acted unilaterally and airdropped supplies on humanitarian grounds, an action that was denounced at that time by many countries including, indeed, Sri Lanka as a breach of international law and violating that country's sovereignty. New Delhi had perhaps no choice, because the government of Tamil Nadu appeared ready to help the fellow Tamils across the straits. The Indian assistance proved crucial, as the Colombo government climbed down and signed a peace accord with India.

The Indo–Sri Lanka Peace Accord of 1987, signed by Rajiv Gandhi and President J. R. Jayewardene, in Colombo, on July 29, 1987, was not to the liking of many Sri Lankans, including Prime Minister Ranasinghe Premadasa. The Indian government agreed to send the Indian Peace-Keeping Forces to make sure that the LTTE was "neutralized." The agreement as well as the IPKF eventually failed because India had misjudged Jayawardene's commitment and the "reasonableness" of the LTTE leaders.

In January 1989, there was a change of guard in Sri Lanka as Premadasa, who had opposed the Indo–Sri Lanka Accord, was elected president of the country. Two parties—the Sri Lanka Freedom Party and the United National Party—in Sri Lanka, who had opposed the Indian intervention, had received 95 percent of the popular vote. Premadasa immediately demanded that the IPKF be withdrawn. The Indian intervention was, at that point of time, unpopular in India as well, because the IPKF operations had involved the death of more than 1,000 Indian soldiers and more than 5,000 Sri Lankan Tamils. The operation had cost the Indian treasury in excess of 2,000 crores of rupees and had attracted considerable criticism of the IPKF's violation of human rights. Rajiv refused to withdraw the IPKF because he did not want to admit the failure of his Sri Lanka policy. One of the early decisions of V. P. Singh, his successor as prime minister in December 1989, was to withdraw the IPKF in March 1990.

India and China Resume Relations

In the liberal atmosphere of post-1979 China, the two countries opened talks on the border question in the early 1980s. As seven years of efforts at the vice ministerial level proved less than fruitful, Prime Minister Rajiv Gandhi, visiting China in 1988, removed a major obstacle by declaring that India would not insist on border settlement as a precondition to broadening bilateral relations. In 1991, an agreement was signed to resume the border trade, and accordingly two routes were opened: via Shipki La near Simla and Lipulekh La near the western Nepal-India border. More visits at the highest level between India and China followed in the 1990s. Significant was the signing, in 1993 during the visit of Prime Minister P. V. Narasimha Rao to China, of the Agreement on the Maintenance of Peace and Tranquility, most important its renouncement of the use of force to settle the border dispute. In November 1996, during the first ever visit of a Chinese president to India, Jiang Zemin, the Agreement on Confidence Building Measures of the Border, including procedures to verify border violations, was signed. The two sides agreed to reduce troop deployment all along the border. Most important for India was the Chinese stance on the Kashmir question: China remained neutral during the Kargil War between India and Pakistan in October 1999.

As could only be expected, the continuation of China's military relationship with Pakistan was an impediment in the further amelioration of India-China relationship. India continued to feel that the Sino-Pak axis was directed toward India's "encirclement." China had continued, though clandestinely, to help Pakistan's nuclear capabilities, including building a nuclear power plant at Chasma. More significant, China supplied Pakistan with nuclear-tipped M-11 ballistic missiles and under an agreement signed in 1988 built an M-11 missile factory in Pakistan. Alarmed by these developments, which were a gross violation of the Nuclear Non-Proliferation Treaty (of which both Pakistan and India were not signatories), the United States suspended all military aid to Pakistan in 1990. For several years, despite its doubts to the contrary, the U.S. administration had been certifying that Pakistan had no nuclear capability. The United States was also concerned with the increasing closeness between North Korea, Iran, and Pakistan's head of all nuclear and missile development, A. Q. Khan, who was then suspected (later confirmed) of selling for profit the centrifuge technology and ring magnets to several countries, including North Korea and Iran. In 1995, U.S. satellites detected Chinese missiles being unloaded in Pakistan, despite China's being a signatory to the Missile Technology Control Regime.

The border question has not still gone away. In 2003, during Prime Minister Vajpayee's visit to China, nine "Memoranda of Understanding" were signed. They included one on expanding trade across the border from Sikkim to Tibet and another on the boundary dispute. The new aspect of the latter was that Vajpayee underlined the politi-cal aspect of the problem and agreed with his hosts to appoint a "special representative" to explore "from the political perspective of the overall bilateral relationship the framework of a boundary settlement." During Vajpayee's tenure as prime minister, there were two meetings, in October 2003 and March 2004, between India's representative, Vajpayee's national security adviser, Brajesh Mishra, and Chinese senior vice foreign minister, Dai Bingguo. The border settlement is the most difficult issue for any political party in power in India, since the 1962 parliament resolution forbidding the alienation of Indian land is still on the statutes.

The 1993 Sino-Indian memoranda emphasized "complementarity rather than competitiveness" between the two countries. Vajpayee was accompanied by a very large delegation from the two premier Indian business organizations, the Federation of Chambers of Commerce and Industry and the Confederation of Indian Industries. Encouraging to the Indian industrial cooperation with China was Zhu Rongji's statement in the previous year in Bangalore that a combination of Indian software and Chinese hardware would be most desirable. In 2003, some of the top Indian corporate entities—Infosys, Tata, Bank of India, and the State Bank of India—made investments in China. By 2003, India-China trade, which was a minuscule $265 million in 1991, had climbed to an impressive $6 billion. A new level of cooperation between China and India was seen at the WTO on the question of allowing foreign direct investment in agriculture, a field of livelihood for the bulk of the people in both countries. Both India and China agree that if the Western countries are allowed an ingress in the field of agriculture, large numbers of people will be so affected that it will certainly bring about wide-scale social disruption, most likely with accompanying dire political consequences.

As China and India are both emerging economies on the global level, there will be, in the not too distant future, increasing areas of competition between the two, sometimes for the same resources. In 2006, the main areas of such competition were identified as FDI funds, energy, and IT markets. In April 2005, the Chinese premier, Wen Jiabao, addressing the Tata Consultancy Services in Bangalore, said that cooperation between China and India in the IT industry will help the two nations lead the world in that sector. Such cooperation between the two neighbors will signify "the coming of the Asian century in the IT field." Would this really mean a Chinese policy of joining hands with India on a strategic level? Or, as is more likely, will the two countries divide the IT field, with China taking the hardware and India the software?

With burgeoning industry, the energy needs of both India and China can be met only with increasing imports of oil from the Organization of Petroleum Exporting Countries (better known as OPEC) to supplement their own efforts

to increase domestic production and refining capacities. Both are aware that competition between them could only contribute to the global spiraling prices in petroleum products. Two months after Wen Jiabao's appeal for cooperation in the IT industry, India's then minister for petroleum, Mani Shankar Aiyar, was persuading China to cooperate rather than compete for oil and gas abroad.[12] Independent of China, a month later, Prime Minister Manmohan Singh and President George W. Bush sought to provide an alternative source of energy for India by establishing new nuclear plants. Another area where the two Asian neighbors need considerable understanding and cooperation is in keeping the sea-lanes open and secure for transporting the energy resources from the Middle East through the Indian Ocean to China. In this, China is aware that India has the capability to block or impede oil supply along the Indian Ocean and the Straits of Malacca.[13]

India and the United States: The Recent Phase

India and the United States—Natural Allies? As India entered the second half of its first century of independence, its foreign policy imperatives changed drastically, one of them being very close cooperation with the United States. The issues were no longer anticolonialism and antiracism from the Indian side and anticommunism from the United States as they were in the middle of the last century. The new issues are centered around global trade and investment opportunities, which can help India overcome poverty and disease for millions of its people. On the U.S. side, the strategic issues of nuclear nonproliferation, war against terrorism, securing the oil supplies of the Middle East, and reining in the historical expansionist urges of China hold the greatest priority.

The termination of the cold war, the fall of the communist system, the end of bipolarity in world affairs, and the lack of a need to balance between the two superpowers freed India from the straitjacket of the previous four decades in its relations with the United States. Almost simultaneously, in 1991, India entered a liberal economic regime, freeing trade and investment of the four-decade-old bureaucratic and legal shackles, which would allow greater economic interaction between India and the United States. The U.S. interest since the 1990s has shifted from containment of communism to expansion of democracy and the free-market system throughout the world. This did not at once open the doors for a close and cordial relationship between the world's two largest democracies. As the State Department states, "The interactions [between India and the United States] continued for a decade to be affected by the burden of history, most notably the long-standing India-Pakistan rivalry and nuclear weapons proliferation in the region."[14]

Two major incidents in 1989–1999 showed how such a "burden of history"

affected the course of relations between India and the United States. In May 1998, when India and Pakistan conducted nuclear tests, the proliferation-related restrictions on U.S. aid became applicable to both South Asian countries. The second incident was the brief India-Pakistan war in the Kargil area of Kashmir in October 1999 when the United States, concerned that it might become a nuclear conflict, intervened very effectively to compel Pakistan to withdraw its forces from the Indian side of the LOC in Kashmir.

Three countries—Israel, India, and Pakistan—all of them suspected of having a small number of nuclear weapons since the late 1980s, had refused to sign the Nuclear Non-Proliferation Treaty in 1965 (renewed in 1995), on the grounds that the treaty restricted their sovereign right to develop weapons for self-defense. The perceptions of the United States and India on the nuclear question have been strikingly different. India has been critical of the NPT because it allows only five powers who had nuclear know-how in 1965 to become the sole holders of nuclear weapons in the future. They also happen to be permanent members of the Security Council, holding veto power. When the NPT was renewed in 1995 for an indefinite period of time, there was no change in the list of nuclear powers. That would shut off all other countries including India from their quest for equity with other countries, particularly the five nuclear powers. To India, it is a clear case of discrimination and smacks of the old colonialism. George Perkovich, a foremost expert on India's nuclear position and capabilities, holds that in India's case, its "moral norms and postcolonial identity have also affected nuclear policy-making much more extensively than military security models would hold."[15] In 1988, several years before the NPT's scheduled renewal, Prime Minister Rajiv Gandhi proposed a time frame for global elimination of all nuclear weapons. When the "nuclear club" did not give it any attention, he ordered weaponization in India. Indian intelligence was aware at that time that Pakistan had either possession of or the capability to produce nuclear weapons. In fact, although the nuclear powers ignored the intelligence, both countries' strategic thinking included the possession of a few nuclear weapons by their rivals. Like China, India has declared it will not have "first use," whereas Pakistan has declared that, although it will not use nuclear weapons against a nonnuclear state, it retains its right to use them against India in case the existence of Pakistan itself is at stake. Most South Asian experts, however, hold that a nuclear conflict between the two countries is least likely and that, in fact, their mutual ability to cause tremendous harm to each other made possible by their nuclear holdings will stand in the way of a major conflict.

Thanks to pressures from their agricultural constituents, some U.S. congressmen urged that the sanctions on the two South Asian countries on agricultural items be removed. More diverse similar pressures resulted in the removal of most sanctions within two years. Then, in the wake of 9/11, the U.S. need of close cooperation of the South Asian countries in its fight against the Taliban regime in Afghanistan and generally against international terrorism led to the lifting of all the remaining sanctions by October 2001.

The United States and the Fourth India-Pakistan War: The Kargil Conflict. In May–July 1999, an armed conflict, an undeclared war, took place between Indian and Pakistani forces in Kargil, a district and town of that name lying near the Indian side of the line of control, which was respected by the two sides as the "international" border since the Simla Agreement of 1972. Kargil's strategic importance was underlined by its location on the Indian National Highway, 1A, connecting Srinagar and Leh. It was the only Muslim-majority district in the predominantly Buddhist Ladakh part of the Indian-held Jammu and Kashmir. The stretch of road that was infiltrated by Pakistani regulars dressed as civilians was about one hundred miles of narrow, two-way, curvy highway with a steep fall, very common in the Himalayas. Not all the peaks had Indian military outposts.

Although the Kargil strategy and its failure are blamed on Pakistan's then (and now) chief of the armed forces, General Pervez Musharraf, the Kargil Plan, including the construction of military supply routes, had been completed during the time of Zia and Benazir Bhutto. The full strategic advantage of the plan would be twofold, cutting Indian access to Ladakh and, during the subsequent negotiations to restore the access, compelling India to give up the Siachen Glacier as well as to resolve the entire Kashmir dispute.

The Pakistan government ascribed the conflict entirely to Kashmiri insurgents, though the captured documents, British Broadcasting Corporation reports, and later the revelations contained in the charges made by Prime Minister Nawaz Sharif against the army chief, Pervez Musharraf, point to the involvement of some units of Pakistan's armed forces in Kargil. Officially, the government kept up the pretense for quite some time, going to the extent of refusing to accept the bodies of soldiers who had lost their lives or denying to their families the postdeath benefits due to them. The government was not always able to keep up the pretense. Thus, there have been at least two occasions when it honored its soldiers for their glorious role in the Kargil conflict: Two soldiers were decorated with the Nishan-E-Haider, and ninety others were given the gallantry award for their commendable acts of bravery in Kargil. And then there is that oft-quoted interview of Prime Minister Nawaz Sharif in Pakistan's *Dawn* on June 13, 2000, in which he placed the Pakistani army casualties in the Kargil conflict at 4,000. There were also some doubts expressed in non-

Pakistani media about the insurgents' capability for high-altitude warfare and for the use of some high-grade equipment such as antiaircraft guns.

The Indian army entered the conflict when they learned that Pakistan infiltrators from the other side of the LOC had occupied some military posts along the mountain ridges in the 16,000- to 18,000-foot range. So far, both the Indian and the Pakistani practice had been to abandon the "forward" posts at those heights during the winter and then reoccupy them in the spring. According to the Indian accounts, Pakistani infiltrators sprang a surprise on the Indians by occupying more than one hundred of their military posts. By the time the Indian army patrols discovered that some peaks had been captured and manned by infiltrators from across the LOC, the peaks had been virtually converted, due to their natural advantage of higher ground, into minifortresses, requiring a very high ratio of soldiers to reclaim them. Moreover, action to reoccupy had to be taken precipitately because of the advancing winter and freezing temperatures.

The Indian army lost a large number of men, estimated between 600 and 800, in reclaiming those peaks, though they used the efficient, but ill-famed, Bofors guns for the purpose. In this somewhat low-level conflict lasting more than two months, Pakistan's oil supplies had come to a dangerously low level, as the Indian Navy blockaded access to the Karachi harbor. U.S. intelligence learned that the

Pakistani Army had been "covertly" planning a nuclear strike at India, which alarmed the United States as well as the G-8 nations and the European Union. In the context of both India and Pakistan conducting nuclear tests in the previous year, there was every possibility of a nuclear conflagration in the Himalayan heights. It is not clear whether Prime Minister Nawaz Sharif was on a visit to Washington, D.C., or whether President Bill Clinton summoned him there. What is certain is that Clinton and Sharif met at Camp David on Independence Day 1999 and that the U.S. president asked his visitor to use his influence fully for the immediate withdrawal of infiltrators and their backers from Kargil to the Pakistani side of the LOC.

Was Sharif aware of the Kargil happenings? Seven years after the conflict, he revealed that he was totally unaware of it until he received a call from the Indian prime minister, Vajpayee. According to him, the Kargil adventure was entirely the work of Musharraf and "just two or three of his cronies."[16]

President Clinton's intervention had the desired effect. Pakistani troops were immediately withdrawn, though some nonmilitary infiltrators refused to leave immediately. The conflict came to an end officially on the Indian side on July 26, the day celebrated in India every year since then as *Vijay Diwas,* or Victory Day. General Pervez Musharraf was furious that Nawaz Sharif's orders should foil his carefully laid plans

in Kargil. Amid charges and counter-charges between him and Sharif, the general staged a coup on October 12, 1999, ousting Nawaz Sharif and taking over power. Kargil thus had a direct dismal effect on Pakistan's fledgling democracy where once again the military had dismissed a civilian government and taken over control of the government. Despite calls for an inquiry, no public commission was appointed for probing into who was responsible for the conflict.

Among the other results of the conflict was a serious setback to Pakistan's economy. In India, defense spending went up substantially, as the military of the two sides maintained a standoff on the LOC for nearly one year, keeping high the tensions in the two countries as well as in the world because of the potential for a nuclear flare-up. The handling of the Kargil crisis lent a tremendous boost to the NDA government led by Vajpayee and gave it a decisive majority in the elections of September–October 1999.

The United States and India: A New Relationship. The removal of most sanctions and the positive role Clinton played in bringing an end to the Kargil war assured him the warmest welcome when he visited India in 2000. Pakistan's downgrading in the White House was underlined by the U.S. president spending five days in India and only five hours in Pakistan. The security risk was advanced as the reason the visiting president used a decoy plane for landing at Islamabad with the lights shut off. Both the public address to the parliament, broadcast live to the country, and his private conversations with President-General Pervez Musharraf emphasized the U.S. expectation that Pakistan would return soon to democracy.

Clinton planned to replace the old relationship with India based on the cold war framework with a new one based on expansion of democracy and globalization. The sanctions imposed in the aftermath of the nuclear testing in 1998 were regarded as an unfortunate interlude that should not be allowed to vitiate the new basis of a close relationship. The itinerary of Clinton's visit to India in 2000 underlined both democracy and India's domination of information technology. He had characterized India as a "strategic partner." In that year's presidential election campaign and thereafter, George Bush's first administration upgraded India's importance in America's worldview, beginning certain dialogues with India that resulted in concrete agreements in the beginning of his second administration. During that first administration, in September 2003, the visiting Indian prime minister, Vajpayee, described India and the United States as "natural allies."[17] The United States followed with the announcement in January 2004 of the Next Steps in Strategic Partnership (NSPP), which included immediate steps toward greater transparency in the U.S. licensing arrangements for Indian imports of sensitive items and technology, enabling a significant rise in high-tech trade between the two countries.

Though Vajpayee lost the 2004 election, which brought the traditionally left-leaning Congress Party into power and Manmohan Singh in as prime minister, the momentum of the India-U.S. initiatives was not lost, nor did it slow down. When Singh first met President Bush on September 21, 2004, in New York on the sidelines of the United Nations General Assembly session, Bush assured him that the "best" in India-U.S. relations was "yet to come." The end of the year saw the two countries working together in the catastrophic situation created by the tsunami in South and Southeast Asia in December 2004. Although it provided an opportunity for the Indian and U.S. navies to work closely together in search, rescue, and reconstruction efforts, the State Department noted that it "underscored the interoperability of the navies of the two countries in a real life situation." During President Bush's visit to India in March 2006, India and the United States concluded a Maritime Cooperation Framework "to enhance security in the maritime domain." This will include prevention of piracy, carrying out search-and-rescue operations, combating marine pollution, and responding to natural disasters. The two countries have been working on finalizing a Logistics Support Agreement.

A number of steps were taken in 2005–2006 to enhance the India-U.S. defense cooperation. In November 2005, the Indian Air Force and the U.S. Air Force held a "dissimilar air-combat training exercise, 'Cope India 05,'" at the air force station Kalaikunda. Much more significantly, it included joint exercises involving the navies, armies, and special forces of the two countries.

The visit of the Indian prime minister, Manmohan Sigh, to Washington, D.C., in July 2005 saw the upgrading of the bilateral relationship between India and the United States to a "global strategic partnership." The United States declared that it favored India's emergence as a major player in the twenty-first century and that it was willing to help India reach that position.

The "global strategic partnership" envisaged cooperation on a wide range of issues. Already the two countries had held numerous and "unprecedented" joint military exercises. There were ongoing discussions of the possible sales to India of major U.S.-built weapons systems and high technology. India was globally the largest weapons buyer in 2005. The U.S. goal clearly is to wean India progressively from Russia and replace it as India's major supplier.

There have been a number of agreements signed between the two countries between 2004 and 2006 with significant economic implications. Thus, the "Open Skies Agreement" of April 2005 provided for appreciable increase in the number of flights, which would boost trade, tourism, and business. The state-owned Air India announced its decision to purchase sixty-eight Boeing aircraft valued at US$8 billion.

The new phase of India-U.S. relations has enhanced the bilateral trade at an annual rate of between 20 and 25 percent, doubling the trade from $13.49 billion in 2001 to $26.765 billion in 2005. The continued policy of economic liberalization has been a boon to U.S. industries, particularly MNCs, making the United States one of the largest foreign direct investors and raising the U.S. FDI from a meager $11.3 million in 1991 to $4.13 billion as of August 2004. The United States is also the leading portfolio investor in India; as of June 30, 2004, the American Institutional Investors had invested $10.2 billion of a total of $25.3 billion in Indian capital markets, accounting for 40.5 percent of the total. The United States is also the most important destination of Indian investment abroad. Between 1996 and September 2004, Indian companies invested a little more than $2 billion in the United States, accounting for 18.7 percent of total.

Capping the India-U.S. cooperation is the Full Civil Nuclear Energy Agreement initiated during Prime Minister Singh's visit to the United States in July 2005 that aims to promote nuclear power and energy security to India to help the latter achieve its industrial goals. The agreement, which separates India's nuclear military installations from the civilian plants, will make India subject to the International Atomic Energy Safeguards. Approved by the U.S. House and Senate separately in 2006, a joint committee was, at the end of 2006, expected to iron out the differences between the two versions. Once approved, India will be free to buy the advanced civilian nuclear technology from any member of the forty-five-nation Nuclear Supplies Group. Importantly, it will also open doors for Indian scientists to all kinds of dual-use high technologies, including nanotechnology, biotechnology, and defense technology. Separately, the United States has supported India's membership in the Jeju, South Korea–based International Thermonuclear Experimental Reactor Project, which combines studies in plasma physics and the future power-producing fusion power plants. Most significant, the U.S.-India Civil Nuclear Energy Agreement acknowledged India's record in the nuclear field as that of a "responsible state," which, though not a signatory to the Nuclear Non-Proliferation Treaty (Pakistan and Israel are the two other nonsignatories), has been most mindful of the perils of proliferation.

———

NOTES

1. Jawaharlal Nehru, *Independence and After* (New York: John Day, 1950), 297.

2. Ibid., 333.

3. For example, see Baldev Raj Nayyar, *American Geopolitics and India* (New Delhi: Manohar, 1976).

4. Lloyd I. Rudolph and Susanne Hoeber Rudolph, "The Making of U.S. Foreign Policy for South Asia: Offshore Balancing in Historical Perspective," *Economic and Political Weekly,* February 25, 2006, 705.

5. Michael Brecher, *Nehru: A Political Biography,* 226.

6. For India's role at Geneva, see D. R. SarDesai, *Indian Foreign Policy in Cambodia, Laos, and Vietnam, 1947–64,* 42–51.

7. J. N. Dixit, *Across Borders: Fifty Years of India's Foreign Policy* (New Delhi: Picus Books, 1998), 75.

8. Ayub Khan, *Friends, not Masters: A Political Autobiography* (Oxford: Oxford University Press, 1967), 143.

9. J. N. Dixit, "The Errors of Simla," July 15, 2001, http://www.rediff.com, n.p.

10. Ibid.

11. Banglapedia, "Simla Agreement," http://www.banglapedia@gmail.com.

12. *New York Times,* June 5, 2005.

13. David Zweig and Bi Jianhai, "China's Global Hunt for Energy," *Foreign Affairs* (September–October 2005): 33.

14. U.S. Department of State, *Document/ B93097,* April 6, 2006.

15. George Perkovich, "What Makes the Indian Bomb Tick?" in *Nuclear India in the Twenty-first Century,* edited by D. R. SarDesai and Raju G. C. Thomas, 26.

16. *Telegraph,* May 29, 2006.

17. Atal Bihari Vajpayee, "India-U.S. Relations in an Emerging Global Environment," speech presented at the Asia Society, New York, September 22, 2003.

———

SELECTED BIBLIOGRAPHY

Adas, Michael. "Twentieth Century Approaches to the Indian Mutiny of 1857–58." *Journal of Asian History* (Weisbaden) 5, no. 1 (1971): 1–19.

Ahmed, Imtiaz. *State and Foreign Policy: India's Role in South Asia.* New Delhi: Vikas, 1993.

Ali, M. Athar. "The Mughal Policy: A Critique of Revisionist Approaches." *Modern Asian Studies* (London) 27, no. 4 (October 1993): 699–710.

Ali, Tariq. *An Indian Dynasty: The Story of the Nehru-Gandhi Family.* New York: Putnam, 1985.

Altekar, A. S. *Rastrakutas and Their Times.* 2d ed. Pune: Oriental Book Agency, 1967.

Asher, Catherine Ella Blanshard. *Architecture in Mughal India.* Cambridge: Cambridge University Press, 1992.

Ashton, S. R. *British Policy Towards the Indian States, 1905–1939.* London: Curzon, 1982.

Austin, Grenville. *The Indian Constitution: Cornerstone of a Nation.* Oxford: Clarendon Press, 1966.

Baker, David. "Colonial Beginnings and the Indian Response: The Revolt of 1857–58 in Madhya Pradesh." *Modern Asian Studies* (London) 25, no. 3 (July 1991): 511–43.

Bakshi, S. R. *Morarji Desai.* New Delhi: Amol, 1991.

Banerjee, Hiranmay. *The House of the Tagores.* 3d ed. Calcutta: Rabindra Bharati University, 1968.

Basham, A. L. *The Origin and Development of Classical Hinduism.* Edited by Kenneth G. Zysk. New York: Oxford University Press, 1989.

———. *The Wonder That Was India: A Survey of the History and Culture of the Indian Sub-continent Before the Coming of the Muslims.* New York: Grove Press, 1954.

Bayley, C. A. *Indian Society and the Making of the British Empire.* Cambridge: Cambridge University Press, 1987.

———. *Rulers, Townsmen, and Bazaars: North Indian Society in the Age of British Expansion, 1770–1870.* Cambridge: Cambridge University Press, 1983.

Beach, Milo Cleveland. *Mughal and Rajput Painting.* Cambridge: Cambridge University Press, 1992.

Begley, Vimala, and Richard Daniel DePuma, eds. *Rome and India: The Ancient Sea Trade.* Madison: University of Wisconsin Press, 1992.

Bhattacharjee, Arun. *Rajiv Gandhi: Life and Message.* New Delhi: Ashish, 1992.

Blake, Stephen P. *Shahjahanabad: The Sovereign City in Mughal India.* Cambridge: Cambridge University Press, 1991.

Bondurant, Joan V. *The Conquest of Violence: The Gandhian Philosophy of Conflict.* Princeton: Princeton University Press, 1958.

Bose, Sugata. *Peasant Labour and Colonial Capital: Rural Bengal Since 1770.* Cambridge: Cambridge University Press, 1993.

Brass, Paul R. *The Politics of India Since Independence.* Cambridge: Cambridge University Press, 1994.

Brecher, Michael. *Nehru: A Political Biography.* Oxford: Oxford University Press, 1959.

_____. *The Politics of Succession in India.* Westport, Conn.: Greenwood Press, 1976.

Brown, Judith M. *Gandhi and Civil Disobedience.* London: Cambridge University Press, 1977.

_____. *Modern India: The Origins of an Asian Democracy.* New Delhi: Oxford University Press, 1985.

Brown, Leslie. *The Indian Christians of St. Thomas: An Account of the Ancient Syrian Church of Malabar.* Cambridge: Cambridge University Press, 1956.

Carras, Mary C. *Indira Gandhi in the Crucible of Leadership.* Boston: Beacon Press, 1979.

Chandra, Bipan. *Essays on Contemporary India.* New Delhi: Har-Anand, 1993.

Chattopadhyaya, B. D. "Origins of the Rajputs: The Political, Economic, and Social Progress in Early Medieval Rajasthan." *Indian Historical Review* (Delhi) 3, no. 1 (March 1976): 59–82.

Chaudhury, K. N. *The Trading World of Asia and the English East India Company, 1660–1760.* Cambridge: Cambridge University Press, 1978.

Chellaney, Brahma. *Nuclear Proliferation: The U.S.-Indian Conflict.* New Delhi: Orient Longman, 1993.

Collins, Larry, and Dominique Lapierre. *Freedom at Midnight.* New York: Simon and Schuster, 1975.

Crawford, S. Cromwell. *Ram Mohan Roy.* New York: Paragon, 1987.

Cunningham, Joseph Davey. *History of the Sikhs: From the Origins of the Nation to the Battles of the Sutlej.* Delhi: Sultan Chand, 1955.

Damodaran, A. K., and U. S. Bajpai, eds. *Indian Foreign Policy: The Indira Gandhi Years.* New Delhi: Radiant, 1990.

Das, M. N. *India under Morley and Minto: Politics behind Revolution, Repression, and Reforms.* London: Allen and Unwin, 1964.

Das, Veena. *Mirrors of Violence: Communities, Riots, and Survivors in South Asia.* New Delhi: Oxford University Press, 1992.

Dasgupta, A. "Indian Merchants and the Trade in the Indian Ocean." In *The Cambridge Economic History of India, c. 1200–c. 1750,* edited by Tapan Raychaudhuri and Irfan Habib, 407–33. Cambridge: Cambridge University Press, 1982.

Davies, Collin. *An Historical Atlas of the Indian Peninsula.* Oxford: Oxford University Press, 1959.

Derrett, J. Duncan. *Religion, Law, and the State in India.* London: Faber, 1968.

Desai, Morarji. *The Story of My Life.* 3 vols. New Delhi: Pergamon, 1979.

Desai, Ramesh. *Shivaji, the Last Great Fort Architect.* Bombay: Government of Maharashtra, 1987.

Dhanagare, D. N. *Peasant Movements in India, 1920–1950.* New Delhi: Oxford University Press, 1983.

Digby, Simon. "The Maritime Trade of India." In *The Cambridge Economic History of India, I, c. 1200–c. 1750,* edited by Tapan Raychaudhuri and Irfan Habib, 125–62. Cambridge: Cambridge University Press, 1982.

Doshi, Saryu, ed. *India and Greece.* New Delhi: Marg, 1985.

Dunn, Rose E. *The Adventures of Ibn Battuta.* London: Croom Helm, 1986.

Eaton, Richard M. *The Rise of Islam and the Bengal Frontier, 1204–1760.* Berkeley and Los Angeles: University of California Press, 1993.

_____. *Sufis of Bijapur, 1300–1700: Social Roles of Sufis in Medieval India.* Princeton: Princeton University Press, 1978.

Elliot, H. M., and John Dawson, eds. *The History of India as Told by Its Own Historians.* 8 vols. 1867. Reprint, Delhi: Low Price Publications, 1996.

Embree, Ainslee T., ed. *Alberuni's India.* New York: Norton, 1971.

_____. *1857 in India: Mutiny or War of Independence?* Lexington, Mass.: D. C. Heath, 1963.

_____. *Encyclopedia of Asian History.* 4 vols. New York: Scribner's, 1988.

_____. *Sources of Indian Tradition I: From the Beginning to 1800.* New York: Columbia University Press, 1988.

Erikson, Erik H. *Gandhi's Truth: On the Origins of Militant Nonviolence.* New York: Norton, 1970.

Fairservis, Walter A. *The Roots of Ancient India: The Archaeology of Early Indian Civilization.* New York: Macmillan, 1971.

Featherstone, Donald F. *Victorian Colonial Warfare, India: From the Conquest of Sind to the Indian Mutiny.* London: Caswell, 1992.

Feldhaus, Anna. "Maharashtra as Holy Land: A Sectarian Tradition." *Bulletin of the School of Oriental and African Studies* 49 (1986): 532–48.

Fischer, Louis. *The Life of Mahatma Gandhi.* New York: Harper, 1950.

Fisher, Michael. *A Clash of Cultures: Awadh, the British, and the Mughals.* New Delhi: Manohar, 1987.

_____. *Indirect Rule in India: Residents and the Residency System, 1764–1857.* New Delhi: Oxford University Press, 1991.

Frykenberg, Robert E. "The Impact of Conversion and Social Reform upon Society in South India During the Late Company Period: Questions Concerning Hindu-Christian Encounters with Special Reference to Tinnevelly." In *Indian Society and the Beginnings of Modernization, c. 1830–1850,* edited by C. H. Phillips and Mary Doreen Wainright. London: School of Oriental and African Studies, 1976.

Gandhi, Mohandas. *An Autobiography: The Story of My Experiments with*

Truth. 1957. Reprint, Boston: Beacon Press, 1993.

Ganguly, D. K. *Ancient India: History and Archaeology.* New Delhi: Abhinav, 1994.

Gascoigne, Bamber. *The Great Mughals.* London: Cape, 1971.

Glazer, Sulochana Raghavan, and Nathan Glazer, eds. *Conflicting Images: India and the United States.* Glendale, Md.: Riverdale, 1990.

Goalen, Paul. *India: From Mughal Empire to British Raj.* Cambridge: Cambridge University Press, 1993.

Gokhale, B. G. "Buddhism in the Gupta Age." In *Essays on Gupta Culture,* edited by Bardwell L. Smith. Delhi: Motilal Banarsidass, 1983.

———. *Poona in the Eighteenth Century: An Urban History.* New Delhi: Oxford University Press, 1988.

Gokhale, Kamal. *Shivaputra Sambhaji* (in Marathi). Pune: Lokmanya Prakashan, 1971.

Gopal, Sarvepalli. *Jawaharlal Nehru: A Biography.* 3 vols. London: Cape, 1975–1984.

Gopal, Sarvepalli, ed. *Anatomy of a Confrontation: The Babri Masjid-Ramjanmabhumi Issue.* New Delhi: Viking, 1991.

Goradia, Nayana. *Lord Curzon: The Last of the British Moghuls.* New Delhi: Oxford University Press, 1993.

Gordon, Raymond G., Jr., ed. *Ethnologue: Languages of the World.* 15th ed. Dallas: Summer Institute of Linguistics, 2005.

Gordon, Stewart. *The Marathas, 1600–1818.* Vol. 2, pt. 4 of *New Cambridge History of India.* Cambridge: Cambridge University Press, 1993.

Gorman, Mel, "Sir William O'Shaughnessy, Lord Dalhousie, and the Establishment of the Telegraph System in India." *Technology and Culture* 12, no. 4 (October 1971): 581–601.

Goyal, Shankar. *Aspects of Ancient Indian History and Historiography.* New Delhi: Harnam, 1993.

Guha, Ranajit. *Elementary Aspects of Peasant Insurgency in Colonial India.* New Delhi: Oxford University Press, 1983.

Guha, Ranajit, and Gayatri Chakravorty, eds. *Subaltern Studies: Writings on South Asian History and Society.* 5 vols. New York: Oxford University Press, 1982–1987.

Gune, V. T. *The Judicial System of the Marathas.* Pune: Deccan College, 1953.

Gupta, Bhabhani Sen. *Communism in Indian Politics.* New York: Columbia University Press, 1972.

Gupta, S. P. *The Lost Saraswati and the Indus Civilization.* Jodhpur, India: Kusumanjali Prakashan, 1995.

———. "Recent Economic Reforms in India and Their Impact on the Poor and Vulnerable Sections of Society." In *Economic Reforms and Poverty Alleviation in India,* edited by C. H. H. Rao and H. Linnemann, 126–70. New Delhi: Sage, 1996.

Gupte, Pranay. *Mother India: A Political Biography of Indira Gandhi.* New York: Scribner's, 1992.

Habib, Irfan. *The Agrarian System of Mughal India, 1556–1707.* New York: Asia Publishing House, 1963.

———. *An Atlas of the Mughal Empire.* New Delhi: Oxford University Press, 1982.

Habib, Irfan, ed. *Medieval India*. Vol. 1, *Researchers in the History of India, 1200–1750*. New Delhi: Oxford University Press, 1992.

Halbfass, Wilhelm. *India and Europe: An Essay in Understanding*. Albany: State University of New York Press, 1988.

Hardgrave, Robert L., Jr., and Stanley A. Kochanek. *India: Government and Politics in a Developing Nation*. 5th ed. Fort Worth, Tex.: Harcourt Brace Jovanovich, 1993.

Hart, Henry C., ed. *Indira Gandhi's India: A Political System Reappraised*. Boulder: Westview Press, 1976.

Haynes, Douglas E. *Rhetoric and Ritual in Colonial India: The Shaping of a Public Culture in Surat City, 1852–1928*. Berkeley and Los Angeles: University of California Press, 1991.

Heimsath, Charles. *Indian Nationalism and Hindu Social Reform*. Princeton: Princeton University Press, 1964.

Hill, John L., ed. *The Congress and Indian Nationalism: Historical Perspectives*. Westwood, Mass.: Riverdale, 1991.

Hirschman, Edwin. *White Mutiny: The Ilbert Bill Crisis in India and the Genesis of the Indian National Congress*. New Delhi: Heritage, 1980.

Hossein, Hameeda. *The Company Weavers of Bengal: The East India Company and the Organization of Textile Production in Bengal, 1750–1813*. New Delhi: Oxford University Press, 1988.

Humbers, Philippe. *The Rajiv Gandhi Years: Sunshine and Shadows*. New Delhi: Vimot, 1992.

Hussain, Muhammed Hadi. *Syed Ahmed Khan: Pioneer of Muslim Resurgence*. Lahore: Institute of Islamic Culture, 1970.

Hutchins, Francis. *The Illusion of Permanence: British Imperialism in India*. Princeton: Princeton University Press, 1967.

——. *Spontaneous Revolution: The Quit India Movement*. Delhi: Manohar, 1971.

Ilaiah, Kancha. *Why I Am Not a Hindu: A Sudra Critique of Hindutva Philosophy, Culture, and Political Economy*. Calcutta: Samya, 1996.

Inden, Ronald. *Imagining India*. Oxford: Oxford University Press, 1990.

Irschick, Eugene F. *Politics and Social Conflict in South India: The Non-Brahman Movement and Tamil Separatism*. Berkeley and Los Angeles: University of California Press, 1969.

——. *Tamil Revivalism in the 1930s*. Delhi: Manohar, 1986.

Iyer, Raghavan, ed. *Essential Writings of Mahatma Gandhi*. New Delhi: Oxford University Press, 1991.

Jalal, Ayesha. *The Sole Spokesman: Jinnah, the Muslim League, and the Demand for Pakistan*. Cambridge: Cambridge University Press, 1985.

Jayakar, Pupul. *Indira Gandhi: A Biography*. New Delhi: Penguin, 1992.

Jeffrey, Robin, ed. *People, Princes, and Paramount Power: Society and Politics in Indian Princely States*. New Delhi: Oxford University Press, 1978.

Jones, Kenneth W. *Arya Dharm: Hindu Consciousness in 18th Century Punjab*. Berkeley and Los Angeles: University of California Press, 1976.

——. *Socio-religious Reform Movements in British India*. Cambridge: Cambridge University Press, 1989.

Joshi, Barbara R. *Democracy in Search of Equality: Untouchable Politics and Indian Social Change.* Delhi: Hindustan Publishing, 1982.

Kapur, Rajiv. *Sikh Separatism: The Politics of Faith.* New Delhi: Vikas, 1987.

Karashima, Noboru. *Towards a New Formation: South Indian Society under Vijayanagar Rule.* New Delhi: Oxford University Press, 1992.

Keay, John. *Democracy and Discontent: India's Growing Crisis of Governability.* Cambridge: Cambridge University Press, 1992.

_____. *The Honourable Company: A History of the English East India Company.* London: Harper Collins, 1991.

Kenoyer, Jonathan Mark. *Ancient Cities of the Indus Valley Civilization.* Karachi: Oxford University Press and American Institute of Pakistan Studies, 1998.

Khilnani, Sunil. *The Idea of India.* New York: Farrar, Straus, and Giroux, 1997.

Kopf, David. *The Brahmo Samaj and the Shaping of the Modern Indian Mind.* Princeton: Princeton University Press, 1979.

_____. *British Orientalism and the Bengal Renaissance: The Dynamics of Indian Modernization, 1773–1835.* Berkeley and Los Angeles: University of California Press, 1969.

Kosambi, D. D. *Myth and Reality: Studies in the Formation of Indian Culture.* Bombay: Popular Prakashan, 1962.

Krishna, Murari. *The Calukyas of Kalyani, from circa AD 973 to AD 1200.* Delhi: Concept, 1977.

Kulkarni, A. R. *Maharashtra in the Age of Shivaji.* Pune: Deshmukh, 1967.

Kulke, Hermann, and Dietmar Rothermund. *A History of India.* Rev. ed. London: Routledge, 1990.

Kumar, Dharma. "The Affirmative Action Debate in India." *Asian Survey* 32, no. 3 (1992): 290–302.

_____. *Land and Caste in South India.* Cambridge: Cambridge University Press, 1992.

Kumar, Dharma, and Meghnad Desai, eds. *The Cambridge Economic History of India, II: c. 1757–c. 1970.* Cambridge: Cambridge University Press, 1983.

Kumar, Deepak, ed. *Science and Empire: Essays in Indian Context, 1700–1947.* Delhi: Anamika Prakashan, 1991.

Kumar, Ravindra, ed. *Netaji Subhas Chandra Bose: Correspondence and Selected Documents, 1930–42.* New Delhi: Inter-India, 1992.

_____. *The Social History of Modern India.* New Delhi: Oxford University Press, 1983.

Kumarappa, Bharatan, ed. *Non-violent Resistance.* New Delhi: Schocken, 1951.

Laine, James W. *Shivaji, Hindu King in Islamic India.* New York: Oxford University Press, 2003.

Lelyveld, David. *Aligarh's First Generation.* Princeton: Princeton University Press, 1977.

Lewis, Martin D., ed. *The British in India: Imperialism or Trusteeship?* Lexington, Mass.: D. C. Heath, 1962.

Lingat, R. *The Classical Law of India.* Translated by J. D. M. Derrett. Berkeley and Los Angeles: University of California Press, 1973.

Mahadevan, T. M. P. *Outlines of Hinduism.* 3d ed. Bombay: Chetana, 1999.

Mahalingam, T. *Administration and Social Life under Vijayanagar.* 2 vols. Madras: University of Madras, 1969–1975.

_____. *South Indian Polity.* 2d ed. Madras: University of Madras, 1967.

Mahar, Michael, ed. *The Untouchables in Contemporary India.* Tucson: University of Arizona Press, 1972.

Malik, Hafeez. *Sir Sayyid Ahmed Khan and the Muslim Modernization in India and Pakistan.* New York: Columbia University Press, 1980.

Marshall, John Hubert. *Taxila: An Illustrated Account of the Archaeological Excavations Carried Out at Taxila under the Orders of the Government of India between the Years 1913 and 1934.* 3 vols. Varanasi: Bharatiya, 1975.

Marshall, P. J. Bengal. *The British Bridgehead: Eastern India, 1740–1828.* Cambridge: Cambridge University Press, 1987.

_____. *Problems of Empire: Britain and India, 1757–1813.* New York: Barnes and Noble, 1968.

Masani, Zaheer. *Indira Gandhi: A Biography.* Farmington, N.Y.: Brown, 1976.

Masselos, Jim, ed. *India: Creating a Modern Nation.* New Delhi: Sterling, 1990.

McGetchin, Douglas T., Peter K. J. Park, and D. R. SarDesai, eds. *Sanskrit and "Orientalism": Indology and Comparative Linguistics in Germany, 1750–1958.* New Delhi: Manohar, 2004.

McLane, John R. *Indian Nationalism and the Early Congress.* Princeton: Princeton University Press, 1977.

Mendelsohn, Oliver, and Marika Vicziany. *The Untouchables: Subordination, Poverty, and the State in Modern India.* Cambridge: Cambridge University Press, 1998.

Menon, V. P. The *Transfer of Power in India.* Princeton: Princeton University Press, 1957.

Metcalf, Thomas R. *The Aftermath of the Revolt: India, 1857–1870.* Princeton: Princeton University Press, 1964.

_____. *Ideologies of the Raj.* Cambridge: Cambridge University Press, 1994.

_____. *An Imperial Vision: Indian Architecture and Britain's Raj.* Berkeley and Los Angeles: University of California Press, 1989.

_____. *Modern India: An Interpretive Anthology.* London: Macmillan, 1971.

Miller, Barbara Stoler. "Presidential Address: Contending Narratives—the Political Life of the Indian Epics." *Journal of Asian Studies* 50, no. 4 (November 1991): 783–92.

Minakshi, C. *Administration and Social Life under the Pallavas.* Madras: University of Madras, 1977.

Minault, Gail. *The Khilafat Movement: Religious Symbolism and Political Mobilization in India.* New York: Columbia University Press, 1982.

Mishra, Jayashri. *Social and Economic Conditions under the Imperial Rashtrakutas.* New Delhi: Commonwealth, 1992.

Misra, Satya Swarup. *The Aryan Problem: A Linguistic Approach.* Delhi: Munshiram Manoharlal, 1992.

Mitchell, George. *Architecture and Art of Southern India: Vijayanagara and the Successor States, 1350–1750.* Cambridge: Cambridge University Press, 1995.

Moon, Penderel. *The British Conquest and the Dominion of India.* London: Duckworth, 1989.

_____. *Divide and Quit.* London: Chatto and Windus, 1961.

Moraes, Dom. *Indira Gandhi.* Boston: Little, Brown, 1980.

Moreland, W. H. *India at the Death of Akbar.* Vol. 1, *An Economic Study.* 1920. Reprint, Delhi: Atmaram, 1962.

Mughal, M. Rafique. "The Harappan Settlement Systems and Patterns in the Greater Indus Valley (circa 3500 B.C.–1500 B.C.)." *Pakistan Archaeology* 25 (1990): 1–72.

Mukhia, Harbans. *Perspectives on Medieval History.* New Delhi: Vikas, 1993.

Muller, Max. *Sacred Books of the East.* 50 vols. Oxford: Oxford University Press, 1879–1910.

Nanda, B. R. "The Kushana State: A Preliminary Study." In *The Study of the State,* edited by Henri J. Claessen and Peter Skalnik, 251–74. The Hague: Mouton, 1981.

_____. *Mahatma Gandhi.* Boston: Beacon Press, 1958.

Narain, Harsh. *The Ayodhya Temple Mosque Dispute.* New Delhi: Penman, 1993.

Narasimhan, C. R. *Rajagopalachari: A Biography.* New Delhi: Radiant, 1993.

Natarajan, S. *A Century of Social Reform in India.* Bombay: Asia Publishing House, 1962.

Nayar, Kuldip, and Khushwant Singh. *Tragedy of Punjab: Operation Bluestar and After.* New Delhi: Vision Books, 1984.

Nehru, Jawaharlal. *Jawaharlal Nehru's Speeches.* 5 vols. New Delhi: Publications Division, Ministry of Information and Broadcasting, 1958–1968.

_____. *Selected Works of Jawaharlal Nehru.* Second Series. 16 vols. New Delhi: Jawaharlal Memorial Fund, 1988–1992.

_____. *Towards Freedom: An Autobiography.* 1941. Reprint, Bombay: Allied Publishers, 1962.

Nelson, David N. *Bibliography of South Asia.* Methuen, N.J.: Scarecrow, 1994.

Nugent, Nicholas. *Rajiv Gandhi: Son of a Dynasty.* New Delhi: UBS, 1991.

O'Hanlon, Rosalind. *Caste, Conflict, and Ideology: Mahatma Jotirao Phule and Low Caste Protest in Nineteenth Century Western India.* Cambridge: Cambridge University Press, 1985.

Oldham, R. D. "On Probable Changes in the Geography of Punjab and Its Rivers." *Journal of the Asiatic Society of Bengal* 50, no. 2 (1887): 305–67.

Omvedt, Gail. *Cultural Revolt in a Colonial Society: The Non-Brahman Movement in Western India, 1873 to 1930.* Bombay: Scientific Socialist Education Trust, 1976.

_____. *Dalits and the Democratic Revolution: Dr. Ambedkar and the Dalit Movement in Colonial India.* New Delhi: Sage, 1994.

Page, David. *Prelude to Partition: The Indian Muslims and the Imperial System of Control, 1920–32.* New Delhi: Oxford University Press, 1982.

Pargiter, F. E. *Ancient Indian Historical Tradition.* 1922. Reprint, Delhi: Motilal Banarsidass, 1962.

_____. *The Purana Text of the Dynasties of the Kali Age.* Oxford: Oxford University Press, 1913.

Pearson, M. N. *Before Colonialism: Theories of Asian-European Relations, 1500–1750.* New Delhi: Oxford University Press, 1988.

————. *The Portuguese in India.* Cambridge: Cambridge University Press, 1987.

Piggott, Stuart. *Prehistoric India to 1000 B.C.* London: Penguin, 1952.

Possehl, Gregory L., ed. *The Harappan Civilization.* London: Arts and Phillips, 1982.

————. *South Asian Archaeology Studies.* New Delhi: Oxford University Press, 1992.

Powell, Avril Ann. *Muslims and Missionaries in Pre-mutiny India.* London: Curzon, 1993.

Prasad, Rajeshwar. *Days with Lal Bahadur Shastri.* New Delhi: Allied, 1991.

Price, Ralph B. "The 'New Political Economy' and British Economic Policy for India." *American Journal of Economics and Sociology* 35, no. 4 (October 1976): 401–14.

Qureshi, I. H. *The Muslim Community of the Indo-Pakistan Sub-continent, 1610–1947.* The Hague: Mouton, 1962.

Ramusack, Barbara N. *The Princes of India in the Twilight of Empire: Dissolution of a Patron-Client System, 1914–1939.* Columbus: Ohio State University Press, 1978.

Ranade, R. D. *Mysticism in Maharashtra.* 1933. Reprint, Delhi: Motilal Banarsidass, 1982.

Rangarajan, L. N., trans. and ed. *Kautilya: The Arthasastra.* New York: Penguin, 1992.

Rizvi, S. A. A. *The Wonder That Was India.* Vol. 2, *A Survey of the History and Culture of the Indian Sub-continent from the Coming of the Muslims to the British Conquest, 1200–1700.* London: Sidgwick and Johnson, 1987.

Robb, Peter G. *The Evolution of British Policy Towards Indian Politics, 1880–1920.* Westwood, Mass.: Riverdale, 1992.

Robinson, Francis, ed. *The Cambridge Encyclopaedia of India, Pakistan, Bangladesh, Sri Lanka, Nepal, Bhutan, and the Maldives.* Cambridge: Cambridge University Press, 1989.

Roy, Asim. "The Politics of India's Partition: The Revisionist Perspective." *Modern Asian Studies* (London) 24, no. 2 (April 1990): 385–415.

Rudner, David W. *Caste and Colonialism in Colonial India: The Natukottai Chettiars.* Berkeley and Los Angeles: University of California Press, 1994.

Sahasrabuddhe, P. G., and Manik Chandra Vajpayee. *The People versus Emergency: A Saga of Struggle.* Translated by Sudhakar Raje. New Delhi: Suruchi Prakashan, 1991.

Samgwan, Satpal. *Science, Technology, and Colonisation: An Indian Experience, 1757–1857.* New Delhi: Anamika Prakashan, 1991.

Sankalia, H. D. *Aspects of Indian History and Archaeology.* Delhi: B. R. Publishing, 1977.

SarDesai, D. R. *Indian Foreign Policy in Cambodia, Laos, and Vietnam, 1947–64.* Berkeley and Los Angeles: University of California Press, 1968.

SarDesai, D. R., and Anand Mohan, eds. *The Legacy of Nehru: A Centennial Assessment.* New Delhi: Promilla, 1992.

SarDesai, D. R., and Raju G. C. Thomas, eds. *Nuclear India in the Twenty-first Century.* New York: Palgrave, 2002.

Sarkar, Jadunath. *Fall of the Mughal Empire.* 4 vols. Bombay: Orient Longman, 1964–1972.

_____. *Shivaji and His Times.* Calcutta: Orient-Longman, 1961.

Sastri, K. A. Nilakanta. *The Colas.* 2d ed. Madras: University of Madras, 1975.

_____. *History of South India from Prehistoric Times to the Fall of Vijayanagar.* 4th ed. Madras: Oxford University Press, 1976.

Schwartzberg, Joseph E., ed. *A Historical Atlas of South Asia.* 2d ed. New York: Oxford University Press, 1992.

Seal, Anil. *The Emergence of Indian Nationalism: Competition and Collaboration in the Late Nineteenth Century.* Cambridge: Cambridge University Press, 1968.

Sen, S. N. *Administrative System of the Marathas.* Calcutta: K. P. Bagchi, 1925.

_____. *Foreign Biographies of Shivaji.* 2d ed. Calcutta: K. P. Bagchi, 1927.

_____. *Military System of the Marathas.* 1928. Reprint, Calcutta: K. P. Bagchi, 1979.

Sen, S. P., ed. *Sources of the History of India.* Calcutta: Institute of Historical Studies, 1978.

Seshan, N. K. *With Three Prime Ministers: Nehru, Indira, and Rajiv.* New Delhi: Wiley-Eastern, 1993.

Sewell, Robert. *A Forgotten Empire: Vijayanagar.* London: Sonnenschein, 1900.

Sharma, Kusum. *Ambedkar and the Indian Constitution.* New Delhi: Ashish, 1992.

Sharma, Ramesh Chandra, Atul Kumar Singh, Sugam Anand, Gyaneshwar Chaturvedi, and Jayati Chaturvedi. *Historiography and Historians Since Independence.* Agra: M. G. Publishers, 1991.

Sharma, Ram S. *Aspects of Political Ideas and Institutions in Ancient India.* 2d ed. Delhi: Motilal Banarsidass, 1968.

_____. *Indian Feudalism, c. 300–1200.* Calcutta: University of Calcutta Press, 1965.

_____. *Light on Early Indian Society and Economy.* Bombay: Manaktalas, 1966.

Sharma, Ram S., ed. *Land Revenuw in Ancient India.* Delhi: Motilal Banarsidass, 1971.

Shourie, Arun. *Indian Controversies: Essays on Religion in Politics.* New Delhi: Manohar, 1993.

Singh, Gopal. *A History of the Sikh People, 1469–1978.* Delhi: World Sikh University Press, 1979.

Singh, Harbans. *The Heritage of the Sikhs.* Columbia, Mo.: South Asia Books, 1983.

Singh, Patwant, and Harji Malik, eds. *Punjab: The Fatal Miscalculation.* New Delhi: Patwant Singh, 1985.

Singh, Surinder Nihal. *Rocky Road of Indian Democracy: Nehru to Narasimha Rao.* New Delhi: Sterling, 1993.

Singhal, D. P. *India and World Civilization.* 2 vols. London: Sidgwick and Jackson, 1972.

Sisson, Richard, and Stanley Wolpert, eds. *Congress and Indian Nationalism: The Pre-independence Phase.* Berkeley and Los Angeles: University of California Press, 1988.

Sitaramayya, Pattabhi. *History of the Indian National Congress.* 2 vols. Bombay: Padma, 1947.

Smith, Donald E. *India as a Secular State.* Princeton: Princeton University Press, 1963.

Smith, Vincent A. *The Oxford History of India.* Edited by Percival Spear. 3d ed. New Delhi: Oxford University Press, 1958.

Spear, Thomas George Percival. *A History of India.* Vol. 2. Baltimore: Penguin, 1965.

_____. *The Oxford History of Modern India, 1740–1975.* New Delhi: Oxford University Press, 1978.

Spencer, George W. "The Politics of Plunder: The Cholas in Eleventh Century Ceylon." *Journal of Asian Studies* 35, no. 3 (August 1976): 405–19.

Stein, Burton. *Essays on South India.* Honolulu: University Press of Hawaii, 1975.

Stein, Burton, ed. *Peasant, State, and Society in Medieval South India.* New Delhi: Oxford University Press, 1980.

_____. *Thomas Munro: The Origins of the Colonial State and His Vision of Empire.* New Delhi: Oxford University Press, 1989.

Stewart, Gordon. *The Marathas, 1600–1818.* Vol. 2, pt. 4 of *New Cambridge History of India.* Cambridge: Cambridge University Press, 1993.

Subrahmanyam, Sanjay. *The Political Economy of Commerce: Southern India, 1500–1650.* Cambridge: Cambridge University Press, 1990.

Subramaniam, Chitra. *Bofors: The Story behind the News.* New Delhi: Viking, 1993.

Tahseen, Rana. *Education and Modernisation of Muslims in India.* New Delhi: Deep and Deep, 1993.

Talwar, S. N. *Under the Banyan Tree: The Communist Movement in India, 1920–64.* New Delhi: Allied, 1985.

Tandon, Prakash. *The Punjabi Century, 1857–1947.* Berkeley and Los Angeles: University of California Press, 1968.

Tarn, W. W. *The Greeks in Bactria and India.* Cambridge: Cambridge University Press, 1951.

Taton, Rene, ed. *Ancient and Medieval Science.* London: Thames and Hudson, 1963.

Taylor, Jay. *The Dragon and the Wild Goose: China and India.* New York: Praeger, 1991.

Taylor, P. J. O. *Chronicles of the Mutiny, and Other Historical Sketches.* New Delhi: Indus, 1992.

Thapar, Romila. *Ashoka and the Decline of the Mauryas.* Oxford: Oxford University Press, 1961.

_____. *From Lineage to State: Social Formations in the Mid-First Millennium* B.C. *in the Ganga Valley.* Oxford: Oxford University Press, 1984.

_____. *A History of India.* Vol. 1. 1965. Reprint, Baltimore: Penguin, 1966.

_____. *Interpreting Early India.* New Delhi: Oxford University Press, 1992.

_____. "The State as Empire." In *The Study of the State,* edited by Henry J. Claessen and Peter Skalnik. The Hague: Mouton, 1981.

Trautmann, Thomas R. *Dravidian Kinship.* Cambridge: Cambridge University Press, 1981.

_____. *Kautilya and Arthasastra: A Statistical Study.* Leiden: Brill, 1971.

Tully, Mark. *India: Forty Years of Independence.* New York: Braziller, 1988.

Tully, Mark, and Satish Jacob. *Amritsar: Mrs. Gandhi's Last Battle.* London: Cape, 1985.

Vincent, Rose, ed. *The French in India: From Diamond Traders to Sanskrit Scholars.* Translated by Latika Padgaonkar. Bombay: Popular Prakashan, 1990.

Wagle, N. K. *Countryside and Society in Maharashtra.* Toronto: Center for South Asia Studies, 1988.

_____. "Hindu-Muslim Interaction in Medieval Maharashtra." In *Hinduism Reconsidered*, edited by G. D. Sontheimer and H. Kulke. New Delhi: Manohar, 1989.

Washbrook, David A. *The Emergence of Provincial Politics: The Madras Presidency, 1870–1920.* Cambridge: Cambridge University Press, 1976.

_____. "South Asia, the World System, and World Capitalism." *Journal of Asian Studies* 49, no. 3 (August 1990): 479–508.

Wheeler, Robert Eric Mortimer. *Civilization of the Indus Valley and Beyond.* New York: McGraw-Hill, 1966.

_____. *Early India and Pakistan: To Ashoka.* Rev. ed. New York: Praeger, 1968.

Wink, Andre. *Al-Hind: The Making of the Indo-Islamic World.* Vol. 1, *Early Medieval India and the Expansion of Islam, 7th–11th Centuries.* 2d ed. Leiden: Brill, 1991.

_____. *Land and Sovereignty in India: Agrarian Society and Politics under the Eighteenth Century Maratha Swarajya.* Cambridge: Cambridge University Press, 1986.

Wolpert, Stanley. *Gandhi's Passion: The Life and Legacy of Mahatma Gandhi.* New York: Oxford University Press, 2001.

_____. *Nehru: A Tryst with Destiny.* New York: Oxford University Press, 1996.

_____. *A New History of India.* New York: Oxford University Press, 2000.

_____. *Jinnah of Pakistan.* New York: Oxford University Press, 1984.

_____. *Tilak and Gokhale: Revolution and Reform in the Making of Modern India.* 1962.

Wolpert, Stanley, ed. *Encyclopaedia of India.* 4 vols. New York: Charles Scribner's, 2006.

Woodruff, Philip [pseud.]. *The Men Who Ruled India.* Vol. 2, *The Founders.* London: Cape, 1963.

Zelliot, Eleanor. *From Untouchable to Dalit: Essays on the Ambedkar Movement.* Delhi: Manohar, 1992.

Zimmer, Heinrich. *The Art of Indian Asia.* New York: Pantheon, 1955.

INDEX